White Mother to a Dark Race

White Mother
to a Dark Race

Settler Colonialism, Maternalism, and the Removal
of Indigenous Children in the American West and
Australia, 1880–1940 | MARGARET D. JACOBS

UNIVERSITY OF NEBRASKA PRESS | LINCOLN & LONDON

Acknowledgments for the use of previously
published material appear on pages xiv–xv, which
constitute an extension of the copyright page.

Library of Congress Cataloging-in-Publication Data
Jacobs, Margaret D., 1963–
White mother to a dark race: settler colonialism,
maternalism, and the removal of indigenous children
in the American West and Australia, 1880–1940 /
Margaret D. Jacobs.
p. cm.
Includes bibliographical references and index.
ISBN 978-0-8032-1100-1 (cloth: alk. paper)
ISBN 978-0-8032-3516-8 (paper: alk. paper)
1. Indigenous peoples—Cultural assimilation—
United States 2. Indigenous peoples—Cultural
assimilation—Australia. 3. Stolen generations
(Australia) 4. Indian children—Cultural
assimilation—United States. 5. Children, Aboriginal
Australian—Institutional care—Australia. 6. Indian
children—Institutional care—United States.
7. Women, White. 8. Women social workers.
I. Title.
E98.C89J33   2009
305.89915—dc22
2009002451

Set in Fournier by Bob Reitz.
Designed by A. Shahan.

To my mother,
        Evelyn Jacobs,
and my children,
        Cody and Riley Lynch

All of the author's royalties for this book will be donated to the Omaha Language and Culture Program of the Omaha Nation Public Schools in Nebraska.

Contents

Illustrations

Maps

Acknowledgments

I have consumed many years and traveled many miles to write this book, and I am grateful to all those who have helped me along the way. Without institutional support I simply could not have done it. The College of Arts and Sciences at New Mexico State University first offered me a small research grant that enabled me to travel to the National Library of Australia in the summer—or winter, actually—of 1998. Another grant from the Southwest and Border Cultures Institute at NMSU allowed me to visit several research facilities in the American West in 2002 and 2003. The University of Nebraska–Lincoln has been similarly generous and supportive; a Faculty Seed Grant from the University Research Council helped me to travel again to Australia in the summer/winter of 2005 and to make additional travels in the American West in early 2006. I also thank the chair of the History Department and the dean of the College of Arts and Sciences for granting me a year off from teaching to complete this book.

Several national agencies and foundations have also made my research and writing possible. An Extending the Reach Grant from the National Endowment for the Humanities and a Fulbright Senior Fellowship transported me to Australia from July to December of 2001. During that time, the Centre for Cross-Cultural Research at Australian National University provided me with a beautiful office and the best intellectual company any scholar could wish for. A grant from the Charles Redd Center for Western Studies sent me to eleven western states in the United States in the summer of 2002. Finally, the Spencer Foundation provided me with essential support to turn my hundreds of pages of notes into hundreds of pages of book manuscript during the 2005–6 year. I am grateful to all of these agencies for their ongoing commitment to research and writing in the humanities and social sciences.

Archives, museums, and libraries have been essential to this project. In the United States, kudos to the hard-working and helpful staff at the National Archives repositories in San Bruno and Laguna Niguel, California, and Denver, Colorado. I extend my heartfelt thanks as well to the archivists at the Smithsonian Institution's National Anthropological Archives, the Eastern Washington State Historical Society at the Northwest Museum of Arts and Culture in Spokane, the Braun Library of the Southwest Museum (now part of the Autry National Center in California), the Wyoming State Archives in Cheyenne, the Special Collections at the University of Arizona Library, the Archives and Special Collections of Cline Library at Northern Arizona University, Special Collections at Boise State University, and the Rio Grande Historical Collections at New Mexico State University. In Australia, I am grateful to the staffs of the National Library of Australia in Canberra, the Mortlock Library in Adelaide, and the Battye Library in Perth. Thanks, too, to the archivists who pulled so many documents for me at the Australian Archives in Canberra and Melbourne as well as at the Public Records Office of Victoria, the State Records Offices of South Australia and Western Australia, and the Northern Territory Archive Service. I also wish to thank the staff at the beautiful library of the Australian Institute for Aboriginal and Torres Strait Islander Studies in Canberra. A very special thank you to Doreen Mellor of the Bringing Them Home Oral History Project at the National Library of Australia for granting me access to this collection.

Others have provided support of a more intellectual and collegial kind along the way. In Australia my first teachers were the feminist historians Vicky Haskins, Ann McGrath, Kat Ellinghaus, and Alison Holland. In 2001, while at the Centre for Cross-Cultural Research, I had the great good fortune to meet and befriend other outstanding scholars, including Bain Attwood, Fiona Paisley, Desley Deacon, Ann Curthoys, Rosanne

Kennedy, and Gordon Briscoe. I was also very fortunate to be invited to join the Modernistas, a women's writing group. Thanks especially to Bain for generously offering me copies of primary sources relevant to my work and to Ann M. and Ann C., Vicky, Fiona, Bain, Alison H., Kat, and Tim Rowse for reading my work and offering such valuable suggestions to improve it. I have benefited particularly from my decade-long intellectual collaboration and friendship with Vicky Haskins.

In the United States, I wish to thank in particular all of my colleagues at NMSU and UNL, in particular Joan Jensen, Jon Hunner, Marsha Weisiger, John Nieto-Phillips, John Wunder, Andy Graybill, Victoria Smith, Donna Akers, and Doug Seefeldt, colleagues in western history and American Indian history who have been good friends and helpful sounding boards over the years. Thanks too to Clifford Trafzer, who organized the Boarding School Blues symposium at Sherman Institute and so generously allowed me to participate with the incredible group of scholars he assembled there. During the last two years that I worked on this book, I also had the great good fortune (or perhaps temporary insanity) to take Mark Awakuni-Swetland's Omaha-language class at the University of Nebraska. I am grateful for the humbling experience of struggling to learn the language and coming to know some of the Omaha people in Lincoln and in the Omaha Nation. A great big thank you to Joe Lamb, research assistant extraordinaire, who persevered in finding the answers to all my obscure research questions. Thanks too to Leslie Working for helping with some of the photographs and to Ezra Zeitler for his maps. In the final stages of writing I also benefited from teaching and learning from my students in a graduate seminar on Women, Gender, and Empire.

Big thanks also go to my family, who accompanied me—sometimes reluctantly, sometimes with great enthusiasm—through all the years and over most of the miles of making this book. I am so grateful to my husband, Tom Lynch, for the steady loving companionship of these years. He also deserves credit and a lifetime of breakfasts in bed for reading and editing the first draft of every chapter. Unlike the many others I have thanked in these pages, my children did not support my research and writing in any way. Instead, they interrupted me when I was writing, abruptly jarred me into the present when my mind was lost in the past, required my presence at their sporting events and concerts, yawned when I discussed my keen insights at the dinner table, and kept asking me if I was done with my book yet. In truth, however, their presence in my life generated the inspiration for this book and the direction it took over time. To them, and my mother, Evelyn Jacobs, this book is dedicated.

Portions of this manuscript were previously published. Some material from chapters 2, 4, and 6 originally appeared in the following: "Indian Boarding Schools in Comparative Perspective: The Removal of Indigenous Children in the U.S. and Australia, 1880–1940," in *Boarding School Blues: Revisiting American Indian Educational Experiences*, edited and with an introduction by Clifford E. Trafzer, Jean A. Keller, and Lorene Sisquoc (Lincoln: University of Nebraska Press, 2006), by permission of the University of Nebraska Press, © 2006 by the Board of Regents of the University of Nebraska; with Victoria Haskins, "Stolen Generations and Vanishing Indians: The Removal of Indigenous Children as a Weapon of War in the United States and Australia, 1870–1940," in *Children and War*, edited by James Marten, 227–41 (New York: New York University Press, 2002). Some material from chapter 3 first appeared in "The Great White Mother: Maternalism and American Indian Child Removal in the American West, 1870–1940," in *One Step over the Line: Toward an Inclusive History of Women in the North American Wests*, edited by Elizabeth Jameson and Sheila McManus (Edmonton: University of Alberta Press, 2008). Some material from chapters 3 and 5 first appeared in "Maternal Colonialism: White Women and Indigenous Child Removal in the American West and Australia, 1800–1940," *Western Historical Quarterly* 36 (winter 2005): 453–76, copyright by the Western History Association, reprinted by permission. Some material from chapter 4 originally appeared in "A Battle for the Children: American

Indian Child Removal in Arizona in the Era of Assimilation," *Journal of Arizona History* 45, no. 1 (spring 2004): 31–62. Some material from chapter 8 first appeared in "Working on the Domestic Frontier: American Indian Domestic Servants in White Women's Households in the San Francisco Bay Area, 1920–1940," *Frontiers: A Journal of Women's Studies* 28, nos. 1 and 2 (2007), by permission of the University of Nebraska Press, copyright © 2007 by Frontiers Editorial Collective.

A Note on Terms

As this book demonstrates, the language we use to refer to groups of people can have devastating consequences as to what policies the majority population finds acceptable to enact on their behalf. There are no perfect terms to describe the groups of people I study in this book, but I have chosen to use the following:

INDIGENOUS PEOPLE refers to the original inhabitants and their descendants on both the North American and Australian continents.

AMERICAN INDIANS (and sometimes *Native Americans*) refers to indigenous people in North America.

ABORIGINAL PEOPLE denotes indigenous people in Australia. Where possible, when I am writing of specific indigenous peoples, I use the tribal or group name preferred by the group.

Some quotations from contemporary sources include terms for indigenous people—such as ABO, SQUAW, LUBRA, GIN, HALF-CASTE, and HALF-BREED—that are considered derogatory and demeaning today. I include these terms only to convey the attitudes of historical actors, not to condone such language.

When speaking of the earliest colonial eras, I refer to *Europeans* or specific European groups (for example, *the British*) to describe the settler population. For later years, I use the term *whites* to refer to the descendants of European settlers. The term *white* should not be understood as a fixed or self-evident category, but as one that settlers developed over time to distinguish themselves from indigenous peoples and some other immigrants. Whiteness, a fluid racial designation, came to signify entitlement to land, authority to govern, and a set of cultural and social privileges denied to those deemed nonwhite.

Abbreviations

AAPA	Australian Aboriginal Progressive Association
AAW	Association for the Advancement of Women
AFA	Aborigines' Friends' Association
ADC	Aid to Dependent Children
AFWV	Australian Federation of Women Voters
APNR	Association for the Protection of Native Races
ASAPS	Anti-Slavery and Aborigines Protection Society
BCL	British Commonwealth League
BIA	Bureau of Indian Affairs
FCAA	Federal Council for Aboriginal Advancement
GFWC	General Federation of Women's Clubs
IRA	Indian Rights Association
IWSA	International Women's Suffrage Alliance
NCAI	National Congress of American Indians
UAM	United Aborigines' Mission
WCTU	Woman's Christian Temperance Union
WNIA	Women's National Indian Association
WNPA	Women's Non-Party Association
WSG	Women's Service Guilds
WWCTU	World's Woman's Christian Temperance Union
YWCA	Young Women's Christian Association

White Mother to a Dark Race

One of my earliest memories is lying on my belly on my mother's back, clutching her shoulders, as we paddled about in a shallow pool of water on the north shore of Oahu, just a hundred steps down the beach from the house we were renting in the mid-1960s. This memory is more sensory than anything else: my skin a bit clammy against hers, the warm sea gently bathing us, the faint taste of salt on my tongue, the brilliant sunlight beaming down on us, the ocean's bracing smell. I also recall sitting under our grand piano, the taste of my well-tempered thumb, the feather weight of my hair as I twirled it around my index finger, the percussive plunking of "Twinkle, Twinkle, Little Star" that seeped down through the hard wood of the piano while my mother's voice occasionally intervened. These visceral memories call up feelings of pleasure, comfort, and security, all the sensations we would wish for any young child.

Margaret Tucker had similar sensory memories growing up with her extended family in the first years of the twentieth century at Moonahculla and Cumeroogunga, neighboring settlements for Aboriginal people along the Edwards and Murray Rivers in southeast Australia, on the boundary between New South Wales and Victoria. Tucker remembers, "My old aunt and others would think nothing of peeling off their clothes, tying them and our clothes on their heads, and with us clinging to them, they would swim across to islands in the lakes. I still remember how scared I was, holding on for dear life, but as we did it often I not only learned to love it, but I learned to swim too—at the age of three." Many of Tucker's early memories involve hunting, fishing, and plant-gathering trips. "On hunting trips," she recalls, "I remember being carried on my old aunt's back in a possum rug, warm and snug, the gentle rhythm rocking me to sleep."[1]

The sensory similarities between my sheltered childhood and that of Tucker's end here. By custom and necessity, Tucker did not spend as much time with her mother when she was a small child, for she had many more caregivers than I had. Even before Europeans arrived in their homelands, it was common and desirable for Aboriginal families to share in child rearing. Once they were dispossessed from their lands, however, it was often impossible for mothers and fathers to participate in the day-to-day rearing of their children. Margaret's father was often away shearing sheep for a living, and her mother had to work. "Our old aunt and uncle cared for us mostly," Tucker remembers. Rather than taking care of her own four daughters, Tucker's mother, Theresa Clements, took care of white women's homes and children. As Tucker remembers, "Mother was skilled in sewing and ironing and worked at these tasks and in caring for the children at several of the stations [ranches] around the Murray-Edwards-Murrumbidgee area." "When Mother was not working and was at home for a while," Tucker recalled, "the days were delightful"; "we loved having her at home with us all."

In my early childhood, I can recall few upsetting memories. Being stung by a bee, being left home because I was too young to tour Pearl Harbor, and not winning all the prizes at my fifth birthday party were the extent of the indignities I suffered. By virtue of being Aboriginal, however, Tucker had more than her share of painful and humiliating memories. She remembered going fishing with her mother, a common means of finding food during drought years, when "station owners and squatters had put fences across the land, and natural food like kangaroos, emus, and even rabbits were scarce." "One day like many others when we were feeling the pinch . . . Mother picked up Old Auntie's fishing line. We [children] all armed ourselves with other lines and followed Mother down to the river. We looked around for bait, which was easily found after years of practice as we used mostly worms. We threw our

1. Theresa Clements and her four daughters, May, Margaret, Geraldine, and Evelyn (seated). Used with the kind permission of Grosvenor Books.

lines into the river and sat quietly waiting for nibbles." But Tucker's idyllic fishing trip was cut short by the arrival of two policemen, who warned Tucker's mother that she could be fined heavily for fishing off season.

As Tucker neared adolescence, she and her family "lived in constant fear." They knew all too well that state authorities had devised plans to remove Aboriginal children from their families to be institutionalized in special homes and missions. When her family lived temporarily at Brungle with her father and his relatives, representatives from the Aborigines' Protection Board visited them and sought to remove Margaret and her three sisters to the Cootamundra Domestic Training Home for Aboriginal Girls. At this point, Margaret's mother and father were able to evade the authorities, but the family knew that the board would continue to pressure them. "We were terrified at the thought of being separated from our parents, and while we listened fear and suspicion grew in our hearts. I edged nearer to Father, who I felt for the first time really belonged to us and would help my mother protect us. My father and mother were fighting to keep us together as a family." When Margaret's father had to go out again to shear sheep and then sent money back to his family, Margaret's mother took Margaret and two of her other daughters back to Moonahculla, hoping to elude the board.

She could not. One day when thirteen-year-old Margaret was at school and her mother was off working in a white woman's home, a motor car pulled up outside the school, a rarity at that time and place. A policeman and another official beckoned the schoolteachers outside and then came in to dismiss all the children except Margaret, her sister May (eleven), and another eleven-year-old girl. When the girls realized what was going on they began to cry, and soon a crowd of forty or fifty Aboriginal women and elderly men gathered outside the school building: "[They were] silently grieving for us. They knew something treacherous was going on, something to break our way of life." When the missionary, Mr. Hill, demanded that the three girls go with the police, the "Aboriginal women were very angry" and suddenly "were all talking at once, . . . but all with a hopelessness, knowing they would not have the last say." The missionary's wife and schoolteacher, Mrs. Hill, tried to stall the inevitable departure of the girls until Tucker's mother could be summoned from her job. When Mrs. Clements did arrive on the scene, having run one and a half miles back to the settlement, still with her apron on, Margaret thought, "Everything will be right now. Mum won't let us go." Indeed, her mother did confront the police officer; she "said fiercely, 'They are my children and they are not going away with you.'"

Yet Theresa Clements could not protect her daughter. Margaret remembers:

The policeman . . . patted his handcuffs, which were in a leather case on his belt, and which May and I thought was a revolver.

"Mrs. Clements," he said, "I'll have to use this if you do not let us take these children now."

Thinking that the policeman would shoot Mother, because she was trying to stop him, we screamed, "We'll go with him Mum, we'll go." I cannot forget any detail of that moment, it stands out as though it were yesterday. I cannot ever see kittens taken from their mother cat without remembering that scene. It is just on sixty years ago.

The authorities did allow Mrs. Clements to accompany her two oldest daughters as far as the police station in Deniliquin. After following the policeman into the station, Clements heard a car motor start up outside. When she rushed out of the station, the vehicle was pulling away with two of her daughters in it. Margaret recalls, "My last memory of her for many years was her waving pathetically, as we waved back and called out goodbye to her, but we were too far away for her to hear us."

Tucker stayed at Cootamundra only a short time before being sent out to work as a domestic servant in Sydney. She learned much later what had happened to her mother after she and May had been taken away:

I heard years later how after watching us go out of her life, she wandered away from the police station three miles along the road leading out of the town to Moonahculla. She was worn out, with no food or money, her apron still on. She wandered off the road to rest in the long grass under a tree. That is where old Uncle and Aunt found her the next day. . . . They found our mother still moaning and crying. They heard the sounds and thought it was an animal in pain. . . . Mother was half demented and ill. They gave her water and tried to feed her, but she couldn't eat. She was not interested in anything for weeks.[2]

Margaret Tucker's story, published in 1977, marked the first moment in Australian history when a significant number of non-Aboriginal people learned of the long-standing and widespread policies to remove Aboriginal children from their families to be raised in institutions or in white families. Since that time—with the publication of additional Aboriginal autobiographies, the historian Peter Read's *The Stolen Generations*, and other histories of removed Aboriginal children, as well as a government inquiry culminating in the publication of the *Bringing Them Home* report—many more experiences of removed Aboriginal children and their families and communities have come to light.[3]

My own children were two and five in 1998, when I began research on the Stolen Generations. Long interested in comparative history between the American West and Australia, I had obtained a small grant to fly to Australia to carry out a research reconnaissance mission for almost two weeks. Having just finished a book on white women's encounters with Pueblo Indians, I was curious to examine the interactions of white and Aboriginal women. I remember boarding the shuttle bus in Las Cruces, New Mexico, for the airport while my boys played in the plastic pool they had set up at the bottom of our porch. My older son, Cody, had rigged up a slide on the porch stairs, and over and over they slid into the pool, laughing uproariously each time they hit the water. Two-year-old Riley's diaper had begun to bulge to huge proportions, dragging him down like an anchor. I felt a pang of fear as the shuttle pulled away. What if somehow I never saw them again? What if my plane crashed or some dreadful accident occurred while I was away? I didn't have to worry, however, that a government agency would remove my children in my absence.

As I began my research in the archives at the National Library of Australia and followed the fallout in the newspapers and on television from the recent publication of the *Bringing Them Home* report, memories of my childhood and my longings for my own children repeatedly visited me. What if I had been snatched from my loving mother and beloved home when I was just a child, to be reared among strangers in an unfamiliar place? What if my own children were taken from me and I was as helpless to prevent it as was Theresa Clements? I often found myself overcome by the enormity of the violation done by Australian governments from the late nineteenth century to nearly the present in stripping Aboriginal families of their children.

After the archives closed each day, I pored through Aboriginal autobiographies in the reading room of the National Library. Although each story was unique, I began to notice similarities to American Indian accounts that I had read. Most dramatically, perhaps, I recalled what had happened to the Hopis. Helen Sekaquaptewa recounted when officials conducted a raid on her village at Oraibi in 1906:

Very early one morning . . . we awoke to find our camp surrounded by troops who had come during the night from Keams Canyon. [The] superintendent . . . called the men together, ordering the women and children to remain in their separate family groups. He told the men . . . that the government had reached the limit of its patience; that the children would have to go to school. . . .

All children of school age were lined up to be registered and taken away to school. Eighty-two children, including myself, were listed. It was late in the afternoon when the registration was completed. We were now loaded into wagons . . . [and] taken to the schoolhouse in

New Oraibi, with military escort. We slept on the floor of the dining room that night.

The next morning three more wagons were hired, covered wagons drawn by four horses. All were loaded in, boys and girls in separate wagons. We just sat on the floor of the wagon, and still with military escort, started for Keams Canyon.[4]

This was not the first time government officials had forcibly removed Hopi children at Oraibi. In 1903 Belle Axtell Kolp, a white school-teacher, witnessed the brutal methods used by Superintendent Charles Burton to obtain children for the schools. On the morning of February 5, Burton made a sweep through the village:

Men, women and children were dragged almost naked from their beds and houses. Under the eyes and the guns of the invaders they were allowed to put on a few articles of clothing, and then—many of them barefooted and without any breakfast, the parents and grandparents were forced to take upon their backs such children as were unable to walk the distance (some of the little ones entirely nude) and go down to the school building, through the ice and snow in front of the guns of the dreaded Navajos. They were kept there all day, until after six in the evening, while clothing could be made or found for the children.[5]

Each rainy, windy Canberra winter evening, as I walked back from the library to my chilly apartment on the other side of the lake, I thought about the many moving histories of the Indian boarding schools I had read. Like the experience of the Stolen Generations of Aboriginal children, many American Indian children had also been removed and separated from their families to attend distant boarding schools.[6] Yet most books on the Indian schools discussed the motivations of their founders or the experiences of the children within the schools, but rarely gave more than passing attention to the way children were brought to the schools or

2. Hopi children, 1912. NAU.PH.643.4.42 (Item 1504). Image courtesy of Cline Library, Northern Arizona University.

the subsequent effect on their families and communities.[7] Many American Indian autobiographies, however, recounted the pain of being taken from or leaving loved ones.[8] During that first week in Canberra, I became morbidly fascinated with how the Australian state governments and the U.S. government could resort to such devastating policies.

As a historian with an interest in cross-cultural relations between white and Indian women, I wondered what white women in both the United States and Australia had thought and done about the separation of indigenous children from their families. I knew that many white women at the turn of the twentieth century had used women's traditional association with motherhood as the basis for political activism and social reform. I also knew that white American women had been some of the most vocal proponents of the assimilation policy for American Indians that promoted boarding schools. When I found during my first research trip to Australia that many white Australian women also had supported the removal of Aboriginal children, I was struck by the paradox of white women upholding motherhood as a sacred institution while simultaneously supporting the sundering of these bonds between indigenous women and their children. How could well-intentioned women have supported such a grievous policy?

When I returned to the United States, I embarked on years of research that took me to three national archive regional centers, one state archive, two historical societies, four university archives, and two private archives. As I delved into this subject more deeply, more questions arose. What was it exactly that reformers and officials hoped to change about indigenous children by taking them from their families? Why did white women focus so assiduously on the homes and bodies of indigenous people? What was the meaning of this experience for indigenous children, their parents, their communities? In the process of being removed from their families and homes, how did indigenous children change? To what extent did they remain tied to their homes, families, and cultures? Did any white women protest this policy? If so, what led them to break away from the dominant position of other white women reformers? This book is my attempt to answer these questions.

As I wrote this book, several themes emerged that flow through the pages that follow. First, Australia's "protection" policies and the U.S. government's "assimilation" program, each of which included indigenous child removal as a key element, have often been characterized as more enlightened approaches, or at least well-intentioned if misguided efforts, that broke with earlier and more brutal methods of colonization. However, these policies shared the same fundamental goal of earlier strategies—that of dispossessing indigenous people of their land—and aimed to complete the colonization of the American West and Australia by breaking the affective bonds that tied indigenous children to their kin, community, culture, and homelands.

Second, it was not simply ethnocentrism, racial prejudice, or a sense of religious superiority that led reformers, missionaries, and government officials to promote the removal of indigenous children; it was also that the persistence of indigenous peoples as distinctive groups within each society threatened nation-building efforts in both the post–Civil War United States and Australia after its federation in 1901.

Third, protection and assimilation policies and practices had a particularly gendered dimension; they especially affected indigenous women and implicated white women. White women in both the United States and Australia generated powerful images that pathologized indigenous families and helped to justify indigenous child removal policies. Moreover, unlike earlier phases of conquest and colonization, in which male settlers deemed their womenfolk in need of protection from indigenous "savagery," both male authorities and white women reformers envisioned an important role for white women to play in carrying out "women's work for women"—that is, helping to "rescue" and "uplift" indigenous women and their children from the supposedly backward and oppressive environment in which they lived. In the eighteenth and nineteenth centuries in the United States, it was common for white administrators and some Indian people to refer to the U.S. president and the federal government as the "Great White Father." In this new phase of colonialism it might be more appropriate to speak of the "Great White Mother," a term the Women's National Indian Association used to describe themselves in 1904.[9] In an era in which women were marginalized from full participation in political life, white women's bids to help draft and implement policies for indigenous people in both the United States and Australia represented a significant means by which white women sought to gain public legitimacy and authority, often at the expense of indigenous women's rights.

Fourth, to accomplish their aims of "rescuing" indigenous women and their children, white women reformers and many male authorities deemed it necessary to invade the most intimate spaces of indigenous homes and families. Reformers and authorities sought to undermine the intimate bonds between indigenous children and their families and to replace them with a new loyalty and affiliation to institutional authorities. As in other colonial contexts, intimate spaces became small theaters of colonialism where colonial scripts were produced and performed.[10] While such intimacies could serve the interests of the state, they could also lead in unexpected directions, as some white women experienced wrenching tensions between their maternalist ideals and state policy directives.

Last, in carrying out this project I found an inordinate amount of attention paid by white women to indigenous homes and bodies. Within the institutions to which indigenous children were taken, white women caregivers focused particularly on enforcing new concepts of the body, especially sensory experience, and home. Caregivers and other authorities sought to sever the intimacy and sensory connections the children had developed with their homelands, a crucial task in consolidating settler claims to the land. Rather than seeing this near obsession with indigenous children's bodies and homes as a fascinating but irrelevant facet of white women's reform efforts, I have come to believe, as the anthropologist Ann Laura Stoler puts it, that "colonizing bodies and minds was a sustained, systemic, and incomplete political project."[11]

This book could be two, or even four separate books—one about American Indian child removal and another about Aboriginal child removal (or one about indigenous histories and another about women and gender)—but I believe that by braiding these many histories together, we gain new insights that would not have been possible by examining each history in isolation.[12] My study of the Stolen Generations in Australian history over the past ten years has profoundly changed the way I view American Indian history, especially the Indian boarding schools. My comparison of white American women's maternalism with that of white Australian women has also irrevocably altered my interpretation of the history of women in the American West. My hope is that this book may contribute to expanding how scholars of both U.S. and Australian history view their respective fields. More important, I hope that this book may play some small part in bringing recognition and justice to all the indigenous children and families who have been fractured by these policies and practices.

White Mother to a Dark Race

Chapter 1

Gender and Settler Colonialism in the North American West and Australia

At the age of five, my idyllic childhood on the north shore of Oahu came to an abrupt end. My father, who had so wanted to live in Hawai'i after he retired from the army, contracted cancer and died, and my mother moved my brothers and me to Kansas City, where she had grown up, to share a small home with my grandmother. After a year of urban life, my mother moved us again, to a place she had always wanted to live: the Rocky Mountains of Colorado. We settled in a 1960s-style ranch home in a tiny town, Chipita Park, up Ute Pass and at the foot of Pikes Peak. In many ways, my childhood seemed a journey from one exquisite location to another. I traded the sands of Sunset Beach and the warm currents of the Pacific Ocean for the chilly waters of Fountain Creek and the imposing mountains of Rampart Range and Mount Esther that rose up on either side of our home.

Looking back from the vantage point of a historian of the American West and of indigenous peoples, however, I now see my childhood as a move from one colonized space to another; I lived in beautiful places from which indigenous peoples had been dispossessed. Unbeknown to me as a child, my family and I were unwitting participants in, but ultimately beneficiaries of, the ongoing colonization of indigenous peoples in Hawai'i and the American West. However, unlike other colonial histories that have been disrupted and exposed by nationalist movements for independence and eventual decolonization, the colonial histories of the places I inhabited were buried and obscured. Through hundreds of subtle lessons I learned as a child, the displacement of indigenous peoples from their lands and their replacement with people of European descent seemed an inevitable and natural process. Through television series and textbooks, museum exhibits and cultural festivals, I imbibed the idea that indigenous people were a part of the past. Their cultures and ways of life might have been interesting and even laudable, I was taught, but ultimately they had to give way to European settlement, "civilization," and "progress."

As a child, I had little exposure to the cultures and histories of the indigenous people European settlers had displaced. In Hawai'i, the extent of my contact with indigenous Hawaiians was to take *haole*-style hula lessons and attend the Kodak Hula Show on Waikiki Beach with our out-of-town visitors. In Colorado only the name of my small town—derived from a Ute Indian "princess" (or sometimes "queen"), the wife of Chief Ouray—signified that Indian people had ever lived in that mountain valley. (As punishment for the so-called Meeker Massacre of 1879, which occurred hundreds of miles to the west of Pikes Peak, the government confined all the Utes to reservations in southwestern Colorado and Utah.)[1] The town where I went to high school, Manitou Springs, appropriated an Algonquin word from tribes of the eastern United States. All that seemed to remain of the local indigenous cultures in these places, at least through the eyes of my protected childhood, was a fragmented figment, a quaint tribute.

Indigenous peoples have long known and told the histories that were hidden from my view, but only recently have historians within the academy (some of whom are indigenous themselves) begun to unearth these subterranean colonial histories. Scholars have given a name to this distinctive kind of imperialism: settler colonialism, a type of European expansion that resulted not in overseas empires but in "societies in which Europeans have settled, where their descendants have [become and] remained politically dominant over indigenous peoples, and where a heterogeneous society has developed in class, ethnic and racial terms." As Daiva Stasiulis and Nira Yuval-Davis explain it, "colonies of exploitation," or extractive colonies, rested on the "appropriation of land, natu-

3. Ute Indians marking the old Ute trail. In 1912, seventy-five Ute Indians were invited back to the Colorado Springs area (from where they had been removed in the previous century) to perform for tourists at the Garden of the Gods and to mark the old Ute trail. The author grew up nearby. Image courtesy of Denver Public Library, Western History Collection, Horace Swartley Poley, P1272.

ral resources and labour" through "indirect control by colonial power through a small group of primarily male administrators, merchants, soldiers, and missionaries. In contrast, settler [colonies] were characterized by a much larger settler European population of both sexes for permanent settlement." Settler colonies entailed "much more elaborate political and economic infrastructures" and eventually obtained either formal or informal independence from the metropole.[2] The distinction between extractive and settler colonies should not be seen as a strict dichotomy but as a continuum; many imperial enterprises have combined elements of resource extraction, forced labor, and the appropriation of land.

Until recently I had been reluctant to use the term *settler colonialism* to describe the ways people of European descent gained dominance in the North American West and Australia. The term seemed so innocuous; it conjured up an image of immigrants and emigrants peaceably spreading across continents, diligently clearing fields and erecting homes on empty land that was theirs for the taking. The concept seemed to reinforce the idea that these lands were not already settled by hundreds of thousands of indigenous people. Yet as scholars have delved deeper into the topic, they have made clear that settler colonialism was anything but benign, and may have been even more deadly to indigenous people than more classic types of extractive colonialism. The ultimate goal of settler colonialism—the acquisition of land—lends itself to violence. As Patrick Wolfe writes, the settler colony's "aim is the replacement of native society. . . . Its governing logic is one of elimination" rather than incorporation of indigenous peoples.[3] In other, primarily extractive colonies, the indigenous population served as laborers on plantations, in mines, on railroads, and in factories; by contrast, settler colonies rested on importing labor, often slaves or indentured workers.[4] Indigenous people in settler colonies were not necessary or desired as laborers; to lay claim to their lands, the state sought instead to effect their disappearance. Therefore, policies of exclusion and segregation became central to the development and administration of settler colonies, at least in the first phase of colonization. As we shall see, indigenous child removal constituted another crucial way to eliminate indigenous people, both in a cultural and a biological sense.[5]

As I learned as a child, a curious feature of settler colonialism is that its founding and enduring narratives often obfuscate conquest and colonization and their attendant violence, instead portraying European settlers primarily as victims and resisters of another kind of tyranny. It is true that many early Anglo-Celtic settlers in both North America and Australia came from peasant families that had themselves been only recently dispossessed, forced off the land they cultivated by enclosure movements and the modernization of agriculture. Ironically, and tragically, in their search for new lands on which to settle and make a living, they displaced others. However, in the retelling of their histories it is this aspect of the story that is so often marginalized.[6]

The standard settler colonial narrative of U.S. history, embedded in our elementary school curriculum and popular culture, focuses on a persecuted European religious minority who founded a colony in the American wilderness. Popular accounts of early interactions between Europeans and Native Americans enshrine the first Thanksgiving, where allegedly peaceful Indians and grateful Pilgrims shared a meal together, as the iconic image of cultural contact. Virginia's origins are largely passed over in this account, except for the mythologized encounter in which Pocahontas allegedly saves John Smith from death at the hands of her "savage" relatives. The popular chronicle of early America culminates in the American Revolution, emphasizing how Britain wronged its American colonists and the oppressed Americans revolted against their British masters. As the historian Carole Shammas has written, "Having practically destroyed the aboriginal population and enslaved the Africans, the white inhabitants of English America began to conceive of themselves as the victims, not the agents, of Old World colonialism."[7] In this enduring vision of American history, conflict with American Indians is represented as a pesky impediment to settlement, not as the central story of conquest and colonization.

Similarly, the conventional settler narrative of Australian history has depicted its early settlers as innocent victims of cruel British authorities who sent their poorest, most benighted people, charged with all manner of petty crimes, to a remote convict settlement in the antipodes. In this case, Australian nationalism "calls up a fraternal contract. . . . Its public persona is a brotherhood summed up as mateship, an ideological representation of rough egalitarianism and 'innocent male virtue.'"[8] In this popular account, Aborigines appear (where they appear at all) as just another obstacle to settlement. (One official lamented in 1929, for example, "Our experience in New South Wales has been that the native population has been treacherous and blocked settlement in the early days.")[9] In these versions of history, it is the settlers—fleeing persecution, being sent to the colonies against their will, and struggling against British oppression and the harsh land—who are the victims of violence and oppression and the heroes who triumph over tyranny. Against all odds, these accounts assert, these spirited settlers—"battlers," in Australian parlance—built new nations.

The concept of the frontier in both countries has also contributed much to heroic narratives of settler triumph that all but erase the histories of violence and conflict with the indigenous inhabitants of each continent. Myths of valiant settlers on the frontier work to obscure colonial histories in both countries. Popular histories of westward expansion cast American settlers as brave individualists who were willing to endure great hardship to take up new opportunities and lands in the American West.[10] Australian pioneer accounts echo American sagas; for example, one historian in 1924 characterized frontier life as "the struggle and the glamour, the *camaraderie* and the fights against uneven odds, the romance of overlanding and mustering, the dirt and droughts and disease."[11] The "struggling bush worker for whom solidarity meant survival" correlates with the white pioneer of the American West.[12] By emphasizing the hardships pioneers endured, such narratives have authorized a sense of entitlement on the part of settlers. We settlers earned our place; we earned our right to the land, such accounts insist.

Settler colonial narratives, where they do acknowledge conflicts with indigenous peoples, often present the demise of indigenous peoples as inevitable. Conflicts with American Indians are immensely popular in narratives of westward expansion, and their eventual capitulation is taken as an inescapable consequence of Americans' superior technology, military prowess, and centralized state. For many, the spread of European American settlers over the North American continent is a sign of divine providence, or, in its secular form, manifest destiny. With a wistful sigh, popular accounts of westward expansion mourn the passing of the Indians as a (perhaps) tragic but unavoidable result of progress.[13] In Australian settler narratives, a similar belief prevails. In 1929 an Australian administrator remarked, "We have the slowly advancing tide of resolute white settlers, and a receding tide of natives, sullen and naturally resentful. That position has been the same in Africa, America, Australia, and the Pacific. We have had massacres and ill-treatment, and there has been the same trouble, where aboriginals were concerned, all over the world. I say it quite frankly, these things end in the same way—in the domination by the whites."[14]

Just as I also learned as a child, another common feature of settler colonialism involves the appropriation of indigenous symbols as emblems of the new nation at precisely the moment when indigenous people are characterized as nearly extinct. As the Australian historian Jan Pettman puts it, "Aboriginal people do now occupy a ritual place as the First Australians, although they are largely contained within the Past, or appropriated as magically spiritual, exotic and good for tourism" and "provide local colour at national celebrations."[15] (Even this jaded historian could not resist purchasing a number of cheap boomerangs to give as gifts to my children's friends when we returned from living in Australia.) Certainly the same could be said for American uses of Indian symbols.[16] (Much to my chagrin, the Hopi flute player, Kokopelli, adorns one of my oven mitts, and a New Age Indian dreamcatcher hangs in one of my sons' bedroom windows.)

Intent on complicating popular narratives that obscure the central stories of colonization and dispossession, scholars have increasingly taken up writing the violent histories of colonialism within their nations. In Australia the anthropologist William Stanner issued a challenge to scholars in his 1968 Boyer lectures when he referred to "the great Australian silence," "a cult of forgetfulness practised on a national scale." Over the next several decades, a number of scholars, including Charles Rowley and Henry Reynolds, sought to amplify these silent histories. This has led to great conflict, dubbed "the history wars" in Australia, over the meaning of the past. Former prime minister John Howard denounced what he calls "black armband history," a portrayal of Australian history as "little more than a disgraceful story of imperial-

ism, exploitation, racism, sexism, and other forms of discrimination."
He and other white Australians bemoan the loss of a historical narrative
of heroic struggle.[17] The historian Henry Reynolds has countered that
Howard prefers "white blindfold" history.[18]

American historians have also challenged cherished settler colonial
narratives, and as a result have unleashed a powerful backlash, primarily
over national history standards and museum exhibits. To counter falling
high school test scores, in 1992 the United States decided to develop
new national standards of excellence in five subjects, including history.
Several prominent professional historical organizations partnered with
about thirty other organizations representing parents, school administrators, librarians, curriculum specialists, precollegiate history teachers,
independent schools, and other educators. Through a long and laborious
process of consensus building, these diverse organizations developed
a set of voluntary history standards that integrated the newest historical scholarship—which has closely examined issues of race, class, and
gender—into more conventional models. Yet even before the group
unveiled their national standards, a well-organized campaign led by
Lynne Cheney, the former head of the National Endowment for the Humanities, which had funded the efforts to draft the standards, attacked
the standards as portraying a "grim and gloomy" version of American
history. The conservative radio talk show host Rush Limbaugh claimed
that the standards represented the "bastardization of American history"
and would indoctrinate students in the belief that "our country is in-
herently evil." Due to this campaign, in early 1995, the U.S. Senate
officially condemned the National History Standards.[19]

A museum exhibit in the 1990s also sparked enormous controversy
over the interpretation and public presentation of history. In 1992 the
Smithsonian's National Museum of American Art presented an innova-
tive show, The West as America, offering well-known paintings by celebrated western artists accompanied by text influenced by the burgeoning
scholarship of "new western historians." Curators "invited viewers to
interrogate the paintings for evidence of romanticizing and mytholo-

gizing subtexts" and "pointed out elements of nationalism, racism, and imperialism that might be discerned in the painters' representations of the frontier." Conservative uproar over the exhibit, including charges that it was "perverse" and "destructive," led the museum's director to rewrite five of the exhibit's labels and the show's tour to other cities to be canceled.[20] Though clearly a politically fraught task, confronting settler narratives is a crucial responsibility in coming to terms with our entangled pasts and mediating multiple interests in the places we now share and each call home.

Additionally, if we are to fully comprehend settler histories, the central role that gender played in settler colonies must be addressed. In any society, gender—the meanings we attach to maleness and femaleness and the practices that ensue from these meanings—constitutes one of the most fundamental organizing principles. Gender systems, especially the sexual division of labor, often underpin the economy of a group; they also provide fundamental mechanisms for the reproduction of the group and assertions of identity.

Up until the 1970s the popular mythologized narratives of settler colonies focused primarily on men, marginalized *all* women, and neglected questions of gender. In early women's history projects to recover and reclaim women's experiences, white women's role as pioneers in American westward expansion and as the "goodfella missus" in Australia took center stage.[21] These works spread far beyond the academic realm. As a child growing up in the 1970s (and an aficionado of Laura Ingalls Wilder books and the TV show based on them), I spent many a day playing "pioneer girl" down by the creek that ran behind our house in Colorado. Many Australian and American women recall dressing up as Annie Oakley and playing cowgirl in the 1960s.[22] These inclusions of white women in the popular and academic settler narratives of the American West and Australia have reinforced, not challenged, settler colonial narratives. Focus on the hardships and travails of white women "on the frontier" and "in the outback" have further confirmed a sense of ownership on the part of white settlers to the lands of North America and Australia. Moreover, feminist appropriation of colonial metaphors to apply to the experience of white women in the two countries has deflected attention away from actual colonial relations and white women's role in them.[23]

New generations of scholars have worked diligently to enlarge our view of women and gender in the American West and Australia. Now considerations of indigenous women and immigrant women, as well as discussions of masculinity, sexuality, and gender, populate the historical scholarship in both countries.[24] Still, the older narratives that celebrate and elevate white pioneer women have maintained their powerful hold on American and Australian imaginations. Nearly every day when I pedal my bicycle to work I pass a statue of a valiant (white) pioneer woman looking stoically toward the horizon. And whenever I travel to national parks and monuments in the American West and browse through their gift shops, there is always a shelf devoted to western women, but it almost invariably includes only white pioneer women (or, occasionally, white prostitutes).

To do justice to and fully understand the settler colonial histories of the United States and Australia, we must move beyond merely adding (white) women to a simple narrative of heroic triumph over adversity. The anthropologist Ann Laura Stoler's concept of the "intimacies of empire" is helpful, indeed indispensable, to understand and reconceptualize the intersections between colonialism and gender.[25] It was not only in the halls of governance or on fields of battle, but also in the most intimate spaces of homes, schools, and missions where colonialism's power and hierarchies were constituted and reproduced. Gender and the intimate figured in the workings of colonialism in several ways. First, to bring indigenous people into the new economic order or the Christian fold, colonizers struck at the most intimate aspect of indigenous societies: their understandings of gender and the sexual division of labor. Second, sexual intimacies between men of the colonizing group and indigenous women helped to facilitate trade and colonial enterprises in extractive colonies. Third, the protection of white women by white men often became a primary justification for violence against indigenous peoples. Fourth, to reproduce European notions of the home and advance the spread of European settlements, colonizers depended on enlisting white women. Finally, through their associations with the intimate domain of the home and with child rearing, white women claimed a role in transforming indigenous homes and bodies.

These intimacies of empire were all apparent in the development of settler colonies in North America and Australia. In the rest of this chapter I piece together the bare bones of settler colonial encounters on these continents up to the late nineteenth century. Such an approach necessarily neglects the unique features that make such encounters much messier in detail than in crude outline. This basic anatomy, however, provides the context for my more fleshed-out examination of indigenous child removal in subsequent chapters.

At first glance it might seem inappropriate to compare the history of the European settlement of Australia with that of the United States. Thousands of miles separate one continent from the other, and Europeans colonized Australia nearly two centuries after they first established settlements in what became the United States. Different motivations and historical contingencies guided the European settlement of each. Yet it would be a mistake to fall under the spell of nationalist narratives of exceptionalism that ignore a common set of relationships that developed in each place between incoming settlers, many of them of Anglo-Celtic origin, and indigenous peoples. While each place developed its own unique form and personality, a similar skeletal frame supported and gave shape to the unique histories that played out in each location.

Interestingly, the founding of the new American nation in the late eighteenth century and its century-long drive to colonize the rest of the American continent coincided roughly with Britain's establishment of its Australian colonies and its own century-long enterprise to take over the Australian continent. The American West, then, understood as both an ever-moving frontier at the outer limits of American colonization efforts and as a fixed place west of the Mississippi River, offers an appropriate settler colony to compare with Australia.

Initially, some European nations sought to establish extractive colonies on the North American continent. In search of the supposedly golden cities of Cíbola, the Spanish first mounted a major expedition under the command of Francisco de Coronado, north from Mexico City in 1540 and then again in 1598, this time led by Juan de Oñate. Disappointed to find no mineral riches, the Spanish instead founded a small settlement in Santa Fe in 1609. However, the Spanish did not recruit large numbers of settlers, and they never outnumbered the local Pueblo Indian population; after decades of proselytization and forced labor the Pueblos rose up in rebellion in 1680 and forced the Spanish out of their homeland, keeping them out for twelve years.[26]

Early colonizing efforts by the French and Russians focused on the exploitation of furs rather than minerals. Well into the nineteenth century many Americans continued to regard the American West in the same fashion. Most Americans who ventured west prior to 1840 were young men in search of quick profit through trapping beaver and trading beaver and bison furs; later, a series of gold and other mineral rushes would attract more Americans and other immigrants. Beginning in the 1840s, and increasingly after the Civil War, many Americans began to regard the American West as suitable for permanent settlement.[27]

In Australia some colonizers also looked more to exploitation of resources and profit making than to settlement. European (and some American) whalers and sealers, many of whom lived with Aboriginal people, established a profitable industry on the south coast of Australia in the early 1800s. Like fur traders in North America, sealers often relied on the skills and labor of indigenous peoples, particularly Aboriginal women, to exploit the region's resources.[28]

Although most of the early trappers, sealers, and traders did not seek to take over indigenous lands, their extractive enterprises had profound impacts on indigenous societies. By depleting resources and introducing new systems of labor and trade (not to mention unfamiliar diseases and alcohol), these European entrepreneurs greatly contributed to the decline of indigenous craft skills and the growing dependence on European goods, at least in North America, as well as the disruption of traditional subsistence activities in favor of increased hunting and trapping for new European demands. As Colin Calloway puts it, "Indians were becoming tied to developing European capitalism as both producers and consumers, and being incorporated into a world market."[29]

New trade relations also altered the most intimate aspects of indigenous societies, the "necessary balance" and complementarity of the gendered division of labor, and thus destabilized indigenous modes of production and reproduction.[30] The trade in furs, for example, undermined American Indian women's prominent role in food procurement and distribution. As Carol Devens argues, Montagnais women in the northeastern part of the North American continent spent increasing amounts of time processing furs once their men became involved in the fur trade; their primary role in providing sustenance for the group diminished and, with it, their status.[31] A similar decline in women's economic independence occurred when the Cherokees became involved in the deerskin trade and Plains tribes began trading buffalo hides.[32]

As in other extractive colonies around the world, sexual intimacy between men of the colonizing group and indigenous women also figured prominently in early colonial encounters in North America and Australia.[33] Colonizers used rape, sexual assault, and forced concubinage as a weapon of conquest, as is evident in accounts of the Spanish colonization of California and in many accounts from Queensland, Australia.[34] Yet consensual forms of sexual intimacy also occurred frequently. The Australian scholars Annette Hamilton and Ann McGrath assert that in early encounters with non-Aboriginal men, Aboriginal women themselves sometimes initiated contact with foreign men, "either out of curiosity and desire or in the hope of receiving goods in exchange."[35] For a time such relationships followed the "custom of the country," that is, of indigenous people, in Sylvia Van Kirk's phrase for fur trade marriages in Canada. In fact, European men benefited from indigenous women's knowledge and skill, and they used their relationships with the women to become integrated into already existing trade networks and gain access to resources.[36]

European Christian missionaries were also involved in early colonial enterprises in North America and Australia, and their religious interests often set them at odds with other agents of colonialism. In California, for example, the Catholic Church, represented by Father Junipero Serra, sought to stop the rape of California Indian women by Spanish soldiers. In Australia missions provided a haven from settler violence, sexual and otherwise, and from dispossession and disease. As Catherine Berndt has written of one mission, "Goulburn Island, like other mission stations, was a place of refuge. It was a community where most people were known individually and all could be sure of personal concern about their health and welfare. In a world that was potentially hostile, and largely indifferent or exploitive, missionary paternalism (and maternalism) had its uses."[37] The Australian anthropologist Annette Hamilton notes that missionaries "were among the very few who raised their voices to protest against the ruthless practices of settler colonists and to champion some kind of rights of indigenous people."[38]

Nevertheless, as Berndt puts it, "the mission was also part of that invading society: it was simultaneously protective and destructive."[39] In particular, Christian missionaries sought to interfere in the intimate circles of indigenous peoples and undermine their conceptions of gender and sexuality. Karen Anderson and Carol Devens, for example, argue that French Jesuit missionaries promoted a patriarchal ideal that overturned Montagnais Indian women's roles in food distribution and family decision making and curtailed their ability to divorce easily.[40] In Australia missionaries sought both to "protect" Aboriginal women from liaisons with white and Asian men and to break down Aboriginal traditions and replace them with Christian notions of gender and sexuality.[41]

Although some colonizers of North America and Australia sought to exploit resources and trade or to convert indigenous people to Christianity, the British primarily aimed to found permanent settlements on these two continents, in part to solve some of their own economic and social problems. Settler colonialism simultaneously rested on displacing indigenous populations from the land and quickly replacing them with incoming Europeans in fortified settlements. Unlike extractive colonies, which involved only a small number of mostly male Europeans who never outnumbered the indigenous population (and who in fact depended on the knowledge and good graces of the indigenous people), settler colonialism required importing large numbers of Europeans, including women, in a short time and ensuring that they would create families.

With a charter from the British Crown, the Virginia Company in 1607 initially envisioned Virginia as an extractive colony that might yield precious minerals or other sought-after goods in Europe. When such dreams of quick riches were dashed, it became apparent that the colony would work well as a mixed settlement colony, where plantations could grow a valuable new cash crop: tobacco. British colonists had hoped that the local Indian groups under the Powhatan Confederacy would supply the labor needed for their new venture, but the Indians in the vicinity quickly dispatched such notions. In 1622 local Indians rose in rebellion, killed four hundred colonists, and bankrupted the company. The new colony turned to indentured English and Irish servants, British convicts, and, later, African slaves to labor on their plantations and instituted a brutal policy of dispossession against the local indigenous people. In an effort to establish a viable settler colony that would reproduce itself, Virginia also struggled to equalize the unbalanced sex ratio. By the end of the seventeenth century, Virginia emerged as a full-fledged settler colony; Indian populations had been destroyed or removed, the increasing importation of African slaves had resolved labor shortages, and British women had migrated there in sufficient numbers to form families and reproduce the settler population.[42]

Farther north, in the Plymouth and Massachusetts Bay colonies, Puritans set out to establish a settler colony from the beginning. Seeking religious refuge beginning in 1620, they migrated as families and promoted small farms rather than large plantations. Puritan families reproduced themselves and their settlements rapidly, and their perpetual quest for land led to great conflict with local Indian groups. Violence erupted frequently, most seriously in the Pequot War of 1636–37 and in the King Philip's War of 1675–76; by the end of the seventeenth century Puritan groups and other English settlers had gained control of most of the eastern seaboard in New England. Farther inland and to the north, in Canada, the French and several Indian tribes still claimed possession of the land, but as a result of the so-called French and Indian War (also known as the Seven Years War) between 1756 and 1763 the British gained control of the territory.[43]

The British had regarded Virginia as a suitable repository for its convicts. When the American Revolution brought an end to this practice, Britain established a penal colony at Port Jackson in Sydney Cove in New South Wales, the eastern portion of Australia that James Cook had "discovered" and taken possession of for England in 1770. As in North America, the British in Australia were not interested merely in trade but also in settlement, and thus land. In contrast to the United States, the British considered Australia to be *terra nullius*, empty land; they refused to recognize Aboriginal title to the land and therefore did not make treaties with Aboriginal people. Instead, Britain immediately claimed all land for the Crown and turned all Aboriginal people into British subjects. Beginning in 1793 officers who administered the colony were eligible for land grants of unlimited size, and freed convicts and soldiers each received small land allotments of up to twenty hectares. While large landowners found the land well suited to grazing sheep and cattle, settlers on smaller plots along the Hawkesbury River concentrated on growing wheat and maize. By 1800 a thousand colonists had taken up land along the fertile river. As in the British colonies in North America, Aboriginal people resisted the taking of their land. In New South Wales they attacked settlers who had taken over their land on the Hawkesbury River. One Eora man, Pemulwuy, organized attacks on several British settlements before being shot and killed in 1802; the British placed his head in a jar and sent it to England. That same year, fearing that the French had designs on Australia, the British established another penal colony on the small island to the south of the Australian continent, which the Dutch had dubbed Van Diemen's Land and would later take the name Tasmania.[44]

As with Virginia, these early Australian colonies suffered from a shortage of British women, a necessary requirement if Britain was to establish a viable settler colony on Australian soil. Men outnumbered women on the First Fleet to Australia by three to one, and until 1820 there was only one British woman for every four British men. Such conditions were not conducive to building a settler colony; relationships between Aboriginal women and British men and the prevalence of prostitution and homosexual relationships would not lead to the dominance of the British settlers. Not until the 1850s, when increasing numbers of British women migrated to Australia and white women bore an average of seven children, did these sex ratios even out.[45]

With expanding populations on both continents, the insatiable British demand for land did not end with initial settlement. In 1763, at the close of the French and Indian War, the victorious but war-weary British had issued a royal proclamation to prohibit settlement on Indian lands west of the Appalachian Mountains. The American colonists still hungered for land, however, and chafed at British restrictions; the Proclamation Line became one of many American grievances against the British that erupted in the American Revolution. At the close of the Revolution, during which many Indian tribes fought on the side of the British, Britain transferred sovereignty to America over all territory south of the Great Lakes, east of the Mississippi River, and north of Florida, ignoring the fact that Indian groups on much of this land had never transferred it to the British in the first place. The new American government sought to expand westward through treaties, if possible, and by war, if necessary. Under pressure from American settlers, in the 1780s representatives from several Indian nations met with American treaty commissioners in New York, western Pennsylvania, and southwestern Ohio and ceded vast tracts of their lands to the newly forming United States.[46]

Still, some Indian groups held out. The Shawnees, already displaced from their original homelands, sought to organize a united pan-Indian movement to prevent further American expansion but were defeated when their leader, Tecumseh, was killed in battle in 1813. Several tribes—the Cherokees, Choctaws, Creeks, Chickasaws, and Seminoles—adopted the trappings of "civilization" to avoid removal from their homelands in the southeast. Ultimately, however, with the passage of the Indian Removal Act in 1830, the majority of these tribes' members were forcibly removed to the new Indian Territory west of the Mississippi in the 1830s.[47]

The battlegrounds of American colonialism then moved to the American West, a region partly claimed by the United States through the Louisiana Purchase of 1802 and partly claimed by the Spanish (and later the newly independent Mexican government). Many Indian peoples of the region, however, did not recognize either of these nations as their ruler. Before Americans arrived on the Great Plains other Indian groups had migrated to and within the area; having acquired the horse and gun from Europeans, they vied with one another for control of the area. In 1848, after a short-lived war with Mexico, the United States acquired a vast tract of land in the present-day southwestern section of the country. That same year the discovery of gold in one newly conquered territory, California, prompted more and more Americans to migrate westward. Indian people in California faced further loss of their lands and the destruction of the habitat on which they depended.

As in earlier eras, the establishment of a settler colony in the American West required not only the displacement of indigenous peoples but also their replacement with the settler population. In the United States, to facilitate settlement of the West the 1862 Homestead Act granted 160 acres of free land to any male settler or single woman who would cultivate the land, erect a home, and reside on the claim for five years. Homesteaders could then obtain full title to the land for a ten-dollar fee. Alternatively, after just six months homesteaders could purchase their land at $1.25 an acre. As a result of these new incentives, homesteaders took up 985 million acres over a seventy-year period.[48]

Still, Indian people on the Great Plains stood in the way of settlement. Conflicts between Great Plains tribes, emigrants, and the U.S. government increased greatly after the Civil War, as more and more Americans headed westward. Beginning in 1867 the federal government negotiated treaties with representatives from many of the Great Plains tribes and agreed to provide rations to replace the bison that these groups had hunted for millennia. Yet not all tribal members agreed to the terms of the treaties, and when the government failed to supply adequate rations, some bands of Indians went outside the bounds of the reservation in search of bison. The U.S. government responded by dispatching the army to attack the recalcitrant bands. A series of bloody Indian wars resulted, ending in 1890 with the massacre of Lakota people at Wounded Knee.[49]

As in North America, the British in Australia continued to expand their settlements into indigenous lands. In the early nineteenth century pastoralists moved westward over the Blue Mountains, southward to the Murray River, and northward toward Brisbane; the population of sheep grew from about 100,000 in 1820 to thirteen million in 1850, leading one historian to assert that these grazers were "the shocktroops of land seizure."[50] Although the government tried to regulate the dispersal of land to colonists, settlers simply moved into areas they coveted, especially near waterholes that Aboriginal people depended on for both material and spiritual sustenance. The pastoralists' livestock ate up indigenous foods, drove away game, and took over water holes, engendering bitter conflict with the displaced Aboriginal people. Dispossessed of their land and cut off from their source of food, many Aborigines killed settlers and speared cattle, only to be met with brutal "punitive expeditions," a form of vigilante violence that Henry Reynolds claims "exacted revenge out of all proportion to the numbers of settlers killed." (Reynolds estimates that while Aborigines were responsible for approximately three thousand settler deaths, settlers killed at least twenty thousand Aborigines.) Some station owners allowed Aborigines to continue to live on their land but treated them much like serfs.[51]

Conflict was particularly violent in Van Diemen's Land, where pastoralists and their livestock had also vastly expanded outward from the initial settlement. After Aboriginal people made more than twenty separate attacks on settlers during just one month in 1828, the governor declared a state of martial law and sent three thousand men to form a "Black Line," two hundred kilometers long, to sweep down the island to drive all Aboriginal people southward to the coast. When this failed to quell Aboriginal resistance, the governor hired a tradesman-cum-missionary, George Robinson, to use more diplomatic means to persuade Aboriginal people to settle on a separate reserve. Between 1830 and 1834 Robinson succeeded in rounding up the remaining Aboriginal population and having them deported to Flinders Island.[52] Queensland, which originated as a penal colony for New South Wales in 1824, gained a reputation as a site of particularly fierce settler violence against Aboriginal people.[53]

The colonies of Victoria and South Australia began on a more equitable footing, when, in 1835, John Batman and a group of tradesmen from Van Diemen's Land crossed the Bass Strait to the mainland of Australia to take up land in the Port Phillip District. Here Batman exchanged goods such as blankets, axes, mirrors, clothing, and flour with the local Kulin people for 200,000 hectares of land. In 1836 the British government, in establishing a new colony in South Australia, stipulated that Aboriginal people should be properly compensated for their land. Yet conditions in these colonies soon degenerated into the same pattern of dispossession, Aboriginal resistance, and settler reprisals present in New South Wales and Van Diemen's Land.[54]

As with the Homestead Act in the United States, all Australian colonies also passed Selection Acts, which were meant to distribute land to small landholders and more effectively settle the land. Beginning with Victoria in 1860 and New South Wales in 1861, the Selection Acts enabled selectors to buy at a cheap rate up to 250 hectares of vacant Crown land or parts of lands held by pastoralists. These laws never achieved their aim of reducing the holdings of pastoralists, but they did promote more settlement by small homesteaders and further the dispossession of

Aboriginal peoples.[55] This process of moving into and taking possession of Aboriginal country occurred over a number of years, beginning in the south and on the coasts and spreading inland intermittently across the continent. Some Aboriginal groups, especially in Western Australia and what became the Northern Territory, remained relatively isolated and were spared the effects of contact for decades.

By the late nineteenth century, in the areas they had colonized Australians had isolated Aboriginal people on missions or reserves to "protect" them. No longer able to hunt and gather on their traditional lands, Aborigines had to replace indigenous foods with government rations. Unlike American Indian groups, however, many of which could claim large reservations, by 1910 nearly all Aboriginal land had been taken by colonists or the Crown.[56] Moreover, unlike in the United States, where the federal government held centralized control over all affairs with Indians, each colony, and then state, in Australia pursued its own policies toward Aboriginal people.

The establishment of settler colonies and their displacement of indigenous people from their land had even more profound effects on indigenous peoples than had extractive colonies. On both continents, while the settler population swelled the numbers of indigenous people declined precipitously. Coupled with settler violence and the destruction of traditional patterns of subsistence, disease, especially smallpox and venereal disease, decimated indigenous peoples. Demographers have estimated the original population of North America north of Mexico to be as low as two million and as high as eighteen million people. By 1890 the U.S. census counted just 248,253 American Indians.[57] In Australia estimates of the original Aboriginal population range from 300,000 to one million; only an estimated 85,000 Aboriginal people remained by 1851, and this number declined to around 60,000 in the 1920s. (The Australian government did not include Aboriginal people in its census until the 1960s, so historians must estimate not only the precontact but also the postcontact population.)[58] Uprooted from their home countries to unfamiliar lands or institutions, many indigenous people found it difficult to subsist as they had for millennia through hunting, gathering wild foods, or horticulture (as many tribes in North America practiced). Instead, by the late nineteenth century in both the American West and in Australia they had become largely dependent on government rations.

Gender and the intimacies of empire again proved important in these simultaneous processes of displacing indigenous peoples and building settler societies. In the early phases of settlement the protection of white women against Indian and Aboriginal depredations became a primary justification for violence and repression against indigenous populations.[59] Moreover, colonizers not only sought to balance sex ratios and promote settlement by European families, but also regarded the reproduction of European gender systems, particularly "the home," as an essential means of establishing dominance in the new settlement. Settler colonies thus relied on the mobilization of white women, who were charged with making and keeping the home, as key figures in promoting settlement.[60]

At the same time, indigenous gender systems, also fundamental to the continued viability of their societies, were under assault. The forced removal of indigenous peoples from their lands changed the terms of intercultural relationships between European men and indigenous women. No longer under the control of indigenous peoples, these sexual relations now met the needs of European settlers. Unable to support themselves from their land and reduced to semistarvation, some indigenous women resorted to prostitution with white men.[61] Moreover, as white women worked to establish new homes and reproduce a settler society, intercultural relationships between white men and indigenous women, once tolerated if not promoted, became unacceptable. The children of such unions lost their status within colonial society as well.[62] This was particularly true in Australia, where authorities became disturbed, as we shall see, by the numbers of children whom the government labeled "half-castes."

Loss of land also threatened one of the most fundamental ways of organizing indigenous societies: the gendered division of labor. Dependence on government rations, for example, meant that Aboriginal women no longer had a primary role in food gathering, nor the independence and value that came from such a role. Among the Walpiri of Central Australia, the anthropologist Diane Bell noted some continuity of gender roles with the past: women's and men's work was still clearly divided after colonization. Nevertheless, the new context for work had weakened women's roles. Bell believes "land is the power base" from which women's autonomy emerged. Thus in those Aboriginal groups that were most displaced, Bell believes, the women lost the most status; by contrast, in Aboriginal groups that were the least displaced the women have retained the highest status.[63] While finding that Cherokee women also held on to some of their power and influence after colonization, the historian Theda Perdue notes that the women's culture and status were tied to the common tribal ownership of land and the women's role as farmers. Following colonization, when much Cherokee land moved to individual, and male, hands, Cherokee women saw a diminution in their authority.[64]

Indigenous peoples also found their most intimate associations and value systems threatened by Christian missionaries (many of them white women), who continued to play a prominent role in spreading European gender ideals, among members of their own group as much as among indigenous populations. As in earlier eras, missionaries consciously sought to change the gender systems of indigenous people through invading their most intimate spaces.[65] As I explore in the pages that follow, white women organized their own reform groups to "uplift" indigenous women, an effort that focused primarily on indigenous homes and bodies.

By the late nineteenth century one phase of colonization—marked by the takeover of land, the forced relocation or dispersal of many indigenous groups, a drastic decrease in population, and the reduction of most indigenous people to a state of dependence—had ended, and another was about to begin. Despite the fact that white settlers had gained access to nearly all the land on each continent by the end of the nineteenth century and isolated indigenous peoples on remote missions and reservations, colonizers still regarded them, literally, as "the Indian problem" and "the Aboriginal problem." In an era of nation building in each country white officials and reformers puzzled over the place of indigenous peoples in the new nations they were creating.

Gender and the intimate would again figure significantly in the solutions both male administrators and female reformers proposed to the "problem" of indigenous people. The gender systems still practiced by some indigenous peoples became crucial markers of difference—or more particularly, of inferiority—that justified conquest, segregation, exclusion, and transformation. The intimate lives of indigenous people—the ways they cared for and raised their children, their dwellings, their sexuality, their marriage practices, their gender relations, even the ways they adorned their bodies and styled their hair—eventually came under the scrutiny and condemnation of their colonizers. By the late nineteenth century many white Americans and Australians deemed these indigenous intimacies to be an impediment to the complete colonization of these peoples and thus designed new policies that included interference into these most intimate aspects of indigenous lives, including the removal and institutionalization of children. This new phase would build on earlier efforts by Christian missionaries to make incursions into the intimate spaces of indigenous families. In the name of fully assimilating or absorbing indigenous people into the emerging American and Australian nations, governments in each country enacted new policies designed to remove indigenous children from their families and communities and to place them in new institutions.

Chapter 2

Designing Indigenous Child Removal Policies

There have been times in the past when the most dreaded enemy of our people were the Indians. . . . The cruelties and the savage fiendishness of their treatment of our frontier settlers has been exceeded only by the brutality and fierceness with which we have retaliated upon them. Fortunately, for all concerned, this period of warfare is probably practically at an end. . . . The hateful adage that found currency in the army, that "the only good Indian is a dead Indian," has been fruitful of harm, discreditable to our Christianity, and a reflection upon our national magnanimity. This, however, is ceasing to be a dominant force in our vocabulary, and it is coming to be generally recognized that the Indians are entitled to consideration and kind treatment. • THOMAS J. MORGAN, commissioner of Indian affairs (1889–93), "Our Red Neighbors," *Baptist Home Mission Monthly* 16, no. 6 (June 1894)

In the late nineteenth century, government officials in both the United States and Australia devised new policies for indigenous peoples: "assimilation" in the United States and "protection" in Australia. As can be seen by Commissioner Morgan's quote, officials often proclaimed that they were ushering in a new age of dealing fairly and kindly with the remaining indigenous inhabitants.[1] Yet these new policies actually entailed one of the most draconian measures possible: the removal of indigenous children from their kin and communities to be raised in distant institutions. Instead of breaking with the past use of violence and force, these new approaches are best seen as part of a continuum of colonizing approaches, all aimed ultimately at extinguishing indigenous people's claims to their remaining land.[2] As the anthropologist Ann Laura Stoler finds, "The politics of compassion was not an oppositional assault on empire but a fundamental element of it"; the "production and harnessing of sentiment" comprised a key "technology of the colonial state."[3]

In both countries, government officials and reformers used a remarkably similar language to justify their policies. They routinely asserted that the removal of indigenous children from their families would "save" the children from lives of backwardness and poverty in their "camps" and "civilize" and make them "useful" in Australian and American societies. Authorities also warned that if children were not removed, indigenous people would become a "burden" or a "menace" to their emerging nations. Just underneath this articulated layer of justification lay a bedrock of concerns about defining and building the nation—as white, Christian, and modern. Policy makers regarded the surviving indigenous populations as standing in the way of national unity, modernity, and progress and envisioned child removal as a means to complete the colonization of indigenous peoples. Significantly, whereas U.S. authorities focused primarily on culturally assimilating Indian children, many Australian officials promoted the biological absorption of Aboriginal children, what they termed "breeding out the colour."

The Genesis of Indigenous Child Removal as Federal Policy in the United States

The systematic removal of Indian children began in earnest with the rise of U.S. assimilation policy in the 1880s. Many reformers and government officials sought a solution to the seemingly intractable "Indian problem," that is, the continued militant resistance to colonization by some Indian tribes and the growing impoverishment and dependence on the government of many other Indian peoples. Through the removal of Indian children to distant boarding schools, along with the individual allotment of communally held land and the suppression of native religious practices, reformers and officials hoped American Indians would be assimilated into the mainstream of society. "There is but one policy possible if we are to do the Indians any good," editorialized one newspaper in Illinois, "and that is to divide them up and get one Indian family away from another and get them mixed up with white people."[4]

Historians trace the origins of a system of government-run boarding schools to two main sources: army officer Richard Henry Pratt's "experiment" with Indian prisoners of war and a new reform movement in the late nineteenth century that regarded military solutions to the so-called Indian problem as ineffective and cruel. In 1875 the U.S. government rounded up seventy-one men and two women from the Kiowas, Comanches, and Cheyennes who had participated in the Red River War and incarcerated them at Fort Marion in St. Augustine, Florida, under the command of Pratt. Pratt decided to "rehabilitate" the prisoners by requiring them to undergo military discipline, Christian teaching, and education in the English language and other subjects. He selected ten of the men, cut their hair, and dressed them in military uniforms. Within two weeks he had shorn all of the male prisoners, replaced all of their native dress with soldiers' uniforms, and begun conducting daily military drills. White women in St. Augustine volunteered to teach the prisoners English and to proselytize them in Christianity. Eventually, in 1878, Pratt arranged for seventeen young men, all of whom were in their late teens or early twenties, to be sent to Hampton Institute, a school that Gen. Samuel Armstrong had established for newly freed African American slaves.[5]

From this "experiment" in rehabilitating his prisoners, Pratt contended, "We have been told there are 35,000 or 40,000 [Indian] children to look after. If we place these children in our American lines, we shall break up all the Indian there is in them in a very short time. We must get them into America and keep them in."[6] Due to Pratt's apparent success, the secretary of the interior, Carl Schurz, gave Pratt special orders to bring fifty Indian children from the Missouri River agencies at Fort Berthold, Standing Rock, Cheyenne River, Crow Creek, Lower Brulé, and Yankton to Hampton Institute. He returned with forty boys and nine girls. (From 1878 to 1888, Hampton Institute brought 320 boys and 147 girls from twenty-seven tribes, each for three years of

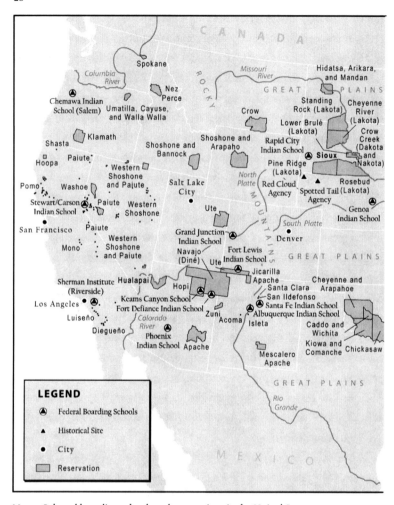

Map 1. Selected boarding schools and reservations in the United States, ca. 1900.

education.)[7] In 1879, with new authority from the government and two hundred Indian pupils, Pratt opened his own school, Carlisle Institute in Carlisle, Pennsylvania, which became the most famous of the boarding schools. Pratt stipulated that Indian students stay for at least five years at Carlisle. Throughout Pratt's twenty-four-year career as Carlisle's superintendent, he institutionalized 4,903 Indian children from seventy-seven different tribes.[8]

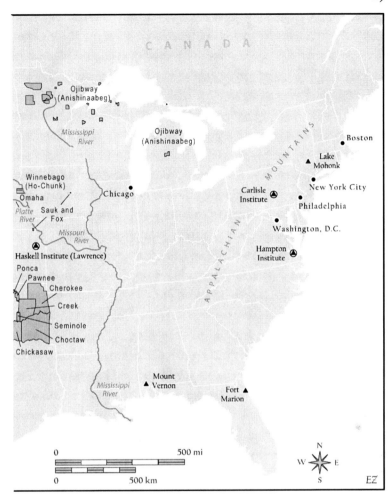

Drawn by Ezra Zeitler.

At the same time that Pratt began his experiment, a number of other white reformers took up the Indian cause. In 1879, for example, the Women's National Indian Association (WNIA) formed to advocate for American Indians; male reformers followed suit in 1882 when they established the Indian Rights Association (IRA). In 1883 reformers, dubbing themselves "Friends of the Indian," began to meet annually at Lake Mohonk in New York to discuss and coordinate campaigns for Indian reform. These reformers, many of whom had been raised in abolitionist families or cut their teeth on other nineteenth-century reforms, were moved deeply by growing accounts of atrocities committed against Indian peoples. Two events in particular nurtured this growing reform movement: an 1879 speaking tour by Chief Standing Bear of the Poncas, in which he recounted the unjust and tragic relocation of his band from Nebraska to Oklahoma, and the publication in 1881 of Helen Hunt Jackson's *A Century of Dishonor*, which documented a litany of injustices and massacres against Indian peoples by the federal government. These reformers challenged the federal government's use of military force against Indian peoples and instead encouraged the government to adopt what they believed to be a more humane policy: assimilation.[9]

Many of these reformers identified education as a necessary ingredient in their program of assimilation, but most did not regard setting up day schools within Indian communities as a viable option. As the commissioner of Indian affairs put it in 1886, "The greatest difficulty is experienced in freeing the children attending day schools from the language and habits of their untutored and oftentimes savage parents. When they return to their homes at night, and on Saturdays and Sundays, and are among their old surroundings, they relapse more or less into their former moral and mental stupor."[10] The government turned to on-reservation boarding schools, but even these did not seem to satisfy administrators' desires to control the education and socialization of American Indian children. Officials still complained of the bad influence of parents and tribal communities on their pupils.

Thus these reform organizations called on the federal government, which held sole responsibility for all Indian affairs, to enact Pratt's vision of off-reservation boarding schools; over the next several decades, Congress appropriated funds for just such a purpose. The Bureau of Indian Affairs (BIA) established a network of institutions, starting with day schools on reservations for the youngest children, who would then ideally graduate to on-reservation boarding schools, and then attend off-reservation boarding schools. Usually government authorities aimed to remove the children from the ages of eight to ten for a period of five to ten years, when they would normally be educated into the ways of their own people, and socialize them instead in Christian, middle-class, white mores.

In the year 1885 alone the government opened twenty-seven off-reservation boarding schools. (Unlike Carlisle and Hampton, however, these schools were all in the American West.) By 1902 the BIA had established 154 boarding schools (including twenty-five off-reservation schools) and 154 day schools for about 21,500 Native American children. Of these children, about 17,700 attended some sort of boarding school. There were also still a number of mission schools operated by various religious organizations that contracted with the federal government to carry out the government's educational mission.[11] By 1911 the numbers had shifted somewhat. Now there were 221 day schools and 98 boarding schools (twenty-two of them off the reservation). Two more boarding schools, Genoa and Grand Junction, closed that year. Although there were fewer boarding schools, roughly the same number of children attended them. In 1911 17,865 children were enrolled in boarding schools, exceeding the official capacity of 15,512. (By contrast, the day schools were underenrolled; only 6,119 Indian children attended day schools, although there was room for 7,589.) An estimated 5,000 Indian children attended mission schools and 4,460 went to public school.[12] Not every Indian child went away to boarding school, but Frederick Hoxie asserts that at least among Plains Indians, "by the early 1900s, it was almost impossible for a family to avoid sending its children away for an education, the principal goal of which was to separate the children from their traditions and their past."[13]

The Origins of Aboriginal Child Removal Policies in Australia

In Australia in the late nineteenth century Aboriginal people were no longer engaged in warfare against their colonizers, as they were in the United States, yet Australian authorities still confronted an "Aboriginal problem." Economic depression and shrinking sources of self-support for Aborigines across the continent drove increasing numbers of Aborigines into dire poverty in need of mission or government support. As in the United States, officials and reformers sought a means to reduce indigenous people's dependence on government aid.[14] Moreover, Australian authorities believed that their Aboriginal problem was exacerbated by an increase in the numbers of so-called half-castes, people of mixed Aboriginal and European (or Asian) descent. To address their indigenous "problem," colonial and state authorities responded by crafting new "protection" policies. Unlike in the United States, where the federal government took responsibility for Indian affairs, jurisdiction over Aboriginal affairs fell to each of the Australian colonies or states, with the commonwealth eventually responsible for the Northern Territory. The first colonies to enact protective legislation for indigenous people were Victoria in 1886 and Queensland in 1897; each developed a distinctive model for managing indigenous people and removing their children. After Australian federation, New South Wales adopted a policy modeled on Victoria's in 1909, while Western Australia (1905), South Australia (1911), and the Northern Territory (1911) followed the Queensland model.[15] Structurally, Victoria and New South Wales each administered their policies through a board for the protection of Aborigines, whereas the other states each appointed a chief protector of Aborigines. By 1911 all states except Tasmania—which claimed (mistakenly) that it no longer had an Aboriginal population—had developed separate welfare systems for Aboriginal children.[16]

Administrators in each state and territory created a two-pronged approach to Aboriginal affairs, based on the division they drew between so-called full-bloods, whom they believed to be dying out, and half-castes. For "full-bloods," the new protection policies entailed strict segregation from white residents (and in some states from "half-castes" as well). Officials routinely justified this as a humanitarian approach to protect Aborigines from the harmful influences of Europeans, but those covered by the Aboriginal acts led severely restricted lives; additionally they were ineligible for citizenship and its privileges (including pensions and maternity allowances).

Policy differences in the states revolved primarily around how to deal with "half-castes." Victoria's and New South Wales's boards for the protection of Aborigines developed policies of dispersal: moving people of mixed descent and an alleged preponderance of "European blood" off of reserves and seeking to "merge" their children into the general population. Such Aborigines of mixed descent would thus cease to be the responsibility of state governments. According to Anna Haebich, Victoria's Aborigines Protection Act of 1886 "forced all persons of 'mixed-race' under thirty-four [years of age] . . . off the stations and missions, regardless of ties of kinship and country or need, and prohibited them from having any further contact with the people who remained behind."[17] In 1893 the New South Wales government built a dormitory for girls on its Warangesda station and until 1909 removed roughly three hundred girls from their families to the institution. At the same time, they provided incentives for the girls' families to leave the mission, offering them free railway tickets to leave the area.[18]

The Queensland model, by contrast, through the Aboriginal Protection and Restriction of the Sale of Opium Act of 1897, empowered a chief protector of Aborigines to remove *all* indigenous people—"full-bloods" and "half-castes," adults and children—to segregated government settlements and missions. (This may have been the intention, but, as Rosalind Kidd points out, administrators never had the funds to implement this policy fully. Moreover, local male settlers who depended on the labor of Aboriginal people or cohabited with Aboriginal girls and women refused to cooperate.) Once Aboriginal families had been removed to the settlement, their children, usually by the age of four, were to be separated from their parents to live in sex-segregated dormitories and later sent out to work (at about age fourteen). J. W. Bleakley, chief protector from 1913 to 1942, became a primary proponent of Queensland's segregation approach. Rather than try to disperse those of mixed descent, Bleakley sought to bring them under the control of the act, to isolate them, and to ensure that they would not mix with whites.[19]

Western Australia's Aborigines Act of 1905 closely paralleled Queensland's legislation, but it was implemented quite differently, beginning in 1915 under the chief protectorship of Auber Octavius Neville. As was done in Queensland, Neville focused on rounding up all Aboriginal people on native settlements and missions, separating children from their parents, training them for domestic and menial labor, and then sending them out as adolescents to work. Unlike Bleakley, however, Neville favored the eventual "absorption" of part-Aboriginal people into the white population, rather than their segregation. His policy diverged from that in Victoria and New South Wales because he sought to maintain control over people of mixed descent for as long as possible.[20] In 1936, for example, due to his agitation, an amendment to the act extended the chief protector's guardianship over Aboriginal children from age sixteen to twenty-one. Neville thought even this was too young and that guardianship should continue indefinitely.[21]

The Northern Territory most resembled Western Australia in its approach to Aboriginal affairs. Under the jurisdiction of the commonwealth government beginning in 1911, its ordinances empowered a chief protector to segregate "full-bloods" on isolated reserves and to summarily remove "half-caste" children to be absorbed into the white populace. Administrators only half-heartedly implemented this policy until Dr. Cecil Cook became the Northern Territory's chief protector of Aborigines in 1927. Serving in this role until 1938, Cook required the fingerprinting and medical examination of all Aboriginal people, who were then issued identification "dog tags" (as Aboriginal people called them) to wear as necklaces.[22] For "half-castes," Chief Protector Cook crafted a policy in line with Western Australia Chief Protector Neville's absorption plan. He warned, "Unless the black population is speedily absorbed into the white, the process will soon be reversed, and in 50 years, or a little later, the white population of the Northern Territory will be absorbed into the black."[23] To promote the speedy absorption of "half-castes," Cook stipulated that "illegitimate children of not less than fifty per cent white blood [should be] removed from the aboriginal camps at an early age and placed in Institutions where they [will be] reared at European standards and given statutory state school education."[24]

At first some state legislation required that only Aboriginal children who were neglected, unprotected, or orphaned could be removed. For example, under its provision for custody of children, the Victorian Aborigines Act of 1890 allowed that "the Governor may order the removal of any aboriginal child *neglected by its parents, or left unprotected* . . . to an industrial or reformatory school." The act further provided that "any half-caste child *being an orphan* and *not otherwise required by the manager of a station* may be transferred to an orphanage or to any of the branches of the Dept. for Neglected Children at the direction of the Board."[25]

In some states, too, legislators at first empowered administrators to remove children only through existing child welfare legislation. In 1909 the New South Wales Aborigines Protection Act gave the Aborigines Protection Board the power to remove any children deemed neglected under its more general child welfare legislation, the Neglected Children and Juvenile Offenders Act of 1905.[26] In South Australia officials began to remove a few "half-caste" children in the early 1900s under the provisions of the 1895 State Children's Act on the grounds that they were neglected. As with non-Aboriginal children, authorities had to have a court order to remove Aboriginal children under this act.[27]

However, administrators often chafed at the restrictions imposed on them to prove neglect and lobbied for new legislation that would enable them to remove Aboriginal children more easily. In South Australia in 1911, the Aborigines Act did away with the requirement to obtain a court order to prove neglect of an Aboriginal child; instead, the new legislation gave the chief protector of Aborigines legal guardianship over every Aboriginal and "half-caste" child.[28] Similarly, the New South Wales Board protested that its powers to remove Aboriginal children were too limited under the initial legislation. Thus the 1915 Aborigines

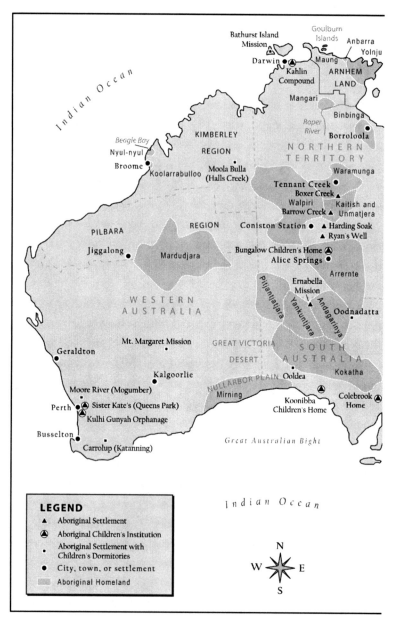

Map 2. Selected institutions for Aboriginal children, Aboriginal settlements and missions, and traditional Aboriginal territories in Australia.

Drawn by Ezra Zeitler.

Protection Amending Act empowered the board to remove children from their families without having to obtain a court order. Now the order of an Aboriginal reserve manager or a policeman would suffice to remove an Aboriginal child.[29] By 1915 the Victorian Aborigines Act too had dropped any references to neglected or orphaned children. It stipulated merely that the governor could remove Aboriginal children simply for their "better care, custody, and education."[30] One state, Tasmania, chose a different route from the others. While the government there did remove indigenous children, it did so under the existing child welfare legislation, including the Infants Welfare Act of 1935. In this case, authorities were more likely to foster out Aboriginal children to white families than to institutionalize them.[31]

Indigenous child removal policy in Australia differed from that in the United States in several key ways. Unlike in the United States, where authorities counted the numbers of Indian pupils in the boarding schools and recorded their names and backgrounds, authorities in Australia compiled little documentation of their endeavors, perhaps because in many cases they intended the children to be "absorbed" with no record of their Aboriginal past. Thus historians have had to estimate the numbers of Aboriginal children taken from their parents and communities. Peter Read figures that one in every six or seven Aboriginal children in New South Wales were taken from their families; he and Coral Edwards calculate that there are about 100,000 people of Aboriginal descent living today who don't know their families or communities due to these past policies.[32]

In the United States, ideally authorities would send an Indian child away to boarding school at around the age of ten. In Australia, by contrast, although there was disagreement and variation among different states, most officials recommended removing children at much younger ages. In 1913 Queensland Chief Protector Bleakley asserted, "Quadroon children should be taken from their mothers as soon as possible . . . at three years of age."[33] The secretary of the State Children's Council in South Australia believed "they should be taken away directly they are born. If they are in a wurlie [an Aboriginal shelter] a week it is bad for them, but it is fatal for them to remain there a year."[34] In contrast, some officials believed that taking infants and toddlers from their parents was particularly cruel. In 1927 an inspector of the Aboriginal Station at Lake Tyers in Victoria asserted, "Whilst probably it would be in the best interest of the children if they were removed as infants to ordinary institutions or to white foster homes, . . . such a policy would be so inhuman [*sic*] from the point of view of the parents that it cannot be contemplated."[35] This official seems to have been in the minority, however. As administrators focused more and more on the color of Aboriginal children and on permanently absorbing "nearly white" children into the white population, they justified the removal of ever younger children.

Here was another crucial difference between policies in the United States and Australia. U.S. authorities aimed to remove children usually for three to five years (though sometimes children were institutionalized for up to a decade), whereas many Australian state governments intended Aboriginal children to be permanently removed from their parents, homes, and communities.

Justifying Indigenous Child Removal

Despite these important differences, it is intriguing to consider the overwhelming similarities between the policies: the overriding decision to separate indigenous children from their families and communities for the stated purpose of being "assimilated" or "absorbed" into the white population. In addition to sharing a *policy* of indigenous child removal, officials on both sides of the Pacific Ocean used remarkably similar rhetoric to justify the removal of children, sometimes appealing to a humanitarian impulse and at other times responding to widespread fears of social unrest or pragmatic economic concerns.

Under criticism from humanitarian movements within their own countries and abroad, officials in both countries were anxious to distance themselves from the overtly violent methods of the past.[36] Therefore, they presented their new policies of protection and assimilation as benevolent approaches that broke once and for all with the harsher methods of the past. Thomas J. Morgan, commissioner of Indian affairs from 1889 to 1893, traced the genesis of this new approach to the presidency of Ulysses S. Grant (1869–77) and his "peace policy," "the essential idea of which was that the Government more fully than ever before was to recognize the Indians as its wards, towards whom it was to act as a guardian, treating them as orphan and dependent children, not with harshness, severity and military subjection, but with kindness, patience, gentleness and helpfulness." Morgan believed that "this was a great change for the better and marked an epoch in" the government's relationship with the Indians.[37]

In Australia some authorities presented new protection policies as an abrupt departure from the violence of the past. In Queensland lawmakers supposedly adopted their new policy of protection in 1897 in reaction to the government investigator Archibald Meston's 1895 inquiry into and subsequent report on the conditions of Aboriginal people throughout the colony. Meston blamed the actions of "unscrupulous and degraded whites" for the cruel and desperate conditions many Aborigines faced. He presented the idea of segregated reserves, overseen by white authorities, as a more benevolent approach to Aboriginal affairs.[38]

Thus, in both countries, reformers and policy makers often insisted that they were engaged in a humanitarian enterprise to rescue indigenous children from the supposedly backward environments in which they lived. Rather than robbing Indian families of their children, Commissioner Morgan claimed the government was offering opportunity, rights, and privileges to them. He wrote in the *Baptist Home Mission Monthly*, for example, that Indian babies, as compared to other American babies, were born as "alien[s], . . . shut off from opportunity, predetermined to degradation." Morgan claimed righteously that no Indian child should be excluded from "the inestimable rights and privileges of American citizenship" and instead should be given "an opportunity for the development of his better nature."[39] A resolution passed at the Indian Institute for schoolteachers on reservations and in boarding schools invoked powerfully resonant terms—*slavery* and *freedom*—to justify the schools, claiming, "The true object of the Indian schools and of the Indian management is to accomplish the release of the individual Indian from the slavery of tribal life, and to establish him in the self-supporting freedom of citizenship and a home in the life of the nation."[40]

In Australia officials likewise framed their efforts to remove indigenous children as benevolent acts of Christian charity. In 1911 the South Australia protector cited the case of an "almost white" nine-year-old girl. "To have left her to the inevitable fate of all half-caste girls brought up in the blacks' camps in the interior would have been, to say the least of it, cruel," he asserted.[41] Thus administrators turned the tables: it was not a brutality to remove children from their mothers and communities; rather, it was cruel to let them stay with their kin. Similar to white American officials, white Australians often presented the removal of children in positive terms—as an opportunity. For example, the minister of the interior stated in 1933, "Children who have only a slight percentage of colored blood in their veins should have the opportunity of becoming white citizens."[42]

American and Australian policies differed on the issue of educating indigenous children. American officials claimed, in fact, that they were rescuing Indian children in order to educate them. Commissioner Morgan, for example, proclaimed, "Education . . . is the Indians' only salvation. With it they will become honorable, useful, happy citizens of a great republic, sharing on equal terms in all its blessings. Without it, they are doomed either to destruction or to hopeless degradation."[43] By contrast, officials in Australia rarely justified removal of children on the basis of needing to educate them, but the issue did come up when idealistic missionaries and reformers challenged the government's failure to provide an adequate education for removed children. One letter from the prime minister's secretary to a reformer clarifies the government's racialized position on education for Aboriginal children in the

Northern Territory: "Half-castes are collected into special Government Homes where education is imparted by trained teachers. The standard of education varies according to the preponderance of aboriginal or European blood in the child. Quadroons and Octoroons usually have more intelligence than cross-breeds with a preponderance of aboriginal blood, and are accordingly educated to a higher standard than the latter. The standard of education is such as will ensure that the half-caste is able to take his place in the community and to engage in the industries carried on in the Territory."[44]

Colonial officials' rhetoric of rescuing and providing opportunity to indigenous children depended on harshly stigmatizing indigenous communities and families. After all, from what did Indian and Aboriginal children need to be rescued? Commissioner Morgan contended, "If they [Indian babies] grow up on Indian reservations removed from civilization, without advantages of any kind, surrounded by barbarians, trained from childhood to love the unlovely and to rejoice in the unclean; associating all their highest ideals of manhood and womanhood with fathers who are degraded and mothers who are debased, their ideas of human life, will, of necessity, be deformed, their characters be warped, and their lives distorted." Appealing to missionaries and humanitarians, Morgan claimed, "The only possible way in which they can be saved from the awful doom that hangs over them is for the strong arm of the nation to reach out, take them in their infancy and place them in its fostering schools, surrounding them with an atmosphere of civilization, maturing them in all that is good, and developing them into men and women, instead of allowing them to grow up as barbarians and savages."[45]

In both the United States and Australia authorities developed a kind of colonial phrasebook that fiercely disparaged indigenous communities. Commonly, they employed the word *camps* to refer to nearly all communities of indigenous peoples. Such a usage connoted lawlessness, disorder, impermanence, and degeneracy, in contrast to the orderliness and control of white institutions. For example, Morgan contrasted the idle, systemless camp with the industrious systematized school. "In the

4. An Aboriginal "camp" on the Richmond River in New South Wales, an original glass plate from the Tyrell Collection taken between 1880 and 1910. In contrast to figure 5, from the same collection, this image may have been meant to convey the supposed "backwardness" of camp life as compared to the mission. By permission of the National Library of Australia, NLA.PIC-VN4085288.

camp, they know but an alien language; in the school, they learn to understand and speak English," he wrote. "In the camp, they form habits of idleness; in the school, they acquire habits of industry. In the camp, they listen only to stories of war, rapine, bloodshed; in the school, they become familiar with the great and good characters of history. In the camp, life is without meaning and labor without system; in the school, noble purposes are awakened, ambition aroused, and time and labor are systematized."[46] Similarly officials in Australia identified camps as "demoralizing." Western Australia Chief Protector Neville justified Aboriginal child removal by raising the familiar specter of "hundreds of [half-caste illegitimate children] living in [Aboriginal] camps close to the country town under revolting conditions. It is infinitely better to

5. An Aboriginal mission in New South Wales, an original glass plate from the Tyrell Collection taken between 1880 and 1910. In contrast to figure 4, this image conveys the sense of order that settlers believed they would impart to Aboriginal people by removing their children from "camps." By permission of the National Library of Australia, NLA.PIC-VN4085278.

take a child from its mother, and put it in an institution, where it will be looked after, than to allow it to be brought up subject to the influence of such camps."[47]

Before and after Europeans invaded indigenous homelands, Aboriginal people and many Indian people *did* often move their communities from place to place—within their clearly defined territories—as part of their subsistence strategies. They carefully selected and often returned to their "camps," however, and often had strict rules governing the placement of dwellings within their movable villages.[48] Ironically, by driving indigenous people from their lands and disrupting their traditional subsistence activities, officials had in fact created the very destitution that they so derided. In Australia, where the government never engaged in treaty making or designated substantial reservations for Aborigines, large numbers of impoverished Aboriginal people who had been "dispersed" formed communities of "fringe dwellers" on the outskirts of towns. Rather than assuring that Aboriginal people had adequate land and a place to establish their communities unmolested from white trespassers, authorities deemed them derelict and advocated taking their children away.[49]

The rhetoric of rescue also rested on beliefs that indigenous families were failing to take care of their children. In 1911, when Leo Crane, the superintendent of the Hopi Reservation, removed fifty-one girls and eighteen boys from the Hopi village of Hotevilla (all the children remaining who had survived a measles epidemic that had decimated the village earlier that year), he wrote indignantly, "Nearly all had trachoma. It was winter, and not one of those children had clothing above rags; some were nude."[50] Crane deemed the children's diseased and bedraggled condition proof of parental neglect and the necessity of removing them from their families, not an indictment of the government for failing to provide the ailing and impoverished Hopis with appropriate aid and support.

In Australia officials used similar justifications and routinely asserted that they took only "neglected" children, not children who were well cared for by their parents. Queensland Chief Protector Bleakley, for example, explained that on his reserves, "Not every child has to be handed over to the charge of the dormitory system. If a mother is able to take care of her children, she is allowed to do so. If she neglects them, we have the power to take them from her, and put them into dormitories."[51] For many settlers and authorities, however, indigeneity itself became inextricably associated with neglect. A police officer at Oodnadatta in South Australia reported to the chief protector, "There are certainly a number of half-caste children in this district, but as, with the exception of a few, they are living with the parents and are generally speaking, very well looked after, I would not consider them neglected." Yet he noted that other whites in the area "would consider any half-caste child outside the Mission neglected."[52] Many authorities also routinely claimed that Aboriginal people particularly rejected mixed-race children. The anthropologist Daisy Bates, for example, wrote about a "half-caste" girl named Adelina, whose "mother was . . . easily induced to part with [her child] to the Mission" because half-castes were allegedly not welcome among Aborigines.[53]

As the South Australia police officer made clear, the notion that indigenous children were neglected by their families often did not hold up under scrutiny. When one Aboriginal man, John Watson, applied for legal custody of the son of his deceased sister, his petition was denied even though officials reported that Watson "and his wife are a fine type of Half Caste and to all intents and purposes are living as white people in a four roomed stone house on 150 acres of privately owned land. Watson is a splendid shearer and makes big money in that employment. The . . . children are being brought up as Methodists." Despite this glowing account, officials ruled, "Although in this case it appears that Mr Watson is a far better guardian for the child than [the white father] it must be remembered that the application is to remove a legitimate child from a white man, and place it under a half-caste aboriginal."[54] Australian officials' claim that Aborigines rejected or neglected "half-caste" children, ostensibly because they were half-white, seems to have been true only in a small number of cases. Elsie Roughsey, a Lardil woman from Mornington Island, explains that families often violently disapproved if their children refused to marry the partners they had chosen for them from within their kin group. If an Aboriginal group could identify the white father of a "half-caste" child, it is likely that child might be rejected. However, Roughsey points out, "should a girl become pregnant while working or visiting on the mainland, the parents accept it as just 'one of those things that happens.'" Thus "the anonymity of the father apparently allowed for non-ambivalent acceptance of the baby into the family."[55]

Ignoring the close-knit extended families and clans from which indigenous children came, reformers and authorities in both the United

States and Australia often further justified indigenous child removal by categorizing many of the children they removed as orphans in need of a home and family. One missionary, Violet Turner, recounted that when "David's" mother died of pneumonia, "the little baby was left to the mercies of anyone in the camp who cared to attend him. His father went off on the usual 'walkabout' after the funeral, caring nothing for the welfare of his two children. . . . The sad little baby grew ill through neglect. But the missionaries went down to the camp, got the permission of the old men, and carried both children back to the Home."[56]

In many cases the children were not orphans at all but either the offspring of unwed Aboriginal parents or "half-castes." In a letter to his superiors, Alice Springs Government Resident Stan Cawood wrote, "[The] suggestion of treating the children of unmarried [Aboriginal] parents as orphans is, I understand, at present in vogue in Queensland."[57] A Victorian administrator informed his superior that a "little Half-Caste boy" had been taken from his mother and "brought to the Orphan Asylum at Brighton, which will be of great good to him, as he never will no [*sic*] anything about the evil ways of the Blacks."[58]

Even in cases where indigenous children had no living parents they were often taken care of by other members of their extended family and were not in need of removal to an orphanage. Intricate indigenous kinship systems assured that no child was ever really orphaned. Buludja, a Mangari woman from the Roper River area near Arnhem Land in the Northern Territory, explained to her white interviewer, "You whites have only one father, but we often have several. . . . All my father's brothers are my fathers, and all my mother's sisters my mothers." She continued, "That is why we call mother's sister's children sisters, whereas you call them cousins."[59] Similarly, among the Navajos, according to Left Handed, "'Mother' refers to a great many other women besides one's real mother. In fact, wishing to distinguish his mother from among all these other women, who stand in different relationships to him and are also called mother, a Navaho must state explicitly, 'my real mother,' or use some such . . . phrase as, 'she who gave me birth.'"[60] Some settlers observed and supported such extended kin relations. A station (ranch) owner in Victoria told a royal commission there, "I do not think it at all desirable to board out the orphan [Aboriginal] children—in fact it would be very difficult to find orphans—as soon as one father dies another claims the child—there are always relations that claim them."[61] Basing their standard on a nuclear patriarchal family model, however, most authorities routinely regarded indigenous family arrangements as unsuitable.

American and Australian reformers and authorities tried to justify their emerging policies not only by appealing to humanitarian impulses but also by playing off widespread fears of indigenous people as a "menace," a term found as frequently in the rhetoric of authorities as is "camp." Here they acted out a common "tension of empire," between "a form of authority simultaneously predicated on incorporation and distancing." Authorities blithely moved from the "inclusionary impulses" of benevolent humanitarian rhetoric to the "exclusionary practices" of segregating indigenous peoples and declaring them a menace.[62] For example, the Aborigines' Friends' Association worried that when Aboriginal youth left school, if they were "allowed to wander at their own sweet will, no attempt being made to direct their energies into proper channels, . . . they [would] grow up to be a menace to the community by living idle, useless, disorderly lives."[63] Similarly, Commissioner Morgan asserted, "To leave these thousands of [Indian] children to grow up in ignorance, superstition, barbarism, and even savagery, is to maintain a perpetual menace to our western civilization and to fasten upon the rapidly developing States of the West . . . an incubus that will hinder their progress, arrest their growth, threaten their peace, and be continually, as long as it remains, a source of unrest and perplexity. To educate them . . . is to remove this burden, this source of perplexity, this menace."[64]

As Morgan's statement shows, alongside the specter of indigenous children becoming a "menace" to society, officials also raised concerns that they would become a "burden," perpetual dependents on government assistance. Herbert Welsh, president of the IRA, queried, "Shall our people let these poor, unhappy creatures remain in our midst—a burden and a care—denied the privilege of acquiring our language and the education in agriculture necessary to support life?"[65] The protector of Aborigines in South Australia asserted in 1910, "If left to wander and grow up with the aborigines[, 'half-castes'] and their offspring will become an ever-increasing burden."[66]

Officials' notion that indigenous people placed a financial burden on society revealed an unwillingness to acknowledge the devastating effects of colonialism on indigenous societies. Obviously, if indigenous people had held on to their lands and been able to continue to subsist as they had for millennia, they would not have become dependent. Moreover, despite a century of violence, dispossession, and paternalism, many indigenous people had adapted to the new social and economic order. For example, in the 1880s a group of disgruntled Aboriginal people who had lived at the Maloga mission took up residence at a nearby government reserve, which they named Cumeroogunga, meaning "my country." Cumeroogunga also attracted Aboriginal families who had been dubbed "half-castes" and exiled from other Aboriginal reserves in the area.[67] It was here that Margaret Tucker's mother, Theresa Clements, grew up, and where Tucker spent some of her childhood. By 1908 Cumeroogunga was a "thriving village" of forty-six cottages, with its own shop, school, and church and nearly four hundred people, many of them farming their own individual blocks of land in addition to the communal farm. Because the small land base could not support all the people who lived there, many men worked for others in the Riverina pastoral stations as drovers, fencers, shearers, and harvesters while their families stayed home to hunt rabbits, fish, and cut timber to earn supplementary income. Despite their small acreage, Cumeroogunga residents created a prosperous wheat-farming community. In fact, up until 1910 Cumeroogunga residents enjoyed equal or greater success growing wheat than did their white neighbors.[68]

Yet the paternalism of government officials, combined with settlers' desire for the fertile land, undermined the efforts of the Cumeroogunga community. In 1907, claiming that the Cumeroogunga residents had improperly rented their land to outsiders, the Aborigines Protection Board of New South Wales revoked twenty of the community's individual holdings and installed European overseers to manage the community's farming efforts. Beginning in 1909, the board also enacted a dispersal policy to evict "half-castes" from the community. (Many became impoverished "fringe dwellers" who barely eked out a living in "camps" on the outskirts of towns.) As a result, Cumeroogunga's population was halved and increasing numbers of white Australians leased the community's lands in the 1920s. By 1959 the government had revoked all but eight hectares of the community's once thriving land base.[69] Essentially, the government, under pressure from white settlers, had turned independent, self-sufficient Aboriginal people into landless, impoverished outcasts who now were, indeed, a potential "burden" on society.

Similarly, after the American Revolution, the so-called Five Civilized Tribes of the southeastern United States—the Cherokees, Choctaws, Chickasaws, Creeks, and Seminoles—developed robust self-supporting communities in what remained of their homelands. The Cherokees, for example, designed a written language, began publishing their own newspaper, drafted their own constitution, and set up their own courts of law. A few Cherokees even adopted the plantation-style agriculture of the white southerners around them.[70] Still, white settlers hungered for the land of the Five Tribes, and eventually the government removed nearly all southeastern Indians to Indian Territory in present-day Oklahoma. Once there, despite internal conflicts left over from the removal and exacerbated by the Civil War, the Five Tribes rebuilt their self-sufficient communities on their new communally held lands in the West. Each tribe reestablished its own government, court of law, and school system. Some of the Five Tribes published their own bilingual newspapers. However, the passage of the Curtis Act in 1898, which abolished tribal governments in Indian Territory and required their land to be allotted, once again undermined the significant economic gains the Cherokees and other southeastern tribes had made once they were relocated.[71] If

Indians did indeed present a "burden" to the emerging nation, it was due in great part to government policies. In both the United States and Australia, government officials intervened to destroy the successes of these indigenous communities.

Explaining Indigenous Child Removal Policies

Given the remarkable similarities between government policies and rationales in both nations, it would seem that American and Australian authorities must have conferred with and influenced one another. I have found no evidence, however, that officials in the two countries were aware of each other's policies. American officials did not discuss or refer to Australian policy, and Australian officials seem to have known only the vague outlines of federal Indian policy in the United States. For example, in 1929, the minister of state for home affairs in Australia, when discussing a proposal to establish reserves for Aborigines in northern and central Australia, declared, "I think the Government would try to exercise control on the lines of the Indian Reservations in the United States and Canada."[72]

Australian officials did look to how other nations dealt with "the coloured problem." The 1937 Commonwealth and State Aboriginal Authorities Conference on Aboriginal Welfare, "realizing that the pursuit of this policy [of racial absorption of 'half-castes'] and its ultimate realization, unless subject to enlightened guidance, may result in racial conflict," explicitly recommended that the commonwealth "should take . . . steps . . . to obtain full information upon racial problems in America and South Africa." Interestingly, however, it was American experience with African Americans, not American Indians, that Australians looked to as a lesson. Northern Territory Chief Protector Cook worried, for example, that violence against Aborigines along the lines of the lynching of African Americans might take place if Aborigines were "elevated to a position almost equal to that of a white."[73] Nevertheless, if there was no direct exchange between Australian and American officials, there was a "modular quality" to "colonial perceptions and policies," as Ann Laura Stoler has noted, a kind of international lexicon of potential strategies for rule that circulated among colonial regimes.[74]

PRECEDENTS FOR INDIGENOUS CHILD REMOVAL

Both Australia and the United States acted on precedents within their own histories for removing children, some of which had a common origin in British law and administration. In the settler colony that became the United States the practice of separating Indian children from their families was common among warring Indian groups even before the invasion of Europeans. Many American Indian tribes took children captive during war parties, often as a means of replacing kin who had died or been killed. Often such captives became fully integrated into their captors' society.[75] However, once Europeans arrived on the scene, the nature of child removal changed. In the American Southwest early Spanish colonizers bought American Indian children from their native captors and seized children themselves from the Apaches, Navajos, and Comanches, primarily to work as servants and laborers in Spanish households. By the early nineteenth century, a brisk trade had developed with American Indian wholesalers selling captive native children to Spanish and Mexican traders on the Old Spanish Trail from Santa Fe to Utah. Thus Indian captives became commodified, valued more for their labor than for their replacement of family members. Nevertheless, following native traditions, captive children might be eventually incorporated into their new Spanish families.[76] Early colonizers also removed Indian children for the purposes of religious conversion. Franciscan friars in the Southwest and California targeted children for removal and conversion, as did some French Jesuit missionaries in the Great Lakes region and Upper Mississippi Valley.[77]

Compared to the Spanish, the English took very few Indian children into their households as servants or slaves, but they did sometimes remove children as part of their sporadic and small-scale efforts at religious conversion. The first two charters of the Virginia Company stipulated that the colonists (mostly of the Anglican faith) must engage in conversion of the Indians; the company offered ten pounds to every colonist who instructed an Indian boy in his or her home. The company also sent some Indian boys abroad to be schooled. The resistance of Indian parents to these practices, however (as well as Virginia's greater focus on commerce), limited the colonists' efforts. In New England, Puritan missionaries varied in their approaches toward converting Indian children to Christianity. In Massachusetts in the seventeenth century, the Reverend John Eliot founded nine Christian Indian villages, but he did not advocate the separation of children from their families.[78] At his school in Connecticut, however, in the late eighteenth century, the Reverend Eleazer Wheelock insisted that his Indian pupils be "taken out of the reach of their Parents, and out of the way of Indian examples, and kept in School under good Government and constant Instruction."[79]

In the nineteenth century early Mormon settlers in Utah also became involved in taking Indian children into their homes and communities, initially "redeeming" dislocated and enslaved Indian (mostly Paiute) children by purchasing them from Indian (mostly Ute) or Mexican slave traders. Eventually Mormon settlers started buying Indian children directly from their parents to fulfill the Mormon spiritual aim of "saving" the Indians. In 1851, in fact, the Mormon leader Brigham Young advised his followers to "buy up the Lamanite [Indian] children as fast as they could, and educate them and teach them the gospel." However, it is clear that the Mormons also intended to use the children as laborers, as the Spanish had. An 1852 law, the Act for the Relief of Indian Slaves and Prisoners, provided that Indian children could be indentured to Mormon families. Young promoted such an act so that "in return for favors and expense which may have been incurred on [the Indians'] account, service should be considered due." In other words, the Indian children were required to pay back their purchase price through laboring for their Mormon family for up to twenty years. Young justified the Mormon purchase of Indian children by claiming, "This may be said to present a new feature in the traffic of human beings; it is essentially purchasing

them into freedom instead of slavery; but it is not the low servile drudgery of Mexican slavery, . . . to be raised among beings scarcely superior
to themselves, but where they could find that consideration pertaining
not only to civilized, but humane and benevolent society."[80]

The Mormons established a precedent that would be followed by the
federal government in the years to come. On the surface they claimed
to be acting out of humanitarian and religious ideals to provide a better
life for destitute and dislocated children, but ultimately many Mormon
benefactors may have simply regarded their Indian charges as a source
of labor. As the historian Sondra Jones reveals, Indian children "were
seldom treated as equals to their white [Mormon] brothers and sisters,"
rarely received any education, and were often traded, bartered, or given
away by their Mormon buyers. One Mormon settler, Jacob Hamblin,
explained that he purchased an Indian boy in 1854 to "let a good man
have him that would make him useful."[81] As we shall see, making Indians and Aborigines "useful" became a primary concern in the removal
of indigenous children.

Settlers in the new state of California also took part in schemes to
remove Indian children to fill labor shortages. Shortly after the United
States took California from Mexico, the new California State Legislature
of 1850 enacted the Act for the Government and Protection of Indians,
which, despite its altruistic title, amounted to allowing Indian children
to be enslaved. In 1860 the state government amended and strengthened
the original act, empowering judges throughout the state to "bind and
put out [any Indian child under the age of fifteen years] as apprentices,
to trades, husbandry, or other Employments." It also allowed for the in-
denturement of any Indian prisoner of war and any vagrant Indians "as
have no settled habitation or means of livelihood, and have not placed
themselves under the protection of any white person." The amended
act also fixed the terms of indenture for male children under fourteen
years of age until they "attain the age of twenty-five years; if females,
until they attain the age of twenty-one years." For those over fourteen
years, their indentures could be set at ten years.[82] William Brewer, an

Early Anglo settler, observed the way this act was put into practice. "It has for years been a regular business to steal Indian children," Brewer wrote in his 1860s journal, "and bring them down to the civilized parts of the state, even to San Francisco, and sell them—not as slaves, but as servants to be kept as long as possible. Mendocino County has been the scene of many of these stealings, and it is said that some of the kidnappers would often get the consent of the parents by shooting them to prevent opposition."[83] Thus precedents for Indian child removal had already been established well before the late nineteenth century.

The Indians were not the only Americans who suffered from the practice of removing children from their families. Slave owners routinely removed or threatened to remove children from their enslaved mothers in order to promote a compliant labor force. This practice raised the particular ire of women abolitionists and was effectively ended with the emancipation of slaves.[84] Child removal was carried out not only by Christian whites against racial and religious "Others," but also by the state against impoverished families. Thus even ostensibly "white" or Christian children could be removed from their parents on economic grounds. In colonial New England, under the doctrine of *parens patriae* the state was the ultimate parent of every child; it had the "power to intervene, on behalf of the child, even in the biological family."[85] If parents could not economically support their children, they were required to forfeit them, sometimes to workhouses but more commonly as indentured servants to other families in the community.[86] By the early nineteenth century dependent children who could not be supported by their parents were more likely to be placed in orphan asylums, even though one or both of their parents were still living. Such institutions, with their emphasis on rigid discipline, military drills, routine, and structure, provided a template for the Indian boarding schools the government would later establish.

In the nineteenth century a movement of middle-class reformers emerged in urban areas to "save" working-class white children whom it believed to be neglected or abused. Linda Gordon asserts that some child savers forcibly snatched poor children from their families. By the late nineteenth century, however, most states had established juvenile court systems in which reformers were required to obtain a court order to remove children they deemed neglected, abused, or delinquent.[87] Arguing that institutional care was an inferior solution, these reformers promoted a return to the practice of placing removed children with families.[88] One child saver, Charles Loring Brace, founder of the New York Children's Aid Society in the 1850s, originated the idea of the orphan trains, a program of "placing out" removed working-class children—rarely true orphans—with rural farm and ranch families, primarily in the rural West. According to Marilyn Holt, Brace's program removed at least 200,000 children (as well as some adults) from the city to the country. As in the case of many of the Mormons who adopted Indian children, however, most host families perceived the program as a modern form of apprenticeship.[89]

Many of these nineteenth-century child savers characterized working-class homes and families in much the same way that other reformers would represent American Indians. One early penologist, G. E. Howe, in fact argued, "In removing a boy from an inadequate or bad home into a better or good one, we are not acting in violation, but in harmony with natural law. . . . So that if we remove a child from parents who have virtually orphaned him by their inadequacy, neglect, or cruel usage, and from a home unnatural and hateful, and bring him into the adoption of a wiser and better parentage, and into the more natural home of comfort and benevolence, then, again, we are not going contrary to, but in unison with, natural principles."[90]

As with efforts to remove American Indian children, white middle-class women were often at the forefront of this social movement. They used the same rhetoric toward poor immigrant women that other female reformers would direct at American Indian women, alleging that "a considerable percentage of foreign-born mothers are too ignorant to feed or care for their children in a wholesome way" and that "they are but children themselves, but with a duller perception."[91] Such reformers believed that if they could Americanize immigrant children, the children would eventually influence their mothers and fathers. As I explore in the following chapter, many women reformers held similar notions regarding the need to "civilize" Indian children.[92]

However, by the first decades of the twentieth century removal of "delinquents" went increasingly out of fashion as a means to solve family problems. The prestigious 1909 White House Conference on Dependent Children, convened by Theodore Roosevelt, resolved that, "except in unusual circumstances, the home should not be broken up for reasons of poverty, but only for considerations of inefficiency or immorality."[93] As Susan Tiffin puts it, in the nineteenth century reformers had been interested in saving children; by the early twentieth century they hoped to save families.[94] Hence, from 1890 to 1930, many Progressive women reformers developed alternatives to full-scale removal of immigrant working-class children, such as opening day nurseries.[95]

There are many parallels between the removal of white working-class children, largely the children of European immigrants, and the removal of American Indians from their families. Rooted in their own Christian (primarily Protestant), middle-class, white norms and standards, reformers deemed both working-class immigrant and American Indian families as deficient and inadequate to raise children properly based on perceived differences of class, religion, and race. (Many native-born Protestant Americans of English or German background considered Irish, Jewish, and southern Europeans to be separate, nonwhite races when they first emigrated to the United States.)[96] Their children, therefore, needed to be "rescued." Ultimately reformers placed the children in institutions or in work situations with families, where they were to be properly disciplined and taught skills appropriate to the emerging industrial order.

What sets the removal of American Indian children apart from the institutionalization of immigrant working class children, however, is that the state never envisioned the removal of *all* children of immigrant and working-class parents as it sought to place *all* Indian children in boarding schools. Moreover, by the late nineteenth century neither reformers nor the state could summarily remove working-class children from their homes without a court order. The state required no such legal intervention to remove American Indian children. The idea of "saving" children by separating them from their families became a solution of last resort for working-class families, not the ubiquitous practice it was for American Indians by the early twentieth century.

Australia had similar precedents in its history. Prior to the imposition of formal state policies aimed at separating Aboriginal children from their families, many settlers throughout the Australian colonies had already engaged in taking Aboriginal children. In New South Wales, colonists began taking Aboriginal children into their homes nearly from the moment they established a colony.[97] In Van Diemen's Land, founded as a penal colony in 1803, some sealers and other colonists made arrangements with parents to "borrow" their children as laborers, paying for them with food and other goods. Increasingly, however, outright kidnapping of children became common. Settlers frequently shot indigenous adults and took their children as laborers in a situation akin to that in California in the 1850s. Aboriginal girls became particular targets as sex slaves or prostitutes. A series of governors in the 1810s issued proclamations against the kidnapping of indigenous children, but to little avail. In 1819 the governor ordered that all children who had been taken without parental consent should be sent to Hobart to be institutionalized and educated by the government.[98]

When New South Wales established the penal colony of Moreton Bay in Queensland in 1824 settlers routinely kidnapped indigenous women and children for labor and for sex. When in 1895 the government commissioned Archibald Meston to report on the government and mission stations for Aborigines, he revealed, "Kidnapping of boys and girls is . . . [a] serious evil. . . . Boys and girls are frequently taken from their parents and their tribes, and removed far off whence they have no chance of returning; left helpless at the mercy of those who possessed them, white people responsible to no one and under no supervision by any proper authority." Although the governor promised to protect Aborigines soon after South Australia was established as a free colony (rather than a convict settlement) in 1836, patterns of settler violence against Aborigines plagued this colony as well. As in many other states, pastoralists often brutally removed Aboriginal children from their families and put them to work as servants and stockmen, especially after the position of protector was abolished in 1856.[99]

In the early to mid-nineteenth century, as humanitarian movements expressed alarm over settler violence and conflict, some colonial authorities worked in tandem with missionaries to establish institutions to "protect" and "civilize" Aboriginal children.[100] Missionaries often condemned the brutal efforts of pastoralists to commandeer the labor of indigenous children, but they too sought to remove children from their families. Most of these institutions, however, met with little success because Aboriginal people resented attempts to take their children and to train them as menial laborers; for example, the Native Institution at Parramatta in New South Wales brought in only thirty-seven children in seven years and closed by 1820.[101] Only in Tasmania, where the Black War had driven nearly all of the Aboriginal inhabitants from the mainland to Flinders Island by 1835, did authorities succeed in rounding up large numbers of Aboriginal children to be brought up in newly established institutions.[102] In other areas, despite decades of assaults on their communities, Aboriginal people still had the resources to resist the taking of their children, and the state at this time lacked the legal apparatus to remove children.

However, from the mid-nineteenth century on, officials began to discuss the merits of removing Aboriginal children from their families. In South Australia, for example, in his 1842 report, the protector of Aborigines argued, "The complete success as far as regards their [Aboriginal children's] education and civilisation would be before us, if it were possible to remove them from the influence of their parents." Australian colonies thus made some efforts in the nineteenth century to bring Aboriginal children under existing child welfare legislation or to craft new mechanisms to allow for the removal of the children.[103] In the late nineteenth century too missionaries renewed their efforts to reach Aboriginal children. In 1874, having convinced the government to set aside reserves for Aboriginal use, Daniel Matthews founded a refuge for Aborigines at Maloga along the Murray River on the border between Victoria and New South Wales. According to Richard Broome, Matthews and his wife, Janet, "scoured the country for neglected Aboriginal children and destitute adults to bring to Maloga."[104]

As in the United States, Australian state governments also engaged in removing the children of white working-class families. Before colonizing Australia, England had regularly removed children of the working classes who were deemed orphaned, destitute, or delinquent. Authorities boarded out some of these children with families or placed them in institutions. Sometimes they transported them to one of their colonies, and Australia itself became one destination for removed children. Between 1830 and 1842 Britain removed and transported approximately five thousand working-class youth, some as young as seven, all allegedly criminals, to Australia. Once there, the children were institutionalized, then trained, then sent out to work for settler families as apprentices.[105]

In the colonies, too, authorities sometimes removed the children of convict mothers. The historian Heather Goodall explains, "Children of convict mothers were separated from them and placed in 'orphan' homes to facilitate employment of their mothers (and often fathers) on remote pastoral runs." These children were routinely apprenticed in their teen years, "with girls indentured to domestic service positions in which their wages were controlled by the State Children's Relief authorities." As they would do later with Aboriginal children, authorities often justified the removal of convicts' children on the basis that they were illegitimate or orphans, a term that "was used loosely to refer to any destitute child."[106]

Increasingly over the course of the nineteenth century, Australian officials targeted many white working-class children for removal and reform. As the legal scholar Antonio Buti makes clear, reformers and authorities envisioned a growing network of industrial schools, reformatories, orphanages, and other institutions in the late nineteenth century as a means to "'rescue the rising generation' from the alleged moral laxity associated with poverty and a lack of parental supervision and control within working class families." Authorities aimed to turn these children into "good and useful men and women" who would be industrious and contribute to the colony's growth.[107] At first, as in the United States, authorities preferred institutions for the care of such "orphans," yet after a series of debates in the 1870s and 1880s reformers came to favor home placements over institutional life for the children.[108] As in the United States reformers established an Australian Society for the Prevention of Cruelty to Children in New South Wales in 1888, with other states establishing their own societies in the next two decades.[109]

Australia had its oceanic version of the orphan trains; in this case a provision of the British Poor Law Act of 1850 enabled authorities to ship British "orphans" or otherwise destitute children to its colonies, including Australia, Canada, Rhodesia, and New Zealand. (Although most such "orphans" were shipped overseas between 1870 and 1915, the program lasted until the 1960s.) Australia was the major recipient of these children in the 1920s. As with the orphan trains in the United States, most of these children were sent to farms, where they were meant to benefit from the supposedly more healthful rural lifestyle.[110]

When speaking of impoverished white children, administrators utilized nearly the same language—minus a racialized component—that they would later use in reference to Aboriginal children. As one reformer put it in 1864, "Every dependent child ought to be separated and removed as far as by any means may be possible from pauper moral influences and pauper physical and social degradation." Worried that poor children "might inherit the vice of pauperism," reformers called for their removal to "respectable homes" where they would be "absorbed amongst other children and go to ordinary schools and take a share in ordinary work." In boarding out such children, reformers hoped to produce a more "industrious class of domestic servants and 'respectable poor.'" "Even before thirteen years of age," the scholar Margaret Barbalet found, such children "were supposed, above all, to be *useful*." The discourse and aims of early child welfare policy in Australia would be echoed in future decades for Aboriginal children.[111]

By the late nineteenth century, as in the United States, new child welfare legislation prevented authorities from summarily removing white working-class children without the consent of their parents. For example, Western Australia's Industrial Schools Act of 1874 required that parents give their legal consent in writing before guardianship of their children could be transferred to an institutional director. Buti notes that in cases where guardianship was legally removed from working-class parents to institutional authorities in Australia, the institutional directors "then acquired all the obligations or duties of guardianship," including providing the child with financial maintenance, protection, education, discipline and punishment, affection, and emotional support. In stark contrast to the laws that affected Aboriginal children, many child welfare laws required that parents be given access and visitation rights and that the child be educated in the religion of the parent's choice.[112]

Australian officials also established a series of Children's Courts over the next several decades, as in the United States, to deal with juvenile "delinquents." The 1907 State Children's Act of Western Australia, for example, stipulated that in order to remove a child from his or her family, the Children's Court must determine that the child was in fact destitute or neglected.[113] As in the United States, by the early twentieth century Australian child welfare advocates had come to believe that they should provide for impoverished children without fragmenting their families; thus the removal of working-class children became a policy of last resort.[114] Moreover, Buti emphasizes that this newer child welfare legislation in Australia did not empower the state, its welfare agencies, or any of its ministers to become the legal guardian of removed white children.[115] By contrast, every Australian state (except Tasmania) created a separate child welfare system for Aborigines that gave the state and its ministers unprecedented powers over Aboriginal families.

Thus by the late nineteenth century many precedents existed for removing indigenous children from their families in both the United States and Australia. Settlers in both countries had engaged in the kidnapping and virtual enslavement of indigenous children in the frontier regions, and missionaries and government officials had made some sporadic efforts to remove indigenous children to institutions. Additionally each country had already used—and then abandoned—child removal as a means to discipline and reform working-class families. These precedents combined with new historical developments at the turn of the century to lead both Australia and the United States to turn to full-fledged systematic policies of indigenous child removal.

NATION BUILDING AND INDIGENOUS CHILD REMOVAL

It is not coincidental that the United States and Australia designed policies to systematically remove indigenous children at the same time that each country sought to become a modern, industrialized nation. As the United States tried to rebuild itself economically and politically after the Civil War and as Australia federated in 1901, nation builders in each country sought to create a unified sense of the nation based on whiteness and modernity. Indigenous peoples, at least as they were denigrated by white observers, stood in stark contrast to these national ideals.[116] Moreover, each nation, as a settler colony, sought to consolidate control over the remaining indigenous populations to assure the final transfer of all land into colonizers' hands. The continued survival, persistence, and resistance of indigenous peoples stood in the way of such claims. Child removal furthered nation-building aims on one level by trying to erase perceived differences of indigenous peoples and ostensibly to bring them into their nations; at the same time, on another level, it sought to undermine indigenous claims to the land by breaking down indigenous children's intimate affiliations with their kin and country.

Articulations of racial ideologies were central to nation building in each country. By the turn of the twentieth century both countries had enshrined "whiteness" as an essential qualification for full citizenship and had enacted immigration policies designed to create "white" nations. Australia did so in an explicit manner, even adopting the "White Australia" policy. Enacted in the same year as federation, the Immigration Restriction Act of 1901 sought to restrict the numbers of Asians and others deemed nonwhite from entering the country while continuing to promote Anglo-Celtic immigration. Initially the act required would-be immigrants to take a "dictation test" in English; later, authorities allowed testing in any European language, but no Asian languages.[117] As a corollary to this policy, the Australian government also pursued a pro-natalist policy for whites only. In 1912 the commonwealth government passed a "maternity allowance" that gave payments to most white mothers on the birth of a child. Nearly all Asian, Pacific Islander, and Aboriginal women were excluded from this allowance. Aborigines faced other exclusions as well; they were denied citizenship until 1948 and were excluded from the census and from voting in federal elections until 1968.[118] In short, as Raymond Evans puts it, "Racial bravado and racial angst, though logically opposed, operated viscerally together to produce a profound sense of racial purpose" in building the Australian nation.[119]

The United States pursued a similar racialized immigration policy. At the turn of the twentieth century anti-immigration societies organized to close the gates to all immigrants but those considered "white" from northern and western Europe. (Anti-immigrant white supremacists considered Jews, Greeks, Italians, and other southern and eastern European immigrants to be separate races, primarily on a religious basis. Thus "whiteness" in the American context was intently bound up with Protestantism.) The Chinese Exclusion Act of 1882 barred most Chinese from immigrating to the United States, and countless laws, such as the Alien Land Acts in California and other western states, prohibited Japanese and other Asian immigrants from owning land.[120] Naturalized citizenship was limited to those who were white, a prerequisite that many immigrants who were denied citizenship challenged in court.[121] In

1924 Congress adopted the National Origins Act, which, without ever mentioning the word "white," enshrined this racialized immigration scheme into law; it restricted the numbers of European immigrants to a small percentage of those already in the country in 1890 (before a large influx of immigrants arrived from southern and eastern Europe) and curtailed Asian immigration altogether on the grounds of forbidding immigration to those who could not naturalize (that is, nonwhites).[122] Shortly thereafter, as Mae Ngai has shown, immigration opponents turned their attention to "undocumented" Mexican immigrants who had been granted an exemption to the 1924 act but now were required to have documentation to enter the United States.[123]

Efforts to build a white America also meant exclusions of other nonwhites. As a result of the adoption of the Fourteenth and Fifteenth Amendments to the Constitution, the United States could not officially exclude African Americans from citizenship in the nation. Nevertheless, Jim Crow segregation and disenfranchisement, mostly in southern states, essentially blocked African Americans from true membership in the nation. Full citizenship eluded American Indians as well; Congress granted the right to vote to Indians only in 1924 (although many Indians were excluded from state suffrage until much later), and extended the protections of the Bill of Rights to them only in 1968.[124]

It was against this backdrop of official and unofficial policies to promote white nations that indigenous child removal played out. The indigenous inhabitants of each country presented a problem to nation builders concerned with whiteness. Although some zealous white supremacists supported outright extermination of indigenous peoples in the nineteenth century, such drastic measures were out of line with the modernizing ethos in each country. Moreover, humanitarian movements in the United States, Australia, and Australia's mother country, England, prevented authorities, even had they wanted to, from resorting to such methods. Instead, each nation proposed to "assimilate" American Indians and "absorb" Aborigines into the majority population. Given that each nation sought to define itself as white, this meant that indigenous people, if they were to be incorporated into the nation, needed to become white, in some sense of the word. In the United States, at least up to about 1900, many reformers and government officials believed Indians could be whitened through cultural assimilation; in Australia many authorities focused instead on the biological assimilation of Aboriginal people.[125]

In both the United States and Australia Darwinism and the emerging field of anthropology influenced white authorities, writers, and reformers. Intellectuals in these fields built on earlier Enlightenment social theories to propose a cultural (or social) evolution model. In the United States the proto-anthropologist Lewis Henry Morgan devised a hierarchical scale of human development, ranging from savagery at the lowest levels up to barbarism and finally to civilization. Morgan applied a set of criteria—based primarily on economics, religion, and gender roles—to measure any given society's degree of advancement on his scale. "Heathen" hunter-gatherers ranked lowest on Morgan's pyramid, barbarian pastoralists represented a more advanced stage, and agriculturalists garnered a higher spot. It will come as no surprise that the top position was reserved for the very group to which Morgan and other social theorists like him belonged: those with a Protestant Christian background and British ancestry.[126] Other social theorists in Britain, including Herbert Spencer and Francis Galton (Charles Darwin's cousin), proposed similar scales of social evolution that were influential in Australia.[127]

These schemata proved popular to white Australian and American settlers who sought to justify their conquest of indigenous peoples. The Australian anthropologist Herbert Basedow declared in 1925, "The Australian aboriginal stands somewhere near the bottom rung of the great evolutionary ladder we have ascended—he the bud, we the glorified flower of human culture."[128] In 1940 the journalist Ernestine Hill contended that Aborigines were "left far behind in the race of the ages, marooned on an island continent of sunny climate." She added, "In the great race of civilisation, he is an outsider. Stone Age man, a savage at heart."[129] In the United States officials and reformers expressed similar sentiments. For example, Alice Cunningham Fletcher, an early anthropologist and reformer, asserted, "The life of the nations and the peoples of the world is like the life of the human being; it has the childhood period, the adolescent period, and the mature period. . . . We speak of savagery, barbarism and civilization,—terms which merely represent these stages."[130]

Both Americans and Australians agreed that "primitive" peoples would prove unfit in the competition for survival and were a "dying race." In the United States, for example, Fletcher declared in 1886, "Many must die. There is no help for them."[131] J. Woodcock Graves, a Hobart attorney, expressed this notion in his poem about Truganini, supposedly the last of the Tasmanian Aboriginal people:

Around the world our conquering Race is sweeping
with firm restless tread,
And everywhere are Nature's children weeping
For those untimely sped:
But though our power be impotent to save,
Our love may smooth their pathway to the grave.[132]

White Australians and Americans differed, however, as to what, if anything, could be done about indigenous people's lowly status on the scale of human evolution. As I shall discuss later, white American reformers in the late nineteenth century tended to adhere to an environmentally determinist view, in line with emerging ideals of the Social Gospel and Progressive movement, that by changing their environment some "savages" could rise up the ladder of civilization in just a generation or two. Most white Australians in the early twentieth century, by contrast, viewed the cultural evolution model to be a biological imperative; thus Aborigines were doomed by their genetic inheritance to be left behind by civilization, progress, and modernity. Considering Aboriginality purely in biological, "blood" terms, white observers interpreted a decline in the number of "full-bloods" as proof of their imminent demise. A 1925 report from Lake Tyers in Victoria noted, "The full-blooded population is now about 60" and "there are no full-blooded girls under 10 years old." The report's author asserted, "In a comparatively short time, say 40 to 50 years, *there will be no full-blooded Victorian Aboriginal in existence. . . .* The race will be extinct."[133] It was thus clear to many Australian policy makers what must be done (or not done). One legislator in Western Australia declared in 1905, "All we can do is to protect them as far as possible and leave nature to do the rest. It is a case of the survival of the fittest but let the fittest do their best."[134]

Not only did Australian authorities believe that "full-blood" Aborigines were a dying race, but many actually seemed to believe such a fate was desirable. A telling exchange occurred between the reformer Charles E. C. Lefroy and the commissioners at a Royal Commission on the Constitution in the 1920s. Lefroy had initiated a campaign to set aside native reserves for Aboriginal people. One commissioner asked Lefroy, "You say that with white care, the aborigines would be not a dying race but one liable to increase. Do you consider that an increase is desirable?"[135] As Patrick Wolfe has pointed out, in a settler colonial society like that of Australia, where the objective of colonizers was to acquire all available land, settlers welcomed the disappearance of indigenous inhabitants.[136]

Australian authorities evinced greater anxiety about miscegenation between whites (as well as Asians) and Aboriginal people, and the resulting progeny, who were not believed to be dying out but increasing rapidly, threatening to prevent the establishment of a white Australia. Ernestine Hill claimed, "Already the steady increase of coloured and half-breed populations threatens an empty country with the begetting of one of the most illogical and inbred races in the world."[137] (Note that Hill regarded Australia as an "empty country," a common strategy, explored in chapter 1, that settler colonialists used to erase the indigenous presence and absolve their own role in displacing indigenous peoples.)

As we have seen regarding different state policies, opinions differed among administrators and reformers about how best to handle this "problem." Some believed in preventing further racial mixing by isolating so-called half-castes from the general population and fining white men who cohabited with Aboriginal women. This potential solution, however, was never popular with white male lawmakers. In 1937, for example, Western Australia legislators debated whether to demand stiffer fines or prison sentences for white men caught having sexual intercourse with Aboriginal women. A. Thomson represented a common viewpoint: "I have no sympathy with any person who will go into a native camp, but I am afraid that we are going to brand a young man who may, in a moment of indiscretion, bring himself under the provisions of this legislation, and render himself liable to a [fine] . . . or three months' imprisonment. Personally, I consider it is going too far." Interestingly, however, many legislators did not find it going too far to severely punish Aboriginal women who cohabited with white men. The Honorable E. H. H. Hall suggested that "action should be taken against such a woman that would prevent her from ever bringing children into the world again." L. B. Bolton agreed: "It would not be too much to suggest that we take steps to sterilise these unfortunate young women."[138]

More commonly, Australian authorities promoted the biological absorption of "half-castes" into the general population; in its most extreme form, officials called this "breeding out the colour." Perhaps its most enthusiastic proponent was Western Australia Chief Protector Neville, who in 1937 raised the specter of whites becoming a minority in Australia. "Are we going to have a population of 1,000,000 blacks in the Commonwealth," he queried a commonwealth conference, "or are we going to merge them into our white community and eventually forget that there ever were any aborigines in Australia?"[139] Neville sought to engineer the demise of Aboriginality by removing lighter-skinned Aboriginal children and restricting marriages to those of "compatible racial make-up"; he dictated that in Western Australia half castes could marry only other half-castes or whites, not "full bloods."[140]

In the Northern Territory, Chief Protector Cecil Cook similarly endeavored to "breed out the colour" by controlling the marriages of Aboriginal and "half-caste" women. He sought to prevent marriages and cohabitation between white men and "full-blood" Aboriginal women but actively promoted such liaisons between white men and "half-caste" women. Cook reported in 1932 that he had also taken steps to keep "coloured aliens" (Asian and Pacific Islander men) from "mating" with Aboriginal women. He concluded, "Every endeavour is being made to breed out the colour by elevating female half-castes to the white standard with a view to their absorption by mating into the white population."[141] Under this scheme, child removal proved indispensable. As Ernestine Hill put it in reference to part-Aboriginal children who were taken to the Bungalow institution in Alice Springs, they would be "encouraged to live white, think white and to marry, if possible, into the white race, or failing that, with each other." In this way, Hill believed, they might be able to "outgrow their heredity."[142]

Cook and Neville were the most vocal and open advocates of "breeding out the colour" through arranged marriages and Aboriginal child removal. Other states pursued the same policy but often without advertising it. For example, in the 1920–21 report of the New South Wales Board for the Protection of Aborigines, members stated, "The process of gradually eliminating quadroons and octoroons is being quietly carried on." Board members explained, "The children are rescued from camp life, and are put through a course of training in the Board's Homes at Cootamundra and Singleton before being drafted out to service. . . . A continuation of this policy of disassociating the children from camp life must eventually solve the Aboriginal problem."[143] A few years later board members admitted that "some criticism of this system has found expression, it being contended that the separation of the sexes will only tend to expedite the passing of the Aboriginal race." The board defended its policies, however, arguing that "its object is to save the children from certain moral degradation on the Reserves and Camps" and to allow for their return later, after they had reached maturity.[144]

Whether administrators favored isolation of "half-castes" or "breeding out the colour," they based their decisions on biologically deterministic notions, sometimes closely correlated with the eugenics movement, regarding the heredity of racial characteristics. Those who argued against "breeding" "half-caste" women with white men claimed that such a racial mixture would only lead to the degeneration of the white race. Queensland Chief Protector Bleakley believed that "half-castes" had "been fathered by a low type of white man. The result is that the half-breed, although he may not have the colour of the aboriginal, has his habits, and consequently cannot happily be absorbed into the white race."[145] Bleakley referred frequently to "throwbacks," a term eugenicists used to refer to mixed-race progeny who "reverted" evolutionally to the "worst" traits (that is, those the eugenicists attributed to nonwhites) of their genetic forebears. "Even admitting possibilities of breeding out [Aboriginality]," he argued, "there were alarming throwbacks, and . . . 90 per cent of such marriages were failures and the progeny unsuitable to build up a moral, virile race necessary to a young country."[146] Of particular note, Bleakley made clear that in promoting the growth of the new nation of Australia it was necessary to "build up a moral, virile race," that is, a white race.

By contrast, those who argued for the absorption of "half-castes" through "breeding out the colour" contended that Aborigines were actually of the Caucasian race and therefore could easily "breed" with whites. In 1931, in an editorial on the native problem in the southwest of Australia, a writer who used the pen name "Araunah" argued that "throwbacks" never occur in the case of "matings" between Aborigines and Caucasians "because the Australian aborigine is Caucasian, springing originally from the same stock as we." Therefore, Araunah continued, "if miscegenation were encouraged instead of being frowned upon, the aborigines would ultimately become absorbed, blending insensibly into the white stock with which they had mated and leaving in their descendants no physical trace of a mixed origin." Araunah lamented that in the camps in the southwest there were "quarter-castes so white as to be indistinguishable from Australians of purely British parentage," yet they were "living like beasts in these camps." Araunah believed, as did many officials and reformers, that if these "nearly white" children were "taken out of the squalid setting of a native camp and seen differently clad in a wholly white environment, [they] would be accepted without question as people of white parentage."[147]

Whether authorities believed that racial theories proved that blacks could be absorbed or that they must remain segregated, they always posed the same solution: the removal of children from their families' care. Bleakley, for example, though he opposed "breeding out the colour," insisted that "the half-breed must be protected," a euphemism for removing and institutionalizing mixed-race children. He told the 1937 Commonwealth Conference on Aboriginal Affairs, at which Cook and Neville were present, "We have found that even the semi-civilized need protection and control, otherwise they become a menace to the white race by reason of their low social conditions, and their susceptibility to disease and illnesses." He added, "We have found it necessary, if we are to protect them, to keep them under constant supervision."[148]

The gendered dimensions of Australian child removal should be obvious by now. As the historian Russell McGregor and others have pointed out, Cook's and Neville's racial order had virtually no place for "half-caste" men, as it was unthinkable to most white Australians that white women should help such men "breed out their colour."[149] As Cook envisioned it, "By elevating the girls to white standard it will be possible to marry an increasing number to white settlers whilst the boys could be safely removed to centres of denser white population where they would be competent to take work on the same basis as white men, thereby reducing the coloured population of the Territory and very appreciably diminishing the coloured birth rate."[150] Thus, at least in the early twentieth century, authorities more often targeted Aboriginal girls than boys for removal. Heather Goodall found that in New South Wales up to 1921, more than 80 percent of the removed children were girls. By 1936 this proportion had dropped only slightly. Moreover, Goodall discovered that by 1928 girls who were twelve years or older accounted for 54 percent of the total children taken, while boys in the same age group accounted for only 14 percent. Goodall reads this as evidence that authorities sought to reduce the Aboriginal birth rate by removing girls who were "approaching the age of puberty."[151]

In sum, Australian officials' belief in the power of biological determinism led them to propose Aboriginal child removal essentially as a means to breed the Aboriginal problem out of existence. Wherever they stood on the issue of "throwbacks," administrators believed that the solution lay in either isolating Aborigines into extinction or in making them white through intermarriage and biological absorption. Thus, to administrators, Aboriginal child removal, together with the control of Aboriginal sexuality and procreation, served as an essential cornerstone to building a white Australia.

By contrast, at least until 1900 influential American reformers and government officials tended to regard the "Indian problem" as more cultural than biological.[152] Whereas these Americans too wished to create a white nation, their model of cultural assimilation suggested that one was not necessarily born white, but could become so. As Pratt put it in a speech to the Board of Indian Commissioners in 1889, "I say that if we take a dozen young Indians and place one in each American family, taking those so young they have not learned to talk, and train them up as children of those families, I defy you to find any Indian in them when they are grown. . . . *Color amounts to nothing. The fact that they are born Indians does not amount to anything.*"[153] Contrast Pratt's beliefs to those of Chief Protector Neville, who wrote, "Our own race has taken thousands of years to reach the point where it is to-day, and we cannot expect this hiatus [between 'half-castes' and 'civilized' whites] to be bridged in a generation. . . . For this purpose of change at least two centuries must be allowed."[154] To Pratt and other reformers, it was the traditionalists who clung to the old ways who would die out (not necessarily "full-bloods") and Indian people who embraced modern, white ways of life who would survive. Thus when the boarding school system was initiated, humanitarian reformers argued that removing Indian children from the influence of such traditionalists and from their home communities was essential to "whitening" the Indians and making them eligible for inclusion in the modernizing nation.

At least in the first twenty years of the boarding school system, reformers and officials tended to believe that individual Indians could quickly advance beyond savagery and barbarism to civilization through social engineering, not through the kind of biological manipulation that many Australian officials embraced. As Commissioner Morgan put it, "A good school may . . . bridge over for [Indian children] the dreary chasm of a thousand years of tedious evolution" from savagery to civilization.[155] Another reformer, Merrill Gates, declared to the Lake Mohonk Conference in 1900, "Education and example, and pre-eminently, the force of Christian life and Christian faith in the heart, can do in one generation most of that which evolution takes centuries to do."[156] Gates's comment also suggests the centrality of religion to American reformers' ideology, a point to which I will return later.

U.S. officials and reformers did not ignore racial makeup; they were concerned with the degree of "Indian blood" for the purposes of allotting tribal lands to individual Indians under the Dawes Act of 1887, and boarding schools did keep rosters of children that listed their percentage of Indian blood. But the federal government deemed assimilation essential to *all* American Indian children, no matter what their descent. Thus they did not target children of mixed descent, as in Australia, and without a desire to biologically whiten Indian children, and thus to control the reproduction of Indians, removal fell fairly evenly on boys and girls.

Increasingly, however, in the early twentieth century some reformers and officials were moving toward a more biologically deterministic view of the so-called Indian problem. For example, at the National Education Association Conference in Denver in 1909 one speaker, Charles Bartlett Dyke, fulminated on "Essential Features in the Education of the Child Races." Dyke declared, "To-day Americans are attempting to educate every race under the sun, with extremely limited knowledge of race differences and possibilities. One very positive school of theorists demands identical education for all, in conformity with the equality postulated by our Declaration of Independence. Another equally positive school pleads for the development of the *best* in the Indian, the Negro, the Filipino, the Hawaiian, instead of trying to make of him a poor white man." Through his own work of teaching various groups in Hawai'i, Dyke claimed, "I became firmly convinced that psychical race differences are not eliminated in any appreciable number of generations, be the education what it may." He concluded that the "child races" lack the intellect to acquire a college education and therefore, "for economic reasons, primitive man must be trained in vocations that fit him for life in the white man's world."[157]

Dyke's views were embraced by a key administrator of Indian affairs, Estelle Reel, who held the influential position of superintendent of Indian education from 1898 to 1910. Emphasizing that it was not environment but genetics that determine human capacity, Reel contended that changing the environment of Indians would not create any measurable change; the best that could be done was to fit such inferior peoples for their appropriately subordinate role in society. She asserted in 1900:

The Indian child is of lower physical organization than the white child of corresponding age. His forearms are smaller and his fingers and hands less flexible; the very structure of his bones and muscles will not permit so wide a variety of manual movements as are customary among Caucasian children, and his very instincts and modes of thought are adjusted to this imperfect manual development. In like manner his face is without that complete development of nerve and muscle which gives character to expressive features; his face seems stolid because it is without free expression, and at the same time his mind remains measurably stolid because of the very absence of mechanism for its own expression. In short, the Indian instincts and nerves and muscles and bones are adjusted one to another, and all to the habits of the race for uncounted generations, and his offspring cannot be taught like the children of the white man until they are taught to do like them.

It was a short step from such biological determinism to support for eugenics, a step Reel freely took in her opposition to intermarriage between Indians and whites. She believed such unions would lead to "more or less a state of degeneracy among the offspring."[158] At least in one state, Vermont, eugenicists targeted the small remaining population of indigenous people, the Abenakis, for investigation and often subsequent institutionalization and sterilization.[159]

The Progressive, environmentalist point of view lived on, however. Elaine Goodale Eastman (see chapter 9), who had worked as a schoolteacher and superintendent of schools in the Dakotas and then married a Dakota (Santee Sioux) man, Charles Eastman, objected to this rising sentiment. "Heaven forbid that these rising young Americans be taught to look upon themselves as an inferior class," she wrote, "set apart by Nature and heredity to be 'hewers of wood and drawers of water' for the 'superior' race!"[160]

Given the ubiquity of scientific explanations for race and the popularity of eugenics in both Australia and the United States, it is interesting to ponder why biological absorption was more prominent in Australia as a solution to "the Aboriginal problem" than it was in the United States for "the Indian problem." Conversely, we might wonder why the cultural assimilation program that flourished in the United States, at least for several decades, did not have more adherents in Australia. In Australia opposition to schemes to "breed out the colour" derived partly from diehard racial purists but also from missionaries and the women's movement.[161] Yet, as I explore in subsequent chapters, these latter two groups enjoyed little influence over Australian policy in comparison with their prestige in American society in the late nineteenth century. And as the historian Katherine Ellinghaus points out, Australia lacked the vibrant reform movement regarding indigenous affairs that propelled much of the turn toward cultural assimilation in the United States.[162]

In the United States religious motivations and the desire to build the nation as a Protestant country were closely tied to the racial politics of Indian child removal. As the historian Francis Paul Prucha has written, the Indian reform movement of the late nineteenth century that so vehemently supported assimilation policy was through and through an evangelical Protestant movement. Although Indian reform groups such as the WNIA and the IRA were not run by any one Christian denomination, they maintained close ties with Protestant congregations throughout the land (but expressed much antipathy toward the Catholic Church). Christianization was central to their agenda; they could not imagine the "civilization" of the Indian without his or her adoption of Christianity. As one religious leader put it, "The first motto of all Indian reformers should be Indian evangelization. . . . The longest root of hope for the Indians is to be found in the self-sacrifice of the Christian Church."[163]

Although the Protestant orientation of the American reform movement may have contributed to the preference for cultural assimilation policies in the United States, the non-Christian status of many American Indians represented another justification for the removal of American Indian children from their families. Convinced that only individual salvation could solve the "Indian problem" and reform society, American reformers concentrated on breaking up tribal life and cultivating individuality. The reformer Merrill Gates put it this way: "If civilization, education, and Christianity are to do their work, they must get at the individual. They must lay hold of men and women and children, one by one. The deadening sway of tribal custom must be interfered with. The sad uniformity of tribal life must be broken up! Individuality must be cultivated."[164] Many reformers seemed to doubt their abilities to Christianize individual indigenous people within their tribal communities, where elders still practiced their religions; thus they often perceived Indian child removal as a necessary means to convert Indian children.

Moreover, assimilation policy arose at the same time that prominent reformers and officials increasingly defined the United States as a Protestant nation. Rooted in the early nineteenth-century revival movements, evangelical Protestantism had fueled the major reform movements of the century and come to dominate the nation. As new immigrants from southern and eastern Europe, the majority of whom were Catholic and Jewish, arrived in the country in the late nineteenth century, many native-born Protestant Americans viewed them as a threat to the emerging religious unity of the nation. To such reformers and policy makers, unconverted Indians also imperiled the religious uniformity they sought in the United States.[165]

In Australia missionaries, whom the state relied on to help in carrying out its Aboriginal child removal policies, could not envision incorporation of Aborigines into their new nation without their conversion to Christianity. An article from the Adelaide *Advertiser*, for example, described the Colebrook Home for Aboriginal children (established by missionary women) as having two objectives: "first, to make Christians of these children, and, second, to merge them into the white population."[166] Violet Turner, a missionary, explained, "One aim of the United Aborigines' Mission is to see every black or native child enjoying the parental care, comfort and Christian training of a Godly home."[167] Yet Christianity seems to have played a lesser role in both the design of Aboriginal child removal policies and in the related project of building the nation. In the discourse of male legislators and administrators, concerns with race far outweighed interest in Christianization, and as we shall see in subsequent chapters, government administrators frequently clashed with and resented the interference of missionaries, particularly women.[168]

Concerns with modernity and progress, however, underpinned indigenous child removal policies in both the United States and Australia. In the model of cultural evolution that influenced both nations, savagery was defined not only racially (as dark-skinned people) and religiously (as pagan), but also economically (as noncapitalist and nonmodern). Civilization was defined as the opposite: as white, Christian (preferably Protestant), capitalist, modern, and industrializing.

Policy makers and reformers in both countries regarded indigenous people particularly as standing in the way of modernity and progress, hallmarks of each emerging nation. Despite the fact that many indigenous peoples had been integrated into colonial economic systems for generations, many white settlers continued to characterize them as peoples who were locked in a premodern, primitive past.[169]

Moreover, many reformers and officials virtually equated modernity and whiteness. Indeed, the specter of "nearly white" children growing up among "primitive" Aboriginal communities deeply disturbed most white Australians. In regard to the establishment of Sister Kate's Home in 1933, Chief Protector Neville declared that the home accommodated "these near-white children who were quite out of place in native settlements and who deserved all the facilities and upbringing usually accorded to white children."[170] "Near-white" children living in Aboriginal camps were "out of place"; they challenged the linkage between modernity and whiteness, raising the unthinkable possibility that white people might be dragged down into a "primitive" state. Further, if "near-white" children lived with and as darker Aboriginal children within their camps, how would racial distinctions and their privileges and restrictions be constructed and maintained?[171]

In some cases indigenous groups did resist modernization. Although indigenous peoples had engaged with European capitalist markets for some time by the turn of the twentieth century, many individuals and groups continued to practice indigenous economic modes, what white observers in both the United States and Australia often characterized as irrational economic activity. That many indigenous people moved from place to place according to the season to follow the source of their subsistence, even long after colonization, set them at odds with a modern, industrializing nation.[172] The persistence of other indigenous economic systems also frustrated administrators. Authorities at the BIA regularly bemoaned the practice of giveaways and potlatches, ceremonies at which Plains and Northwest Coast Indian families, respectively, honored a special occasion and displayed their status by giving gifts to other community members. Indian peoples in such groups gained status not by how much they accumulated, but by how much they gave away, a practice that BIA officials believed discouraged industry and thrift. Such traditions also had the effect of redistributing resources in a manner that diverged significantly from capitalist emphases on wage work and production for the market.[173] Because indigenous peoples often avoided full-scale integration into capitalist economies and instead patched together disparate economic strategies—a fledgling craft industry, seasonal wage work, the gift economy, traditional foodways, and dependence on government rations—they represented an anomaly to the modernizing nation.

Where indigenous people still held on to their lands in a communal fashion, such lifestyles remained more viable, and it thus proved more difficult for officials to realize the goal of forcing indigenous inhabitants to participate in the modern economy. In a letter to Alice Fletcher, Pratt insisted, "The Indian would be far better off financially, physically and morally if his right to land had never been awarded. . . . It is . . . a curse to him in every aspect. . . . I am sorry the Indians are not all bootblacks, or washer men, as well as women, or barbers, hotel waiters, etc. These qualifications would bring them into fellowship with the world."[174] Opposing both the reservation system and the allotment of communally held lands to individual Indians, Pratt on another occasion wrote, "I would blow the reservations to pieces. I would not give Indians an acre of land. When he strikes bottom, he will get up."[175]

The perceived failure of many indigenous families to participate fully in the modernizing economies of their nation-states, at least on white terms, made those families even more vulnerable to child removal. Just beneath the surface of benevolent justifications for child removal lay another layer of discourse that had to do more with economic concerns: that if left to their own devices, indigenous people would become dependents on their respective nations, but if properly trained they could become "useful" in the industrializing economy. In 1909, in a typical comment, the protector of Aborigines in South Australia believed that, if removed, "half-caste" children "will as a rule, grow up useful, self-supporting members of the community, instead of developing into worse than useless dependants."[176] In similar language, Herbert Welsh, president of the IRA, supported the removal of Indian children to boarding schools: "The probabilities are that many Indians will thus be saved to honorable and useful, though humble, lives, which otherwise would inevitably sink into hopeless, gypsy-like vagabondage and decay." The subheading of the article in which Welsh was quoted proclaimed that Indian children would be "saved for useful lives."[177]

Notably, most officials and reformers envisioned only a limited usefulness on the part of indigenous workers. Queensland Protector Bleakley claimed that "education *of the right sort* should enhance the natives' value, making them more intelligent and *useful.*" Bleakley explained, "It is argued that education spoils them, making them cunning and cheeky. The trouble probably is that they become enlightened and as a result, dissatisfied with conditions." He contended, "The right education, with improved working and living conditions, should make for better service."[178] Similarly, Superintendent of Indian Education Estelle Reel stressed, "All teaching should be of such a nature as will best fit the child to cope with his environment." She added, "Teaching that is not practical and useful is of little value."[179] In these sentiments Reel and Bleakley echoed other colonial administrators. In the Dutch East Indies, for example, as Stoler writes, "Education was to modulate [métis children's] desire for privilege, temper aspirations deemed above their station, and remind them that colonial privileges did not follow because European 'blood flowed in their veins.'"[180]

To this end of making indigenous children "useful," reformers and officials promoted what was called "the outing system" in the United States and "apprenticeship" in Australia. In many of the Indian boarding schools half of each school day was devoted to "industrial training." Once children were trained, outing programs then placed Indian girls and boys as workers with white families for half of each school day—the boys to carry out manual labor, usually agricultural, and the girls to labor as domestics. After their industrial training in homes such as Cootamundra in New South Wales, Aboriginal girls were placed as apprentices in white homes. Like Indian boys, Aboriginal boys often were apprenticed as stockmen or other types of manual laborers. In both countries the youthful indigenous workers were given a small spending allowance, but employers deposited the remainder of their wages in trust accounts under the control of institutional officials or the chief protectors. As Inara Walden explains, the Aborigines Protection Board instituted a system of indentured servitude that had long since been abandoned among whites.[181]

Authorities envisioned outing and apprenticeship as essential in converting indigenous children from "useless" dependents on government handouts to "useful" participants in the modern economy. Reel claimed that the outing system "places the student under the influence of the daily life of a good home, where his inherited weaknesses and tendencies are overcome by the civilized habits which he forms—habits of order, of personal cleanliness and neatness, and of industry and thrift, which displace the old habits of aimless living, unambition, and shiftlessness. It places him in the midst of the stir of civilized life, where he must compete with wide-awake boys and girls of the white race. . . . It removes the prejudice between the races by showing each to the other in its true light."[182]

Ironically, in places like Cumeroogunga and Indian Territory, many of the indigenous people who lost their land were self-supporting, presumably useful members of the community. But the correlation between removing indigenous people from their land and taking their children away to make them useful reveals the assumptions behind white rhetoric. A useful indigenous person meant an Aboriginal or Indian who was in service to a white employer specifically, and to the settler economy more generally.[183] Thus indigenous child removal was necessary to properly integrate indigenous people into the modern nation, albeit in the lowest, most marginalized positions.

Perhaps the most crucial goal of the nation builders in each settler country was to gain complete control over the land; authorities looked to indigenous child removal, in part, to help them achieve this objective as well. By the turn of the twentieth century white Australians had secured title to virtually all the land on the continent. Still, authorities sought to undermine indigenous land ownership. In New South Wales, for example, the historian Heather Goodall found that between 1911 and 1927 Aboriginal peoples lost 13,000 acres of their land, half of the total Aboriginal reserve land in the state. While white farmers took most of this land, the Aborigines Protection Board itself claimed some of the land in order to establish new institutions in which to place removed Aboriginal children.[184]

Indigenous control of land was a greater problem to authorities in the United States, where, through the reservation system, American Indians still retained a significant amount of land. Most settlers and even some humanitarian reformers regarded the American Indian retention of any land as thwarting the nation's ultimate development. The reformer Lyman Abbott told the Lake Mohonk Conference, "Three hundred thousand [Indian] people have no right to hold a continent and keep at bay a race able to people it and provide the happy homes of civilization. We do owe the Indians sacred rights and obligations, but one of those duties is not the right to let them hold forever the land they did not occupy, and which they were not making fruitful for themselves or others."[185] U.S. authorities garnered more land from American Indian reservations at the turn of the century by allotting reservation land. As part of the assimilation policy, Congress passed the 1887 General Allotment Act, also called the Dawes Act, to break up tribal lands and allot each male head of household 160 acres of land. This land was to be held in trust by the BIA for twenty-five years to prevent its sale. After the allotment of all reservation lands, any remaining surplus land would be transferred to the U.S. government for sale. All told, Indian peoples lost about ninety million acres through the implementation of the Dawes Act.[186]

As Australian and American authorities secured the transfer of more land to their governments, and thereafter to settlers, they also engaged in policies of removing indigenous children from their families. Rather than regarding these as distinct and separate policies, we should more properly view them as policies that worked in tandem to divest Indian peoples of their last remaining lands. As long as indigenous people were identified as part of a distinctive group with a long historical association with a particular area, they could make claims to particular territories and lands. Disconnecting children from both their group identity and traditional land association contributed to this primary aim of settler colonialism.

Indigenous child removal served authorities in one final way in their quest to build unified modern nations: by pacifying any remaining military resistance to colonization. Aboriginal families who protested their children's exclusion from public school or petitioned against the revocation of their land were more likely to have their children removed by the chief protectors or the Aborigines' protection boards. For example, in the 1920s in Moree in New South Wales children were removed from families who openly opposed the town's new segregation of Aborigines in a separate school.[187]

This practice seems to have been far more prevalent in the United States than in Australia, where well into the late nineteenth century Indian peoples organized armed resistance to U.S. colonization. Assimilation policy, in fact, arose in the midst of the nineteenth-century Indian wars on the Great Plains, and reformers and officials regarded child removal as a means to prevent further resistance from Indian peoples. Commissioner Morgan asserted, "It is cheaper to educate a man and to raise him to self-support than to raise another generation of savages and then fight them."[188]

It was not education per se, however, that officials believed would deter resistance, but the taking of children from their families. Historians have commonly asserted that Pratt developed the idea of educating Indian children from his experience with rehabilitating Indian POWs, but he learned something else from his experiment. He recognized that breaking up Indian families could work wonders in controlling Indian resistance to American conquest. During their first year of imprisonment, the POWs asked Pratt to arrange a conference for them in Washington in order to be reunited with their women and children. Quoting from their appeal, Pratt wrote to the U.S. Army adjutant general on their behalf: "We want to learn the ways of the white man, first we want our wives and children and then we will go any place and settle down and learn to support ourselves as the white men do." The prisoners further begged Pratt, "Tell 'Washington' to give us our women and children and send us to a country where we can work and live like white men." They ended their appeal by reiterating, "Only give us our women and children." After the venerable reformer and author Harriet Beecher Stowe visited St. Augustine, she commented on an old chief who "wears the little moccasin of one of his children tied round his neck."[189] Pratt discovered from this experience that separating Indian people from their kin could serve as a powerful means of compelling their obedience and squelching their resistance; Indian child removal worked as a tool of control as powerful, if not more so, than outright warfare. Reformers and government officials took their cues from Pratt. On one occasion the commissioner of Indian affairs expressly ordered Pratt to obtain children from two reservations with hostile Indians, the Spotted Tail and Red Cloud agencies, "saying that the children, if brought east, would become hostages for tribal good behavior."[190]

Clearly, despite Australian and American authorities' attempts to characterize their new policies of indigenous child removal as benevolent programs to rescue and uplift Aboriginal and Indian children, other, more primary concerns motivated policy makers to resort to these drastic measures: a desire to entrench control over indigenous lands and peoples in order to build ethnically and religiously homogeneous and modern settler nations. Far from being a kinder, gentler approach to the administration of indigenous affairs, assimilation and protection policies—with indigenous child removal as their centerpiece—were meant to serve as extensions of and supplements to violent aggression.

These new policies did, however, represent a break with the past in at least one crucial way. Prior to this era colonizers had regarded indigenous affairs as an entirely masculine endeavor. White men were to carry out trade, diplomacy, and warfare with the indigenous inhabitants of their colonies. A few white women were involved in missionary enterprises, but they played more of a symbolic function in earlier eras, as potential victims of indigenous male violence and sexual assault who needed the protection of white men. Now, as the contested territory of colonialism encompassed the intimate realm of indigenous communities and families, white women—as moral guardians of this intimate domain—had a particularly valued role to play in colonizing and building the new settler nations, as the next chapter explores.

Chapter 3

The Great White Mother

Who will carry the light to these dark sisters? Who will go to them and teach them of the love that can turn their night to day, their sorrow to rejoicing. The Indian women, old and young, need to be taught that their highest, holiest duty is the intelligent management of the home and the children that God has given to them. Not until the Indian women become good nurses, good housekeepers, intelligent Christian women, will the Indian problem be solved. • *The Indian's Friend* 12, no. 4 (December 1899), publication of the Women's National Indian Association

As government officials developed indigenous child removal policies in both the United States and Australia, white women in both countries clamored for a greater voice in public policy. They justified their increased public role, often condemned as outside their proper sphere, by identifying their activism with motherhood, women's traditional domain. Through this emerging maternalist politics, they offered to mother other seemingly disadvantaged women and advocated policies designed to strengthen mothering. Such a maternalist agenda might have led white women to defend indigenous women against state authorities who sought to remove their children (as it did in their campaigns for single white working-class mothers). Paradoxically, however, most white women activists who crusaded for indigenous women endorsed indigenous child removal.

As can be seen in the epigraph from *The Indian's Friend*, white women reformers in the United States often cast Indian women as deficient mothers and homemakers; white Australian women characterized Aboriginal women in a similar manner. By depicting indigenous women as the degraded chattel of their men who failed to measure up to white,

middle-class, Christian ideals, many white women missionaries and reformers created a pathological view of indigenous women and gender
relations that became yet another justification for the removal of indigenous children. At the same time, many white women reformers cast
themselves as important political players who would solve the Indian
and Aboriginal "problem" by metaphorically and literally mothering
indigenous people and their children. In particular, they claimed a role
for themselves as surrogate mothers who would raise indigenous children properly in more wholesome environments.

Thus, instead of watching from the sidelines as male government
officials designed and carried out policies of indigenous child removal,
many white women reformers campaigned for a greater role in setting
public policy for indigenous peoples and became deeply implicated in
this phase of settler colonialism. In the United States the women found
a receptive audience for their views among male government officials
and used their newfound influence to gain increased public authority.
In Australia, by contrast, where male officials routinely rebuffed white
women's efforts on behalf of Aboriginal women, white women struggled
to attain a greater voice in government policy.

Maternalist Politics

A particular kind of women's movement, what historians have called
maternalism, swept across North America, Western Europe, and Australia in the late nineteenth and early twentieth centuries. At a time
when nation builders conceived of their emerging nations not only as
white and modern but also as embodying a particular masculine ideal,
maternalists contested the exclusion of women and what were coded
as women's concerns from political and public life. While some white
men in both the United States and Australia defined the nation in part as
muscular masculine entities that would provide protection to dependent
white women against "a rising tide of color," many maternalists sought
instead to assert themselves as independent subjects.[1]

Although the term *feminism* was not used in the United States at least until the First World War, maternalism can be considered a type of feminism, concerned as it was with mobilizing women to address the disadvantages of other women and gain greater political authority. The politics of maternalism usually embodied four characteristics: (1) elevating motherhood as woman's most sacred occupation; (2) justifying women's presence in public reform as a natural extension of their experience or socialization as mothers; (3) acting in a motherly manner toward other women they deemed in need of rescue and uplift; and (4) upholding a maternal and domestic role as most fitting for other women, not for themselves.[2] In some sense, while rejecting the role of dependent woman in need of protection, white women maternalists articulated their own role as one of protector to dependent "other" women.

Most scholarship on American maternalism has focused on middle-class white women reformers during the Progressive era who labored to reduce infant child mortality rates, limit child labor, protect women workers, and develop mothers clubs, child care facilities, and playgrounds. Progressive maternalists in the United States also campaigned for mothers' pensions, which enshrined in legislation the notion that poor single mothers belonged in the home with their children, not in the paid workforce. This legislation eventually formed the basis for Aid to Dependent Children (later Aid to Families with Dependent Children), a centerpiece, along with Old Age Insurance, of the Social Security Act and New Deal welfare state.[3] When it came to single white mothers, maternalists agreed that, barring any overt neglect or abuse, children belonged with their mother. A 1912 cover of the *Delineator*, a popular women's magazine at the turn of the century, featured the headline "Our Christmas Wish for Women: That Every Decent Mother in America Could Have Her Babies with Her." At the 1908 National Congress of Mothers, one speaker opposed "breaking up families unnecessarily" and called for making a "clear distinction between pecuniary incapacity and moral incapacity" before removing any child from his or her mother.[4]

After Australian women gained the vote in the commonwealth in

1902, Australian women's organizations also sought to create a welfare state by extending what they believed to be women's maternal values and priorities into the newly federated nation. They developed new institutions such as free kindergartens, nurseries, schools for mothers, special hospitals for mothers and babies, and playgrounds. As the birth rate dipped precipitously among Australian white women between 1890 and 1900, the maternalist movement also aimed to reduce infant mortality.[5] Similar to the movement in the United States, Australian maternalists were concerned with supporting single white mothers and ensuring that they could keep and care for their children. In 1927 the feminist publication the *Dawn* noted approvingly that the Tenth International Congress of the International Alliance of Women for Suffrage (which included Australian delegates) resolved that "every effort should be made to enable the unmarried mother to support and keep her child under her own guardianship." The *Dawn* also praised new legislation in South Australia whereby an illegitimate child would "become a ward of the State only if voluntarily given up by the mother, and if the Children's Court decided that it is in the best interests of the child."[6]

Australian maternalists also particularly campaigned for white women to gain custody rights to their children after divorce. For example, the South Australia Women's Non-Party Association protested in September 1924, "By the very laws of Nature the bond existing between mother and child must perforce be stronger than that between father and child. Yet, in the eyes of the obsolete law on the question of child-guardianship, a mother has no authority over her own children, except by the courtesy of her husband."[7] This campaign finally met with success beginning in 1940 in South Australia.[8] Australian feminist groups also campaigned for mothers' pensions, resulting in the passage of the first maternity allowance in 1912. Covering both married and single white mothers but excluding Aboriginal and Asian women, this allowance bolstered the White Australia policy.[9]

As one of their primary tenets, maternalists considered motherhood to be sacred and the maternal bond between a woman and her children to be inviolable. Ellen Key, a Swedish feminist thinker influential in both the United States and Australia, asserted, "The time will come in which the child will be looked upon as holy . . . a time in which all motherhood will be looked upon as holy, if it is caused by a deep emotion of love, and if it has called forth deep feelings of duty."[10] In a 1932 play written by Millicent Preston Stanley, leader of the Australian mothers' custody rights campaign, the lead character, who has lost custody of her child, makes her case to the bar of Parliament: "Have you forgotten that Nature has welded the mother and her child into one spirit and one flesh through the great drama of birth—or if remembering, how justify the law which has sundered so often and so pitilessly the mother from the child?" The character further proclaimed "mother right the highest moral law."[11]

Maternalists used women's traditional association with motherhood to justify their participation in reform politics, a male-dominated realm, by arguing that they were merely extending their natural role as potential mothers who had values and skills that were necessary to solve the major problems of the day. Hannah Schoff, president of the National Congress of Mothers in the United States, wrote in 1905, "There is a broader motherhood than the motherhood that mothers one's own; there is the spirit of the Lord that is the mother that mothers all children, and it is because the world lacks that, that the conditions of the children of this country [have] not been better."[12] Such sentiments prevailed in Australian women's reform circles as well. When asked why she had become involved in federal politics, the Australian feminist Edith Jones told the Women's Service Guild, "I believe that the best home is run by the man's and woman's mind co-operating. Federal Parliament represents a million homes, but the woman's mind has never played its part."[13]

Maternalists argued that the needs of women were often overlooked by male policy makers, and therefore women had an indispensable role in public life. One woman who helped to rescue Chinese prostitutes in California proclaimed, "[Women] are united in that tenderest of ties, a common sympathy for the oppressed of our own sex."[14] In Australia

Edith Jones queried, "Who can look after women and children as well as women?" and asserted, "Women in public life would be able to remember matters affecting women and children that men are too apt to forget."[15]

Maternalists also sought to mother women they perceived as disadvantaged and in need of protection. Australian maternalists were especially concerned with protecting girls and women from male sexual exploitation, and the attendant venereal disease, out-of-wedlock pregnancies, and sexual assaults that accompanied unchecked male sexual license. To that end they promoted the appointment of women to a variety of influential posts, such as justices of the peace, police officers, jail matrons, factory and school inspectors, magistrates, doctors, and lawyers.[16] In the United States female moral reformers and missionaries also sought to mother women they viewed as oppressed. In the American West, for example, they opened rescue homes for Chinese prostitutes, unwed mothers, and Mormon women in polygamous marriages.[17]

Historians' studies have shown that maternalism also entailed the promotion of motherhood and domesticity as the most fitting occupations for women, at least for those women whom maternalists sought to rescue. (Many American maternalists never married or had children and pursued highly visible careers; many Australian reformers remained childless and also eschewed domestic cares for public activism.) Through their campaigns for maternity allowances in Australia and mothers' pensions in the United States, maternalists upheld the notion that mothers belonged in the home with their children and that the state should properly value motherhood and compensate women for the labor involved in mothering.[18]

White women's maternalism toward indigenous women took a different turn. Although they still glorified motherhood, used it as a platform for political activism, and tried to mother other women, most white women reformers represented indigenous women as unfit mothers and in fact promoted policies to remove their children from them. Moreover, white women reformers added another dimension to maternalist thinking and politics: a fervent belief that transforming the indigenous home

and woman's role within it would solve the "problem" presented by indigenous people to rapidly industrializing nations. Hence white women
created a unique strain of maternalism toward indigenous women that
would intersect with and reinforce their governments' aims in dealing
with indigenous people.

— maternalists fight 4 W Rights while taking motherhood from Ind. women

White Women's Organizations

Veteran women reformers in the United States established the foremost
white women's organization concerned with Indian affairs in 1879; it
started as the Central Indian Committee of the Women's Home Mission
Circle of the First Baptist Church of Philadelphia, then became an independent organization, the Woman's National Indian Treaty-Keeping
and Protective Association, and later, simply, the Women's National
Indian Association (WNIA).[19] In its first two years in existence, the group
sent petitions to Congress to demand that the United States live up to
its treaty obligations; members gathered thirteen thousand signatures
for the first petition and fifty thousand for the second. By 1883 the WNIA
had twenty-six auxiliaries in New Hampshire, Massachusetts, Maine,
Connecticut, New York, New Jersey, Pennsylvania, Delaware, Maryland, Washington DC, Ohio, and Michigan.[20] The following year the
group expanded to Indiana, Illinois, Wisconsin, Minnesota, the Dakotas, Iowa, Nebraska, and Kansas and established its first mission at the
Ponca Agency in Nebraska for Poncas, Otoes, and Pawnees. By 1885
they had initiated eighteen new auxiliaries as well as a second mission at
Round Valley, California.[21] By 1889 they boasted of establishing seventeen missions among fifteen tribes. Rooted in Christian missionary and
reform efforts, the WNIA affiliated with Protestant church organizations.
Other white women concerned with Indian affairs worked through their
churches and missionary societies. For example, the Women's Executive Committee of the Presbyterian Church had established twenty-four
Indian schools in Arizona by 1897, ten of which were boarding schools.
About two thousand Indians attended these schools.[22]

In its first few years, as witnessed by the tenor of its petition campaigns (and its original name), the WNIA focused more on promoting Indian rights than on a maternalist agenda. When a group of male reformers founded the Indian Rights Association in 1882, however, some WNIA members believed they should turn to more gender-appropriate maternal reform, what they often referred to as "uplift." In New York in 1883, for example, several members wanted to establish a school and dedicate the organization to missionary work. Notably, other members objected because they believed it "unwise to divert to any extent our attention from the effort to secure civil and political protection for the Indian." They insisted, "We should use all our Association's resources in urging Government to give to the Indian truth and justice *practically*, before offering him a religion whose fruits, as he thinks, are robbery and cruelty towards himself." Those in favor of uplift activities won out in New York and nationwide, declaring that the newly formed "gentlemen's association," the Indian Rights Association, could pursue civil and political reforms, "thus leaving our own society free to devote . . . a portion of our work to uplifting Indian homes; to aiding the vastly needed work within Indian hearts, minds and souls."[23]

Thereafter, as a full-fledged maternalist organization, the WNIA concentrated on reaching Indian women and children, first through sending women missionaries and field matrons to remote Indian communities. Emily Cook described the field matron program as embodying "mother love and sister influence" and expressed admiration for a matron in Washington state "who has done much toward putting Indian girls in white families and getting under sheltering care those who have gone astray until they can have an opportunity to rebuild their lives."[24] As a second step in their maternalist program, the WNIA focused on promoting schooling for Indian children. They believed, along with Richard Henry Pratt, "that the education of Indians . . . will most justly, quickly, and economically solve the Indian problem." The Massachusetts branch of the WNIA, for example, set up a school for the children of Apache prisoners in Alabama and arranged for eight of the older Apache children to be sent to Hampton Institute.[25] Although there was never unanimity among WNIA members about whether day or boarding schools were best, Amelia Stone Quinton, a long-standing president of the organization, promoted boarding schools over day schools for Indian children.[26]

As maternalists, WNIA members contrasted their approach to that of men, asserting, "While the men of the last few generations were oppressing the aborigines, . . . the women were forgiving them . . . and pitying them for their ignorance, sins and sufferings. . . . The daughters of those women have developed compassion into action . . . and have . . . organized a great reform."[27] Members also emphasized that they were carrying out "women's work for women," a phrase that linked them to white women worldwide who, as missionaries and reformers, ventured into colonized areas everywhere to carry out their mission of rescuing women they deemed in need of uplift.[28] The WNIA readily invoked family metaphors, calling themselves mothers and sisters to Indian women, to establish a sense that they knew what was best for these women, even though few of them had spent any time in the presence of actual Indian women or solicited their concerns. Members represented their endeavors as the "noble efforts of the women of America in behalf of the deeply wronged children of the forest."[29]

In Australia white women did not take up Aboriginal women's issues as an organized campaign until several decades after American women had become concerned with Indian women. Moreover, no white women's organization akin to the WNIA, focused only on Aboriginal people, formed in Australia. Instead, already existing feminist groups addressed the issue, usually when one of their members had taken up the issue as a personal cause. The Women's Non-Party Association (WNPA) of South Australia led the way in 1920. This group sought the participation of the Women's Service Guilds (WSG) of Western Australia in the "protection of aboriginal women against the vices of white men," especially along the east-west railway that connected South Australia with Western Australia. The WSG decided to work with the WNPA, lobbying for harsher penalties against white men who engaged in sexual liaisons with Aboriginal women. It was not until the late 1920s, however, that women's groups became more actively involved in advocating for Aboriginal women, beginning with the WNPA in 1926 and the Australian Federation of Women Voters (AFWV) in 1928. The AFWV also affiliated internationally with the British Commonwealth League (BCL), a subgroup of the International Women's Suffrage Alliance based in London, which also began to speak out on Aboriginal women's status in the late 1920s.[30] The Woman's Christian Temperance Union (WCTU) became involved in advocating for Aboriginal women in the 1930s. Other women's groups, including the Victorian Women's Citizen Movement and the National Council of Women, also occasionally joined in efforts to lobby for the greater protection of Aboriginal women.[31] (If you are having trouble keeping all these organizations straight, see the list of abbreviations following the table of contents.)

Once mobilized, white Australian women used much of the same rhetoric of "women's work for women" that their American counterparts had first employed decades earlier. At a 1929 conference Edith Jones spoke out regarding the need for more white women to be appointed to official positions on the basis that only women could understand the plight of and properly care for Aboriginal women and children. She declared, "The question of the half-caste is a big problem because the aboriginal woman is behind all the troubles which have been mentioned here today. We want to help that woman, and I believe that help can only be achieved by the direct application of the mind of [white] women to this problem."[32] In a letter to her feminist colleague Bessie Rischbieth in 1932 the activist Mary Bennett underscored her belief in white women's role at Mt. Margaret Mission: "[It] particularly appeals to me—an Australian woman's work for native women. It is grand, beautiful! an inspiration!"[33]

White Women Reformers

In the United States the white women who became involved in reforming Indian policy and uplifting Indian women emerged primarily from maternalist women's groups, Christian missionary societies, and the new discipline of anthropology. Three white women in particular stand out as powerful spokespersons for the movement: Amelia Stone Quinton, Alice Fletcher, and Estelle Reel. Together these three women created, reinforced, and promoted images of Indian women and families that gained wide currency in both popular culture and government circles and wielded significant influence over the direction and implementation of Indian policy in the late nineteenth and early twentieth centuries.

Amelia Stone Quinton, one of the founders of the WNIA and its long-time president, embraced both the Christian missionary and maternalist traditions. Born in 1833, Quinton grew up in a fervent Baptist household in Syracuse, New York, the virtual epicenter of the religious revival known as the Second Great Awakening and of women's reform movements. Following the path of many other nineteenth-century women reformers, she did volunteer work in New York City's asylums, alms-houses, infirmaries, and women's reformatories. She married Reverend James F. Swanson and lived in Georgia for a number of years. After his death she taught at the Chestnut Street Female Seminary in Phila-delphia and became a state organizer for the WCTU in New York in the 1870s. In 1877, exhausted from her maternalist endeavors, she traveled to England, where she met and married Richard Quinton. The couple settled in Philadelphia, where Quinton renewed her friendship with the founder of the Chestnut Street Female Seminary, Mary Lucinda Bonney. Bonney took an active part in the Woman's Union Missionary Society of America for Heathen Lands, which dispatched women missionaries to Asia, and served as president of the Women's Home Mission Circle of the First Baptist Church, a group that supported missions among American Indian communities. Quinton eagerly joined Bonney's new campaign to defend Indian lands and treaty rights, carrying out much of the research needed for the Central Indian Committee's first petitions to Congress and later serving as president of the WNIA for seventeen years. As the primary spokesperson for the WNIA, Quinton created and reproduced popular representations of American Indian women and influenced public policy. In the year 1880 alone, Quinton presented 150 addresses to women's groups and church and missionary organizations.[34]

Alice Cunningham Fletcher played an equally significant role in white women's efforts to reform Indian policy in the late nineteenth and early twentieth centuries. Fletcher had close ties to the WNIA, frequently speaking at their meetings and supplying them with information for their journals, petitions, and other publications. She also, however, became increasingly interested in studying Indians as an anthropologist. As a young woman, she cut her political teeth on women's reform, first participating in Sorosis in New York, one of the earliest women's clubs in the United States, and then helping to form the Association for the Advancement of Women in New York in 1873. Serving as one of the association's secretaries for four years, Fletcher learned how to run an organization, participate in public debate, and petition public officials. In 1878, because of her dire financial circumstances, she refashioned herself as a public lecturer, speaking to women's groups on topics related to American history. Finding much interest in her lectures on "prehistoric" America, she developed a series called "Lectures on Ancient America."

Fletcher's lectures led her to a more profound interest in Indian peoples. First through correspondence with and then through informal tutoring from Frederic Putnam, the director of Harvard University's Peabody Museum of American Archaeology and Ethnology, she began her study of anthropology, an altogether new field. Fletcher longed to carry out research among American Indians, a proposition that was unheard of for a single woman in the late nineteenth century. Some single women had served as teachers or missionaries among Indian peoples, but only one other woman, Matilda Coxe Stevenson, had carried out such scientific research (among the Pueblos beginning in 1879), and she had been married to the leader of the research expedition. Fletcher finally found her chance to pursue her unprecedented endeavor in 1881 through her association with Susette La Flesche, a Western-educated

Omaha Indian woman, and Thomas Tibbles, a white journalist. Fletcher had first met La Flesche and Tibbles in Boston in 1879, when they sponsored a lecture tour of the Ponca Indian leader Standing Bear, the event that galvanized the Indian reform movement in the East. In 1881, when La Flesche and Tibbles traveled to Boston again, Fletcher told them of her interest in going to live and study among Indians; later that summer the couple, now married, invited Fletcher to go camping with them among the Lakota Indians the following autumn, after which she could travel on by herself. At the age of forty-three Fletcher took up their offer and decided to make a particular study of Indian women.[35]

During the next several decades, Fletcher shuttled between studying and reforming Indians. She wrote dozens of articles for popular journals and reform publications to advocate assimilation for American Indians, including individual land allotment and boarding schools. On periodic trips back to the East, she lobbied the government and lectured to both professional anthropological societies and reform groups. In 1882, for example, after spending a brief period of time studying the Omaha Indians, she advocated to Congress that their land be allotted in severalty. The following year, Congress approved such a bill and requested that she carry out the land allotment program among the Omahas. That same year, Richard Henry Pratt hired her to "recruit" Plains Indian children for Carlisle Institute (see chapter 5). In 1888 she published a 693-page report for the U.S. Bureau of Education and the Department of the Interior entitled *Indian Education and Civilization*. The following year, the commissioner of Indian affairs hired her to conduct land allotments among the Nez Perces in Idaho.[36]

Having begun her reform within women's groups, Fletcher established close ties with the WNIA. At the Friends of the Indian meeting at Lake Mohonk, New York, in 1884, she proposed a revolving loan fund for young Indian couples who had returned from boarding school, enabling them to borrow money to build American-style homes and thereby to model "civilization" to other Indians. The Connecticut branch of the WNIA enthusiastically took up this proposal.[37] Quinton singled out

Fletcher for special mention in her articles on white women's reform work for Indians. She lauded Fletcher for bringing thirty-six Indian children to Carlisle and Hampton, "herself raising $1800 with which to meet the expenses of other Indians who begged to join the party and seek an education," and for persuading General Armstrong to "undertake at the Hampton school, the training of young Indian married couples, in cottages built by funds she raised for their training, and by the success of this experiment introduced the department of Indian Home Building into the Women's National Indian Association."[38]

Fletcher also became an ethnographic researcher; she published many articles and reports for academic journals on various aspects of Indian culture among the Omahas, Winnebagos, Pawnees, Osages, and Lakotas. Together with Susette La Flesche's Omaha brother Francis, she would eventually publish an extensive ethnography of the Omahas and a significant study of Omaha music. In fact, Francis La Flesche and Fletcher established a forty-year professional and personal collaboration. In the 1880s, when not in the field, the two rented houses next to one another in Washington DC. They spent nearly every day in each other's company, carrying out their research and writing, but also attending receptions and dining out together. In 1891 Fletcher bought a home in Washington, which she shared with La Flesche for the next sixteen years. (During part of that time, Fletcher's colleague from Idaho, Jane Gay, also lived with them.) Speculation abounded as to the nature of the relationship between Fletcher and the Indian man who was seventeen years younger than she. In 1891 Fletcher formally adopted La Flesche as her son. He married a Chippewa woman in 1906 in the parlor of the home he shared with Fletcher, but the marriage did not last a year. La Flesche continued to live with Fletcher until her death in 1923, and she left the bulk of her estate to him.[39]

On many occasions it was difficult for Fletcher to reconcile her reform impulses with her anthropological orientation. As she advanced in her career and these tensions became more intolerable, she increasingly disengaged from reform efforts.[40] However, the damage to Indian peoples had already been done. Considered an expert on Indian issues by virtue of her ethnographic work among Indians, and prolific in her writings and public speaking engagements, Fletcher had exerted enormous influence on government policy makers to divide up Indian lands and remove Indian children from their families.

Born a generation later than Quinton and Fletcher, Estelle Reel likewise had accrued a number of maternalist reform credentials before becoming involved in Indian reform. She was born in Illinois in 1862 and educated in Chicago, St. Louis, and Boston. At age twenty-four she moved to Cheyenne, Wyoming, where her brother had been elected mayor; there she taught school for a few years and then held local office as the superintendent of schools for Laramie County. From 1895 to 1898 she served as the state superintendent of schools, another elected position, and was appointed secretary of the State Board of Charities and Reform of Wyoming, through which she concentrated on improving asylums and prisons. In 1896 the Republican Party considered selecting her as their candidate for governor of Wyoming. She demurred and worked for William McKinley's election to the presidency. As a reward for her work, McKinley appointed her to the post of superintendent of Indian education in 1898, which she held until 1910.[41]

Though she had no history of involvement in Indian reform, Reel sought to gain experience and knowledge quickly. In her first three years on the job she allegedly traveled 65,900 miles by train and wagon to visit all the Indian schools.[42] During her tenure she focused on two main efforts: pushing for a compulsory school law for American Indian children and devising a uniform course of study for the Indian schools, which was published in 1901.[43] At the close of her career in the federal government, Reel married Cort Meyer of Washington state, whom she claims to have met when she arrived by train for an inspection of the Indian School at Fort Simcoe. When they married and moved to Toppenish, Washington, Reel declared that her "zeal was transferred to beautifying her home, which was soon one of the show places of the area," and which she bequeathed upon her death in 1959 to the Toppenish Garden club "to be used as a resort area." She lived to the age of ninety-six.[44]

Like Quinton and Fletcher, Reel helped to shape the discourse about Indian women and children that would in turn affect Indian policy. The WNIA naturally embraced her, regularly reporting on her activities and including excerpts from her reports.[45] While serving as superintendent of Indian education, she waged a vigorous public relations campaign, penning numerous articles about herself and her efforts—in the third person—and sending them out for syndication in newspapers throughout the country. She even wrote her own obituary, which the editor of the *Toppenish Review* wryly noted "was written several years ago by Mrs. Cort Meyer, with the apparent intention that it be used as her obituary. It was completed except for a blank space where the date of her death was to be inserted."[46]

In addition to these three key figures in the United States, an informal network enabled like-minded white women to convene, share their views, and develop programs for American Indian women and children. A number of white women, particularly those who served as missionaries, schoolteachers, and matrons, wrote columns for and letters to the WNIA newsletter, *The Indian's Friend*, their religious denomination's missionary society journals, or their boarding school's newspapers. They detailed their experiences and perspectives working among American Indian women, thus contributing to this growing discourse. Annual meetings of the Friends of the Indian at Lake Mohonk, though including men, also provided a forum for white women reformers to exchange views, as did Indian institutes organized by Estelle Reel for schoolteachers.

White women reformers' maternalism toward Indian women was animated by and linked inextricably with their evangelical Christian orientation. Quinton, for example, in chronicling the founding of the WNIA, commented, "The motives were Christian, and the inspiration had its birth from the missionary spirit. . . . Even the first movement though for five years wholly devoted to gaining political rights for Indians, was as truly from the missionary spirit as was afterward the planting [of] missions in the tribes." In 1893 she declared, "Rich in mental, moral and spiritual power, it should be easy for American Christian women to finish the solution to the Indian question."[47] Most American maternalists believed that Indian women could not be "rescued" without conversion to Christianity. Mrs. Egerton Young put it this way in *The Indian's Friend:* "May the [missionary] work continue among the Indian tribes . . . until the Gospel shall so subdue and soften all hearts that tyranny, despotism, and oppression shall cease, and men and women, created in God's image, shall all be lifted to the highest conditions of life, where for God's glory they shall spend their days."[48] This orientation was particularly evident among the older generation of reformers, Fletcher and Quinton, for example.

A network of white women reformers also emerged in Australia. While speaking out for the protection of Aboriginal women and children, these women generated and reproduced enduring images of indigenous women that served to support child removal policies. Many such white women in Australia, like their counterparts in the United States, derived their interest in Aborigines from their activism in women's groups or through missionary activity. I focus here on Constance Cooke, Bessie Rischbieth, Edith Jones, and Mary Bennett. Another group of white women activists—ethnologists akin to Fletcher—also became prominent and outspoken campaigners on behalf of Aboriginal womanhood. Of this group, I feature Daisy Bates and Olive Pink.

Born into a middle-class Anglican family in Adelaide, Constance Cooke (1882–1967) was educated at home; in 1907 at the age of twenty-five she married a professor of chemistry at Adelaide University. The couple had two children before Cooke became involved in feminist campaigns. Active in maternalist politics as a justice of the peace and as a member of the WNPA in the 1920s Cooke became the association's president in 1924 and steered the group to take up the cause of Aboriginal people. As a result of her efforts the WNPA was the first feminist group to promote the welfare of Aboriginal women and children. Nevertheless, Cooke failed in her attempt in 1924 to lobby the AFWV, a group with which the WNPA was affiliated, to pass a resolution to set aside protective reserves for Aborigines. Despite her defeat, she pressed on. In 1926 she was a founding member of the Aborigines Protection League, a South Australian organization, and in 1928 she formed and then led an Aboriginal welfare committee within the WNPA. In 1929 she and her colleague Ida McKay were appointed as the first women to serve on the South Australia government's consultative body, the Aborigines' Advisory Council.[49]

Originally from a working-class family in Adelaide, Bessie Rischbieth (1874–1967) grew up in her uncle's progressive household and eventually married a wealthy wool merchant and settled in Perth. Rischbieth played major roles in a number of feminist groups, including the WSG from its inception in 1909, the National Council of Women beginning in 1911, and the AFWV, which she founded in 1921. After being widowed in 1925, she increased her activism, becoming involved in the international women's movement, including the International Alliance for Suffrage and Equal Citizenship and its subsidiary, the BCL, from 1926 to 1953, as well as the worldwide theosophy movement, a spiritual program that "predicted a utopian future in which all races and creeds would participate in a world civilisation." A maternalist through and through, Rischbieth dedicated herself to aiding women and children. In the Perth area she was instrumental in establishing the Children's Protection Society in 1906, free kindergartens in 1912, and a hospital for women that accepted unmarried mothers in 1916. Like many Australian feminists, she became a justice of the peace in her bid to improve child welfare. Rischbieth became more involved in the "Aboriginal question" in the late 1920s through her involvement in the WSG, the AFWV, and the BCL, focusing particularly on securing federal, as opposed to state, control over Aboriginal affairs.[50]

Another reformer, Edith Jones, became involved in Aboriginal issues through both feminism and missionary activity. She had been a secondary school teacher and a lecturer in education at a teachers' college in Glamorgan, Wales, before she married John Jones, an Anglican minister, in 1904. She accompanied him as a missionary to Thursday Island, off the tip of the Cape York Peninsula in the far north of Australia, where they were based for six years. They returned to England in 1910, but then two years later went back to Australia when John became chairman of the Australian Board of Missions. For ten years they lived in Sydney, where Jones founded the Women's Auxiliary of the Australian Board of Missions and chaired the girls' department of the YWCA in Australia and New Zealand. During that period she traveled extensively across Australia. The couple moved in 1921 to the Melbourne area, where John became the vicar of the All Saints' Church in St. Kilda, a suburb of Melbourne, and Edith took a leading role in the Victorian feminist movement, serving as the second president of the Victorian Women Citizens' Movement and becoming one of the first women justices of the peace in Victoria. She also held a position on the executive board of the National Council of Women and as a member of the Social Hygiene Board.

In the late 1920s Edith Jones became interested in advocating for Aboriginal issues, first testifying before the 1927 Royal Commission on the Constitution that Aboriginal affairs should be made a federal rather than a state responsibility, and then attending the 1929 federal conference to consider the findings of Queensland Chief Protector J. W. Bleakley regarding the condition of Aborigines in the Northern Territory. At this 1929 conference she called for greater protection of Aboriginal women against the abuses of both Aboriginal and white men. In 1929 the Joneses returned to England, where John was appointed vicar of Marlborough. There Edith became active in the BCL and the Anti-Slavery and Aborigines Protection Society.[51]

Through their activism, Cooke, Rischbieth, and Jones became well-acquainted with one another. When they took part in meetings of the BCL in London in the late 1920s, Cooke and Jones met another zealous reformer, Mary Bennett, who derived her interest in the Aboriginal cause from her childhood experiences, the British humanitarian movement, and missionary activity. Though not active in feminist politics before her immersion in Aboriginal issues, Bennett brought a feminist analysis to her advocacy for Aborigines and sought to mobilize feminist groups to take up their cause. Born in 1881, Bennett had a childhood divided between her family's home in London and a pastoral property called Lammermoor in northwest Queensland, on the traditional lands of the Dalleburra people. She was educated from 1903 to 1908 at the Royal Academy of the Arts in London and returned to Australia with her father after her education. In 1914 she married Charles Douglas Bennett, a sea captain, and returned to England in 1921. Widowed in 1927, she published two books that year, *Christison of Lammermoor*, which lionized her father and his benevolence to the Aborigines on his property, and *The Dalleburra Tribe of Northern Queensland*. That year also marked the beginning of her activism in human rights organizations, beginning with the London-based Anti-Slavery and Aborigines Protection Society.

In 1930, at nearly fifty years of age, Bennett published *The Australian Aboriginal as a Human Being* and returned to Australia. She hit the ground running when she arrived, touring Aboriginal reserves and settlements and working on missions in the northwestern region of Western Australia. In 1932 she took up work as the resident teacher at the Mt. Margaret Mission near Kalgoorlie in Western Australia with Reverend R. M. Schenk and his wife, Mysie Schenk. Bennett returned to England during the war years and attended college there, earning a degree from the University of London in 1944. After the war she returned to Western Australia, retiring in Kalgoorlie, where she died in 1961. Of the four women activists featured here, she became the most outspoken critic of government policies toward Aboriginal people.[52]

These Australian women activists kept in close communication with one another, but they did not always agree; nor did they particularly like one another. Seasoned reformers at first welcomed Bennett into the fold, even if they believed her to be a bit naïve. In 1930 Jones wrote of her to Rischbieth, "Poor dear, I wonder if she realises what a job she is taking on."[53] Bennett initially warmed to the other women campaigners. Once in Perth, she wrote to Rischbieth, "It is [good] to feel that while I am at work in the wilds (as I hope to be soon) I shall have good friends engaged in the harder task of spreading enlightenment and educating a better, sounder public opinion."[54] Very quickly, however, other reformers' enthusiasm for Bennett turned to caution; by 1931 Jones was characterizing Bennett as "a bit of an extremist on the native question" who emphasized the "darkest side" of Aboriginal affairs. Jones particularly objected when Bennett criticized mission activities.[55] Yet she appreciated Bennett's sharing of information, telling Rischbieth, "Mrs. Bennett is indefatigable in sending us the result of her research work amongst the Abo's esp. in relation to 'wages,' witchcraft and polygamy—all very valuable. She has also sent specimens of handcraft, photos, etc."[56]

Despite these behind-the-scenes differences, white women activists in Australia presented a fairly uniform vision of Aboriginal women and solutions to the "Aboriginal problem," at least until the mid-1930s, when Bennett broke away decisively from her sister reformers. As prominent activists who tried to steer the government toward what they viewed as a more effective and humane policy toward Aborigines, Cooke, Rischbieth, Jones, and Bennett wrote many articles and delivered many speeches that included vivid descriptions of Aboriginal women and family life. Together with anthropologists and missionary women, they were most responsible for projecting a particular image of Aboriginal women that, as I will show, contributed to pathologizing indigenous society and promoting Aboriginal child removal.

Some early women anthropologists, including Daisy Bates and Olive Pink, reinforced these negative representations of Aboriginal women. Bates, an iconic and elusive figure in Australian history, has a murky past. Historians generally agree that she was born in 1859 to a poor Catholic family in Ireland, even though she later claimed to be from a wealthy Protestant family. In 1883 she arrived in Queensland and became a governess. The following year she married a stockman on the station, Edwin Murrant (later known as the legendary Breaker Morant who fought in the Boer War). The marriage did not last, and just a year later she married John Bates, a drover, though she was still formally married to Murrant. (At the time, there was no possibility of divorcing Murrant or annulling the marriage to him; for bigamy, however, she could have been sentenced to seven years in prison.) During her first year of marriage to Bates she herded cattle with him. In 1886 she bore a son, Arnold, after which she is believed to have spent little time with her husband and instead traveled to New South Wales and Tasmania, possibly working again as a governess. In 1894 Bates ensconced her seven-year-old son in a boarding school, left her husband behind, and returned to England, where she spent five years working for a reporter. When she returned to Australia she had reinvented herself as a journalist.

For a time Bates reunited with her husband and son in Perth and tried to live as a conventional wife and mother, but she could not maintain the pretense for long. Fostering out her son, Bates, now in her early forties, joined her husband as he traveled around the rugged Northwest buying cattle. She became increasingly curious about the Aboriginal people she met along the way, and she wrote a series of articles about them for the Perth newspapers. To satisfy her growing interest she accompanied a Catholic bishop to the Trappist Mission at Beagle Bay in the Northwest of Australia, where she spent three months learning about the Nyul-nyul and other local Aboriginal people. Following this visit, she settled for eight months with the Koolarrabulloo people near Broome, continuing to write about Aboriginal people for the popular press.

In 1904 Bates broke off her relationship with her husband for good and returned to Perth, where she was commissioned by the Western Australia government to collect ethnographic data on Aboriginal people between 1904 and 1912. She began her task by working out of a government office in Perth, where she gathered as much existing information as possible on Aboriginal languages and cultures and then spent the next two years living out of a tent in nearby Aboriginal communities outside Perth. She then traveled through the goldfields of southwestern

Australia for the next two years, collecting more information about Aboriginal people in the region. In 1910 she was invited to join an expedition to northwestern Australia led by the renowned anthropologist A. R. Radcliffe-Brown, whom she later accused of plagiarizing her research. Bates returned to Perth in 1911, and by 1912 had produced a huge three-volume manuscript on the Aboriginal people of Western Australia. However, the new Western Australia government refused to publish it and terminated her position.

Bates then moved eastward, eventually ending up in 1918 at Ooldea (at age sixty), near the transcontinental railway, where she stayed for the next sixteen years. In 1934 she moved to Adelaide, where she lived for six years off a small stipend from the government to work on her manuscript. From 1941 to 1944, now in her eighties, she returned to her camp at Ooldea. According to the historian Jim Anderson, in 1945, "suffering from malnutrition, she had to be rescued by ambulance and returned to Adelaide." Bates died at the age of ninety-one in 1951.[57]

Bates never achieved the acclaim she sought in the male-dominated anthropological field, but instead gained notoriety as an eccentric. Her views of Aboriginal people, however, became very influential. In particular, Bates was one of the foremost popularizers of the fiction of the Aborigine as the "last of his race," which contributed so much to the Australian fixation with "full-bloods" and "half-castes." The title of her book, *The Passing of the Aborigines,* conveys her emphasis on the inevitable extinction of "full-blood" Aborigines. (Like nearly all of her contemporaries, Bates did not consider "half-castes" to be real Aborigines.) As we shall see, her views of Aboriginal women and gender also had enormous bearing on creating justifications for child removal policies.

Like her predecessor Bates, Olive Pink tried to pursue a career in anthropology but became known more for her eccentricity. Born in 1884 in Hobart, Tasmania, Pink studied and later taught art. After her father's death in 1907 she and her mother and brother in 1911 moved to Perth, where she resumed teaching art. In 1914 she and her mother relocated to Sydney. During World War I she volunteered for the Red

Cross and obtained a job as a drafter with the Department of Public Works. After the war she participated in the bohemian artistic life of Sydney and joined the Association for the Protection of Native Races, a humanitarian organization that spoke out against ill treatment of Aboriginal people. Unlike many of the other Australian women featured here, Pink never married, though she appears to have been engaged to a captain who died at Gallipoli during World War I. In 1926 at age forty-two, she decided to use her annual vacation to visit Daisy Bates, whom she had met at a science congress. Pink and Bates developed an almost instant compatibility. While staying with Bates at Ooldea, Pink made several sketching expeditions and also carried out a rudimentary ethnographic study of Aboriginal kinship and language.

In 1930, having read an article by Professor of Anthropology A. P. Elkin, Pink arranged to accompany Elkin on a new expedition he was planning to Central Australia. But when she arrived at the scheduled point of departure, Oodnadatta, in a remote part of South Australia, Elkin was nowhere to be found. (He later told her he had changed his plans but had no means to communicate with her.) Thus Pink was left to her own devices for six months in Central Australia, where she traveled throughout the area (with a side trip up to Darwin) and camped extensively among various Aboriginal groups. In 1932 she began the study of anthropology at the University of Sydney, which brought her in contact with Elkin again. After passing her exams she embarked on her fieldwork among the Arrernte people of Central Australia, which was to be the basis for her dissertation. But after spending a few months among the Arrernte, she shifted her attention to a neighboring group, the Walpiri, who had been less studied by anthropologists.

Returning to Sydney in 1934, Pink not only worked on writing up her research but also began to speak out against government policies toward Aboriginal people, reserving special wrath for pastoralists and missionaries and supporting the concept of "secular sanctuaries" for traditional Aboriginal people. In the process, she alienated Professor Elkin (who was also an Anglican minister), whose support she needed in order to obtain funding for further research. In 1936, despite Elkin's opposition, she finally secured funding for additional monies to conduct fieldwork among the Walpiri at the Granite goldfields. Here, however, her promising field research was cut short when officials questioned her safety as a single white woman, refused to extend her grant, and insisted she return from the field. Pink returned to Sydney for a few years, struggling to write up her research, to make a living, and to promote secular sanctuaries for Aboriginal people. She decided to abandon academic anthropology and to withhold access to her research data for fifty years. She moved to Alice Springs in 1940, at age fifty-six, where she continued her activism and her research until her death in 1975 at age ninety.[58] Unlike Bates, Pink did not publish a major popular book or a set of articles on Aborigines, yet she wrote extensive letters to other white women reformers and public officials about her observations and beliefs.

Bates and Pink had a complicated relationship with other white women who campaigned for indigenous women's rights. Unlike these other reformers, they opposed missions and their attempts to convert Aboriginal people to Christianity. Of course, this alienated reformers such as Cooke, Rischbieth, Jones, and Bennett. On the other hand, many of these same reformers seemed to admire Bates and Pink and to consider them experts on "the Aboriginal question," and they often incorporated Bates's and Pink's observations into their own speeches and writings. Despite their differences, these six white Australian women contributed most visibly and vocally to white women's maternalist campaigns for Aboriginal women. As in the United States, Australia had its share of other white women, primarily missionaries, who wrote regularly for their mission's journals, often propagating many of the same images of Aboriginal women that more well-known white women also circulated.

White Women's Representations of Indigenous Women

It was not only a maternal agenda that linked American and Australian white women activists, but also the remarkably similar images that they created of indigenous women. To begin with, in scripting themselves as mothers, white women cast all indigenous people as children to be simultaneously nurtured and disciplined, gently guided and closely monitored. Upon first observing the Omaha Indians, Alice Fletcher wrote, "They seemed pleased and glad a Christian woman has come. The tales of oppression are pitiful. . . . They are children as faced toward us, know nothing of the power of law and organization."[59] Estelle Reel asserted in 1899 that because they had not adopted Western scientific notions, "the Indian mind is as the child's mind, or the minds of an era when science was in its infancy."[60] Daisy Bates asserted similarly that Aboriginal people were perpetual "children," who would "never be able to stand by themselves and must be protected to the end."[61]

The tendency of white women to represent indigenous peoples as a "child race" derived partly from their maternalist sensibilities but also from racial and colonial currents. In the era of cultural evolution, as was explored in the previous chapter, some theorists compared the "savage" and "barbaric" races to children who had not yet matured into adults. Moreover, it was not uncommon for colonizers to similarly infantilize the people they sought to subjugate, and once infantilized, indigenous peoples were robbed of their ability to speak for themselves. White women thus took upon themselves the role of spokespersons for indigenous peoples. In one 1933 article concerning Aborigines with leprosy, for example, a reformer claimed to be writing "on behalf of these poor natives, who like dumb animals cannot speak for themselves."[62]

In addition, as was common in colonial discourses around the world, nearly all white women portrayed indigenous women as the degraded slaves of their cruel and lazy men. Making such colonialist connections, Daisy Bates believed "the subjection of women in Africa, India, etc. is not to be compared to the dreadful slavery of the wild Australian woman and the young girl throughout their whole lives." She contended, "Given his choice, the native would be a derelict loafer all his life, living on the prostitution of his women and girls." In the same memorandum she asserted, "The native has been for centuries the lord and master of his women and girls, and all females in camp must wait on their menkind, forage for them and carry all burdens."[63] Bates's depiction of Aboriginal women as slaves became common currency among white women activists.

In the United States white women generally projected a similar image of Indian women as the "squaw drudges" of their men. This was an oft-repeated refrain among white reformers, even when presented with evidence to the contrary. For example, the WNIA journal *The Indian's Friend* extracted a report from a male missionary, Howard Antes, who worked among the Navajos. He acknowledged, "As a property-holder, the Navajo woman, doubtless, does hold a higher position in her tribe than do the women of some other tribes, for she is commonly credited with being the owner of the flocks of sheep and goats." However, Antes countered that she was expected to do all the work associated with her sheep and was "but a chattel herself, to be traded off as a wife for ponies by her father or husband." Antes also objected because the Navajo custom of burning the hogan in which a person had died "deprived [Navajo women] of both privilege and opportunity of exercising the mother and wife instinct to build up a home."[64]

Believing indigenous women to be oppressed, most white women reformers on both sides of the Pacific were convinced that, by contrast, white women occupied a privileged position within their societies. Edith Jones, for example, declared in a 1936 speech, "In the first year of this century, Australia led the world in the enfranchisement of women; yet during the whole of the past century, while the white woman has advanced in status in Australia, the position of the aboriginal woman has gone from bad to worse."[65] American women commonly attributed their supposedly lofty status to Christianity. Mrs. Egerton Young waxed at length in the pages of *The Indian's Friend* on "tyranny and oppression [as] universal sins of fallen humanity." "Not only is this seen in the conduct of strong nations in their dealings with the weaker ones," she wrote, "but saddest of all, it is more vividly seen in the dealings of men towards women in nearly all lands where the Bible has not become an open volume."[66]

These depictions of indigenous women as "chattel" and "burden bearers," as contrasted with white women as "elevated in status," reveal white women's adherence to a sexual division of labor based on a nineteenth-century model of middle-class, Christian, white gender norms, a model in which "true women" oversaw domestic duties and guided affective relationships in the home while their husbands worked outside the home for pay. Although of course most white middle-class women did carry out labor in the home, this nineteenth-century ideal rested on obscuring women's actual work and romanticizing domestic labor.[67] Thus white women reformers who had grown up shadowed by such an ideal perceived indigenous women's work as evidence of their lowly status in comparison to that of indigenous men. When they saw indigenous women engaged in the kind of physical labor that they coded as masculine, they believed indigenous men (who more often engaged in hunting and the defense of their groups) to be idle loafers who virtually enslaved their women.

Indigenous writers as well as some nonnative scholars have since refuted these interpretations of indigenous women's work. Ruth Roessel, a Navajo, writes, "Navajo women do not feel that the work and labor required is something that is too much or too hard, but, rather, they feel that it is something that is right, necessary and good. Their work in the fields gives them meaning and pleasure as well as allowing the close identification of these women with Changing Woman [a Creator] and with the Holy People who . . . gave to the Navajos corn and the other crops." Roessel points out, "The Navajos always have said that as long as they have cornfields and *Kinaaldá* [a puberty ceremony for girls] they have nothing to worry about. . . . In both elements the women play the primary role."[68] Writing in 1939, the anthropologist Phyllis Kaberry notes of Aboriginal women's work, "This state of affairs can . . . be approached positively as the fulfilment by the woman of an important role in economics, and not as the imposition of the heavier work on the weaker sex."[69] Many scholars today believe that indigenous women's activities were highly valued and that men's and women's roles complemented one another; researchers have come up with a range of terms for these gender systems, including *balanced reciprocity*, a *vital symmetry*, a *necessary balance*, and *interdependent independence*. Under such complementary gender systems, "the efforts of both women and men are acknowledged as necessary for the well-being of society."[70]

White women linked indigenous women's supposedly low status not only to their work but also to customary marriage practices among many indigenous peoples. In Australia many groups practiced polygyny and infant betrothal; when a girl was born its parents arranged for it to be married to an adult man. In return, the man had important obligations and responsibilities to the girl's family. Sometimes the girl went to live with her future husband's family as early as the age of nine, although, according to Kaberry, "full sexual intercourse was not allowed until after puberty."[71] These practices shocked and outraged many white Australian reformers who tied polygyny and the infant betrothal of girls to sexual slavery.[72] "Polygamy is founded on the old men bespeaking the girls before they are born," Bennett wrote. "The girls have no voice in choosing their life's partners—they are 'property.' A clean and clean-living half-caste girl has been appropriated by an old witch-doctor three times her age, whom she loathes."[73]

Notably, Bennett and other white women reformers referred to young Aboriginal (or "half-caste") girls as "clean," a term drenched with meaning for white women maternalists. Another reformer questioned whether Aboriginal girls, "having committed the crime of being born *girls* are foredoomed to give their clean little bodies to dirty old men in the bush who can claim them by native right. . . . I ask you, is such polygamy defensible in a British country where white women are, perhaps, the freest in the world?"[74] Above all, as we shall see, white women valued "cleanness"—of women's bodies, in both a sexual and a hygienic sense, and of women's homes. While their bodies were still "clean" and unsullied by Aboriginal men, white women reformers implied, Aboriginal girls should be rescued and protected.

The WNIA similarly portrayed Indian sexual and marriage practices as particularly cruel to young girls. "When a Navajo girl goes to her camp on vacation" from boarding school, *The Indian's Friend* reported, "she is always in more or less danger of forming those associations which result in trouble. If she goes out to herd the sheep some reckless young fellow riding across the country is likely to chase her and throw his lasso over her head, then he will strike the muscles of her arms so that she is powerless and he can accomplish any design for evil he may have in his heart." The writer added that in one such case, a girl's parents "connived . . . as they have come to the Mission and asked the missionary to unite these young people in marriage, which, of course he indignantly refused to do." "How our hearts hurt when we think of the life of this promising young girl being thus spoiled when she was half way to a beautiful Christian womanhood," the WNIA member lamented. "The end will probably be a heathen wedding and a life lived in the usual careless, unclean and superstitious heathen way."[75] As in Australia, white women reformers in the United States also evinced great concern with living a "clean" life.

Indigenous people understood their own marriage practices in quite different terms than white women. All indigenous societies had developed their own systems to carefully regulate who could marry whom and how marriages would take place. Marriage functioned primarily as a means to assure proper care, sustenance, and protection for all members of the group. While white Australian reformers regarded infant betrothal as proof of Aboriginal women's lowly status, Aboriginal people such as the Mornington Islanders regarded marriage as "sharing, raising, and . . . taking care of [each other]." After all, an older man had serious responsibilities to care for his promised wife and her family prior to and after his marriage to her.[76] Nevertheless, in most Aboriginal societies, as the anthropologist Ian Keen writes, "marriage practices defined women, not men, as bestowable. Although not mere objects, women were mainly reactive to marriage arrangements made by others, though they gained control with age. Men tended to deploy women's sexuality in wider relations."[77] Although infant betrothal seems to have restricted younger Aboriginal women's (and men's) choice of partners, this marriage system gave Aboriginal women greater latitude in later life. Once widowed, a woman often was free to choose a series of husbands or sexual partners, many of them younger than herself.[78] It thus seems to have been differences in age more than gender that structured hierarchies in indigenous Australian societies; indigenous women gained status, independence, and authority with age. Moreover, as in any society, actual practices did not always follow ideals; elopement and extramarital relations seem to have been "more common than the ideal picture allows for."[79] It would, in fact, take a multivolume work, perhaps an encyclopedia, to present the complex, varied, and changing nature of Aboriginal marriage practices and gender relations over time.[80]

American Indian groups had developed their own equally intricate and multifarious marriage customs and gender relations. According to the Nakota (Yankton Sioux) anthropologist Ella Deloria, the ideal nineteenth-century Lakota (Teton Sioux) marriage, the "most glamorous kind," was marriage by purchase, what white women reformers deemed evidence of Indian women's property status. "A woman who married in that way was much respected," Deloria writes. Yet marriage practices within Indian societies did not always follow the ideal, and they proved to be contested and somewhat elastic. Deloria explains that the Lakota had two other types of marriage: when two families mutually agreed that their children should marry and elopement. While Indian women were not the abject victims of male tyranny that white women reformers portrayed them as, neither were they fully liberated women in the twenty-first-century understanding of the term. Deloria's book *Waterlily* makes it clear that a sexual double standard existed among the Lakota; men went unpunished for sexual transgressions, but women could be shamed and ostracized for failing to remain a virgin before marriage or engaging in extramarital affairs. Marriage customs among indigenous groups were thus considerably more complicated than white women maternalists in the United States and Australia allowed.[81]

Like colonizing women around the world, white maternalists in the

United States and Australia reduced the heterogeneity and intricacy of indigenous gender relations to a homogenized image of indigenous women as the oppressed victims of their tyrannical men.[82] This appears to have been an early variant of and historical precedent for what the feminist theorist Chandra Mohanty calls "the Third World Woman," a creation of Western feminists in the 1970s and 1980s that similarly positioned non-Western, nonwhite women as always and everywhere the powerless and dependent victims of male violence, patriarchal families, and male-dominated religions.[83]

In Australia white women reformers believed that the status of Aboriginal women had only gotten worse with the coming of "civilization," particularly as a result of widespread interracial sex between white men and Aboriginal women. As Bennett put it, Aboriginal women were just "property" under tribal law; now wholesale prostitution of them by their own men had made them "merchandise."[84] As Bennett's remark makes clear, white Australian women commonly cast indigenous women as the passive victims of either their own cruel men or of lecherous white men.

At times, in contradiction to this view of indigenous women as passive victims of sexual exploitation, some white women in both nations portrayed indigenous women as the instigators of sexual immorality. The journalist Ernestine Hill, for example, wrote, "The black woman understands only sex, and that she understands fairly well. She is easy for the taking. . . . The lubra [a derogatory term for an Aboriginal woman] has no moral ethics whatever. . . . The half-caste girl, with her laughing eyes and sensuous lips, [is as] unmoral as her mother."[85] Some white women reformers in the United States also condemned what they perceived to be sexually immoral behavior among indigenous women. Mrs. Dorchester, reporting from the Navajo Agency, asserted, "The [Navajo] mothers to-day are the strongholds of paganism; they are conservative, superstitious," and involved in promoting early marriage of Indian girls, "selling of young girls for wives," and "tolerating a plurality of wives."[86] Ironically, white women seemed oblivious to the contradictions between their representation of indigenous women as the hapless victims of male degradation and this contrasting image of native women as active sexual agents. In either case, white women judged indigenous women as degraded in their bodies and in need of uplift and rescue.

It was not only white women's conceptions of indigenous women's sexuality, marriage, and work lives that led them to condemn indigenous societies and to advocate removal of indigenous children; it was also their beliefs that indigenous women were deficient mothers.[87] American Indian ways of rearing children often appeared alien to white women observers, so much so that white women often accused them of abuse or neglect, prime factors in justifying the removal of their children. Mrs. Weinland, a missionary in southern California, reported to the WNIA, "There are a great many little children here." When she drove over to visit several families, Weinland "found two new babies: one only two days old, and one nearly two weeks old and neither had on any article of clothing. One baby was wrapped in a piece of cheese-cloth, and crying with colic; and the baby two days old was wrapped in a piece of old calico and lying on the ground on a piece of an old quilt. The mother also was lying on the ground, covered with a gray blanket. This family lives in a brush-hut, called a 'wickyup.' The women do not seem to make any provision for their little ones."[88]

White female reformers and missionaries particularly condemned the ubiquitous use of cradleboards by a large number of Indian tribes. One missionary, Miss Howard, wrote, "I found a woman with a sick baby not yet three weeks old; of course it was strapped upon a board; and it was moaning with fever." A doctor told Miss Howard, "Get the babies off the board; that is what kills them." Howard believed the WNIA "would do a good work if [they] accomplished only [the cradle board's] abolition." She "succeeded in getting [this Native American woman] to hold her baby in her arms, and to put him upon a bed to sleep, 'as white squaws do.'"[89]

While white women perceived cradleboards as evidence of poor

6. An Indian woman on the Mescalero Apache Reservation with her infant in its cradleboard. New Mexico State University Library, Archives and Special Collections, MS 323.0027.

mothering skills, many Indian cultures utilized them for both practical and sacred purposes. Soon after giving birth, most American Indian women went back to their daily work of gathering or growing food, as well as collecting water and firewood, and so they devised means of carrying their infants while working. In many North American Indian cultures, mothers bundled their infants onto cradleboards that they wore on their back or leaned against a bush or tree while they engaged in their daily work.

Native cultures often infused the cradleboard with sacred meaning. Among the Navajos, soon after a child's birth "the father or some relative makes a cradle board from a perfect tree—one not struck by lightning." According to Irene Stewart, a Navajo, "Every bit of material [used for the cradleboard] is touched with corn pollen and sheep tallow with red ochre as the maker prays" to provide divine protection for the child. This sacred and blessed cradleboard, believed to have been given to the Navajos by the Holy People, would become the child's home for the next year. Countering white women's concerns, Stewart asserts, "The cradle board is convenient and safe and comfortable. I was raised in one."[90] Cradleboards were often passed down through generations, sustaining connections with the past and with ancestors.[91] For white American women, however, cradleboards appeared to be a wholly foreign method of carrying infants that demonstrated Indian women's supposed incompetence at mothering.

In Australia white women similarly portrayed Aboriginal women as inadequate mothers. At Ooldea the missionary Annie Lock criticized Aboriginal women: "[They were] very careless with their babies [who] were sleeping cosy in my arms & cried when their mothers took them, they carry them so uncomfortable."[92] As in North America, Aboriginal women kept their babies with them nearly all the time and devised a variety of methods to carry them. The Berndts observed that an Aboriginal baby "spends most of his time with his mother, or someone who deputizes for her. She breast-feeds him, carries him with her when she goes looking for food. He may lie in a curved wooden dish at her side,

7. A white and a Hopi girl with their dolls, January 1926. Clashing notions of how to raise children properly are vividly illustrated in this photo. Not only does the Hopi girl stray from white maternalists' bodily ideals, with her bare feet, but she also holds her doll inappropriately on her back. NAU.PH.99.54.166 (Item 7165). Image courtesy of Cline Library, Northern Arizona University.

in some areas lined with a pad of soft paperbark . . . or he himself may be wrapped in paperbark. In other areas he may be carried in a netbag, slung from her forehead."[93] In simply carrying their infants differently than white women did indigenous women became marked as inferior mothers.

Some white women claimed that indigenous women engaged in a more serious offense, infanticide, especially against mixed-race children. Daisy Bates alleged that "half-caste" children were unwanted and that Aboriginal mothers routinely killed them.[94] Even in the United States, where there was not such an obsession with part-Indian children, the belief prevailed that mixed-race children were rejected by their mothers. In Arizona Miss F. S. Calfee, a field matron among the Hualapai Indians, accused them of mistreating a "little half-breed girl." Calfee asserted, "[The girl, about twelve,] seems to have a nice disposition, and were she taken away and kindly treated, would, I feel sure, make a good woman." According to Calfee, "These Indians hate half-breed children, and whenever they dare, smother them at their birth. This little girl has been treated worse than a dog by the Indians with whom she has had to stay, and they allowed her to go almost naked, until I made clothes for her." Calfee wrote the WNIA in hopes that someone would volunteer "to take this poor, abused child and care for her." She also commented, "If the boarding school which the Massachusetts [Women's] Indian Association hopes to have on its ranch in Truxton [Canyon] . . . were in operation the right thing would be done for this forlorn child."[95]

There is, in fact, evidence that some indigenous women in some groups may have practiced infanticide in some circumstances. Bennett explained such a practice in an empathetic way: "A woman can carry one child in her long hunting day's trail; and that is a severe test of enduring love. It may be twenty miles to the evening meeting place." Her husband, if successful in his hunting, would be required to carry up to eighty pounds of meat to their evening rendezvous. "If there are a child of two years and a new baby, what is their mother to do? She knows that if she tries to carry both children none of them will reach the meeting place. She kills the baby rather than leave it to the crows. She carries the two-year-old throughout the long day's journey and digs for roots and lizards and grubs and gathers seeds for her provision towards the evening meal."[96]

Some American Indian women probably carried out infanticide as well. Theda Perdue notes that among the Cherokees, "infanticide may have been practiced . . . as the only acceptable means by which people could control population growth. Apparently the mother alone had the right to abandon a child; for anyone else to kill a newborn constituted murder."[97] The practice of, and apparent harsh necessity for, infanticide represents a facet of traditional indigenous life that challenges our present-day tendencies to romanticize indigenous societies and tempts us to adopt some of the same attitudes of white women reformers at the turn of the twentieth century. Yet the use of infanticide suggests, as Bennett sought to convey, the difficulty of subsistence for some indigenous peoples, not the callous indifference of the mothers. Moreover, as we saw in chapter 2, the notion that Aboriginal people rejected mixed-race babies was a common but largely unsubstantiated claim that was used to justify the removal of part-Aboriginal children.

Some white women went to extremes in creating sensational portrayals of poor Aboriginal mothering. Daisy Bates routinely asserted that Aboriginal women in Ooldea ate their unwanted babies. For example, she declared in 1929, "There is no time to lose in getting [a] new system in force" because "the groups still untouched by civilization are eating their own kind, and cannibalism is intensifying in the [central] Reserve."[98] The historian Jim Anderson found that in 1930, Bates "sent the bones of what she claimed were the remains of a cannibalistic feast to Adelaide University for investigation. They turned out to be 'undoubtedly those of a domestic cat.'"[99] The anthropologist Isobel White contends that Bates lost respect among scholars and some reformers when she made such accusations.[100]

This notion of Aboriginal women eating their babies was picked up and repeated by other prominent white women. Jessie Litchfield, a settler who lived in the far north of Australia, claimed that although there were many white men who cohabited with Aboriginal women, "there were very few half-castes in the north," because they were "invariably killed at birth," to be eaten at "cannibal feasts."[101] Remarkably, American women made similar fanciful claims about Indian parenting. In 1915 Matilda Coxe Stevenson, an early anthropologist among the Pueblo Indians of the southwestern United States, alleged that the Pueblos routinely fed unwanted babies to large snakes that they kept in captivity. Although Stevenson's sensational claims could not be substantiated and Indian agents protested to the commissioner of Indian affairs, no public retraction appeared in any of the newspapers across the country that had originally carried Stevenson's comments.[102]

As in the case of "child savers," who took urban children from their impoverished parents, these reformers regarded any family relationships that deviated from their nuclear patriarchal family ideal—of male bread-winning and female domesticity in a middle-class home—as aberrant.[103] Marie Ives described her version of the ideal home to the Lake Mohonk conference: "[It] is the husband and wife loving each other, mutually helpful and considerate, and the little children trained by wise love. That is the ideal which I would set before the Indians."[104] Indigenous families came up short in many white women's eyes because, as explored in chapter 2, extended families with elaborate kin networks rather than nuclear families were the norm in indigenous societies.

Still other reformers disparaged indigenous family life simply because of the great poverty they witnessed, much of it induced by European colonization. In one sod house among the Omaha Indians, a WNIA member, Mrs. Frye, "found a mother with a young infant wrapped in rags, sitting alone on a little straw on the damp ground with most meagre food and no comforts."[105] Similarly in Australia, white women often criticized Aboriginal women for feeding their children a "monotonous diet of damper [a type of bread cooked in a Dutch oven] and tea."[106] Such reformers seemed oblivious to the fact that whites had taken over lands on which indigenous people used to hunt and gather wild foods and had replaced that nutritious diet with rations of coffee, tea, and flour.[107]

White women reformers particularly dwelled on what they believed to be the inadequate home environment of indigenous women and children. Loulie Taylor, describing her experiences at Fort Hall Reservation in Idaho, wrote:

> We had . . . the advantage of seeing just how the Indian lives in his tepee, and what had been the life of these children before coming to the mission.
>
> What a contrast! The smoking fire in the centre of the tepee, and on it the pot of soup stirred by the not over-clean squaw, whose black hair fell in as she stirred; men, women, and children lolling on the ground, a few blankets the only furnishing of the tepee; and then to think of the neat, comfortable home at the mission, with the uplifting of its daily prayer offered to their Great Spirit, our Heavenly Father. We realized what a blessed work these faithful missionaries . . . were doing in giving to these poor, neglected children . . . some of the light and blessing that had been given to them.[108]

Similarly, Australian white women routinely condemned Aboriginal housing as a sign of indigenous women's supposed degradation. Violet Turner, a missionary and writer, described one Aboriginal home near Oodnadatta in South Australia: "Just behind the group was—well, what was it? Not a house, surely? It looked like a crazy patchwork quilt worked out in tin of all shapes, stuck together at any angle. Where there was not enough tin a row of old barrels did duty as part of the wall. It would be difficult to describe the collection of rubbish that formed the roof. This was the home of one of these native families."[109] Turner and Taylor can barely conceal their contempt for the people who live in dwellings that are so alien to their experiences.

The white, middle-class home occupied a central place in white maternalists' identities and priorities. Without a clean, orderly, fixed abode that included all the trappings of modern middle-class life—furniture, decorations, curtains, tablecloths, and other accoutrements—indigenous women appeared to white women reformers to be utterly inadequate not only as housekeepers, but as mothers. White women regarded the home as an extension of a woman; if her home was "unclean," disorderly, or lacking in Western material goods, it reflected poorly on the woman's moral character.[110]

An indigenous woman's morals were allegedly on display through her body as well. If she did not conform to white women's dress and hygienic codes, an indigenous woman might be labeled "unclean." The concerns of white women reformers are captured and packaged together in one WNIA article, "The Indian Girl," which began by describing the girl's bodily appearance as beyond the pale of white women's standards: "In her ears are earrings half a yard long. Her bare arms are generally ornamented with wide bracelets. Around her neck are numerous strings of beads and a necklace of elk teeth." The author then laments that the Indian "girl has never had a bath in her life; she has never slept in a bed or eaten from a table; was never in childhood taught to say a prayer or tenderly kissed and snugly tucked into bed. But with or without sup-per . . . and, in the same clothes she had worn for months, [she] curled herself up under a blanket and slept. She does not know a single letter of the alphabet, or a hymn. She has never been to a birthday party, nor a Thanksgiving dinner, nor a Fourth of July celebration; she has never heard the sweet story of Christmas."[111] Violet Turner echoes the WNIA in her description of an Aboriginal boy, "Jack," who "had never been in a house, had never seen a table set for a meal, and knew no food but the flour-and-water damper of the camp."[112] Neither Jack nor the Indian girl had experienced the world—through their bodies or homes—as white middle-class women believed they should. These seemingly mundane matters, the intimate details of these children's lives, accumulated enor-mous significance to these women as signs of deficient and inadequate mothering and homemaking.

As these white women's laments make clear, cleanliness of the body

8. Daisy Bates and Aboriginal women, 1911, postcard. This image conveys the starkly contrasting conceptions of the body between many white women maternalists and many Aboriginal women at the turn of the twentieth century. P2044/2. By permission of the National Library of Australia.

and home was not simply about an absence of dirt or even just a trope for morality; it was also tied to middle-class consumption, to promoting an aesthetics that required the adornment of the home and the body in a way that signified one's class status. Most white women reformers could not escape their constellation of middle-class aesthetics, values, and consumerism to recognize the different sensory universe that many indigenous people inhabited.

In fact, many white women invested their vision of home with great significance, as the foundation of "civilization," and believed that if indigenous women simply adopted such homes, the "problem" of indigenous people would be solved.[113] In 1890 one WNIA member, Mrs. Dorchester, asserted, "No uncivilized people are elevated till the mothers are reached. The civilization must begin in the homes."[114] Estelle Reel concurred: "The homes of the camp Indians are to be reached mostly through our school girls, who are to be the future wives and mothers of the race, and on their advancement will depend largely the future condition of the Indian. All history has proven that as the mother

is so is the home, and that a race will not rise above the home standard."[115]

Perhaps the home and body took on such significant dimensions
among white women because the establishment of white homes throughout the land and white women's reproductive bodies were vital to the
settler colonial enterprise. Where white men (primarily) set up only
camps in places from which they sought to extract resources and then
move on (as in mining camps), the building of solid homes demonstrated in no uncertain terms an intention to stay and to settle. In laying
claim to the land, government officials and boosters alike promoted
home building. It is no accident that in the 1860s both the U.S. government and all the Australian colonies passed legislation (the Homestead
Act in the United States and the Selection Acts in Australia) to promote
homesteading on small plots of land by yeoman farm families.[116] In the
1930s the journalist Ernestine Hill concluded in her book *The Great
Australian Loneliness* that in the Northern Territory, still sparsely settled
by whites, "the dominant need is for the great national stimulus of home
life. . . . In a word, its crying necessity is more white women."[117] The
home and its keeper, invested with material and political significance,
would act as the stimulus to nation building.

Further, through their bodies white women would literally reproduce
the settler population necessary to establishing dominance over the invaded territory. Far from being intimate matters that were insulated
from the public world of nation and empire building, the home and the
body, and women's association with them, functioned as indispensable
building blocks for the settler colonial project. White women were thus
endowed with a special role to play in the reproduction of the settler
colony.[118]

Given the similarities between American and Australian white
women's maternalist sentiment and their representations of indigenous
women within their own nations, we might assume that the two groups
had frequent contact and communication with one another, but there is
little evidence that they did. While white women surely relied on strong

female networks within their own countries, it is difficult to find any direct contact between white women activists in the United States and Australia. Australians maintained closer contact and ties with England and its other colonies than they did with the United States. Through the London-based organizations, the BCL and the Anti-Slavery and Aborigines Protection Society, as well as the Pan-Pacific Conferences that were first held in 1928 in Honolulu, Australian women connected their maternalist movement to others around the world.[119] American women who advocated for Indian issues seemed less internationally aware and connected.

Australian feminists did seem to keep abreast of the United States and its racial and gender politics by reading. (I have found no evidence that American women made any similar effort to learn from Australian experiences and events.) Bennett read avidly, telling Pink how much she enjoyed Booker T. Washington's autobiography, using familiar terms to make sense of his experience. She told Pink, "Though a half-caste, [he] remained a negro at heart with all a negro's wonderful spirituality and other gifts." Perhaps referring to W. E. B. Du Bois's famous remark that "the problem of the twentieth century is the problem of the color line," in her 1930 book Bennett declared, "The founding of a just relation of the white and the dark races is not our problem alone. It is a world problem. It is described as the most important business of this century." Later in her book Bennett remarked, "We want an . . . Australian Harriet Beecher Stowe."[120] It is interesting to note, however, that Australian women activists such as Bennett looked more toward ideologies and policies involving African Americans than they did to those directed at American Indians.

Despite little direct connection, this shared commitment to maternalist reform in both the United States and Australia may have emanated from an Anglo-American women's internationalism that began in the late nineteenth century and spread across English-speaking nations and colonies through the activism of the World's Woman's Christian Temperance Union (WWCTU), women's foreign missionary societies, and the Young Women's Christian Association.[121] The WWCTU's global organizing efforts in particular brought American and Australian activists together. For example, Jessie Ackermann, an American activist who became one of the WWCTU's international missionaries, toured Australia extensively four times and claims to have organized more than four hundred branches of the WCTU there.[122] Mobilizing for suffrage worldwide, often through the WCTU as well as the International Woman Suffrage Alliance (IWSA), also brought women together across international borders and allowed maternalist notions to be disseminated widely in disparate regions. When the American suffragist Carrie Chapman Catt spoke at an IWSA banquet given in her honor in London, she promoted the maternalist vision to her international audience: "It remains for women to unite in something greater than nations,—in the motherhood of the world."[123]

— white women promoted the notion of dirty - unsuitable women in NA & Ind. comm, in order to justify child removal

From Representation to Action

For white women who worked on behalf of Aboriginal and Indian women, indigenous women seemed to be wholly unequipped to raise their children. Whereas white women depicted white motherhood as sacred, they portrayed indigenous motherhood as virtually pathological. These derogatory representations did not just operate in the field of abstract discourse, however; they had very real consequences for indigenous women and their families because they helped pave the way for or affirmed proposals to remove indigenous children to institutions where white women would raise them "properly." White women themselves put their beliefs into action and used their considerable organizational powers to promote policies to remove and institutionalize indigenous children.

In the United States, based on their oft-repeated view that Indian women and girls were degraded, particularly in sexual matters, white women reformers often advocated the removal of Indian children. Amelia Stone Quinton, for example, claimed that Navajo women were promiscuous, and therefore "good morals [within the home] are next to impossible. For children from such homes, the day school can do far less than the boarding school."[124] Like Quinton, Alice Fletcher became a primary proponent of Indian child removal. According to the WNIA, Fletcher "had found [Omaha and Winnebago] pupils returned from Eastern Indian schools, to be among the tribes the leaven of hope, progress and civilization in almost every instance. . . . She thought we could not too highly value the atmosphere of civilization and right faith in the East, which, constantly absorbed, forces rapidly forward the progress and development of Indian pupils here. This culture, she says, is needed to . . . redeem them from the monotony and sleepiness of uncivilized ideas and methods."[125]

Fletcher often justified her support for removing indigenous children by invoking the ideology of cultural evolution. In her speech, "Our Duty toward Dependent Races," Fletcher fulminated:

> In this march of progress thru the centuries the victory has been with the race that was able to develop those mental forces by which man is lifted above his natural life, which enabled him to discern the value of work.
>
> Looking back over the ages, there is little doubt that to the white race belong the great achievements of human progress. The religions of the world have sprung from this branch of the human family, the higher arts and sciences are its children, and it is also true that this race has held possession of the best portions of the Earth's surface.[126]

Given this "march of progress," Fletcher contended. "Civilization or extermination are the solemn facts which face the Indian. There is no middle course for any race. Isolation is practically extermination, if we honestly mean to offer the chances of life to the Indian, he must be brought in amicable contact with our daily living."[127]

As we shall see in chapter 5, Fletcher took her support for child removal to the next level; in 1881 she hired on with Captain Pratt to "recruit" Indian children for Carlisle. After meeting with the famed Lakota leader Sitting Bull, Fletcher supposedly gained his consent to take all seventy-six of the children from his band. She wrote to the secretary of war for his permission to have the children taken to mission schools: "I lay this matter before you hoping you will be able to help these little ones who in their nakedness of mind and body plead to the benevolence of our race. Sitting Bull has learned his first lesson, submission, and seems now willing and ready to be led toward a better way of living, he proves his sincerity in this request." Fletcher signed her letter, "With earnest wishes that these children may be given into Christian hands."[128]

Perhaps the white woman in the United States with the greatest authority to turn white women's negative representations of Indian women into the policy and practice of Indian child removal was Estelle Reel. In her position as superintendent of Indian education from 1898 to 1910, Reel enthusiastically led efforts to remove increasing numbers of Indian children from their homes to boarding schools. She presented herself as having a special talent—because she was a woman—for coercing Indian women to give up their children. In one of her press releases, reprinted verbatim by a newspaper, she asserted:

No man superintendent of Indian schools could have done what Miss Reel is doing. Her strongest hold is to go into the wigwams of the Indian women, gain their confidence and liking and make them see how much better it is to trust their children to the training of civilization. Among the wildest, most degraded peoples it is still the mother who has the say concerning the children, and the lower in the scale of intelligence the woman is the more surely she will trust a woman rather than a man of any kind. It has remained for civilized woman to turn from her own sex and declare she would trust a man before a woman.

At any rate these wild women trust Miss Reel utterly when she goes into their wigwams and tells them that their children will have

9. Estelle Reel, superintendent of Indian education, 1898–1910, with Indian students at Sherman Institute, Riverside, California. ER6.30.4, Estelle Reel Collection (MS 120), Northwest Museum of Arts & Culture, Spokane, Washington.

power to cope with the white man and get their own back again if they learn to use the white man's own weapons. As woman to woman she appeals to them, and they listen and acquiesce.[129]

Reel also provided newspapers across the country with other upbeat accounts of her role in taking Indian children to boarding schools, declaring in one such account, "Miss Reel is popular with the Indians. She is known as the 'Big White Squaw from Washington.' So fond of her are some of the Indians that they are willing she should take their children away, and one Indian woman insisted that she should carry a pair of fat papooses to President Roosevelt. She doesn't have to bribe the Indians with promises and presents to send their children to school now."[130]

Despite her bravado, Reel probably had little to do with the actual removal of children, but she would have learned from her agents and superintendents of the difficulties they often encountered from women who resisted the taking of their children. Therefore she promoted a compulsory law to force Indian parents to send their children to school (see chapter 4). Again, writing in the third person, Reel wrote of herself:

Miss Reel is of the opinion that a general compulsory law is indispensable to any considerable degree of progress in Indian education, and that such a law should be enacted and enforced. The average attendance at the Indian schools is some 20,000, but it is not obligatory upon the father or mother of the child to send the little one to the school, and if the parents so will, the child need never attend. . . .

The Indian child must be placed in school before the habits of barbarous life have become fixed, and there he must be kept until contact with our life has taught him to abandon his savage ways and walk in the path of Christian civilization.[131]

In her zeal to promote a compulsory school law for Indian children, Reel announced, "If the Indian will not accept the opportunities for elevation and civilization so generously offered him, the strong hand of the law should be evoked and the pupil forced to receive an education whether his parents will it or not."[132]

Reel justified such drastic measures in part by appealing to maternalist images of Indian girls as exploited victims within their tribes. She and a small group of teachers at the Indian school in Grand Junction, Colorado, petitioned the government to pass her compulsory schooling law in 1900, offering this rationale: "The training the young Indian girl desires is sometimes denied her by the greed of gain that may and does accrue to her parents because of her sale; you know that such parents refuse their consent to the child going to school either on or off the reservation; thus taking advantage of the only law in our land that in any direct way provides for the government and control of the more progressive by the more ignorant and prejudiced."[133]

Reel also relied on the maternalist notion that the civilization of Indians depended on transforming the home and the Indian woman's role within it. If Indian girls could be taken away and trained in the boarding schools before they learned the poor habits of their mothers, they would become the vanguard of reform. As Reel put it, "Industrial training will make the Indian boy a useful, practical, self-supporting citizen. It will make the Indian girl more motherly. This is the kind of girl we want,—the one who will exercise the greatest influence in moulding the character of the nation. . . . Thus will they become useful members of this great Republic, and if compulsory education is extended to all the tribes, there is little reason to doubt that the ultimate civilization of the race will result."[134]

Thus in the United States white women reformers not only created ubiquitous images of Indian women as unfit mothers, but also worked intently to promote, and sometimes even to carry out, policies to remove Indian children from their families. In this endeavor, powerful white women such as Quinton, Fletcher, and Reel seem to have had the ear of the federal government and to have been regarded by government officials as a powerful tool to aid them in their assimilation policies. A different situation prevailed in Australia, where white women had a more embattled position in relationship to their state governments and Aboriginal policy.

Protecting Aboriginal Women and Girls

Like their American counterparts, many white Australian maternalists promoted the removal of Aboriginal girls to institutions. In 1924, for example, a large coalition of women's groups across Australia led a campaign to reform the Bungalow home for Aboriginal children in Alice Springs, alleging that conditions there fostered sexual immorality. At an interstate conference of the National Councils of Women of Australia in Melbourne that year, Mrs. A. K. Goode condemned the Bungalow and contended, "There should be a training school in the Territory, and flaxen-haired children taken further away, perhaps to South Australia."[135] After the conference, many women's groups began agitating for reform. On the surface, the women seemed to oppose child removal. The Tasmanian WNPA wrote angrily, "The children were taken from the protection of their mothers, and placed in a galvanized iron shed."[136]

Yet the WNPA and other women's organizations did not propose returning the children to "the protection of their mothers" or ending the practice of indigenous child removal altogether. Instead, the WNPA "arranged a deputation to the Minister of Public Works and asked him whether . . . the government would place some of the youngest and whitest (quadroons and octoroons) [at the Bungalow] under the care of the South Australian State Children's Department." The group also promoted building a new home for children at the Bungalow based on the cottage system rather than dormitories. "One of its advantages," the WNPA wrote, "is the possibility of really guarding inmates, a matter surely to be seriously considered in the half-caste home." In addition, the association asked for white women to be consulted regarding Aboriginal policy and to be made protectors in the northern areas of the country. Other women's organizations—the WSG in Western Australia, the WCTU, the Feminist Club in Sydney, and the Women's League and the Women's Union of Service in New South Wales—joined the WNPA in its campaign to reform the Bungalow in 1924.[137]

During this campaign Constance Cooke wrote to the minister for the interior "to ask [the] Government to do something for the younger and whiter children." "Sir," Cooke pleaded, "we recognize that the institution to be built in the North is most desirable for those half castes whom it is impossible to absorb into our own populations (partly because many of them are already immoral through their past environment, and partly through their aboriginal characteristics). But we do beg that our Government . . . will give the younger and whiter children the chance of a fuller citizenship." Cooke ended by repeating her request that "those female children (the quadroons and octoroons), who are more white than black, be placed, at about the age of two years, in decent civilized homes with foster mothers" in South Australia.[138]

Interestingly, some white men challenged the women's organizations on this point. John Sexton of the Aborigines' Friends' Association (AFA), a South Australian missionary organization, told the commonwealth government's minister for home and territories, "Strong opposition was shown at the [AFA] meeting to the proposal to raid native camps in the interior and take half-caste children from their mothers in order that they may be brought to [South Australia] and trained in the State Children's Department. It was contended that this procedure would violate natural instincts, and it was agreed that such children born in the interior should be trained and disciplined in Federal Territory, and be placed in such localities that native mothers would be able to gratify their maternal feelings by seeing their children occasionally." Thus Sexton proposed rebuilding the Bungalow in a more "suitable locality."[139] Other white men joined the chorus of protest against the women's proposals. Alfred Giles wrote to a newspaper in Adelaide, "I do not think I have ever heard or read of such a cruel, shocking, and un-Christian proposal as that submitted by a group of people calling themselves Christian." He continued, "The proposal placed before the Minister is neither more nor less than slavery," and "to separate [the children from their mothers] indiscriminately and for ever would be a barbarous cruelty." (It may be that these male critics opposed white women's efforts more to stifle their budding political activism than to take a principled stand against child removal. Both Sexton and Giles still supported the removal of "half-caste" children to an institution even if they did advocate that "parents of the inmates should have free access to them at stated intervals.")[140]

When Sexton's criticism became public, the women's groups defended themselves: "At the time, our aims were somewhat misrepresented, and it was fancied that we advocated a wanton separation of mothers and children. It is now, I think, well understood that we referred to the neglected and orphaned children and those of depraved mothers—children who are already rightly parted from unfit guardians."[141] Even in backpedaling from their original stance, however, the groups revealed a close adherence to the rhetoric of neglect, moral depravity, and unfit motherhood, charges that, as we have seen, were unfairly associated with *all* Aborigines.

The government rejected the white women's proposal out of hand. Tellingly, however, a few years later government authorities proposed a similar plan. A representative for the prime minister promoted removing young "quadroons" and "octoroons" from the Bungalow to South Australia, arguing, "If these babies were removed, at their present early age, from their present environment to homes in [South Australia], they would not know in later life that they had aboriginal blood and would probably be absorbed into the white population and become useful citizens."[142] Thus male government authorities did not oppose white women's scheme because they disagreed with it, but because they believed the women to be meddling in public policy making that was outside their proper sphere.

After this episode, the women's organizations seem to have become wary of organizing a strong public stand on Aboriginal child removal, but some individual women occasionally raised the issue. At the 1927 BCL conference, for example, Constance Cooke asked, "Should the children who are racially more European be left amongst the children who are racially more aboriginal?" She contended, as did the authorities, that they should be removed: "These children have already been taken from their mothers, and if the younger and whiter ones were sent away from the native environment they could be absorbed easily into our population, and thus given the chance of a fuller citizenship. . . . We should do all in our power for these victims of a white man's depravity."[143] In 1932 Cooke again supported the removal of indigenous children, in this case recommending the establishment of a "hostel for neglected female full-blood native children."[144]

As these examples demonstrate, white Australian women reformers often did not object to official policy, including the removal of Aboriginal children, but to how male officials carried it out. This was nowhere more evident than in the women's criticisms of officials' efforts to deal with interracial sex and "half-castes." Australian women's groups condemned authorities who turned a blind eye to interracial sex or even encouraged it through "breeding out the colour." The Women's Section of the United Country Party registered their strenuous objections to Northern Territory Chief Protector Cecil Cook's policy encouraging marriages between white men and "half-caste" women. "It is greatly to be deplored that the Federal Government is so far lost to the knowledge of our deep rooted sentiments and pride of race," they wrote, "as to attempt to infuse a strain of aboriginal blood into our coming generations." Thus they resolved, "The Women's Organisations of Australia [should] be urged, that for the race heritage that we hold in trust for the generations to come, for the sanctity of our age old traditions, and the protection of our growing boys, to combat with all their power this insidious attempt to mingle with the community, women of illegitimate birth, tainted with aboriginal blood, the offspring of men of the lowest human type, many of who are Asiatics and other foreign nationalities."[145] Interestingly, in this case the women's group objected to Cook's policy not on the grounds that it demoralized Aboriginal women, but because they believed it was tainting the white race with Aboriginal and other nonwhite blood.

Other longtime women activists objected to Cook's policy because they believed it failed to properly protect Aboriginal women. Bennett opposed Cook's plan because it involved "the extermination of the unhappy native race, and the leaving of the most unfortunate native women at the disposal of lustful white men." She wrote, "This policy is euphemistically described by Australian officialdom as 'the absorption' of the native race and the 'breeding out of colour'!!! We shall be better able to evaluate this policy when another race applies it to ourselves as 'the absorption of the white race' and 'the breeding out of white people'!!!"[146]

Olive Pink raised feminist concerns with interracial sex to the level of an obsession. "I am sorry for half-castes and would get them all the justice I could (now they have been born—through the lack of sexual self-control of men of the white race)," she wrote. "It is no use calling our race more civilized and then blame the black women. . . . We should try to educate and absorb those half-castes already born. But try to prevent the breeding of more."[147] Like Bennett and many other feminists, Pink despised the government's absorption plans. She believed, "An 'ABSORPTION' policy is substituted for the almost obsolete lethal instruments of poison and gun. It is an equally dastardly means. Looked at, stripped bare of verbal camouflage it amounts to a Church-and-State approved licentiousness, by white men, WHERE BLACK WOMEN ARE CONCERNED."[148] Many male officials regarded Pink as a nuisance, as "so obsessed with matters of sex" and as a "self-appointed guardian of humanity's morals," who "for years . . . has bombarded people in all parts of Australia with unsolicited and interminable correspondence, unrestrainedly defaming large numbers of . . . people associated . . . with aboriginals."[149] To her many critics, Pink retorted, "I know perfectly well I have been and shall be accused of being a) a rabid feminist or b) with a 'complex' on sex. But I am guilty of neither."[150]

Although Pink was perhaps the most vocal and frequent critic of interracial sex, she was not alone; virtually all white officials and reformers agreed that unregulated interracial sex was a problem. They posed three main solutions: (1) control and limit white men's access to Aboriginal women; (2) import more white women into remote frontier areas; and (3) "protect" (that is, control) Aboriginal and "half-caste" women. Many feminists originally sought to restrict white men's sexuality by increasing penalties against those who engaged in sex with Aboriginal women and to assure the enforcement of such laws. "Male licentiousness is responsible for the fact that there is a native problem at all," Pink asserted. "Were there no white males there would be no 'native problem.'"[151]

As we have seen, white male authorities never took this feminist proposition seriously, but in an interesting twist on the "problem" of interracial sex in Australia, they often blamed white women for failing to move to the outback to become the partners of white men. J. W. Bleakley contended, "Efforts to check the abuse of these defenceless [female] aborigines and the breeding of half-castes will have little likelihood of success until conditions can be developed that will encourage white women to brave the hardships of the outback. One good white woman in a district will have more restraining influence than all the Acts and Regulations."[152] Such a belief seemed stronger among white men, but was shared by some women, such as the journalist Ernestine Hill, who, after journeying through Australia beginning in 1930, concluded in her book *The Great Australian Loneliness*, "If there is any blame for Australia's present half-caste problem, it lies at the self-contained flat door of the white woman of the overcrowded cities, for men are only human."[153] Bennett objected to such a stance in a letter to the editor of the *Western Australian:* "With regard to the widespread abuse of black girls and half-caste girls, it is time that the wickedness of the white men was charged to them."[154]

Bennett and her sister reformers had to admit defeat, however; they did not have the power or influence to stop white men from having sex with Aboriginal women in the outback. Thus they turned, as did many white male officials, to "protecting" Aboriginal girls and women, in effect monitoring and controlling their sexuality, through their decades-long campaign for the appointment of women protectors. Daisy Bates had applied for the job of protector of Aborigines in Western Australia in 1912 but was rejected on the grounds that a white woman would be unsafe traveling and living among Aborigines. However, the state government did reward her with the unpaid position of honorary protector of Aborigines.[155] A few other women had also gained such "honorary" positions; government authorities directed them "to take a particular interest in the protection of the Aboriginal and half-caste children, especially in the rescuing of half-caste girls under the age of sixteen years from immoral and vicious surroundings." However, officials did not allow female protectors the broader powers they gave to male protectors to issue permits for employment to their Aboriginal charges; instead, it limited them to providing basic medical attention and referring Aboriginal people to health care authorities.[156]

A desire for greater involvement and influence over state policies coalesced into a campaign for women protectors that began in the late 1920s and continued throughout the 1930s. White women activists believed that male authorities were failing to protect Aboriginal women and that therefore white women should become their protectors. Bennett accused male police officers of fathering many half-caste children and of protecting other white men who consorted with native women.[157] She argued, "There is little hope for safety of the person for female natives until the evil of placing defenceless native girls under the '*protection*' of alien white men is done away with, and women are appointed to care for women. This is asked by Women's Associations in Australia."[158] As can be seen in Bennett's comment, the campaigns for women protectors undertaken by white women's groups epitomized their notions of women's work for women. At a 1929 conference Edith Jones argued, "[White women] can understand . . . [the] needs [of Aboriginal women and children] far better than men, however kindly disposed they may be. It is for that reason we feel that women protectors are urgently needed."[159] There was some disagreement among white women advocates as to what qualified a woman to serve as a protector. Some believed missionaries qualified; others supported only women with some anthropological training.[160]

At least one Aboriginal woman agreed that white women would make better administrators of Aboriginal policy. When asked if white women should participate in administration of the Native Act of Western Australia, Gladys Prosser replied, "I think that is essential. . . . Our native mothers have all the natural feelings of mothers the world over, and to many of them the administration of the Native Department by men only, is a stark tragedy."[161]

Some male reformers concurred that white women were needed as protectors of Aboriginal women. Reverend Rod Schenk, for example, of the Mt. Margaret Mission, asserted, "It would be difficult to find a man who could not condone to some extent the treatment of native women by native and white men, but a good [white] woman stands in with her native sister and wins the day."[162] In his 1929 report to the government on conditions of Aboriginals in Central Australia, J. W. Bleakley wrote that "a good missionary mother with common sense and medical knowledge" was needed there. However, Bleakley and others did not approve of single women serving in such a capacity.[163]

Most officials, however, routinely rebuffed the women's calls for women protectors. Baldwin Spencer recommended that every official working with Aboriginal people, especially government protectors, should be a married man.[164] The minister for the interior in 1936 reacted with indignation to charges that Aboriginal women were being brutally treated and declared that "the demand that women should be appointed as protectors . . . was absurd."[165] In 1937, when chief protectors and other officials from all the states and the Northern Territory met in Canberra to consider Aboriginal welfare, the group of men declared that the widespread appointment of women protectors "is not considered practicable, because of the very scattered nature of native camps, the difficulties of travel and the isolation."[166] White women were successful in having women appointed in some states, but not always as they had imagined. The South Australia WNPA convinced the state government to appoint an "official lady visitor" to inspect Aboriginal girls placed in homes in the state, but the government appointed Mrs. Olive Owen, already a matron at the Home for Aboriginal Women and Children in north Adelaide, not the hand-picked choice of the WNPA.[167] Overall, the decade-long campaign for women protectors came to naught.

Here was a crucial difference between white women's efforts to advocate for indigenous women in the United States and Australia. White women in the United States were integral to reform efforts and policy making. Senator Henry Dawes (architect of the 1887 Allotment Act) reportedly declared, "[The] new Indian policy . . . was born of and nursed by the women of this association [the WNIA]."[168] Alice Fletcher was remarkably influential on government policy. In 1887 she successfully convinced Senator Dawes to amend his proposed allotment act to prevent the patenting of any Indian land to tribes as a whole. She insisted that only Indian individuals should receive allotted land. Joan Mark asserts, "The dramatic increase in federal appropriations for American Indian education in five years—from $475,000 in 1880 to $992,000 in 1885—was due in good measure to Alice Fletcher's efforts." Fletcher also deeply influenced Commissioner of Indian Affairs Thomas Jefferson Morgan (1889–93), one of the most ardent proponents of compulsory education for Indian children. He quoted her at length in his annual reports.[169] And of course Estelle Reel's twelve-year tenure as superintendent of Indian education also attests to a significant collaboration between white women reformers and government officials in the United States.

Australian white women activists, on the other hand, more often worked at odds with government authorities and were excluded from real influence. While attending a 1929 conference, Mrs. Britomarte James summarized the perspective of white women reformers: "We feel that we are at a disadvantage in that at present we can only come and ask the men to do what we would like to be in a position to do if we had more power."[170] Even though many white women spoke out against the abuses of Aboriginal women and proposed a greater role for themselves in policy making and implementation, Australian authorities minimized their contribution. Western Australia Chief Protector Neville, for example, wrote condescendingly, "The women of Australia could do a lot for their less fortunate coloured sisters if they really wanted to, but they have so much they want to do, have they not?" He added snidely (and disingenuously), "One would have thought that where contact between their own men and native women became the rule rather than the exception, as in some parts of Australia, our women would have made their presence felt. On the contrary, very few white women have ventured to speak out."[171] A comparison of Neville's remarks with that of Senator Dawes reveals two very different relationships between white women and the state.

Whether in tandem with their government or not, maternalists in both the United States and Australia who campaigned for indigenous reforms generally supported a policy of indigenous child removal that seems to be fundamentally at odds with other maternalist efforts. In the late nineteenth and early twentieth centuries white American maternalists sought the uplift of African American, Asian American, and Mexican American women, whom they also deemed in need of rescue, but no one seriously entertained that all of the children of any of these groups of women should be taken away and institutionalized for at least a portion of their young lives.[172] And both American and Australian maternalist reformers in urban areas no longer advocated the removal and institutionalization of white working-class children; instead, they sought to ensconce white working-class women in the home through the state's provision of a maternity allowance in Australia and mothers' pensions in the United States.

Why, then, did so many white women reformers promote a policy that undermined indigenous women's maternity? Certainly these women did not set out with cruel intentions; they truly believed they were advocating policies for the good of indigenous children. Bound by their own maternal assumptions of what was good and necessary for children, many white women were sickened by the poverty they witnessed in indigenous communities. The missionary Violet Turner, after touring an impoverished camp at Oodnadatta, felt immensely guilty: "I could scarcely speak to these people for the shame that I felt that our civilization had done nothing better for them than this."[173] Constance Cooke, upon seeing conditions among Aboriginal groups in Central Australia for the first time in the 1920s, admitted, "I was appalled by the misery, want and degradation that I saw. I felt ashamed of our treatment of these original owners of the land."[174]

On many occasions, too, white women reformers evinced great sympathy for indigenous mothers. One WNIA member who witnessed the death of a Navajo child wrote, "It was pathetic to see the grief of the mother." She quoted the Navajo mother: "I never thought a mother felt so sorry when she lost her children, but I am very sorry to lose my baby—that's why I cry so. I wonder if American woman sorry, too, when lose children? I am a poor Indian woman and all I have is this baby."[175] Turner wrote of one Aboriginal woman with her two-day-old baby, "Mother love knows no colour distinction. . . . Wonderful and precious in the eyes of her mother is this wee babe."[176]

How could the good intentions and sympathetic tendencies of white women have led them to support policies that, as we shall see in the following chapters, had such traumatic effects on so many indigenous families and communities? White women could feel ashamed of the treatment of indigenous people and recognize the "strong mother love" that indigenous women felt for their babies, but in almost every instance their adherence to the racial, religious, and economic mores of their times trumped their sense of empathy. Despite her sympathetic portrait of the Aboriginal woman, for example, Turner went on to suggest that white women's intervention was still necessary because "the mother is powerless to save her [daughter] from sprawling about, later on, with the dogs and the dirt, like the other children of the camp."[177] As was true of their countrymen, concerns with whiteness, civilization, and modernity exerted a powerful force on white women maternalists. Religious impulses also especially animated white women reformers.

The ways in which well-meaning white women became intimately involved in promoting a policy that tore apart indigenous families demonstrates the limits of a politics of maternalism. Most maternalists lacked the capability to imagine indigenous women as at once very similar to and quite different from themselves. Conceiving of indigenous women as savage and heathen, many maternalists did not recognize their full humanity; they could not seem to imagine that indigenous women had the same rights to their children as white women did. On the other hand, white women maternalists, convinced of the superiority of their culture, also failed to imagine that women from very different cultures would have their own worthy systems of value and order. Another hallmark of the maternalist mentality—a belief that indigenous people were like children and did not know what was good for them—prevented many white women from being able to listen to indigenous people about what they needed and wanted. Thus, paradoxically, white women maternalists contributed to policies that were designed to undermine indigenous women and their families and to bring them under increasing state control.

Yet it was not just the inherent ethnocentrism of maternalism that led well-meaning white women to endorse and promote policies to dispossess indigenous families of their children. Through their campaigns for indigenous women, white women maternalists also sought to prove themselves fit for policy making and governance, to gain full membership in their emerging nations. To do so, they hitched their maternalist wagons to the train of the settler colonial state. Ultimately, white women's maternalism served the larger goals of settler colonialism, producing two divergent tracks of womanhood: a pro-natalist route for white women that would help to establish and reproduce white settlement on "the frontier" and an antinatalist path for indigenous women that was meant to lead to the eventual demise of distinct indigenous identities and claims to land. Though these tracks did not always lead where they were intended, they caused untold sorrows for indigenous families for decades, as the following chapter demonstrates.

Chapter 4

The Practice of Indigenous Child Removal

I am convinced that force is the only method to be pursued in order to uplift these people. • ESTELLE REEL, superintendent of Indian education, *Report of the Superintendent of Indian Schools for* 1898 (1899), Box 2, Folder 70, MS 120, Estelle Reel Papers, EWSHS

The half-caste is intellectually above the aborigine, and it is the duty of the State that they be given a chance to lead a better life than their mothers. I would not hesitate for one moment to separate any half-caste from its aboriginal mother, no matter how frantic her momentary grief might be at the time. They soon forget their offspring. • JAMES ISDELL, traveling inspector and protector of Aborigines in the Kimberley, Western Australia, 1909, quoted in Christine Choo, *Mission Girls*

While recognizing the ethnocentric bias of officials such as Estelle Reel and James Isdell in calling for the forced removal of indigenous children, we may be tempted to conclude that they and other authorities and reformers ultimately had good intentions; after all, they claimed that they wanted to uplift Indian people and give "half-caste" children "a chance to lead a better life than their mothers." Yet, whether well-intentioned or not, a closer examination of the actual practice of indigenous child removal reveals that the implementation of these policies had much in common with the brutality of each nation's past colonial history. It was the element of removing indigenous children from their families and communities that made the boarding schools in the United States and homes and missions for Aboriginal children in Australia instruments of violence, punishment, and control, and, in fact, often more effective ones than military conquest alone. Indigenous child removal thus functioned not as a benign alternative to the earlier policies of military subjugation, but as a more nuanced weapon in the arsenal of administrators as they sought to consolidate control and complete the colonization of indigenous peoples.[1]

As administrators began to implement their new policies, indigenous families in the American West and Australia rarely sent their children to institutions voluntarily. Authorities thus had to engage in intense "recruitment" efforts, and if those failed they often resorted to trickery, threats, withholding of rations, bribes, or the use of force to achieve their aims. In the United States, Congress briefly granted the commissioner of Indian affairs authority to forcibly compel Indian children to attend boarding schools, but the harsh methods used by some Indian agents to procure children led to public debate and changes in legislation. This enabled Indian people to gain some leverage in their dealings with federal authorities over their children's removal. By contrast, Australian state governments gave much greater power to state officials to take Aboriginal children without the consent of their parents. As a result, many Aboriginal families had far fewer options to evade state authority than did American Indian people.

Because many indigenous people resisted the removal of their children to distant institutions, authorities often claimed that Indians and Aboriginal people were opposed to education and "progress." Officials in fact offered indigenous resistance to child removal as proof of their backwardness, superstitious bent, and savagery, rather than as an understandable reaction to being parted from their loved ones and having their parental authority undermined. Such reasoning by officials became further justification for removing the children from such allegedly "backward" environments. In reality, many indigenous families did not oppose Western-style education for their children; they simply wanted schooling that did not involve the removal of their children. Officials in both countries could have provided more day schools within indigenous communities; the fact that they did not, and instead proposed removing children from their families, provides further evidence that their ultimate goal was not to "protect," "assimilate," or "absorb" indigenous people but to punish them for past resistance, deter further militancy, and gain greater authority over them and their lands.

The Practice of American Indian Child Removal

Over many decades American officials used a variety of means to obtain Indian children for the boarding schools. They much preferred to use persuasion, not force, yet their practices often engendered distrust and resistance on the part of many Indian people. In response, many U.S. authorities turned to more coercive means to obtain the children, including the withholding of rations and the use of military force.

As in other matters pertaining to the boarding schools, Richard Henry Pratt's recruiting methods served as the prototype. Pratt claimed to rely solely on cajolery to obtain children, first for Hampton Institute and later for his own institution, Carlisle. On Pratt's first recruiting mission for Hampton, when he visited the Indian agencies along the Missouri River, he sought to undermine the resistance of some Indians by appealing to others who disagreed. At a council held at Fort Berthold, for example, he writes, "One of the old chiefs . . . assumed at once to answer through the interpreter for all of them with an emphatic no. I was looking the crowd over while he was talking and asked Mr. Hall [a Congregationalist missionary] . . . if there was not a younger man among them anxious for this Methuselah to pass on. He said there was and pointed him out." Pratt asked that all sides be heard at the council. "This younger man got up at once, emphatically opposed the position taken by the old chief, and said what was needed was education." Then Hall helped Pratt come up with a list of ten children whose parents, he believed, could be convinced to allow their children to go with Pratt back to Hampton. Pratt used this formula wherever he went: playing on divisions within tribes, using the resentment of some young tribal members against their elders' authority, and counting on the help of Christian missionaries and Indian agents to help him recruit children.[2]

Pratt also tried to convince Indian parents that by sending their children to school the children would learn how to stand up for Indian rights. When Pratt first met with Spotted Tail, the Brulé Sioux (Lakota) leader at the Rosebud Reservation adamantly opposed the taking of any of his band's children, saying, "The white men are all thieves and liars. We do not want our children to learn such things. . . . We are not going to give any children to learn such ways." However, after Pratt spoke at length about how educated Indian children could help prevent Spotted Tail and his band from losing their land and their rights, Spotted Tail relented. He offered up ninety children from Rosebud, although Pratt was authorized to take only thirty-six from each agency. (Pratt ended up with sixty-six children from Rosebud). Before the children embarked on their journey to Carlisle, Spotted Tail's group held a special giveaway ceremony at which parents of departing children gave away horses and other goods to honor their children. (After visiting Carlisle Institute, however, Spotted Tail reversed his position again and sought to have the children returned.)[3]

After they set up their network of boarding schools, modeled on Pratt's Carlisle Institute, U.S. government officials continued to prefer persuasion to more forceful means. Commissioner of Indian Affairs Thomas J. Morgan (1889–93) proposed that Indian agents and superintendents overcome the "great difficulty in filling the non-reservation schools . . . if possible, by kindness, by persuasion, and by holding out the advantages, both to the child and to the parent, to be derived from a course of training at the industrial school."[4]

Some Indians willingly sent their children to boarding schools. Hopi Edmund Nequatewa's grandfather, who had "put a claim on [him] when [he] was sick" and had therefore gained the right under Hopi custom to guide the boy's upbringing, decided to send Edmund to Keams Canyon School because, he told Edmund, "You must learn both sides, otherwise you will never find out who is right and what the truth is in this world." Edmund's grandfather believed that the elders had told of the coming of the Bahana (European Americans) and that "the *Bahana* is supposed to have a great knowledge of wisdom that he was to come and teach the people—the truth." Therefore, he told Edmund, "whatever you do here at school, try to learn all you can, because you have only a limited time."[5]

As Edmund's story makes clear, those Hopis who supported the boarding schools did not necessarily do so out of a desire to assimilate or modernize. Rather, they saw the boarding schools as a manifestation of an earlier prophecy. Later, when Edmund's grandfather sent him to Phoenix Indian School, he reminded him, "Don't forget what I am sending you down there for. And if that book really contains the truth, you will surely learn something. And when you do, come back someday and study the people here. Study the Hopi and get into all the ceremonies. . . . Find out all you can and listen to everything that is being done or said in any ceremony."[6]

Some white officials recognized that it could be most effective to have Indians themselves recruit other Indian children. Pratt, for example, sent Etahdleuh, one of the Fort Marion POWs who had gone on to Hampton Institute, to recruit children from his own people, the Kiowas.[7] Annie Dawson, after being removed herself to Hampton Institute, later brought Indian children from her reservation, Fort Berthold, to Hampton and Carlisle. Dawson also imbibed many of the lessons of her teachers. After her eastern education, she went to teach on the Santee Sioux Reservation, where she promoted "the idea that the homes of the Indians ought to be elevated." Later she worked as a field matron "to carry industrial education into the homes of the older people, who have not been able to have school advantages." Like many of the white women reformers, Dawson boasted, "I have preached the gospel of soap."[8]

Building on Indian conceptions of reciprocity, church-and state-run schools often obtained children by creating a sense of obligation among indigenous families toward white authorities. This was common when white reformers or missionaries were helpful in treating illness in a family. Early in the 1900s, for example, the white women missionaries who were just starting the Woman's American Baptist Home Mission Society's boarding school among the Navajos hoped to bring four little girls to the school as their first pupils, but no families would allow their girls to attend. One missionary explained, "In a providential way the first two girls came to us. A family appealed to us for medical help. We visited their camp and found the mother, a boy of nine years, and a girl of seven, all in need of the doctor's care. . . . There were two other girls and a baby in the home. We told them that the sick ought to go to the hospital at once and we could care for the two well girls in our own home. The parents gladly fell in with our plan." As a result of the aid they offered this family in their time of need, the parents seemed to feel indebted to the missionaries and allowed their daughters to attend their school. "We took the girls for our school as our first pupils," the missionary exulted. "The parents were grateful indeed for the help we gladly gave in caring for the two girls and helping the sick to the place of healing. We trust that all this will open their hearts to receive the Gospel message and that they may soon experience also the healing of the soul."[9]

Such schemes could backfire when white officials failed to properly care for the children. Native parents were particularly appalled at the numbers of their children who contracted serious diseases or even died at the schools. For example, Lot, a leader of the Spokane Indians, said that he had willingly sent many of his own children and the tribe's children to be educated back east. But out of twenty-one children sent to school, sixteen died. To add insult to injury, the school officials did not send the children home to be buried. "I don't know who did this," Lot asserted, "but they treated my people as though they were dogs." Lot then pleaded with the government to establish a day school on his reservation. The government did not respond for three years, then it contemplated building a school ten miles from the center of the reservation. "My people are now scary [*sic*]," Lot continued. "They do not want to send their children so far away to school."[10]

Other parents reacted with particular vehemence when epidemics broke out in the boarding schools. A Quaker missionary, Thomas Battey, remembered that when a "sickness" spread among his students, a "strong opposition" developed to his on-reservation boarding school. "This morning," he wrote in his journal, "while several children were quietly sitting around, attentively engaged, an old man came in, and in a very violent manner, took the slates and pencils from them, and drove them out of the tent, thus winding up the school for this morning rather abruptly. In the afternoon, as the children began to collect for school, some young [Indian] men came in and drove them out."[11]

When they failed to convince Indian families that sending their children to distant boarding schools was "for their own good," white officials often resorted to trickery. Once authorities had enrolled children in on-reservation day or boarding schools, they often spirited them away to nonreservation schools without their parents' knowledge or consent. Angel DeCora, a Winnebago (or Ho-Chunk), reveals how she was taken from her community school to Hampton Institute:

> I had been entered in the Reservation school but a few days when a strange white man appeared there. He asked me through an interpreter if I would like to ride in a steam car. I had never seen one, and six of the other children seemed enthusiastic about it and they were going to try, so I decided to join them, too. The next morning at sunrise we were piled into a wagon and driven to the nearest railroad station, thirty miles away. We did get the promised ride. We rode three days and three nights until we reached Hampton, Va.
>
> My parents found it out, but too late.
>
> Three years later when I returned to my mother, she told me that for months she wept and mourned for me. My father and the old chief and his wife had died, and with them the old Indian life was gone.[12]

Such trickery bred greater distrust among Indian people toward government officials.

Hence many Indian families tried to prevent authorities from taking their children, often by hiding them. Polingaysi Qoyawayma's mother hid her behind a roll of bedding and then covered her with a sheepskin the first time authorities came to her family's door in search of Hopi children. (Her sick brother, lying on a pallet beside the fireplace, was taken that day.) As white authorities commonly sent policemen (often of Navajo descent) to round up Hopi children for school, some of the Hopis "devised a scheme whereby the still uncaught children were warned to run for cover at the sound of a certain high-pitched, prolonged call."[13] Tall Woman (Rose Mitchell), a Navajo, recalls in her memoir what happened after the government opened an on-reservation boarding school for the Navajos at Fort Defiance in the 1880s: "The agents were sending out police on horseback to locate children to enroll there. The stories we heard frightened us; I guess some children were snatched up and hauled over there because the policemen came across them while they were out herding, hauling water, or doing other things for the family. So we started to hide ourselves in different places whenever we saw strangers coming toward where we were living."[14]

Similarly, Charlie Cojo, a Navajo, recalled, "People used to come around in a wagon getting children to go to school. When the Indians heard a wagon was coming the older people would take all the children up into the rough places, into the mountains and hide them there until the wagon went on so they wouldn't have to go to school."[15]

Many mothers took desperate measures to prevent their children from being taken away. Marietta Wetherill, a white trader who lived on the Navajo reservation, recalled that a number of Navajo mothers resorted to burying their children. Wetherill witnessed the women digging a trench and laying their children in it. "They covered the children's faces with wool and stuck oat or wheat straws from the barn in their mouths and covered them with sand," she recalled. "The children had their instructions before the police came." She added, "I'd do it if they were my children."[16] Among the Mescalero Apaches, "every possible expedient was resorted to by [the women] to keep their children from school." Agent V. E. Stottler claimed that Mescalero women "would brazenly deny having children despite the evidence of the accurate census rolls and the ticket on which they had for years drawn rations. Children were hidden out in the bushes; drugs were given them to unfit them for school; bodily infirmities were simulated, and some parents absolutely refused to bring their children in."[17]

Some Indian parents resigned themselves to having to send their children to school, but preferred some of the mission schools to the government-run institutions. In some cases missionaries sided with the parents. During one of his recruitment trips in 1883 Pratt complained, "I am in the midst of a hard fight. Catholicism has shown its hand to-day through one of its priests appearing in one of the councils of Indians and speaking against the Indians sending their children to Carlisle, or away to school." Pratt was determined, though: "I shall get the children, however, and good ones, too."[18]

Well into the twentieth century resistance among some tribes continued to frustrate officials' attempts to fill their schools. For example, in 1926 Agent E. E. McKean of the Ute agency told the commissioner of Indian affairs, "The 36 eligible Ute children . . . for enrollment at the Ute Mountain School . . . have been very difficult to get. It must be remembered that these children are scattered over four states, . . . and upon several occasions when I visited their camps, there were no children in sight nor could they be located. . . . Recently when I brought this matter to the attention of the Indians, their excuse was that most of the children were sick and that if they were going to die they wanted them to be at home."[19] Thus, filling the Indian boarding schools remained a perpetual problem.

Some Indian children did not share their parents' opposition to the schools, however, and white officials often tried to capitalize on this generational split. For example, Hopi Polingaysi Qoyawayma, who was intensely curious about the new day school at the foot of the Oraibi mesa and had tired of trying to evade government authorities, "wondered if perhaps it might be better to allow herself to be caught and have the worry over. It was an irritating thing to have to be on guard every minute." When her sister and several other Hopi friends eventually were caught and taken to the school, Qoyawayma disobeyed her mother and went down the trail to the schoolhouse, "dodging behind rocks and bushes when she met villagers coming up the trail, then sauntering on, nearer and nearer the schoolhouse." Qoyawayma admitted that "no one had forced her to do this thing. She had come down the trail of her own free will. If she went into that schoolhouse, it would be because she desired to do so. Her mother would be very angry with her."[20]

Qoyawayma was not just curious; she also wanted to share in the material wealth she saw among white people: "The white man had abundant supplies of food, good clothing, and opportunities to travel. [Qoyawayma] had a desire to share the good things of the white way of living." It was, in fact, the promise of oranges in southern California that led Qoyawayma to dream of attending the Sherman Institute boarding school in Riverside. When her parents would not sign the consent form enabling her to go, Qoyawayma stowed herself away on the wagon bound for the train station at Winslow, Arizona, where the children would then travel on to Riverside. Although the driver discovered her and summoned her parents, she refused to budge and "won her weaponless battle for another sample of white man's education."[21] As Qoyawayma's case illustrates, by appealing to the curiosity of the youth and playing on generational conflicts, the government's system of schooling deeply undercut the authority of Indian parents and guardians.

Administrators also benefited when family members disagreed over the best course for their children. A Navajo using the pseudonym "Bill Sage" recalled that his older brother had been trying to persuade him to attend boarding school for some time, though his parents opposed it. Finally, Sage remembers, "My brother took me to another hogan and told me he wanted me to go to school. . . . He told me it would be a good thing for me to do. He said the white man would get me to talk English. He said he didn't have enough money to buy clothes or food for me, and it would be 'Lots better for you to go there.' He asked me 2 or 3 times and then I said, 'Yes, I'll go.' He told me I would wear nice shoes, a coat, hat, pants, shirt. That made me go, I guess."[22]

In the case of Irene Stewart, a Navajo girl who was living with her grandmother in Canyon de Chelly after the death of her mother, her father decided to have her taken to the Fort Defiance boarding school against the wishes of her grandmother. One day, when her grandmother "had gone to the canyon rim to pick yucca fruit and cactus berries to dry for winter food," a mounted Navajo policeman carried Stewart on horseback all the way to Fort Defiance. "My father said that Grandmother wouldn't give me up to be put in school," Stewart recalled, "so he had told the agency superintendent . . . to send a policeman to pick me up. Years later I was told that Grandmother took this very hard, and that her dislike for Father increased."[23]

When authorities could not compel Indian people to send their children to boarding schools, many officials resorted to brutal means to achieve their ends. One common method was to withhold rations, which had been guaranteed by treaty to replace the Indians' traditional means of subsistence. At the Mescalero Apache Reservation in New Mexico in the 1890s, the acting Indian agent found, "The greatest opposition came from the objection of the men to having their hair cut, and from that of the women to having their children compelled to attend school." However, "the deprivation of supplies and the arrest of the old women soon worked a change. Willing or unwilling every child five years of age was forced into school," he boasted.[24] Still, in many cases parents refused to send their children off to a distant school. Estelle Reel noted in 1899, "Some reservations withhold the rations until the parents place their children in the schools, and so strong is the opposition to this that in many cases they [Indians] have held out against it until their families were on the verge of starvation."[25]

A related strategy on the part of Indian agents involved using money, goods, or so-called gratuity funds—compensatory payments that were made to entire tribes and then distributed to members on an individual basis—as bribes. In 1890 Commissioner Morgan recommended that in the case of the Utes the gratuity fund "be largely used for distribution as a reward to those who actually send their children to school, and especially to those who send them to the school at Grand Junction or some Eastern school, such as Carlisle, Pa. or Haskell, Kansas."[26] One agent among the Utes, meeting bitter opposition from the Weminuche Ute leader Ignacio to sending children to the off-reservation school, offered him two hundred dollars in 1883 if he would agree to send his band's children to boarding school.[27] In 1893 Agent S. H. Plummer offered axes, coffee pots, and pails to any Navajo parents who sent their children to school.[28]

Many Indian people were not moved by the withholding of their rations or the offer of bribes. Thus some authorities resorted to the threat of physical force. Lame Deer, an Oglala Sioux (Lakota) from the Rosebud Reservation, recalled:

> I was happy living with my grandparents in a world of our own, but it was a happiness that could not last. . . .
>
> . . . One day the monster came—a white man from the Bureau of Indian Affairs. I guess he had my name on a list. He told my family, "This kid has to go to school. If your kids don't come by themselves the Indian police will pick them up and give them a rough ride." I hid behind Grandma. My father was like a big god to me and Grandpa had been a warrior at the Custer fight, but they could not protect me now.[29]

When threats did not work, many agents enlisted military or police forces, sometimes made up of native people themselves, to physically compel Indians to comply. Marietta Wetherill recalled that in 1907 Superintendent R. Perry came to Pueblo Bonito in northwestern New Mexico with four or five Navajo policemen to take children to school. Wetherill was shocked that Perry needed police to get the children to go to school and that he received five dollars for each child he procured. "They didn't tell Uncle Sam they used force," Wetherill asserts. "I've seen those police pull the children away from their mothers, they just screamed and cried."[30]

Government authorities became particularly brutal against the Hopis, a sedentary group based in northeastern Arizona who had practiced agriculture for centuries. When some of the Hopis refused to send their children to boarding school in 1890, Commissioner Morgan wrote to Agent David Shipley, "In regard to the demoralized condition of the Keam's Canon [*sic*] School in which you state that but four children remain, and that something must be done to induce the people to send their children to school, you are directed to visit each of the Moqui [Hopi] villages . . . and to take such steps as are authorized to induce them to place their children in school."[31] Shipley responded by dispatching troops to Oraibi on Third Mesa, the most recalcitrant of the Hopi villages, to summarily remove 104 children on December 28, 1890.[32]

The use of force only increased the Hopis' bitterness and distrust. In the winter of 1893–94 the Hopis on Second Mesa refused to send their children to boarding school. The new acting agent at Fort Defiance, Lieutenant Plummer, ordered the Navajo police "to compel Moquis [Hopis] of the three villages . . . to furnish their quota of children for . . . school." (Plummer added that he would not take more than the quota because Keams Canyon School was already overcrowded.)[33] A few weeks later, with two feet of snow on the ground, a temperature of 17 degrees below zero, and twenty-five cases of mumps at the school, Plummer reconsidered; he ordered the superintendent of Keams Canyon School to "suspend all issues of Annuity Goods and all work on houses and wells for the Moquis of the second mesa."[34]

Despite these attempts to literally starve the Indians into submission, problems with the Hopi, especially those at Oraibi, persisted. In 1894 there were still only ten Hopi students at Keams Canyon School.[35] Over the next several decades the BIA repeatedly sought to force the Hopis of Oraibi and other villages to relinquish their children to the boarding schools. Many of the Hopis became so embittered by the government's methods of forcing their children to school that they even began to oppose day schools.[36]

Just as they employed Navajo policemen to compel Hopi children to go to boarding school, the BIA commonly used native police forces to round up other children. However, this practice did not always work; on many occasions Indian police balked at removing children of their own tribes. In Lander, Wyoming, because of "great difficulty . . . in landing [Shoshone] children in the government schools," Agent Herman Nickerson sent out Indian policemen to round up children whose families had hidden them in the brush. When found, the children often scratched and kicked their pursuers. According to a newspaper report, three native policemen resigned "rather than oppose the wishes of their people."[37]

The BIA and other arms of the federal government vacillated on the issue of whether it was permissible to use force to compel Indian children to attend school. Up until 1886 Congress made no mention of the issue in its annual appropriations bills for the BIA. In its 1886 bill, for the first time, Congress stipulated, "No part of the money appropriated by this act shall be expended in the transportation from or support of Indian pupils or children off their reservations . . . if removed without the free consent of their parents" or guardians.[38] The BIA then proceeded cautiously. In 1886, when the frustrated Ute agent wrote to the BIA asking how to compel resistant Utes to send their children to school, Commissioner of Indian Affairs John Atkins called upon the agent to use restraint: "Referring to your communication relative to the obstinacy of the Indians in refusing to send their children to school, and recommending that their rations be withheld, and that a sufficient military force be stationed at the Agency for protection in case the Indians should resist the measure, you are directed to continue to use every means in your power to induce the Indians to send their children to school, without resorting to the extreme measures suggested. If they still refuse, you will report the fact to this Office, when the matter will receive further consideration."[39]

Yet to continue to receive congressional funding for the schools, the BIA required that agents meet strict quotas to fill the boarding schools.[40]

Atkins's successor, T. J. Morgan, pressured his agents, writing in 1890 to Agent Charles Bartholomew of the Southern Ute and Jicarilla Apache Agency:

> This Office desires to impress upon you the fact that the most impor-
> tant work entrusted to agents is that of bringing the children of the
> reservations under their supervision into the schools. . . .
>
> The large government training schools off reservations must be
> filled, and filled so far as possible by promotions from the reservation
> day and boarding schools. . . .
>
> The reservation boarding schools must be filled to their utmost
> capacity. The places of those sent to non-reservation schools will be
> taken by pupils from the camps. Agents are instructed to exert the
> authority vested in them to so fill these schools.[41]

To meet these quotas, Morgan reversed earlier attempts at restraint and empowered agents to use withholding of rations and physical force, hence evading the congressional mandate of parental consent.[42]

To bolster his efforts to remove children, Morgan gained new author-ity from Congress's Appropriations Bill in 1891, which authorized him "to make and enforce by proper means such rules and regulations as will secure the attendance of Indian children of suitable age and health at schools established and maintained for their benefit."[43] In 1893, Mor-gan's last year as commissioner of Indian affairs, Congress strengthened the government's powers, explicitly allowing that the "Secretary of the Interior [who oversaw the commissioner of Indian affairs] may in his discretion withhold rations, clothing and other annuities from Indian parents or guardians who refuse or neglect to send and keep their chil-dren of proper school age in some school a reasonable portion of each year."[44]

Morgan used these new laws to broaden his authority. In 1892 he wrote to the Ute agent about filling the new Fort Lewis Indian School in Durango, Colorado: "Begin immediately the work of collecting Ute children for the school. You will use such means as may seem to you best. . . . If you find that they will not consent willingly to having their children go, then use such compulsion as may seem to you wise. I have no doubt at all that if you use proper efforts you can secure at least 100 children from the Utes for the school as soon as it is prepared to take them."[45] Ultimately, Morgan was not content with the agent's efforts, writing to him in November of that year, "The office is not satisfied that you have used proper means, or made the necessary effort to secure Indian children for Fort Lewis school."[46]

Morgan's more aggressive approach angered many Indian people, and at least one influential white man, Charles Lummis, a journalist who, when offered a job as the city editor for the *Los Angeles Times* in 1884, decided to "tramp across the continent" from his home in Ohio to take up his new position. During his journey Lummis encountered the Pueblo Indians of New Mexico and even sojourned briefly at San Ildefonso Pueblo. After taking his new job, he was overcome by a paralytic stroke at age twenty-eight; in 1888 he hoped to cure himself by going to live in the village of Isleta Pueblo. He stayed there off and on for five years and thereafter dedicated himself to defending the lands and cultures of the Pueblos and educating the public about Indians generally.[47]

In the summer of 1891 elders at Isleta Pueblo summoned Lummis to a meeting in an attempt to get their children, whom they referred to as *cautivos* (captives), back for the summer from Albuquerque Indian School. Lummis wrote on their behalf to Commissioner Morgan, who allowed just three children to return, and then only one at a time. In 1892 Isleta parents again asked for the return of their children for the summer, but Morgan "bluntly refused" and told the Isleta families their children were to remain at the Albuquerque Indian School for nine more years. Lummis accompanied one Isleta man, Juan Rey Abeita, to court to get his three children back. An Albuquerque newspaper reported, "[Lummis] declares that he will see the Isletans protected in their legal and humane rights, if he has to devote the rest of his life to it." When the judge ordered that the three children be returned to their father, other Isleta parents went to demand their children. Finally fifteen more children were returned.[48]

Lummis then took the experiences of the Isleta Pueblos to a national audience, writing in a Boston newspaper:

> The filling of a Government Indian school in the southwest is a constant wrangle—as its progress is a serial scandal. The principal—whose stipend shrinks if he have not the full capacity of grist, I mean pupils—descends upon the various Pueblo villages to impress recruits. He does not hesitate to attempt bribery of the Indian officials to order children given him; nor to bear upon the parents all pressure due or illegitimate, that he dares. He takes a number of tearful timid children from their bulldozed and weeping parents, and dumps them into his salary-mill. If they run away from their slavery there, he hunts them down as he would convicts. . . . In cases within my personal knowledge, boys who had escaped were captured and carried back at the point of a six-shooter . . . by the salaried teachers of a paternal government, and restored to the prison; their brief taste of freedom was rewarded with a ball and chain. I have also known a poor lad to walk a thousand desert miles to get from the "school" back to the huts of his fathers.[49]

Like many indigenous writers, Lummis compared the boarding schools to prisons and removed children to captives and slaves. He wrote to the *Albuquerque Times*, "It may occur to American fathers and mothers to inquire when Mr. Morgan purchased his chattels, or under what charge of crime he imprisons them. It is true that the Indians have had the ill taste to be born with browner hides than ours; but after reading over the constitution; after remembering a somewhat heavy national price we paid to prove the Negro a man and give him control of his children, most of us have brains and hearts adequate to understanding that even an Indian should not be forcibly robbed of his children."[50]

Perhaps as a result of Lummis's assault, even some government officials in the 1890s began to question the wisdom of forcibly removing children. In 1893 Thomas Donaldson, in his census bulletin and report on the Hopis, queried, "Shall we be compelled to keep a garrison of 250 to 300 men at the Moqui [Hopi] pueblos in order to educate 100 to 200 children at a distance from their homes? We began with soldiers and Hotchkiss guns. Are we to end in the same way? Such civilizing has not heretofore been a pronounced success."[51]

Due no doubt in part to this national publicity, Morgan's successor, Daniel Browning (1893–97) backed down from Morgan's hard-line position. He wrote to all Indian agents in 1893, "You are advised that hereafter no children are to be taken away from reservations to non-reservation schools without the full consent of the parents and the approval of the agent. The consent of the parents must be voluntary, and not in any degree or manner the result of coercion."[52] And in 1894 Congress's Appropriations Bill reversed its earlier positions and stipulated, "No Indian child shall be sent from any Indian reservation to a school beyond the State or Territory in which said reservation is situated without the voluntary consent of the father or mother [or guardian] of such child." Congress also ruled it unlawful to withhold rations as a means of compelling Indian parents to send their children to boarding school.[53] In reaction to the new policy, Browning wrote to the new Ute agent, David Day, in 1895, "You can not, under the act of Congress, use any coercive measures, such as withholding annuities or rations to force attendance at the [Fort Lewis] school, nor do I desire you to do so."[54]

Congress left a gaping loophole in this new parental consent requirement, however: such consent was necessary only if a child was to be sent off the reservation *out of state*. Since by 1889 every western state had at least one reservation boarding school and many had nonreservation schools, agents still could compel parents and guardians to send their children to these schools without their consent. (These schools too were often quite distant from Indian communities.) Congress's 1894 stipulation, repeated in subsequent annual appropriation acts, did not stop the Indian agents to the Hopis, for example, from their relentless pursuit of

Hopi children for Keams Canyon School from the late 1890s up through the 1920s. Because the children were not to be removed from the state of Arizona, authorities did not have to obtain parental consent.[55] In addition, in 1906 Congress gave the commissioner of Indian affairs another tool for forcibly removing Indian children from their families; it allowed him to designate certain boarding schools as Indian Reform Schools and did not require the consent of parents or guardians to place youth in these schools.[56]

Yet, even with this loophole, attendance in the boarding schools fell markedly in the late 1890s and early 1900s, and the BIA reverted to pressuring its agents to fill the schools.[57] Such pressures encouraged intense competition for students. Agents and superintendents who had difficulty filling their own day schools and reservation boarding schools were reluctant to send pupils to nonreservation schools.[58] Such a system resulted in much younger children being removed to the schools than was originally intended. Supervisor of Schools Millard F. Holland found that at the Navajo Agency Boarding school "a little boy was enrolled during his stay . . . that there being no clothing small enough for him he was put in dresses, and his clothing had to be changed two or three times a day, that several of the employees estimated his age as three years or under, that the superintendent entered him on the record as five years, that he (the supervisor) had him sent back to his mother."[59] Superintendents of the schools also routinely admitted very unhealthy children as a means of filling their quotas, a practice that contributed to the high rates of disease in the schools.[60]

The issue of using force to remove Indian children resurfaced in the early 1900s under the administration of Commissioner of Indian Affairs W. A. Jones and Superintendent of Indian Education Estelle Reel, who sought a compulsory school attendance law for Indian children. Reel's timing was poor, as both Constance DuBois, a member of the Connecticut branch of the WNIA, and Charles Lummis waged fierce campaigns against Indian child removal in the early 1900s (see chapter 9). Moreover, President Theodore Roosevelt, who traveled in many of the same social and intellectual circles as Lummis, appointed Francis Leupp, a journalist and reformer who favored the preservation of Indian culture, to the position of commissioner of Indian affairs in 1905.[61] Reel's efforts thus came to naught.

Although Leupp retained Reel as his superintendent, he had a markedly different approach to Indian education than his predecessors. In 1905, for example, he told his agents that it was not appropriate to fill quotas for schools by enrolling unhealthy children. "Do not forget that Indian schools are *for the benefit of the children and not the employees*," Leupp declared. "Indian children should be *educated*, not *destroyed* in the process."[62] In 1908 he introduced two forceful circulars opposing the quota system. In the first he asserted:

> The worst abuses of the practice permitted in past years could be checked, I believed, by cutting off the privilege of sending irresponsible canvassers into the field to collect children and ship them in to the schools; for out of that custom had grown up a regular system of traffic in these helpless little red people. The schools are supported by appropriations based upon the number of children who can be gathered into them, at the rate of $167 a head; in other words, the more children, the more money. Therefore the successful canvasser occupied to all intents the position of a commission merchant or supply agent who received his pay in such favors as were at the disposal of his superintendent. How many grades higher in moral quality was such commerce in human flesh and blood than that once conducted on the Guinea coast, which was broken up by making it piracy?[63]

These were strong words—reminiscent of those of Charles Lummis—that resonated deeply in a country that had only recently outlawed slavery. The second circular demanded, "No pressure must be brought to bear . . . to force any child into a nonreservation school."[64] In 1909 Leupp issued an order prohibiting nonreservation school superintendents from sending "agents into the field to win the consent of parents for the sending away to school of their children."[65] In general, Leupp hoped to phase out the boarding school system altogether, writing in his annual report for 1908, "The whole method of conducting these schools is conducive of unwholesome conditions for young people who have been always accustomed themselves, and are descended from ancestry always accustomed, to the freest open-air life."[66]

Leupp's successors, however, did not maintain his position on the boarding schools; in fact, a circular issued to all BIA superintendents in 1924 reveals that the federal government continued to pressure superintendents to enroll and retain children in the boarding schools or to get them into public schools.[67] Obtaining consent from unwilling parents remained a perennial issue for Indian agents. It was not until the 1920s that a new generation of reformers—who opposed assimilation—raised the issue again. In the 1930s newly elected president Franklin Delano Roosevelt appointed one of this new generation, John Collier, to head the BIA, resulting, for a time, in a challenge to and retreat from the removal of Indian children to boarding schools. With the passage of the Indian Reorganization Act of 1934 Collier shifted Indian education toward day schools. When Collier's new policies went into effect there were only six day schools in Navajo country, for example, but in the autumn of 1935 thirty-nine new day schools opened, and before the end of the 1930s Collier had built eleven more. Moreover, the schools emphasized a curriculum that taught Indian language, culture, and history in addition to more conventional subjects.[68]

Many readers may wonder why it was wrong to compel Indian children to attend school at the turn of the twentieth century. After all, weren't all American children required to attend school? Indeed, by 1900 thirty-two states had passed compulsory school attendance laws, and by 1918 such laws were universal.[69] There is a crucial difference here, however. Nonnative children were expected merely to attend schools in their neighborhoods and nearby towns, not to be separated from their families in the name of education. American Indian children, by contrast, were forced to travel great distances and to live for many years away from their homes and families to attend boarding schools. And in many cases, Indian children were barred from attending local public schools near where they lived.

For many readers the concept of a boarding school conjures up images of an elite and privileged education. Many well-off families in England and its colonies, including the United States and Australia, have sent their children—quite voluntarily—to boarding school. Wasn't this government plan, then, an attempt to extend this same type of opportunity and privilege to one of the most disadvantaged groups in American society? For a time, some Indian educators, including Pratt, did envision an elite, classical education for Indian children, yet, as we saw in chapter 2, by the early 1900s most reformers and government authorities had rejected Pratt's vision, instead asserting that Indian children were capable of only a rudimentary education and eventual employment in an unskilled occupation.[70] Moreover, as the historian Tsianina Lomawaima has pointed out, whereas elite boarding schools were dedicated to "cultural reproduction and the training of elites," Indian boarding schools were "devoted to cultural obliteration and transformation."[71] Authorities claimed that they were extending a benevolent hand to American Indians, offering their children an education, an opportunity to join the mainstream of American society. Yet in insisting that their children be removed from their homes and families for such education, authorities often traumatized and undermined the families. If education had been the aim of American policy, it could have been accomplished without the strife and turmoil (and expense) generated by the BIA's efforts to cajole, trick, bribe, starve, or physically force Indian people to relinquish their children to distant boarding schools.

The Practice of Aboriginal Child Removal in Australia

In Australia many officials characterized the practice of removing Aboriginal children as a smooth process whereby officials easily convinced Aboriginal people of the desirability of relinquishing their children and

Aboriginal mothers dutifully, and even gratefully, complied. Western Australia Chief Protector Neville, for example, presented himself as able to calmly persuade Aboriginal women to part with their children. "Many working half-caste girls having infants fathered by white men came to me to discuss the disposal of their children," he wrote after his retirement. "When I explained to them that separation was inevitable for their children's sake, most of them saw the matter as I did." Neville further asserted that "most of the mothers especially will be glad" to part with their children "because they wish their children to adopt white ways."[72]

Officials routinely told removed Aboriginal children, many of whom had been too young to remember the circumstances of their removal, that their mother couldn't take care of them and had voluntarily placed them in a home or mission, and some children accepted this explanation. Ivy Kilmurray, whose family was from the Gibson desert area of Western Australia, told an interviewer, Vera Whittington, "My mother, Genevieve . . . heard of Sister Kate and she *brought* us down—we were only briefly at Mogumber [Moore River]—to Sister Kate's [institution for half-caste and quarter-caste children]. . . . *My* mother gave away her children—two girls and a boy—so that they would have an education and the girls would not be the 'playthings' of the shearers."[73]

We cannot really know how many Aboriginal mothers voluntarily gave up their children to institutions. No statistics exist as to even how many children were removed, let alone how many came voluntarily versus how many were coerced.[74] Yet when Aboriginal mothers and children, such as Theresa Clements and Margaret Tucker, tell their own stories a picture quite different from the official narrative emerges. Aboriginal memoirs and oral histories are full of haunting and poignant stories of removal. Iris Burgoyne, a Mirning-Kokatha woman of the west coast of South Australia, who "saw countless children stolen from their mothers on the mission" recalled:

[A Sister] would visit the mission every month or so in a shiny black car with two other officials and always leave with one or two of the fairer-skinned children. . . . We wised up! Each time that car pulled into the mission, our aunties, uncles and grandparents would warn the older children and they grabbed the little ones and ran into the scrub. We took anyone's fair-skinned child, sat them down quietly and watched the visitors go from house to house. The Sister would bark at the mothers, "Where are your children?"

This Sister went to the old folks in search of the children. The old people never lied, but they could not be straight with this woman. I shed tears when I remember how those children were ripped from their families, shoved into that car and driven away. The distraught mothers would be powerless and screaming, "Don't take my baby!" The mother struggled with the policeman.

"You hang on, Linda. We will let you know where we put him. We will look after him better than you can," said that old bastard of a Sister. "Prove yourself with those other children, and you will have your child back!" I hated that Sister and her cronies.[75]

Other Aboriginal people reveal similarly traumatic stories. Bessie Singer of Western Australia remembers being stolen from her mother: "We were playing by a water tank when these two guys came up to us. We lived at Murgoo Station—down the bottom in corrugated [iron] huts . . . whole families of us. This day my mother was working at the big house (the 'white house' we called it because of the people there). . . . These two guys said, 'Come here you, we want you.' We ran up to the cemetery. They caught us and put us in a cattle truck. I saw my mother come running. They drove past her. I was seven years old. It took about three days to reach Mullewa." Singer remembers, "In Perth they separated us. Agnes went to Mogumber [Moore River]—she was dark. Me, my sister and nephew went to Sister Kate's."[76] Sam Lovell, growing up in the Kimberleys of Western Australia, recalls the terror of his removal to Moola Bulla, a government station, at age three or four: "I can remember this police man chasing me down the creek and grabbing hold of me and taking me back and putting me on the vehicle and taking me to Fitzroy [Crossing]."[77]

In Queensland, where entire families were brought to settlements, child removal took a different form than in other Australian locales. In some cases Aboriginal families voluntarily came to the settlements; when Ruth Hegarty's grandfather could no longer find work on sheep and cattle stations during the Great Depression, he decided to move his entire extended family to Barambah settlement (which later became Cherbourg). Local authorities assured Hegarty's grandfather that his family would find help and support to get them through the hard times and that they could return home later. Upon arrival at Barambah, however, the superintendent immediately split up the family, sending Hegarty's grandparents to the Aboriginal camp, the boys to the boys' dormitory, and Hegarty's mother and Ruth (just six months old) to the girls' dormitory. When Hegarty turned four officials took her from her mother to live in a different wing of the dormitory and eventually sent her mother out to domestic service. The family never returned to their ancestral country.[78]

It is clear from the archival record as well as oral histories and Aboriginal memoirs that a large number of Aboriginal families were subject to the brutal forcible removal of their children. Because Australian state governments invested Aborigines Protection Boards and chief protectors of Aborigines with much greater power over the children than the commissioner of Indian affairs enjoyed, the issue of consent did not bedevil the Australian administrators. However, Aboriginal resistance did frustrate officials' attempts to carry out their policies.

As in the United States, indigenous people sought any means available to prevent the removal of their children. Commonly, as Iris Burgoyne mentioned, parents hid their children when authorities came calling. Mona Tur of the Andagarinya people in the northern desert region of South Australia would go out in the bush with her mother for two or three weeks when police were looking for children. "But one day," she recounts,

> everybody was sitting down [in our camp] because it was very, very hot that day. And as we were sitting in our *ngura* [shelter] . . . I could

hear all this commotion going on. "Policeman, policeman, police-man." . . . And Mum said, "Now the policeman has come and I have to dig a hole inside this *ngura* so the policeman won't take you away, and when I dig this hole, I'm going to put you inside and just cover it up so your head will be showing, but you must not sneeze, cough, cry or anything because you'll be taken away and we will never, ever see you again."

And so she did this to me. . . . On that particular day they must have shooed about twenty dogs into this little *ngura*, so the dogs would be lying around where I was and mother would put a blanket around me as well. I was just striving away there for breath, . . . it was so hot I thought I was going to die.[79]

Tur's experience is reminiscent of how some Navajo women buried their children. Concealing children proved to be successful in some instances; many administrators noted the absence of Aboriginal children on their tours of the camps. Most believed that this was "a strong indication of the existence of venereal disease," but it may have been a sign that communities carefully hid their children when authorities came on the scene.[80]

As in the United States, some indigenous people turned to privately run missions, some of which allowed parents to see their children, to avoid having their children permanently removed. For example, in South Australia, many Aboriginal parents brought their children willingly to the Koonibba Lutheran Mission, as they could still have regular contact with their children there.[81] In Western Australia many Aboriginal families enrolled their children at the Mt. Margaret Mission before they could be taken forcibly by the government to the Moore River or Mogumber Settlement.[82] Not all the missions were so accommodating to Aboriginal parents, however, and many worked in close cooperation with the government, but some of the more lenient missions seemed far preferable to many Aboriginal parents than having their children removed to a more distant location where they might never see them again.

In another effort to prevent their children from being taken, many Aboriginal people refused to live on settlements or missions that were set aside for them. In New South Wales, for example, Heather Goodall contends that policies of child removal led many Aboriginal families to flee from government-controlled reserves and areas to the outskirts of country towns. She found that in the 1910s and 1920s "there were never more than 15 per cent of the Aboriginal population under Board managerial control." However, with the advent of the Depression of the 1930s more Aboriginal people, lacking employment and barred from receiving benefits or work relief in the state, were forced to rely on the Protection Board's rations and resources. By 1935, Goodall found, "over 30 per cent of the known Aboriginal population was under the direct and dictatorial control of Protection managers and many more were on reserves under the surveillance of the police."[83]

Families also tried to avoid all interaction with authorities because any encounter with a white official might lead to the removal of a child. Mary King, born in 1921, remembers the traumatic events that led to her removal at age eight from her Queensland home. Her mother had gone out to get groceries one morning while the children were still asleep. "While she was away," King recalls, "my stepfather came into my room and raped me that morning and Mum come home and caught him in the act. So, that's how come she sent for the police. And then the police found out that we lived there where there was no school, so the government said that we had to be taken away so we could go to school somewhere." The next day the policeman returned to take the three oldest children away. "We thought we were going for a holiday when we got into the car. Never been in a car before. And I can still see my mum sitting on the ground there. . . . I can see her crying."[84]

Australian officials were empowered to summarily remove Aboriginal children in such a fashion, but due to Aboriginal resistance and the obvious trauma the policy caused, authorities were sometimes reluctant to do so. In South Australia administrators lamented the "disinclination on the part of the police to take action" to remove children from their families. The secretary of the State Children's Council explained, "I do not mean that the men are cowards, but they have been afraid that it would lead to disaster."[85] On the front lines, police officers sometimes intervened on behalf of Aboriginal families. In Victoria in the late 1890s, for example, one constable who had been charged with removing several children deemed destitute and neglected and living with unwed parents reported that it was inadvisable to remove the children. He found the children "strong and healthy, and . . . apparently better fed and clothed than some white children I see in my district." He concluded his report, "I might add that if people are doing their best to feed their children, it would be a harsh action on the part of the police to deprive them of the company of their offspring, again it must not be lost sight of, that the times are hard even for white people, and some that I know find it difficult to feed and clothe their families. But while they can manage to do so they would not like to have their children placed in a government institution."[86]

Hence, although Australian authorities had the power to forcibly remove Aboriginal children to institutions, they often could not do so in a simple, straightforward manner; instead, they resorted to a number of methods similar to those used in the United States to remove Indian children. As in the United States, some missionaries obtained children for their homes by treating or curing illnesses in the families. Toomoo came to Ooldea in South Australia when she became ill with pneumonia at age three. Her parents first sought treatment from the "witch doctor," as missionaries called him, but when she failed to get better her parents reluctantly brought her to the mission. When she recovered, "Toomoo's parents were so overjoyed," according to the missionaries, "that they had now no hesitation in allowing their little one to remain at the Mission."[87]

When such gentler methods failed to bring children to the institutions, some authorities turned to withholding rations or using them as bribes, as in the United States. In South Australia officials gave an extra four hundred pounds of flour to an Aboriginal community at Encounter Bay "as a reward for the children attending school." Officials also requisitioned blankets to be "given [only] to those parents who send their children to school."[88] Dependence on rations thus made Aboriginal people more vulnerable to child removal.

As in the United States, authorities commonly resorted to trickery to separate children from their parents. Victoria Archibald's mother mysteriously disappeared one day when she and Victoria went into Sydney to get food vouchers:

> The last day I seen my mother, we went to Sydney from La Perouse. . . . They used to get vouchers in to travel on the train or the tram or buses. . . . And they also get . . . a voucher for food, meals, because there's a lot of rationing down there. So anyway, I waited at the office [of the Aborigines Protection Board] and they said she'd just gone down there to get something. I waited there, and waited there, and when it started getting late in the afternoon I found out she wasn't coming back, I started to look for my mother then. They said, "She'll be back soon, she'll be back soon," and then I discovered that she wasn't coming back. I was locked in the office, Aboriginal Protection Board office.[89]

Nita Marshall recalls that the station boss at Frazier Downs in the northwestern corner of Western Australia took Nita and her mother to La Grange to get the mail. Nita was playing outside when she saw a truck come. The police got out of the truck and asked her if she wanted to go for a ride. She said yes. "Oh, I'm in that for a ride, yeah. He gave me some lollies [candy] and 'Jump in the back of the ute [pickup truck]!' My mother seen it from the window. She was upstairs. She come down. She said, 'Where you taking my daughter?'" The police told Nita's mother that she was being taken to a school in Broome. Nita's mother wanted to come too, and at first the police allowed her to accompany Nita, but on the drive to Broome the police pulled Nita's mother out of the truck. "[They] throw [her] out on the ground. . . . I jumped on my

mum and they was swinging me around. I just about killed my mum
from holding her tight in the neck. They beat her anyway. And then
they took us back to Broome." After two weeks there, they sent Nita
to Sister Kate's, farther south in Perth.[90]

These frightful scenes of separation are more common in Aboriginal
oral histories and memoirs than in American Indian accounts. This may
be due to differences in how authorities in each nation carried out indigenous child removal. American ambiguity about the need for parental
consent granted Indian families some room to maneuver and some respite
from relentless attempts to interfere in their families. In contrast, the presence of explicit state legislation transferring guardianship of Aboriginal
children to the state put Aboriginal families and communities at a greater
disadvantage than American Indians in their bids to hold on to their
children. Moreover, because Australian officials intended separation of
children from their mothers and other kin to be permanent, these parting
scenes may have been particularly traumatic remembrances.

Yet the distinction I make here between Aboriginal and American Indian experiences of child removal would have mattered little to families
at the time. When a child was removed, both Aboriginal and Indian parents and guardians worried—with good cause—that they might never
see their beloved son or daughter, grandson or granddaughter, again.
Often cut off from all contact with their children for years, indigenous
families, according to officials at the time, sometimes came to regard
their children as forever lost to them or even dead. One official, Ernest
Mitchell, told an interviewer, "[When Aboriginal children are removed]
the mothers regard the children as dead: rarely, if ever [do they] see, or
hear of the children again."[91] Many Indian parents came to feel much the
same. As Agent Plummer told his supervisors, "The violent prejudice
now existing among the Navajos to the removal of children to non-
reservation schools is due, in a great measure, to the feeling that when
children are taken off of the Reservation they are lost to the parent as
much as if buried."[92] Moreover, not realizing the tight control that officials had over their children, some Aboriginal women simply thought

their children had become uninterested in them. Mondalmi, a Maung woman from western Arnhem Land, criticized "half-caste" children for rejecting their black mothers. "They don't like to think they have mothers with black skins," she told the anthropologist Catherine Berndt.[93]

Parents whose children were taken—whether at the point of a gun or with their signature of consent—could not know if they would ever see their children again. They surely worried about how they could protect their children from harm so far from home. If they had consented to their child's removal—for an extra bag of flour, a blanket, or simply an official's assurance—they certainly doubted if they had made the right decision. For *all* indigenous parents, separation from their children was undoubtedly a deeply painful experience.

Once their children were removed, indigenous parents and guardians often felt a despairing sense of powerlessness against the strong arm of state authority. Think of what Lame Deer remembered when a policeman came to take him away to school: "My father was like a big god to me and Grandpa had been a warrior at the Custer fight, but they could not protect me now." How devastating it must have been for indigenous families who could do so little to prevent their children from being taken. On both sides of the Pacific many indigenous parents and guardians sought to overcome this sense of powerlessness and to take action to regain custody of their children, maintain regular contact with them, or gain some modicum of control in the situation. Many Indian and Aboriginal groups organized to protest the removal of their children or to promote alternatives to removal and institutionalization. Once again, it appears that American Indians may have been more successful in these endeavors, in part because authorities did not explicitly intend for separation of children from their parents to be permanent.

On an individual basis, many Aboriginal parents sought to get their children back by petitioning officials. Australian archives are full of poignant letters from distraught parents who begged officials to return their children. An Aboriginal mother wrote to officials in Victoria in 1912:

Dear Sir,

Please I wont you to do me a favour if you could help me to get my two girls out of the Homes as they were sent there as neglected children. . . . When they were sent away it was said by the Police Magistrate that they were to be sent to the Homes till we were ready to go on to a Mission Station. They were to be transferred . . . as it was no place of ours to be roaming about with so many children. . . . I then come out to Coranderrk Mission Station with a broken heart not seeing my own flesh and blood which God has given to me as a comfort & I would like them to live with me till death does part us. . . . Trusting in your help and in the Grace of God help I may be able to see my too dear girls again.

In 1914 this woman wrote again to the Aborigines Protection Board in Victoria. As in so many cases, the authorities were indifferent to this woman's desperate request. On her letter someone scribbled "I consider the girls are much better off where they are"; "No promise has been made to return them and it is better they should learn to earn their living outside"; and "It is not advisable to remove the girls [from the Homes]."[94]

Walter and Irene McHughes, an Aboriginal couple of South Australia, found themselves in dire straits and asked the Colebrook Home to take in their two older children, ages eleven and thirteen. The home refused, declaring the boys were too old, but did offer to take the four younger children. The McHughes agreed, with the understanding that they could retrieve their children once they had improved their economic condition. When Walter McHughes found employment and housing he wrote to the board to regain his children. His letter reveals the deep trauma that child removal caused among so many Aboriginal families: "I am working and have a big nine roomed house living in I want to know if we can have the 4 little kiddies home again as you promised we could have them when we settled down. As the wife cant seem to settle down without them. I am afraid she will break down in Health as she feels it very hard without them." The board, however, rebuffed McHughes.[95]

When Mrs. Robinson's two boys, Willie and Paddy, ages nine and seven, were taken to an institution in South Australia in 1910 without the knowledge or consent of her or her husband, Mrs. Robinson wrote to the protector, "This note is an appeal to you to endeavour to regain possession of my children which was taken from me under false pretenses. . . . I can assure you they were never neglected." Robinson obliquely pointed out that charges of neglect should really be leveled against authorities who failed to fulfill promises they had made to Aboriginal people. "I beg to inform you," she wrote, "that some time ago I was confined of a fine boy and it died through cold and [I] nearly died myself and when the nurse spoke to Mr Panton [the police corporal] for blankets he said we would have to buy our own blankets and after the baby died he was spoken to about a coffin his answer was you can bury it in a cocoa box."[96]

Some Aboriginal people took matters into their own hands; rather than write to authorities, they simply tracked down their children and sought to take them back themselves. While their daughter, "Jane King," languished at the Cootamundra Girls Home in New South Wales for eight years to be trained for a domestic apprenticeship, her parents, unbeknown to her, tried to regain custody of their daughter. Jane learned much later in life that her mother had "slept out in the open paddock [near Cootamundra] through an entire and freezing winter," hoping to take her back.[97] As these examples show, few parents seem to have been successful in their efforts.

If Aboriginal parents could not get their children back entirely, many mothers at least sought to make contact with their removed children. Rose Foster wrote respectfully to the Board for the Protection of Aborigines in Victoria to request a pass to visit her daughters in Melbourne. She pleaded with the board, "I have not seen them For a long time. . . . It Hurts my feelings Very much to know that They are so far away From me a Mother Feels for her Children."[98] Authorities rarely granted such requests.

Many people of part-Aboriginal descent tried to prevent the removal of their children or to get their children back from institutions by claiming that they were exempt from the "Act"—legislation in each state that defined Aborigines based on their degree of Aboriginal "blood" and regulated the treatment of Aborigines. Some mothers contacted state officials and went to court to prove they were not covered by the act and that therefore their children should not be removed. In 1933 in the Northern Territory Christina Mary Odegaard wrote to C. W. Martens, a member of Parliament, to ask his advice. "Mr Cook Chief Protector of Aborigines has classed me as an abo, also my daughter Florrie and wants to take Florrie from me and place her in the Compound among a lot of half castes and blacks," she explained to Martens. "I want you to let me know if Cook has this power, and the best way to act under the circumstances." Odegaard placed Florrie in a convent to keep her safe from Cook, but Cook had made arrangements to prevent Florrie from being returned to her mother. Thus, Odegaard declared, "I am anxious to get my daughter home again."[99]

Odegaard's association with an influential government official was unusual; most Aboriginal or part-Aboriginal women would not have had such recourse. Martens took her inquiry seriously, writing to his associate in Parliament, H. G. Nelson, "I know this woman very well and I have . . . told her I would do anything I could, in conjunction with yourself, to prevent what is suggested." Martens vouched for Odegaard: "This woman lived for some time on Thursday Island [a mission] and I know she has given this child a good upbringing, and it would be a shame in my opinion to attempt to put this girl into the aborigines compound. She has had a good home life as well as attending a Convent School at Thursday Island."[100] Cook contested Martens's claim that Florrie "had a good home life" by alleging that Odegaard had deserted her Norwegian husband and cohabited and had children with a number of Asian and Pacific Islander men. He recommended that Florrie should be permanently removed from her mother.[101] Cook contended, "In view of the fact that she is practically white, and it is suspected that her mother intends that she should become a prostitute in an environment of coloured aliens and low-grade whites, it is recommended that no action be taken to remove the girl from the Convent."[102] Cook utilized much of the maternalist rhetoric regarding Aboriginal women that was explored in chapter 3; he sought to associate Odegaard with sexual immorality and thus discredit her as a fit mother.

When her petition to state officials failed to obtain her daughter's release, Christina Odegaard filed suit to regain custody of her daughter. At the trial the judge did not wish to hear from Odegaard, but, revealing the importance attached to paternity, "said he would like to hear what the girl's [white] father had to say about the matter if he were sufficiently interested." Odegaard's attorney claimed that the girl's father "had deserted her in 1919 when about a month old and had had nothing to do with her upbringing."[103] Still the judge persisted and delayed the trial for a month, at which time the father, Olaf Odegaard, a stock camp cook, finally appeared and "said he was prepared to maintain his daughter . . . at the Convent but if she did not wish to remain there he would take her with him and make arrangements to leave her with some people." Christina was still not questioned, but authorities continued to condemn her as immoral on several occasions. Olaf claimed "his wife now had several other children of which other men were the fathers." A police officer testified that she "was at present living [out of wedlock] with a man named John Thomas. The home would be a very undesirable place for a growing girl to be kept in."[104]

Florrie herself was called to the witness box, but because she appeared shy, the judge questioned her separately in his chambers. He concluded that she "did not have any idea . . . as to what she wanted to do except to go back to her mother. Apparently she thought a lot of her mother but that was all she knew about the matter." Believing "it would be a disadvantage to her to be returned to her mother," the judge ruled that she should stay at the convent another year, while Cook obtained employment for her.[105] Even if neither Christina Odegaard nor her daughter had the requisite amount of "blood" to be classified as Aboriginal and therefore subject to the act, the mother's alleged immorality and her association with nonwhites marked her and her daughter as Aboriginal and brought them under the control of the state.

Other people of part-Aboriginal descent also turned to the state to challenge their categorization as Aborigines, a strategy that, as the Odegaard case shows, was fraught with peril. Such an approach, though sometimes successful in keeping families intact, also entailed cutting off all contact with Aboriginal kin and community. Many Aboriginal families in such situations faced a devastating choice: sacrifice other family relationships in order to keep their children or give up their children in order to maintain family and community ties.[106]

Once their children were institutionalized in boarding schools, some Indian parents sought to take them back. One angry Caddo mother, whose son had been punished harshly for hitting another student, visited the boarding school and demanded that her son be released to her. When the school's superintendent, Thomas Battey, refused, she stayed all night hoping to spirit her son away. Although the woman left in the morning, unsuccessful in her quest, one of her older sons succeeded in "stealing" his brother back, as Battey put it.[107] Interestingly, Battey and others were so infused with a sense of their righteousness that they failed to see their own actions in the same light as Indian peoples did, as virtual kidnapping, and instead characterized the Indians as "stealing" their own children.

Like Aboriginal parents, if Indian mothers and fathers could not bring back their children, at least they hoped to visit them. An old Navajo man and his wife traveled hundreds of miles from western New Mexico to the Santa Fe Indian School to see their boy and bring him home for a visit. Superintendent John DeHuff refused to release the boy, saying that he "had been enrolled [at the school] for a period of three years and . . . his enrollment term had not yet expired."[108] The boy ran away from school the following December.[109]

Many Indian parents and guardians sought to at least recover their children during holidays and summer vacations. For example, the Navajo man "Warrto," knowing that the boarding schools wanted to make sure Indian children worked during the summers, wrote to his superintendent, "I would like very much to have all my boys come home this summer as I have work for them. Some of them will have to work on the farm and others tend the sheep."[110] Boarding school officials rarely granted such requests, primarily because if they let children return for the summers they found it was "an endless job trying to get them all back by September first." Although some parents dutifully returned their children in the fall, one official wrote, "It takes a policeman to get [other children] back with a fuss included."[111] To prevent the loss of their inmates, boarding school superintendents routinely sent them off in the summers to work with white families or as teams to do farm labor.[112]

In fact, many American Indians whose children were returned to them in the summer did refuse to let their children return in the fall. During Leo Crane's harsh administration among the Hopis, sometimes when puberty-age girls returned to Hopiland for the summer they became pregnant and married, perhaps in part as a way to avoid returning to boarding school. The reformer Gertrude Lewis Gates (see chapter 9) testified, "Early marriages are common [among the Hopis] but the age limit is being lowered to escape family separation—Witness: several hasty marriages at Oraibi this fall."[113] Crane attempted to try several Hopi men in Arizona courts for the statutory rape of two young Hopi girls who had become pregnant and who "were not more than thirteen years old." As "there are no maternity wards in connection with class-rooms," Crane lamented, these girls "could never be cared for in the schools now." He sought to "have guilty married men punished for wilfully continuing what I have been pleased to term 'child prostitution' among the Hopi—a method adopted to defeat education." The courts declined, however, to charge the men with rape, and the Hopi girls were able to evade boarding school.[114] According to another superintendent, "[The Navajos] want their girls to marry and thereby get away from the necessity of sending them back to school."[115]

Australian Ind. people had less success fighting child removal because parental consent was not nec. for removal

Collective Action

Indigenous communities sometimes acted collectively to oppose the removal of their children. In the United States, at least one Indian community may have resorted to arson and murder to prevent their children from being taken to school. At the Pechanga Reservation near Temecula in Riverside County, California, in 1894 Mrs. Mary J. Platt, a forty-year-old widow and the government school teacher, was murdered in her home. Mrs. Platt's murder confounded her colleagues in the WNIA. They speculated that she might have angered liquor interests whom she had sought to keep from selling alcohol to the Indians. "There were [also] rumors that a chief had been angered because of some alleged severity in school discipline," the WNIA wrote, but these rumors were quickly dismissed as "wholly impossible." Another missionary in the area, William Weinland, wrote, "Upon [Mrs. Platt's] arrival the Indians told her plainly that they did not care for school, and that she might as well go home again. But nothing could turn Mrs. Platt from her duty," even though in 1891 the school house had been burned to the ground.[116]

More commonly, Indian people sought nonviolent means to keep their children. Many did not so much resist the American system of education as they resisted the separation from their children. Violet Pooleyama, a young Hopi woman who witnessed the government's heavy-handed attempts to force Hopi children to go to boarding schools, wrote, "Do you wonder now that the people of Hotevilla tremble when they see white people coming to our village? Why don't they leave us to ourselves? . . . But if we must go to school, why don't they build us a school with all the grades somewhere near our villages so that we can see our children every day?"[117]

Some tribes consented to or even promoted on-reservation boarding schools, especially on reservations where the great distances between settlements made day schools impractical. For example, the Pit River Indians in northern California requested that the government "establish an Indian boarding school at or near [the] village (Fall River Mills), it being a common centre to which they could all, within a circuit of fifty miles, send their children." The WNIA reported, "If such a school cannot be had, they earnestly desire two district schools about fourteen miles apart." The Navajos, according to WNIA president Amelia Stone Quinton, favored on-reservation boarding schools, where they "can see their children when hungry for the sight of their faces, . . . while the plan of taking the children off the reservation meets their utter disapproval and bitter hostility." In fact, when Quinton spoke with Navajo soldiers at Fort Wingate in 1891 they were cordial with her until she brought up the education of their children. She wrote, "[This] revealed the angry fear of a non-reservation school, or the suspicion that I had come to steal their children for one of the latter."[118]

Aboriginal communities also sometimes engaged in collective action against the taking of their children. In 1919 authorities had rounded up several children from Cumeroogunga. In response, Herbert and Florence Nicholls (whose son Doug would become a major Aboriginal leader) petitioned the Aborigines Protection Board on behalf of the community and received assurances that it would not happen again. A member of the board wrote to the Nicholls, "No more girls shall be taken away from Cummerogunga [*sic*] or elsewhere to be placed in the Board's home or in service unless with the consent of the parents, or until after the full facts have been considered by the Board, and its sanction to such removal obtained." The board also offered to give parents a free railway pass to visit their girls at Cootamundra "*at least* once a year." And the board promised, "In regard to the matter of the girls recently taken by the Police at Cummerogunga, the Board will give further consideration to their case at its next meeting."[119]

Like American Indians, many Aboriginal people did not oppose education, but questioned why their children must be removed for that purpose. In 1913 Matthew Kropinyeri stated to the Royal Commission on Aborigines in South Australia, "In regard to the taking of our children in hand by the State to learn trades . . . our people would gladly embrace the opportunity of betterment for our children; but to be subjected to complete alienation from our children is to say the least an unequalled act of injustice; and no parent worthy of the name would either yield to or urge such a measure."[120] Susie Wilson, another South Australia Aboriginal person who testified to the same Royal Commission in 1914, told the commissioners, "We would like to have a school here, so that our children could be taught to read and write. We do not want them to live in the camps all their lives." Commissioners asked Wilson if she would prefer to go away to a "big farm in some other part of the State where there were only half-caste people, and where [her] children could be taught." She answered, "We would sooner stay here and be near our own people." She concluded her testimony by declaring, "We would like our children to go to school, but we do not want them to go too far away."[121]

Indigenous communities in both Australia and the United States also pursued a related strategy of agitating for their children to attend local public schools. For example, "at Upper Lake [in northern California] where the Indians [mostly Pomos] refused to send their children to the local day school, which caused its close," one Indian agent "learned . . . that the Indians won their suit against the public school trustees" to force the public school to allow them to attend.[122] When Norman Harris learned that the Australian Aborigines Amelioration Association was sympathetic to Aborigines, he wrote them to discuss his belief that Aboriginal children should be able to attend state public schools with other Australian children. "It is the right to come among respectable people we want, which is our birthright," he contended. "Our education and training do not want to be in some isolated school or place such as those run by the State now. Our children are not aliens, and our children should get Christian justice and equity."[123] On the southeast coast of New South Wales, the Aboriginal community at Bateman's Bay successfully campaigned to enable their children to attend the local public school.[124]

Over time, the American Indian experience of child removal diverged from that of Aboriginal people. Due to a number of differences in policy and practice, American Indians eventually exerted greater control over the practice of child removal. The U.S. government's vacillation on parental consent gave Indian families somewhat greater leverage with authorities. Additionally, American reformers leaned toward a more cultural understanding of supposed Indian deficiency and reform; if they could change the "backward" environment of Indians, they believed, they could solve the "Indian problem." With such an orientation, reformers promoted only the temporary removal of Indian children; they hoped to inculcate in the children new values and lifestyles so that they would eventually return to and transform their communities.

Thus, in this context, American Indian families seized the initiative where they could. For example, if they could not prevent the removal of their children or bring them back in the summers, some tried to exert control over the process. The Navajo (Diné) girl Kaibah hid behind her mother's skirts when the superintendent of the boarding school at Toadlena came to take her away. When the superintendent tried to give Kaibah an apple, she threw it at his forehead and then bit him when he caught her by the hand. Her mother, disliking her daughter's discourtesy and realizing the futility of resistance, offered to send her son to school instead, insisting that she "must prepare [Kaibah] before sending [her]." Mother Chischillie, as she was known, wanted to prepare her daughter to "take care of herself when she is among [strangers]." She told the superintendent, "I shall start at once to teach my daughter to herd sheep, to weave, to cook, and to take care of the hogan, so she will be self-reliant. I shall take her with me to the meetings of our people, so she will not be afraid of strangers. I have treated her as a child too long."[125] Mother Chischillie thus sought to set the terms of the removal of her children.

Indian parents also sought to exercise some choice as to which school their children would attend. In his work on the Rapid City Indian School in South Dakota, the historian Scott Riney points out that Indian parents preferred that *all* of their children attend the boarding school if the oldest one was taken there, rather than separating them into different schools. Riney also reveals that Indian parents were selective about which boarding schools they wanted their children to attend, dependent on the school's health record. Moreover, some parents secured employment at Rapid City Indian School, taking up their jobs only when assured that their children would be enrolled there. Thus they found a means to keep the family intact.[126]

It was not only Indian parents who sought to gain some control over their children's boarding school education, but the children themselves. For example, Hopi Don Talayesva (called Sun Chief in his autobiography) had witnessed Navajo and African American policemen dragging many Hopi children off to school from his village of Oraibi. He also observed that the white teachers cut the children's hair, burned their clothes, and gave them new names. He decided to take matters into his own hands. "In 1899 it was decided that I should go to school," Talayesva recalls. "I was willing to try it but I did not want a policeman to come for me and I did not want my shirt taken from my back and burned. So one morning in September I left it off, wrapped myself in my Navajo blanket, . . . and went down the mesa barefoot and bareheaded." When Talayesva reached the New Oraibi School at the foot of the mesa, he "entered a room where boys had bathed in tubs of dirty water." Talayesva remembers, "I stepped into a tub and began scrubbing myself." From New Oraibi, Talayesva went to Keams Canyon School until returning to Oraibi the following summer. At the end of the summer, before he could willingly return to school, he reports, "The police came to Oraibi and surrounded the village, with the intention of capturing the children of the Hostile families and taking them to school by force. They herded us all together at the east edge of the mesa. Although I had planned to go later, they put me with the others. The people were excited, the children and the mothers were crying, and the men wanted to fight." Again Talayesva did not wish to be herded like an animal. Rather than riding in the wagon with the other children, he asked if he could ride double with one of the policemen on his horse.[127]

Among some Indian tribes compulsion eventually proved unnecessary to fill the boarding schools. More parents actively sought out boarding school education for their children, thinking that it would prepare them to deal with future problems between their tribe and the U.S. government. Still others simply lived in such dire poverty that boarding school was a chance to stave off starvation and poverty for their children.[128] As Commissioner John Collier's Indian New Deal policies took effect—allowing Indian languages to be spoken and taught in the schools, eliminating the military system, and infusing more money into the schools—Indian communities more readily sent their children to school. By the late 1940s, Sally Hyer writes, attending Santa Fe Indian School had become a "time-honored custom," especially among the Pueblo people north of Santa Fe. Collier's reforms also eventually led to the hiring of more native people to run the schools; by the mid-1950s Indians made up 60 percent of the staff at the Santa Fe Indian School. When this school closed in 1962, Indian people even protested.[129]

Even as American officials continued to control Indian people and assure their dependency, some Indian parents and children eventually could exercise greater choice. Having more options diminished feelings of powerlessness and enabled some families to take a more active role in the boarding school education of their children. At least for some American Indian peoples, journeying to boarding school eventually became less of a brutal removal and more of a joint enterprise between family and state (and often church), even a rite of passage for Indian children. In Australia, where authorities generally intended the removal of children to be a permanent separation, indigenous families rarely claimed particular homes or missions as their own (though indigenous people who grew up in the institutions often expressed great ambivalence about the experience, as explored in chapter 6); removal of Aboriginal children to institutions remained a coercive state measure.

Although government officials and reformers touted assimilation in the United States and protection in Australia as compassionate policies designed to lift indigenous children out of poverty and give them greater opportunity, the approach by which they set out to accomplish this goal undermined their claims of benevolence. Governments in both countries resorted to a number of means, from verbal pressure to creating a sense of obligation, from employing older children as recruiters to trickery, and, most brutally, from withholding rations to using military and police forces. Although some indigenous people undoubtedly cooperated with authorities and brought their children in voluntarily, they did so within an extremely coercive context. These policies cruelly traumatized indigenous peoples with methods that were akin to the forcible seizures of land and removals of indigenous people from earlier eras of colonization. Now there was no place indigenous people could hide from the state, as authorities invaded the most intimate spaces of indigenous people's lives and challenged their sovereignty even over their own kin. Given their associations with the intimate realm, the home, and raising children, white women ultimately became instrumental in carrying out these policies, as the next chapter explores in more depth.

→ Child removal became a way to promote colonialism, instead of a benevolent action to uplift the Ind. People

Chapter 5

Intimate Betrayals

Have you ever thought how much more harm is done in this world by "good people" than by scoundrels? • CHARLES LUMMIS TO ALICE FLETCHER, March 4, 1900, Alice Cunningham Fletcher and Francis La Flesche papers, NAA

Although authorities frequently used force to remove indigenous children from their families, they much preferred to bring American Indian and Aboriginal children to institutions through persuasion. After all, marching children off to school at gunpoint or whisking them away in police cars while their parents wailed did not square with either the U.S. or Australian government's attempts at the turn of the twentieth century to distance themselves from the more violent colonization methods of the past. Such persuasion, however, involved colonizing the intimate realm, coming into close personal association with indigenous peoples in their homes and communities, a task that many reformers and authorities believed to be the province of women. Thus government entities, reform organizations, and missionary societies regularly enlisted white women to carry out child removal.

Often white women's maternalist convictions converged with official policy goals; as shown in chapter 3, many white women reformers and missionaries supported the removal of indigenous children. To carry out their goals, maternalists also believed it essential that they gain admittance into the intimate circle of indigenous families and serve as surrogate mothers to indigenous children. In many cases, white women overcame initial suspicions and secured a degree of trust from the families, who sometimes incorporated them into their existing kinship systems as mothers, aunts, or grandmothers. Some white women sincerely sought long-term associations with indigenous families, but others understood their first allegiance to be to the state, their reform organization, or their missionary society or church. For these white women maternalists, their ultimate goal was not simply to befriend indigenous people and advocate for their cause, but to transform them religiously, socially, culturally, and economically through a process that included removing their children. Such women engaged in tactical intimate associations with indigenous families, to be abandoned when their aims had been achieved.

To the families that white women befriended, these associations carried different meanings: they signified bonds of reciprocity, trust, and responsibility. When white women failed to fulfill the motherly obligations and responsibilities they had assumed, the families' trust often gave way to feelings of betrayal. Moreover, many indigenous women came to resent and contest white women's assumption of the maternal role.

In this chapter I look particularly at the complicated intimacies formed between the reformer and anthropologist Alice Cunningham Fletcher and the Omahas and Winnebagos of Nebraska and between the missionary Annie Lock and Aboriginal people in Central Australia. Acting on her maternalist impulses, her desire for an official position of authority, and her need to financially support herself, Fletcher hired on with the government in the 1880s to "recruit" Indian children for the Carlisle and Hampton boarding schools. Her intimate experiences with Omaha and Winnebago families and their growing distrust of her eventually forced her to examine her role in separating Indian children from their families. In Australia, where white women had a more conflicted relationship with government officials, Annie Lock set out on her own to Central Australia to "rescue" Aboriginal children. In the process she developed a critical assessment of Australian colonial policies and ran afoul of government officials. Ultimately, however, she also betrayed the intimate associations she had formed with Aboriginal children.

These stories highlight the complicated nature of white women's participation in the colonial enterprise. At the very moment the U.S. and Australian governments were articulating their assimilation and protection policies in order to gain increasing control over their indigenous populations, white women in both countries were agitating against their unequal status and their exclusion from full participation in civic society. Through their work in support of the colonial project of assimilating American Indians, white women such as Fletcher acquired significant influence in American society at the turn of the twentieth century. Yet Fletcher and other white women accrued status at the expense of the indigenous people they allegedly sought to support. In Australia, where they never gained as much influence over Aboriginal affairs, white women nevertheless campaigned for a greater role in Aboriginal policy making. Government officials simultaneously resented the women's interference and recognized their usefulness in carrying out the government's aims. Although many white women reformers may have possessed their own seemingly benevolent reasons for engaging in aspects of indigenous child removal, in many cases their efforts ultimately contributed to state policies.

In the United States white women played integral roles in implementing indigenous child removal. White women reformers themselves sought opportunities to carry out this maternal work, and government officials recognized that white women could be more effective than men as "recruiters" of Indian children. Richard Pratt readily utilized white women to gather children for Carlisle Institute, perhaps because he believed they would have greater success than former military men like himself in convincing Indian people to send their children eastward. When Pratt made his initial trips west to "recruit" Indian students for Carlisle, Sarah Mather, who had taught Pratt's POWs in St. Augustine, "urgently desired to accompany" him as assistant to the Indian girls. Although sixty-three years old, Mather joined Pratt on this mission as well as on a later expedition to Wichita, Kansas, to bring back Cheyenne, Kiowa, and Pawnee children to Carlisle.[1] On Hampton Institute's behalf, Cora Folsom made many trips west to "recruit" students.[2]

Alice Fletcher, who, as we have seen, became an influential proponent of child removal, hired on with Pratt in 1882 to "recruit" Plains Indian children for Carlisle and Hampton Institutes. On her way west she was to accompany a group of children from Carlisle back to their homes at Rosebud, Pine Ridge, and Sisseton Agencies. Pratt gave Fletcher precise orders: "You are authorized to proceed as far as Pine Ridge agency and to remain at Pine Ridge and Rosebud agencies as long as the best interests of the children whom you return home may seem to demand. Instructions will be forwarded to you at Rosebud in regard to your bringing back with you a delegation of Omaha and Sioux children."[3] A few weeks later Pratt asked Fletcher to accompany another "thirty-eight Ind. Ty. [Indian Territory] children mostly Cheyenne, Kiowas, Arapahoes, and Comanches" to their homes. Pratt stipulated, "All the desirable ones are to return after six or seven weeks at home."[4]

A peculiar notation is present in the upper lefthand corner of one letter that Pratt sent to Fletcher: "x Desirable 1 Immaterial o Don't Want." Each child listed in the letter was then coded with an x, a 1, or a o, but in a different ink than the original letter.[5] Fletcher appears to have used this code to categorize the children as to whether or not they should return to Carlisle. This notation reveals several aspects of Indian child removal in the late nineteenth century. First, unlike subsequent government officials, Pratt did not wish to remove every Indian child but just those he deemed desirable. Concerned as he was with creating a new model for the assimilation of Indian children, Pratt was intent on the success of Carlisle, which could come about only if he could transform Indian children into poster children for assimilation. Perhaps he did not want to take any chances with children he thought would not make Carlisle look good.

This code tells us more, though. It offers a haunting portrayal of how cavalier and callous both Pratt and Fletcher could be in their efforts to "recruit" children. These lists of children do not reveal anything more about them or their communities and families than whether they would be desirable to Pratt's overall plan. With these terse notations, Fletcher and Pratt seemed to erase all the precious richness of each child and the community from which he or she came.

In a similar vein, Pratt also gave Fletcher explicit quotas for each tribe or band. "Authority is given me for sixty-five Sioux children," he wrote to Fletcher, "into which must go the Sitting Bull party. Suppose we say eight (8) from S. B., thirty (30) from Rosebud, and twenty-seven (27) from Pine Ridge, but allow it to be flexible." Pratt asked Fletcher to bring the party of children east by about September 1 and told her she would be paid fifty dollars a month.[6] (Many Omaha people living today assert that Fletcher was paid by the head for each child she "recruited.")[7] Samuel Chapman Armstrong, the director of Hampton Institute, asked Fletcher to bring some Omaha students back to his institution as well.[8] Fletcher was quite successful in recruiting children among the Omahas, with whom she had been living and carrying out anthropological studies, but the government agreed to pay transportation for only fifteen Omahas to Carlisle, not for ten additional Omahas to Hampton.[9] So Fletcher used her connections with the WNIA to raise the money to bring the additional children.[10]

Fletcher may have been less successful with tribes with whom she had no sustained relationships. By the end of July Pratt had decided to join Fletcher, telling her he wanted to recruit Pine Ridge and Rosebud students himself. He told her, "You may limit your effort to the Sitting Bull and Omaha children. Should you find it too difficult to get your Sitting Bull and Omaha children together, you may leave the Sitting Bull children to me to look after."[11] In her dealings with Sitting Bull, Fletcher was warned by Agent George Andrews of Fort Randall, "I have had one interview with Sitting Bull and a number of his people . . . and find there is a great reluctance to let the children go; the subject is being discussed very thoroughly among the Indians. . . . The death[s] of [several of their children at mission schools] appear to be the great objection, and the long stay of the band at this post, with the uncertainty of their ultimate disposition, is much talked about, and used as another great objection."[12] According to her diary, however, Fletcher claimed to have great success with Sitting Bull: "In one of these interviews Sitting Bull asked me if his young children could not be sent to the mission schools; he said they were ill clothed and that he wanted them to begin to learn the better way of living while they were little. He desires them to learn to read and become 'like the people who loved God.' . . . Sitting Bull begged me 'to pity his women and children' and that I might 'remember to pity and help them,' he drew off his ring and gave it to me."[13] Despite her upbeat tone, it is unclear how many children she was able to recruit from Sitting Bull's band. Later, according to Pratt, Sitting Bull declined to send any children eastward with another recruiter, "Miss B," probably Miss Marianna Burgess, another loyal teacher of Pratt's.[14]

In their role as recruiters white women often witnessed the pain and anguish of indigenous families who were to be separated from their beloved children, and it may be that this experience introduced a first hint of doubt about their mission. In 1884, for example, when Cora Folsom went to a Minniconjou Lakota (Sioux) community in the Dakota Territory, the "fine looking old men" who met in council told Folsom and the other recruiters with her, "They have taken away our tobacco and we will give up our rations; we will not give up our children." Folsom recounted that when they came out of their council,

> crowds of men and women had collected around the tipi and when we came out feeling like chastened children we had to pass down a long line of blanketed Indians, some of whom responded to our smiling "How" while others looked pained and grieved to see women so young and so apparently innocent ready to tear little children from the loving arms of their parents. They had seen to it, however, that there was nothing to fear, for not a child of the five hundred appeared in sight to tempt us. Where so many could have hidden in tipis so devoid of hiding places we shall never know, but the children must have been in the game for no sound of them reached our ears.[15]

Even Alice Fletcher, so seemingly assured of her righteousness, seemed to falter a bit as she took her first party of Indian children eastward. On August 13, 1881, she started for Carlisle with eleven girls and fourteen boys, most of them Omahas, from the train depot in Sioux City, Iowa. "The parents of the children gave up their little ones for five years willingly," she wrote.

> Some [parents] came forty miles on the way. The parting was most pathetic. As I looked on the group where stood mothers with their little ones clinging about their necks, the tears falling plentifully, the father near by, red-eyed but resolute. I wished that all who find it difficult to see a man in an Indian might have been there with me. One old woman who was parting from her elder boy, mingling her grey hair with his glossy black locks as she bent over him, he was her only son save the baby in her arms, several little graves filled the space between these two, this woman said to me: "Ah! Friend, it is best my boy goes, but my heart cries, and it will cry, but no one shall hear it. By and bye [*sic*] I will be able to keep back the tears, I shall think, my boy is learning and will do much in the future when he comes back and will be happy and good!"[16]

Clearly, Fletcher realized the profound grief that child removal brought to the families. Yet, as expressed through the old woman's lament for her son, she also conceived of the enterprise as one that would ultimately serve the larger cause of "civilizing" the Indians.

In her recruitment efforts Fletcher came to rely on an intimate network of indigenous people—some returned boarding school students, others local Indians—to aid her. Among the Omahas, the La Flesche family became key contacts. As described in chapter 3, Fletcher came to know the La Flesche family through her association with the young, well-educated Susette La Flesche in Boston in 1879, when she served as a translator for the Ponca leader Standing Bear on his speaking tour to protest the removal of the Poncas from the Dakota Territory to Indian Territory. Fletcher used her association with Susette and her white husband, Thomas Tibbles, to organize her first trip among the Indians of the Great Plains.[17]

When Fletcher first arrived in Omaha, Nebraska, in 1881 Susette and her husband took Fletcher in a carriage eighty miles north to the Omaha Reservation, a trip that took two days. There the La Flesche family, led by the patriarch, Joseph La Flesche, welcomed Fletcher. The elder La Flesche, of mixed Ponca and French parentage, had grown up among the Omahas and been chosen by an older chief to be his successor. Joseph had long been a proponent of selective assimilation; in 1854, when the Omahas moved to their reservation on the Missouri River, he established a settlement of frame houses near the new Presbyterian mission and school that some other Omahas called Make Believe White Men's Village. (Other Omahas moved to two other villages of more traditional earth lodges located to the west and south of La Flesche's settlement.) Joseph promoted farming on new, individually owned tracts of land and set up a police force to keep order. In 1866 he converted to Christianity and sent his children to the mission school. He made sure that all his children were well educated in American schools. His daughter Susanne eventually became a medical doctor and his son Francis had just secured a position as a clerk in Washington with the Bureau of Indian Affairs when Fletcher first came to the Omaha Reservation.[18]

Fletcher depended on several La Flesche family members as her proxy recruiters who routinely reported to her. One La Flesche daughter, Rosalie, told Fletcher, "I saw John Webster and told him what you said. He said he would do as you said about his daughters going back [to school] in the fall."[19] On another occasion Rosalie wrote Fletcher that her brother Noah was also working to recruit children for schools and that her father, Joseph, had made a speech on the Fourth of July "about sending children off to school." According to Rosalie, however, other Indians did not commit.[20] Noah La Flesche reported to Fletcher on his difficulties rounding up children: "I want to tell you about the scholars for Hampton. It has been very hard work looking for children. I haven't as many as you wanted." He had found three under twelve years old and seven over twelve. "I told the Headmen and policemen about wanting their help in getting children, but they didn't help me at all."[21]

10. Alice Fletcher (dark dress) seated in the middle of a group of white and Omaha women at the Omaha Mission, Nebraska, ca. 1883–84. BAE GN 4473, National Anthropological Archives, Smithsonian Institution.

Clearly Fletcher had developed sustained relationships with the La Flesches, but there seems to have been an instrumental quality to her growing intimacy with the family. At least in her first years of association with them, Fletcher seems to have used them to further her aims: to study their culture as an anthropologist and to carry out the policy and mission of the government and reform organizations. Eventually conflict developed between Fletcher and some members of the La Flesche family. While she became closer to Francis and Rosalie, Susette and Tibbles grew distant, as they opposed assimilation and the removal of children to boarding schools.[22]

Among the Winnebagos of Nebraska, who resided on a reservation neighboring the Omahas', Fletcher relied extensively on one returned Hampton student, Julia St. Cyr, who, while experiencing great tragedy, nevertheless tried to carry out Fletcher's bidding. When St. Cyr arrived home from Hampton Institute she found that her mother had just died. She wrote poignantly to Fletcher, "My dear darling mother died last week Tuesday morning about four o'clock. It was the time I was just coming back . . . from Hampton. . . . Oh it is so lonely here. If I had gotten here in time it will not be so hard, but I came three days after Tuesday after my darling mother died. My father has sore eyes very badly and our mother's loss is so great to him." In her grief, however, St. Cyr promised, "Miss Fletcher I forgot to tell you that I am going to get the children and send them all right. I am going to get sound bright children."[23]

In return, St. Cyr and her ailing father beseeched Fletcher to help them send her brother David home: "I didn't tell you while I was in Washington that I wished you would help David my brother that he can come home."[24] A few weeks later St. Cyr again wrote to Fletcher: "I had five children to go to H[ampton] and just as they were ready two of them backed out—at least their parents backed out." St. Cyr complained, "There is not much going on here now. It is quite dull to me. I have gotten so used to the School," but she asked Fletcher again that her brother David be sent home.[25] The records do not indicate if Fletcher ever helped to have David sent home, but this correspondence does suggest that many indigenous people looked to Fletcher as a mediator. Moreover, they seemed to regard their relationship with her as a reciprocal one. St. Cyr worked to carry out Fletcher's recruitment goals, and in return she expected Fletcher to advocate for her needs.

There is evidence that other indigenous people regarded Fletcher in a similar fashion. Because she had recruited so many of their children for the boarding schools, and seemingly made many promises regarding their safety and well-being, many other Winnebago and Omaha people sought her mediation with the schools. Some recruited students looked to Fletcher to help them leave school. One Omaha boy, Eli Sheridan, wrote to Fletcher in 1885, "I want to go home this month. I am tried [*sic*] of this school." Sheridan repeated his request emphatically: "Miss Fletcher, I want you to let me go home this year. When we come to Carlisle school you say to me [my] brother when ever you want your brother come home I let come home Your promes [promise] to my brother. If you don't let me go home I *will* run of[f] this school to go home." He insisted, "I think go home this year. That is my *will*."[26]

Fletcher appears to have promised the Omahas that their children could return whenever they wanted. Expecting that she would help them, many parents and family members sought her aid in bringing their children home for the summer. John Big Elk, for example, wrote to Fletcher, "I want Steward Plack and his brother to come home during vacation to help me with my harvest. . . . I wish you would speak to the man who has the care of them and let me know what he says."[27] Ultimately, however, Fletcher lacked such power and will. Thus, far from contracting a reciprocal relationship with Omaha and Winnebago families, she made empty promises in an effort to gain more children for the boarding schools.

As some Omaha children at Hampton and Carlisle became sick and died, Fletcher was forced to confront the gravity of what she had done in removing the children. After he became seriously ill at Hampton, authorities returned Noah Webster to his family, but he died after being at home just ten weeks. Seemingly powerless against the boarding school bureaucracy, Noah's father, John Webster, pleaded to Fletcher, "I have lost two boys this was the older. I feel very sorry. I do not know what to do with myself, that is why I write to you. . . . I cannot eat, and I cannot do anything. . . . My wife and family do not feel well. We want you to help us to get our girl (Etta) back home again. If we have her back I think we will feel better."[28] In another letter, Webster placed his faith in Fletcher: "I am an Indian and could do not [*sic*] wonderful thing but although you are a woman you can do more than any Indian can do and so we ask you to help us in all our wrong ways."[29] Records do not indicate how Fletcher responded or if Etta was returned to the Websters.

Although Webster remained polite to Fletcher, another Omaha family, the Springers, became outraged by her role in the removal of their children to Carlisle and the death of their daughter. The Springers wrote in anger and despair to Pratt:

We feel very sorry that we did not hear about the sickness of our daughter, in time to have her come home. We did not get the letter you sent to the agent till a long time after it came to the agency. . . . We feel that those who profess to have the management here of our children, feel but little interest in their welfare. and that when we make a request, it is not attended to. We would like the body of our daughter Alice sent to us. . . .

We also want Elsie and Willie sent home, as we have good schools here on the reserve. one a girls school, and one for boys and girls. . . .

We are anxious to have our children educated, but do not see the necessity of sending them so far away to be educated, when we have good schools at home, where we can see them when we wish, and attend to them when sick. Please send them as soon as possible, so as to get them home before cold weather.

I had no idea of sending my children there, but Miss Fletcher got round Elsie and persuaded her to go and then Alice wanted to go with her. It was Miss Fletcher's doings that they went, and now my husband is grieving all the time. I do not see why the government put so much power and confidence in Miss Fletcher, as we think she does no good to the Omahas but much harm. She cannot be trusted. Please do not deny our request, if you have any regard to a Father's and Mother's feelings.[30]

Unfortunately, the Springers met with callous indifference from Pratt, who replied that their letter surprised and pained him. He told them he could have sent Alice home if he had received information from them that they wanted him to do so. (Since they had never learned she was ill, however, they could not have requested this.) Pratt then refused to transport Alice's remains home to her Omaha family. "Her body is now in such a state of decomposition as renders it wholly impracticable to send it home," he told them. "It has been kindly and tenderly laid away, and it seems to me, that when you consider it fully you will feel that it would be better to let it rest there." As a final blow to the Springers, Pratt refused to send their other children home:

> About returning Elsie and Willie, that can only be done with the consent of the Department. I think if you could see their improvement you would be better reconciled to their absence. Elsie is quite strong in her desire not to return. Willie has, now and then, seemed desirous of going home, but latterly has been contented. They are having extraordinary opportunities of observation and experience, just what all civilized people desire for their children, and it seems to me that if you consider the matter more thoroughly, you would desire them to continue, rather than narrow them down to the limited sphere of a reservation school.

Pratt added that it seemed "unwise to send them back before the time" of their period of study expired. He closed his letter by stating, "The loss of Alice is very sad, and I sympathize most sincerely with you, but yet people die everywhere. She had the kindest treatment, a good nurse and physician, and was cared for as tenderly as possible by the teacher and everyone at the school."[31]

Pratt sent his correspondence with the Springers to Fletcher. If she felt any guilt or misgivings about her role in the death of Alice Springer, Fletcher did not reveal it to the girl's parents. Nor did she attempt to console them or express any sympathy to them for their loss. "I can only repeat his [Pratt's] words," she wrote to them. "'I am surprised and pained at what you say.'" Fletcher added:

> Life and Death are in God's hands. . . . God called Alice away and altho it is very sad and hard we must accept his will. He only can comfort your hearts and He will, for his love is [illegible] all his children.
>
> As to Elsie and Willie I hope you will think over all the Cap[tai]n says. . . . The words you wrote about me and my efforts in behalf

of the Omahas. I am sure you did not realize in your grief what you were saying or you would not have written so unjustly.[32]

If Pratt and Fletcher seemed impervious to the pleas of the Springers, another white woman, "Mrs. Springer's intensely sympathetic friend," empathized with the couple and also wrote to Pratt to have Elsie and Willie returned from school. Pratt relented a little; he told Fletcher, "If they send money to pay travel expenses, I will ask the Dept. and send Wm and Elsie home tho they both are anxious to remain."[33] Not surprisingly, the Springers lacked the funds to pay for the return of their children. Two years later, in 1885, after Mr. Springer died, Mrs. Hamilton, presumably the sympathetic friend, wrote to Willie Springer, "You must come to help your Mother care for her little ones. . . . Surely they will not refuse now. . . . They *must* send you both home. We wrote of your father's failing health in time for you to see him, had you been sent as you *should have been*. Your mother will always feel sore about it. . . . I feel *sure* Christian people cannot keep you from your dear Mother a day."[34] As Mrs. Hamilton's plea makes clear, not all white women adhered to the notion that the strict separation of children from their families for a fixed number of years was necessary or desirable.

Nevertheless, Mrs. Hamilton surfaces briefly in the historical record only to fade into obscurity, while Fletcher continued to hold great power over indigenous families. Fletcher's power derived from both the maternalist reform organizations she represented and the state, which, through Pratt, had authorized her to recruit Indian children for the boarding schools. In her adherence to their convergent goals of removing and transforming Indian children, Fletcher ultimately betrayed the trust and intimacy she had established with many Indian families.

On the other hand, Fletcher's intimacy with Indian families—her knowledge of their grief and anguish—may have led her to envision another possible model of Indian education. Although she did not express any regret in her diaries or letters regarding her role in separating the children from their families, her growing unease with the practice can be seen in a new program that she promoted. According to the WNIA in 1884, "Her favorite plan is to bring young husbands and their wives East, to be educated as families, and then to be returned to their tribes, and provided with homes, that they may educate their people by precept and example."[35] (See chapter 7 for more on the enactment of this "model family program" at Hampton Institute.) This was perhaps the inherent risk in the state's project to colonize the intimate: that empathy and compassion might complicate and ultimately triumph over state goals of controlling indigenous people.

In Fletcher's case, this risk never materialized; she never publicly opposed indigenous child removal or assimilation policy. Instead, her personal, professional, and maternalist goals all intersected with the government's assimilation policy. Pratt and the government found her useful in pursuing their efforts to remove and institutionalize Indian children, and Fletcher gained a stage on which to act out her maternalist impulses, make a living, and pursue a scientific career. The WNIA and the women's movement also embraced Fletcher for advancing the cause of all (white) women. At the turn of the twentieth century white women's participation in the assimilation of American Indians served as a means to elevate the status of white women. As the Omaha Indian John Webster wrote to Alice Fletcher, "Although you are a woman you can do more than any Indian can do." Unfortunately, as Webster knew all too well, white women earned their advancement through supporting, not challenging, the policies that had such tragic consequences for many Indian families.

In Australia, white women also became caught up in the policy of removing Aboriginal children. However, given the tension between white women reformers and male authorities over Aboriginal affairs, most white Australian women acted more independently of and even in opposition to the state than did American women. Most white women reformers still supported the removal of children, but they believed they could better implement this policy than the government. Thus their interventions into the intimate realm of indigenous families brought them into the same kind of complicated relationships with indigenous women and children that vexed Alice Fletcher.

As we saw in chapter 3, many white Australian women desired to have official government positions—protectorships—that would enable them to carry out child removal. When state governments dragged their feet in assigning women to such positions, some women simply volunteered. Nellie Campbell, who lived in Melbourne, wrote to the minister of the interior, "Should you require a woman to assist in transporting, etc., may I step in?"[36] A few women did gain official positions of authority over Aboriginal women, including Miss Lappidge, a nurse who worked for the State Children's Department in South Australia, and an unidentified policewoman, both of whom were instrumental in removing the baby of a nineteen-year-old Aboriginal woman, Priscilla Karpanny.

Adhering to maternalist notions that Aboriginal women were incapable of caring for their children and their homes, Lappidge came to inspect the home of Karpanny at Point McLeay and declared, "Your baby is dirty, and so is the house." Lappidge also objected that the baby slept with Karpanny in her bed and threatened to take the baby unless Karpanny got a separate bed for him. Karpanny complied, but a few months later authorities insisted that she bring her baby to the hospital even though he was not sick. Karpanny told a newspaper reporter, "I thought it was cruel to take my baby from my breast, when he was quite well, and put him in a hospital with sick babies, . . . but when the policeman said my baby must go, I brought him. I did not know he was made a State child until we got to the Adelaide Railway Station. When we got out of the train the State lady [Lappidge] said to the policewoman who was there: 'The baby has to be taken away from the girl, as he is a State baby.' . . . Then they took my baby from me." Karpanny was dumbfounded: "The State lady never came back to see if I got a bed for him, and I do not know why they took him away."[37]

Lappidge's and the policewoman's actions did not go unchallenged in this case, however. Karpanny seems to have gained the support of several male missionaries in South Australia. C. E. Taplin, who identified himself as honorary protector of Aborigines, wrote to the chief protector, "That a woman should have her own baby recklessly dragged from her arms, and taken entirely away from her, at the behest of a Government Official, because some female inspectress thought the mother an *unsuitable guardian*, is shocking to contemplate. What does the female official know of the right way to treat an aboriginal baby?" Taplin added, "To forcibly remove an infant in these circumstances from its natural protector, I contend is a grave outrage."[38] Another male missionary, Reverend H. E. Read, who dispensed medicine at Point McLeay, testified to the newspaper, "Priscilla always appeared to have great affection for her child and wherever she went she took the baby with her. . . . The child always appeared to be clean, and . . . well nourished and well cared for. I know of *no* neglect on the part of the mother, towards the child." Read concluded, "I am quite at a loss to understand why the child was removed from its mother[']s care."[39]

Perhaps with the help and encouragement of Taplin and Read, Karpanny's case gained rare coverage in the local newspaper, the *Adelaide Sun*, which reported in 1924, "There is at present in Adelaide a young aboriginal mother breaking her heart because a heartless Parliamentary Act [the Training of Aborigines' Children Act of 1923] has enabled the servants of the Chief Protector of Aborigines to figuratively, if not literally, drag a babe out of the arms and from the breast of its mother." Although the term "stolen generations" originated in the 1980s, this 1920s reporter recognized the experience of Priscilla Karpanny as theft and the act as a law "under which an aboriginal mother may ruthlessly have her babe stolen. The word 'stolen' may sound a bit far-fetched, but by the time we have told the story of the heart-broken mother we are sure the word will not be considered out of place, especially by women who know the instincts of motherhood."[40]

This article is also unusual in that it allowed Karpanny to tell her own story and reprinted it verbatim. She described her family, including details about two brothers who fought in World War I, a father who died five years before, and siblings who earned wages to help support Karpanny and her mother at the Point McLeay station. Karpanny's account of her family highlighted their hard work, respectability, and service to the nation. She then told the story of her mother, a "woolpiece-picker" who went with two other native women to the shearing sheds in Wellington. As there was no room for Karpanny and her brother in the small hut supplied to the workers, Karpanny stayed in Portalloch, where she met a "young native," Terence Wilson, who promised to marry her. She bore a son in August 1923. When the baby was three weeks old, according to Karpanny, "My mother took my little brother and myself and baby [back] to Point McLeay." She contended that neither the superintendent nor the police ever "complained to me about my conduct, or that I neglected my child." Her mother added her objections to the newspaper article: "We were never given a chance to show in a court of justice whether we were right or wrong. Can we not have a judge to say if we are right or wrong? Two of my sons fought at the war for England and Australia. Is there to be one law for the white people, and another for the black?"[41]

As a result of this negative publicity, Chief Protector Garnett was forced to defend Lappidge to Reverend John Sexton of the Aborigines' Friends Association, who joined Taplin and Read in advocating for the return of Karpanny's baby. Garnett claimed, "[Miss Lappidge] complained to me generally of the poor results of her work amongst illegitimate children at Point McLeay, with special reference to Priscilla Karpany and her baby which she said was dirty, neglected and ill and that the mother would not carry out her instructions." Garnett concluded, "It seemed to me a clear case for action under the Aborigines Children's Training Act." He claimed that the matron of the hospital where the boy was taken found that he was dirty and had a slight fever and cough. Garnett did concede that the manner in which the child was taken from its mother by a "Lady Police Officer" at the Adelaide railway station "was most tactless and unfortunate. Why they did not first take the mother and child away from the crowd to the Police Station I do not understand." Due to the furor over the incident, the State Children's Council eventually decided to return the baby to Karpanny.[42]

This case, so unusual in the publicity it garnered and in the return of the child to his mother, illustrates a number of important dimensions in the role white Australian women played in the removal of Aboriginal children. First, it shows another instance of a white woman justifying the removal of an Aboriginal child on the basis of whether its mother conformed to white women's standards of keeping house and caring for children. Second, it illustrates that many Aboriginal women contested such portrayals of themselves as unfit mothers and homemakers. Third, the case illustrates the hostility many white women faced, not only from indigenous women, but from many of their fellow male reformers. Some of these male reformers—Reverend Sexton, for example—may have genuinely opposed Aboriginal child removal (see chapter 9). Others may have simply used the issue to prevent white women from gaining any official power or authority. Thus, unlike Fletcher and other white American women, who generally enjoyed the support of government officials and their fellow white male reformers, Australian white women were more likely to meet opposition from all sides.

More commonly than in the case of Lappidge, white Australian women became involved more informally in child removal through living for long periods in close proximity to Aboriginal peoples. Some of these women, promoting themselves as experts on Aboriginal people, sought a role as intermediaries between government officials and the indigenous communities they had come to know. Daisy Bates, for example, told the Royal Commission on Aborigines in South Australia in 1914, "There are two children that I now want to get away from their mother, because she is rather a drunken woman."[43]

White women missionaries also often played this intermediary role. The state often relied on these women to carry out its aims; in turn, missionaries gained the state's seal of approval and some material aid (a small stipend per child) in removing children for their own purposes.

For example, white women missionaries working at Oodnadatta in South Australia wanted children "to merge into the white population" and believed they never would as long as they were close to "camp." Thus "it was decided to remove the children to a place further south, where there were no aborigines." The missionaries chose Quorn, four hundred miles away, as the site for Colebrook Home. They identified children to be removed from Oodnadatta to Colebrook, and then enlisted the police constable's assistance in trying to forcibly take the children.[44]

Missionaries often portrayed their efforts in the most glowing terms. Some white women missionaries claimed, for example, that Aboriginal people wanted, even begged them to take their children. Ruby Hyde, who worked in South Australia, went to retrieve the "half-caste" children of a white man who had asked missionaries to take them. When she arrived, the "lubras" welcomed her. Hyde asserts that one would have willingly given up her children, ages sixteen months and three years, but the three-year-old was frightened: "It would have been disastrous to the interests of the Mission had she [Hyde], on this first visit, carried off a couple of screaming, protesting children, and she prayed that the little girl might keep quiet when the time of departure came."[45]

Despite their often positive portrayals, many Australian missionaries sometimes revealed that Aboriginal people were not always so welcoming or willing to have their children taken from them. Like the American Cora Folsom, Hampton's schoolteacher and recruiter, the Australian missionary Violet Turner experienced distrust and suspicion from indigenous people, who instructed their children to hide from missionaries. After Turner asked a police constable if she could take a little "half-caste" girl, Eva, from her community to Quorn, Eva's community became wary of Turner. "As I came near the camp on the day of our ride there was a sharp word of command in the native lingo, and off went all the children. Some ran to their mothers and hid their faces in the shelter of the mother's arms, others hid in an old-disused hut. They were all afraid of me." Turner, like Folsom, saw herself as a maternalist savior and found it discomforting to be "regarded as an ogress who would rob them of their children."[46]

Although maternalists commonly asserted that Aboriginal communities rejected their "half-caste" children, Turner and other missionaries more often reported great resistance to taking such children. Turner would see Eva many times with her community, and each time the community would keep her away from Eva. Seeing that Eva and her friend, Gracie, had "wandered off by themselves," away from a group of Aboriginal women, Turner sought to make contact. "A sudden sharp word of warning from the [Aboriginal women] sent the little girls scuttling off like rabbits, to hide behind an iron fence, for safety from the terrible white lady who had come to take them away."[47] Again Turner realized with dismay how the indigenous women saw her, as a "terrible white lady."

Like Alice Fletcher, Australian missionaries also experienced some of the profound resentment of indigenous families when they established relationships with them but failed to fulfill the promises or obligations that such intimacies entailed. Turner recounts the story of Ethel, a "full-blooded" girl whose parents had brought her at age twelve to the Oodnadatta mission to keep her safe from white men until her marriage to a full-blood man. The missionaries promised to return Ethel to her parents when it was time for her to marry, but in the meantime they sent her farther away to their mission in Quorn. Missionaries regarded Ethel as a favorite who they hoped would follow in their footsteps and become a missionary. "God was . . . preparing her for something better than an aboriginal camp," Turner wrote. When Ethel contracted a lung infection and was sent home to die, her parents felt betrayed. According to the missionary Iris Harris, "The parents are most bitter against us and blame us for the girl's death. They have turned the natives against us." Harris and Turner seemed to see no reason for the family's bitterness, believing that they had "saved [Ethel] from darkness and superstition." Their intimation that it was better that she died than return to live in an Aboriginal camp must have deepened the anguish her parents already felt at their daughter's death.[48]

Intimacy between missionaries and indigenous families could also yield more complicated outcomes. The story of one Australian missionary, Annie Lock, illuminates how white women who developed intense intimate relations with indigenous people, particularly in the care of children, could come into conflict with the state and begin to question the implementation of its policies. Lock's eventual friction with state authorities illustrates how female missionaries in Australia occupied an ambiguous position in relation to the state in carrying out Aboriginal child removal.

Born in 1876, Annie Lock had been working as a dressmaker in Riverton, South Australia, when she "received her call" at age twenty-four. After training as a missionary at Hope Lodge, she worked with the United Aborigines' Mission (UAM), a missionary group founded and dominated by women, in New South Wales, Western Australia, and South Australia. She later set out on her own to Central Australia in the 1920s and then returned to South Australia in the 1930s. All in all, Lock lived and ministered among Aboriginal people from about 1903 to 1937.[49]

Throughout her more than three decades in the field, Lock became involved in the policy of removing Aboriginal children on many occasions. In 1910, when she worked at the Dulhi Gunyah orphanage in Western Australia, she wrote the *Australian Aborigines Advocate*, "An Aboriginal man called and told me of neglected children at Busselton, and on the following day I consulted several members of the Council, when a course of action was decided upon, the outcome of which has been several additional children handed over to us for training." A few days later she reported that she had visited Busselton and brought home "eight additional inmates, one a baby about twelve months old." At this stage in her career, when referring to Aboriginal children, Lock utilized a language that obscured the true horror of the enterprise in which she was engaged. Children were "inmates," "a course of action was decided upon," children "came," were "handed over," or "were received" by Lock and the orphanage. Like many other maternalists, Lock also often asserted that Aboriginal parents "gave" her their children. When she met a group of children near Marree in South Australia, for example, she claimed that one said to her, "Mother said you can have me for your little girl."[50]

While in South Australia in the 1920s, Lock also helped to establish the Colebrook Home for Aboriginal children. According to Violet Turner, Lock was traveling to Oodnadatta in 1924 when she stopped at Marree. There she learned of Rita, a ten-year-old Aboriginal girl who had been dismissed as a useless domestic servant by two white women. Turner alleges that Rita had been turned over to an Afghan man to marry and asserts that "instantly all the mother-love of [Lock's] heart was stirred to action, and she went to the police and offered to take Rita herself." When the police agreed, Lock took Rita to Oodnadatta with her. Three years later, Lock brought Rita and other "rescued" children to Quorn for the founding of the Colebrook Home. The chief protector brought other children in, including Rita's sister Bessie, whom, he said, "has no one to care for her, and is becoming uncontrollable."[51]

When she moved to Central Australia in the late 1920s, Lock seemed to become more explicit and public in her support for child removal. In 1929 she wrote to the reformer Constance Cooke, "We are trying to solve the problem with the natives up this way. The only thing I can see would [be] to get the children right away from their parents and teach them good moral, clean habits & right from wrong & also industries that will make them more useful & better citizen[s] by & by. We could get the very old blind ones & the helpless ones & keep them in one quarter & have the children in another place on the same reserve & let the young couples work on the stations. The parents are willing to give them over to me & they go & work on the stations."[52] During that same year, she also wrote to the activist Mary Bennett of her solution to the "problem" of Aboriginal people in the Northern Territory:

If natives are taught to work young they are good workers. . . . The problem up here is the children. If we could get a piece of country and get the children and train them while they are young and at the same time teach them useful trades, the girls to sew, cook, wash and clean, the boys to be horsemen, cowboys, shearers, and trades like making up wood and tin cans and iron work, and to be useful at gardening and general work about a home, they would need good, firm, kind persons to train them and not to spoil them or make too much fuss of them. The only education they need is to read and write and do arithmetic, so that they may know the value of money and how to get change.[53]

On occasion, Lock facilitated the placement of Aboriginal girls into service. "Some [of my children] are very bright and would make good girls for any home," she wrote to the AFA. "I just received a letter asking me for two girls they thought I was still in the Oodnadatta home. I sent two girls out while I was there to stations and this is another lady asking me for girls. That is my one aim to try & train the girls to be useful."[54]

Like other white women who portrayed indigenous families as willing to give up their children, Lock tended to downplay her conflicts with the families, but she experienced her share of opposition. While in Katanning (Carrolup) in Western Australia in May 1913, she attended the funeral of an Aboriginal woman. "One little girl and two boys and a husband are left," Lock remarked. "We tried to get the little ones, but the father clung to them." To Lock's dismay, she was told, "We cannot take them if they are cared for by the others."[55] Just a year later "an Aboriginal woman complained that Lock had threatened to take her children away if she did not come to Katanning." Lock claimed she did not threaten the woman, but simply offered to take the "three dark ones."[56] At Ooldea in the 1930s she again struggled with Aboriginal families over the removal of their children. "The past two months we have had trouble with the young girls," Lock wrote to the *United Aborigines' Messenger* shortly after a measles epidemic. "The adults have tried to get them away. One [of the girls] went away, but returned; two of the girls, Pansy & Dossie, again ran away, but were brought back."[57]

Additionally Lock used child removal as a way to punish Aboriginal people in the same way officials often did. In 1936 she caned several children at Ooldea for disobeying her. In retaliation, Harry, the father of one of the girls, attacked and beat Lock, bruising the left side of her face. After this incident, Lock "recommended that 'to teach them a lesson & to punish Harry, Dossie [his daughter] should be taken away from him by the Police and put in [the] Quorn home or the Coast home.'"[58]

Lock's support for and participation in Aboriginal child removal did not, however, translate into wholesale support of government policies. In fact, she outspokenly criticized other state policies toward Aboriginal people, such as the right of settlers to Aboriginal land. "The poor natives are just hunted from their hunting grounds and cannot get their usual food," she wrote. "Where they used to camp near waterholes and wait for their wild animals to come in for water, now these water holes are taken up by the squatters for their cattle and sheep." Lock understood why the Aborigines with whom she lived resorted to raiding settlers' camps for livestock: "They do not like to see their little ones dying and crying for food." She further blamed the government, which received "rent from these squatters and [did] not give the natives food in place of their country."[59]

Like many of her compatriots in women's groups, Lock also condemned what she saw as the sexual exploitation of Aboriginal women by white men. In 1925 she wrote, "Sin, sin all around. White men with their black wives just camping under the starry sky with their camp sheet, their only dwelling, sometimes under a dray or old shed. Half caste children and quarter caste and some almost white run around their camps. What is Australia coming to? Are there no laws to protect the natives, and can these white men do what they like with the black men and women?"[60] She wrote to Mary Bennett, "The greatest trouble is that the white men seem to delight to get the young girls from ten years up, and will even come and ask for them and offer money, tobacco and all sorts of things to the women for the girls." Thus, Lock's mission included "civilizing" unruly white men as well as uplifting Aborigines.

As she wrote to Bennett, she believed she had "to protect the white man and try to uplift them and at the same time try to teach the black men what is right."[61]

Joining in the chorus of white women who promoted female protectors, she reiterated, "The Policemen are not the right ones to be Protectors of Aborigines. Many of them are as bad as any other white men with the young [Aboriginal women]." Instead, Lock saw herself as a rightful protector of Aborigines, especially the girls.[62] In correspondence with Constance Cooke, Lock wrote, "You mentioned women protectors yes I would like to be made a protector but voluntarily position not paid & if we are made so in this way we can have a greater power to act."[63]

Lock particularly challenged male privilege and behavior when she testified against male officials in the inquiry into the horrific Coniston massacre. In 1928, after four years of severe drought and dispossession of their watering holes and hunting grounds, a group of Aborigines killed a white guard and dingo hunter at Coniston Station, sixty miles from Harding Soak, where Lock was living near an Aboriginal community. In retaliation, the police, led by Constable George Murray, and other local whites murdered dozens of Aborigines—the official count varied from thirty-one to thirty-four—and arrested two Aboriginal men, Padygar and Arkirtra.[64] An ensuing outcry against the violence led to an official investigation, and authorities summoned Lock to give evidence to a board of inquiry to determine whether white settlers had given Aborigines any provocation for their attack. Lock testified that indeed they had: a white dingo hunter had refused to let go of an Aboriginal woman and was murdered by two Aboriginal men in retaliation.

The board of inquiry, however, found "no provocation" by whites for Aboriginal depredations and no evidence of police misconduct. Instead, the board took seriously the testimony of the superintendent of the Hermannsburg Mission near Alice Springs, who "disapproved of women missionaries working among blacks." He asserted, "The spectacle of a white woman moving about among nude blacks lowered her in their eyes to their own standards" and claimed that Lock wanted to marry a black man. The board concluded by blaming the "rising of the natives" on "unattached missionaries wandering from place to place having no previous knowledge of blacks and their customs and preaching a doctrine of equality." Further, they impugned Lock as a "woman missionary living amongst naked blacks thus lowering their respect for the whites." The police were exonerated. The newspapers covered the sensational charges against Lock rather than the violent raids that had been conducted against Aboriginal people in the area.[65]

It is perhaps difficult to reconcile these two visions: Lock the blithe supporter of child removal and Lock the ardent critic of state policies. How could she simultaneously deliver such a devastating critique of white Australian conquest, both territorial and sexual, and at the same time support a key aspect of this conquest: child removal? An in-depth examination of another of Lock's experiences in Central Australia in the late 1920s offers an opportunity to analyze how these two contradictory strains could come together in the practice of maternal politics.

After twenty-four years living among various Aboriginal groups in Western Australia and South Australia, Lock struck out on her own, first for Ryan's Well, then to Harding Soak, to work among the Kaitish and Unmatjera peoples about one hundred miles north of Alice Springs in Central Australia in May 1927.[66] An acquaintance told her of the native people in the area "and how they were suffering." Lock explained, "So I made it a matter of prayer and felt led to come up."[67] Shortly after she arrived at Harding Soak, she applied respectfully to the government for a mission lease in order to establish a hospital and training school for Aborigines there. She also requested a supply of rations and medicines to distribute.[68]

Thus began Lock's conflicted relationship with state authorities. One government administrator viewed Lock charitably: "[She is] an earnest Christian woman of respectable character, with great sympathy for the natives, who seem to have confidence in her. She has the reputation of being somewhat eccentric but I do not think more so than might be expected of any middle-aged single woman who has taken up work of this kind."[69] But other officials regarded her as an interfering nuisance. Government Resident for Alice Springs Stan Cawood declared, "Miss Lock is an eccentric woman and her ideas of Missionary work and the methods employed are certainly degrading not only to herself as a white woman but to the blacks that she has gathered around her."[70] Sgt. Robert Stott, Central Australia's police protector of Aborigines, regarded Lock as "simply a Crank."[71]

Based on negative recommendations from Stott, who alleged that Lock's camp would take up valuable pastoral land, discourage Aborigines from working for pastoralists, lead them to become "a menace to stock holders," and expose them to "contamination by Afghan carriers and unscrupulous travellers passing North and South" on the nearby overland track, the government refused her humble requests.[72] Lock claimed, "[This is the] first refusal I have had from any Government for the natives, during my 25 years among them."[73]

Despite this rejection, Lock pressed on with her original plan of ministering to sick Aborigines and taking in and caring for Aboriginal children. During her first six months at Harding Soak in 1927 she cared for a diseased Aboriginal man who had shown up at camp with two women and their children, including one "half-caste" girl known as Dolly. According to Lock, "[Dolly] was going about naked and hungry and as the father was too ill to work on any station, the mother gave me little Dolly, as she had two other children and found it hard to get food for them and a sick husband. Dolly soon found she was better off and had no desire to go bush with her mother." Lock claimed that she gave Dolly schooling and "cared for [her] as well as any white child." Lock also took in two other girls—Betsy, a baby, and Neta, age seven—as she treated their father's arm: "[Their] aunt went to work on a station, so I kept the two little girls and fed and clothed them, and never let them go back to the camp [with their father], as it made so much unpleasant work every morning for me." According to Lock, "[He] was pleased to let me have his little girl [Neta], as I was the means of saving her and his arm. He was also proud of his baby because of her training."[74] Thus, in

11. Annie Lock with Dolly and Betsy, Northern Territory, Australia, ca. 1928, CRS A1/15, Item 1929/984–93, National Archives of Australia, Canberra, Australian Capital Territory.

explaining how she acquired Dolly and Betsy, Lock lapsed into familiar maternalist discourse: Dolly was "naked and hungry," her father ill, her mother unable to care for her. Aboriginal men and women were grateful to Lock and "pleased" to let her have their children. Dolly soon "had no desire to go bush with her mother." Lock cared for Dolly "as well as any white child."

Perhaps no conflicts would have developed over Lock's taking of Dolly and Betsy had Lock stayed put at Harding Soak, but she moved within a few months to a new location at Barrow Creek. Lock claims that after her two adult patients had healed, she was called to minister among the Aborigines at Barrow Creek. Conflicting accounts, however, attribute her move to either the waterhole drying up at Harding Soak or Aboriginal people moving en masse from the area due to the Coniston massacre.[75] In any event, Lock claimed that she had the permission of Dolly's mother to take the child with her when she left Harding Soak. "When I left Harding Soak the mother was there and wished Dolly goodbye," Lock would later testify, "and said, 'bring her back to see me when she is big girl.'" When she arrived at Barrow Creek, Lock claims, "the officials had sent the natives out bush, because they were killing [white settlers'] stock." Lock decided to continue north by train to Darwin with the girls, in part to help Dolly and Betsy find treatment for a disease called yaws. She claimed that she asked the Barrow Creek natives if she should leave Betsy with them, and "they replied, take her, we have no food and she will get sick again and starve."[76]

When authorities from Central Australia learned that Lock had taken the children out of their administrative area, they quickly acted to stop her, seemingly regarding Lock as a dangerous threat to their authority. A flurry of correspondence regarding the case ensued between Government Resident Cawood, Police Protector Stott, Constable Murray, the chief protectors in Central Australia and Darwin, and the Home and Territories Department in Canberra. Suddenly government authorities positioned themselves as protectors of poor Aboriginal mothers whose children had been torn from them. Stott claimed that when he visited

Lock's camp in January 1928 he met Dolly as well as Dolly's mother. Stott alleged that the mother "requested Dolly be taken to the Halfcaste Home at Alice Springs." According to Stott, Lock "very much resented the Mothers wish." When Stott informed Lock that the "Halfcaste home was the proper place for Dolly . . . [the girl] commenced crying and clinging to Miss Locks dress." Lock told Stott "it was her desire to adopt Dolly and take her to Quorn," in South Australia, and she asked Stott to be allowed to keep the girl. He "agreed to leave Dolly temporary in her charge." Cawood alleged that an Aboriginal woman had complained that Lock had taken her child, presumably Betsy.[77] Constable Murray asserted that "suitable action be taken to have the [Aboriginal] child [Betsy] returned to its mother, the mother is very grieved over the loss of her child."[78] Professing himself in sympathy with grieving Aboriginal mothers and accusing Lock of illegally taking the children, Cawood asked Constable Murray to apprehend Lock in Darwin and retrieve the children.[79]

Apparently, at nearly the same time as Lock was traveling north with Dolly and Betsy, Constable Murray was escorting his two prisoners, Padygar and Arkirtra, who were alleged to have killed the white dingo hunter prior to the Coniston massacre, to Darwin for trial. Up in Darwin with Dolly and Betsy, Lock in fact attended the trial of Padygar and Arkirtra, who were acquitted for lack of evidence.[80]

While Lock attended the trial and found treatment for Dolly and Betsy, she housed the girls at the local compound for "half-caste" children. When she went to retrieve them there on November 18, they were gone. Lock rushed to the railway station, where she found the girls. As she hugged and gathered the girls to her, Constable Murray appeared on the scene and demanded that she return the children. According to newspaper reports, Lock exclaimed, "Take them, but take them from my arms!" Murray responded that it was his duty to do so. Lock retorted, "Duty! I did your duty for you. I rescued a starving, motherless babe suffering from sores, even to her very mouth, right under your very nose . . . as you well know, I fed and cured during twenty months as one of my own charges at my own expense and brought her here for final injections." Newspapers reported that a sizable crowd had gathered by this time, in sympathy with Lock. The constable decided not to press the issue, and "Lock bore away her charges amid cheers."[81] Here, Lock objected not to the policy of Aboriginal child removal; she herself believed Dolly and Betsy were better off in her care. Instead, her objection was to the way authorities carried out the policy. She believed the state had failed in its duty to "protect" the children. Like many of her compatriots, she believed white women maternalists could do a better job.[82]

This conflict also gives us a glimpse at the dynamic of the relationship between Lock and the two girls. From both the newspaper and Lock's account, it appears that the girls had developed genuine affection for Lock and regarded her as their mother. According to Lock, "[The girls] called out 'Mummy, Mummy,' and clung to me. I took them to the back of the railway station and told them that Murray was taking them away from me, and we all had a cry." When Constable Murray tried to take the children, "they clung to [Lock] and screamed." Authorities tried to make Lock put the girls on the train. She challenged them instead to take the children from her: "By this time a lot of onlookers had collected, . . . a lot of people present . . . were in sympathy with [me]."[83] Lock now positioned herself as the wronged mother. Effacing the Aboriginal mothers who had been dispossessed of their children, she claimed the role of a mother whose children were being taken from her.

Lock won this battle, striding off the train platform with the two girls amid the cheers of onlookers. (It is doubtful that the crowd would have been so supportive of an Aboriginal mother in the same circumstances. No such uproar ensued, after all, when Nurse Lappidge and a police-woman took Priscilla Karpanny's child away from her at the Adelaide train station.) Ultimately, however, Lock lost the larger war with male officials after she and the children returned to Central Australia. In early January 1929, Lock was summoned before another board of inquiry and fined three pounds and five shillings for taking the girls from Central to North Australia without state permission. Authorities took Dolly into custody and put her in the Bungalow for "half-caste" children in Alice Springs. They left Betsy in Lock's care, presumably because she was a "full-blood," not a "half-caste." However, when Lock sought to take Betsy to Adelaide, authorities refused to grant her permission. Lock claims, "I had to come back into the bush again and find her father and sisters and aunt to see if they would care for her, [but] they did not want to take her because they say she would cry for me and the father said, 'You grow her up now.'"[84]

Lock then decided to stay in Central Australia for a time with Betsy and other Aboriginal children. She returned to an area near Harding Soak (Ryan's Well) with Betsy. Lock reportedly "sheltered" more than a dozen children, including Dolly's sister, Leach, and Betsy's sisters, who came to "sit down along mummy's camp," while their parents hunted for food. When the station owner at Ryan's Well asked Lock and the Aborigines to leave his land, Lock set off north with four children.[85] She stayed in Central Australia at Boxer Creek, where she taught a group of children on the station of Mr. Curtis, a "half-caste" man, until 1933. At that point, she decided to leave. She arranged for the "half-caste" girls she was teaching to be sent to the Bungalow and left Betsy and two of her sisters with the Curtises. Lock's departure proved traumatic for Betsy, who allegedly cried to Lock, "Mummie, you won't go away and leave me? You know you growed me up." According to Turner, Lock reportedly replied, "brokenly," "I can't take you Betsy."[86]

The relationship between Lock and Betsy had become very intimate, but seemed to have drastically different meanings to "mother" and "daughter." Although Lock proudly portrayed herself as the "mummy" to the many Aboriginal children she cared for and objected when authorities sought to remove "her" children, she ultimately saw herself as a temporary, surrogate mother who could abdicate her role when she received a new "call" to go elsewhere. It seems that to Lock, the children she cared for were fungible. It didn't matter who exactly they were; what mattered was her work in caring for them. For Betsy, however, Lock had become her mother. Betsy had already been separated from her birth mother (as well as all of her kin); now she was to lose her adoptive mother. Mothers were not easily replaceable to Betsy, but many other daughters remained in need of Lock's mothering. Perhaps I am being too critical in my assessment of Lock; no doubt it was a difficult decision for her to leave Central Australia and Betsy behind. Yet there is an element to Lock's maternalism, as there was to Alice Fletcher's relationship to the Omahas, of undermining the intimate relationships within indigenous communities, of developing new intimate relationships with indigenous children, and then failing to carry out all the responsibilities associated with such intimacy.

In 1933 Lock set out for a new mission, to Ooldea, Daisy Bates's territory, in South Australia, where she apparently competed with Bates in "looking after the Aborigines." Missionaries had long objected to Bates's secular approach and championed Lock's work. After a visit to Ooldea in 1934, Reverend Sexton of the AFA declared, "[Bates] looked pathetic wheeling a little go-cart with some parcels. She has lost touch with the natives who say that granny has gone in her mind. I learnt that she was jealous of Miss Lock's influence over the natives. . . . Mrs. Bates is a journalist and her interest in aborigines is literary and academic, but Miss Lock's is in sacrificial service." Sexton asserted that 350 natives were assembled in Ooldea for ceremonial purposes and that they had made Lock their "queen," giving her the honor of opening their ceremonies. Nevertheless, he also documented some of Lock's troubles, revealing that a newcomer to camp threw a bucket of water on her when she told him to do something.[87]

Lock also faced opposition from Daisy Bates herself, who objected to the missionary's presence at Ooldea and asked for government assistance to relocate to Adelaide. "I have had to endure here the humiliating spectacle of an illiterate mission woman coming suddenly here," Bates wrote to a government minister, "and, with Government, Railway, and Police support—taking over my natives whom I have controlled since 1914."[88] Thus these two white women, who championed different means of advancing the cause of Aborigines, nevertheless both acted out their maternalist visions, Bates "controlling" "my natives" and Lock offering "sacrificial service."

Lock finally left Ooldea and the mission field in 1937. All in all, she had spent thirty-four years working as a missionary among Aboriginal people. When she retired at the age of sixty she married James Johansen, without the required permission of her sponsor, the UAM. (Missionaries with the female-dominated UAM had to pledge to remain single; if they wished to marry, they had to gain permission from the Mission Council, and their spouses had to undergo training if not UAM members.) The new couple acquired a caravan, which they used to conduct itinerant mission work. Lock died just six years later, in 1943.[89] Unfortunately, I have not been able to find out what happened to Dolly or Betsy.

In carrying out policies of child removal, white women maternalists often insinuated themselves into the intimate lives of indigenous families, hoping to take over the role of mother and to form new intimacies with the children. Although white women such as Alice Fletcher and Annie Lock portrayed themselves as selfless surrogate mothers, their intimate invasions seem to have been based more on strategic decisions—related to fulfilling their maternalist ideals, professional aspirations, or state goals—than on long-term commitments to indigenous people. For many indigenous families, these new intimacies seem to have represented something more: an act of inviting white women into their intimate worlds, of adopting them in some sense into their families. As such, families like the Springers expected the white women to behave as good family members. When the women failed to live up to these expectations, indigenous people often felt betrayed and used, or, as in Betsy's case, perplexed and abandoned. They learned that white women's interest in their lives was often instrumental and not always genuine, that intimacy with white maternalists was not a deep well from which they could draw at will but a spigot that could be turned on and off at the women's whim.

Still, as Fletcher's and Lock's cases suggest, the intimate liaisons that white women established with indigenous families could introduce doubt into the women's commitment to the maternalist enterprise and the state's policies. When Fletcher witnessed the "pathetic" scenes of Indian children parting from their parents at the train station in Sioux City and received the Springers' anguished letter, she confronted a profound contradiction between the maternalist rhetoric of white women reformers and her own experience and everyday relationships with Indian people. And when Lock had to leave a distraught Betsy behind in Central Australia, she also faced a cruel discrepancy between maternalist visions, state priorities, and a little girl's longing for her mother. As we shall see in chapter 9, such contradictions and tensions—ever present in the intimate relationships of colonialism—could inspire white women's opposition to the entire colonial enterprise.

While white women such as Fletcher and Lock endured a crisis of conscience, indigenous children who found themselves in the grip of the state suffered a different kind of ordeal. Once removed from their communities, indigenous children traveled long distances from their homes and families to intimidating institutions, where they were inducted into an exacting new regime. Ideally, they were also to be drawn into new intimacies, often with white women teachers and matrons as their caregivers. Here too such intimacies could be employed in the service of the state, turned to white women's maternalist ends, or transformed into something new altogether. It is to indigenous children's experiences within these institutions that I now turn.

Chapter 6

Groomed to Be Useful

You thought it would cripple you for life, but it didn't cripple your tongue.
• MARGARET BRUSNAHAN, on her experience in an orphanage in South Australia,
quoted in Mattingley and Hampton, *Survival in Our Own Land*

Once they had brought indigenous children to the institutions, officials and reformers labored to undermine the connections that tied them to their families, communities, and homelands. Although an ocean apart, American Indian boarding schools and Australian institutions for Aboriginal children subjected the children to a remarkably similar set of initiation rituals and daily routines, designed in part to replace the children's prior sensory conceptions of season and place with a new sensory regime founded on more abstract notions of time and space. Moreover, in both countries indigenous children in many of the institutions had to endure the same conditions: overcrowding, poor sanitation, an inadequate diet, a high incidence of disease, and often brutal and dehumanizing abuse. In fact, the experience of many of the children in the institutions makes a mockery of the rhetoric of rescue and lays bare the punitive nature of indigenous child removal. Both Indian and Aboriginal children resorted to similar strategies, including running away and relying on their new families of peers, to cope with life in the institutions.

However, when it came to whether children maintained contact with their kin and communities, Indian and Aboriginal children's experiences diverged. Although American authorities frowned on children going home for the summers, they did allow the children to correspond with their families, and many children, especially those in on-reservation boarding schools, did manage to see their families periodically. Furthermore, many Indian children eventually returned to their communities. Australian officials, by contrast, more often sought to prevent all contact between Aboriginal children in the institutions and their families. Although some children were able to circumvent these restrictions, a large number grew up without knowledge of or contact with their families, and many believed, as authorities told them, that their mothers had abandoned them. Consequently, whereas both Aboriginal and American Indian people who spent their childhood in an institution express great ambiguity about their experiences, some American Indians were more likely to eventually claim the boarding schools as their own and turn them to their own purposes.

From the moment indigenous children arrived in the institutions, white authorities sought to abruptly scrub away the children's prior identities and to immerse them in a new way of life. They carried this out by focusing on the children's bodies, including their sensory experiences, and on closely monitoring and regulating the most mundane activities. Indigenous children on both sides of the Pacific were forced to endure a hauntingly similar set of bodily rituals designed to initiate them into their new homes. Authorities focused primarily on bathing—washing off the outward signs of "camp" life—cutting hair, destroying old clothing and dressing the children in new uniforms, renaming the "inmates," introducing the children to new foods and dining rituals, and requiring them to sleep in unfamiliar beds in large dormitories. The quotidian and the intimate became premier sites of colonization, not mere backdrops for more dramatic political and military events.

Perhaps appropriately, due to this focus on dirt as a sign of savagery and cleanliness as civilization, new arrivals at the institutions were required to take a bath as soon as they arrived. Jean Carter was taken as a child to a home in Bidura, New South Wales: "I remember we were in this place, it was a shelter sort of thing, and this big bath, huge bath, in the middle of the room, and all the smell of disinfectant, getting me hair cut, and getting this really scalding hot bath."[1] Navajo Irene Stewart remembers, "Upon being brought into the girls' home [at Fort Defiance Boarding School], I was taken to a huge bathtub full of water. I screamed and fought but the big girl in charge was too strong. She got me in and scrubbed me."[2]

Next, authorities also sought to effect a transformation in indigenous children by disposing of their old clothes and dressing them in new. Pratt stipulated that the Indian children in his care wear military uniforms. Other boarding schools and institutions also required their children to wear uniforms. Irene Stewart remembers, "[The 'big girl'] put me into underwear and a dress with lots of buttons down the back. I remember how she combed my hair until it hurt. And the shoes she put on my feet were so strange and heavy. I was used to moccasins."[3] Similarly, Jean Carter recalls, "I remember being taken down to this place where there was all these clothes. I remember getting fitted out."[4]

Some children resisted parting with their familiar clothing and its intimate associations. When a five-year-old girl from San Juan Pueblo was taken to the Santa Fe Indian School, her mother "put her best shawl" on her daughter. A white woman employee from the school tried to take the shawl from the girl as they rode the train to Santa Fe, but the girl refused. "I held it to me because that shawl touched my mother and I loved it," she remembered. "I wanted it to touch me." Even after her bath and new clothes, the girl would not give up her shawl.[5]

Most officials also ordered that the children have their hair cut. For many American Indian children, such a move caused great consternation. At Carlisle Institute, when barbers cropped the hair of the first group of Indian boys, one boy woke Mrs. Pratt with "discordant wailing." He told her that "his people always wailed after cutting their hair, as it was an evidence of mourning, and he had come out on the parade ground to show his grief." Mrs. Pratt recalled, "His voice had awakened the girls, who joined with their shrill voices, then other boys joined and hence the commotion."[6] Mrs. Pratt understood and represented the children's actions as a quaint but superstitious act. We might better understand it as an act of mourning for being uprooted and being shorn of one's identity, both literally and figuratively.

Zitkala-Ša, or Gertrude Bonnin, a Nakota or Yankton Sioux, devoted an entire chapter of "The School Days of an Indian Girl" to "The Cutting of My Long Hair." Seeing other Indian girls at her new school, White's Institute, a Quaker school in Indiana, with their cropped hair and warned by a friend that she would soon have her own hair cut, Zitkala-Ša rebelled: "Our mothers had taught us that only unskilled warriors who were captured had their hair shingled by the enemy. Among our people, short hair was worn by mourners, and shingled hair by cowards!" So the eight-year-old Zitkala-Ša hid under a bed, unwilling to submit to the indignity. "I remember being dragged out, though I resisted by kicking and scratching wildly. In spite of myself, I was carried downstairs and tied fast in a chair." Then, she continues, "I cried aloud, shaking my head all the while until I felt the cold blades of the scissors against my neck, and heard them gnaw off one of my thick braids. Then I lost my spirit." She felt, "Now I was only one of many little animals driven by a herder."[7] (Other children likened the experience of being initiated into new institutions to being treated like a domesticated animal.)

Though seemingly mundane, hair held other crucial meanings in American Indian societies. When it was time for an Omaha Indian boy to be inducted into his clan, the Omahas performed a ceremony, Wé-bashna, meaning "to cut the hair," which involved ritually cutting the boy's hair in a certain pattern according to the clan into which he was being initiated. Fletcher and La Flesche describe this ceremony as consecrating the boy to Thunder, "the symbol of the power that controlled the life and death of the warrior." "The hair of a person was popularly believed to have a vital connection with the life of the body," Fletcher and La Flesche explain, so "by the cutting of a lock of the boy's hair and giving it to the Thunder the life of the child was given into the keeping of the god."[8]

Cutting hair also had significant meaning for Aboriginal peoples.

12. Aboriginal girls at the Roper River Mission, Northern Territory, with their heads recently shaved, ca. 1915. Photo from Church Missionary Society—Australia Collection— H. E. Warren (NTRS 690), held by the Northern Territory Archives Service. Courtesy of the Church Missionary Society—Australia.

When the missionary George Taplin sought to cut the hair of the local Ngarinyeri children that he brought to boarding school at Point McLeay in South Australia in the 1860s, "their parents were very averse to the hair-cutting process for the bigger boys." "It is the custom of the natives to let a youth's hair grow from the time he is ten years old until he is sixteen or seventeen," Taplin explained, "that is until he is made a young man. . . . But I insisted that my pupils must have their hair cut, and after some scolding from their mothers I carried the point."[9] Because hair was such an important aspect of indigenous identity for many groups, authorities' insistence on cutting hair constituted an often traumatic assault on the children and their affiliations.

After undergoing such a drastic bodily transformation, the children were expected to eat unfamiliar, often revolting foods, with tools that many of them had never encountered before. Willie Blackbeard recalled, "When I first come to school in [it] was Sunday at dinner time. First they cut off my long hair and then dressed me in school clothes. At the table I could not eat hard bread and hard meat and strong coffee."[10] Bertha Sheeply remembered her experience at the first school she went to in New Mexico: "At the table I couldn't eat with knife, fork and spoon, cause I was used to eating with my hand."[11] The historian Nancy Rose Hunt has noted that introducing cutlery, "the knife-and-fork doctrine," was a central part of promoting hygiene and a new conceptualization of domesticity to the Congolese.[12] The enforced use of these new colonial objects in the setting of the boarding schools and Aboriginal children's institutions functioned in a similar way.

Children new to the institutions also experienced great difficulty adjusting to the sleeping arrangements, often in a large dormitory with lines of unfamiliar twin beds. Beds themselves were often a source of anxiety. Bertha Sheeply recalled, "In the night when we were going to bed I was afraid to lay on that high bed, because I might fall off in the night."[13] Navajo Irene Stewart also recalled, "[The beds] seemed so high. Some of us fell out during our sleep." Moreover, the children were simply scared, lonely, and homesick. Stewart recalled that at night in the dorm, "there was always someone crying, mostly because of homesickness."[14] Jim Hart, who lived in the dormitory at Cape Bedford, a Lutheran mission in Queensland, also remembered that children frequently cried at night: "You know, you three, four year old you want your Mother, . . . to sit on your mother's lap, go to sleep, feel your mother, your warm mother, you know. It's not there."[15] Children, particularly siblings, often slept with one another to ease the fear and loneliness. Willie Blackbeard recalled, "When I first went [to] sleep I was kind [of] scared, but my brother was in school and he sleep with me."[16] Thus, from the moment the children stepped into the institutions, matrons and other school authorities sought to enforce a bodily regimen on them that was often quite foreign to their own ways of living.[17]

13. Indian girls praying by their beds in a dormitory at Phoenix Indian School, Arizona, June 1900. Still Pictures Branch, NWDNS-75-EX-2B, National Archives and Records Administration, College Park, Maryland.

Within a few days, sometimes even within hours of their arrival, indigenous children could expect to be given a new name, or sometimes just a number, the next step authorities took in seeking to divest the children of their indigeneity. Marjorie Woodrow asserted that Aboriginal children at Cootamundra were addressed by their numbers, not their names, "like a prison camp."[18] Soon after his arrival at Carlisle, Ace Daklugie, a Chiricahua Apache, recalled,

the torture began. The first thing they did was cut our hair. . . . The bath wasn't bad. We liked it, but not what followed. While we were bathing our breechclouts were taken, and we were ordered to put on trousers. We'd lost our hair and we'd lost our clothes; with the two we'd lost our identity as Indians. Greater punishment could hardly have been devised. That's what I thought till they marched us into a room and our interpreter ordered us to line up with our backs to a wall. . . .

Then a man went down [the row]. Starting with me he began: "Asa, Benjamin, Charles, Daniel, Eli, Frank." . . . I became Asa Daklugie. We didn't know till later that they'd even imposed meaningless new names on us, along with the other degredations [sic]. I've always hated that name. It was forced on me as though I had been an animal.[19]

Like rituals for hair and clothing, naming was also an act of profound significance in many indigenous cultures and often associated with rites of passage. When a child could walk by itself, the Omahas celebrated with the ThikúwiNxe, the "turning of the child" ceremony. As Fletcher and La Flesche explain it, "Through this ceremony the child passed out of that stage in its life wherein it was hardly distinguished from all other living forms into its place as distinctively a human being, a member of its birth gens, and through this to a recognized place in the tribe." In this ceremony, which took place for all the new toddlers in the springtime, each child received a new name and was given new moccasins to prepare it for the long journey of life.[20]

In many Aboriginal communities, family members chose names for their children based on a "significant happening around the time of conception." Connie Nungulla McDonald explains, "In the tribal custom, a child is 'found,' having come from the Dreamtime in the form of something from nature such as an animal, plant, landform, or the like." During a drought, one of Nungulla McDonald's female relatives went walking in search of water. "After walking some miles, she heard a noise which sounded like water. She followed it and to her amazement found not just water but a running stream. Around that time she became pregnant. . . . When the baby, a girl, was three weeks old the tribe decided to call her Mindigmurra, meaning flowing stream."[21] Names often bore associations with particular places that linked indigenous peoples with their land. Thus the institutions' practice of renaming children worked symbolically and materially to sever their connections with kin and home country.

Naming practices in the institutions diverged markedly from indigenous practices in another significant way as well. In indigenous societies individual names, though important, were secondary to other forms of identification and might be used only rarely as a form of address or term of reference. Instead, indigenous naming practices sought to affiliate the child to larger collective identities within her or his group. As Maria Brandl explains, "The personal name that is the prime identification label of European Australians is of much less importance for Aborigines. . . . More important labels are a child's local descent group identity, which allots him a place in his society's order of things, in ceremonies, and relationships."[22]

Even in their early childhood, indigenous girls and boys needed to learn what to call and how to behave toward their many relatives. As Nakota (Yankton Sioux) Ella Deloria writes in her ethnographic novel of nineteenth-century Lakota (Teton Sioux) life, "The first thing to learn was how to treat other people and how to address them. . . . You must not call your relatives and friends by name, for that was rude. Use kinship terms instead. And especially, brothers and sisters, and boy cousins and girl cousins must be very kind to each other. That was the core of all kinship training."[23] New institutional naming practices thus profoundly violated some indigenous codes of conduct.

Daily Routines

Once they had passed their first stage of initiation, the children then had to learn the daily routine, a regimen often punctuated by bells and whistles and rigidly choreographed. Ruth Hegarty at Cherbourg in Queensland recalls, "Mornings we were awakened by the sound of an old bullock bell." Once the children had quickly bathed and dressed, "a bell rang for [them] to assemble in a line on the veranda outside the dining room door." When the children had finished their breakfast—in total silence—they "formed into very orderly army-type rows to be inspected by the matron," who checked them for sores and head lice and required the girls to lift their dresses and show their underclothes. Cherbourg's inflexible schedule included "very strict meal times, three meals a day at exactly the same time each day." As with breakfast, the children "were never allowed to make a sound" during meals.[24]

Such regimens varied somewhat among Aboriginal institutions, but were standardized at the Indian boarding schools. "Bill Sage" (a pseudonym) remembered that his Navajo mentor at school told him, "When you hear the first whistle blow, that means for the boys to get up. The second whistle means everybody go down stairs and wash. The third whistle means to line up outside. . . . When we lined up outside, there were a lot of boys there. . . . They told us that when we started to walk we should watch their steps so we could go that way. When . . . I started to go, [I] didn't know how to do it like the other boys. The biggest boys were in front, and the little ones behind."[25]

In an attempt to "rehabilitate" his prisoners of war, Pratt originated the idea of organizing the Indian children into military-like companies and drilling them as the military trained its recruits.[26] Other boarding schools followed Pratt's lead. Lame Deer recalled, "In those days the Indian schools were like jails and run along military lines, with roll calls four times a day. We had to stand at attention, or march in step."[27] One woman from Santa Clara Pueblo described the military atmosphere of the Santa Fe Indian School: "They used to drill us. . . . Drill us to school, drill us to the dining room, and drill us back to the dormitory. We were just like prisoners, marching everyplace."[28]

Beyond military discipline and frequent marching, the children also had rigid timetables for school and work. Irene Stewart recalled:

> During the day we were always being put in line to march to school, to meals, to work, to the hospital. Four hours of each day were for school work; four hours for industrial education. . . . Getting our industrial education was very hard. We were detailed to work in the laundry and do all the washing for the school, the hospital, and the sanitorium. Sewing was hard, too. We learned to sew all clothing,

14. Indian children in companies for military-style drilling at Albuquerque Indian School, n.d. "Albuquerque Indian School," File 609, General Correspondence File, 1911–35 (Entry 90), Southern Pueblos Agency, Record Group 75, National Archives and Records Administration, Rocky Mountain Region, Denver, Colorado.

except underwear and stockings, and we learned to mend and darn and patch. We canned food, cooked, washed dishes, waited on tables, scrubbed floors, and washed windows. We cleaned classrooms and dormitories. By the time I graduated from the sixth grade I was a well-trained worker. But I have never forgotten how the steam in the laundry made me sick; how standing and ironing for hours made my legs ache far into the night. By evening I was too tired to play and just fell asleep wherever I sat down. I think this is why the boys and girls ran away from school; why some became ill; why it was so hard to learn. We were too tired to study.[29]

Victoria Archibald remembers the arduous work that was required of all Aboriginal inmates at Cootamundra and the cruelty of administrators. Before breakfast the girls had to scrub the floors, but the matron

15. Indian girls in the laundry, Oneida School, Wisconsin. ER8.12.4, Estelle Reel Collection (MS 120), Northwest Museum of Arts & Culture, Spokane, Washington.

would "come along and she'd put her foot on you [to] start right back there again. She'd put her foot on your back."[30]

Such an educational regimen differed markedly from indigenous concepts of education. Although great variation existed, in both North America and Australia children learned through example, by observing how others acted—in stories and in everyday life—and through emulating others in hands-on practice and play. Each indigenous group had its own set of knowledge it sought to convey, but common to each group was a need to teach children a deep knowledge of the land (and often the sea) in order to live from it. Such knowledge required that children learn to use all their senses to perceive and experience their world. The classroom encompassed the natural world, and their schooling entailed learning time-honored ways of living in and with their environment, even after generations of colonization had moved many indigenous peoples off their land. Emily Margaret Horneville, a Muruwari, remembers that in her community in northwestern New South Wales on the Culgoa River, "many activities took place on the river," including fishing, swimming, canoeing, tree climbing, and swinging. As a child, Emily also "accompanied the women to the swamp to gather nardoo seed" or would hunt possums and other nocturnal animals in the moonlight. She also engaged in hunting goannas in the winter. As her biographer, Lynette Oates, explains it, "She learnt the way of all wild things: how to tell the tree where the native bee hid its honey; where emus' nests were hidden; when the quandong were ripe in the bush; how to predict climate changes from the behaviour of ants and insects or by the pattern of clouds." Emily considered her outdoor experiential education a kind of school (one that would be the envy of my two sons). She told Oates, "There were schools around, but I didn't attend any. Mumma took me to the bush. I learnt my ABC, but that's all. I wouldn't have that schooling. I went to *my* sort of school—in the bush!"[31]

Similarly, American Indian people gained an intimacy with and an education from the land and the natural world. From her infancy in a cradleboard, Dilth-cleyhen, a Chiricahua Apache, learned the secrets of her people's land. When it was time to harvest a special root, blossom, or fruit in a distant location, Dilth-cleyhen would accompany her mother and other women and their children. Propped in her cradleboard against a tree or bush or "suspended from a sturdy branch," Dilth-cleyhen watched as the women went about their work. As she grew older, her mother told her, "You will learn . . . that most of the things we eat grow in a special place and in a special season. So we move about, following the bountiful food supply." Women gathered mesquite bean pods in the flat lowlands, picked the red fruit of the three-leaved sumac in the foothills, cut the stalks of the narrow-leafed yucca and the mescal from the agave or century plants in the mountains, and plucked juniper berries, piñon nuts, and acorns from the mountain trees. Plants yielded important medicines as well. Dilth-cleyhen learned from her mother of the osha root that her people found at higher elevations to treat headaches and colds. Moreover, her band shared with their children the knowledge of "every spring of sparkling water, every waterhole," as well as "the most sequestered camps and the shortcuts to reach them, ... the wide arroyos, the dangerous washes."[32]

Sedentary tribes that practiced agriculture also transmitted their knowledge of the land to their children. Maxi'diwiac, or Buffalo Bird Woman, a Hidatsa who lived on the Missouri River in today's North Dakota, learned from her mother and other female relatives when it was time to plant the first seed of the spring—sunflowers—after ice broke on the Missouri and the soil could be worked. Maxi'diwiac learned "when corn planting time came by observing the leaves of the wild gooseberry bushes. This bush is the first of the woods to leaf in the spring. Old women of the village were going to the woods daily to gather fire wood; and when they saw that the wild gooseberry bushes were almost in full leaf, they said, 'It is time for you to begin planting corn!'"[33]

To survive, it was critical that indigenous children developed a particular sensory connection to and intimate link with the land. Children learned to take visual cues from the natural world—where the emus had their nests, when the gooseberries leafed out—and to listen for its signals, the night sounds that could tell them how many animals were out and about. By fingering the soil as it warmed in the spring, or inhaling the aromas of steaming mescal, or savoring the sweet wild honey children built up intimate associations with the natural world around them. In short, they learned to read the land through their senses and to experience their world in a very physical and tactile way. Interestingly, at the time the governments in the United States and Australia enacted their new policies of assimilation and protection, when Emily Margaret Horneville, Dilth-cleyhen, and Buffalo Bird Woman were adolescents or young women, indigenous people still conveyed such knowledge to their children despite a century of colonization. Because the project of indigenous child removal was linked to efforts to dispossess indigenous peoples of their remaining land, we perhaps can better comprehend why authorities sought to remove children from their learning environments and to break their intimate connections with the land of their ancestors.

A New Sensory Regime

Through regimentation authorities aimed to profoundly transform how indigenous children experienced the world. Reformers and officials often regarded the community life of the children as chaotic and disorderly and sought to impose a new order on them. Violet Turner wrote, "One appreciates Colebrook Home at all times, but more so after a visit to a native camp, when the contrast between camp children running wild and camp children rescued strikes one so forcibly."[34] Authorities particularly aimed at redirecting how the children conceived of time; rather than living to the rhythm of the natural world, now children had to conform to the clock. At Sister Kate's in Western Australia Sandra Hill recalled having to go to bed at the same time every night, even when it was still daylight in the summer.[35] Elsie Roughsey was "locked in from seven o'clock at night to seven in the morning" in her Mornington Island dormitory in northern Australia.[36] In the United States, Gertrude Golden, a schoolteacher, lauded the new time discipline in the boarding schools: "It helped the children overcome habits of procrastination and slovenliness, so inherent in their natures. They had the *mañana* trait, often attributed to the Mexicans. Any time was time enough. Punctuality meant nothing in their lives. They ate, slept, worked and played only when the spirit moved them. The industrial education provided in the schools was also a strict necessity because there was absolutely nothing in the home to take its place."[37] Of course, this new time discipline was related to capitalist values of thrift and industry that the institutions sought to instill.

Children were no longer to be guided by the rising and falling of the sun, the circle of the seasons, or even the feeling in their own belly that they were hungry. Now children were to answer only to a new abstract authority—represented by bells and whistles—that determined when they must waken, when they must learn and work, and when they could eat and sleep and even defecate. "To the Indian kid the white boarding school comes as a terrific shock," Lame Deer commented. "He is taken from his warm womb to a strange, cold place. It is like being pushed out of a cozy kitchen into a howling blizzard."[38]

The new sensory regime in the institutions also required strict spatial arrangements to tightly control the activities of the children. Many authorities designed the institutions to prevent any unregulated contact between indigenous children and whites who lived near the institutions. Pratt claimed that the curiosity of whites about the Indian children at Carlisle "interfered with the work," and thus he erected a seven-foot-high picket fence around the perimeter, encompassing some 27 acres, "in order to keep the Indians in and the whites out except as they passed through the gate at the guardhouse."[39] Moreover, as the scholar Jacqueline Fear-Segal has explored, Carlisle Institute was designed as a series of buildings surrounding a quadrangle, with a bandstand in the middle from which the students could be observed at all times, a plan of surveillance remarkably reminiscent of Jeremy Bentham's panopticonic penitentiary.[40]

In many Aboriginal settlements in Queensland and Western Australia, where entire families were brought in, the dormitory system enforced new spatial arrangements as well. Up until a certain age, usually around five, the children lived with their mothers in a women's dormitory or home. Thereafter they were housed in girls' or boys' dormitories in the Aboriginal settlement, forbidden to have sustained contact with their families who lived in nearby "camps." Living so close and yet so far from one's parents could be deeply painful to children. Lyn Hobbler, born at Mona Mona Aboriginal Reserve in Queensland, lived with his mother in a cottage until he turned six or seven; then he was put in the boys' dormitory. "We were all fenced around," he recalls. "It was the boundary and I couldn't see my mother. That was the saddest part in my life."[41] Jean Sibley, taken at age three to Palm Island in Queensland, concurred; she was seven when her mother died: "I was on the verandah, . . . in the dormitory, looking through the wire as the funeral was going down."[42] For Ruth Hegarty at Barambah Settlement in Queensland (later renamed Cherbourg), separation from her mother at age four was her "deepest recollection." Hegarty concludes, "The most dreadful part of it was that the mothers were still living there. But we were under the care and control of the government. So I would have nothing to do with my mother in the dormitory; nothing at all." In fact, Hegarty was once belted for trying to get her mother's attention.[43]

In addition to the trauma of being separated from their loved ones, confinement and indoor seclusion within dormitories represented yet another blow to children used to ranging over miles of territory and spending a great deal of time outdoors. The new sensory regime cut the children off from their intimate associations with the natural world and their ancestral lands. Now the children, especially the girls, spent an inordinate amount of time indoors in school or at work. Instead of gathering water and fuel, helping to grow or gather food, assisting with hunting, or helping with the preparation of food—tasks that seamlessly blended learning, working, and playing, often in an outdoor setting—children were educated at a fixed time and location and carried out their work "details" at a separately scheduled time and designated location. Indigenous girls not only had to mold their feet to fit into new hard shoes and to button up their bodies in new clothes, but they had to train in a host of new, mostly indoor tasks—sweeping and scrubbing floors and washing windows, for example—that would have been senseless in many of their homes. Doris Pilkington likened Moore River Settlement in Western Australia to a prison. "I think the most devastating thing for me was looking at . . . the bars on the windows," she recalls, "a kid born on the ground under a tree and everything was your playground . . . you had this freedom of movement and everywhere you went there was somebody there who loved you and would give you something and be aware of you and look after you."[44] For Pilkington and other indigenous children, their experiences of home—where "everything was your playground"—were inseparable from their connections to kin, family, and community.

Many indigenous children did not just miss the possibility of being able to roam about unfettered in the outdoors with their kin; they also longed for the *specific* lands from which they came. Navajo Ruth Roessel writes that when she went to a school near her home, she still felt connected to the land she knew. "When I was at Lukachukai I knew where I was and knew how to get home," she wrote. "Many times I had walked with the sheep from right above the little community of Lukachukai to Round Rock [her home]. So I never felt that I was away, even when I stayed in the dormitory at Lukachukai that one year." Yet being removed to a much more distant boarding school proved to be disorienting. As Roessel put it, "At Fort Wingate I felt I had gone to a new country or at least to some place far, far away." She was not allowed to go home frequently as she had been able to do at Lukachukai.[45]

White authorities' attempts to substitute European foods for native sustenance represented yet another attempt to break the hold of family and homeland. As the examples of Emily Margaret Horneville, Dilth-cleyhen, and Buffalo Bird Woman demonstrate, the growing, hunting, and gathering of traditional foods linked indigenous peoples to their lands and often served as the basis of the group's sexual division of labor. When Europeans introduced new foods, beginning with rations on reservations and settlements, they not only created new dependencies but undercut indigenous people's close association with the land as well as their gender system. Food, though seemingly a mundane and everyday matter, became yet another powerful tool of the colonizers in their attempts to transform indigenous children.

Thus the tongue became as significant as hair. For many Indian children the lure of new and exotic tastes offered at boarding schools served as a recruiting tool. Missionaries first lured Zitkala-Ša to school at age eight by telling her and her friend Judéwin "of the great tree where grew red, red apples; and how [they] could reach out [their] hands and pick all the red apples [they] could eat." "I had never seen apple trees," Zitkala-Ša related in her autobiography. "I had never tasted more than a dozen red apples in my life; and when I heard of the orchards of the East, I was eager to roam among them." She begged her mother to let her go east, and her mother eventually relented.[46] Thus falling prey to the temptation of white men's apples, Zitkala-Ša left her edenic existence. The promise of oranges in southern California convinced Hopi Polingaysi Qoyawayma to defy her parents' wishes that she stay in Hopiland; instead, she tried to stow away on a wagon bound for Sherman Institute in Riverside, California. "Land of oranges! She visualized ground covered with great, golden oranges, sweet to the taste, pungent to the nostrils. How wonderful it would be to live in such a land!"[47]

For some Aboriginal children too, who came from communities where their subsistence patterns had been irrevocably disrupted, the potential of a full belly attracted them to new institutions. Joy Williams remembered this about Lutanda Children's Home in New South Wales: "I think I was converted six million times—was saved. That entailed another piece of cake on Sunday! Had nice clothes, always had plenty of food."[48] Bessie Singer claimed that at Sister Kate's in Western Australia, the students "were better fed than the local community in the Depression days."[49] Elsie Roughsey remembers her life at the Mornington Island Mission: "We were well fed, as in those days the Mission had a garden and cows, goats, and cattle. We'd have porridge with fresh milk. At noon we'd have a big meal of rice with meat and things from the garden: pumpkin, cabbage, carrots, beets, beans, shallots, tomatoes, pineapples, custard apples, lemons, papaws."[50] Institutions varied considerably, however; as we shall see, many other children experienced inadequate and poor quality food.

For some children, however, the tastes and textures of new food was unpleasant and even frightening. Ruth Roessel describes her early encounters with food at her school: "I didn't know much about the food they fed us. I particularly remember cocoa, which I was afraid to drink it because I thought it was muddy water. Also, I remember we were afraid to eat macaroni and spaghetti. It looked like worms. We feared that it was something that was not good for us. On the other hand, I remember loving ginger-bread cookies in the shape of ginger-bread men which the school's cooks made."[51]

The tongue also required another kind of transformation; authorities in the institutions sought to disconnect indigenous children from their communities by suppressing their language. Pratt and most other boarding school officials in the United States required that students speak only English; Pratt even turned down the services of interpreters in an attempt to force the students to speak English.[52] A few school officials believed it was more effective to allow students to occasionally use their native language. During the first decade that Hampton Institute enrolled Indian students teachers relied on older children to help translate, and even allowed students to use their own language before breakfast, after dinner, and all day on Sunday.

By 1888, however, the government had pressured all Indian schools to institute an English-only rule.[53] Many indigenous people have related that they were punished for speaking in their own language. Charlie Tallbear wrote to his former teacher Gertrude Golden about his first days at a boarding school: "The teacher was trying to talk to me. I didn't say a thing because I don't understand them what they mean. In the school was very hard lesson for me. When my teacher try to make me read, I won't do it, and so she sometime whip me."[54] Teachers also criticized Navajo children for failing to show proper emotion when reading and reciting, and lowered their grades accordingly, even though in the Navajo language, "everything is just kind of monotone. There's no exclamation or excitement."[55]

Children also suffered punishment for other forms of communication the authorities deemed improper. For example, in Navajo culture shaking hands represented a means to show kinship, affection, and compassion to another person. According to one Navajo woman, "When you shake hands with somebody, you say, 'I want to be your friend.' 'I acknowledge you as my relative.'" Yet Navajo children were punished for shaking hands with one another in boarding school.[56]

These myriad means of breaking indigenous children's bodily and sensory habits might seem to be basic components of assimilation and absorption, of making indigenous children more like whites. Yet the imposition of new bodily and sensory regimes served another purpose as well. Undermining the transfer of knowledge from indigenous adults to children—knowledge about the land, gained through bodily and sensory experience—weakened indigenous claims to certain lands, thus making way for colonists to take over any land that still remained in indigenous hands. One story from South Australia illustrates the consequences of institutional efforts to colonize indigenous children's bodily experience of the world. The Ngarinyeri people of South Australia believed that if the local *panpande* and *palye* trees were burned, the *ponde*, or Murray River cod, would disappear. The missionary George Taplin was delighted when some of the local boys he had brought into the mission collected such wood for firewood. "I could not help thinking today that a load of firewood which the boys fetched bore witness that superstition was losing its hold upon them. It was composed almost entirely of *panpande* and *palye* wood. Three years ago, the boys would not have dared to burn such wood, as the old men would have been so angry." Taplin also noted, "The schoolboys are glorying in the fact that they have done several things in defiance of native customs, and have received no harm."[57] What Taplin regarded as superstitious native customs most likely constituted ecological insight honed over thousands of centuries of observation and experience within a particular place. Taplin celebrated that the boys had rejected their intimate cultural knowledge of the land—and their culture's knowledge bearers.

As Taplin's account makes clear, attempts to deaden the sensory connection between the children and their lands also served to undermine indigenous religions. In both Aboriginal and American Indian cosmologies, a people's long ties and responsibilities to particular places were at the core of religious belief and ceremony. As Ian Keen puts it for Aboriginal people, "According to a very widespread conception, ancestors left traces of their actions, being, and powers in the land, waters, and sky, creating consubstantial links between people, country, and the sacred objects and ceremonies, which followed ancestral precedents."[58]

Christian proselytization in the institutions encouraged the children to abandon their land-based religious beliefs and their older associations and intimacies; at the same time, it reaffirmed new conceptions of race. Jean Begg, who was brought up in the Bomaderry Children's Home, remembers:

We were . . . brought up to think that Aborigines were dirty and bad. . . . We were taught how wicked they were—sinful—evil. . . .

I remember in the night I was terrified to go into the dark, because we were taught that Jesus was nailed to the cross, to cleanse us from our sins, so that we wouldn't be bad any more and we would know Him by the nail prints in His hands and I remember I was terrified of going into the dark. . . . Besides that kind of religious fear, I had fear of Aborigines, knowing that they were evil, wicked and not understanding black, but only relating it to sin and drinking and cruelness.[59]

Authorities also denigrated indigenous cultures by teaching their pupils prevailing racial ideologies. As the scholar Ruth Spack discovered, Hampton Institute used William Swinton's *Introductory Geography*, which purported, "There are differences among men far greater than differences in complexion and features. We ask which kinds of people are the best educated, and are the most skilled in finding out and doing things which are useful for all the world? Which are making the most progress? And, when we find a people very much noted for all these, we say that they are a highly civilized people." By contrast, "When we find people who are not so enlightened, but who still are not savages, and seem to be on the way to become civilized people, we call them semi-civilized, which means half-civilized." And at the bottom, "The races who, in their way of living, are the least civilized, who have no written language, and only the rudest arts,—are called savage races." Spack also uncovered a telling teacher-question/student-answer recitation carried out at Hampton. Teachers began by asking, "To what race do we all belong?" Students responded, "The human race."

"How many classes belong to this race?"

"There are five large classes belonging to this race."

"Which are the first?"

"The white people are the strongest."

"Which are next?"

"The Mongolians or yellows."

"The next?"

"The Ethiopians or blacks."

"Next?"

"The Americans or reds."[60]

(The alert reader may note that only four "classes" of the human race are accounted for.)

Many indigenous people absorbed and reproduced such lessons. In 1908 in a speech to the Friends of the Indian, Simon Redbird, who had studied at Haskell Institute in Kansas and then went on to work as a carpenter at several boarding schools, opposed any effort to close the schools. Redbird agreed with white reformers that "the grown-up Indian in his primitive state is simply a child and his children are therefore simply infants." In concurrence with his white patrons, he also pointed out, "Schools are the greatest weapon to use when you want to subjugate any nation; when educated they will come under the law and when under the law, they will not need looking after."[61] In Australia indigenous children similarly learned and internalized prevailing racial ideologies. Hilda Evans, who concluded that it was a good thing that she was separated from her family to get an education at Sister Kate's, learned, "[There are] quarter-caste and quadroons and then something else before you were out of it [Aborigine], because I think it's Australians and Maoris that don't throwback, but being mixed up you did a throwback."[62] Nancy De Vries, having been in foster care until the age of six, was scared by the other Aboriginal children at the Bidura home when she first arrived. "I happened to turn around and there was this girl who was very dark-skinned and curly hair like an Afro hairdo," she explains. "I got a hell of a fright and screamed and screamed. I cried, I screamed, I screamed. This nurse came running up, shook the hell out of me and she said, 'What are you crying for you stupid little thing, don't you know you're the same as her?' I suddenly found out I was a Koori [a term for Aborigines in southeastern Australia]! I was about six, 1938."[63]

Discipline and Punishment

By requiring that children sever connections to their families and lands, give up their language, dress, and foodways, adopt a regimented and highly controlled life, and accept Christianity as well as their place in the racial hierarchy, authorities sought a near total transformation in indigenous children. To make sure the children conformed, staff at the institutions set up elaborate systems of surveillance and discipline and often punished children not only for offenses such as disobedience, speaking their own language, running away, fighting, and swearing, but also for failure to conform to bodily expectations.[64]

Some children remember being punished for wetting their beds. Ruth Hegarty recalls that at Cherbourg children who wet their beds at night were made to sleep outside on the verandah, even in the coldest weather.[65] Similarly, Sandra Hill claims that when she once wet her bed at Sister Kate's she was forced to stand on a milk crate and "drape the wet sheet over [her] head as kids used to walk past on their way to church." "No matter how small [they] were," children who wet their beds had to wash their sheets.[66] A Navajo remembered that children who wet their beds had to carry their mattresses around in the public square at their school for an entire day.[67]

Picking at one's food could also result in severe punishment. Annie Mullins lived with her family at Doomadgee Mission in Queensland, but at age six was separated from them to live in a dormitory. One day when she was fourteen or fifteen and was picking weevils out of her porridge, the white matron told her to stop: "[She] told me to drop the spoon, stop eating and go and face the wall. . . . And I wouldn't move. I never dropped the spoon, I was just still pulling out the weevils, and . . . she came down. And she tried to push me. I wouldn't move. . . . She started tearing my clothes then, and that's when I . . . swung round and grabbed her and pushed her against the wall, and tore her dress." For her offense, authorities tied Mullins naked to a post under the house and flogged her with a hose.[68]

In at least one home, children were punished for making any noise at all during the matron's afternoon nap. Daisy Ruddick, taken from her mother when she was about six and placed in Kahlin Compound in Darwin, explained how total silence in the dormitory in the afternoon was maintained: "You had a wooden post, and we had to stand in the hot boiling sun with our hands behind our back because we woke [the matron] up from her sleep. That was our punishment. You wouldn't believe it, would you? It sort of reminds me of a concentration camp. You'd stand in that hot boiling sun for . . . I don't know what . . . it seemed like a lifetime." "She had a riding whip you know—we used to get it over the back," Ruddick continued. "Flogging was every day."[69]

Corporal punishment such as that experienced by Ruddick and Mullins was common. Elsie Roughsey recalled the forms of punishment at the mission at Mornington Island: "We'd have to stand in front of the group, be hit on the fingers with rulers or write something a hundred times. If someone did something very bad, she'd have to lie on the scales and be hit on the backside until there were red marks. Sometimes we'd have to go without a meal."[70] Margaret Brusnahan of South Australia remembered vividly, "At the orphanage I was always told that I was bad, wicked. . . . I'd always hold my own, even though I knew what I'd get at the end of it. I was locked in broom cupboards and made to kneel on split peas with my hands on my head."[71]

Laura Dandridge, the matron at Keams Canyon School in Arizona between 1899 and 1902, bore witness to the harsh disciplinary measures that were used there. She alleged that two teachers, W. W. Ewing and C. W. Higham, "each carried a club varying in size at times from three-fourths of an inch to one and one-half inches in thickness and two to four feet in length, when marching the Hopi children to the school-room from the place of line up. Should any of the children get out of step, or take hold of his or her companion's hand, or for any other slight and trivial offense, the offending boy or girl in the company would receive a whack from the club thus carried." Dandridge also complained that a school employee, Mr. Commons, whipped a child named Leslie for "acting smart," then dragged him by the hair. Dandridge later learned that Leslie had been choked by Commons until he fainted. Several of the other children ran to Dandridge to tell her, "He is gasping for breath and has fainted." She claimed that Hopi children were punished for speaking their language by having to carry heavy rocks or by being whipped.[72] Other punishments for indigenous children in both the United States and Australia included the "deprivation of food, usually breakfast or dinner, the whitewashing of faces, tying inmates to their beds or hard physical labours."[73]

Such methods of discipline were alien and undoubtedly harrowing to many indigenous children. Lame Deer explained in his book, "It is hard for a non-Indian to understand how some of our kids feel about boarding schools. In their own homes Indian children are surrounded with relatives as with a warm blanket. . . . Children have their rights just as the adults. They are rarely forced to do something they don't like, even if it is good for them." American Indian families seem to have rarely used corporal punishment to discipline children. Lame Deer explained, "Like all Indian children I was spoiled. I was never scolded, never heard a harsh word. '*Ajustan*—leave it alone'—that was the worst. I was never beaten; we don't treat children that way."[74] Researchers have witnessed a similar permissive style of Aboriginal parenting in which "restrictions are few for children, and punishment of a severe or prolonged kind is rare." In western Arnhem Land, for example, adults preferred not to use physical punishment on their children; instead, a "mother may threaten her child with a thrashing 'in spirit.' This means, simply, hitting his footprints or a tree, making a fine display of rage without touching him at all. It is a warning of what she *could* do, if provoked, but would prefer to avoid."[75]

The frequency and intensity of physical punishment in the institutions far exceeded anything the children had experienced in their own communities. Many children understandably sought to escape from such brutal conditions; however, running away could result in more such humiliating punishments. In 1923 Superintendent Stacher at Crown Point Agency in New Mexico described "one large girl that has run away 5 or more times since she entered school in September, sometimes taking small girls with her being out all night and . . . hungry and cold with danger of freezing to death." The superintendent claimed that her people brought her back each time, "and there seemed no other way than to put hobbles on her."[76] Many institutions had special jails for returned runaways. "Bob" (a pseudonym), a Navajo, remembered, "When anybody ran back home and was brought back to school they would punish him by putting him in jail. . . . A boy could be kept there 3 days before they put him back in school. Around the school, if you made a little mistake you could be put in jail, too. . . . They used to whip some school boys."[77]

Aboriginal children who ran away and were caught endured similar confinement. Moore River in Western Australia was notorious for its jail, referred to by the inmates as "the boob." One young Aboriginal woman told the reformer Mary Bennett, "I often tried to get away [from Moore River] because I didn't get enough to eat, and I didn't like the way the black trackers used to treat us." She accused them of swearing at the children and hitting them with sticks. The young woman continued, "Many times I was in the boob. The boob was a little tin house with stakes all around the inside, barbed wire on top, no windows, and a big iron door locked with handcuffs." She testified that she had been confined to the boob for two weeks, allowed to see no one, and given only bread and water. As a result of Bennett's attempts to publicize this treatment, a royal commissioner warned the Department of Native Affairs in Western Australia that incarceration in the boob constituted "barbarous treatment."[78]

Discipline could also involve attempts to reverse gender roles. Navajo Irene Stewart witnessed the punishments "meted out to runaways. They were spanked and either locked up in a room or made to walk back and forth in front of the girls' and boys' dormitories. If a boy, he was dressed in girls' clothing; if a girl, in boys' clothing."[79] Shaving girls' heads as a punishment was also common. In Queensland, at the Cherbourg Reserve, one woman remembered that as a girl she and two other girls each took a peach from a tree when they thought no one was looking, but the matron saw them: "They put us in jail for two hours and shaved our heads."[80] At a boarding school for the Navajos in Toadlena, Arizona, four girls who ran away and were caught were subjected to a similar penalty. As Kay Bennett remembered, "All of the girls [at the school] were assembled at the playground, a chair was brought, and the guilty girls, one by one, were told to sit on the chair while an attendant cut off all their hair and shaved their heads. The girls watched in shocked silence, thinking what if this should happen to them. To have one's hair cut short was a drastic break in Navajo tradition, but to have it all cut off, was a great disgrace."[81]

Conditions in the Institutions

Officials regularly justified indigenous child removal as a means of rescuing children from impoverished environments where they allegedly suffered from malnourishment, poor sanitation, neglect, abuse, and exposure to sexual immorality. Such conceptions of indigenous societies were often based on white, middle-class, Christian standards that had little meaning in indigenous contexts. Ironically, however, indigenous children routinely endured such degradations in the government- and church-run institutions set up for their care. Ruth Hegarty remembered that at Cherbourg, when the girls turned thirteen and entered the fourth grade (their last year of schooling before being sent out to service), the headmaster "would sit behind a girl as she sat at her desk, straddling her with his legs and pressing his body against her back. On the pretence of helping her with her writing, he would press his right arm against her breast."[82] Of the Aboriginal witnesses called before Australia's National Inquiry into the Separation of Aboriginal and Torres Strait Islander Children from Their Families in 1996, "almost one in ten boys and just over one in ten girls allege they were sexually abused in a children's institution." The report of the inquiry carefully noted that "witnesses were not asked whether they had had this experience," so they estimate that many more Aboriginal people may have been abused but chose not to disclose this.[83] American Indian children also experienced sexual abuse. Helen Sekaquaptewa described a male teacher, "who when the class came up to 'read,' always called one of the girls to stand by him at the desk and look on the book with him. . . . He would put his arms around and fondle this girl, sometimes taking her on his lap." When it was her turn and this teacher rubbed her arm and "put his strong whiskers on [her] face," Helen screamed until he put her down.[84]

Many indigenous children suffered at the institutions in other ways as well. Although U.S. officials often lured children with the promise of exotic and abundant food, malnourishment was an all too common feature of boarding school life. A Ute boy wrote to his agent in 1884, "As you are father, I write to you to tell you that we are almost starving at the Albuquerque School, and because of that, I and 3 other Ute boys had already left that place; but at the Pueblo Agency that told us it was best for us to return and write to you about this, which we now do. . . . Four Pueblo boys also left with us. . . . Please write soon as to what we shall do. We cannot afford to starve at school when we have plenty to eat at home." The boy added in a postscript, "Four Zia [Pueblo] boys also left the school the other day—and four Apache boys—all because they were starving."[85] Similarly, although some Australian institutions provided a decent diet, others failed miserably to properly feed the children. Many Aboriginal people refer frequently to what seemed to be a staple in their institutional diet: "weevily porridge." Marjorie Woodrow vividly recalls the "cold dripping on toast" and the "weevily porridge."[86] Ken Colbung, perhaps trying to soften his words for his white interviewer, declared, "Sometimes we had weevils in the porridge. Who would worry about it really? . . . I was at that stage eating grass-hoppers."[87] Like many others, Hegarty also remembers the miserable food: weevily porridge and damper, a bland bread, for breakfast, stew with damper for lunch, and pea soup with weevils and damper for tea time (dinner). "Children were so hungry," she recalled, "that they often would steal turnips at night."[88]

Ironically, even though an alleged lack of sanitation and hygiene in indigenous communities constituted one of the reasons officials and reformers deemed the children in need of rescue, many institutions were notorious for their poor sanitation. To prevent the children from running away or engaging in "immoral" activities, many authorities locked them into their dormitories at night, often without any kind of sanitary facilities. Daisy Ruddick recalled the procedure at Kahlin Compound in Darwin: "We were locked up at night. . . . We had to take the kerosene tin to use it as a toilet in the building. Just imagine! At summer time, somebody had diarrhoea or something—well you can imagine what the smell was like!"[89] Edmund Nequatewa revealed in his memoir that when Indian boys in the locked dormitory at Keams Canyon School had to urinate at night, they tried to go through holes in the floorboards. One night several desperate boys taught officials a lesson: they "decided that they will just crap all over the floor." Authorities still would not unlock the dormitories at night; instead, they supplied the children with buckets.[90] Even with the buckets, conditions were little better. While serving as matron at Keams Canyon School, Laura Dandridge complained that the policy of locking boys in their dormitory from 7:30 p.m. to 6 a.m. was dangerous to their health. "I have seen the pails running over with filth in the morning, the odor, even after cleaning the floor, being unbearable," she testified.[91]

The children also had to cope with other unsanitary conditions in the institutions. A young Aboriginal woman told Mary Bennett that the Moore River dormitory was cold at night and full of bugs. The royal commissioner who investigated the treatment of Aborigines in Western Australia in the 1930s confirmed in his final report that the dorms at Moore River were vermin-ridden and called for reforms. However, in 1944, ten years after his report, nothing had changed. According to Bennett, a white woman who worked at Moore River commented, "I have seen the children covered with red bites which irritated them terribly, and I have heard them crying in the night at the prospect of spending another night in that bed."[92] Overcrowding plagued many of the Indian boarding schools. For example, although the Phoenix Indian School could accommodate only 700 Indian children, an agent reported that at one point in 1903 725 pupils were in attendance at the school.[93]

In many cases, the homes to which so many indigenous children had been summarily taken—allegedly because they were neglected or poorly cared for—subjected the children to much worse conditions than they experienced in their own communities. A matron in the girls' dormitory at Fort Defiance, Mary E. Keough, testified, "My north dormitory, where twenty-seven girls slept all winter, and my clothing room where sixty-one girls dressed and undressed for school, church, etc., went without stoves when the thermometer often registered fifteen and twenty degrees below zero. The children would beg to be allowed to sleep in my private room or their sitting room that they might not suffer from the cold." When pipes burst in the girls' bathroom, "the whole year the bath room floor was submerged from one to six inches in water. I repeatedly asked [Superintendent] Mr. Levengood to have the necessary repairs made, but to no avail."[94]

Health, Disease, and Death

Such conditions may have contributed to the high rates of illness, disease, and death that became a tragic constant in institutional life. In his study of Barambah in Queensland the historian Thom Blake found that unsanitary conditions, poor diet, and overcrowding led to population decline at the settlement well into the 1920s.[95] Many oral histories, memoirs, and life stories of Indian people include their encounters with disease and death in the schools. Navajo Irene Stewart revealed, "During my first winter in school I became very ill with double pneumonia which nearly took away my life."[96]

As we saw in chapters 4 and 5, the frequent incidences of death in the Indian boarding schools became a point of particular contention for the families. Many Indian people believed that most officials at the boarding schools were indifferent toward their children's deaths and the families' grief. Navajo Rose Mitchell (Tall Woman) claimed, "From what I heard, when some of the children who were at the Chinle Boarding School, and at Fort Defiance and other schools, got sick and passed away from the flu, they got the students who were strong to help with burying them. . . . They'd dig big holes and wrap them up and put lots of them in there together. At the schools, they used tractors for that; they made one big ditch when lots of children died overnight, put them in there, and then covered them all up like that."[97] Marietta Wetherill, a white trader's wife, also commented on the callousness of school officials regarding illness and death. The son of one of her Navajo friends, Tomacito, was sent to boarding school, first in Albuquerque and then to Fort Lewis in Colorado. Wetherill "traced him there and learned he [had] died of diphtheria." To Wetherill's amazement, "nobody ever notified Tomacito." Wetherill railed against the schools, "It just breaks my heart because I was so helpless to do anything. I wrote letters I hunted children, and I'd have to tell their folks they were dead." She also deplored the government for treating the Hopis in the same way.[98]

When agents did try to act respectfully and responsibly toward Indian parents, they were often reprimanded by their superiors. The superintendent of the Albuquerque Indian School objected when the agent sided with Ute parents who wanted their children returned after many deaths at the school. "A letter from the Commissioner raises the question whether or not the Ute children should be taken home," the superintendent wrote to the agent. "You seem to have put it on the ground of the large number of deaths and the consequent anxiety of the parents. You should have based it on the ground that it was the agreement that they were to remain two years." The superintendent insisted, "Agent Patten promised that the children should go home in two years and I want that promise made good."[99]

Institutional Variation

As the example of the Ute agent shows, policy administrators differed in their attitudes and approaches toward indigenous people, and therefore conditions within the institutions varied as well. Not all caretakers of in-digenous children sought to undermine all aspects of their culture. Ken Colbung, a one-time inmate at Sister Kate's, maintains, "Gran [Sister Kate] let us be ourselves. She let us eat food we knew about but she said about bird's eggs 'three there, make sure there's one left.' ... When *she* saw us eating grasshoppers, she just said, 'Are they nice? Do you like them?' I said, 'Would you like one, Granny?' She replied, 'No, thank you, I've got false teeth.'"[100]

Administrators varied as to how much contact they allowed between parents and children. When Gertrude Golden worked at the Indian Boarding School on the reservation for the Umatillas, Cayuses, and Walla Wallas in Oregon under the tyrannical principal, Miss Goings, "the pupils [had] never [been] allowed to go home for extended visits during the school year." But when Miss Goings was deposed, the agent, according to Golden, "always a weak man, began to court the favor of the Indians by allowing parents to take their children from school and keep them out long periods of time."[101]

Conditions at the boarding schools could also vary according to the staff. At another one of Golden's assignments, which she referred to as the School of Hard Knocks, in Montana, she experienced indiffer-ent authorities and "entirely neglected" children. "Lazy employees sat about eating, drinking and playing cards," she wrote. "The plight of the children did not in the slightest degree trouble the consciences of my shiftless co-workers—or should I say 'co-shirkers.'" Golden ex-claimed, "Talk about Indians 'going back to the blanket' when left to themselves! Here was a group of white people left to themselves for a few months without a head or supervisor, reverting to gross neglect of duty, to dishonesty and even worse."[102]

Unfortunately, far too many of the institutions suffered from the types of staff Golden encountered. Lame Deer claimed that the teachers at his day school taught only up to the third grade. "I stayed in that goddam third grade for six years. There wasn't any other. The Indian people of my generation will tell you that it was the same at the other schools all over the reservations. . . . In all those years at the day school they never taught me to speak English or to write and read. I learned these things only many years later, in saloons, in the Army or in jail."[103] Thus, as explored in chapter 2, even though the BIA declared that it was removing Indian children in order to educate them, most institutions failed miserably to extend a viable education to them. Australian state governments never pretended to remove Aboriginal children in order to school them. For its first six years of operation, Palm Island provided no schooling whatsoever. By 1928 they had hired one teacher and found two unpaid assistants to teach 220 children. In other Queensland Aboriginal settlements children were given just four years of schooling and only half the normal school hours.[104] Sam Lovell contends, "We never had much education [at Moola Bulla Native Settlement in Western Australia]. Our education was all work."[105] Indeed, as chapter 8 explores, the institutions in both the United States and Australia primarily focused on preparing their inmates to take up unskilled manual labor and domestic service.

Coping Strategies

Due to the often poor conditions in the schools as well as the shock of being so abruptly uprooted from their homes and thrust into what Ace Daklugie called "a vicious and hostile world," the children developed myriad coping strategies, some quite drastic.[106] Despite the severe punishment that authorities meted out to runaways, many indigenous children simply tried to escape the confines of the institution rather than submit to its rigors. Archival records in the United States, as well as Indian autobiographies and oral histories, attest to the ubiquity of running away, especially by boys. In 1925, for example, the superintendent of the Southern Ute Boarding School informed the commissioner of Indian affairs that out of seventy-three students at his school, "during the months of June, July and August, there were fourteen deserters."[107] Seventy-five Carlisle students ran away between 1907 and 1909, only one of them a girl.[108] (Although Brenda Child found a larger number of girls running away from Flandreau and Haskell, she notes that running away may have been harder for girls because they were more likely to appear suspicious if seen unchaperoned outside the school.)[109] In Australia running away from the institutions was also very common, for both girls and boys. The historian Heather Goodall estimates that one in five Aboriginal children who were removed by the New South Wales Aborigines Protection Board "escaped or 'absconded,' for which they were pursued by the police" and often severely punished with further institutionalization in homes, prisons, or, in some case, psychiatric institutions; of these runaways she asserts that three-quarters eventually returned to an Aboriginal community.[110]

Indigenous children were willing to bear thirst, hunger, and extremes of temperature to escape the institutions. Several Navajo children ran away from the boarding school in Grand Junction, Colorado, and "traveled overland in winter, many suffering from frost bite and exposure," wrote Agent Edward Plummer in 1893. Plummer informed his supervisors, "This has prejudiced the Navajos very much against leaving the Reservation and I am still contending with this prejudice in securing pupils for the school here."[111] After his principal teacher, Flora Harvey, hit him across the face with a ruler for rushing out of his class when he became ill, Edmund Nequatewa said, "[I] was always thinking of how I could get away" from the Phoenix Indian School. Eventually, Nequatewa and a friend made their break, traveling hundreds of miles across the desert from Phoenix in southern Arizona to Hopiland in the north of the state. In addition to relying on their intimate knowledge of the land, Nequatewa and his friend met Yavapai people and a few "cowpunchers" who fed them and helped them on their way.[112]

In Western Australia, Doris Pilkington's mother, Molly, then age fourteen or fifteen, and her two sisters made a similar cross-country escape that has been immortalized in Pilkington's book and the movie *Rabbit-Proof Fence*. Shortly after being taken to Moore River in the south, Molly fled with her two younger sisters, Gracie and Daisy, and walked over one thousand miles, much of it desert, over seven weeks back to Jiggalong in the north along the north-to-south fence that settlers had erected—futilely—to keep rabbits from invading the western part of Australia. Like Nequatewa, Molly and her sisters relied on the help of native people they met on the way as well as a settler family. Pilkington writes, "Molly, Daisy, and Gracie were very much at home in this part of the country. They evaded capture by practising survival skills inherited from their nomadic ancestors." (Gracie eventually decided to leave her two sisters and turn herself in.)[113] "[I was] running away from [Cootamundra]," Nancy De Vries remembers, "and drinking bore water because it was so bloody hot out on the road and thinking, 'God I've poisoned myself,' and I was that glad when the police came along in their car and caught me and took me back."[114]

Some indigenous children, including De Vries, also attempted suicide. As she was recovering from her illness at Cootamundra, she swallowed half the contents of a bottle of aspirin. On other occasions, she recalls, "I tried the quick death of pills or hanging. I always tell people I cut my wrists here cutting a jam tin, because it's very embarrassing admitting that I tried to commit suicide. I tried to kill myself. I was lonely, I was unhappy, I wanted my mother, I wanted my identity, I felt cheated, I wanted to be me."[115] De Vries's story as well as that of countless other runaways who risked injury and death and endured freezing cold or blistering heat to get away from the institutions attest to the deep discontent that pervaded the lives of many indigenous children who had been separated from their families.

Most children did not resort to such extreme measures to escape their institutions, but many engaged in daily acts of disobedience. At boarding school from the age of fourteen, Lame Deer remembered, "I felt so lonesome I cried, but I wouldn't cooperate in the remaking of myself. I played the dumb Indian. They couldn't make me into an apple—red outside and white inside. From their point of view I was a complete failure. I took the rap for all the troubles in the school." He concluded, "I think in the end I got the better of that school. I was more of an Indian when I left than when I went in. My back had been tougher than the many straps they had worn out on it."[116]

Other Indian children also refused to cooperate in the efforts to re-make them. Thomas Battey, a Quaker teacher who taught at a boarding school among the Caddos in the early 1870s, complained, "I have great difficulty in making them understand that they should keep still, without talking or laughing aloud." Without an interpreter and unable to speak their language, Battey could not control his students. Furthermore, they refused to conform to his Franklinesque schedule of early to bed and early to rise. Even after the lights went out, the Caddo children talked, sang, and laughed until midnight or after, and then slept late in the morning.[117]

Some children turned activities in the schools to their own purposes. Sports, for example, carried many Indian youth through the hardship of being separated from their families.[118] (Aborigines do not appear to have engaged in competitive sports in their institutions until after World War II.)[119] Many children even used sports to keep their native ways alive. Daklugie remembered, "The thing that pulled me through was the athletic training at Carlisle. I enjoyed the sports and, although the conditioning didn't measure up to my father's and Geronimo's training routine, it kept me active and fit." He points out, "To celebrate the victory [after football games], we had a party in the gym. Some of us did our native dances."[120]

Other children found a degree of comfort by forming a close-knit family of their peers. Sam Lovell remarks, "[The government] broke all that tie between you and your family, taking you away. My family is the kids that I grew up with."[121] Ruth Hegarty observes, "I grew up with all these girls [in the dormitory]. The thing is, I think, whilst it was the government's policy to institute us, we became one family. We became a family of all of us in there. We still take care of each other." When she turned fourteen and was required to go out to work, Ruth was frightened to have to leave the mission and dorm and her new family of peers: "It might have been an institution, but at least it provided me with some comfort, when you knew that there were people around you that supported you."[122] Irene Stewart fondly recounts playing with other Navajo children, at least on Saturday afternoons. "By the time I entered fifth grade," she writes, "I had forgotten about my grandmother and other relatives. I was no longer lonesome and homesick. And when I was home on summer vacations, I missed the fun I had at school."[123]

This family of peers, however, should not be romanticized or considered an equivalent substitute for the traditional family life of indigenous groups. Cruelty was also a feature of this peer culture. Elsie Roughsey recalled "unhappy times in the dormitory" when other girls teased her or fought with each other.[124] Helen Sekaquaptewa experienced insidious harassment from an older girl who threatened to pull her hair when she was supposed to be brushing and braiding it unless Helen gave her some of her food. She also recalled how the Navajos and the older Hopi children at Keams Canyon School always got more food than the younger children. "It seemed . . . the Navajos would have their plates heaping full, while little Hopi girls just got a teaspoonful of everything. I was always hungry and wanted to cry because I didn't get enough food." She further recalled, "Sometimes the big boys would even take bread away from the little ones."[125]

Of course, administrators never envisioned such a peer-based family; they had intended the children to establish new intimacies with their caregivers, primarily white women. Perhaps recognizing the potential of relationships between peers to undermine their mission, many institutional authorities sought to create hierarchies of children within the institutions, often appointing older children to oversee younger ones. Like Sekaquaptewa, many indigenous inmates recalled these "native helpers" as cruel and brutal to the younger children. Doris Pilkington described one such helper as a "cruel spinster" who beat the girls with a strap.[126] Victoria Archibald claimed that the "Aboriginal lady that grew up there" and became a matron at Cootamundra "was worse than the [white] matron."[127] Intentionally or not, the institutions fostered a new type of intimate relationship among peers. Both a source of support and of abuse, these peer cultures replaced the children's prior reliance on parents, family members, and elders for support and socialization.

Staying Connected

Although most authorities tried to prevent it, institutionalized children sought to maintain meaningful contact with their families and homelands. In the United States children were allowed to correspond with their families, but officials routinely tried to interfere in what children wrote to their parents. Alice Fletcher told children at Hampton Institute that they shouldn't write anything negative in their letters home: "Don't spend your time saying to your parents 'I want to see you.' . . . Try to make little pictures in your letters of your happy, busy life here." However, children did not passively accept such advice. Hampton's director, Samuel Armstrong, often complained that students had caused "mischief" by the letters they wrote home.[128]

Some Indian children managed to spend summers at home, which allowed them to stay in touch with their family's and culture's ways of living. During her summer vacation from boarding school, for example, Irene Stewart was schooled in Navajo ways. Although her "attempt to live the traditional Navajo way of life was chopped up with school life," she still maintained crucial contact with her family and community.[129] Except in a few rare cases—Mt. Margaret Mission in Western Australia, for example—Aboriginal children rarely were allowed to even correspond with their families, let alone spend their summers with them. Although institutional life was very similar for Indian and Aboriginal children in many ways, this marked a crucial difference in their experiences. Officials intended the separation of Aboriginal children from their families to be permanent and therefore sought to limit contact as much as possible between the inmates and their parents and other family members.

Nevertheless, Aboriginal children did find ways to maintain some sense of connection with their families and cultures. Much to the dismay of authorities, some children who lived in institutions close to Aboriginal communities still participated in initiation ceremonies at puberty. John Sexton, a missionary with the Aborigines' Friends' Association, lamented, "It is disquieting to know that the tribal laws cover even the half-caste children of the Bungalow [in Alice Springs], who are claimed by natives and over whose lives a shadow is cast. It is common knowledge how young men are captured by the old natives and taken into the bush to undergo four weeks of terror and suffering, from which they emerge with broken and maimed lives."[130] As in the writings of other white officials, Sexton's comment assumed that white institutions were the rightful guardians of Aboriginal children and that their families were "capturing" them and rendering them "broken and maimed" through their own puberty initiation rituals. Despite its bias, Sexton's observation makes clear that some Aboriginal children, even "half-caste" children who authorities claimed were rejected by Aboriginal communities, were able to maintain this key association with their kin.

In those areas where children lived in dormitories on Aboriginal settlements, they also found it possible on occasion to connect with kin and "camp." Ruth Hegarty remembers that when she was ten years old, her grandmother's brother (her grandfather in her group's kinship system)—a "clever man," or healer—came to visit her at the girls' dormitory at Cherbourg. Hegarty and her friends in the dormitory often "told each other stories about clever men" and their powers. On Saturdays, the "big girls" at Cherbourg were allowed a small measure of freedom to play at the duck pond outside the dormitory yard. Unbeknown to their keepers, who stipulated that the dormitory girls could fraternize only with dormitory boys, the girls sometimes met up with Aboriginal boys from the nearby camp. The boys often brought them "gifts of small wild birds, already plucked and cleaned," that Hegarty and her friends would mix with "bits of vegetable peels that [they] dug out of garbage bins" to make a "delicious stew."[131]

As a means of staying linked with their kin and the land (and to supplement the often meager diet in the institutions), other institutionalized children also obtained native foods. During the rare occasions when they could leave the institution, Daisy Ruddick and her friends learned from Aboriginal people near Kahlin Compound about what they could eat in the bush. At other times, "[they] used to experiment with things to eat." "There was a lot of bush food around in those days," she writes. "We used to test it . . . and we learned what not to eat."[132] Like their Aboriginal counterparts, American Indian children also kept connections with their families and cultures by procuring native food. One night two Omaha boys snuck out of their mission school and headed back to their village to obtain some pemmican, a rich delicacy made by pounding together berries and the oil rendered from buffalo bones. Returning to the school, the boys shared their prize with a group of their fellow students. "We had built a fire in a vacant room adjoining our dormitory; into this warm room we repaired with our bag, and sat in a circle on the floor, Indian fashion," Francis La Flesche recalled. After the pemmican had been divided evenly among the boys, one boy "took a tiny bit of the pemmican, and held it toward the sky for a moment as a thank offering to Wakonda [the Creator], then placed it with great solemnity on the floor in the centre of the circle. This done, we fell to eating, telling stories as we feasted, and had one of the most enjoyable nights of our lives."[133]

Other Indian children were also willing to steal away from school just to eat their favorite native foods. Navajo Ruth Roessel attended the Lukachukai Day School: "Many of the parents would bring food, such as watermelons, corn, mutton, and fried bread. That certainly was what we liked and knew how to eat." When she was later boarding at the Lukachukai School (which had become a boarding school for students who lived far away), Ruth and her friend Angela so wanted to feast on familiar food that they walked through a snowstorm to Angela's home. "One Sunday afternoon it was snowing, and my friend Angela wanted to go to her mother's home because she knew they were butchering sheep and we could get some mutton and bring [it] back to school," Roessel recalls. "So we left the school that afternoon and walked through the snow and the cold. Finally we reached her hogan. We had a wonderful meal of roast mutton and fried bread." Unfortunately, when they returned on horseback that night with Angela's brother, the horse shied, threw the girls off, and ran away, scattering the prized mutton and fried bread (better known today as fry bread). The girls had to walk the rest of the way in the snow and did not arrive until about midnight. Later, when Ruth attended the Fort Wingate Boarding School, she looked forward to the rare occasions when her family would send a package of mutton and fried bread. "We would sit and eat the mutton and fried bread and think of home."[134]

Negotiating Identity

Given that the children had limited, if any, contact with their home and families once institutionalized, many struggled to gain a sense of identity. For some removed children, especially those Aboriginal children who were removed as babies, the institution was the only home they had ever known, and therefore it seemed "natural." Leonard Ogilvie, who had been removed to Moore River, explains that his peers there "didn't know any different, that was their home, they loved it there, it was their home."[135] Alfred Neal explained that he was happy in the boys' dorm, separate from his mother on Palm Island: "That's the only world I knew, see."[136] Asked what he thought of being separated from his family, Martin Dodd replied, "We just thought it was part of our life, when you got split up like that."[137] In the United States Indian children often experienced the same sense of naturalization. "Bill Sage," a Navajo, told his interviewer, "I got used to the school and only thought about my people once in a while. The school was just the same as my home."[138]

For Aboriginal children who had never known anything but institutional life and did not see themselves as Aboriginal, it could be a shock to realize that other Australians did not consider them to be white. Removed to Bomaderry Children's Home at the age of fourteen months, Alicia Adams regarded Matron Barker and the other "all lady staff" as her family. "I never knew I had a mother or a father. I just thought Mum [Matron Barker] was my mum, you know, my white mum and I thought all the ladies were my real aunties." Moreover, the Bomaderry staff sought to completely distance the children there from knowledge of their Aboriginal heritage. Adams explained, "We were never taught about Aborigines. I never even knew the word Aborigine." At Bomaderry, she says, "I was scared of Aborigines. I was real scared of [the Aborigines who occasionally came to the home]. . . . I used to cling [to Mum, the white matron], and nearly pull Mum's dress off her because of this Aborigine." When she turned twelve, authorities transferred Adams to the Cootamundra home for domestic training, a move that proved traumatic. "I really loved this Home at Bomaderry, and I really cried every night just because I missed home here you know." For the first time, too, Adams found out that she was considered Aboriginal, not white. "I was real hurt because I didn't want to be brown, you know, I wanted to be white. And ever since I was little I always thought I was white."[139] Adams's experience illustrates the contradictions inherent in New South Wales's absorption policy. Though her early caregivers pretended she was white, officials ultimately regarded her as an Aboriginal girl who must be trained to be a domestic servant. Even if raised as white, there was no guarantee that once out of the institutions indigenous children would be treated by other Australians as such.

A similar dilemma confronted many Indians who had been removed as children. After years of study to become a medical doctor, the Santee Sioux Charles Eastman was disheartened to find that he could not attract patients to his medical practice in St. Paul, Minnesota. After passing the state's medical examination—a three-day ordeal that about half the applicants failed—Eastman "opened an office, hung out [a] sign, and waited for the patients." Rather than seeking Eastman's expertise as a Western medical doctor, "a large number [of local residents] came to [him] for Indian medicine and treatment." Defying their expectations, Eastman said, "[I] told them, of course, that I had no such medicine. . . . Finally, a prominent business man of St. Paul offered to back me up financially if I would put up an 'Indian medicine' under my own name, assuring me there was 'a fortune in it.'" Eastman declined, "determined that the good men and women who had helped [him with his education] should not be betrayed."[140]

Like Eastman, many more Indian than Aboriginal children either had
been removed at an older age and therefore had memories of their Indian
childhood or had managed to sustain contact with their family despite their
removal. Faced with myriad and often clashing influences in their young
lives, these Indian children also struggled to gain a positive sense of identity. Irene Stewart relates, "As a child I was shifted back and forth from my
Navajo life to the white man's schools, and I think this accounts for some
of my varied characteristics. It was in my early years that I began to give
way to feelings of inferiority and insecurity. It seemed as though hardly
anyone cared for me after I was taken away from Grandmother."[141]

Many removed indigenous children neither became "white" nor remained a full member of their particular tribe or clan, but created a different identity altogether. The peer culture of the institutions led many
children to develop an affiliation with other Indians and Aborigines in a
broad sense. Essie Horne, a Shoshone, attended Haskell from the time
she was fourteen:

> For me, one of the things that the boarding school fostered was an
> understanding of different tribes. . . . I think of the boarding school
> as a kind of cultural and historical feast. I was tremendously enriched
> by my association with people from other tribes.
>
> The schools were trying to take the Indianness out of us, but they
> never succeeded. Not completely, anyway. They actually ended up put-
> ting a lot of Indianness into the Indian, just by throwing us all together
> in a group. The boarding school may have contributed to the break-
> down of the family and may have increased the rate of alcohol abuse . .
> . but it also unwittingly created a resistance to assimilation, which might
> take shape in very subtle or quite rebellious forms. The experience of us
> boarding school students strengthened our resolve to retain our identity
> as American Indians and to take our place in today's world.[142]

Institutionalized children shared a distinctive history that also contributed to this new identity. Interestingly, Ruth Hegarty of the Cherbourg

mission in Queensland coined the term "dormitory girl" to capture the essence of this experience: "Our lives were governed by the same policies and what happened to one, happened to all of us. No one was treated as special or given special privileges. We were treated identically, dressed identically, our hair cut identically. Our clothes and bald heads were a giveaway. We were dormitory girls."[143]

Moving On or Going Home

Eventually the children left the institutions. Most Indians returned to their families and communities, at least for a time. Sometimes this proved to be as traumatic as the initial separation had been. When Irene Stewart returned to Navajo country after four years at Haskell, she felt as disoriented as when she had first left her home. "Father looked at me for some time. I think he wondered about my bobbed hair and all the new style, perhaps even my actions. I felt out of place again," she writes. "When I had left the Navajo country years before, I felt heartbreak; now I was disappointed in it. I could not make up my mind to stay on the reservation. Hogan life — once a great pleasure to me, and in later years so satisfying — was not for me. I looked forward to the white man's ways and decided to go back to school, this time to Albuquerque Indian School." Stewart graduated from the Albuquerque Indian School in 1929 and then headed for California to "enter a nine months' Bible study course." Along her journey she acquired "the missionary zeal." After Christian training in Berkeley she was assigned by the Presbyterian mission to work in one of their hospitals in Redrock, Arizona, a place which at that time "was absolutely isolated." Stewart recalled, "It was a lonely experience after tasting the city life, and I wished I were back in California." Within less than a year, however, the hospital closed due to lack of funds, and Stewart headed back to Oakland, California, where she worked for a year before marrying an Oneida man.[144]

Realizing the estrangement that had taken place when their children were removed, many indigenous communities sought ritualized ways to reintegrate them into their culture. Navajo "Bill Sage" remembers that after several years away at boarding school he finally went home. His father came to pick him up in Fort Defiance. "When we came to where my father was," Sage remembers, "there were three men and one woman there. After I shook hands with these people, I knew one of them was my father, but I didn't remember him." "When I got home," he recalls, "my two sisters and my brother were there. I remembered my brother but had forgotten all about my two sisters." Not only had Sage forgotten what some of his family members looked like, he had also forgotten some of his Navajo ways. "After I had been to school I wasn't trying to believe the Navajo way. I believed the American way. I didn't know any more of the Navajo way than when I went to school."[145]

To reincorporate Sage back into his family and community, his family wanted to have a "sing" for him, a performance of the Blessing Way, a Navajo ceremony meant to keep the individual in balance with the physical, social, and spiritual worlds. At first, Sage was not interested and refused. (Such is the nature of Navajo society that children were not forced to take part in rituals, as they were in boarding schools.) Eventually, however, after his family members continued to ask him, he agreed. Sage granted an account of the sing to the anthropologists Dorothea and Alexander Leighton:

At the start of the Sing, the Medicine Man talked to him, saying that Bill had been to school and learned a lot of white man's ways. But he was not a white man and what would he do with learning all that? It wouldn't make him white, he would still be Navajo. White man's ways are one thing and Navajo ways are another, and he had better learn the Navajo way. . . . All through the Sing he thought about how he would tell the boys about it when he went back to school. Lots of the boys used to have stories to tell about Navajo ways, but when they asked Bill for some, he didn't know any.

Sage later asked his father why they had had a sing for him. His father replied, "We didn't want to put you in school, your brother did that. We all were so glad to get you back here without anything wrong with you. All the Navajo do the same thing when [they] have sent children to school—they put on the Blessing Way for their children. That's the way we Navajos work it when our children go to school."[146]

Unlike most Indian children, many Aboriginal youth never returned to their communities or families, or did so only many years later. Aboriginal people were often dispersed far from their home territories and nearly all officials stringently sought to completely cut off all contact between institutionalized children and their parents. They therefore often misled children by telling them that they had been removed because their parents didn't want them or had hurt them. At Tuffnell Home in Brisbane, where Laurette Butt was the only indigenous child, the nuns told her that her mother was no good and had abandoned her. Butt learned otherwise from the "greeter" who routinely allowed other mothers to visit their children but had been ordered not to allow Butt's mother to see her. Much later in life, Butt reunited with her sister, who set the record straight that their mother always talked about her and sought to find her. According to her sister, "She didn't know how long it would take but [Laurette] would come home one day. Laurette will come back one day and there has to be a place here for her when she comes back." Unfortunately it was too late; Butt's mother was already dead.[147] Doris Pilkington believed authorities when they told her that her mother had given her away. When she eventually reunited with her mother in 1962 at the age of twenty-five, she recalls, "I actually blamed my mother for giving me away to the government and accused her one time, you know, asked her, 'Why did you give me away?' She just broke down and cried. She said, 'I did not give you away, you were taken away, the government took you away to send you to school.'"[148]

When first institutionalized, Sandra Hill recalls, "I started to hate my mother." She felt abandoned and betrayed: "From the minute we got into that receiving home and we were de-liced and processed, like prisoners, that's when I let go of my mother, that's when my hatred for her started, and it continued right up until I got my documents, basically, because I knew no different. Someone had to take the rap and she was the sucker that had to take the rap," Hill told her interviewer. "I spent all my life blaming mum for not wanting us and all of that, but I didn't know about the assimilation policy and I didn't know about the 1905 act and I didn't know about her childhood experience and the level of her removal. That's made all the difference in the world to how I perceive my mother." She recognizes that many stolen children hate their parents "instead of seeing that it was a government policy and a government department that did it." In Hill's case even knowing the truth did not help her gain intimacy with her birth mother. Hill tried to restore a relationship with her but felt guilty that she didn't feel close to her. "There's this cultural perception that you really have to love your mother because she gave birth to you," she explains, "and it is just that, it's a perception."[149]

Such separation and estrangement from one's family often became a multigenerational phenomenon. Helen Baldwin was one of seven children of Nellie Darby who were all removed and placed in orphanages in Victoria. Baldwin comments, "It's just a sad case. . . . You know . . . [my mother] was taken away from her parents at Lake Tyers. And then I was taken from her."[150] In her oral history Doris Pilkington reveals the epilogue to her mother Molly's famous story of removal to and escape from Moore River. After Molly had two children, Doris and her sister Anna, authorities took the two girls to Moore River in 1941, when Doris was just four years old. Officials also took Molly on the trip for surgery. Molly lived in the camp at Moore River; Anna, who was still nursing, was allowed to live with her mother, but Doris was confined in a dormitory. Molly escaped with Anna and journeyed back to Jiggalong—as she had first done when she was fourteen—but she could not take Doris because she was too big to carry. Authorities later tracked down the family again, removing Anna to Sister Kate's.[151] Cycles of child removal also played out among Indian peoples, but as we saw in chapter 4, over time many Indian families came to claim the boarding schools as their own and more willingly sent their children to the schools.

As they look back to their past, indigenous adults who were removed as children have had varying reactions to their experiences. While Doris Pilkington longed to reunite with her mother and to make sense of the experience through her writing, her sister, Anna, according to Doris, is not interested in reuniting with either her mother or Doris. "I don't need the past, it means nothing to me," she allegedly told Doris.[152] Geoffrey Parfitt thinks "the government did the right thing at the right time." He concludes, "We were lucky in a way that we were sent to Sister Kate's. . . . They don't have to say 'sorry' to me, I thank them a bit. I thank them for getting me out of the gutter a bit."[153] Suspecting her parents "could have been real drunks," Alicia Adams contends, "Maybe they were wise to take us away from them. . . . I'm glad, I wouldn't be a missionary, I could be in the gutter, I could be a drunkard. I was real glad I was put there in the Home."[154] "Bob," a Navajo who was removed as a child, told an interviewer in 1940 that he believed his experience was good for him and that the new day schools introduced by John Collier in the 1930s had set the Navajos back. He told his interviewers:

They used to teach a lot of things to the school boys and girls then. The government used to have a good school. The boarding school was very good for Indian children. Nowadays they're trying to start day schools. . . . Our children will get no place that way. When I was in school, they watched us pretty closely. They wouldn't allow us to talk our own language, made us speak English, made us speak quietly in the dining room when we were eating and also in the bedroom. If anybody talked in the school room, they tied a rag around his mouth and the back of his head. In that way the children used to mind and learn their lessons. Nowadays when I go through these day schools, they may be yelling in their own language, hollering. At night time they can be singing in their language as loud as they can. They are doing all this instead of learning their lessons. The teachers and employees just watch the children hollering and singing and don't say a word. All they do is watch and listen.[155]

Carlos Montezuma, a Yavapai Apache who was a close friend of Pratt's and became a medical doctor, defended the schools and staunchly recommended getting "Indians out of the reservation as far and as fast as possible, and to take the children at any cost."[156]

Other indigenous people, however, have felt bitter and resentful. Leonard Ogilvie, who was brought to Moore River, contends, "We went there to be brought up as white kids . . . but when we left there we were Aborigines, second-class citizens and we were nothing actually."[157] Helen Baldwin concludes, "[There was] nothing positive about being taken away from your mother. No, I don't care if she was an alcoholic. Or what she did. She was my mum. You know, and I had the right to stay with her. . . . The government. You know. It wasn't going to make us white. Like they hoped."[158] Florrie Springs, who had been taken as a child to Sister Kate's, spoke bitterly: "I met my mother for the first time when I was forty-six, right? I cried. I have no children. . . . I miss not having a family."[159] Laurette Butt asserts:

> I cannot understand the mentality of the do-gooders in those days because of how I suffered and I haven't got a family. . . . I loathe Mother's Day, only because I know I had one and she looked for me and I was looking for her. And I think of her and how my mother must have suffered. And all the other mothers that carried their children for nine months and who loved them and then somebody come along and just take them, and say, "We know what's best for your child." And they ruined my life in that respect. . . . I have got on and done the best what I can for my life. But there's only one thing that I really missed, . . . LOVE. I starve for it.[160]

Similar to Butt, Zitkala-Ša felt cheated. In an essay she wrote in the *Atlantic Monthly* in 1900, she lamented:

For the white man's papers, I had given up my faith in the Great Spirit. For these same papers I had forgotten the healing in trees and brooks. On account of my mother's simple view of life, and my lack of any, I gave her up, also. . . . Like a slender tree, I had been uprooted from my mother, nature, and God. I was shorn of my branches, which had waved in sympathy and love for home and friends. The natural coat of bark which had protected my oversensitive nature was scraped off to the very quick.

Now a cold bare pole I seemed to be, planted in a strange earth.[161]

For some indigenous adults, the experience of removal and institutionalization was complex and not easy to categorize as wholly good or wholly bad. Danny Colson, son of a Pitjantjatjara woman and a white camel man, was taken at age ten from Ernabella Mission, where he lived with his mother, to Colebrook Home in Quorn, South Australia. "While I am grateful for what I learned and the opportunities that life and the education gave me, I wouldn't wish it on anybody," he explained. "As a small child, being taken away from your mother to a place far away with people of another race, is terribly traumatic. I couldn't even speak English and I thought they were going to eat me." He adds, "I appreciate the opportunities I had when young, so I can now live a reasonable lifestyle and help my people to better themselves. But the separation of those years was heart-breaking."[162] Irene Stewart concluded enigmatically, "I was . . . caught in the middle between the white man's way and the Navajo way. It was the result of my being kidnapped for education. This I am grateful for."[163]

It may be tempting to read the remarkable resiliency of people such as Irene Stewart and Danny Colson as proof that indigenous child removal policies weren't really so bad after all. If some children eventually became successful participants in the dominant society, wasn't child removal, traumatic though it might have been at the time, worthwhile in the end? One response is to ask why indigenous children were not given an education and opportunities without "being kidnapped" and having to endure "heart-breaking" years of separation. The experience of children in the institutions suggests, once again, that providing education and opportunities for participation within each settler society—despite all the benevolent rhetoric—was never the true aim of the institutionalization of indigenous children. That some children eventually seized such opportunities and succeeded, on white terms, should not blind us to the foremost goals of administrators: divorcing the children from their indigenous heritage—and thereby erasing their claims to specific lands—and preparing them to take up "useful" labor.

As in other aspects of indigenous child removal, gender played a prominent part in the efforts of institutions to break the children's sensory connections to kin and homeland. The next chapter examines how officials designated white women as the most appropriate caretakers for removed indigenous children. Moreover, as a key component of their attempts to undermine the children's intimacy with their families and homelands, the institutions sought to transform one of the most fundamental aspects of the children's background: their gender systems.

Chapter 7

Maternalism in the Institutions

At the Home they were such strong women we knew when we were young. We
knew nothing of men. • IVY KILMURRAY, resident of Sister Kate's Home,
Western Australia, quoted in Vera Whittington, *Sister Kate: A Life Dedicated to
Children in Need of Care*

As we have seen, the gender systems of indigenous people served as a
marker to reformers in both Australia and the United States of indigenous people's alleged inferiority and backwardness. It is no surprise,
then, that the institutions sought to steer indigenous children toward
new conceptions of men's and women's proper roles in society. The
institutions themselves modeled the new patriarchal families that authorities and many reformers promoted among indigenous families.
Generally, the state conceived of a kind of sexual division of labor in
which white men—as administrators of policy, superintendents, or dis-
ciplinarians—were meant to perform the role of stern authority figures,
while white women were to act the part of nurturing caregivers.

The state, in effect, became the "father" to indigenous children in
both the United States and Australia; it became the head of the new
"family." To remove and raise the children, however, the state needed
"mothers" as well, women who would, as matrons and schoolteachers
within the institutions, carry out the intensive hands-on, day-to-day
work of dressing and bathing the children, feeding them, and social-
izing them into their new roles. Put another way, the state became a
legal or fictive guardian to the children, and then subcontracted many
of its guardianship responsibilities—providing protection, education,

discipline and punishment, affection and emotional support—to white women.[1]

Yet in this period in which gender roles in white society were under contestation, white women within the institutions often operated uneasily in relationship to the state and its patriarchal authority. Critical of both the male administration of indigenous policy and of patriarchal families—whether Aboriginal, American Indian, or white—many white women sought to create alternative women-centered homes where children were, ideally, nurtured and mothered. To a certain extent, according to some testimony by removed children, these women were successful in creating more humane institutions, even as they struggled to obtain adequate funds.

In the end, however, white women's work supported the state's aims of controlling indigenous children and the communities from which they came. Most white women still sought to utterly transform the children, particularly the girls, in their care. Changing indigenous gender roles, transforming indigenous homes through promoting domesticity, and monitoring girls' bodies and containing their sexuality figured prominently in white women's agenda. To achieve these aims, the women resorted to measures of surveillance and control that differed little from the state's approach.

While some indigenous girls seem to have internalized these new conceptions of gender, others resisted attempts to "domesticate" and control them. Moreover, the experience of removal and institutionalization—and assaults on indigenous gender systems—led many indigenous women to articulate an alternative maternalism that rested on restoring the dignity of indigenous women, honoring indigenous mothers, and asserting indigenous women's desires for and rights to the custody of their own children.

White Women in the Institutions

By relying on white women to carry out much of his program, first at Fort Marion and later at Carlisle Institute, Richard Henry Pratt es-

16. Sarah Mather (left) and the first group of Sioux Indian girls from Rosebud and Pine Ridge Reservations immediately after their arrival at Carlisle Institute, 1879. For a full list of all the girls in the photo, see Richard Henry Pratt, *Battlefield and Classroom: Four Decades with the American Indian, 1867–1904* (New Haven CT: Yale University Press, 1964). Photo 12-20-01, 309B #1, Cumberland County Historical Society, Carlisle, Pennsylvania.

tablished the practice of employing women as schoolteachers within the Indian boarding schools. He lauded the "excellent ladies, who had in their earlier years been engaged in teaching," who "volunteered to give daily instruction to the [Indian] prisoners in classes." In particular, Pratt singled out Sarah Mather, who was one of the first women to graduate from the women's college Mt. Holyoke and who had opened a girls' boarding school in St. Augustine, Florida. Mather would continue to work with Pratt at Carlisle, where white women, including Pratt's own wife, composed a large majority of the teachers. Many other white women volunteered time, donated money, or raised funds for Pratt's efforts. Speaking of some of these women, Pratt remarked, "These ladies until their death were among my most invaluable aids and helpers in promoting the prosperity of the school."[2]

The Women's National Indian Association also praised white women's work in the Indian schools. Amelia Stone Quinton remarked, "In the educational work of various types done for the native Indians, noble women have been engaged, and this is notably true of the Hampton, Virginia, and Carlisle, Pennsylvania Indian schools, where gifted women of high culture, have devoted some of their best years to the elevation of the red race."[3]

When the U.S. government set up its own system of Indian boarding schools, it continued Pratt's tradition. In his study of the schools, David Wallace Adams found that "the average teacher appears to have been a single woman in her late twenties."[4] The historian Cathleen Cahill discovered that the proportion of women employees in the Indian School Service "held steady between fifty-five and sixty-two percent" from 1890 well into the twentieth century.[5] The Bureau of Indian Affairs also hired white women to serve as matrons within the schools, a position that entailed "directing the household departments of the institution; supervising or directing or promoting the social life of students, training or guiding them in correct habits of health, self-discipline, ethics of right living, physical training or recreational work; teaching vocational guidance, housekeeping, care and repair of clothing."[6]

The BIA agreed with the WNIA that white women possessed innate maternal characteristics that fit them for these positions. When Julia Carroll set out for Genoa Indian School in Nebraska in 1923 to become a matron, her employer told her, "I am glad to appoint you. I think you will be a very nice mother to those children."[7] (The only requirement for the matron's position was an eighth-grade education, passage of a civil service examination, and six months of training or experience in related occupations.)[8]

In Australia male authorities also deemed women the best caretakers of removed indigenous children, but given the greater antipathy between female reformers and male officials, as seen in chapters 3 and

5, authorities in charge of Aboriginal affairs usually preferred to hire married couples to run institutions, reserves, and stations, the husbands to serve as superintendents and managers while their wives worked as teachers or matrons. For example, when Ella Hiscock's husband became the manager of an Aboriginal station in New South Wales, she became the station's matron.[9] Authorities generally believed it inadvisable for white women to "reside alone and unprotected at any of the reserves"; the historian Katherine Ellinghaus attributes this attitude to a fear that white women might become intimately involved with Aboriginal men, as a few missionary women had.[10]

Western Australia Chief Protector Auber Neville made some exceptions; he claimed, "I always advocated the appointment of married couples at all Northern institutions, both partners as workers. At Southern institutions nurses and female attendants or teachers might be single, but it is preferable that they should belong to the married state, too."[11] (Undoubtedly, Neville regarded the more remote and less populated north as unsuited to single white women.) By contrast, Chief Protector Cecil Cook in the Northern Territory preferred to employ single women. "The Matron [of the] Half-Caste Home, must be a woman sympathetically disposed to the Half-Caste child," Cook wrote, "eager to undertake the arduous duties involved in the elevation of the Half-Caste to the white standard and at the same time she must be a fully qualified general and obstetric nurse who is prepared to give full service to Aboriginal patients however revolting their condition!" Cook believed most of the married women were not qualified (and possibly distracted by their wifely duties), and thus more often chose to hire single women, especially nurses from the Northern Territory Medical Service.[12]

While they were sometimes excluded from government positions, many single white Australian women found means to work within mission institutions for indigenous children. By 1900, according to Catherine Bishop, women were the majority of personnel in mission fields worldwide. In 1902, Bishop found, single women constituted 67 percent of the missionary force in Australia; by 1917 this proportion had risen to

78 percent. Yet, Bishop notes, most mission societies were very patriarchal. Hence in Australia women founded their own groups, the United Aborigines' Mission (UAM) and the Aborigines' Inland Mission, which were "predominantly female." Moreover, missionaries with the UAM were required to remain single.[13]

What prompted so many women to enter careers in institutions for indigenous children? Certainly women's professional opportunities were limited at the turn of the twentieth century, and teaching, missionary work, and nursing had become coded as women's professions that built on women's "natural" nurturing abilities. However, not all of the American women teachers who hired on with the BIA did so out of a maternalist mission; some saw it instead as an opportunity to break away from restrictive gender norms, to have an adventure, or simply as a way to make an independent living.[14]

In this, many suffered disappointment. Gender biases still pervaded the BIA hierarchy. It was difficult for women to gain a foothold in the upper ranks of the agency's education bureaucracy; although many women became principals of Indian schools, few rose to the rank of superintendent or assistant superintendent. According to Adams, in 1900, out of ninety-nine superintendents in the BIA, only eight were women.[15] Instead, most women labored for little pay under difficult conditions in the schools. As one teacher, Estelle Aubrey Brown, put it:

These women work long years on inadequate salaries on which they must deny themselves, not only of small luxuries, but of essentials. In no other way can they make some small provision for old age. No retirement pay awaits them when they are dismissed for age or ill-health. These underpaid old maids and widows are the vertebrae of the sprawling spinal column which unifies the field service. They are earnest, sincere women: barren, unloved women. They are the privates in the infantry of a bureaucratic army. To them falls the hand-to-hand fighting against odds. They suffer the casualties, receive the wounds.[16]

Many other female Indian Service employees echoed Brown's grim assessment of their work lives and resented their limited roles within the schools.

Australian women who worked in the institutions were also often overcome by the hard work and frustrated by the way the homes were run by male officials. The experience of Ida Standley in establishing and running the Bungalow home in Alice Springs mirrors that of American women who worked for the BIA. According to her official (though muddled) story, Standley originally hailed from Adelaide. Apparently at a very young age she had three daughters and a son, whom she left when she was twenty-four "at the call of duty" to take up reform work. She worked briefly for the South Australia Education Department before she "was loaned to the Federal Government to open the new school at Alice Springs." From 1914 to 1929 she ran the Bungalow for "half-caste" children in Alice Springs while also teaching school to white children. She retired in 1929, allegedly at age thirty-nine, a Sydney newspaper claimed, "to take up her duties as a great-grandmother to the family which she had to leave at the call of duty." She died at the age of forty-four of appendicitis in Darwin in 1934.[17]

This popular narrative of Standley's life is remarkable not only for its assertion that she became a great-grandmother at age thirty-nine, but also because it presents her as giving up the mothering of her own children in order to play a maternal role to Aboriginal children and ostensibly to teach Aboriginal girls proper domesticity and mothering. Perhaps it was because this was done in the name of Christian duty that official accounts withheld any judgment. The unofficial story seems a bit more believable. According to Eileen Park, an Aboriginal woman who grew up at the Bungalow, Standley's grown daughter owned the Stuart Arms Hotel in Alice Springs, and as a child Park used to play with Standley's granddaughter after school.[18] It seems that Standley was quite a bit older when she set out on her "call of duty" and that her family accompanied her.

Given the mystery surrounding Standley's background, we cannot know what motivated her to take off for the Northern Territory, but it was a bold move with or without her family. She may have been exerting an independent streak and seeking a meaningful career, or at least a self-supporting job, in becoming a surrogate mother to dozens of Aboriginal children. Instead, she found low pay and a grueling schedule. She taught white children for four and a half hours every morning and Aboriginal children in the afternoon for one and a half hours. She also supervised the sixty-one Aboriginal children at the Bungalow and their meals. She was given no free days or holidays. Consequently, Standley tried to get transferred in 1925. Instead, from 1925 to 1927 Parliament raised her salary three times. For all their reliance on Standley, authorities also kept nearly as close a watch on her as they did on the Aboriginal girls she supervised. Chief Protector Cook once reprimanded her for going into Alice Springs from the Jay Creek site of the Bungalow (where it was located between 1928 and 1932) without his permission.[19]

Despite these hardships (or maybe in part because of them), many reformers and officials imbued white women's employment with a maternalist sense of mission. Standley's maternalist experience may not have lived up to her hopes, but she did receive accolades for her work. Reporters lauded her for "slaving her life out for those girls." When she retired in 1929 she was made a Member of the British Empire for "spread[ing] a maternal wing about the unwanted half-castes who were in a sorry plight," and a beautiful rocky chasm (or canyon) in the McDonnell Range west of Alice Springs was named for her.[20] Observers frequently mentioned Standley's maternalism; some referred to her as the "mother of Alice Springs," others as "Ma" Standley. One visitor to the Bungalow commented, "One would naturally think Mrs. Standley was a mother of these Halfcaste children of which she has full control, on account of her kindness and motherly love which she has shown towards them." A reporter claimed, "To the native 'boys,' in fact to the entire male population, Mrs. Standley was affectionately known as 'Mum.'"[21]

Eleanor E. Bryan, a matron at the boarding school in Grand Junction, Colorado, elevated her labor in a similar manner:

> There is a higher aim in this great field of labor, and to this I would raise the dignity of matronhood and compare it favorably with that of motherhood. . . . [The mother] is, or should be, the character builder of her child.
>
> So it is with the matrons of our Indian Government schools; she must try to accomplish the same for her Indian girls and boys as the sweet and noble mothers of our land achieve for their children. When a little child at the tender age of 3 or 4 years is taken from its Indian mother, placed within a boarding school, and kept there until he has attained the age of 21, if, during that period, he has been deprived of a good school mother's refining influence and love, he has necessarily missed from his character an additional force he should have known.[22]

Estelle Reel also ennobled women's work within the Indian boarding schools. "The true mother-teacher will strive to secure before all other things the happiness of the children," she encouraged the BIA's women teachers, "for the sunshine of the schoolroom is to them what sunshine is to young plants."[23]

Creating Maternalist Institutions

In the United States, as we have seen, many white women who worked in the schools resented carrying out the difficult day-to-day work in the schools for low pay and little opportunity of advancement while distant male administrators with higher salaries sat in judgment of them. Mary Dissette, for example, while working at Zuni Pueblo in New Mexico, lamented, "The poor teachers have risked their lives daily to help the people while the Agent was in Pueblo, Colorado attending to his banking interests and the Supervising teacher sat in his office chair assisting the clerk with the Agent's office work and writing peremptory letters to these same long suffering little appreciated women."[24]

Some American women thus established their own women-centered maternalist institutions. In fact, Dissette acquired a "commodious house, surrounded with garden and orchard," in Santa Fe, New Mexico, to bring young Indian women to live. She explained, "It is designed that here will be taught cleanliness, the art of plain cooking and housekeeping; simple hand-spinning wheels and looms will be introduced and the making of blankets, rugs and carpets taught by a person competent to the work, the inmates all combining in one large family, a Christian home, thus providing the urgent need of the hour, upon all reservations, support to the returned students from the government schools, and strength to resist the evil influences of reservation life, and the better equipping them for all life's duties."[25]

To many maternalists such as Dissette, who sought to bring indigenous and white women together "in one large family" in "a Christian home," adult men were dispensable; female reformers believed they knew best how to raise the children and run the institutions. Largely critical of patriarchal families, either indigenous or white, they created alternative maternalist institutions that bear a striking resemblance to the maternalist utopia envisioned by one of their contemporaries, the feminist writer Charlotte Perkins Gilman. (In Gilman's *Herland*, no adult men are present, motherhood is deified, and children are raised communally by professional caretakers, freeing up most women to engage in other occupations. Extending motherly values into society at large, Herlanders had eradicated inequality, poverty, and war.)[26] By creating women-centered maternalist institutions, women such as Dissette may have been seeking ways to create autonomous spheres of female influence and authority.

In Australia, where white women reformers endured an even more strained relationship with the state and male-dominated church organizations and reform groups, many white women also sought to create their own maternalist institutions for indigenous children. In Western

Australia, Kate Clutterbuck, a member of the Anglican Sisterhood, established the Parkerville Children's Home, primarily for orphaned white children, in 1903. Forced into retirement in 1933 by a hostile archbishop, Sister Kate then established a home for "half-caste" children that later become known as Queen's Park Children's Home (or simply, Sister Kate's).

With her focus on providing motherly care to Aboriginal children in a home-like setting, Sister Kate developed a maternalist institution, run only by women and attracting the attentions of white women in the community. Women's groups in Western Australia wrote approvingly of Sister Kate and the other women who worked with her. One woman proclaimed, "What wonderful women they are, mothering and loving all who come their way."[27] A local group, the League of Women Helpers, visited the home weekly, bringing special treats for the children or hosting parties. Girl Guides and women's religious organizations also became involved. Mary Durack, an author and a member of a prominent pastoralist family, also took a personal interest in Sister Kate's. The home did not openly exclude men; several adult men who had once been orphans in Sister Kate's Parkerville home routinely helped out there, as did men associated with several Western Australian newspapers. Nevertheless, Sister Kate and her associates created a woman-centered place where they could enact their maternalist ideals.[28] For Sister Kate, Ruth Lefroy, and other white women who worked in the home, working with Aboriginal children and other white women appeared to provide a satisfying alternative to life in a conventional patriarchal marriage. And despite the many power imbalances that existed between the white women and the Aboriginal children in their care, we might also view such institutions as attempts to create viable interracial communities that few other whites were interested in at the time.

The ability of white Australian women to work independently of the state in carrying out their maternalist agenda was limited, however, as we saw in the case of Annie Lock. From the very beginning, Sister Kate's mission became inextricably entangled with Chief Protector Neville's. In 1934 she told a leader of the Women's Service Guilds (WSG) that she and her long-time associate, Ruth Lefroy, "really wanted to go up the Country & take the poorest and most degraded of the poor Native children." However, "Mr. Neville was anxious we should start a Home for Quarter Caste children so that they could be removed from the native camps." Sister Kate brought "nearly 50 half caste children" to Parkerville, but, she told the WSG leader, "It is not the work we really want to do but are assured by Mr. Neville it is wanted most."[29] Neville used Sister Kate's Home primarily as an institution for lighter-skinned children from the Moore River (or Mogumber) Native Settlement.

For a time Neville's needs and aims coincided nicely with Sister Kate's mission. He stood to gain enormously from her work. Although his department paid a "maintenance" fee for each child (which was far below the fee paid for white children in state care), he did not have to pay wages to Sister Kate or the other women who worked in her home. Moreover, Sister Kate raised her own money to build new cottages and other buildings to house more Aboriginal children, all at no expense to Neville.[30]

Gradually, however, a tense relationship developed between Sister Kate's Home and Neville's department. The chief protector and Sister Kate often clashed over whether she could admit other children that he had not sent to her. She also continually did battle with Neville over increasing the maintenance for her children, arguing that her children's amount should be the same as that of white children in orphanages.[31] When Neville refused her requests, she had to find a way to make up the difference between the meager maintenance and the actual cost of caring for the children. Sister Kate came to resent that she and other women of the home were contributing their labor with no charge to Neville's department, yet he was unwilling to give them adequate support for the children. In 1939 she wrote to Neville, "I have given my money and myself to help the cause of these children and it seems very hard that now when I am old that I should die in debt." Neville recoiled at the letter and asserted that the department would eventually have to take charge of the home. Given his dictatorial ways, Sister Kate's associate, Ruth Lefroy, believed that a board should advise and "if necessary . . . control [Neville]. [It] is too much for any human being to have absolute control . . . over 50 or 60,000 human beings."[32]

Perhaps because of their experiences with Neville, Sister Kate and Lefroy often contrasted their daily, intimate work for Aboriginal children with that of the more distant administrative work of male authorities. Lefroy, for example, writing a letter to the editor of the *West Australian* to set the record straight on the origins of Sister Kate's home, asserted, "Anybody with money can put up fine buildings, but very few can build up children's characters. That is Sister Kate's abiding work, which will bear fruit not only among the 800 children she has already reared or trained in the home, but also among their descendants long after the last building in Parkerville Home has crumbled into dust."[33]

As part of their claim to creating better institutions through their maternal qualities, many white women reformers made similar claims, often asserting that they had created more home-like institutions for removed indigenous children. Many such women believed that dormitories could not re-create a proper home and so promoted the "cottage system" instead. Acting on a proposal by Alice Fletcher, Hampton Institute in Virginia enacted a unique and experimental system; from 1882 to 1891 it introduced cottage housing for married Indian couples and their children. Overall twenty-three families participated in the program, including two Winnebago couples, six Omaha families, and fifteen Lakota couples, eventually living in cottages the Indian husbands themselves helped to build. Many of the couples were already active missionaries within their home communities. Hampton's program was one of a kind and short-lived; it failed to live up to the expectations of its initiators (with only one student actually graduating from Hampton and almost half leaving Hampton after less than a year in the program), and administrators phased out the program and turned the cottages into demonstration homes to teach Indian girls how to keep house.[34]

More commonly, those schools that enacted a cottage system followed a maternalist model: each cottage included one white woman who tended to a small group of Indian children. Miss Worden of the Santee Mission School in Nebraska, for example, claimed in 1893, "The first thing . . . that impresses the children when they come to us is that they come to a home. We have five cottages where the pupils live. Each one of these is presided over by a Christian woman."[35] White women reformers also reasoned that such cottages would provide better training for Indian girls. After visiting Booker T. Washington's Tuskegee Institute in 1906, Estelle Reel promoted Tuskegee's "practice cottages" for Indian girls at Indian schools.[36]

Sister Kate utilized a similar cottage system that she believed provided a more humane institution for Aboriginal children. She told a newspaper reporter, "There is not a trace of institution life here."[37] The *West Australian* characterized Sister Kate's first brand-new cottage home as "almost stark in its newness, yet radiating, already, after a fortnight, a 'homey atmosphere.'" The newspaper lauded Sister Kate's cottages: "This is the first of many she hopes to establish for the little dark-skinned sons and daughters of Western Australia—the quarter-caste and half-caste children who do not belong in the squalid atmosphere of native camps, but, when taken from them are given nothing in return for mother love, except, perhaps regular food, clothing and an inadequate education. These are the children who, like the octoroons of the Northern Territory . . . might develop into useful citizens if placed under proper care." With a not-so-veiled criticism of Neville's institutions, the newspaper represented Sister Kate's as a better alternative, where the staff treated the children as a "family" and gave them "a touch of real home life, endowed with love, personal interest in their well-being, and a sincere desire that they should have the best that life has to offer them." The paper further asserted, "These affectionate children . . . are blossoming into a natural, happy childhood in the sunshine of Sister Kate's unique personality—these little Australians who have made the wonderful discovery that somebody wants them after all."[38]

We cannot really know from white women reformers' pronouncements or journalists' hyperbole whether the women's efforts to create maternalist institutions did in fact result in providing a more loving, home-like environment for removed indigenous children. We must turn instead to indigenous people's experiences and accounts to assess these efforts. Certainly Hampton's family cottage system, no matter what its intentions, actually allowed Indian parents to reunite with their children. In 1885 Daniel and Emma Fire Cloud from the Crow Creek Agency arrived at Hampton to live in a cottage and to join their two sons there. "The joy of these little ones on being told that their father and mother would soon be with them was most touching and the meeting between the long separated parents and children was a scene not easily forgotten," wrote the *Southern Workman*, the school's newspaper.[39] Yet even being present at the school could not shield Indian parents from one of the most tragic aspects of the boarding school experience. As the scholars Roger Buffalohead and Paulette Fairbanks Molin discovered, "Six of the Indian children associated with the model family program at Hampton died at the school," including one of Daniel and Emma Fire Cloud's sons. Parents too succumbed to disease; at least twenty-four parents left the school due to contracting tuberculosis, and "over half of the adults from the model family program died within a few years of their return home."[40]

Some Indian accounts and surviving letters reveal that white women did become "like mothers" to some Indian children, and the institutions did become their "homes." Howard Kirchazzy, for example, who joined the navy in 1921 and lost track of his Indian family, told his former teacher Gertrude Golden, "You seemed a mother to me at school, that which I've never known to this day. The way you tried to teach me at school."[41] Alice Awa, a Hopi girl at Keams Canyon Boarding School, wrote to her former teacher, Laura Dandridge, who had been fired (see chapter 9), to tell her how all the girls cried when they found out Dandridge had left. Awa called her "Mother Dandridge" and ended her letter by saying, "I love you the best and I always think you are my own mother."[42]

As Awa's poignant letter suggests, although many white women may have sought to provide motherly care within home-like institutions, they often could not fulfill their ideals or the expectations they had created among indigenous children. As we saw with Annie Lock and Betsy in chapter 5, this could be extremely painful and confusing to the children. Emma Chooro, a Hopi girl, also wrote to Dandridge: "Dear mother . . . I never can forget you, so I am still feeling bad all the time yet, and here Miss Anderson is going away that she made me feel worse again. It seems like every body is going to leave this place that I cries when I think of it. . . . I wish I was with you. At night we'll be feeling bad when we are getting ready for bed when we think of how we[']ll be crowding around in your room."[43] Even if white women did ennoble their work in institutions with a higher maternalist purpose, their positions within the institutions were ultimately jobs, jobs that they could (and often did) leave or jobs from which they could be (and often were) transferred or fired. Here again white women had forged new intimacies with indigenous children, intimacies that they could not always sustain to the expectation and satisfaction of the children they cared for.

Other Indian children felt no affection for their women teachers. Lame Deer declared that his teacher at boarding school was "a mean old lady," and he sought to harass her at every turn. "I once threw a live chicken at her like a snowball," he recalled. On another occasion he "fixed an inkpot in such a way that it went up in her face." The harsh corporal punishment Lame Deer received did nothing to deter him.[44]

In Australia some indigenous inmates experienced none of the maternal nurturing reformers and officials claimed that white women would render their charges. "Del," a young Aboriginal woman who worked for Joan Kingsley Strack as a domestic servant in the 1930s, described the matron at Cootamundra as viciously cruel to the young inmates; she "beat them with sticks & whips & blackened their eyes" so severely that the cook at the Home contacted the police.[45]

Others remembered their matrons in more positive terms. Many former residents of the Bungalow recalled Ida Standley fondly. Clarence Smith, who lived at the Bungalow until sent out to a cattle station at

17. Children and staff at the Bungalow, Alice Springs, Northern Territory, 1928. The figure with the hat in the center of the back row appears to be Ida Standley. CRS A263; 6a, National Archives of Australia, Canberra, Australian Capital Territory.

age twelve, asserted that Standley was a "very nice lady."[46] Eileen Park told her interviewer, "We all learned to love Mrs Standley. She was like a mother to us as well as a teacher; she was a beautiful woman."[47] Yet interviewees said very little specifically about Standley.

Former inmates of the Bungalow differed in their assessment of the institution as a "home." For Eileen Park, the Bungalow did become her home, and Standley and the other children her family. Park told her interviewer that she was never lonely: "There [were] so many children there, we weren't lonely at all."[48] For other inmates, the Bungalow was a miserable environment. Emily Liddle recounted that the Bungalow at Jay Creek "wasn't even fit for a dog to live in, in those days. . . . it was just concrete floor, no beds, one big shed was built there." She remembered, "At night time we used to get no mattress—only blankets to sleep on. We used to put all the stools up and we used to sleep on those concrete floor[s]."[49] Others commented on the lack of any real education despite Standley's purported efforts. Clarence Smith remarked, "The schooling was very poor," as children were in school for only about one and a half hours a day.[50]

There is much evidence that Sister Kate's home differed in many ways from some of the other institutions to which Aboriginal children were taken. At least until the 1940s, Sister Kate did not believe in cutting off all contact between the children and their birth families, and she tried to keep siblings together. Ken Colbung remembers that Sister Kate allowed his aunts and uncles from Moore River to come visit him: "She'd invite them to come any time [but] Native Welfare didn't like them coming. Wouldn't give them permits to travel to visit, see?" Gradually, however, because she wanted the children to be able to pass for white when they left her home, Sister Kate came to feel that it was inadvisable to allow children to see their relatives.[51]

Sister Kate also sometimes did battle with local whites who looked down on the Aboriginal children. Colbung recalls that when Sister Kate took the children into the city, they were not allowed to use "white" toilets. "But when you were with her you'd be alright . . . she'd take you up to the lavatory . . . and she'd stand there . . . no-one dared say anything . . . Miss Lefroy, too." Sister Kate also advocated that the children should attend the public school near the home, a scheme that many officials and white parents throughout Australia strongly opposed. To her credit, she was successful in placing her children in the state school beginning in 1934.[52]

Some indigenous people did look on Sister Kate as their mother or grandmother and agreed that she had indeed created a loving home environment. Gerald Warber, removed at age two to Sister Kate's, regarded her as "mum to her children" and highly praised Ruth Lefroy, whom he called "Friend." He declared, "I think as far as she could, she and Ruth Lefroy gave us as wonderful an upbringing as any kid could [get] under the circumstances." Sister Kate "was very loving" and "devoted to the children." The housemother, on the other hand, "didn't have that motherly quality," and, according to Warber and many other interviewees, life at the home deteriorated after Sister Kate's death in

1946 and Lefroy's in 1953.[53] Other indigenous people who grew up at Sister Kate's did not have such pleasant memories. Although Hilda Evans portrays Sister Kate as a "lovely person," she claims that she was distant from the daily running of the home. She asserts, like Warber, that the housemothers at Sister Kate's were cruel, dishing out "beltings" and confining girls in a "linen press" where there was "not much breathing space."[54]

Curiously, perhaps, most indigenous autobiographies and oral histories have little to say, good or bad, about the white women who cared for or taught the children in institutions. Understaffed as most of the institutions were, white women actually had limited contact with the children. No matter what their intentions, they rarely had the opportunity to re-create intimate home-like settings where they played a motherly role to the indigenous children in their care. More often indigenous people's memories of institutional life focus on peers and the indigenous staff members who worked in some of the homes, missions, and schools.

What stands out among interviews of children who lived under Standley's care at the Bungalow, for example, is the frequency with which they mention other Aboriginal women who lived and worked there. Ada Wade, who was taken at age six with her mother to the Bungalow in 1914 and lived there until she was sent out to domestic service at age eleven, reminisced in her interview not about Standley, but about her own mother's role in the running of the Bungalow. According to Wade, "[My mother] cooked for us, worked for us, do the sewing for us, dress us, look after us when we were sick. Everybody's kids. Brought one child in when the mother died—about a fortnight old—and fed her with her own breast, as well as her own little son. Anyone'd think she had twins." Her mother kept goats, too, and fed the children with them. Unlike Standley, who was paid (if meagerly) for her work, Wade's mother "never got a penny out of it." "She only done it for goodwill."[55]

Emily Liddle recounted the work of her Aunt Hettie, who served as both cook and teacher. Rather than Standley or another white woman,

Emily remembers, "[Auntie Hettie] used to teach the girls how to do things properly. She had more patience I think . . . than the matrons. She used to teach us how you are to do things the proper way. . . . That's where we learned a lot of it—how to set bread, how to cook bread, do things around the house and clean up the cupboards, and wash clothes the proper way and iron it properly."[56] In official and popular accounts of Standley and the Bungalow, the presence of Aboriginal women like Wade's mother and Hettie is erased. Perhaps Standley and others regarded them merely as helpers or servants, handmaidens to the real "mother" of the house, Ida Standley. The prominence of these Aboriginal women, and not Standley, in the oral histories of former residents of the Bungalow suggests, however, that such women played key but largely invisible roles in the institutions.

Similarly, in the girls' dormitory at Cherbourg, Ruth Hegarty lived in fear of the white matron, who "always carried a small whip around with her (the sort that jockeys use)," but "had great admiration" for three "aunts"—Mattie, Connie, and Mabel—who "had spent the better part of their lives in the dormitory." Mattie and Connie worked as cooks in the girls' dormitories, and all three aunts took the little girls (if they had behaved well) on occasional bush walks. Hegarty reveled in these outings, especially when they collected gum from the eucalyptus trees, visited local farms, or went swimming in nearby creeks. The matron remains an unidentified menacing presence in Hegarty's memoir, but the aunts emerge as important mentors to the girls.[57]

Some Indian women appear to have played a similar role in the Indian boarding schools. In 1906, under the administration of Commissioner of Indian Affairs Francis Leupp, the BIA hired Angel DeCora, a Winnebago (or Ho Chunk) artist, to teach art at Carlisle. DeCora had been removed herself to Hampton Institute. Her interest in art led her to study at the Burnham Classical School for Girls, to the Smith College Art Department for four years, to Drexel Institute in Philadelphia to study with the renowned illustrator Howard Pyle for over two years, and on to Boston, where she studied first at the Cowles Art School and then at the Museum of Fine Arts. DeCora first opened a studio in Boston and then in New York, where she engaged in portraiture, landscape painting, illustration, and design, which she found to be "a more lucrative branch of art" and "the best channel in which to convey the native qualities of the Indian's decorative talent."[58]

Once hired by Carlisle, DeCora sought to infuse the curriculum with a respect for Indian experience. "The educators seem to expect an Indian to leave behind him all his heritage of tribal training," she declared, "and in the course of five years or more to take up and excel in an entirely new line of thought in mental and industrial training whose methods are wholly foreign to him. An Indian's self-respect is undermined when he is told that his native customs and crafts are no longer of any use because they are the habits and pastimes of the crude man."[59] DeCora spoke somewhat from experience. She told the Lake Mohonk Conference in 1895, "I went first to the reservation school, but I must confess that I spent a good deal of my time there running away. If they had taught me drawing, I do not think I should have run away."[60]

Having experienced the pain of removal herself as well as the denigration of her culture, DeCora sought to compensate for the hardships young indigenous children faced. "I found one of the necessary things to do," DeCora later told a meeting of the Friends of the Indian, "was to impress upon the minds of my pupils that they were Indians, possessing native abilities that had never been recognized in the curriculum of the Government schools." She designed a course of study that would introduce students to the art work of each tribe. "Here in the school," she asserted, "nearly every Indian tribe is represented, and each one contributes his share of artistic thought, and the ones who have been deprived of the home training by reason of having been sent away to school so young have the chance to learn from the more talented ones of the class."[61] Not all of indigenous children's relationships with their peers and older indigenous staff were positive, as we saw in chapter 6, but the presence of indigenous women on the staff, such as Hettie at the Bungalow and DeCora at Carlisle, could soften the blow of removal and institutionalization, and often these older women became more influential mentors to indigenous children than the white women charged with their uplift.

Mothering in a New Home

A focus on whether white women created home-like institutions and provided indigenous children with motherly care is not sufficient to understanding the nature of these institutions. "Home" and "mothering," as I explored in chapter 3, are not enacted or experienced the same way across time, space, and culture.[62] In the new homes to which indigenous children were brought, as examined in the previous chapter, authorities endeavored to radically transform the children's bodies and how they experienced the world through them. As part of this effort, many white women teachers and matrons identified the transformation of indigenous gender roles as a key component of the children's resocialization.

Believing that indigenous boys had been taught to oppress women, the teachers and matrons labored to change boys' as well as girls' behavior. Writing of the mission home at Ooldea in South Australia, Violet Turner claimed that newly arrived Aboriginal boys resented having to cart water from the well to the house because they saw it as "woman's work." "No man ever carried water in the bush, and when these boys were asked to carry water for the Home girls to use for their washing they were highly indignant," she asserted. But the boys apparently learned their new roles when they "heard the missionary speak to his wife as to an equal, and saw him actually lift a burden for her, and open a door for her, though she was of the sex they had always looked on as the burden-bearers."[63] Miss Shepard, a teacher among Geronimo's band of Chiricahua Apaches who were imprisoned at Mt. Vernon, Alabama, promoted the idea that boys should guard girls' honor. "One striking instance of the new light thrown upon the young Indian's life by these teachers," she wrote, "is the formation among the older boys of a guard of honor for the girls. . . . This is a true order of chivalry, and shines out upon the dark background of the ordinary savage contempt for women."[64]

White women believed they were uplifting indigenous women by sparing them hard physical labor, such as carrying water. In the United States the schools ignored Indian women's traditional roles in farming, and instead insisted that men take up the plow and the hoe. At the same time as this potentially emasculated Indian men, it threatened Indian women's crucial economic and social role and their independence. White women in the schools instead promoted "protection" for indigenous women by "a guard of honor" of boys, a "true order of chivalry."

Ironically, given that they wished to evade male protection and embraced an alternative, woman-centered family, many of the white women who worked in the institutions identified the patriarchal home—with men as breadwinners and women as domestic dependents—as the foundation of their efforts to transform indigenous gender roles. "For almost the first time in the history of government dealings with the Indian," Estelle Reel wrote, "there is now a serious attempt made to foster in the wild red soul the instinct for a fixed home, a home that the male Indian must maintain by his own labor, while the female Indian keeps the house and makes the home. When you can make a young Indian feel that he must support his family or do without one, you've got him for civilization."[65]

Indeed, in the United States, where officials expected Indian children to eventually return to their communities, women teachers, matrons, and reformers put an inordinate amount of emphasis on transforming Indian girls' conceptions of and experiences of the home. Once the home was transformed, the women believed, Indian children would learn the rudiments of the new civilized order and other aspects of civilization would follow. "The first thought to impress upon the [Indian] mind is this," Reel wrote in the *Uniform Course of Study*, "a home is not a home unless it be a permanent abiding place and a house. . . . It must be governed by habits of neatness, promptness, and order." She counseled Indian teachers to "develop the thought that the child's first lessons in vice or virtue are learned in the home."[66]

18. Girls at the Mescalero Apache Reservation playing with their dolls, wickiups, and
tepees. Within their own communities, Indian girls learned how to care for children
and homes, but to many white women maternalists, Indian notions of domesticity were
deficient. New Mexico State University Library, Archives and Special Collections, MS 110,
RG 81–38.

19. Indian girls at Santa Fe Indian School, ca. 1904. With proper cradles for their dolls, these girls are learning white maternalists' notions of how to be good mothers. Courtesy of Palace of Governors (Museum of New Mexico/DCA), Negative #1035.

By installing indigenous women in the home and investing them with the responsibilities for introducing and maintaining a new order, white women believed they were elevating indigenous women to a privileged position. Mrs. Mead declared to the Lake Mohonk Conference in 1898, "I have been intensely interested in the Indian home question, because it is the woman that makes the home and exalts the family." She added, "Until we reach the Indian woman in her tepee, until we rouse her aesthetic and moral nature, and develop her mental power, we shall never have an Indian civilization worthy of the name of humanity."[67]

White women reformers often claimed that they could transform indigenous homes and thereby solve the so-called Indian or Aboriginal problem simply by teaching removed girls middle-class domestic skills. "We cannot lay too much emphasis on the value to these girls of learning cooking and nursing," Miss Worden of the Santee School told the Lake Mohonk Conference. "When they learn to understand these things, their home life will be revolutionized. The telling work must be done in the homes, and the women have the most important part of the home life to see to. When you get a woman to understand that it is her highest duty in this world to take care of her family and home in a Christian and intelligent manner, you have got near the heart of the matter."[68]

Some native students became converts to such sentiments and took up the white woman's burden. Elizabeth Bender (tribe unidentified) declared, "[The] unkempt homes [of Indian families] are breeding places for filth and disease." She queried readers of the Carlisle publication, *The Redman*, "Can we expect to develop great, strong Christian leaders in spite of such home conditions?" Her answer: "Yes, we can. We can take our youth away from home, send them off to such schools as Haskell, Carlisle, or Hampton for a period of years, give them an even better education than these now offer, and have them associate with high minded instructors who shall teach that the home is the very core of any civilization, that the ideal home shall permeate its environment and bring it into keeping with that of their school. When we shall have done this no girl will be ashamed of her people or disgusted with her lot." Given domestic training, Bender believed, the Indian girl "will look upon her lot as a sacred calling and appreciate the dignity and nobility of labor." Invoking a cliché, Bender declared, "As no people advance any faster than their women and the home is conceded to be the core of the Indian problem, my plea is that these Indian girls should receive a fair chance."[69]

Not all Indian girls accepted this new domestic order so readily. When the Lakota girl Zitkala-Ša was punished for disobeying a rule by being sent to the kitchen to mash turnips for dinner, she took her revenge: "I took the wooden tool that the paleface woman held out to me. I stood upon a step, and, grasping the handle with both hands, I bent in hot rage over the turnips. I worked my vengeance upon them." When the white woman came to retrieve the turnips, "the pulpy contents fell through the crumbled bottom to the floor!" Later, as Zitkala-Ša sat eating her dinner, she recalled, "I whooped in my heart for having once asserted the rebellion within me."[70]

Not all American women reformers subscribed to the tenet of maternalism that indigenous girls should be taught domestic skills merely to improve their homes. Some white women, acting on their own experience of work, sought to impart valuable skills to indigenous girls and women so they could support themselves. Sybil Carter, for example, a southern white woman who had been left destitute by the Civil War, sought to train adult indigenous women to make lace: "This is what we must do for our Indian sisters. We must give them industries and let them work for wages."[71] She elaborated, "I go after the women, and . . . I preach to them that a woman who does not work neither shall she eat. . . . I put it to her plainly that it is their duty to work, that I have spent money and time and a great many prayers that they may learn to be industrious, and to be clean and sweet and pure."[72]

In reality, much of the domestic training of Indian girls did, indeed, aim at preparing them for wage work—primarily as domestic servants in white women's homes, as shall be explored in the following chapter. Estelle Reel told a reporter in 1899, "In one school in southern California the Indian girls are being taught cooking, and already they have turned out a large number of efficient cooks. The demand for these Indian servants is very great in southern California and Arizona, and indeed the supply is not equal to the demand."[73] White women reformers did not regard the training of Indian girls as servants to be at odds with their loftier goals of sending the girls back to their communities as civilization's revolutionary agents. Instead, they rationalized the girls' domestic service as another means of training them to maintain a proper home.

In contrast to this ubiquitous rhetoric of transforming the home life of Indian girls, white women reformers, missionaries, and matrons in

Australia rarely expressed such sentiments regarding Aboriginal girls. Institutions for Aboriginal children more blatantly focused on training girls for service—to make them "useful"—and seemed uninterested in the girls' long-term prospects.

In both American and Australian institutions, white women caretakers were interested in transforming, or at least controlling indigenous girls' bodies, and, as explored in chapter 3, closely linked proper homes with proper bodies.[74] As the historian Nancy Rose Hunt has argued, "Colonial domesticity, as a discursive field and thus a realm of social practice, was often indistinguishable from colonial hygiene." She found that in the Belgian Congo, hygiene became a "colonywide enterprise to remake, sanitize, and discipline native space, homes, gender and sexual relations, and eating and elimination practices."[75]

White women envisioned the ideal female body first and foremost as clean, a word that signified not just being free from dirt, but being free of disease and being virginal, Christian, and industrious. Cleanliness was more than a physical condition; it also entailed a new way of thinking, acting, and appearing in the world. After living at a boarding school for a number of years, some indigenous children internalized such prescriptions. For example, Margaret Beauregard, a Chippewa who attended Chilocco, wrote in the WNIA's journal, "Cleanliness, in the home and of the body, is essential to keep a family well and happy, and so you will always find the true woman looking after the sanitary condition of her home. . . . The husband, as I see it, is the one to go out and make the living, and the wife or mother tries to be as saving as possible and yet not stingy." She added, "The husband and the wife, together, should take the responsibility of training the children to be good, clean, moral, upright, God-fearing men and women, but too often this duty is left for the wife and mother to perform. How very essential, then, that the women should be clean in thought, word, and deed."[76]

American white women also stressed the need for new forms of dress that they believed would help to clean and protect indigenous women and be more suitable to their transformed role within the home. Indian women who had worn loose clothing that was adapted to their work of growing and gathering food also needed to be fitted into more appropriate attire. Some of the new clothing promoted as cleaner and more healthful actually imposed new restrictions on indigenous women's movement, and was even opposed by women's dress reform advocates. For example, Walter West, a Southern Ute Reservation superintendent, requested funds from the government in 1916 to buy corsets for Indian girls to improve the "general health and appearance of the girls."[77] White women reformers and male officials believed that by altering the girls' bodies, they could civilize them. A Carlisle publication boasted, for example, that due to boarding school education, "the clear-eyed, intelligent, clean-limbed, progressive, and talented Indian woman of today is as different from the humble, plodding, dull-eyed squaw of the Western plains in days agone as is the 'finishing school' graduate from the women who followed the Forty-Niners to California."[78]

In Australia many white women were equally concerned with indigenous girls' bodies but less confident in their ability to transform them. They believed that fundamental bodily differences existed between white and Aboriginal women that could never be rectified through environmental or cosmetic changes. Thus, to many white Australian women, Aboriginal children who had some "white blood" had different bodies than "full-blood" Aborigines. Violet Turner, for example, regarded half-caste girls such as "Eva" as "too frail for the rough, hard existence of a native camp. . . . The native children's thick skulls could withstand the heat, but Eva's more delicate European descent required shelter and care."[79] Nevertheless, like their American counterparts, Australian white women evinced great concern with controlling Aboriginal girls' bodies.

Monitoring Girls

Transforming indigenous girls' bodies to conform to white ideals and "keeping them clean" required careful monitoring of and "protection" of the girls' sexuality. Daisy Bates believed that "the half-caste problem should be more firmly grasped." She contended, "A diary of the women and girls movements should always be kept at mission and institution." Bates asserted, "I have kept such a diary through all the years of my work amongst the groups and this has been a great help in lessening the caste menace."[80] The institutions readily put their own systems of surveillance into place. Ruth Hegarty remembered that at Cherbourg, "to keep the dormitory girls and women from sneaking out to meet their boyfriends, a six-foot high barbed wire fence was strung around the dormitory, with very thorny rambling roses growing on it." To further guard the girls, at night authorities locked the doors and employed native police to patrol the dormitories. Moreover, before bed each night, matrons required the girls to take off all their clothing, put on white nightgowns, and "lift their nighties in the light of a torch or lantern to reveal that [they] had nothing on underneath."[81]

Alice Fletcher kept tabs on Indian women once they returned to their reservations after boarding school to make sure they continued to adhere to white bodily standards. She utilized white contacts who lived among the Omahas, including Rosalie La Flesche's husband, Ed Farley, to monitor newly returned students, even other members of his wife's family. In 1885 Farley wrote to Fletcher that Philip La Flesche and his bride, Minnie, were building a house with funds from Sara Kinney and the Connecticut Women's Indian Association. "They both said it was so hard to live the way they had to live after their life at Hampton," Farley told Fletcher. He reported that Minnie had digressed from the bodily norms taught at Hampton: "Minnie is two shades darker since I saw her last spring but no wonder having to live in a tent when out here, she will bleach out when she has a house of her own to live in." Farley also reported that Minnie was wearing her hair in braids rather than pinned up. He assured Fletcher, "I told her how you wanted them to do when they live in their house."[82]

This letter is revealing on a number of counts. Both Fletcher and Farley seemed to believe that living in a wooden frame house (not a tent or tepee) could "bleach out" Indian women. American women reformers inextricably linked the adoption of Western-style housing to changes in the body. Both were worried that Minnie, by virtue of not living in a proper home and reverting to Indian bodily fashions, might go back to her "uncivilized" ways of living and thinking. This letter reveals the intense scrutiny that Indian people endured under the gaze of white women who sought to monitor and manage many details of their intimate lives.

Much of white women's concerns with indigenous girls' bodies and their sexuality centered around menstruation. The onset of menses was a point of pride and honor within many of the girls' indigenous communities; many groups held (and still hold) special puberty ceremonies for girls that involve physically and mentally challenging rituals that emphasize their fitness for adulthood.[83] In the institutions, however, a girl's first menses became a source of shame and mystery. When Ruth Hegarty got her period and was accompanied by a friend to see the matron about it, the matron simply handed her a sanitary belt and six flanelette rags. "For a moment," Hegarty remembers, "I thought I would get some instructions but . . . all she said was: 'Take care of them, you'll not get any more.'" Hegarty relied on other girls to teach her how to use and keep clean her new supplies. She learned nothing from the matron about sexuality and reproduction. When she was discovered watching a cat giving birth in a washroom, Hegarty was "told [she] was dirty and made to sit in a corner for the afternoon."[84] For many indigenous girls, accustomed to puberty ceremonies and other important rites of passage, the white women's way of teaching about hygiene but not about reproduction was a particularly significant step in disengaging girls from the important socialization offered by their families and communities.

Signs of a girl's period also went from being a cause for celebration to becoming yet another aspect of an Indian girl's body that had to be closely monitored. Ruth Roessel remembered that at the dormitory at Fort Wingate Boarding School, "the matrons had a book with every girl's name in it, so that when each girl had her period they would mark it down. In this way they kept track of each girl's period, and if one missed her period they would know about it and they would call the girl in and ask what happened."[85]

Despite this system of monitoring, white women's attempts to control the sexuality of young Indian women often proved unsuccessful. Roessel, for example, recalls the following episode:

One morning, when I was in about the eighth grade, I remember the matrons called all the girls together and said there would be an inspection. They would do this whenever something was wrong—that is, bring all the girls together. It was after breakfast, and the girls were told to line up. The girls who were thirteen years or younger were told they could leave. Because I was one of those younger girls I did not have to stay there, but I did.

The matrons told the girls that no one could leave until they found out who had the baby which they had found in the bathroom that morning. Someone had left a new-born baby in the toilet bowl, and they were trying to find out whose it was. . . .

. . . One of the girls admitted that the baby was hers; so they let the others girls go. . . .

. . . I never did learn what happened to the baby.[86]

Incidences of Indian girls becoming pregnant, and sometimes killing their newborns in a desperate attempt to escape shame and punishment, seem to have been all too common in the boarding schools. Gertrude Golden witnessed an incident when she worked as the principal at Fort Defiance. Ada, the oldest girl in the 1915 graduating class, had returned from a summer among her family members "like a different girl, not her cheerful, friendly self."

About a month before the closing of school, and our graduating exercise, Ada appeared in line for breakfast one morning looking very white and weak. The assistant matron noticed her and helped the girl back to bed. The doctor who called a little later immediately saw what had happened, although the poor girl denied vigorously that she had given birth to a child in the night. Examination of her trunk revealed a dead infant, newborn. Then, and only then, did Ada give way. She confessed fully, telling what had happened during the summer at the home of her cousin and how she had suffered during the following months in an effort to conceal her condition. She had tried to stop the cries of the child and, in doing so, had choked it to death.

Golden blamed the matron, whom she believed had "plainly neglected her duty, or she would have been alert to Ada's condition and at least saved her from the crime she committed." Ada transferred to another school but died within the year of consumption.[87]

To avoid such tragedies, once young indigenous women reached what white women regarded as a marriageable age, the women sought to contain and channel their sexuality into an appropriate (that is, Christian) marriage. Officials had long sought to usurp the indigenous family's role in arranging marriages. In both nations authorities believed securing a respectable Christian spouse for their charges in a proper Christian marriage was key to promoting assimilation and preventing reversion to primitive ways. For example, the Indian agent James McLaughlin of the Standing Rock Agency in Dakota Territory declared, "In our own school we have always taken the position that . . . we will not allow one of our school girls to be sold by her parents, or to marry one who had never been to school. It is not difficult to manage." He added, "We knew the only hope for the girls was in marrying them to some of our educated and civilized young men. If they returned to the camp, they would return to their Indian life." McLaughlin rewarded (or bribed) those who married in Christian fashion with 160 acres, wagons, and cattle.[88]

In Australia, in addition to the "breeding-out-the-colour" schemes of Chief Protectors Cook and Neville, Bishop F. X. Gsell, based at the Catholic Bathurst Island Mission, proudly dubbed himself the "Bishop with 150 Wives." Between 1921 and 1938 Gsell allegedly bought

150 girls to prevent them from being betrothed to elderly men in their group. He brought the girls to the mission to be raised and aggressively pursued any girls who ran away or were taken back by tribal members.[89] Elsie Roughsey, a Lardil woman who grew up with missionaries at Mornington Island in Queensland, explained how the male missionary there sought to control Aboriginal marriage:

> Marriage was arranged and agreed on in several ways. The young man might express to the Missionary his desire to marry a certain young woman. Then the Missionary, if this seemed suitable to him, . . . would tell the girl. The girls apparently had the privilege of refusing, but rarely did. While right-head or straight-head marriages were part of the Lardil tradition, there were probably not more than eight dormitory girls who married men according to their traditional kinship rule. . . . The Missionary decided when his charges were of marriageable age, and that a couple had some qualities that might make them compatible mates. He then arranged the union of the young man and woman.[90]

White women, too, sought to control the marriage of indigenous girls. Sister Kate, for all her conflict with Chief Protector Neville, seems to have shared his penchant for racial engineering. In one letter to Neville she opposed the marriages of "quadroons" to one another, hoping instead that the girls would marry white men.[91] Missionary women at the Home in Ooldea in South Australia attempted to prevent Myra, living at the home but betrothed since infancy to an older man with three wives, from marrying him. When she turned sixteen, her parents came to take her from Ooldea. The missionaries believed it was for the purpose of marriage and confronted her parents, telling them Myra would not go. Then a boy at the mission, Walter, proposed to Myra. When a missionary presented this to her parents, they became angry and said "they would never allow their daughter to marry a *boy* (with scornful emphasis on the word). She must marry a *man*." The parents also objected because Walter had refused to go through with initiation and was therefore ineligible to marry. "It was a fight for the happiness of many other girls besides Myra," Violet Turner asserted. "Were other babies to be given in betrothal to old men, and were young girls to be forced into hated marriages for all time?"[92]

White women in the United States also sought to control the marriage choices of the Indian girls they "protected." For example, missionaries at Ganado among the Navajos were upset when a girl they had adopted, Grace Segar, went home on vacation at age sixteen. According to a missionary, "Her relatives used every effort to reinduct her into heathenism and to marry her to a heathen man. They kept her in hiding for a year and a half and tried every expedient they could think of to keep her from getting back among Christian people." After eighteen months of her seclusion, the missionaries "secured her release and she completed her education." Furthermore, the missionaries found a suitable mate for Grace Segar. "The greatest joy that [Ganado] has known in the past summer is that we are able to keep our young people until they form those attachments which result in marriage and the establishment of Christian homes."[93] Thus white women sought to supplant the authority of the indigenous family and community in regulating marriages. Notice too that white women routinely positioned themselves as the ones whose children had been taken. In this case, Grace Segar's family "kept her in hiding" and it was missionaries who "secured her release."

Although white women couched their concerns for indigenous women in terms of rescue and uplift, there is a strong hint of a desire for control in their remonstrances. Critical of the patriarchy of Aboriginal societies, as well as their own, white women sought to wrest control of marriage away from men of all races. But they did not intend to allow indigenous women to freely choose their own marriage partners. Instead, they aimed to assure that Indian and Aboriginal women would marry the young Christian indigenous men they deemed fit and appropriate.[94]

At times indigenous customs could coalesce with institutional priorities. When it came time for Elsie Roughsey to marry, for example, missionaries at Mornington Island considered Dick Roughsey, who had also been raised in the dormitory system there, to be a suitable mate. Their Aboriginal families also encouraged Elsie and Dick to wed, but for quite different reasons: "The idea that they should marry had been fostered by the fact that Elsie's older sister had married Dick's older brother. In their kinship way of relating they were already in-laws. In addition, they were 'grannie' cousins. Their parents and other relatives had suggested to Dick that he should marry Elsie."[95]

Sometimes indigenous girls consented to institutionally arranged marriages just to escape from the institutions. Another resident of the dormitory on Mornington Island, Catherine Elong, remembered that one day "the Missionary asked her if she would mind marrying Vernon, and she replied that she would [marry him]; so the wedding took place in less than a week. Her husband, Vernon, had been raised in the boys' dormitory." Catherine never loved Vernon; she told her interviewer, "I married him to get my freedom from the dormitory." Later, having left her husband, Catherine concluded, "The marriage was wrong from the beginning; he was suspicious and accusing."[96] Still other Aboriginal youth may have used the white authorities' attempts to control their marriage in their own power struggles with Aboriginal elders.[97]

Some young indigenous women and their families understandably resented and resisted white women's (and men's) attempts to govern their marriage practices. In 1934 a group of "half-caste" women in Broome in northwest Australia testified before an investigatory commission in Western Australia that one of their top concerns was the chief protector's control over whom they could marry. The group wrote, "Sometimes we have the chance to marry a man of our choice who may be in better circumstances than ourselves. A white man, or an educated Asiatic, but we are . . . rejected because that man does not wish to ask the Chief Protector's consent. We are worse than aboriginal, they can marry amongst themselves and no questions asked." The group also pointed out, "The result of such marriage being refused gives some of us fatherless children." "Therefore," they pleaded, "we ask for our freedom, so that when the chance comes along we can rule our lives and make ourselves true and good citizens." Interestingly, the group also objected to being told by the mission to marry "natives." The women wrote, "The half-caste wife cannot live the life of a full blood native. The exposure is too great, and the food insufficient or unwholesome. Also the native is looked down upon by his tribe and the half-caste wife cast aside because of her broken spirit, by having to walk behind her husband obediently and humble herself to him."[98] Raised in the missions, these women appear to have embraced many of the messages of white women regarding the oppressed position of Aboriginal women. Nevertheless they resisted efforts to control their intimate lives.

The Rise Of Indigenous Women's Activism

The remarkable petition by the "half-caste" women of Broome demonstrates that indigenous women had begun organizing efforts to fight against the injustices they faced. Not only did these women oppose efforts to control whom they married, but they also spoke out against the removal of Aboriginal children. The group lamented that they did not know their parents: "We educated halfcastes who have been sent to the missions have been taken from either our fathers or our mothers when we were children by the advice of the Department. And by so doing that has been the end of father and mother to us. Do you not realize the cruelty of this, would you white people like to think when you send your children to school that you would never see them again? That is one more reason why we want our freedom."[99]

To make their concerns heard, however, indigenous women often had to rely on forging alliances with white women reformers, the very women who often sought to control them. In fact, this petition from the Broome women shows the hand of white women's intervention (it was forwarded on behalf of the women by Alice Sawdon, a white reformer who lived in Broome), as the group asked the commission "for a paid

Lady Protector." Their reasoning: "So that we can be in a position even should our freedom be gained, we could be councilled and guided until we older ones have properly gained the knowledge of the white man's law." We should not view this petition, however, as wholly manipulated by white women. After the above statement, the tone of the writing changes dramatically, reflecting the voice of the Broome women again, who make clear that they do not want a "Lady Protector" who is in the typical maternalist mode:

> We would like someone who understands us and our native women. One that we can go to when we are in doubt in confidence. One who would talk to us for our good. Not a person whose attitude and look would give us the shivers to look at only because she thought we might have done wrong that made us go to her. One that would listen and not try to put the fear of God in our hearts, before we have had time to speak to her. Some of us may want guidance also a little control, and we want someone that we could trust so that they would be out for our interest and not abuse.[100]

Other Aboriginal women activists faced the same problem: they resented white interference in their lives but needed white allies to advance their cause. They subtly tried to steer white women away from a maternalist mission of "rescuing" and "uplifting" indigenous people. In 1935, for example, the Aboriginal activist Anna Morgan spoke to a meeting organized by the International Women's Day Committee. As reported in the Sydney newspaper, Morgan, a "full-blooded" woman of over sixty years, remarked, "The blacks of Australia are trying to emancipate themselves. The authorities are hindering them at every turn, and keeping them in enforced ignorance and poverty. All my life I have been reading books, searching for knowledge and fighting against those who want to draw a line between me and my white neighbors. Now I am determined to put my people's case before you."[101]

Morgan, born in Victoria around 1875 and raised with her family at

Ebenezer Mission until 1890, when authorities forced them to move, had suffered many indignities over her life. When she spoke to the white women's group she described the most recent injustice she had faced: "When I was 60 I applied for a Commonwealth old age pension, but was informed that I was regarded as an aborigine and therefore not entitled to one. On the other hand, we have been unable to get any assistance from the State Aborigines' Board, because that body considers we are not true blacks."[102] Within months of delivering this speech, Morgan died. In the last years of her life she had come to know the white woman reformer Helen Baillie, who was probably responsible for scheduling Morgan's speech. Baillie wrote Morgan's obituary for *Woman Today* and later published several Aboriginal stories that Morgan had told her. Baillie concluded in her obituary, "Surely the life of Anna Morgan is a challenge to white Australians to take up the case of their dark sisters, so that an enlightened public opinion will amend those laws which inflict such injustice on our aboriginal race."[103]

Just a few years later another Aboriginal activist, Pearl Gibbs, struck up a friendship and brief activist partnership with Joan Kingsley Strack, a white woman in Sydney who had become distressed by the experiences of her Aboriginal servants. Perhaps with Strack's assistance Gibbs also sought to mobilize other white women as potential allies through writing to *Woman Today:* "Ah! my white sisters, I am appealing to you on behalf of my people to raise your voices with ours and help us to a better deal in life."[104] Interestingly, both Gibbs and Morgan sought to cast their relationship with white women in terms of equality, not hierarchy, as sisters and not daughters. Morgan made it clear to her white audience that she was on an equal footing with them — she had been reading and searching for knowledge all of her life — and that blacks wanted emancipation, not protection. Pointedly, Gibbs asked her "white sisters" to raise their voices *with* Aboriginal women, not *for* them.

In the United States too Indian women activists sought out white women as allies in their campaigns for indigenous rights. Zitkala-Ša, for example, approached the million-member women's organization the

General Federation of Women's Clubs (GFWC) in the early 1920s to form an Indian Welfare Committee. Like Gibbs and Morgan, she sought to lead the GFWC women in a direction different from the maternalist agenda of other women's groups, such as the WNIA. Rather than supporting "rescue" and "uplift," Zitkala-Ša urged the women to work for citizenship and land rights.[105]

Indigenous Women's Maternalism

Alliances with white women could be risky, however, as indigenous women struggled to advance a different agenda and to redefine their relationship with white women on more equal terms. Indigenous women found that they had much work to do in dismantling white women's powerful maternalist discourse. In doing so they articulated alternative indigenous maternalisms. In the United States Indian women's maternalism sought to counter white women's ubiquitous negative images of them, their homes, and their communities and to honor Indian mothers. In Australia Aboriginal women projected a maternalist agenda that claimed their rights to homes and motherhood.

Because so much of white American women's maternalism hinged on denigrating indigenous women and their homes, many well-educated Indian women devoted some portion of their adult lives to fighting the misrepresentations and stereotypes of Indian women. Ella Cara Deloria, a Nakota or Yankton Sioux, who later became a writer and worked with the anthropologist Franz Boas on Dakota texts, worked as a director of physical education at Haskell in 1921 and published a report on Indian girls' health in 1922. Deloria began by outlining the traditional life of a Sioux woman. Far from presenting traditional Indian women as "plodding" and "shiftless" (as Carlisle's newspaper did), Deloria asserted:

The great-grandmother seemed to have unusual vitality and endurance. It could not be otherwise under her conditions of life, for she had continuous exercise from her childhood to her grave. Yet she exercised not because she knew that it would increase her circulation and induce deeper respiration, but because camp had to be moved every third day or so, the tipi had to be taken down and erected again, the wood had to be gathered and chopped for fuel, the water had to be carried from the spring or river, the fur had to be scraped off the buffalo hide, the corn had to be hoed, mushrooms and berries, wild turnips and rice had to be provided for the winter if her family was to live.

According to Deloria, the Indian woman's clothing was also conducive to her health: "There were no constricting garments about the waist. Her moccasins were correct, following the natural lines of the foot." Now, in the 1920s, according to Deloria, Indian girls' and women's bodies were changing, and for the worse, with colonization. Far from becoming more industrious and useful, Indian girls had lost something valuable: "Life is radically different [for Indian girls] than what it used to be. The Indians for the most part live in houses now, and the need for tipi building and camp moving does not exist. Food and wearing apparel are to be had at the trader's store, no need now to forage for wild fruits and to tan the animal hides for clothing. . . . As a matter of actual fact therefore, the Indian girl is not being trained at home for anything in particular which involves vigorous muscular activity." Now, in her physical education program Deloria had to compensate for Indian women's loss of vitality; the girls now had to learn "how to stand, walk, and sit."[106]

Other well-educated Indian women also fought back against the portrayal of Indian women as oppressed toilers compared to their idle men. In a speech she gave before the first conference of the Society of American Indians in 1911, Chippewa Marie Baldwin spoke on "Modern Home-Making and the Indian Woman." "One of the most erroneous and misleading beliefs relating to the American Indian woman," Baldwin stated, "is that she was both before and after marriage the abject slave and drudge of the men of her tribe." Instead, she argued, "in a large number of tribes she was on an absolute equality with her sons and brothers in the exercise and enjoyment of the several rights and patrimony of her people." Moreover, "the woman was industrious, frugal, loving and affectionate and performed her duties willingly and cheerfully. She was not a drudge and slave of her husband and the men of her tribe. She was treated with the respect, the esteem, gentleness and loving consideration she so richly merited and appreciated."[107]

Angel DeCora also sought to restore the dignity of native women. In a speech given at the annual convention of the National Education Association in 1907 she remarked, "In looking over the native design work of my pupils, I cannot help calling to mind the Indian woman, untaught and unhampered by the white man's ideas of art, making beautiful and intricate designs on her pottery, baskets and beaded articles, which show the inborn talent."[108] DeCora described to her largely white audience how she trained herself for her new job by visiting tribes across the nation, "with the view of getting an insight into the Indian woman's life and her natural tendencies in domestic life; not with the purpose of giving her instruction in the improved methods of domestic science, but to find out the kind of work she does in which she employs her native designs."[109] DeCora subtly suggested that Indian women had something to teach white women and that they possessed "natural" abilities both in the domestic realm and in making art. She thus played to but inverted increasingly popular views of Indians as possessing fixed biological traits.

Indian women also called on white women's maternalism by emphasizing mothering as a universal experience that cut across the borders of culture and race. Marie Baldwin, for example, asserted that the Indian woman was "above all a mother — fond, loving, careful, religious, — whose tireless devotion and self-sacrifice to home, husband and dependent children yield the first place to that of no other woman."[110] At an annual meeting of the WNIA, the Indian secretary of a local branch of the Woman's Christian Temperance Union in Warm Springs, Arizona, stressed, "The mother, be she white or red, has the same heart-aches over her boys."[111]

Honoring Indigenous Mothers

Deloria's, Baldwin's, and DeCora's statements all point to a developing alternative indigenous maternalism among Indian women that sought to honor rather than denigrate Indian mothers and the way they raised their children. This was apparent among some Indian girls as well. For her speech at Hampton's Commencement, the graduating student Lucy Conger subtly countered the litany of negative representations of Indian women, their homes, and methods of raising children. She proclaimed that an Indian "child is always welcome and enters life the possessor of the most passionate love of its parents," and she told her audience, "Indian children were early trained for hardihood." Belying the notion that Indians lacked morality, she asserted, "To be modest and industrious were the virtues set before [Indian girls]. This produced an energetic and a very feminine type of woman." Conger continued to stress the importance of "the intricate line of relationships" and the "social obligations of an Indian." "From babyhood the children were taught to respect their elders. . . . They must always be patient, truthful, self-controlled," she declared. Moreover, "hospitality too must both be offered and accepted without a question." She concluded by remarking on the clash between the values of her upbringing and her schooling: "These two social requirements of generosity and hospitality make it almost impossible for the educated Indian to have a home by himself and live like a white man, for as soon as he gets a little ahead his friends make him a visit or are in need and he feels in duty bound to share with them."[112] Even as she graduated from Hampton as a supposed model of assimilation, Conger put her newly acquired Western education to use to dignify Indian family life.

American Indian women's maternalism also took a quite different shape than white women's by connecting with powerful traditional roles in many tribes. For example, Creek, Cherokee, Choctaw, and Chicka-saw Indians who opposed assimilation and the allotment of communally held land formed the Four Mothers Society around 1895, a group that included both men and women and attracted up to twenty-four thousand members. Desirous of reviving the women-centered ceremonies and values of their tribes, they brought back the Green Corn Ceremony (which honored the Corn Mother Selu) and stomp dances (which paid homage to the matrilineal clans and power of Cherokee women).[113]

Aboriginal women's maternalism differed significantly from that of American Indian women. Except for some early accounts such as Margaret Tucker's *If Everyone Cared*, we find little evidence of the kind of rehabilitative work in which American Indian women writers engaged. Often removed before they could even remember their home community or family, many Aboriginal children seem to have become more estranged from their families and cultures. Like the "half-caste" women of Broome, some removed children came to accept many of the platitudes—such as Aboriginal men's oppression of women—they were taught about their culture in the institutions. Removed to Bomaderry Children's Home when she was just fourteen months old, Alicia Adams imbibed from her caretakers images of dirty Aboriginal homes. She disclosed to an interviewer, "When I used to go and visit [Aboriginal people] I used to hate eating off their plates and drinking out of their cups." When Adams finally reunited with members of her own Aboriginal family, her institutional upbringing made her uncomfortable in their homes. "I wanted to get to really know them, but I wanted to get home," she admitted. "I didn't want to stay too long. . . . Some of the houses had all holes in the walls, it was really terrible. I was thinking in my mind, 'Hope I'm not sleeping here tonight.'"[114] Moreover, as we saw in chapter 6, Aboriginal children were often told that their mothers had abandoned them, and many found it difficult to reconcile with, let alone come to honor, their mothers.

Thus in Australia Aboriginal women's maternalism seemed instead to rest on asserting their rights to home and motherhood. In their appeals to white women, they stressed mothering and the desire for a home as common links between indigenous and white women. This is best expressed in a speech that Margaret Tucker gave on an International Women's Day in the 1950s, which, although outside of the time frame of this study, grew out of her experience of child removal and speaks to the indigenous maternalism that Aboriginal women developed. Tucker told her audience of sympathetic white women:

> Since I came to Victoria we've had ups and downs. [My sister and I have] been made to feel that we are aboriginal women. . . .
>
> It is true we meet some charming people, who are most sincere. Even these people are inclined to pity us. We would rather they try to understand us. . . .
>
> I know what [Aboriginal] women want. They want homes. Is that strange for a woman? Our women are homeloving and want to bring up children as you do. They want to give their children advantages and want them to take their place in the community.[115]

So often taken from their own family and denied their own children, other Aboriginal women reiterated Tucker's position. Margaret Brusnahan, for example, an Aboriginal woman of South Australia who was brought up in Roman Catholic orphanages and foster homes, declared, "All I ever wanted was a home and a family."[116]

Some Aboriginal women activists linked their opposition to child removal policies with Aboriginal women's desires for a home. In 1934, for example, Anna Morgan wrote to the *Labor Call*, "At the age of fourteen our girls were sent out to work—poor, illiterate, trustful little girls to be gulled by the promises of unscrupulous white men. We all know the consequences. But, of course, one of the functions of the Aborigines Protection Board is to build a white Australia." Morgan contended, "We want a home. We want education."[117] When given a public forum, Aboriginal women activists also asserted their right to their own children. Gladys Prosser of Western Australia, who had managed to regain custody of her son, Gradie, after he had been removed from her, asserted forcefully, "In no circumstances should the separation of mothers and children be permitted except in circumstances where it is proved that the children are neglected. The same law that applies to the white race should apply to the native race in that regard."[118]

Thus, like white women, Aboriginal and Indian women also utilized a politics of maternalism as a basis for their political activism. However, their maternalist ideologies asserted — explicitly and implicitly — the right of indigenous women to raise their children as they saw fit within their own homes. Indigenous maternalisms also sought to advance a common experience of mothering and homemaking that put them on an equal footing with white women. As Tucker put it, Aboriginal women did not want pity but understanding. Indigenous women's developing maternalisms were therefore fundamentally at odds with the maternalist agenda of many white women.

In their efforts to create more intimate home-like settings for indigenous children in institutions, many white maternalists viewed themselves as critics or opponents of the state and its patriarchal foundation. Through their roles as surrogate mothers, many white women undoubtedly developed relationships of genuine affection and respect for some of the children within their care. Yet these new homes were neither benevolent nor benign institutions. The children's new "mothers" sought to profoundly alter how indigenous children, especially girls, experienced the world. White women attempted to "clean" the girls: to strip them of their old associations and ways of living. Now they were to be confined and restricted within new forms of dress and new homes. By donning the garb of "civilized" women and occupying a new type of home, white women believed, indigenous girls and women were signaling their acceptance of new ways of perceiving and acting in the world. Now they would no longer be the supposedly slave-like drudges of their men, but the useful servants of civilization. Instead of serving as the sexual chattel of their men, as white women believed, they would become the domestic dependent wives of Christian men (a scenario virtually all maternalist women had avoided or abandoned themselves).

Of course, all did not go according to plan. Indigenous girls looked to each other for guidance and support and sometimes to older Indian and Aboriginal women who worked in the institutions. And although white women often portrayed them as lacking voice and agency, indigenous children were not pawns to be moved about on the stage of a maternalist drama. Many Aboriginal women who had been removed as children—such as Angel DeCora, Zitkala-Ša, and Margaret Tucker—became powerful activists who labored to undo some of the damage that had been done to indigenous families. And as indigenous girls moved from the institutional life to yet a new intimate setting—the homes of white families—to work as domestic servants, the ability of white women maternalists to monitor and guide them further eroded.

Chapter 8

Out of the Frying Pan

The increasing difficulty in obtaining white girls for domestic service has created what, at first, was regarded as a heaven-sent opportunity for native girls to secure a good home with food and clothing, and receive motherly care and domestic training: not forgetting, of course, the saving to the State of the cost of their upkeep. Many of these girls were half-castes and there should be the further advantage of the civilised home background and preparation for their assimilation into the white community that their half-white blood entitled them to. With this in view, large numbers of these girls, many of them fresh from leaving school, some as young, even, as ten years of age (when the average white girl would still be playing dolls) had been brought to the metropolis and placed in service with employers.

• J. W. BLEAKLEY, chief protector, Queensland, 1913–42, quoted in Huggins, "'Firing On in the Mind': Aboriginal Domestic Servants in the Inter-War Years"

In both the United States and Australia, the "heaven-sent opportunity" of placing indigenous girls into domestic service seemed to fulfill many of the state's ultimate aims in removing indigenous children. While authorities and reformers in both countries touted such placement as providing the girls with "motherly care and domestic training" in a "civilised home" and "preparation for their assimilation," they also revealed that such placement saved the state money and filled a labor shortage. Placing indigenous girls in domestic service constituted a key part of the outing and apprenticeship programs developed by American and Australian institutions for indigenous children. Institutions first trained their female inmates to perform domestic service (and their boys to carry out manual labor) and then placed them as workers with white families. Due to a shortage of domestic and unskilled labor as well as the lower wages that indigenous child workers were paid, white families readily employed them.

Outing Indian girls and apprenticing Aboriginal girls to perform domestic service created another intimate arena in which white women and indigenous girls interacted. Both the state and white women reformers ennobled this domestic service by characterizing it as an essential element of the civilizing mission and invested white women employers with a maternal role to play toward the girls. Some white women claimed that their servants did become just like members of their family, and some indigenous servants undoubtedly developed bonds of affection and intimacy with the families for whom they worked. Yet for other employers and girls there was little pretense of maternalism in this new intimate setting. Although the state and white women employers tried to maintain some control over indigenous servants, maternal monitoring and control broke down, thus sometimes affording the girls greater freedom but also making them more vulnerable to abuse and exploitation.

Many white women reformers supported apprenticeship and outing as a vital next step after institutionalization in the program of uplifting indigenous girls. Australian authorities promoted apprenticeship as a primary means of assimilating Aboriginal girls and providing them with moral training. "The home of every applicant for an Aboriginal servant has been inspected," asserted the New South Wales Board for the Protection of Aborigines in 1915, "and the girls are consequently employed by people who help to uplift them in every possible way."[1] In the United States Estelle Reel declared that the outing system "places the student under the influence of the daily life of a good home, where his inherited weaknesses and tendencies are overcome by the civilized habits which he forms—habits of order, of personal cleanliness and neatness, and of industry and thrift, which displace the old habits of aimless living, unambition, and shiftlessness."[2] Although she used male pronouns, Reel's comment makes clear that outing was meant to continue the institutional program of remaking Indian girls' bodies and homes.

Of course, training indigenous girls for and placing them in domestic service also contributed to the colonial project of making indigenous people "useful." In "The Field Matron's Work," Lida W. Quimby of Puyallup, Washington, urged, "It is to be most devoutly wished that the Government make it obligatory on superintendents and agents to encourage the outing system of wage-earning for young Indians — for girls and women, who are in school years beyond the time when school is a necessity for them, or are leading idle lives on reservations — where a little urging on the part of agents would influence them to take positions as wage-earners."[3] Domestic service, reformers hoped, would make indigenous people less of a burden on the public treasury.

Given the maternalist discourses in both the United States and Australia that pathologized indigenous women as "dirty," it might seem unthinkable that any white women would employ them as servants. In fact, in some communities white women did refuse to employ Indian women. Although white settlers in northern California had once relied on Pomo women to wash their clothes and dishes and clean their homes, by the 1920s white women did not consider Indian women fit to work in their homes. In the 1930s the white interviewer Elizabeth Colson found that only one Indian woman could find employment within Ukiah, and that was at a convent. Colson wrote, "Whites commonly explain the exclusion of Indian women from town work by saying that they are too lazy to work at all or that they prefer to work as fruit pickers."[4]

Yet white women elsewhere were more than willing to take advantage of indigenous servants, in part because other help was becoming less available. In Australia the commonwealth official R. C. Urquhart reported in 1922, "There is considerable demand for girls from 'The Bungalow,' and Sergeant Stott has already placed seven females in good situations in Adelaide, and could place more in the same city if they were not too young as yet to be available." Urquhart made the case that a better institution in Alice Springs was needed in order to train half castes for these situations.[5] Sometimes authorities themselves directly benefited from the child removal policy. Herbert Basedow, an anthropologist and former protector in the Northern Territory, secured Aboriginal women as domestics in his home in Adelaide. (After his death, his widow could not afford to pay their return fares to Alice Springs, so the women "remained in employment" with Dr. Basedow's sisters.)[6]

There was a particularly high demand for Aboriginal girls as domestic servants in areas of the continent where it was considered unsuitable for white women to engage in labor. In her 1930 speech to the British Commonwealth League, Edith Jones acknowledged the important role Aboriginal domestic servants had played in allowing white women to "civilize" the Northern Territory. She quoted Bleakley's 1929 report that contended "white women were only enabled to live in Central Australia by the help of their Aboriginal sisters" who worked as servants for them.[7] Dorothea Lyons, a Northern Territory settler, claimed that without Aboriginal servants "[she] couldn't have stayed here [in Darwin]—the heat was so bad and just the work. One was always enervated from the heat. It was quite trying." (Curiously, Lyons later claimed in her interview that her domestic staff could handle only one job per day: "Because genetically they're not built like us to cope with things.")[8] At one point, Chief Protector Cook bemoaned the "tendency to utilize aboriginal women as much as possible in duties connected with the Darwin Aboriginal Compound, and not train and place them in domestic service." He explained, "This is particularly unfortunate at a place like Darwin where no other domestic service is available. It means that the white women who are expected to maintain the White Australia Policy are forced to carry out, unaided, all the heavy and enervating duties of household management in a [severe] tropical climate." Because of a shortage of Aboriginal women as domestic servants in the Darwin area, white families employed Aboriginal men as house servants as well.[9]

In the United States there was an equally high demand for Indian girls as domestic servants. Robert Trennert found that the Phoenix Indian School's outing program evolved into a "method of supplying cheap labor to white employers." According to Trennert, Superintendent Samuel McCowan had once been wary that outing might become a simple labor supply program, but embraced it once he learned "how fashionable it had become for Phoenicians to have an Indian servant." McCowan was also influenced by Estelle Reel, who reviewed the Phoenix outings in May 1900. Meeting with prominent families, she was impressed by how much they valued their Indian help. She applauded when told that the wives of leading local citizens traveled about the country taking schoolgirls with them to serve as maids and nurses. To Reel this type of maternalism was the essence of Indian education. It gave the girls a chance to travel, "and they acquire in one year as much cultivation and civilization as could be engrafted upon them in four or five years of ordinary intercourse in the school."[10]

Indian women were in demand as domestic servants in other parts of the American West in the first decades of the twentieth century. By that time most domestic servants were women of color or newly arrived immigrants; white native-born women virtually had abandoned the occupation once other employment options became available.[11] African American women, who worked extensively as domestic servants in the East, did not make up a sizable pool of laborers in western locations until World War II, and at that point they eschewed domestic service for better paying jobs in ship-building and other defense industries.[12] Mexican women immigrants and Chinese and Japanese immigrant men had served as domestic servants from the late nineteenth century up through the 1920s. Yet immigration from Asia had been curtailed due to the 1882 Chinese Exclusion Act and the 1924 Immigration Act. Moreover, at least 500,000 Mexicans were deported and/or repatriated during the Depression. Therefore, there was a scarcity of domestic servants throughout the American West.[13]

Additionally, white employers may have preferred indigenous girls as domestic servants because they could pay them so much less than other women. In Australia Inara Walden found that in 1910 the wages for a second-year Aboriginal girl were two shillings and six pence a week, far below the standard wages for servants, which ranged from ten to twenty shillings a week. Moreover, the protection board allowed the girls only six pence as "pocket money" and required the rest to be paid into trust accounts under the board's control. Some former servants testified, however, that they were not given even their rightful pocket money by their employers, and few ever received their wages in trust after they had finished their apprenticeships.[14]

It is difficult to compare American Indian domestic servants' wages with that of other racial groups in the United States, as no agencies kept track of domestic servants' earnings by race. Moreover, since by the early twentieth century domestic service in the United States was dominated by nonwhite and non-native-born women, all of whom were paid considerably less than "white" women in other occupations, wages for all domestic servants were low. If we compare American Indian women's wages in domestic service in the San Francisco Bay Area with that of the national average for domestic service in the 1920s, we find that the wages such young women could command—fifty to sixty-five dollars a month—were within the national range of fifty-five to sixty-three dollars a month. However, the average wage for domestic servants was considerably higher in the Bay Area than in all other regions of the United States. In 1900 (the last year for which such statistics are available) domestic servants in California and Oregon earned $4.80 a week, while those in the Midwest, Middle Atlantic, and New England made $3.00 to $3.48 a week, and southern domestic servants only took in $1.86 to $2.60 a week. Even with this regional disparity, American Indian women domestic servants were making the same amount as women in other parts of the country, suggesting that they were paid considerably less than other domestic servants on the Pacific Coast. In the 1930s Indian domestic servants in the Bay Area, who averaged just twenty dollars a month, fell well below the national average of thirty-eight dollars a month.[15] Outed American Indian servants received only two-thirds of their pay; as in Australia, the remainder of their income was deposited in trust funds under the control of boarding school superintendents. Moreover, just as with apprenticed Aboriginal women, many American Indian servants had great difficulty in later years obtaining their trust monies.[16]

In addition to the economic incentive, white women employers may also have wished to employ indigenous girls out of a wish to participate in the maternalist mission. Many women employers in fact often expressed a desire to mother the girls they hired as domestics. In 1883 Alice Fletcher wrote to Mary Bonney of the WNIA about "an Indian girl needing a friend." Fletcher told Bonney and her WNIA sisters, "If you would like to take the girl write directly to Capt. Pratt."[17] Mrs. Young replied to Fletcher's request: "I was seriously thinking it was my duty to take one of the Indian girls—to train for usefulness East [*sic*]."

> [As] Miss Fletcher wants Mary to have a friend that will be a mother to her perhaps you had as well send her to me.
>
> There is only one thing that I do require, that is, an honest girl. . . . She is but a child and needs play as well as work. And several years more experience before I would expect her to bear any responsibility.
>
> I do not keep servants, my family is small. . . . I can teach the Indian girl all the lessons she will want. And I will teach her all kinds of house work by having her assist me, also dress-making.[18]

In her letter Mrs. Young shuttled between maternalist sentiment and a more pragmatic orientation. She simultaneously envisioned her relationship to this Indian girl as that of a mother to her daughter, a teacher to her pupil, and an employer to her servant.

Similar impulses are evident among white Australian women who sought to "take in" Aboriginal girls.[19] In 1934 the minister of the interior, Mr. Perkins, called publicly for any institution in Australia's cities to "care for 50 octoroon children of either sex, so that they may be rescued from an environment in which they will be treated as full-blooded blacks." According to a newspaper article, "Mr. Perkins said that when he visited Alice Springs he was struck with the sight of these attractive and apparently pure white little ones, living the lives of aborigines, although their white blood and instincts overwhelmingly predominated."[20]

As a result of such newspaper articles, the minister received requests for the girls from eighteen white women, seven white men, and several mission homes. Some expressed a desire to care for the girls; Alice Sleswick seemed to desire an adoptive daughter: "I would love to have one [of the little girls] but it must be a nice child. . . . I do hope I can get one the younger the better so I can bring it up so that it will look on me as its mother." Most writers, however, were more clearly oriented toward finding a cheap and reliable domestic servant; Mrs. Clifford Smith just wanted to "procure a girl."[21]

Other women evinced a combination of loving maternalism with practical concerns. Mrs. Griffiths included a newspaper photo of a group of children, marking the girl she liked, who was the lightest in skin color, with an x. "I like the little girl in the centre of the group," she wrote, "but if taken by anyone else, any of the others would do, as long as they are strong." In her accompanying letter, Mrs. Griffiths inquired, "I was just wondering if the Govt intend to pay something to anyone who might take one or two of these unfortunate little girls, I would like to take one but, of course could not afford to do so without payment. I am not at all well off and am getting the old age pension. . . . I live alone am healthy but lonely & often wish for the companionship of children whom I love." She included letters of reference (all written in her own hand), which testified that "she is a most motherly woman who loves children, & is a splendid housekeeper and manager."[22] Like Mrs. Griffiths, many writers focused on color. N. L. Baker wished the child to be "nearly white."[23] Mrs. Philp asked for a "girl about 12–14 years of age to train in domestic duties." She had had an aboriginal servant from Palm Island for two years, but she thought an "octoroon" from Alice Springs would be more suitable, "having more of the white man's characteristics."[24] Mrs. A. H. Barnes requested an "octoroon" child because she would feel more comfortable taking her out with her.[25]

The mixed messages that come through in these requests for indigenous servant girls suggest elements of both exploitation and affection that could coexist within the relationships that developed between white

Homes Are Sought For These Children

A GROUP OF TINY HALF-CASTE AND QUADROON CHILDREN at the Darwin half-caste home. The Minister for the Interior (Mr Perkins) recently appealed to charitable organisations in Melbourne and Sydney to find homes for the children and rescue them from becoming outcasts.

I like the little girl in Centre of group, but if taken by anyone else, any of the others would do, as long as they are strong

20. Newspaper clipping of Aboriginal girls available for apprenticeship or adoption. One white woman marked with an x the fair-skinned girl she would prefer to take into her home. CRS A1, 1934/6800, National Archives of Australia, Canberra, Australian Capital Territory.

and indigenous women and girls. This was expressed in official rhetoric as well. In 1913 Queensland Chief Protector Bleakley admitted that an Aboriginal girl working as a domestic "may become one of the family, but at the same time she remains a servant." He added, "When you place those quadroon children with private people, you can never be quite sure that those people will care for them as they would care for their own children. They very often become purely menials and servants."[26]

Another important dimension motivated white women to acquire indigenous domestic servants: doing so enabled them to uphold middle-class standards of purity and cleanliness while escaping the drudgery that such standards required. As Phyllis Palmer puts it, "Maintaining high standards of cleaning and laundering enabled the family's appearance to exemplify its inner state of purity and 'godliness.'"[27] Scholars of domestic service in the United States have pointed out the racial and class inequalities that are built into such employment. Perhaps Pierrette Hondagneu-Sotelo puts it best: "Even among wealthy white women born and raised in the United States in the late twentieth century, few escape the fetters of unpaid social reproductive labor. . . . Their reliance on housecleaners and nannies allows well-to-do women to act, in effect, as contractors. By subcontracting to private domestic workers, these women purchase release from their gender subordination in the home, effectively transferring their domestic responsibilities to other women who are distinct and subordinate by race and class, and now also made subordinate through language, nationality, and citizenship status."[28]

In fact, employing an indigenous girl as a domestic servant made it possible for white families in Australia and the American West to claim middle-class status even if they often struggled economically.[29] In the tropical climate of Darwin in the Northern Territory, which white women routinely described as "enervating," Aboriginal women's servitude enabled white women to maintain or attain a higher class status and to live out a colonial fantasy. Ruby Roney described how white women created "a sort of gracious living." "When a newcomer came," Roney explained, all the ladies in the area "called on her and left their cards. . . . If she wanted to be friends, she called on you. On your card was what day you'd be home. . . . It was quite a day, the ladies whose day it was; they'd be cooking up, all the morning. And everybody dressed up in their best, and their hats and gloves, and went along to their afternoon tea and chat." Roney recognized that this lifestyle would not have been possible without domestic servants:

Of course, there's one thing the ladies had—cheap labour, the natives worked. And those days you didn't pay them wages, you fed and clothed them, and their dependents, and bought them extras, whenever they asked you. Their needs were simple, not like they'd be today. But that was it, and they done the rough work—the sweeping and the cleaning, and the washing and the ironing. . . . I've seen the native women laundresses; I could never iron as good as they could. They learnt well, and they were taught by the early settlers correctly. They could cook too, and they were very good.[30]

White women's call for domestic servants and the desire of authorities to out and apprentice young indigenous women seemed to coalesce nicely. However, the demand for indigenous girls as servants sometimes conflicted with white women reformers' goals of uplifting the girls. Controversy over outing erupted in 1902 at the Phoenix Indian School under the superintendency of Charles Goodman. Goodman learned that many employers did not supervise the Indian girls during their leisure hours, that the girls were gathering with "undesirables" (that is, reservation Indians), and hence the girls' morals were jeopardized. The superintendent responded by allowing girls to work in homes only on weekends, but still accusations of immorality continued.[31]

Matron Schach recommended that even the weekend work for girls be stopped, but Goodman's "main concern seems to have been the great hardship it would work on the people of Phoenix, 'who for years have had much help from this school. Other help is almost unobtainable in this country, and especially the mothers with little children, most of whom have been very kind to the girls, find it a great trial to have to do without assistance even one day in the week.'" The matron resigned, telling Goodman, "I can not permit myself to be made instrumental in the moral downfall of the girls whom I am here to guide and uplift." Schach's resignation led to the end of the school's outing program for girls. In its place, the school decided to open an "Industrial Cottage" program to train girls in domestic work, since domestic service employment was no longer available to them. As a result of this controversy, the federal government decided to investigate the outing program at other boarding schools.[32]

Domestic service for Aboriginal girls also often conflicted with white Australian women reformers' maternal agenda. Frequently, apprenticeship exposed Aboriginal girls and young women to sexual exploitation, the very fate from which so many reformers sought to protect them. Victoria Haskins found that 17 percent of Aboriginal girls apprenticed in urban situations in New South Wales from 1912 to 1928 became pregnant, and Inara Walden discovered that 8.5 percent of the Aboriginal girls in the New South Wales Ward Register became pregnant during their service. Both Walden and Haskins argue that given the tightly restricted world of the servants, it was unlikely they could have become pregnant by men other than their own employers. Haskins contends that despite its rhetoric of "protection," the New South Wales Aborigines Protection Board was fully aware of the likelihood of sexual exploitation of Aboriginal domestic servants but continued to place the girls in such homes because the birth of lighter-skinned children would help to "absorb" Aborigines into white Australia. The state routinely removed children born to the apprenticed girls; only about 5 percent of the girls kept their babies.[33] Haskins thus asserts that the board "colluded in, condoned and indeed encouraged the systematic sexual abuse and impregnation of young Aboriginal women in domestic apprenticeships with . . . the ultimate aim of eradicating the Aboriginal population." She adds, however, "This could not be openly acknowledged because to do so would have alienated the white women whose participation as employers was crucial to the success of this policy."[34]

Australian state policies and practices thus clashed with white maternalists' desire to protect young Aboriginal women, adding fuel to the fire of white women's campaigns for female protectors and leading some white women to advocate that Aboriginal girls, especially those of a very young age, should not work in domestic service. In Western Australia, for example, white women reformers in the early 1930s often cited the following statistic: "Out of 33 coloured girls sent out to employment during the past three years, no less than 30 have returned pregnant."[35] Thus Sister Kate as well as the Schenks and Mary Bennett at the Mt. Margaret Mission attempted to prevent Aboriginal girls in their care from going out to domestic service before they were sixteen or seventeen.[36]

Complaints of moral impropriety led some administrators to call for more regulation and supervision of young Aboriginal women placed in domestic service. Chief Protector Cook sought to more carefully monitor and control the allocation of domestic servants to residents in the Northern Territory. This led the prominent settler Jessie Litchfield to protest to the minister of the interior in 1938 about the new difficulty of acquiring Aboriginal servants in that area. She longed for the good old days, when the former protector of Aborigines came around to white homes: "If you had no aboriginal working, he would supply you with one, on request."[37]

Similar concerns prompted administrators in the United States to issue stern declarations about the need for suitable homes for outed Indian girls. John Holst, supervisor of Indian schools for the Sacramento Agency, reported on the work of the Los Angeles Outing Center and its diligent outing matron, Frances Hall, declaring that Indian girls "must be placed in homes which typify the higher ideals of American life." To this end he mentioned that Matron Hall's work included the inspection of homes for the placement of Indian girls. The homes "must meet certain standards," he asserted. "They must represent worthy ideals, the attitude toward the student must be sympathetic and helpful, and certain conditions must be maintained and regulations enforced."[38]

Despite these tensions, white women's involvement in outing and apprenticeship dovetailed productively with government authorities' aims and white women reformers' maternalist agenda. Yet once indigenous girls moved to this new intimate setting—at once both a home and a workplace—what transpired? To what extent did white women employers take on a maternalist role toward the girls, seeking to care for them but also to control and monitor their bodies and homes? To what extent did white women employers abandon this agenda? And what did this new work and life mean to indigenous girls and young women?

Aboriginal Apprentices

For some indigenous girls and their white women employers there was
no trace of a maternalist relationship; apprenticeship constituted merely
a job. Aboriginal servants clashed with their white women employers
over money matters, work details, and control of their personal lives.
One roster of Aboriginal servants and their employers in South Australia
reveals the conflicting perspectives of servants and mistresses. Although
women employers were ostensibly expected to provide additional training and "protection" to their servants, Mrs. Shuttleworth clearly hoped
for a servant who required little intervention on her part: "She had no
complaints regarding 'Joan' personally but found her too inexperienced
and too young. Too much of her time was taken up in supervising Joan
and trying to teach her," the very responsibilities ostensibly assigned to
maternalists. Joan had different concerns. She claimed that Shuttleworth
had dismissed her without fully paying her. The two could not resolve
their differences. When Shuttleworth asked Joan "if she would like to
stay for another week to see if she could make a better fit of the job . . .
Joan said she would leave and go to her grandmother."[39]

Similarly, Glenyse Ward's employer, Mrs. Bigelow, abandoned all
pretense of a maternalist attitude toward her. When Ward, just sixteen,
arrived after a long journey at the new home where she was to work,
Mrs. Bigelow prepared tea for her husband and herself in "beautiful
cups and saucers," while serving Ward tea in "an old tin mug." Ward
recalls, "I politely asked her if I could have a cup and saucer to drink
from, as I wasn't used to drinking out of tin mugs and had never done so
at the mission." Ward was unprepared for the response. "The answer I
received back was in a very irate and furious tone of voice," she recalls.
"She stated to me that I was there as a dark servant, that I was to obey
her orders, and do what she told me to do!" Ward was unprepared as
well for her dirty quarters in a garage, which contrasted sharply with
the opulence of the main part of the house. Mrs. Bigelow did not allow
Ward in the dining room "while any member of the family was there,"

unless she was summoned by a bell to serve the family. In this case, as compared to the stated intent of maternalists to rescue Aboriginal children from their degraded lives, Mrs. Bigelow made no attempts to expose Ward to the finer things of life. Ward described her position in Mrs. Bigelow's home alternately as a shadow and a dummy, revealing the ways her white mistress did not regard her as a real person. Indeed, Ward wrote that Mrs. Bigelow often referred to her as her slave.[40]

Other employers also looked on and treated their Aboriginal servants as virtual slaves. One lengthy report by a policeman on the "alleged cruelty" to a servant named Amanda by the Schwartzes of Black Hill in South Australia reveals evidence of gross physical abuse. Neighbors alleged that the Schwartzes had been cruel to Amanda "by way of making her done [*sic*] work that is generally performed by a man." Heinrich Christopher Dohnt claimed, "[I] was at Schwartz's place one day and Amanda was then out in the garden digging a trench and it was very hot, and I said to Mr Schwartz that he should send the girl inside that it was too hot for her to be doing that work, Schwartz said 'Shes alright she only a nigger.'" Dohnt felt "sure the work she was doing was too hard for her, as she was only a child." Another neighbor, Mrs. Goesling, believed "that through giving her hard work to do, she has lost all her vitality and hence became very tired and unable to do the work about the house." Some neighbors testified that the Schwartzes had "thrashed" the girl and sent her to school with insufficient food.

Anton Alwin Schwartz countered some of the testimony of his neighbors, claiming that Amanda's "work was household duties and milking cows" and that she had also helped him with his sheep and to cart hay. However, Schwartz admitted, "I have found her very untruthful and disobedient, either my wife or I would thrash her, we always beat her over the hands or across the backside, I understood that I had to punish her in the same manner as I would punish my own child." He insisted, however, "She has never been knocked down by either my wife or me. She broke her arm by slipping down when turning over the water tap in the garden about fourteen days before she went away, she also slipped over on the back verandah two days before leaving. . . . She has not been illtreated by us, but she has received the same treatment as our own children for being untruthful and disobedient, she was always beaten with a strap." (Schwartz's testimony gives new meaning to the common refrain by employers that they treated their servants like one of the family.) When Mrs. Schwartz testified to the police official, she showed him the strap they used to thrash Amanda ("about 2 feet long on a short piece of stick").

Most indigenous girls who received the treatment that Amanda did probably never made it into the official record. But the chief protector of Aborigines went to the hospital where Amanda had been taken, after a pastor in the district informed him that Amanda "was suffering from venereal disease," and Mrs. McKay, a member of the Advisory Council of Aborigines, called the chief protector to tell him that she had learned that Amanda "had sustained a broken arm through being knocked down by her employer."

Amanda's situation was unusual in that she got to tell her own story and that it became visible in the public record. In her testimony she documented the abuse meted out to her by Mrs. Schwartz. She noted first that Mrs. Schwartz refused to acknowledge that Amanda's arm was broken:

She would not believe me and made me carry on with my work. About two or three days later I was sent to get wood with a wheel barrow. Mrs. Schwartz thought I was away too long so hit me all over with a piece of wood.

That same day she pricked me on the bare back with a fork.

A week or two later she pushed me over while I was washing clothes because she thought I was not working fast enough. I fell right to the ground which made my arm worse than ever.

I still had to carry on with my work.

She used to knock my head against the wall. . . .

She . . . hit me on the head with a broken broom handle and also with a shovel. . . .

On another occasion Mr. Schwartz came to me and said that Mrs. Schwartz had told him that I had been mumbling . . . that she should do all the work herself. I told him I had not said that. He then went out and got a whip and hit me about the legs while I was washing up.

Amanda's case was also atypical in that authorities sided with her rather than with her employer. A police constable concluded that the punishment meted out to the girl was "severe and overdone." He told the inspector, "I would not under any circumstance recommend Schwartz's to have the care of another native girl, he has the reputation of being a nigger driver and has a job to get anyone to work for him."[41]

Other Aboriginal servants also complained of abuse. Fourteen-year-old Mavis Mackey complained to a white inspector about her employer: "[She] hits me . . . nearly every day, she hit me with sauce pans and anything she gets hold of. And the little boy always hits us three girls . . . and calls us black and Beast and blames us for everything if he does wrong. And she never lets us go out at all. Every morning she wakes us up at hafe past five or quarter to four and its too early for us. We all wish we wasent hear. I rather go back than stay down hear. they all call us blacks in this house and we sleep on the floor." In this case, the inspector dismissed Mackey's complaint as untrue.[42]

Finding little respite and "protection" through official channels, some Aboriginal servants refused to take such abuse. Victoria Archibald, who was sent out to service in Albury at the age of fifteen or sixteen, came into great conflict with her white mistress. The mistress had ordered Archibald to stir the jam she was making on the stove and also to take care of the children. She was angry when she caught Archibald away from the jam. Archibald recalls, "I turned around and I hit her, and of course she grabbed me then we were wrestling there." Archibald ran away from the confrontation, but then her employer's husband returned: "[He] started roughing me up. Well, I start kicking you see, and he said,

'I'll fix you.'" He put Archibald in a bath with all of her clothes on, but she continued to resist by trying to pull his head in the bath. She managed to get away, change her clothes, and run away from the home, but police found her. She was eventually sent back to Cootamundra and placed at another home in Moree. At her new job, her mistress frequently made her scrub a long verandah and accused her of stealing rings. Archibald escaped out a window and ran away to a police station. Again she was brought back to her employer. As Archibald puts it, "I was jumping the frying pan and the fire there."[43]

As is clear from the statistics compiled by Haskins and Walden, many Aboriginal servants not only faced physical abuse but also suffered frequent sexual abuse. Rarely did these cases become public, however. In one case in the Northern Territory, Alice Mindle confided to a white man, Charles Priest, that her employer, George Leonard Alfred Don, allegedly raped her. Priest wrote a pamphlet detailing and condemning the case, but was then sued for libel. A constable in the case was eventually dismissed, but Mindle found no justice.[44] Understandably, with little recourse in the legal system, many Aboriginal servants took matters into their own hands, as Victoria Archibald did, and simply ran away from their employers. Walden found that in fact 14 percent of all recorded apprentices in New South Wales absconded. If apprehended, however, the apprentices, especially repeat "offenders," were subject to harsh punishments, including placement in reformatories, convents, or even mental asylums.[45]

The experience of domestic service for other Aboriginal girls was not so overtly brutal or relentlessly oppressive. Adherence to the notion that white women should act on the maternalist ideal of mothering and "uplifting" their Aboriginal servants could result in somewhat better treatment for apprentices. Dorothea Lyons, for example, noted that along with paying each Aboriginal servant a very small wage of five shillings a week and putting "two and six into their trust fund," "You were responsible wholly for them—their medical side, their health—you always cared for them." Responsible employers realized that if they didn't properly care for their servants, "[their] own children would be affected."[46]

As a result, complicated intimacies could develop between white families and their indigenous servants. Whites routinely declared that their Aboriginal servants had become members of their family. What exactly did this cliché mean, however? For white women, it appeared to signify loyalty on the part of their servants. Dorothea Lyons, for example, noted that some of her family's domestic servants "stayed with [them] for thirty years." She declared, "They were very fine people and they were very loyal to you."[47] For some Aboriginal servants, the phrase meant being treated more as an equal. Eileen Park, for example, who grew up at the Bungalow in Alice Springs and was sent to work as a domestic in Adelaide when she was twelve years old, claimed of her employer, "I wasn't treated as a domestic, I was treated as her own daughter."[48] Rae Miller, whom Glenyse Ward ran into at a fair, told her "how the white people she worked for made her one of the family. She ate with them, played with the kids, went to the pictures with them."[49]

While some Aboriginal servants may have enjoyed such intimacies, other Aboriginal servants measured their satisfaction in quite different ways. At one of Emily Liddle's placements, she complained, "[It] was just like Bungalow again. You was on a routine." However, the Riley family, another placement, "were lovely people," and Perkins asserted, "We had freedom there."[50] In this case, what mattered to Perkins was not whether she felt like one of the family, but that she was not rigidly controlled.

Negotiating the fine line between honorary family member and domestic worker required a complex balance on the part of Aboriginal apprentices and their white women employers. One of the most complicated intimacies developed between Aboriginal women servants and the white children they cared for. Jackie Huggins explains, "Most European children in the north were reared by Aboriginal house servants, and some were suckled at the breasts of black wet-nurses."[51] One Aboriginal

21. An Aboriginal woman taking care of a white child. The original caption reads: "This is the Lubra who wanted to borrow a camel to go to the Oodnadatta races . . . Patricia Kempe, aged 2 years." By permission of the National Library of Australia, Plate No. 7-A.

servant, Mary Griffith, told Walden that "one of the women she had cared for as a child, and with whom she has maintained contact, had told her she was her 'second mother.'"[52] Kim Mahood, growing up in the outback near Alice Springs, remembers the black women who took care of her. Looking back on her childhood, she writes of herself, "She had two mothers, the white one who had borne her and the black one who named her and dreamed for her. The one who dreamed for her, her skin mother, gave to the child the dreaming of Pintapinta the Butterfly and named her for her own child which was never born." Of her own mother, Mahood writes, "For a restless young woman unused to babies, [Aboriginal women] were a priceless source of childminding, and she readily relinquished the little girl into the black women's capable hands." Mahood even spoke the Aboriginal language of her caregivers before she learned English.[53]

Yet young Aboriginal women were often mothering their white mistresses' children at the expense of their own, engaging in the phenomenon of what Sau-ling Wong calls "diverted mothering," whereby "time and energy available for mothering are diverted from those who, by kinship or communal ties, are their more rightful recipients" to care for the employers' children instead.[54] Jackie Huggins writes of her mother, Rita Huggins, that she "was unable to keep her first-born daughter Mutoo with her when she was sent away to domestic service work." Mutoo grew up with Rita's parents on the Cherbourg Aboriginal settlement. Huggins insightfully points out, "Like other Aboriginal women, Rita was denied her own maternity while forced to wash, change babies' nappies and play with her white employer's children."[55] Huggins notes that when Aboriginal servant women had children of their own, "the extended family play[ed] a very important role in child care arrangements."[56]

Such complicated intimate configurations were a marked feature of the practice of indigenous child removal. In removing indigenous girls from their mothers and communities, white women could become like mothers to the girls in the institutions. When sent out to service, indigenous girls could then become mothers to white women's children. However, when they had their own children, it was often impossible for young Aboriginal women to care for them, since they had to work to support themselves. So their aunts or grandmothers took over their children's care, or sometimes the state removed their children, thus continuing the cycle of child removal and displaced mothering.

When Ruth Hegarty became pregnant while working as a servant in north Queensland, authorities quickly brought her back to Cherbourg. "I'd come home from work pregnant and so gone the way of most other girls from the dormitory," Hegarty writes. "I was painfully aware that our lives were beginning to mirror those of our mothers." Hegarty spent two years with her daughter in the dormitory, as she had done with her mother, then arranged to have her daughter live with her newly wed best friend and husband while she went back out to service. Although she spared her daughter her own fate of growing up in an institution, Hegarty "lost out—just like [her] mother did—on parental bonding."[57]

Intimacy with their employers' families also entangled young Aboriginal servants in maternalistic expectations. In return for treating a servant as a member of their family, white women employers expected to tightly control their servants' personal lives. Mrs. Crittenden of Melbourne had employed Sarah, a "half-caste" from Alice Springs, for four years in her home when she asked authorities for the right to withhold Sarah's wages for a year in order that she could be sent to night school. A government memo reported, "[Sarah] is a very refined and splendid type of girl; in fact . . . it would be difficult to distinguish her from an ordinary Australian child. . . . Mrs. Crittenden is the mother of five children, the eldest being 17 years. Sarah is treated the same as her own children."[58]

Yet many Aboriginal servants resented the tight control that both the state and their employers had over their wages, labor, and leisure. Sarah resisted Mrs. Crittenden's plan for her. Instead, she applied to the minister of home and territories to be released from service; she had become engaged to a "respectable young man." In November 1927 the minister approved arrangements whereby "certain half-caste girls in service in South Australia" who were over eighteen could be released from control, "except in cases where the Chief Protector is of the opinion that it is undesirable in the interest of the half-caste that she should be granted her freedom." The minister determined that Sarah should be released from employment to Mrs. Crittenden, in part because she "shows no indications of aboriginal blood."[59]

Once they turned eighteen many Aboriginal women sought to leave their apprenticeships. Topsy Fitz wrote to her former protector in Alice Springs to retrieve her bank book after working for three years in South Australia. "I feel now that I would rather work for higher wages," she told him. "I am just fed up with working for almost nothing. . . . I don't think that it is a fair thing to keep us girls working hard like this for paltry 3/ [shillings] a week when we are old enough to earn more. . . . I don't even want to go back to Alice Springs to live because that life would not suit me after been down here all these years. . . . I don't think myself a child any longer and I don't think it is fair to treat me like one all the time." Perhaps to demonstrate her capacity for independence and to persuade him to release her, she professed her gratitude for being sent to Adelaide: "[It gave] me a chance to be decent and learn to be a useful woman instead of living up there and be useless and good for nothing and ignorant." Fitz's request generated a long correspondence among officials regarding their interpretations of the South Australia and Northern Territory ordinances, but the record does not reveal if she received her money or her freedom.[60]

Aboriginal servants also sought to evade state control by pursuing alternative careers. While enduring removal from one family and institution to another, Nancy De Vries states, "All this time I knew I did not want to be a maid to white people. I had other ideas. Maybe a bit high for my station in life according to the white society, but I wanted to be a nurse."[61] As we have seen, however, officials had very low expectations for the indigenous children in their care and often thwarted their efforts to "better" themselves. Penny Everaardt comments, "We were told a lot of times that because we were Aboriginal, there was no future for us. We would end up as maids in a motel or looking after children on a farm, so what was the use of an education."[62]

Ironically, despite constantly insisting that they were "uplifting" Aboriginal girls, white women reformers and employers rarely envisioned lifting them any higher in the social scale than as "maids to white people." Daisy Bates, for example, declared, "The best education will raise them [Aborigines] no higher than domestic workers." She added, "At the best the caste can only fill domestic situations."[63] Maternalism required a hierarchy of white women as mothers who protected, monitored, and guided their indigenous children. Although the maternal ideal of uplift often broke down in the private homes in which Aboriginal girls worked, the hierarchy underlying the ideal remained, providing a source of ongoing tension and contradiction in the relationships between white women and indigenous girls and women. A similar dynamic played out among American Indian servants who worked in the homes of white American women.

Outing Girls in the San Francisco Bay Area

Just as in Australia, U.S. authorities attempted to monitor and control young Indian women even after they had left training institutions and gone to work in private homes, primarily through employing white women as "outing matrons" to keep track of the young women. In the San Francisco Bay Area the BIA hired a series of outing matrons from 1918 to 1946, who, beginning in 1925, compiled copious files on each girl and young woman they supervised. Testifying to the intense scrutiny under which these young Indian women lived, these files have inadvertently provided historians with a revealing picture of Indian women's domestic service in white women's homes.[64]

Like Phoenix, the Bay Area suffered from a shortage of domestic servants, yet no boarding schools existed within a convenient distance

22. Indian girls at Carson/Stewart Indian School, ca. 1935. Many of the Indian girls who worked as domestic servants in the San Francisco Bay Area came from the Carson School. Photo 11, Records of the Carson Agency, Decimal Subject Files, 1925–1950, Record Group 75, National Archives and Records Administration, Pacific Region, San Bruno, California.

for Indian girls to be outed on a daily basis. Thus matrons recruited young Indian women from the nearest boarding schools—Stewart Indian School in Carson City, Nevada; Sherman Institute in southern California; and the Chemawa School in Salem, Oregon—as well as nearby Indian communities, including those of the Pomos, Hoopas, Shastas, Monos, Paiutes, Klamaths, Washoes, and Western Shoshones.

Interestingly, rather than originating from the top of the BIA hierarchy, this outing program seems to have been initiated by a disgruntled female employee in the bureau, Bonnie Royce, who had worked for fifteen years among Indian people and served closely with her husband at the Carson School in the position of field matron. In 1916 Superintendent James Royce had written to the commissioner of Indian affairs to clarify his wife's duties: "Mrs. Royce does not care to do regular field matron work and in fact she could not do regular field matron work from this school as we are not on a reservation."[65] A special agent also wrote to the commissioner, recommending that a new outing matron position be created and Mrs. Royce be appointed to it.[66] The commissioner agreed to hire Bonnie Royce in this newly created position, but by June 1918 became suspicious that she had not done any work and that Superintendent Royce had appointed his wife to the position simply to increase his salary. Commissioner Cato Sells questioned why Bonnie Royce was in Oakland, in the Bay Area, that summer rather than at Carson Indian School in the Sierra Nevada mountains. Superintendent Royce rushed to defend his wife and worked with the commissioner to clarify her position.[67] Perhaps Bonnie Royce had been derelict in her new duties and was just using her post to relocate from the isolated Sierra Nevada to the cosmopolitan Bay Area, but Sells's accusations galvanized her into action.

By September 1918, Commissioner Sells had redefined Bonnie Royce's position in a true maternalist fashion; she was now to "give special attention to procuring [employment in] homes for Indian girls after they have left school or for any other Indian women of Nevada and Northern California . . . in order that they may be protected from the degrading moral conditions which are found in the small mining towns of Nevada and the country adjacent thereto." He gave her explicit instructions: "The field [outing] matron should ascertain the character and reputation of the parties wishing Indian help and make regular visits to the homes where such employment is given so that no mistake may be made in placing these girls in homes only where helpful influences are radicated [radiated]." "I feel that there is a great work to be done in Nevada for these Indian women," Sells concluded, "and from the experience that Mrs. Royce has had in Indian work believe that she will be able to give the girls the motherly advice and encouragement which will prove an uplift to those placed in her care."[68]

Royce began her work in earnest by opening a placement office in Berkeley, which later moved to Oakland, and later still across the bay to San Francisco. She convinced the BIA to hire Jeannette Traxler as her assistant in 1929, and Traxler appears to have taken over from Royce sometime in the early 1930s. In 1934 the BIA hired a new matron, Mildred Van Every, who worked at the post until 1946.[69] Whereas the backgrounds of Royce and Traxler are murky, Van Every seems to have emerged from a women's reform organization with maternalist orientations. She had close ties to the Young Women's Christian Association, and in fact served as industrial secretary for the Oakland branch in the 1930s. She also appears on their Indian Girls' Work Committee for 1942.[70]

Young Indian women learned of employment opportunities through the placement service in one of three ways: through referrals from boarding school or reservation officials, through word of mouth among the young women themselves, or through recruitment efforts by the matrons. Matron Van Every visited Sherman Institute every summer and traveled frequently around northern California to recruit young Indian women. The BIA records also indicate that the matrons often corresponded with officials on the reservations and in the girls' former boarding schools.[71] Other young Indian women found domestic employment in the Bay Area through a competing private placement service or on their own initiative.[72]

Unlike most Aboriginal servants and younger outed Indian girls, these young Indian women had some choice in the matter of whether to travel to the big city and take up employment in a white woman's home. However, their agency should not be overstated; their options were also limited. Due to prejudice and lack of real education, they could find little employment except for domestic service. The Great Depression seemed to narrow Indian women's options even further. "Winona" wrote to Matron Royce in search of a position: "I am quiet [*sic*] interested, as we certainly feel the depression. I will quit school in a minute to secure a job for fifty dollars per month as a cook."[73]

Apart from the scarcity of jobs, young Indian women had a variety of their own reasons for taking these positions. Many wanted to help their families. "Elsie," a Washoe Indian from Stewart Indian School, "wished to get more money because she [was] responsible for her little sister."[74] Others had been deserted by or had left their husbands and needed work to support their children. "Daisy," a Klamath Indian who had three children, wrote to Matron Royce in 1930, "I have had so much trouble . . . have left my husband, he is worthless and cruel. . . . I tried to stay with him for the childrens sake but he is just impossible. I am at home with mother now. . . . Must get some work to do soon as my three children and I are without shoes or clothes."[75]

For other young Indian women, work in the big city seemed like a ticket to new adventures. "Irene," from Salt Lake City, "was particularly interested in seeing the Golden Gate International Exposition and to find out whether she could make and sell Indian articles there."[76] Some of the Indian women seemed to regard domestic employment as a route to some form of independence. "Clara" wanted to work for a while in order to save money to go to Willamette University.[77] "Edith," a Winnebago, had studied nursing for two years at Haskell Indian School and then for two years at the general hospital. She had come to the Bay Area to "train voice." According to Van Every, Edith had "a fine contralto voice."[78]

Many young Indian women sought out these jobs in part for the social opportunities they afforded in a bustling urban area. The YWCA sponsored the Four Winds Club in Oakland for the young Indian women and men in the Bay Area, where they met every Thursday night and held chaperoned dances once a month.[79] Others relished dancing and drinking in the city out from under the watchful eyes of the matron at the YWCA or their employers. The employer of "Lydia," a Pomo, complained that she was "out too many nights."[80]

So important was this social life to the young Indian women that many of them refused or resigned from particular jobs if they cramped their opportunities to meet their friends regularly. For example, "Fern" and "Amelia" wrote to Royce in 1929 about how unhappy they were working at the Mt. Diablo Country Club (inland from the Bay Area). They pleaded with her, "We can't stand it here any longer. Too hot, lonesome, and everything. We would like to work some place else, where we can see the girls on our day off. It feels terrible not to see them, and that were [*sic*] way off. . . . Can you please get us a better place. We can't stand the heat. and we can't cook to suit them. . . . We would rather work there [in] the city than out here. Please get us a place there."[81] In the surviving documentation of Aboriginal domestic service, as well as oral histories and memoirs, Aboriginal women did not seem to enjoy the same possibility of freewheeling sociability among their peers that these young Indian women found in the San Francisco Bay Area.

Nevertheless, although Indian women may have taken the jobs for adventure, independence, or social opportunities, the majority of their time was spent carrying out the duties assigned to them by white mistresses and expected of them by the matrons. As "May" put it in a letter to her friend "Amelia," "I guess you know that Royce lady make you work. I've been working like hell every since I got here."[82] Indian girls and women who worked as domestics were charged with basic housecleaning as well as caring for children, cooking, ironing, serving at table, and answering the door bell and telephone. The outing matron kept files that rated the girls on each of these tasks. For Elsie the matron noted:

Care of Children	Poor
Cooking	Assist, no experience
Ironing	Yes
Answering Door Bell	Yes
Answering Telephone	Yes
Serving the table	No Training[83]

Wages varied considerably for young Indian women. In the 1920s "Jane," a Washoe, made fifty to sixty-five dollars a month, whereas in the depression of the 1930s "Susan," a Klamath, earned just twenty dollars a month and "Opal," at one low point, took in only twelve dollars one month.[84] At least for the Indian girls who were still in school, authorities stipulated that two-thirds of this meager income was to be deposited to a trust fund under the control of the boarding school superintendent. It is not clear from the record if Indian servants who were out of school were given their full wages directly.[85]

The agendas of employers often clashed with the priorities of the young Indian servants. White women employers wanted obedient and dedicated servants who would work long hours for low wages. After her servant "Hannah" left because "she would rather work in Oakland where she knew someone and where it was a larger place," Dorris Taft of San Mateo wrote to Matron Traxler to request a new servant, but one who would work for fifteen dollars a month instead of the minimum of twenty-five that Traxler usually required. Taft implored Traxler, "I would like awfully to get a good girl, but one who will stay, this changing and training is a very hard thing both on the girl and on me."[86]

Because most of the girls boarded with their employers, they also had to contend with efforts to limit their leisure time, a perennial problem for all domestic servants who lived in their workplaces.[87] Mrs. Parlier of Berkeley was annoyed when her servant "Sylvia" went with her girlfriends to San Francisco in a taxicab. She was "indignant that people who did household employment should spend their [money] in that way."[88] Indian domestic servants experienced an additional layer of restraint on their free time due to the added maternalist mission expected of white women employers. Mrs. Harrington asked Matron Royce, for example, to clarify how late her servant could stay out at night: "She has a friend in the city—an Indian girl and last Sunday they went to a dance. I feel [she] is a fine girl and one to be trusted, but I simply wanted to know whether I am responsible for her hour."[89] In these cases, the white women often claimed to be not only employers but uplifters who needed to protect and shape the morals of the young Indian women in their employ and care.

As was common in other domestic service arrangements, white women also sought to command deference and strict obedience from their employees. Many young Indian women seemed unwilling to conform to their mistresses' demands. Mrs. Whittaker, for instance, complained that Opal "did not put forth any effort to learn to cook or to 'take hold' in general until she had become very severe with [Opal]."[90] Grace Cresap complained that her Indian girls "have been sullen. They do their work, but not in a happy manner." Thus Cresap decided to return the girls to Matron Royce.[91] As these cases illustrate, white women employers were disappointed in young Indian women who refused to play the role of obedient, cheerful, and humble servant in need of guidance, protection, and "civilization."

For their part, the young Indian women merely sought employment with reasonable hours and decent wages with greater control over their leisure time. They routinely objected to the low salaries white women tried to pay them as well as white women's frequent refusal to pay their full salaries. In 1934, for example, Opal wrote in exasperation to Van Every of her Berkeley employer, "Mrs. . . . David owes me ten dollars and she won't pay me for it. She accuses me of taking things which I didn't do. Do you remember when I left last July you told me to tell you if I didn't receive my pay to tell you. Well I didn't receive it and besides she accused the girl before me . . . of the same thing. I think it's just a stunt to get out of paying me. . . . I wrote several letters to her, but finally gave it up as hopeless. She only paid me twelve a month." Opal added in a postscript, "I need the money terribly and I earned it, more than earned it so please make her pay me."[92]

The type of work the young women were asked to do also grated on them. Opal lamented, "[When Mrs. David] did let me go to Oakland for the dances she always wanted me to go up to the house to mow the land and kill fleas. The house was just infested with them. That is a terrible job by itself. That meant scrubbing all the ten rooms."[93] The servants seemed to particularly dislike caring for children. "Hannah" complained, "[Mrs. Wright] expected me to take care of the kids and do house work at the same time—which I just could *not* do. They [the kids] wouldn't mind." Moreover, Hannah protested, "I had no privacy whatever—the kids slept in my bed—used my things—sassed me back."[94] Hannah's experience suggests that many young indigenous servants, far from developing a motherly intimacy with the children in their care, resented the expectation that they should care for children in addition to their other household duties. Would the Wright children, however, remember Hannah fondly, thinking of all the times they slept in her bed? We cannot know for sure, but research from other colonial sites may provide a clue. Ann Laura Stoler and Karen Strassler found a disconnect between the memories of Dutch colonialists and the Indonesian women who served them. While the Dutch called up childhood memories of "sensuous evocations of bodily intimacy" with their servants, who were "like family," the servants only remembered dull and monotonous "routines, tasks, and commands," regimented schedules, and being relegated to "out back."[95]

Indian girls also chafed at the restrictions their employers placed on their social lives. "Myra's" intercepted letter to her boyfriend is revealing in this regard. After staying out late with her "dearie," Myra wrote to him:

> I am writing to tell you what a time I had last night. . . . I was locked out so I couldn't come in, I sure wished I stayed with you then. I am here at the YWCA now writing you these few lines. Well, Honey, so I might not get to see you Sunday. . . . Maybe I have to stay Home all-day. It certainly will be tough. If I can't see you. . . .
>
> Well, Mrs. J. call Mrs. Royce up this morning, and told her I was locked out and she told Go right Back to Mrs. Johnson, But I haven't started yet. Hell with Johnsons. They make me sick all over. I might be going Home to Ukiah, on the next Train that pulls out for all I know.[96]

Such conflicts between domestic servants and their employers over wages, hours, type of work, and leisure were not uncommon in many historical contexts. In this case, however, the additional mission to uplift the young women further complicated the unequal class and race dynamics inherent in servant-employer relationships. Most of the young servants seem to have resisted their employers as maternalistic and uplifting figures. Winona, for example, according to Royce, was "going with associates whose influence we think is bad; she ignores all our advice and that of her employer."[97]

To deal with these conflicts, some young Indian women simply ran away from their jobs, just as Aboriginal servants commonly did. Matron Royce wrote to the mother of one young woman, "I am sorry to report that [Amelia] ran away from a very good place, and I have just learned that she is with [May] at Clovis Calif."[98] Myra threatened to do the same; she wrote to her boyfriend, "I'll tell the wide world, sure as the sun raises, I am going to run away if they treat me like a jail bird."[99] Other Indian women servants called upon the mediating position of the outing matron to gain greater leverage with their white women employers. When Opal's former employer, Mrs. Whittaker, refused to pay her the $3.82 she was owed, Van Every "urged her to write Mrs. Whittaker about the money." A few days later "Mrs. Whittaker called [Van Every] on the telephone and later came into the office protesting that she would not pay [Opal]. [Van Every] maintained that the amount was due to [Opal]." Just two days later, "Mrs. Whittaker left a check for [Opal]."[100]

Some young Indian women, however, seem to have resented the interference, control, and monitoring of the matrons as much as that of their employers. "Etta" wrote to her father to protest "against Mrs. Royce having anything to do with her while she is working in Oakland." The superintendent at Etta's reservation countered, however, that it was Royce's job "to look after the interests of young Indian women who work in the coast cities." "While [Etta] may be 22 years of age," he noted, "I do not think she should resent any supervision that Mrs. Royce may have over her."[101] Etta and her father disagreed. Her father wrote to Royce in 1925, "I wish you would leave [Etta] alone. She's all right when you leave her alone, she old enough to look after her self." Royce seemed to object to the man that Etta had chosen to marry. "If that boy love her and she loves him leave them alone," Etta's father admonished Royce. "We can't pick out her husband and his wife for them so just leave them alone, let them get married if they love each others." Etta's father noted a double standard: "These people here just leave the young paleface alone, they don't but in when they want to get married, they just let them get married. I thought any people I mean Indians could get married any time as long as they're old enough. If they have their folks consent, But I'm mistaken I see."[102]

In fact, like Etta, many young women defied the matrons and their employers over the gender roles and sexual standards they sought to instill in the girls. Rather than abiding by the outdated Victorian standards that were often promoted in the schools, many of the girls embraced the new, freer sexual expression for women that had begun to appear in American popular culture around the 1910s. New hairstyles, music, movies, and books lured the young women away from boarding school fare. Elsie told Matron Van Every that "she wished to stay a while [in a new job] until she got some things she needed including a permanent wave."[103] While hospitalized, Sarah asked Van Every for "two new movie magazines and one Western Romance.": "If you would please send them to me. Is all I would like to have."[104]

As with Aboriginal servants in Australia, the young Indian women particularly resented the control that authorities had over their money. "Sharon" challenged Royce's control of her trust fund. "[Sharon] called me on [the] phone last week and demanded the funds I had in my office," Royce wrote to the superintendent of the Western Shoshone Agency. "When I told her I had transferred same to you she was very abusive and talked as no other girl had ever done. All this is very humiliating; considering the patience I have had with her and all the trouble and care she has caused." Royce lamented, "I have done all in my power to advance these girl's [sic] welfare and have to acknowledge defeat for the first time, as [Sharon] is the first girl to positively refuse my supervision."[105]

Also like young Aboriginal women, many of the young Indian women aspired to a higher calling than domestic service. Yet in the United States they also bumped up against the low expectations of their employers, matrons, and reservation and school officials. In 1933 "Margaret" told John Collier, the newly appointed commissioner of Indian affairs, of her frustrating experience. In her impeccably typed letter, Margaret wrote, "I am an Indian girl and a graduate from Sherman Institute. . . . I was sent out to that school to get an education. When I graduated I found I could not get any other job but as a housekeeper. Any girl knows how to do that sort of work I'm sure. My four years wasted. I found I could have accomplished more if I had attended a regular public high school." Margaret also told Collier that her family had lost their land and become destitute. Her grandmother had sold the family's land, and they were living off the money from its sale. When her grandmother died, however, Margaret's family could not get the rest of the money because her grandmother had not left a will. Margaret lamented, "The reason why we Indians in the middle part of California are backward is because we have nothing to get started with. The little we have doesn't amount to anything. We have no money to go to college to be somebody. Why doesn't somebody give us a break?" She explained further to Collier, "I am working here in Hollywood as a housekeeper. My salary is twenty a month. My ambition was to become a nurse; as I am lacking some credits, I can't get in any nursing school. That means I just have to go back and start my four years over again." She concluded, "This is just a glimpse of one Indian family, but there are many more in California."[106]

Collier proved to be of little help to Margaret.[107] She continued to work throughout the 1930s as a housekeeper. Later she became pregnant and married, but then separated from her husband. When she could not find a place to board the baby while she worked, she decided to leave the child with her mother and make her mother its legal guardian. Margaret remained resentful that after years of boarding school she could not find work other than domestic service. In 1941, according to Van Every, a man came into her placement center and told her, "[Margaret] . . . and [her friend] . . . are violent in their attitude toward our office. . . . They lose no opportunity to make remarks and criticisms and say that we keep Indian girls down." Finally in 1942 Margaret was able to complete a course at the hospital and gain a temporary position there.[108]

Like Margaret, many young Indian women—roughly one quarter of my sample of ninety-seven cases—also became pregnant while working as domestic servants.[109] Unlike the situation in Australia, however, it seems that many of the young women became pregnant not as a result of their employers' sexual abuse, but in relationships of their choosing. While the outing matrons' efforts to control Indian women undoubtedly frustrated the young women's ambitions and desires to be free, the matrons' inspections of employer homes may have shielded young Indian servants from the sexual predation that seems to have been more common in the white Australian households where Aboriginal women worked. Young Indian servants, however, did find a way to evade the matrons' control of their leisure outside of white homes. Freed from the constraints of the boarding schools, many young women seemed to revel in new social opportunities and the chance to flirt and socialize with boys. Some of their relationships culminated in formal or common law marriage, to both Indians and non-Indians, and almost always outside their tribes. "Ruth" married a Portuguese man in 1934. Winona "married a white man with the Radio-Post at San Francisco Beach." "Eunice," a Winnebago, began living with a "Negro" in 1938.[110]

Some Indian servants, like Margaret, became single mothers. This presented a new challenge to them: How would they support and care for their children? Like Aboriginal women in domestic service, some young Indian women left their children back home with relatives. "Mary," a Pomo, had two children who stayed with her mother while she went to work as a domestic servant for nine months of the year. Mary came home in the summers, where she could find work picking hops and see her children.[111] Other Indian women gave up their domestic jobs altogether and returned to their communities. When "Stella" had her baby, she first left her child with its grandmother while she worked as a domestic, but eventually Stella quit her job and went back to her home, which a Ukiah field nurse described as "the camp where her family is staying." Interestingly, despite their maternalistic bent, white women often disapproved of young Indian women's decision to stay at home with their children. A field nurse in Ukiah lamented to Royce about Stella, "So another effort to help her has gone wrong. I still believe the girl wants to do right. It was a lot to expect of her to leave her baby and all her relatives to go out alone to earn a living."[112] It is unlikely that this nurse would have expected or encouraged a white woman to leave her baby to work outside the home.

Other Indian women boarded out their children while they worked. "Ethel," a Paiute, "arrived in Oakland, July 23–1931 With small baby girl." Royce placed Ethel as a domestic and put her baby in a boarding home, but admitted to a field matron among the Paiutes, "I am sure I do not know how we are going to pay for the baby's board, for I fear [Ethel] cannot make enough to support herself and child. The price of the baby's board is $25.00, and [Ethel] has started to work for that amount."[113] Indeed, boarding out one's baby while working was a costly proposition and illustrated that young Indian women were subject to the same type of diverted mothering that Aboriginal servants faced.

The matrons also put pressure on young Indian women to give their children up for adoption, thus renewing the cycle of child removal all over again. The case of "Nellie" is a poignant one. When Van Every first began her work, she and Matron Traxler encountered Nellie, who had a twenty-two-month old boy, "Sammy," who lived with Mrs. Upson while Nellie worked. Nellie had since married and had had another baby but hoped to bring Sammy to live with her new family once her husband found a steady job. Van Every reported that Nellie "does not wish to place the child [Sammy] in an institution." Despite Nellie's reluctance to part with her son, Van Every and Traxler called upon Marie White of the California Children's Home Society, "urging steps to be taken immediately in giving [Sammy] a home rather than longer continuing with Mrs. Upson, who is getting too old to care for him longer." Van Every reported, "Mrs. White said that unless [Nellie] can assume the responsibility of the child or some of the girls' family can see the child thru, the child must be adopted out," but the mother must "sign a relinquishment or a consent before an agency can do the work need[ed] to take over the case."

Traxler and Van Every then went to visit Nellie again. By now economic exigencies seem to have convinced Nellie that she had no other choice but to give up her son. "When asked what she intended doing about [Sammy] she said that she would have to let him be adopted out. . . . We told her of Mrs. Marie White of the Children's Home Society of California and of the work the Society did. She seemed to understand the steps necessary to placing [Sammy] in a Home. She agreed that she would cooperate fully with Mrs. White." A few weeks later Van Every learned that "[Nellie] is expecting another baby and is quite willing to give [Sammy] up, not knowing what else to do about him. She signed the relinquishment papers."[114]

In other cases the matrons and other BIA officials sought to have some children removed from their Indian mothers and institutionalized, just as many of them had been parted from their own parents to attend boarding schools. Losing their children in such a way was often a source of intense pain and anguish for the young women. Etta, for example (the woman whose father had protested against Royce's intervention into her relationship), had been separated from her parents and raised at the Carson Indian School. When authorities removed her four children and sought to place the oldest, a six-year-old boy, at the Carson School, Etta objected stringently. A probation officer reported, "[Etta] is most unwilling for this placement, stating that she had been very unhappy there and that she could not possibly consider placing her child there."[115] Despite Etta's wishes, Royce conspired with the superintendent to place Etta's son at the Carson School. In fact, Royce declared that Etta's "wishes should not be considered in this case, as she is incapable of judging what is best for her boy."[116]

Authorities not only removed Etta's children but took steps to have her placed in a mental institution, claiming that a psychological test had "rated [her] as borderline, mental age 11 years." The matrons' outing records reveal that three other Indian women who had several children out of wedlock and resisted officials' attempts to remove their children were also eventually committed to mental institutions.[117] As the Australian historian Victoria Haskins has found, young Aboriginal women servants who defied authorities were also subject to committal to mental institutions.[118] These cases are a sobering reminder of the ways the BIA continued to wield child removal as a weapon of great power against Indian peoples.

Thus, as with young Aboriginal servants, the cycle of state intervention to separate Indian women from their children continued. Yet Indian parents sought to maintain contact with their daughters who had been outed, often through the outing matron. "Maureen's" mother, for example, frequently contacted the superintendent of the Indian agency in Bishop, California, to learn of her daughter's whereabouts and to seek her return. The superintendent wrote to Royce, "[The mother] is greatly worried regarding her daughter [Maureen]. . . . [She] has received a letter from [Maureen] . . . in which she states that she has left her place where she is working and is looking for another place. . . . [The mother] came to me with the intention of immediately placing a ticket for [Maureen] to come home as she didn't want her to be drifting about in this way. [She] fears that something might happen to her [daughter]."[119]

Although many young Indian women clearly enjoyed aspects of their time in the Bay Area, ties to their communities still tugged at them. When Victoria left her place of employment she received all of her personal items except her photo album. She wrote with alarm to Royce, "That means the world to me because its got my passed away relatives picture in it, my grand ma's was the [only one]."[120] After being let go by her employer, twenty-two-year-old Elsie came to Van Every's office, suitcase in hand, and told Van Every that "she did not like living so far off in the hills and she would rather return home to Nevada." According to Van Every, "[Elsie] said that she did not fit very well in the city."[121] Here again the experience of young Indian women servants diverged from that of Aboriginal apprentices. Young Indian women like Elsie could and often did go back to their homes. In fact, for many young Indian women, engaging in domestic work became part of a seasonal economic strategy. Many young Pomo women, for example, worked picking hops in the summers and served in white women's households in the Bay Area for the remainder of the year.[122] Young Aboriginal women, by contrast, who were often removed at a very young age and whose families had been "dispersed," had greater difficulty finding and reconnecting with their kin and rarely had communities to which to return.

To white women reformers and state authorities, placing indigenous girls in domestic service through the outing and apprenticeship programs represented one more means of distancing the girls from their homes and severing ties with their families, or, in the euphemistic parlance of the times, assimilating and absorbing them. In this process white women were key players, both as outing matrons in the case of the United States and as employers in both countries.

Here, however, more than in the tightly controlled setting of the institutions, the maternal mission became increasingly difficult to maintain. Although state authorities and reformers expected white female employers to act in a maternal manner to their charges by continuing to "protect" them, it rarely worked out this way. White female employers tended to be more concerned with issues of labor than with uplift, with whether the girls carried out their work properly than with whether they were sexually pure. Moreover, the placement of indigenous girls in white homes subjected them (especially in the case of Australia) to sexual predation by white men in the household. Many white mistresses thus failed to fulfill the maternalist role the state and white women reformers envisioned for them.

Young indigenous women too resisted the continued surveillance and control over their lives that officials and reformers sought to extend into the private homes of white women employers. In the United States, especially in urban areas, many young Indian women quickly abandoned the strict sexual codes that white women had sought to instill in them in boarding schools; others jettisoned all pretence of deference toward white women. In some cases outing afforded young Indian women greater individual and sexual freedom. By contrast, in their memoirs and oral histories Aboriginal women rarely represented their experience of domestic service as a carefree period in their lives. The state continued to exert stricter control over Aboriginal girls and young women. Even Indian girls, though, operated within significant constraints. Due to prejudice, most could not pursue educational opportunities, and only the most unskilled jobs were open to them. And once they had their own children, authorities often claimed their children for the institutions or as adoptees into white families. Increasingly, however, many indigenous women and men had begun to speak out against the removal of their children. A few white women also grew to oppose the practice and abandon the maternalist agenda altogether. I continue their story in the next chapter.

Chapter 9

Challenging Indigenous Child Removal

Our mistakes of the past four years have been those of centering efforts on the reservation, and this is due to women,—sympathetic, and I guess I had better say meddlesome—who not having practical knowledge and experience, are guided by the tender qualities of their natures. My expectation is that the present administration will be more common-sense and that there will be a reaction. I count Indian Rights Associations and National Indian Women's Associations foremost now among the harmful influences in Indian management. • RICHARD HENRY PRATT, 1893, in Larner, *Papers of Carlos Montezuma*

As Richard Henry Pratt lamented, relying on white women to carry out maternal colonial aims did not always result in bolstering the state's aims of containing and controlling (or, euphemistically, "assimilating" and "protecting") indigenous people. Enlisted to carry out key aspects of indigenous child removal, white women sometimes developed an ambiguous attitude toward their prescribed jobs. The new intimate relationships they created with indigenous children often complicated their allegiance to policy makers and their agendas. In fact, intimacy between white women and indigenous children, particularly in the institutions, could utterly shatter white women's confidence in the colonial and maternalist agenda. Real ties of affection and growing familiarity with indigenous experience led some white women to question and then condemn the actual *policy* of removing indigenous children. And a few white women moved beyond registering their individual opposition to actually allying with indigenous women and organizing campaigns against the practice. In doing so, these women found it necessary to break away from prior maternalist conceptions of and agendas for indigenous women.

As in the past, white women in the United States enjoyed greater influence in reform and government circles than did their Australian counterparts. In the 1920s, together with like-minded white men, anti-assimilationist white women worked with Indian activists to orchestrate a sustained and successful assault on assimilation policy, including Indian child removal. By contrast, in Australia the few white women who organized against Aboriginal child removal found themselves rebuffed by government officials and often by other reformers as well. Still, their opposition to the practice and their alliances with indigenous women laid the groundwork for post–World War II campaigns for Aboriginal rights.

Growing Opposition to Indigenous Child Removal among White Women in Australia

The first signs of opposition to the practice of Aboriginal child removal by white women show up in what seem at first to be unlikely sources: among white women who served as agents of the state and missionary women. Given that their positions of authority and influence derived from their adherence to the goals of their government agency or church missionary society, we would not expect to see opposition developing from these positions. Yet through sustained contact with Aboriginal families, some of these white women became aware of the devastating injustice of child removal. The clash between indigenous realities, white women's maternalist priorities, and government and missionary goals led some white women to retreat from their support for Aboriginal child removal.

In Victoria Anne Bon was the only woman to serve on the Board for the Protection of Aborigines, first appointed in 1904 and serving until 1934, when she died at the age of ninety-nine. She became sympathetic to the many Aboriginal people who wrote to her of their plight. Their surviving letters suggest that although Bon was limited in what she could do, she became a trusted ally to many indigenous families and used her influence to soften the worst aspects of removal. For example, in 1918 she intervened to help a dying child be returned to its "poor mother." "The changes [the parents] so much desire will not prove a cure," Bon pleaded, "but will afford happiness to parents and child to get away from a home where, I fear in cases of sickness very little sympathy is shown."[1] Bon also interceded later in the 1930s on behalf of a group of part-Aboriginal people who were being evicted from their land at Framlingham because, as "quadroons and octoroons," they did not qualify as Aborigines.[2] Through her frequent mediations on behalf of Aboriginal people, Anne Bon earned a reputation as a thorn in the side of authorities. One member of the board wrote, as early as 1886, of "the trouble and annoyance Mrs. Bon and her protegés give the Board." Bon in fact was censured for disloyalty three times during her tenure on the board.[3]

Although many white women missionaries, such as Annie Lock (see chapter 5), clung to the belief that they knew what was best for Aboriginal people, others were moved by their experiences with Aborigines to reconsider their support for child removal. Upon first encountering Mrs. E. McKenzie Hatton, for example, in the archival record, I judged her to be of the same mold as Annie Lock. Hatton wrote to the prime minister for a special permit and commission to investigate the conditions of Aboriginal and "half-caste" girls of the commonwealth. She told him of her work as a missionary in Queensland for sixteen years, "I had frequently to act as protector to many poor aboriginal girls, and am proud to say had the pleasure of helping them to a better condition of life."[4]

However, long-term association with an Aboriginal woman she referred to as Mrs. Charles fractured Hatton's confidence in the maternal agenda. As a girl, Mrs. Charles had been parted from her family to be "uplifted" by Hatton. She then went on to work as a missionary for fourteen years in the Solomon Islands. After her stint there, Mrs. Charles returned to her original home island in Queensland and, "by a series of remarkable circumstances," reunited with her Aboriginal family, married, and had her own children. In her own community, according to Hatton, Mrs. Charles came to serve as a model native missionary, initiating classes and meetings for Aboriginal women. But even this acculturated Christian woman and her family could not avoid the strong arm of authority. Hatton explained that Mrs. Charles's family, "comprising the father and five children—three girls aged 17, 14, and 12 years, and two small boys,—were seized by the police for removal to the Aboriginal government settlement. The unfortunate people implored to be allowed to remain on the island; their entreaties were all in vain. . . . This hapless family, for no crime, other than that of being black," were jailed for three days to await transit to the settlement.[5] In this instance, Hatton's ongoing friendship with an Aboriginal woman enabled her to experience firsthand the injustice and the lie of child removal policy. Mrs. Charles was a good mother by Hatton's standards; Hatton herself had rescued and brought her up. Yet even she was vulnerable to the state's dispossession of Aboriginal children. Hatton's association with Charles must have led her to ask whether there might be other Aboriginal families who suffered a similar fate.

Hatton also was horrified by the story of her friend Miss Ayers, a missionary who worked on an Aboriginal settlement in New South Wales. During one periodic visit by a policeman, Ayers asked him, "'Where do you take these girls, and what do you do with them when you remove them from the Station[?]' The answer was—'We take them to the city and *lose* them'!" Hatton wrote the prime minister of Miss Ayers's story as well as that of another missionary colleague, Miss Murray, who witnessed "the sorrow of an old man wailing for the loss of his little daughter, who, with no gentle hand, was being dragged off before his eyes by the officer of the law."[6]

Given these circumstances, Hatton and her white women associates requested a special permit from the prime minister to investigate the conditions of Aboriginal girls, declaring, "No wonder some of us cry out with longing and ask to be allowed to *save* them."[7] In this remarkable letter, Hatton shifts back and forth between a maternalist agenda—a longing to protect and save Aboriginal girls—and a critical assessment of state child removal policies. She did not entirely break with the maternalist agenda, but her plaintive letter reveals her growing discomfort with its central tenets. Predictably, state authorities were not responsive to Hatton's criticism. The minister informed Hatton that the issues she raised were matters for states, not the commonwealth government: "It is regretted, therefore, that advantage cannot be taken of your kind offer to investigate the conditions of natives in Australia."[8]

Disillusioned with missionary and state aims and practices regarding Aboriginal families, Hatton instead developed closer contacts with the Aboriginal community in Sydney and worked with the Aboriginal activist Fred Maynard and his newly established Australian Aboriginal Progressive Association (AAPA) in the 1920s. Through this sustained interaction with Aboriginal activists in the AAPA, as documented by the Australian historian John Maynard, Hatton experienced a remarkable transformation. "I came over here from another state expecting to preach to heathen people," she revealed. "But I found an eager keen people who demanded a voice in their own destiny." Listening to this voice, Hatton lost faith in both missionary organizations and the government.[9]

Institutions themselves could be breeding grounds for white women reformers' and missionaries' opposition to Aboriginal child removal, especially when the dismal conditions in the homes and missions and on the reserves undermined white women's desire to transform indigenous homes and bodies. As a result of the miserable state of affairs at the infamous Mogumber or Moore River Settlement in Western Australia, three white women employees there developed a tentative opposition to removing Aboriginal children. Miss Jones complained to officials that Aboriginal children "are herded together like cattle" in the dormitories. She pointed out, "There is no waterproof sheeting for children's beds and no drying facilities at all, so wet beds are simply made up and remain wet." Jones also objected that the children were "locked up like fowls after an early tea [dinner] every night, winter and summer. No light, no fire, no recreation at all . . . no wonder they run away." She also opposed incarcerating the girls in the "boob" (which "measure[d] six feet by four and [was] infested with rats") for fourteen days as punishment for running away. Jones's associate, Miss Birt, also complained of "bug-infested beds" and dirty mattresses, with no sheets and pillowcases provided. She concluded, "There seemed to be very little psychological knowledge or understanding of boys and girls in the adolescent age—one felt at times it would have been better to have left them to their more moral and tribal customs in many ways." Notably, officials' failures to provide decent conditions in the institutions undermined white women's efforts to help Aboriginal children to live "cleaner" lives.

Birt's and Jones's colleague, Sister Eileen Heath, an Anglican deaconess who came to Mogumber in 1935, also spoke out against conditions there. Heath complained to her bishop of the high turnover of staff at Moore River, which she attributed to such disillusionment with the Department of Native Affairs that "fair-minded and decent people do not care to be associated with the odour which surrounds it." She deemed immorality to be rife at Moore River, contending, "[The mission] has developed into an all night and all day brothel." Yet she laid responsibility for this condition at the feet of officials, not Aboriginal people. She called the bishop's attention to the fact that at both Moore River and Carrolup, another native settlement, there had been no schools in operation for months and that at Moore River, "about 150 children . . . are growing up without even the first rudiments of education. . . . The adolescents are a tremendous problem, and are fast degenerating into an immoral loafing camp life, and they will be condemned in later years for the very tendencies we are encouraging in them to-day." Interestingly, Heath's incisive critique noted that it was officials who were creating the very conditions—"an immoral loafing camp life"—they so often used to justify the removal of children in the first place.

Like her colleagues Miss Jones and Miss Birt, from her bitter experience at Mogumber Heath came to question the entire policy of rounding up Aboriginal people on government settlements. She soundly condemned the Department of Native Affairs for its "apathetic attitude which is content to spend thousands annually to keep the natives out of sight and out of mind, without any regard for their development and responsibility as citizens." She added that officials regarded Moore River as "an orphanage, reformatory, penal settlement, vocational training centre (so called), a camping place for indigent natives and a general dumping place for all the undesirables who are unwanted elsewhere." She concluded, "I feel ashamed that our Church is identified with this place as it exists to-day. . . . I honestly think we are doing more harm by herding people together under such impossible living conditions than allowing them to live out their own lives outside."[10]

Nearly sixty years later, when interviewed for the Bringing Them Home Oral History Project, Heath recalled Mogumber in much the same way. She explained that the staff at Mogumber "were frustrated. They came up full of hope . . . but they were limited to how they could do things because there was a policy set and . . . we all had to conform to that particular policy." Heath depicted this policy as dictatorial and tyrannical. Without the chief protector's permission, an Aboriginal person could not leave the settlement, write letters, marry or be baptized, work, or drink alcohol. Children could not leave their dormitories without permission, and contact with their parents in the nearby "camp" was discouraged and infrequent. Like many Aboriginal people, Heath characterized Mogumber as a prison with many runaways who were punished by being "locked in [the boob] for varying periods." She remembered one night when a girl in the boob "had gone completely berserk," and consequently had to be put in an insane asylum, from which she "never came out."

Heath may have developed her critical stance on Mogumber through her close associations with the children and her ability to appreciate rather than completely vilify Aboriginal culture. "Like all children," she remembered, "they made the best of things." She recalled that the children loved singing, swimming, and hunting, and she frequently swam with them in the Moore River. She observed that they supplemented their poor diet with bush food and that many Aboriginal people in the settlement continued to practice other aspects of their culture, such as "sorry cuts," wailing, and other grieving rituals.[11] Not surprisingly, Aboriginal people who remember Heath, including Doris Pilkington, liked her. Leonard Ogilvie remembers that she took children on outings to the city and the bush.[12]

Other white women also developed a critical perspective on Aboriginal child removal through intimacy with indigenous individuals or communities. At least one white woman employer of Aboriginal domestic servants became aware of and opposed to the policies and practices of Aboriginal child removal. The historian Victoria Haskins writes of her great-grandmother, Joan Kingsley Strack, or "Ming," who became politically radicalized through her conflicts with the Board for the Protection of Aborigines in New South Wales over her Aboriginal apprentices. Ming's growing frustration with the board and its treatment of Aboriginal girls eventually led her to join the Aboriginal activist Pearl Gibbs and the Aborigines Progressive Association, albeit briefly, in the late 1930s.[13]

The white woman who developed the most vocal and sustained opposition to Aboriginal child removal was Mary Bennett. In her earliest work that touched on Aboriginal issues, Bennett shared the common maternalist view that it was often necessary to remove Aboriginal children to "protect" them. She described her pastoralist father's failed attempts to guard an Aboriginal woman, Rosy, and her daughter, Topsy, on his station from sexual exploitation by a white man. "Christison was wrung with pity for the miserable myall [Aboriginal woman] Rosy," she wrote. "But no power on earth could turn him from doing what he believed to be his duty." He summoned the police to arrest Topsy and to await orders from the protector of Aborigines. "The order came back promptly to send the child to the Aboriginal Home on the coast," Bennett wrote with admiration for what she understood as her father's difficult but principled stand.[14]

When Bennett returned to Australia she sought out intense interactions with Aboriginal people and sympathetic whites that would eventually challenge her maternalist sentiments. In the early 1930s she traveled to the north of Western Australia, where she met the missionary Mr. Love at Port George, or Kunmunyu, who told her, "We shall not build Christians by teaching people to despise and neglect their parents." Bennett admired Love's school, where the children learned English and other white Australian school subjects, but lived with their parents and thereby "gain[ed] their own language, their tribal history and traditions, knowledge of tracking and hunting, of nature and the resources of their country."[15]

In 1932 Bennett arrived at the Mt. Margaret Mission with two spinning wheels and two looms that she had ordered from Sweden. She contracted with the mission for six months to teach spinning and weaving to Aboriginal women, but stayed on as resident teacher with the Reverend R. M. and Mysie Schenk for eight more years.[16] In 1933 she opened a school for the forty Aboriginal children at Mt. Margaret, using the correspondence school curriculum that Mysie Schenk was using with her own children. In many ways, Mt. Margaret was similar to other institutions for Aboriginal children. In 1928 the Schenks had established a dormitory system, the "Graham Homes," that was designed to separate Aboriginal children from their parents. An Aboriginal "camp" existed nearby. Moreover, the Schenks, and later Bennett, were concerned with controlling marriages of "their" children to mates they deemed suitable. As in other contexts, this created great conflict with Aboriginal families. According to the historian Margaret Morgan, opposition to placing girls in the Graham Homes developed from older men who believed the homes interfered with the practice of betrothing young girls to older men in polygamous marriages.[17]

During her first months at Mt. Margaret, Bennett maintained common maternalist assumptions, arguing for the "protection" of native girls and women. For example, in 1933 she told the Women's Service Guilds (WSG) in Perth that the Aboriginal girls at Mt. Margaret "are unwilling to go to the old men. They may be kept as wives or may be sold to a white man for a plug of tobacco." The girls were equally threatened by white men, according to Bennett. "Wherever there is a white man's camp there is need for protection for these girls," she told the WSG.[18]

Over time, however, Bennett's experience at Mt. Margaret reoriented her views; she dropped her support for "protection" and developed a vehement opposition to the removal of Aboriginal children. At Mt. Margaret she became schooled in the tyrannical ways that Chief Protector Neville administered Aboriginal affairs in Western Australia and also witnessed several alternative approaches to living and working with Aborigines. Though Mt. Margaret was engaged in separating Aboriginal children from their families, it differed substantially from other institutions for Aboriginal children. As a private mission, Mt. Margaret could not compel students to attend, as government institutions could. Bennett wrote, "We can only hold them by sheer appeal, or we cannot hold them at all." Thus, perhaps out of necessity, Mt. Margaret allowed frequent contact between Aboriginal children and their families. Some children lived in the mission homes, some in the "camp." The mission regularly held parents' nights and arranged a two-week holiday every year for parents to take their children away.[19] Thus, when faced with the threat of removal of their children to the government-run institution at Moore River, many Aboriginal families preferred to bring their children to Mt. Margaret. This situation created long-standing conflict with Chief Protector Neville and other government authorities, who believed Mt. Margaret failed to properly remove the children from all camp influence and considered the mission to be in competition with Moore River.[20]

At Mt. Margaret, Bennett also witnessed alternative maternalist approaches to Aboriginal affairs through her friendship and collegial relationship with Mysie Schenk. Although she bore and raised her own children (with the help of Aboriginal women), Schenk took an active part in the affairs of the mission. She disapproved of the conditions that faced Aboriginal girls who went into domestic service in white homes, so Mt. Margaret did not send their girls out for employment. Instead, Schenk started a program to teach Aboriginal girls and women arts and crafts. In many ways, she created a maternalist utopia in the Charlotte

23. Mary Bennett, left, teaching Bessie and Nardie how to cook in her home at Mt. Margaret Mission, ca. 1930s. BA 1340, 009792d, Schenk Family Collection of Photographs of Mt. Margaret Mission, 1921–1990. Courtesy of Battye Library, Perth, Western Australia.

Perkins Gilman mode at Mt. Margaret, spending most of her days with Aboriginal women and children. While some women took care of children, others were freed to carry out other duties. According to Margaret Morgan, Schenk "was never short of nursemaids who loved and cuddled her children when she was busy."

Mysie Schenk's maternalist utopia, however, was under constant threat by Neville's policies and practices. Schenk became quite attached to several young Aboriginal women and girls, only to see them taken by government authorities. In one instance, an Aboriginal mother brought her teenage girl, Lallie, to Mt. Margaret to prevent her from being taken by authorities. According to Morgan, "Mysie took Lallie into her home and loved her. Lallie in turned [sic] loved Mysie's two babies." Yet five days after Lallie gave birth to a stillborn premature baby, authorities took her away to Moore River. "Mysie was shattered," writes Morgan. Such experiences seem to have led Bennett down a more radical path than that followed by many other white women reformers.

During her tenure at Mt. Margaret Bennett developed a scathing critique of colonial policies regarding land, labor, and the breaking up of Aboriginal families. She protested that white pastoralists had been given access to hundreds of thousands of acres of land, leaving Aborigines with just a scant remnant of their original country. She concluded, "Parliament will have to raise vast sums for rations to avoid the frightful reproach of starving the natives to death in their own country, or else restore the land, where, safe from molestation by whites . . . , our natives can settle in homes and earn their own living and develop what is morally their country as well as ours." Bennett estimated that at least fifty native territories should be established throughout Western Australia to meet the needs for land of Aboriginal people.[21] Hoping to strike a nerve in a nation founded on the transportation of convicts to a penal colony, Bennett contended, "Aboriginals are deeply attached to their own country, and should not be 'transported.'"[22]

Yet Bennett recognized that white settlers had little incentive to restore lands to native peoples so that they could live self-sufficiently. She contended, instead, "It pays the white man to dispossess the natives of their land wholesale, because the Government permits them to impress the natives as labour without paying them."[23] In calling for the restoration of native land and full rights for Aborigines, Bennett insisted that Aborigines were deserving of praise, not slander:

> Throughout the north [of Australia] people told me, "the nigger is an animal, he's a monkey, he can't reason, he's got no brains, you've got to treat him like a child." . . . Yet the natives have a very wonderful culture of their own, a marvel of humanity and mathematics. . . . Actually the wild aboriginals are better Christians than we are, for white culture is overwhelmingly competitive, whereas aboriginal culture is co-operative. . . . They founded their social structure on the sentiment of the *family*, . . . and worked out their social system to unite individuals into groups and provide for collective action BY EXPANDING THE PRINCIPLE OF FAMILY SOLIDARITY TO INCLUDE THE WHOLE TRIBE AND OTHER TRIBES.[24]

Though her remarks seem romantic in our own times, they provided a much needed corrective to the more common pathologizing of Aboriginal cultures in her era.

Bennett came to connect the policy of removing Aboriginal children to the government's other policies regarding land and labor. When Neville told her that Olive Pink supported the removal of half-caste children, she wrote to Pink:

> I do not know you, but I am taking the liberty of writing to you to implore you NOT to condone or justify taking half-caste children from their aboriginal mothers. The unfortunate mothers are only victims of starvation and to separate parents and children is to destroy both in the most cruel way. . . . The recent Land Act Amendment of W.A. takes away from natives the right to hunt over their tribal lands when these are *enclosed*, and as all the native waters are fenced in the squatters have them in a [illegible]. Their game is destroyed and their dogs are destroyed and the only way they can come by a meal is by selling their women. So I say that W.A. is deliberately starving their natives to death in their own country. *But* members of Parliament declare in Parliament "THE IMPORTANT thing is to breed out colour," and as long as "colour" is being bred out, that is all that matters.[25]

Through her experience working at Mt. Margaret, Bennett developed a comprehensive critique of settler colonialism in Australia—including the practice of removing Aboriginal children from their families—that diverged sharply from the maternalist analysis of the "Aboriginal problem."

Growing Opposition to Indigenous Child Removal among White Women in the United States

In the United States too, through their sustained contact with indigenous people, some white women came to question and oppose Indian child removal. And as in Australia, this growing opposition to the practice emanated primarily from missionaries, schoolteachers, and matrons. Speaking before the Lake Mohonk Conference of 1899, Mary Collins, a Congregationalist missionary for twenty-five years among the western Sioux, or Lakota, objected to the notion that "the way to civilize the Indian is . . . to take these children away from the reservation and the influence of the old people." She continued, "Whenever the children are taught to despise their home and parents it is a great mistake. I cannot too strongly protest against that." Collins also admonished her audience, "The only one of the ten Commandments with promise is, 'Honor thy father and mother,' and we cannot drop that out of the Indian decalogue. The children are not to despise their father[s] and mothers, but they are to walk along together." Claiming intimacy with the indigenous people in her community, Collins insisted to her white audience, "There is good in the Indian."[26]

Furthermore, Collins realized that in order to convince her audience to oppose Indian child removal, she must also counter the negative stereotypes of Indian homes and mothers. She told her audience of reformers, "The Indian mother teaches her little child in the home. She takes care to teach what she thinks is right; as much care as you do what you think is right. You would be surprised to go into the Indian home and see how careful they are in the training of the children." Though intent on converting to Christianity the Indians she encountered, Collins nevertheless recognized that they had their own system of education and knowledge in place: "No one can live so close to nature without being educated to some extent. They love to study nature, and they are instructing themselves constantly with regard to certain things."[27]

Like Collins, many women day school teachers promoted day schools within Indian communities as a feasible and preferable alternative to removing Indian children to boarding schools. For example, a report in *The Indian's Friend* highlighted an Indian school in Death Valley that "differs from most others in that it has sought to carry its training to the child in his home environment and to his parents also, instead of uprooting the pupil and separating him as abruptly as possible from his traditional habits." The report also lauded the new teacher, Nell Henderson, for her efforts to "study the Indian language" and concluded, "The success of this modest venture suggests the practicability of community schools for the Indian."[28] Marion Moore concurred with this report; she wrote to the WNIA in 1905, "There is crying need of day schools for these people [the Navajos near Crystal, New Mexico]. These are the only hope for the coming generation. They would keep the little ones at home and give them their right to 'mothering,' and these little ones between four and ten years of age suffer in being taken from parents and relatives and being placed in school with hundreds of other children who are as complete strangers to them as would be Sioux or Choctaws."[29]

Elaine Goodale Eastman became a firm proponent of day schools through her work as both a teacher and a superintendent of Indian education for the Dakotas. Although she remained a maternalist committed to the assimilation of Indian children (and a strong defender of Pratt), she nevertheless broke from the mold in promoting day schools and Indian-language retention rather than a complete separation of children from their families and cultures. After taking a brief trip to the West during her tenure as a teacher at Hampton Institute, Eastman came home inspired to engage in new work. Writing about herself in the third person, she exclaimed, with typical maternalist zeal:

One young woman came home in spirit deeply committed to her task as she saw it. She had made up her mind to begin at the beginning, in the heart of a newly transplanted, leaderless, bewildered little community. Others could carry on in more solidly established institutions where there was ample support and companionship. Few, perhaps, would care to blaze a new trail in the obscure corner of a wild land, among recent "enemies" speaking an unintelligible dialect. Behind such considerations lurked, no doubt, a taste for adventure and a distinct bent toward pioneering, possibly handed down through a long line of American forebears.

Despite opposition from some male officials, at age twenty-two, Eastman and one of her sister teachers at Hampton, Laura Tileston, established a day school at White River Camp on the Lower Brulé Sioux Reservation.

"Most people then believed that it was necessary to separate the children entirely from their home surroundings in order to accomplish results," Eastman remarked in her memoirs, but by the time she returned to the East after three years at the White River Camp, she had become a staunch advocate of community day schools. She spoke frequently to the IRA and the WNIA and met the highest authorities on Indian affairs. According to Eastman, Commissioner of Indian Affairs Thomas Morgan (who forcefully promoted Indian child removal), "asked [her] for [her] program for community day schools and gave it full approval." Morgan was so impressed with Eastman that he created a new office for her to fill, that of supervisor of Indian education in the Dakotas. (However, Eastman was expected to pay her own salary as well as that of her two assistants.) Morgan received "considerable criticism" for selecting a young (twenty-six), unmarried woman to fill this position, but apparently he believed that Eastman "would make a more striking impression upon the Indians than a man."

In this post Eastman continued to favor day schools, partly for pragmatic reasons. "Believing that day schools could be made efficient for elementary training at less than half the cost of boarding schools and with little or no opposition from parents," Eastman asserted, "I urged that they be better equipped to help adult Indians as well as children." She also promoted day schools because "it was rarely necessary to compel, or even to urge, attendance at day schools. The Indian's need of the white man's tools was obvious enough." Indian leaders often showed Eastman the locations they had picked for future potential day schools.

As for boarding schools, Eastman drew comparisons between good and bad schools. When she visited the boarding schools in the Dakotas, she found "the boarding school routine in general drab and lifeless, and the military discipline needlessly harsh. The children had too much drudgery and too little relaxation. They were frequently unhappy and homesick. Some regimentation is no doubt unavoidable in large groups, but one could not but compare these depressing institutions with Hampton, where each individual was loved and studied, with Bishop Hare's homelike, small, church schools, and with the famous 'Outing' at Carlisle, giving opportunity for normal home and school life in association with good American farm families." Many Indian students found Hampton, Carlisle, and many of the mission schools just as "drab and lifeless" and full of "drudgery" as the government boarding schools Eastman visited; Eastman, however, had been a teacher at Hampton and a close associate of Pratt and Bishop Hare. Undoubtedly she did not want to offend them. She did find the boarding schools inappropriate for young children and "advised them only for young people prepared to make good use of wider opportunities—never for small children with a day school at hand." By the time she wrote her memoir in the 1930s, Eastman favored the changes that resulted in more Indian children attending public schools.[30]

Beyond her advocacy for day schools over boarding schools, Eastman was unusual in other ways. Rather than trying to wipe out all vestiges of Indianness through assimilation, she seemed to believe it was possible for Indians to take on some aspects of white culture and yet retain their Indian language, clothing, and other markers of Indianness. In fact, through her intimate acquaintance with Lakota people, she became a fluent speaker of their language and adopted some of their dress. On the one hand, as she very well realized, this facilitated her job of assimilating; it "proved an instant passport to their confidence." On the other hand, Eastman's fluency in the language and her adoption of some Sioux clothing and housing accorded the Sioux a respect that they seldom encountered among other government officials. "There was implied compliment to the Sioux in the very fact of my choosing to speak their tongue although it was not required of me," she wrote, "in my frank enjoyment of their company, my habitual wearing of moccasins, and my choice of the Dakota lodge over every other form of canvas house."

For Eastman assimilation was not a one-way process, and according to her, many reformers and government officials were misguided in their approach to Indian affairs. "Fifty years ago, a few strait-laced individuals needlessly rejected everything characteristically native without regard to intrinsic values," she wrote in her memoir. "I was once taken to task by a good missionary of my acquaintance for habitually wearing moccasins in the house and about the camp. I am sure that same clergyman . . . would have rebuked me even more severely for taking part in an inter-camp game of 'shinny' with a hundred or more yelling and excited men and women! Perhaps we placed undue emphasis on surface indications of conformity."

Perhaps due to her open-minded attitude, Eastman took intimacy with Lakota Indians to a new level when she married Charles Eastman, a boarding school–educated Dakota (Santee) medical doctor whom she met at Pine Ridge Reservation just prior to the Wounded Knee massacre in 1890. Perhaps her opposition to boarding school education as expressed in her memoirs resulted in part from bearing six children with Eastman, children who were considered Indian and therefore potential candidates for removal themselves. Her intimacy with Eastman may have enabled her to develop an empathy with the plight of Lakota mothers whose children could be so easily separated from them.

As with Mary Collins, Eastman's long-time contact with the Lakotas also led her to challenge many damaging representations of Indians. "As usual, the official statements were patronizing in tone, addressing the Indians as if they were children incapable of reason," she noted. "In reality, . . . their [the Sioux's] attitude was not one of awe or childlike trust—far from it!" Going against the maternalist grain, Eastman also countered the commonly held view of Indian women as drudges:

The women's labors were many and cheerfully performed. I have never seen them treated as "slaves" or "beasts of burden," but always as equals and companions. They laughed and chatted freely with husbands and near relatives. . . . It was certainly no hardship for them to fetch the wood and water, take down and put up the tipi, or even water and harness the ponies upon occasion. . . . When the ordinary work of the camp was done, my Dakota "sisters" set about gathering, pounding, and drying wild cherries, picked mint and balm, scraped and tanned skins, and made or mended moccasins. . . . Their method [of tanning skins] took but a short time and left the skin beautifully soft and white.[31]

Interestingly, developing opposition to Indian child removal derived not only from white women like Eastman who worked in day schools on reservations, but also from women schoolteachers who worked in the boarding schools. For some white women, opposition began when their observations of Indian life failed to correspond with prevailing maternalist representations. When Gertrude Golden became a schoolteacher and principal at the Fort Defiance School on the Navajo Reservation, she developed an admiration of Navajo gender roles and, like Eastman, challenged the dominant narrative about downtrodden Indian women: "The social position of the women is of wide independence. Most of the wealth of the tribe belongs to them, and they are the managers of their own property and also the owners of the children. Marriage gives the man no claim whatever to his wife's property or even to the children. Fathers have little or nothing to say in regard to their children, even by way of correction, except to agree with the wife on measures of her own choosing." Countering accusations that Indian women were neglectful mothers, Golden remarked, "The Navajos, as do all the other tribes that I have known, possess a deep affection for their children."[32]

Estelle Aubrey Brown experienced a similar epiphany after years of working at boarding schools in the Southwest. She declared:

It is a proven fact that Navajos are more moral in their sex relationships than white people. Among them there is less promiscuity and there are fewer divorces than among us, in proportion to numbers. Their customs regulating marriage were in force before ever a Christian marriage was performed in the Northern Hemisphere.

These customs are more uniform than are our own varying state laws.
. . . More than other tribes the Navajos recognize the rights of their
woman [*sic*]. It is the woman who takes the initiative in divorce proceedings, usually after seeking the advice of her clan.[33]

From a growing appreciation for (if not outright romanticization of)
Indian cultures, some white women schoolteachers also developed a
pointed critique of the boarding schools. As with Sister Eileen Heath
and her colleagues at Moore River, white American women, armed
with maternalist ideals when they went to work in institutions for indigenous children, were often appalled by the miserable conditions in the
boarding schools, and thus their inability to truly teach the children new
conceptions of home and body. When she took a civil service examination and was required to write on whether the United States should establish penal colonies, Brown devilishly added a postscript to her essay:
"If the United States needed a penal colony at once, if it would install
some plumbing and greatly improve the kind and amount of the food
served, the Crow Creek school for Indian children could be made to
serve the needs of two hundred criminals." Brown's experience with the
BIA, traveling from institution to institution, led to her disillusionment
and anger. She was incredulous that at one school the boy's dormitory
was locked every evening with little ventilation and no toilet facilities
save for three slop buckets. She knew that "truancy was frequent and
troublesome" and that the "boys had to be locked in if any were to be
present for morning roll call." Nevertheless, she was greatly disturbed
by the dormitory and unlocked the door at eleven one night to observe
the conditions there. "The stench of urine was sickening," she wrote.
"Back in my room I was possessed of an urgent desire to transport that
evil dormitory, boys, buckets, and smell—particularly the smell—into
the office of the Honorable Commissioner of Indian Affairs."[34]

In addition to poor sanitation, white women schoolteachers witnessed other gross negligence on the part of school officials. In 1923
Julia Carroll, a matron at Genoa Indian School, was shocked by the

lack of adequate food for the Indian children there. "When I was detailed [to supervise the] dining room," she testified, "there were four or five hundred children or over to be fed, all the way from 2 or 3 years up to grown men. They had bread but no butter; half-cooked oatmeal with no milk; the sloppiest coffee I ever saw. . . . And there was not enough bread." Carroll was moved by small boys who told her they were hungry and asked if she could get them more bread. "That went through me like a knife, being a mother," she asserted. Even more galling, Carroll discovered that there was plenty of food in the bakery, but it was locked up. She also found that Superintendent Sam Davis was hoarding the food to give to Indian children he took from the school to labor (without pay) on his nearby farms. When Carroll confronted the superintendent, he allegedly barked at her, "I want you to distinctly understand that I am the superintendent here, and I do not want any meddlers; and if you are going to come here and meddle, I will see that you are put out of here."

Such indifference and hostility from their white male superiors led some white women to greater opposition to child removal policies. When Carroll went over the superintendent's head to complain, the BIA sent out an investigator whom Superintendent Davis "wined and dined." When the investigator did talk to Carroll, he then relayed her complaints to Davis, who promptly had her transferred. But Carroll did not give up. She persisted in her criticisms of Davis, testifying to a Senate subcommittee in 1929 that he physically abused children at the Genoa School: "I have seen those children beaten up until the blood would flow out of their noses. . . . This brute would conduct a religious ceremony and when he got out he would beat and club those little Indian children. It is a positive shame."

Carroll's testimony before the subcommittee also revealed that authorities were aware that intimacy between white women employers and the Indian children in boarding schools could undermine their aims. Carroll testified that she was told, "You are not to talk so much with the children. They are Indians and you cannot trust them."[35] The superintendent to the Hopis in the early 1900s, Charles Burton, deemed one of his schoolteachers, Laura Dandridge, a liability in his work because she had clearly developed a profound intimacy with Indian girls in her care. She described to the reformer Gertrude Lewis Gates the students' reaction when she was transferred: "My Dear little and big girls cried and clung to me so I felt my heart should break to leave them."[36]

Here in a nutshell was the key contradiction in employing white women as maternal agents of the state. Whereas state authorities sought white women to establish intimacy with and "mother" indigenous children in order to further their colonizing aims, such maternal intimacies could lead white women to actually challenge their government's policies. Thus Pratt could bemoan "meddlesome" women who, "not having practical knowledge and experience, are guided by the tender qualities of their natures." On the one hand U.S. government officials favored the employment of white women as "recruiters" and as matrons and teachers within the institutions for these supposed "tender qualities," yet they also regarded them as a danger to their colonial enterprise. Indeed, just by talking to the children and coming to trust them — what maternalists valued — Carroll and Dandridge had deviated from their role as agents of the state. Their cases suggest that for some white women, once they developed relationships with indigenous children, all did not go according to colonial plan.

Real affection could arise between women and their charges, affection that could lead the women to challenge conditions in the institutions, and sometimes could erupt into full-blown opposition to the policy of child removal. Bertha Wilkins, a former teacher in the Indian schools, came to reject one of the central premises of maternalism. She objected to the schools because "any institution is a sorry home for a little child. Children need above all else love, and nothing but love will satisfy them."[37] In 1899 at the newly inaugurated Indian Institute for BIA schoolteachers, Wilkins declared, "Taking the children away from the home is against nature. We wouldn't stand it; we would fight to the end." Reminiscent of Mary Bennett's analysis of "the Aboriginal problem," she asserted that the problem of the Indian was the problem of poverty.[38]

Perhaps the most articulate of white women schoolteachers who grew to oppose the policy of removing Indian children was Estelle Aubrey Brown:

> From the first I had been surprised by the tender years of the Navajo children in the school. When it was opened, few parents brought their children in. Employees had been sent out to search hogans, to scour the reservation for children. Few girls as old as thirteen were found who were not married. Navajo tribal custom permitted marriage at puberty. There were few older girls here to do the heavy work of laundry and sewing room and kitchen. Girls of ten years had to do this work. Many of the children were only five years old. They had known only the free nomadic life of the desert. They had never sat on chairs, slept in a bed, used knives and forks. They did not know how to wear their new clothes. . . . They were in school against their own will and, in most cases, the will of their parents.
>
> For the first time in this work I asked myself: What right have we to take these children from their parents? What right have we to break up Indian homes? Why do we deny Indians the rights we claim for ourselves?

Brown became more adamant in her condemnation of "the inept and erroneous policy of Indian education, a policy that destroyed family life, disregarded the human right, recognized by all men, of parents in their own children. It was a policy that ignored the necessity of building upon what was good and fitting in the tribal way of life. Instead, it attempted to destroy what the Indians already had." Near the close of her memoir, Brown grew even more vehement:

> I charged the Bureau with kidnaping.
>
> It's [*sic*] inept and largely ineffectual system of Indian education was based on kidnaping, the separation for long periods of young children from their parents. Aside from its inhumanity, this system

failed to recognize the fact that the family must furnish the foundation of any successful structure of racial betterment.

I charged the Bureau with being accessory to the death of many Indian children. . . . I held these commissioners responsible for every undernourished and overworked boy and girl I watched sicken in their schools, later to be sent home to die in the squalor of their reservation homes.[39]

Several white women employees in the boarding schools became uncomfortably aware of their own complicity in the colonial project of indigenous child removal. Gertrude Golden became sickened by the messages she and other white women were imparting to Indian girls. After a Navajo girl, Ada, secretly gave birth to a child and then suffocated it rather than be found out (see chapter 7), Golden came to blame herself for "Ada's misfortune and sad end":

I had been very, *very* emphatic in stressing the wickedness of doing anything that would bring illegitimate children into the world—children who would be without father, home or name and who should suffer the disgrace all through their lives.

Poor Ada had taken my admonitions to heart and, paradoxically enough, what I had intended for good turned out to be evil. I felt that, had I not driven the point home so forcefully, she might have confided in someone who would have arranged to send her home where she at least would have been spared from committing the worst of crimes.[40]

Golden resigned her position soon after this incident.

Brown also was self-critical. "I entered the Indian Service believing implicitly in the Bureau's wise and honorable aims," she wrote. "Disillusionment came slowly. I was one of a poorly educated, untrained group of people. I learned that dissent meant loss of a means of livelihood. But I saw something of the destitution and disease on reservations. I saw sick, hungry, and overworked children. And I did nothing. I was cowardly and acquiescent."[41]

Indeed, for white women who faced limited employment opportunities and depended on their schoolteacher incomes, it took real courage to confront and challenge the conditions in the boarding schools and child removal policy. In protesting, white women often risked their jobs. Cecile Carter was fired for interference and insubordination when she complained of the diseased and dirty condition of children at Fort Defiance.[42] Like Julia Carroll, when Laura Dandridge criticized Hopi Superintendent Burton, she was transferred to another institution.[43] Carroll, Carter, and Dandridge may have been in a minority; many white women did not speak out because they feared for their positions. For example, Julia Carroll's colleague, Ina Livermore, although she witnessed many of the same abhorrent conditions at Genoa Indian School, kept quiet. "I had two boys depending on me," Livermore later told an investigatory Senate subcommittee, "and I could not afford to do anything that would jeopardize my position."[44]

Most schoolteachers who became critical of the schools did so in memoirs or by testifying to investigatory committees after their tenure as teachers had expired. Few had the wherewithal or the resources to take on the school system while in the employ of the BIA. One notable and significant exception is the case of Belle Axtell Kolp, who in 1903 taught briefly at the Oraibi School among the Hopis. As the niece of S. B. Axtell, the late governor and chief justice of New Mexico, Kolp appears to have come from a wealthier background than the average BIA employee. She therefore had less at stake in going public with her criticism.

Kolp resigned in protest from her position just seven weeks after taking the job. She sought out Charles Lummis (see chapter 4), a renegade reformer, and his Sequoyah League. Kolp submitted an affidavit to Lummis concerning the situation at Oraibi School, which Lummis then published in the July 1903 issue of his magazine, *Out West*. In her affidavit, Kolp called herself "a sympathizer with these oppressed people." "Although there a trifle less than seven weeks," she wrote, "I witnessed more of 'Man's inhumanity to man' than I ever saw before or hope to see again." Her first run-in with Superintendent Charles Burton occurred over Hopi dances, which Burton sought to prohibit as licentious and immoral. Kolp attended one to see for herself and concluded, "I saw nothing immoral or improper. . . . They are as sacred and as solemn to these people as religious ceremonies in our churches are to us." From the first, it appears, Kolp refused to see the Hopis as sexually immoral.

Like other schoolteachers, Kolp was appalled at the conditions in the school. Although between 125 and 174 children attended the Oraibi School, there were only two teachers. Kolp also objected that children under five were too young to be removed from their family. She complained of the dangerous condition of the school, inadequate supplies of food, cutting boys' hair to punish them, the use of corporal punishment, physical abuse, and lack of health care. Primarily, however, it was the methods used to compel the children to attend school that led Kolp to resign in protest. "These children, with others, were taken forcibly from their homes by an armed body of Government employees and Navajo Indians under leadership of C. E. Burton," she claimed, "not for the purpose of 'making better Indians,' but for the benefit of those in charge." She explained, "Mr. Ballinger [the principal of the school] wanted to establish a boarding school at Oraibi to take the place of the day school. This would permit drawing more rations and a better salary; also allow him a clerk—which position his wife was to take; so that instead of being school-cook at a salary of $30 per month, or teacher at $52 per month, she would draw from the Government $100 per month. I know these things, for it was all discussed in my presence." After witnessing the brutal methods used by Burton and Ballinger to obtain children for Oraibi (see the introduction), Kolp simply quit.

Even though she had been with the Hopi children at Oraibi School for just a few weeks, Kolp had striven to create bonds of intimacy with them that proved to be stronger than any loyalty she felt to state authori-

ties or the BIA. She regularly had welcomed children into her room to
look at paintings and photographs. When Principal Ballinger chastised
her for this, she asked him why he objected, "since they were learning
of things outside their little world. His reply was, 'We do not want them
to know too much, and they must stay away.'" Ballinger went so far as
to threaten the children with whippings if they went to Kolp's room.[45]
Burton wrote to Kolp that she "must not sympathize aloud to the Indians
when they are punished as this makes them sullen and hard to manage."[46]
As was the case of other women schoolteachers, male superiors tried to
prevent intimacy from developing beyond a mere expedient. Kolp resisted her superior's edicts, however, noting, "I could not be with those
Hopi people and withhold my sympathy from them, as I was ordered to
do by Mr. Burton. . . . I never found that being sympathetic and friendly
made these people 'sullen and hard to manage.'" She concluded, "These
people need neither guns, clubs, force, nor brutality to make them 'better
Indians.' Justice and mercy—kindness and friendship—will lead them
any place. It will cost less; and these abused, embittered people will love,
instead of hate, the name of 'Washington.'"[47]

Other white women who developed close associations with indigenous people also sometimes grew to oppose child removal policies.
Marietta Wetherill, a trader with her husband on the Navajo Reservation, developed her opposition to child removal through long and sustained contact with the Navajos. At first Wetherill went along with the
concept. "I thought I would be smart and sent one little girl to school
when she was five," she recalled. "When she came back at sixteen I
took her to see her mother and there she stood dressed up in a cute little
dress she had brought from school. She didn't know her mother and
her mother didn't know her. Tears rolled down the mother's cheeks.
'This isn't my daughter. She's yours, not mine.' I never got over that."
Wetherill concluded that removing Indian children to boarding schools
"was the most terrific, unjust way of education that ever was in this
world."[48]

White Women Organizing against Indigenous Child Removal

For such growing sentiments among missionaries, schoolteachers, and other close associates of indigenous children to have had an impact on changing child removal policy, white women needed to ally with indigenous women to organize campaigns against child removal, either through white women's groups or through participation in other organizations dedicated to advocating for indigenous rights. In the United States white women more readily engaged in this activism and had a greater impact on changing federal Indian policy in this regard. Only a few white women in Australia came out forcefully and in a sustained manner against Aboriginal child removal before World War II, and, as in the past, male officials routinely dismissed their challenges.

Organized white opposition to the removal of indigenous children erupted sporadically on both continents. As far as I can tell from the existing records, this opposition first emanated from white men's organizations, but some white women soon became involved in these efforts (of course, many indigenous people had organized against child removal from its inception). After his experience of advocating against child removal for Isleta Pueblo families (see chapter 4), Charles Lummis, now back in Los Angeles, launched a new magazine in 1894, which eventually became *Out West*, one of the most popular publications in the American West. In 1901 he founded the Sequoyah League to campaign for Indian rights and "make better Indians," a motto that reveals the limits of Lummis's support for Indian self-determination.[49]

Beginning in 1899 Lummis again raised the issue of Indian child removal nationally when he took up the Hopis' cause against the coercive methods used by Superintendent Burton. In this case, a white woman, Gertrude Lewis Gates, teamed up with Lummis to gather information about Burton's intimidation of the Hopis. Gates described herself to Lummis as the daughter of a "Pioneer in the West, closely identified with the opening days of Minnesota, Montana, and Idaho." She told him, "My education was begun on the Montana hills, continued in Iowa, Idaho, Mass. and Arkansas, and I hope will be finished in Arizona and California."[50] She originally visited the Hopi Reservation "in pursuit of health" and an "initial study of Ethnology," but soon became a representative of Lummis's Sequoyah League. She arrived on July 5, 1902, and set up camp on Third Mesa near Oraibi, where she stayed until November 15.[51] According to Lummis, Gates returned from Hopiland "pretty well loaded for bear. She is a high-minded, fine horse-sense woman, a lady in every way and not a 'sissy.' I have strong hope that her report, which she will give me in a few days, will be the club we need to put that brute and tyrant, Burton, out of the place that he disgraces."[52]

Indeed, Gates's report proved to be the damning document that Lummis had hoped for. She documented case after case of abuse by Herman Kampmeier, a teacher at the Oraibi day school, including one incident in which Kampmeier sought to retrieve a truant child of five or six from his home:

> When Mr. Kampmeier dragged the crying, struggling child away from his mother vainly protestant, the father intervened to save his child injury by accompanying the two to school, and upon Mr. Kampmeier's beating the boy in the back with clenched fist, the father interfered receiving a blow on the head and a sickening kick in the side just below the ribs, while Mr. Kampmeier continued shaking, jerking, and dragging the boy. . . . The two men fought, each trying to get possession of the boy, until the lad got free and ran to his grandfather; the schoolteacher overcame the father and led him captive to the school village, where his hands were bound behind his back with baling wire, his hair rudely cut close to his head, . . . and . . . [he was] later imprisoned half a day. . . . Mr. Kampmeier told the parents if they didn't send the boy to school he would send him to Keam's Canon [*sic*] and keep him there all his life, never letting him return to his parents: "I won't let you see your boy again!" said he.

In her report Gates also criticized Superintendent Burton for the cruel punishments he sanctioned. "*All* Hopis object to corporal punishment of their children," she asserted. "Mr. Burton allows it. Boys and young men of 16 and 18 years of age are slapped, struck with wooden paddles, and rawhided at the boarding school. One boy was whipped until he fainted and was detained in the teacher's room over night to recover. His back was so sore he moved with difficulty for several days, and complained of being hurt internally. This because he used a word of Hopi at the table."

Echoing the sentiments of Eileen Heath regarding Chief Protector Neville, Gates claimed also that Burton was a virtual dictator: "No one enters the Reservation by his knowledge without his consent, nor remains without it; and no Indian leaves seeking work, or for any other purpose, by his knowledge without a permit. And yet he will take a minor away from his home without either verbal or written consent of his guardians, in the face of their protests, removing him to a distant school in another state!"[53] Gates claimed that due to such tyranny, the Hopis had asked for the removal of both Kampmeier and Burton.

As a result of Gates's report and Lummis's campaign, the government conducted an investigation into Burton's administration. As was typical of government officials when they were criticized by white women, the investigator, James Jenkins, sought to discredit Gates and impugn her reputation:

Mrs. Gates has the appearance of being a well-meaning Christian lady, and I have no doubt her intentions were the best when she took up the work of investigating how a reservation should be managed, although her methods of procedure were peculiar, to say the least. She went to Oraibi, . . . camping on the mesa alone in a tent, where she remained five months, devoting most of her time, as she states in her testimony, to the study of ethnology. About a half hour per day, she says, was spent investigating the management of the reservation. Her method of doing this was to write down complaints of two or three hostile Indians and of several discharged and disgruntled employees.

In fact, Jenkins trivialized all the testimony given by women in the investigation. He dismissed Laura Dandridge as a "mulatto woman" and a "mischief maker." Belle Axtell Kolp, he claimed, "couldn't do the work" and was removed; she filled out an affidavit just for revenge. Jenkins concluded that Gates was "a no-doubt well-meaning woman of a sentimental turn of mind," who was friendly with Burton until he called for an end to dances and prevented her from attending. "These dances . . . are not of proper character for a woman to take part in," he wrote in boldface, implying that Gates's presence at the dances was proof of her low morals. "Not one of the persons named is competent to judge in the case," he asserted, "and . . . none of their statements were reliable or trustworthy."[54] As a result of Lummis and Gate's campaign, authorities only reprimanded Burton, and the report vindicated him to some extent. Nevertheless, Gates and Lummis had accomplished at least part of their aim: the BIA dismissed Kampmeier and the school's principal.[55]

Another white woman, Constance Goddard DuBois, also became involved in protesting Indian child removal during the first decade of the twentieth century. A would-be ethnologist and a successful novelist who lived in Connecticut, DuBois worked with the Connecticut Indian Association, a branch of the WNIA. In 1897 she ventured to southern California for a summer, where she encountered the Luiseño and Diegueño peoples (often dubbed "Mission Indians" as a result of having been missionized by the Spanish). Thereafter she spent almost every summer with them and almost every winter in Connecticut advocating their cause. In the early 1900s she conducted fieldwork on the Diegueños and other Mission Indians off and on under the direction of Alfred Kroeber, the renowned chair of the University of California's Anthropology Department in Berkeley, and also recorded songs and myths and collected "specimens" for Clark Wissler of the American Museum of Natural History.[56]

24. A portrait of Constance Goddard DuBois by Charles F. Lummis, 1900. P.32206,
Courtesy of the Braun Research Library, Autry National Center, Los Angeles.

Through her close association with a group of Indian people, and no doubt through her exposure to the new anthropological theories of her day that promoted cultural relativism over a belief in cultural evolution, DuBois became vehemently opposed to child removal and, in particular, Estelle Reel's proposed compulsory education law for Indian children and her emphasis on an industrial curriculum. Instead of relying on maternalist rhetoric, DuBois employed an equal rights discourse to counter Reel's insistence that the state must compel Indian children to attend school. Linking child removal to economic dispossession (as Mary Bennett did), she wrote, "This is, in sober truth, what such a bill proposes: To remove the child from his home, forcibly and without the consent of his parents; to break up the family, and in the last result to turn the Indians into a scattered remnant of homeless vagrants, cheap laborers, or paupers, without land, without a settled occupation, and with no opportunity of using to their profit the smattering of arithmetic, geography, history, and arbitrarily chosen manual trades for which all else has been sacrificed."

DuBois agreed that Indians should be provided with education, but insisted that "the school should be brought to the Indian, not the Indian to the school." Furthermore, she asserted, "We have devised formal and petty standards under which the minds of our children are moulded after set patterns, varied from time to time according to fad or fashion or the growth of public opinion, but uniform enough to level all exuberance of native endowment into one dull level of mediocrity. . . . The Indian, savage and uncivilized as we consider him, is still nearer this ideal of an unfettered individuality than are nine-tenths of our high school graduates." She also challenged the notion that extending a compulsory school law to Indians was equivalent to that for white children. "No white child can be forcibly carried from his home without the consent of his parents," she wrote, "taken to a school inaccessible and remote, and kept a prisoner under close restraint during the term of his education. This has already been done illegally in the case of Indian children, but not, as yet, with the consent of the law." She concluded, "Let no law be placed upon our statute books that shall mete out to the Indian treatment which would outrage every sentiment of humanity if applied to ourselves."

In opposing Indian child removal, unlike many of her compatriots in the WNIA, DuBois recognized the inherent right of Indian families to their children. In particular, she evoked the image of the Indian mother who was victimized by the state and those reformers who supported Indian child removal. She asserted dramatically, "We have robbed the Indians, persistently, systematically, under process of law, and without law; but never has there been such bitter robbery as this. They have been driven by force, like herds of cattle, from the lands the white man coveted; yet even then the Indian mother might keep her child if only to see it die within her arms. No State can prosper if it undermines by law the foundation of every State—the home, even though it be the home of the poorest and most ignorant of its citizens."[57] Like many other white women reformers, DuBois upheld the home as the "foundation of every State," but unlike others, she accorded respect and legitimacy to the Indian home and rights to the Indian mother.

In the early 1900s Gates and DuBois appear to have been lone voices rather than spokeswomen for influential women's organizations. It was not until the 1920s that a full-fledged reform movement against assimilation and its attendant emphasis on boarding schools for Indians blossomed. In 1922 the American Red Cross hired Florence Patterson, a public health nurse, to carry out an extensive investigation into Indian health conditions. Patterson especially criticized the high rates of tuberculosis and trachoma in the boarding schools, blaming poor diet, lack of sanitation, and overcrowding for the spread of diseases. But Patterson went further; she condemned the whole concept of boarding schools:

This program, combined with the strain of bells, bugles, and horns, forming in line five or six times a day, and the mental struggle to combat physical fatigue, could not fail to be exhausting, and the effects were apparent in every group of boarding school pupils and in marked contrast to the freedom and alertness of the pupils in the day schools. One gained the impression that the boarding school child must endure real torture by being continually "bottled up" and that he somehow never enjoyed the freedom of being a perfectly natural child. One longed to sweep aside his repressions and to find the child. As a small child he had undergone a terrific shock in adjusting himself to the school life and routine so different from any previous experience in his life. Again, after several years of nonreservation boarding school life, he would have to face a similar shock in returning to reservation life, from which every effort had been made to wean him.[58]

By the 1920s another women's organization had also become active in the field of Indian affairs, the General Federation of Women's Clubs (GFWC). The highly educated and talented Lakota woman Zitkala-Ša (who is featured in chapters 6 and 7) sought to involve the GFWC in Indian affairs in the 1920s, and under the leadership of Stella Atwood the group's Indian Welfare Committee became a leading advocate of reform in Indian policy. Atwood hired a young and zealous reformer, John Collier, who had become interested in the Pueblo Indians as a result of a visit to the Southwest in the early 1920s. Together Atwood and Collier waged a successful campaign against several specific measures they believed were designed to defraud Indians of their lands and cultural heritage. Moreover, along with a new generation of feminists—including artists, writers, and anthropologists, primarily based in New Mexico—Atwood and Collier assaulted the policy of assimilation generally.[59]

Not all branches of the GFWC and its Indian Welfare Committee were as radical as Atwood and Collier, but even the more moderate branches had begun to oppose the policy of removing Indian children to boarding school. In 1925 Mrs. Wiegel, chair of the Colorado GFWC and a teacher on the Flathead Reservation in Montana for five years, wrote to the superintendent of the Ute Indians at Ignacio, Colorado, telling him that, unlike Atwood or Collier, she did not want to meddle in BIA affairs but did want to see some improvements for the Indians. "The situation is this," she told the superintendent: "We [the GFWC] are here, three million and a half strong, and must be reckoned with. You should be thankful that you have a woman who knows a little about the subject she has tackled. Some in my place could cause a great deal of unpleasantness, as you know very well." She added, "We do not want any John Collierism in our peaceful valley. But you and yours, as well as I and mine, are looking to the betterment of the situation."[60] For Wiegel, the situation could be improved by stopping the practice of removing Indian children to boarding schools. Having heard of Ute children who were taken away to the Santa Fe Indian School only to contract deadly diseases, she wrote to the Utes' superintendent, "I want our Ute children to be allowed to remain at home and go to the public school at Ignacio [Colorado]. If the school is not large enough at present, it must be made a first class school with equal accommodations of other rural schools of the state and at the expense of the state. The Indians are now recognized as citizens of the state in which they live and should receive all the benefits thereof that any other citizen receives."[61]

As a result of the growing agitation against the boarding schools and other aspects of assimilation policy in the 1920s, the federal government commissioned an inquiry into Indian affairs from the Brookings Institution, led by Lewis Meriam, which published its findings in 1928. In the Meriam Report, as it came to be known, investigators criticized many aspects of federal Indian policy. As for boarding schools, the survey staff found "that the provisions for the care of the Indian children . . . are grossly inadequate" and condemned dietary deficiencies leading to malnutrition, overcrowded and unsafe dormitories, substandard health care, poor sanitation, high incidences of tuberculosis and trachoma, poorly qualified teachers, an overly uniform curriculum (that had been established by Estelle Reel), routinization, and cruel discipline and punishment. The report also questioned the work the children did for half of each day to maintain the school, asking "whether much of the work of Indian children in boarding schools would not be prohibited in many states by the child labor laws, notably the work in the machine laundries."

The report did not just condemn the schools, however, but also lambasted the practice of removal. "The long continued policy of removing Indian children from the home and placing them for years in boarding school largely disintegrates the family and interferes with developing normal family life," the report contended. The Meriam Report even drew comparisons between the forcible removal of Indian children and the practice of institutionalizing some white children: "Even in institutions for the care of dependent white children the children are there because they have no homes or because normal home life is impossible, and very few are taken forcibly from their parents. But many children are in Indian schools as the result of coercion of one kind or another and they suffer under a sense of separation from home and parents." The authors also noted, "Among no other people, so far as is known, are as large a proportion of the total number of children of school age located in institutions away from their homes as among Indians under the boarding school policy." The report concluded forcefully, "Whatever the necessity may once have been, the philosophy underlying the establishment of Indian boarding schools, that the way to 'civilize' the Indian is to take Indian children, even very young children, as completely as possible away from their home and family life, is at variance with modern views of education and social work, which regard home and family as essential social institutions from which it is generally undesirable to uproot children. . . . Indian parents nearly everywhere ask to have their children during the early years, and they are right."[62]

Under Franklin Delano Roosevelt's administration the Meriam Report and continued political organization against assimilation resulted in the appointment of one of assimilation's foremost critics, John Collier, to the post of commissioner of Indian affairs. Under the so-called Indian New Deal of 1934, Collier opened more day schools, stressed bilingual and bicultural education, recruited Indian teachers, and reduced the numbers of boarding schools from forty to thirty-one. The Johnson-

O'Malley Act of 1934 gave federal aid to states that enrolled Indians in public schools.[63] Thus, for a time at least, policy and practice toward American Indian children diverged dramatically from that of Australian state governments.

In Australia, the first rumblings of organized resistance by whites to the policy of Aboriginal child removal also occurred, it seems, among white men and not women. In 1921 the Aborigines' Friends' Association (AFA), a male-dominated missionary organization, proposed a clause in the new South Australia Aboriginal bill to prevent the chief protector of Aborigines there from taking children from their parents before they reached the age of fourteen. Members of the AFA had even met with Aboriginal people at Point McLeay about this issue; they had wanted the age to be set at sixteen. The president of the AFA declared that the Point McLeay Aborigines did not object to the "betterment" of their children, including their attendance at mission schools, but they opposed the removal of young children.[64] John Sexton of the AFA wrote to South Australia officials in 1921, "The passing of the Bill in its present form would give the Chief Protector powers which the natives fear might be exercised in taking their children at an early age to some locality away from the station, so that they would lose touch with their children, and their desire is that any system of training and discipline should begin on the station."[65] The group reiterated its opposition to indigenous child removal in 1924.[66] The AFA seems to have been one of the few white reform groups that solicited the opinions and input of Aborigines before proposing plans for their betterment (even though they did not promote the exact wishes of the Aboriginal people they consulted at Point McLeay).

Women's organizations worked at times with the AFA, but not in full cooperation and harmony. As we saw in chapter 3, the AFA led the opposition to white women's widespread campaign to remove lighter-skinned children from Central to South Australia in the mid-1920s. Nearly at the same time, the Women's Non-Party Association of South Australia sought the help of the AFA in obtaining the official appointment by the South Australia government of women "visitors" to Aboriginal girls in service. The AFA struck a deal: if the WNPA would support the AFA's bid to the South Australia government to "hand over to it the care of these girls," the AFA would support the WNPA's nomination for the first "lady visitor." The WNPA later objected, however, when the AFA sought to nominate several women as visitors and the South Australia government appointed an AFA nominee to the position. Moreover, later in the 1920s the AFA disapproved of the WNPA's scheme to move the Bungalow from Alice Springs to Jay Creek and wrote behind the back of the WNPA to register their opposition to the plan.[67]

Two other primarily male organizations also took a stand against child removal in the 1920s. Testifying on behalf of the Association for the Protection of Native Races to the Royal Commission on the Constitution in 1927, the group's leader, Reverend William Morley, wanted an independent investigation "into the practice alleged to exist of forcibly taking children of certain age to those Government stations, however desirable it may be, in many cases that the children being well cared for by their aboriginal parents, should be left in the custody of those parents."[68] Charles Genders, head of the Aborigines' Protection League, also spoke out against the removal of "half-caste" children. Firmly entrenched in prevailing racial ideologies, Genders asserted, "Perhaps the most difficult problem is that of the half-castes—how to check the breeding of them and how best to deal with those now with us." Despite these views, however, Genders included a plank in his program for a Model Aboriginal State that opposed removing children and suggested keeping "half-castes" with "full-bloods" on an isolated reserve.[69] In his manifesto, he argued:

These young people . . . are taken from their country, their home, their parents, from environments where they should have an opportunity of settling down and marrying and they are placed in strange surroundings with people of alien habits and speech, ostracised from association on equal terms with white children, shut off from the hospitality of white people generally and not permitted to marry, and unable to share in national traditions which are held to be most powerful factors in creating character. Even with the greatest kindness from those in whose charge they are placed, what sense of loneliness, or exile, even of slavery must they constantly feel?[70]

Although we find these scattered instances of opposition to Aboriginal child removal, none of these white men or their organizations waged sustained campaigns against the removal of Aboriginal children. And in the 1920s, as explored in chapter 3, white women's organizations supported the policy of removing Aboriginal children to institutions.

This changed in the 1930s, primarily due to the efforts of Mary Bennett, who hoped to put pressure on Australia to reform its Aboriginal policies by mobilizing both national and international feminist groups. In 1933 her paper "The Aboriginal Mother in Western Australia" was read at the British Commonwealth League (BCL) Conference in London. This speech included the statement, "The greatest injustice, which causes the bitterest suffering, is the taking of children from their mothers without their consent." Bennett explained, "Many children are parted from their mothers, whose love and care they miss. They feel they are never safe from police interference, for they may be removed at all ages. Aboriginal mothers before their children are born, go in fear of having their half-caste children taken from them, and their children bear the marks of such fear." Perhaps more startling to her readers, Bennett claimed in her speech that Aboriginal workers in Western Australia were virtually enslaved, an accusation that garnered many headlines in the London newspapers and so alarmed government officials that one of them sent a copy of Bennett's speech to the Western Australia premier in 1934.[71] The international embarrassment over Bennett's allegations helped to bring about the appointment in 1934 of Henry Doyle Moseley, a Perth stipendiary police magistrate, to head a royal commission to investigate the conditions of Aborigines in Western Australia.[72]

The appointment of the Moseley Commission, as it was known, offered reformers the opportunity to voice their criticism of how the state administered Aboriginal affairs. Bennett seized this opportunity and ardently sought to rouse white women's organizations to join her campaign for Aboriginal rights (including the right to retain custody of their children). In 1933, for example, she told a joint reception of the WSG of Western Australia and the Woman's Christian Temperance Union (WCTU), "If white women only knew the facts, . . . they would not tolerate what is going on for one moment. I make an earnest appeal to you to do something to improve the appalling condition of aboriginal women."[73] Together with the WCTU, the National Council of Women, the Labour Women's Organisation, the YWCA, the Country Women's Association, the Housewives' Association, the Women Justices Association, and three other women's groups, the WSG petitioned the Western Australian government to include at least one woman on the royal commission, as "psychologically it is only [white] women who can measure up the needs of the native women." The women's petition added, in maternalist language, "We trust that the Government will make it possible for our women who are feeling a very definite responsibility towards their less favoured sisters, to render this service in the interests of humanity."[74] However, as in the past, white women's groups were unsuccessful in attaining an official position on the commission.

Rather than accepting defeat, Bennett and the network of white women's groups she had organized played a crucial role in giving testimony to the commission, a significant departure from previous government investigations. Twice before in Western Australia, in 1904 and 1927, the government had conducted inquiries into the treatment of Aborigines. In 1904 no women testified, and in 1927 only one woman, who was Aboriginal, gave evidence to the commission.[75] White women's organizations' insistence on testifying to the Moseley Commission represented the increasing demand on the part of white women to play a role in administering Aboriginal policy.

The testimony to the commission of some white women built on familiar maternalist priorities. The WSG, for example, submitted a statement focusing on the status of Aboriginal women and the need to "give the woman the sanctity of her own person." Sticking to the maternalist agenda, the WSG also called for women protectors and inspectors and demanded that the Aborigines Act make "a single act of sexual intercourse [between an Aboriginal woman and a white man] an offence, if a halt is to be called on the breeding of a large half-caste population." The WSG concluded, "The direction of a common native policy should be towards the break-down of every form of domestic slavery, and marriage bondage. The native mind in the process of assimilating Western 'white civilization' should be enlightened as to the true value of human freedom, especially as regards women." Although it briefly mentioned the need to provide more education to all people of Aboriginal descent, the WSG's official statement avoided the subject of child removal.[76]

However, some white women activists deviated from the WSG's predictable stance. In fact, in addition to their official statement, the WSG asked Bennett to give evidence on their behalf, but as the Australian historian Alison Holland notes, "Her evidence moved far beyond what even the Service Guilds would have expected." Her outspoken and radical critique would eventually drive a wedge between her and the WSG.[77] Taking the baton from women's organizations, Bennett began in a typical maternalist mode: "The deplorable *social and economic position of aborigines and people of aboriginal origins* is caused and conditioned by the victimization of aboriginal women." She darted very quickly, however, in new directions to link Aboriginal women's lowly status with colonial economic practices: "Two chief contributing causes of the increase in first-generation half-castes are: 1., starvation by dispossession, and 2., the condonation of the 'property-status' [of women] by the squatters and administration." Bennett then chose to point out the hypocrisy of many pastoralists and officials who "say, '*Don't interfere with native customs*,'" but who "do not mean the very strong and indeed vital bond that correlates the natives to their territory which is their livelihood; no, the 'native customs' which the squatters choose to support are comprised in the 'property-status' of women and young people under the patriarchal system, which the squatters have commercialized, bartering with the old native men for the old men's surplus property in wives, and for the unpaid labour of the young men."

Bennett then tossed away the wsg's maternalist baton altogether and presented another way in which Aboriginal women (and men) were victimized: when their children were arbitrarily removed from them. She quoted an Aboriginal man from Western Australia, Norman Harris, who forcefully claimed, "Under the Aborigines Act everyone of us is a prisoner in his own country. Any police officer can come along and take all of our children at any time and we cannot object or we are committing an offence under the Act." Bennett continued her testimony to the Moseley Commission by relating the story of Wulleen, a "half-caste girl, who suffers from eye trouble as so many half-castes do." When the police came to her community to round up children, Wulleen

> was caught when the others escaped and was sent away to the remote Government institution. Year by year her mother Morel used to beg the missionaries to apply for Wulleen's return. At last the great day came when the request was granted, and I had the pleasure of bringing Wulleen back to her own country. . . . Once we got north from Kalgoorlie the news ran along like wildfire, and at each station when the train pulled up groups of natives collected to welcome the poor child back. In their joy at seeing her again they would stretch up and take my hands in theirs with such affectionate confidence. It was a triumphal journey.

Building on her own intimate experience with Aboriginal women and children, Bennett now connected the allegedly low status of the women to the policy of child removal, for the first time introducing a radical *public* critique of the practice by a white woman reformer. She testified dramatically:

Many of these poor children are parted from their mothers who are the only ones who do really love them, and their hearts are starved for want of love, but first for years they suffer the misery of hunted animals, always running from the police, in the hope of hiding in the country which they know, among their own people, but always in fear that at any moment they may be torn away, never to see them again. They are captured at all ages, as infants in arms, perhaps not till they are grown up; they are not safe until they are dead. If they are not caught and deported as children, because their mothers have been victimized by white men, one day they will be caught and deported with *their* children because *they* have been victimized by white men, but the weary round will go on; from Moore River they may be sent out to serve, and back to Moore River many of them will be sent again, because they have been victimized again. The native woman NEVER gets justice.[78]

Bennett did not let the subject rest; she brought it up over and over again in her testimony:

Section 8 [of the Native Administration Act of Western Australia] should be altered so as to prevent the Native Commissioner from splitting up families. . . . No department in the world can take the place of a child's mother; the Honorary Minister does not offer any valid justification for the official smashing of native family and community life when he said, "The removal of half-caste children is a necessity for so many reasons that it seems almost futile to mention them." Mothers with infants, individual children, sometimes whole families, are mustered up like cattle and deported to the Government Native Settlements, there to drag out days and years in exile.

She concluded forcefully, "No child except for hospitalisation should be compulsorily and permanently removed from the custody of its parent or parents except upon the order of a Magistrate under the Child

Welfare Act, and on the same conditions which apply to white children also."[79] Shedding the last vestiges of the conventional maternalist platform, Bennett insisted, "Our aim should be to raise the native camps into thriving self-respecting village communities, rather than to break them down materially by knocking their homes down and spiritually by taking their children and women from them."[80]

When questioned by Neville as to whether "there is no case [of an Aboriginal child] bad enough to take out of the bush and put into a settlement," Bennett also broke from the maternalist belief that "(white) mother knows best." She replied to Neville, "A native's own will should be consulted. His desire to improve his own position should be studied. His co-operation ought to be sought for the improvement of his own life. I do not believe in gaoling a man. He is not a nut to put upon a screw and give an extra twist to. He is a human being and his co-operation must be sought and encouraged in any welfare scheme."[81]

In addition to Bennett, several other white women testified to the royal commission. Mrs. Nesbitt-Landon, an employment broker and president of the wsg, advocated for Aboriginal girls who were apprenticed into domestic service. She gave evidence to the commission, she said, "at the request of a number of girls and women who are controlled by the Aborigines Department," who were "too terrified . . . to step forward and speak before the Commission." Nesbitt-Landon had gotten into trouble with the Department of Native Affairs for placing Aboriginal girls as domestics independently of the department. Girls complained to her of the low wages the department required their employers to pay them and the fact that a large portion of their wages was given to the department to be held in trust. Nesbitt-Landon told the commission that all the girls who came to her "say they cannot get a statement of their financial position or a bank book or any satisfaction." She advised that "at the age of twenty-one they should be allowed to handle their own money and handle their own affairs."

Nesbitt-Landon also objected to the department's attempts to control the girls' marriages. Like many other white women, she believed, "If greater punishment were given to the white man and he was traced and made to pay there would be far less of the awful grief of the half-caste mother having her child, very often a near white child, placed in the native compound without prospect, very little training and separation from her." She asserted that Aboriginal women "should be owners of their own person and of their own children if born out of wedlock." Unlike many other white women, Mrs. Nesbitt-Landon added, "As an old Suffragist and one of the women who helped obtain the vote in England, [I] feel that there is great power in this vote and I am always instructing these girls that they should demand their vote."[82] Such a concern with Aboriginal women's political rights does not appear to have been on the radar screen of many other white women suffragists.

What was remarkable about the Moseley Commission too was that Bennett and Nesbitt-Landon solicited actual testimony from Aboriginal women rather than merely speaking for them.[83] Some Aboriginal people, such as the "half-caste" women of Broome who were featured in chapter 7, actually testified to the Moseley Commission; others brought their concerns to Bennett, Nesbitt-Landon, and other white women. One Aboriginal man even wrote to May Vallance of the WCTU to thank her and Bennett for their testimony. "The Half caste and Aboriginals of the collie district wish to conveay their Heart felt thank[s] on your evidence on their behalf at the Royal inquiry, which they very much apriceated," Frank Davies Collie wrote to Vallance. "They also wish you to thank Mrs. Mary Montgomery Bennett on Her grand evidence on their behalf. And to thank Her very much for the great work she has done for the colored race."[84]

To some extent, Moseley's report from the royal inquiry did vindicate Bennett and white women's groups. Moseley praised the Mt. Margaret Mission and condemned Moore River. He remarked, "The question arises as to what should be done with the children. Unless the mothers are of a dissolute nature and unlikely to mend their ways, I should not care to part them from their children, but would rather see them sent with their children to the Mission at Mount Margaret, where at least the children will have a better chance than they have at present." At Moore River, by contrast, Moseley wrote, "the care of the half-caste child is hopelessly inefficient. It is a pathetic sight to see these children, in many cases so fair in complexion as to be scarcely distinguishable from white children, living in a hut worse by far than the kennel some people would provide for their dogs — whole families of 9 or 10 being huddled together in abject squalor, with no beds to lie on, no cooking or eating utensils worth the name, no proper facilities for washing, and dressed in clothes a tramp would despise."

Ultimately, however, Moseley's report proved to be a disappointment to Bennett. He was not primarily concerned with the clear neglect of Aboriginal people at Moore River but with the threat he believed they posed to the future of Western Australia. He asserted, for example, "At the present rate of increase, the time is not far distant when these half-castes, or a great majority of them, will become a positive menace to the community, the men useless and vicious, and the women a tribe of harlots." Despite the clear contrast he drew between Mt. Margaret and Moore River, Moseley ultimately envisioned Mt. Margaret as a haven for "full-blood" children and recommended that "greater control be given [to Neville] over half-caste minors." He dismissed Bennett's critique, declaring, "I emphatically do not agree with the statement of the missionary that 'the conditions of to-day are only modern slavery.'"[85] As in the past, Australian white women reformers' efforts to influence government policy regarding Aborigines seemed to have little effect.

Despite this setback, Bennett hoped to maintain the momentum that the women's groups had gained through organizing for the Moseley Commission. She wrote immediately afterward with great passion to another major reformer, Bessie Rischbieth, "Mrs. Rischbieth! I appeal to you: WHAT MADNESS 'PRIUS DEMENTAT' our fellow whites in Australia? I cannot see how white supremacy in the Pacific can last out this decade even. We, I mean, white supremacy, is in the most imminent danger, and everybody is blind. In my view, our only chance of survival is to put our 'spiritual' house in order, and do it mighty quick."[86]

Yet far from creating a sustained and united white women's campaign against child removal as a result of the Moseley Commission, Bennett's outspoken condemnation of white Australians and their colonial practices alienated the more patriotic and nationalist white feminists, including Rischbieth. Very few other white women joined Bennett in her radical aggressive stance, and Bennett felt the rebuff intensely. In 1936 she complained to Edith Jones, "Mrs. Rischbieth is a real rotter. . . . She has been such a beast to two different friends of mine who have taken up work for the natives, and she [wants] to keep the natives out of sight on every possible occasion, though she is much too cunning to show this in front of people like myself who have no other interests except these despised and rejected ones."[87]

Moreover, in an unintended and subtle way, white women's testimony at the Moseley Commission may have led to greater indifference on the part of white women toward Aboriginal affairs elsewhere in Australia. Bennett's and other white women's focus on the miserable conditions in Western Australia enabled white women in other parts of Australia, such as Queensland, Tasmania, and New South Wales, to claim that compared to Western Australia, they had no problems with Aboriginal affairs. Mrs. Scott Mullin, representing the Queensland Women's Electoral League at the BCL Conference of 1934, claimed to be "surprised to hear . . . of the treatment of the aborigines in Western Australia. The condition of affairs was very different in Queensland, where there was a Reserve in which the children were taught carpentering and plumbing, sowing and reaping, fishing and other useful occupations. . . . The boys were taught trades and the girls were being taught to serve, and were serving, as ward-maids in hospitals, pupil teachers in schools, and monitors in dormitories. Girls were also taught domestic work and the care of children."[88] Mrs. Hornabrook of the Australian Federation of Women Voters painted a bright picture for New South Wales, claiming, "The Aborigines received wonderful treatment; they were free there to do what they wished. There were camps for them, and the children were educated on the same principle as the white children."[89] Thus to some extent, but certainly due to no fault of her own, Bennett's campaign backfired by allowing some white women to gloss over Aboriginal injustices that existed in areas beyond Western Australia.

Although Bennett failed to created a united and sustained campaign against Aboriginal child removal and other facets of colonial practice with which she linked it, she did gain some converts to her radical agenda by the late 1930s. After the Moseley Commission, May Vallance and Ada Bronham moved their affiliation away from the WSG (Rischbieth's organization) to the WCTU, which more unreservedly championed Aboriginal citizenship rights and eventually (in the 1950s) came out forcefully against Aboriginal child removal.[90] Bennett also gained an ally in Helen Baillie, who had moved to Australia from London in 1932, been inspired by Bennett to work on behalf of Aboriginals, and had headed the Aboriginal Fellowship Group in Melbourne.[91] In the early 1930s Baillie did not stray far from the conventional discourse regarding the need to separate Aboriginal children from their parents and make them useful. In her 1933 book, *The Call of the Aboriginal*, she advocated for "compulsory education for all half-caste children up to the age of 16" and the need to "train . . . [Aborigines] into useful citizens."[92] By the late 1930s, however, Baillie seemed to have developed a new orientation, proposing that "the solution of the colour problem lies not in absorption but in co-operation."[93] Her friendship with the Aboriginal activist Anna Morgan (as mentioned in chapter 7) may have led her down a different path. She had also befriended three prominent Victorian Aborigines—Margaret Tucker, William Cooper, and Doug Nicholls—and drove them to Sydney for the first major public demonstration by Aborigines, the Day of Mourning, in 1938 to protest Australia's sesquicentenary. (Bennett also attended this protest.)[94] Moving beyond speaking for Aboriginal people, Baillie asserted, "I feel we can help best by assisting the aboriginal people to press for their rights."[95] Perhaps taking further inspiration from Bennett, Baillie had moved into a more intimate position of alliance with Aboriginal people.

Thus by the 1930s the Australian white women's movement was divided on Aboriginal issues between those who continued to embrace maternalist values and those who, like Bennett and Baillie, had sought out relationships with Aboriginal activists based on equality rather than a mother-child relationship. Whatever their stance on Aboriginal child removal in the late 1930s, however, white women had little impact on influencing state policy on the issue. This was most evident when, in April 1937, a Conference of Commonwealth and State Aboriginal Authorities was held in Canberra to discuss and coordinate Aboriginal policy. Here Chief Protector Neville promoted his policies of "breeding out the colour" and suggested that other states should take up his strategy. He boasted to the conference, "I know of 200 or 300 [Aboriginal] girls in Western Australia who have gone out into domestic service and the majority are doing very well. Thus these children grow up as whites, knowing nothing of their own environment. Our policy is to send them out into the white community, and if a girl comes back pregnant, our rule is to keep her for two years. The child is then taken away from the mother, and sometimes never sees her again. At the expiration of the period of two years, the mother goes back into service, so it really does not matter if she has half a dozen children."[96]

White women's and other reform organizations objected to such a callous stance, referring to it as "absorption into the white community no matter what the cost" and "degeneracy through absorption." Yet many white women opposed the policy because they believed that it encouraged immorality and because they opposed "miscegenation," not because, like Bennett, they regarded it as cruel, inhumane, and restrictive of the rights of Aboriginal people. These white women reformers would have agreed with Bleakley of Queensland, who objected to an absorption policy because "there is danger of blood transmission or 'throw-back.'"[97]

The 1937 conference did not daunt Bennett, who kept up her virtually one-woman campaign to undermine Neville and his policies. While Neville seemed to bask in his central and influential role at the 1937 Commonwealth Conference, Bennett escalated her campaign against him. In 1938 she referred to him as a dictator. "The new Native Administration Act places all coloured people, thirty thousand native born Australians, and some whites, at the disposal of a dictator [the chief protector], in this professing democracy of Western Australia," she wrote to him, "enabling him [the chief protector] to 'take any coloured child from its mother at any stage of its life, no matter whether the mother be legally married or not'; to refuse permission to any coloured people to marry; to take charge of the earnings of coloured people." Bennett asserted, "All people . . . ought to be free to work for whom they like, and be free to marry whom they like." She pointedly charged, "The policy of the Department aims at THE DISAPPEARANCE OF THE NATIVE RACE," what later scholars and activists would label genocide.[98]

By the 1930s U.S. policy toward Indian peoples had diverged significantly from that of Australia toward its Aboriginal population. Whereas a sweeping and well-organized anti-assimilation reform movement in the 1920s had brought about a change in the administration of Indian affairs—and its promotion of Indian child removal—Australian state governments largely ignored the fledgling reform movements in their nation (and abroad) and continued their assaults on indigenous families. If anything, by meeting together in 1937 Australian state authorities signaled an effort to better coordinate, not to reform, their absorption efforts.

Moreover, white women's maternalist politics in the United States and Australia had also diverged. By and large the maternalist orientation of white American women reformers, in evidence since the 1880s, declined precipitously in the 1920s and 1930s. Organizations such as the WNIA lost their influence in government circles, while the GFWC, with the anti-assimilationist Stella Atwood at the helm of its Indian Welfare Committee, joined forces with a new generation of feminists, white male activists such as John Collier, and Indian activists such as Zitkala-Ša to move the government in a new direction.[99] In contrast, white women's organizations in Australia had just begun to take up the cause of Aborigines in the 1920s, and, as we saw in chapter 3, they brought the same kind of maternalist zeal to the task as had white American women for many decades. Bennett's efforts in the 1930s to steer white women's organizations away from their maternalist stance to a position of alliance with indigenous women in order to oppose indigenous child removal and other colonial practices did not take root.

This chapter leaves us with two questions: What influenced some white women in each country to abandon the politics of maternalism in order to champion indigenous rights in concert and alliance with indigenous activists? In particular, what led some white women to dissent from the powerful maternalist discourse of their times and instead to oppose indigenous child removal? And why did American white women seem to more readily move in this direction?

Ironically, sometimes the very factors that promoted white women's "rescue" of indigenous children could also lead them to oppose the practice. For example, strong Christian convictions had led many white women to support indigenous child removal, but those convictions could also influence some, such as Mary Collins and Mary Bennett, to take the opposite stance. Anthropological interests had led women such as Alice Fletcher, Daisy Bates, and Olive Pink to promote indigenous child removal, but other women with an interest in ethnology, such as Gertrude Lewis Gates and Constance Goddard DuBois, developed a radical critique of the practice. The rising tide of the new anthropological theory of cultural relativism particularly seemed to influence American women.[100]

The influences of radical political movements, especially socialism and communism, may have also altered some white women's views. Many American women in the 1920s who opposed assimilation policies were influenced by socialism and communism. And perhaps Bennett's strong stand can be attributed in part to her growing interest in radical politics generally. In the late 1930s Bennett teamed up with Jean Devanny, a communist and Labour Party member who adamantly opposed indigenous child removal.[101]

Changes in sexual norms, at least in the United States, may have led some white women to a different view of indigenous women and an opposition to the removal of their children. In the United States, as Victorian sexual norms gave way to calls for women's "sex expressiveness" in the 1910s and 1920s, many white women no longer represented Indian women as downtrodden, but often instead as sexually liberated. In researching my book *Engendered Encounters*, I found a close correlation between growing appreciation of Pueblo Indian cultures and declining adherence to Victorian sexual norms. By contrast, in Australia, where no such movement for women's sexual liberation occurred in the early twentieth century, according to Marilyn Lake, late Victorian codes of morality were sustained well into the twentieth century and may have continued to shape many white women's maternalist responses to Aboriginal people.[102] As they began to emphasize the rights of indigenous people to their land and labor and to connect such issues to child dispossession, white women activists like DuBois and Bennett seem to have put less emphasis on sexual morality.

A final unmistakable factor in moving some white women to oppose indigenous child removal emanates from the tensions that developed between white women's maternalist ideals, their intimate experiences with indigenous women and children, and the state's ultimate goals. It is no coincidence that much of the opposition to child removal arose from white women—primarily missionaries, schoolteachers, and matrons—who worked closely with indigenous children. In places like Moore River in Western Australia, the Hopi village of Oraibi, and Fort Defiance Indian School in Arizona, white women witnessed firsthand the often tragic consequences of indigenous child removal. In many cases, they also came to know and befriend indigenous children and their families. White women's very appeal to the state as colonizing agents—their traditional role as nurturers who could invade the intimate realm—proved also to be their greatest drawback to the state. Still, it was a rare white woman who could set aside her own belief that "(white) mother knows best" or jeopardize her fragile professional position or emergent political authority to listen to and follow the lead of indigenous women.

American white women who began to doubt and speak out against Indian child removal found a more hospitable climate than did Australian white women. Through the WNIA as well as annual Indian institutes for BIA schoolteachers and matrons, white women who worked in the institutions and as missionaries came into greater dialogue with one another than white women in similar positions in Australia. They could compare notes and find kindred spirits. American white women who developed opposition to Indian child removal, such as Belle Kolp and Gertrude Lewis Gates, could also count on the support of some like-minded white men, such as Charles Lummis. Australian white women, by contrast, often worked at odds with white men, whether those men were state officials like Chief Protector Neville or fellow reformers like those in the AFA. In the United States challenges to the racial ideologies of cultural evolution, especially through the growing popularization of the anthropologist Franz Boas's theory of cultural relativism, fostered a movement against assimilation where white women opposed to child removal could find a home.[103] By contrast, biological determinism appeared to remain the racial order of the day in Australia until World War II. Those few white women who dared to challenge Aboriginal child removal in Australia were marginalized and unable to create a viable campaign against the practice.

Ultimately, it may be impossible to determine what multiple factors—some unique to individuals, some a result of larger social trends—combined to propel some white women to take a strong stand against indigenous child removal. Benefiting as they did from their position in the racial, class, and colonial order, most white women reformers failed to develop an analysis that linked indigenous women's victimization to settler colonialism, not to their alleged deficiencies as housekeepers and mothers. In fact, it seems inescapable, if not paradoxical, that maternalism—a political movement founded on the sanctity of motherhood—became a central mode in which white middle-class women became ensnared in the colonial enterprise.

Epilogue

After decades of removing indigenous children to institutions up to the outbreak of World War II, neither the United States nor Australia had solved their "Indian problem" and their "Aboriginal problem." This was because, ultimately, they had misdiagnosed the ailment; it was settler colonialism and its insatiable demand for land that was the problem, not indigenous people. It was a desire to build homogenized nations founded on whiteness, Christianity, and modernity that caused strife and hardship, not indigenous people's survival. Maternalists too had misinterpreted the problem; rather than recognizing displaced peoples with disrupted lives who were trying their best to survive, they saw unfit motherhood and unkempt homes.

Some changes in indigenous policies did come after World War II. Australia's opposition to Nazi racial engineering made its own "breeding out the colour" policies increasingly untenable. Long-time reformers seized on this contradiction to shine a critical light on Australian Aboriginal policy. From her base in London, where she spent the war, Mary Bennett pressured the Australian commonwealth government to create an equal education system for all Australian children, without removing Aboriginal children from their homes. She wrote to one official, "The final overwhelming reason for giving education to Aboriginal children, as well as half-castes, is: our survival demands this justice. As we hope to win the war against Nazism, so we must get rid of our Nazi complex that withholds education from full-blood Aboriginals."[1] For once, facing international embarrassment, officials could not blithely dismiss Bennett and other white women reformers. Thus after World War

II Australian officials finally moved away from an absorption policy. Now the government turned to a policy of cultural assimilation.[2]

In the United States, even though the BIA had abandoned much of its assimilation policy under the administration of John Collier as commissioner of Indian affairs from 1933 to 1945, by the postwar era its policies were tilting again toward assimilation and converging with Australia's new approach. During World War II Collier faced increasing opposition and shrinking budgets from Congress. Moreover, dissatisfaction with the paternalism of the BIA generally led many returning Indian veterans to question the purpose of the bureau and the dependent status of Indian reservations. Up to the 1960s federal Indian policy shifted away from Collier's approach toward congressional attempts to "terminate" the tribal status of dozens of tribes (and with that the government's legal and financial responsibilities to them as well as their land claims) and to "relocate" thousands of reservation Indians to urban areas. In short, much like the earlier assimilation era, the postwar era focused on breaking Indian people's ties to their land by erasing any distinctions between them and the dominant majority population.

For indigenous families who faced state intervention into their most intimate lives, however, these shifts in policy meant little. Though they no longer spoke in the language of biological absorption, Australian states still engaged in the removal of Aboriginal children from their families and communities. A 1947 policy statement for the Northern Territory continued to promote separate policies for "part-aboriginal" people (which replaced the term "half-castes"), including institutionalization, versus "full-blood" Aborigines, who still faced segregation. The statement asserted, "Subsidised provisions shall continue to be made in appropriate homes and institutions for near-white children likely for various reasons to be more suitably reared, educated and provided for [in the] South, than in the Territory."[3] Increasingly in the postwar era, however, Australian governments more often removed children to individual white families through fostering and adoption rather than to institutions. Officials now almost exclusively justified removal based on unacceptable living conditions as determined by social workers—still focused on indigenous women and the home—rather than on the combination of concerns present before the war.[4]

In the United States a somewhat similar trajectory was followed. The nature of removal changed as forced institutionalization receded. Many indigenous people proudly claimed the schools as their own; the boarding schools became more indigenized in curriculum and eventually in management, and became powerful tools for cultural preservation rather than assimilation.[5] However, as in Australia, indigenous child removal continued in a new form: fostering or adopting children out to white families. In the mid-1950s, for example, the Mormon Church revived its program of fostering Indian children (see chapter 2). The Church's Indian Placement Program placed children into Mormon families, where for nine months they went to a public school and were also catechized into the Mormon religion.[6] Social workers too, as in Australia, wielded enormous influence in removing Indian children from their homes. Mary Crow Dog, a Lakota woman (who ended up attending the Catholic boarding school her mother and grandmother had both attended, hated, and run away from), describes the experience of children growing up in the 1950s and 1960s: "Many Indian children [are] placed in foster homes. This happens even in some cases where parents or grandparents are willing and able to take care of them, but where the social workers say their homes are substandard, or where there are outhouses instead of flush toilets, or where the family is simply 'too poor.' A flush toilet to a white social worker is more important than a good grandmother."[7]

Postwar Activism

World War II also unleashed other changes. The character of the movement for Aboriginal and American Indian rights altered—radically—after World War II. Prior to the war, American Indian and Aboriginal activists such as Charles Eastman, Zitkala-Ša, Fred Maynard, and Pearl Gibbs had established their own indigenous rights organizations, but reform groups led by whites had been dominant in setting the reform agenda. After the war, indigenous activists became more vocal and visible and began to demand rights, not reform. Military service during World War II emboldened many indigenous people to actively challenge their second-class status, and postwar decolonization and human rights movements around the world set the tone and context for a different kind of activism, led more often by indigenous people themselves than by well-intentioned but often paternalistic (and maternalistic) whites.

In the United States activists established the National Congress of American Indians (NCAI) to push for Indian rights, particularly land claims, and to oppose termination. Under the leadership of Vine Deloria Jr. (Ella Deloria's nephew) in the 1960s, the NCAI and other Indian-led groups would usher in a new era of Red Power, with militant calls for Indian self-determination. Although some high-profile whites (such as Marlon Brando) and blacks (such as the comedian Dick Gregory) played a role in calling attention to and supporting the Red Power movement, this was a movement led by and carried out by Indians. White women assuredly played behind-the-scenes roles but did not take the active leadership that they had at the turn of the twentieth century.[8]

In Australia after the war, while many Aboriginal activists continued local and regional protests against the discrimination they faced, new national approaches emerged as well. In 1958 a coalition of Aboriginal and non-Aboriginal activists formed the leftist Federal Council for Aboriginal Advancement (FCAA). (This group later added the concerns of Torres Strait Islanders to its agenda and title, becoming FCAATSI). Up to the late 1960s the FCAA agitated primarily to obtain equal citizenship rights for Aborigines, and their campaign culminated in the 1967 referendum that extended greater citizenship rights to Aborigines and brought Aboriginal affairs under the jurisdiction of the commonwealth rather than the state governments. In the 1960s the FCAA and other Aboriginal rights groups also increased their demands for land rights. Taking inspiration from the African American civil rights movement in the United States, many Aboriginal activists engaged in freedom rides, sit-ins, and other acts of civil disobedience to call attention to the continued discrimination they faced. Several prominent Aboriginal activists also emulated other developments in the black rights movements in the United States, calling for Black Power, forming a Black Panthers of Australia, questioning the role of whites in Aboriginal rights organizations, and setting up a "tent embassy" in front of Parliament House in Canberra to call for Aboriginal land rights and Aboriginal sovereignty.[9]

Unlike in the United States, where white women's leadership in Indian rights movements seems to have all but disappeared after World War II, white Australian women continued to play important roles in the Aboriginal rights movement. Now, however, they shifted their attention from indigenous women alone, and instead focused more generally on issues of labor, land rights, and sovereignty. Instead of working solely through white women's groups, they worked more in mixed groups like the FCAA that included both men and women and whites and Aborigines and concentrated solely on indigenous human rights.[10] The old maternalist call of women's work for women faded, with both positive and negative consequences. As maternalism declined, so too did white women's emphasis on monitoring and controlling indigenous women's homes and bodies. (Monitoring continued among social workers at the government level, however.) With white reformers' and indigenous activists' attention now focused more generally on indigenous issues—often defined as those most affecting men—the problems that severely affected indigenous women, including child removal, tended to be less visible. It would take a movement of indigenous women to raise this issue.

In the United States Indian women activists fought for many years to prevent the continued removal of their children through adoption out of the tribal community to white families. Their efforts culminated in the Indian Child Welfare Act of 1978.[11] In Australia Margaret Tucker's daughter actively campaigned in New South Wales for the adoption of the Aboriginal Child Placement Principle, which was eventually in-

corporated into the 1987 Children (Care and Protection) Act of New
South Wales.[12]

Today, the scars of our settler colonial histories remain to remind us
of the past. Many indigenous individuals and families grapple with the
legacies of decades of child removal. A number of Aboriginal authors
have come forward with their stories since Margaret Tucker's first book
on the subject in 1977. Sally Morgan's powerful *My Place,* about her
family's experience in Western Australia, became a best-seller. In 1981
the historian Peter Read coined the term "Stolen Generations" and
initiated extensive scholarship and increased public debate about the
practice. Together with the Aboriginal filmmaker Coral Edwards and
several other Aboriginal activists, Read helped to establish Link-Up
around 1980 to help reunite Aboriginal families who had been torn apart
by past government policies.[13]

Faced with mounting criticism of its past policies, the Australian government (under the Labour Party leadership of Paul Keating) responded
in 1995 by establishing the Human Rights and Equal Opportunity Commission Inquiry into the Stolen Generations. After traveling the country
and gathering the testimony of hundreds of Aboriginal people who had
been affected by the policies, the commissioners published their report,
commonly called the *Bringing Them Home Report,* in 1997, which soundly
condemned as a form of genocide the government's policies of removing
children and called on the government to issue a formal apology. The
report's findings and recommendations were rejected out of hand by the
new conservative government led by John Howard as well as many other
white Australians, especially the recommendation that the government
apologize for its past policies. However, other white Australians were
so moved by the report's findings that they organized a "Sorry Day" to
show their support for reconciliation.[14] Many other white Australians have
signed "sorry books." When I lived in Canberra in 2001 and rode my bike
to work each day, I cycled over "Sorry" after "Sorry" chalked into the
bike trail. Finally, on February 13, 2008, after a change in government,

newly elected prime minister Kevin Rudd apologized on behalf of the Australian Parliament in a powerful and moving ceremony.

In addition to writing their histories and giving oral testimony, several Aborigines have brought lawsuits against the government for the policy of removing indigenous children. The first of these cases was *Kruger v. The Commonwealth*, brought by Alex Kruger and a small group of other indigenous Australians in 1995 who sought to establish that the Aboriginals Ordinance of 1918 for the Northern Territory was invalid because under the Australian Constitution, the commonwealth was not granted the power to make such a law.[15] In 1999 Lorna Cubillo and Peter Gunner, both of Aboriginal descent, brought individual suits against the government, claiming that, in removing them as children from their parents without consent, the government did not protect them as it was supposed to do.[16] Both of these cases proved to be unsuccessful for the Aboriginal litigants, but they both contributed to greater public awareness and debate about the Stolen Generations.

The widely released movie *Rabbit-Proof Fence*, based on Doris Pilkington's book, has also made visible one of the stories of the Stolen Generations. (Australian officials reacted testily when its promotional poster in the United States asked potential viewers, "What If the Government Kidnapped Your Daughter?" and then followed with, "It Happened Every Week in Australia from 1905 to 1971." Australian politicians lambasted Miramax for "misleading and grossly distorting what actually happened.")[17]

The issue of Indian child removal has been much less visible and less debated in American history. Because the early policy was never meant to permanently separate Indian children from their families, it has had somewhat less harsh consequences—at least over the long haul—for Indian families. Indians who had had good experiences in the schools or needed financial assistance to raise their children often sent their own children to boarding schools. This eventually led many Indian people to seize control of the boarding schools, and they became a symbol of Indian perseverance rather than of assimilation.

Still, for many American Indians, removal and institutionalization (or fostering and adoption) has had dreadful consequences, and some are trying to rectify past injustices. They are telling their stories, often of horrendous abuse at the hands of boarding school authorities. Hundreds of American Indians in South Dakota have filed a twenty-five-billion-dollar class-action lawsuit in Washington DC against the federal government, which contracted with the Catholic Church to run several South Dakota schools in the 1970s. The suit alleges widespread physical and sexual abuse.[18] In 2004 several of these former students also brought lawsuits against specific religious institutions in South Dakota, fifty-seven students against St. Paul's School in Marty and sixteen against St. Francis Mission School (where Mary Crow Dog, her mother, and grandmother had all been sent) on the Rosebud Sioux Reservation.[19] In 2000 the head of the BIA, Kevin Gover (himself a Pawnee Indian), apologized on behalf of the BIA at its 175th anniversary commemoration, but made clear that he was not apologizing on behalf of the entire government.[20]

Though these damaging policies have now been retired, some of the vestiges of older attitudes still remain. In 2000 a Navajo couple residing in Kansas used a traditional cradleboard for their infant son both at home and at his day care center. A health care inspector, however, threatened to pull the license of their day care provider if the child was allowed to continue to take his nap on his cradleboard. When the father arrived to pick up his son, the inspector, who was still present, told him that use of the cradleboard amounted to child abuse.[21]

Just as older ethnocentric prejudices have persisted, many indigenous beliefs and practices, including the use of cradleboards, have also survived. Despite a century of efforts to undermine indigenous child-rearing practices, many indigenous people have maintained or revived some of their customary ways of raising and nurturing children. Winona LaDuke (who identifies herself as Ojibwe/Anishinaabe and Jewish), a long-time environmentalist, Native American activist, and Green Party candidate for vice president in the 2000 elections, told her interviewers,

"In the Native community, and my community at White Earth, we parent through extended families and clan relations. . . . So parenting is not done by you. It's done by everybody, though I'm obviously the most active of the parent people in my kids' lives. My kids spend a lot of time with me, but so do a lot of other children. That practice is an essential piece of our culture. . . . We do not largely operate in nuclear families. We operate in extended families. And that's how we parent."[22]

Much as many Americans and Australians today might wish to avert our eyes from the violence and pain of our histories, two settler colonies that became two settler nations cannot ignore the injuries of the past; settlers not only removed most indigenous people from their land but also sought to remove indigenous children from their families. And much as a women's historian and feminist like me might want to believe that most white women challenged these colonial policies and found common cause with indigenous women, we must face the paradoxical truth that in their own quest for independence, public authority, and equality, many white women undermined Indian and Aboriginal women through their support for the removal of indigenous children. Such wounds of history cannot heal by covering them with happy-face Band-Aids or, worse yet, refusing to recognize the injustice that was done. History has had enough such concealments. It's time to discard the Band-Aids, remove the blindfolds, and squarely confront our pasts.

It's a warm day in April with neither a hint of wind nor a wisp of cloud. Our Omaha (UmóNhoN) language class at the University of Nebraska is caravaning up to the Omaha Reservation from Lincoln. On our way out of town we stop to pick up Aunt Alberta (now deceased) and Emmeline (TesóNwi), two Omaha-speaking elders who have been integral to the class and to the university's Omaha-language program. We are headed for Big Elk Park, about twelve hundred acres on the banks of the Missouri River, to find the remains of the Presbyterian mission and school that Francis La Flesche attended and wrote about in his memoir, *The Middle Five*. After driving for more than two hours we come into the diving and pitching hills that belie the notion that Nebraska is completely flat. (In fact, the Omahas had it right; the name Nebraska derives from their phrase, *ni btháska*, flat water, not flat land.) We stop briefly at Blackbird Hill, named for a former leader of the Omahas, on a bluff overlooking the Missouri River and farm fields below. Ever the settler colonialist, I start to imagine myself living in that peaceful, beautiful place. Orlando speaks my thoughts out loud, saying he would love to have a home here; as a member of the Omaha Nation, maybe he will someday. As we head back to our vans we fill a bag with discarded beer cans and head north to our intended destination.

At Big Elk Park we meet Vida, the language instructor at the Omaha Nation Public Schools, and some of her high school students. Vida has also brought two other women elders who speak the Omaha language, as well as her daughter and her dog Blue. We spread out our lawn chairs, blankets, and picnic fixings under a large cottonwood tree on the west bank of the Missouri River. As we eat, Mark, our class's primary teacher (WagóNze), tells his grandfather's story of how he could stand Genoa Indian School for only a brief time before running away. Donna, an Omaha elder, tells of her grandfather's stories of Carlisle Institute. We talk about Francis La Flesche's experience at the mission and his book. In the languid heat one of the Omaha Nation Public School's students lies down on her friend's lap. I have the same drowsy impulse. *Ażhón gonbtha.* Later, as we clean up our lunch, the four Omaha women elders talk and giggle about farting, effortlessly moving in and out of the Omaha language.

Together with Mark and Vida, we students head up into the hills in search of the mission. Joe, Sam, Dave, and Matt break away into the lead, and the rest of us string out into several groups behind them. We all take a wrong turn and end up hiking far to the north of the intended site. Some of us backtrack and muster our energy to head up a likely looking hill. There among the pines we finally find signs of the old mission, first the cemetery where the gravestones of the missionaries and their children lie. Some of the stones are overturned and broken; some small ones peek out from between weeds; some larger ones still stand strong. We can't find headstones for any Indian children, though many died while attending the school.

We scramble (or, in my case, trudge) up to the top of the ridge, finding the foundations of two buildings and an old well. The wild rose bushes rip at our pant legs and scratch Kalene's flip-flopped feet. It's hard to believe that these small foundations once shored up three-story buildings that housed dozens of Indian children. The resplendent oak and black walnut trees, though just beginning to leaf out, provide much needed shade after our climb. An old log makes for a perfect seat to look out over the ridge down in the direction of Macy, the Omaha Nation's tribal headquarters. After cooling off in the gathering breezes, I head down to join the others. We find everyone in our group except Rory, our stalwart linguistics expert and assistant teacher, who remains lost in the hills. Back at the river, under the cottonwood, we gather again, guzzling down cold drinks. Lorene's cell phone rings; it's Rory, wondering where everyone is.

Too soon, I have to drive back to Lincoln with others who have to be back by the evening. The rest of the class goes to the tribe's casino for a buffet dinner with more Omaha elders. My van load comforts itself with pit stop at the truck stop in Fremont.

All that remains: stones and stories. All that continues: the river, the trees, the people, their stories.

Notes

Abbreviations

AIATSIS Australian Institute for Aboriginal and Torres Strait Islander Studies, Canberra

ANC/SM Braun Library, Autry National Center's Southwest Museum of the American Indian, Los Angeles

BTH Bringing Them Home Oral History Project

CIA Commissioner of Indian Affairs

CRS Commonwealth Record Series (Australia)

EWSHS Eastern Washington State Historical Society, Northwest Museum of Arts and Culture, Spokane

GRG Government Record Group

LWVSA League of Women Voters of South Australia (formerly Women's Non-Party Association)

NAA National Anthropological Archives, Smithsonian Institution, Washington DC

NAA-ACT National Archives of Australia, Australian Capital Territory, Canberra

NAA-VIC National Archives of Australia, Victoria, Melbourne

NARA-DEN National Archives and Records Administration, Rocky Mountain Region, Denver

NARA-LAG National Archives and Records Administration, Pacific Region, Laguna Niguel, California

NARA-SB National Archives and Records Administration, Pacific Region, San Bruno, California

NAU Northern Arizona University, Flagstaff

NBAC Noel Butlin Archives Centre, Australian National University, Canberra

NLA National Library of Australia

NSW New South Wales

NT Northern Territory

NTAS Northern Territory Archive Service, Darwin

NTRS Northern Territory Record Service

PROV   Public Record Office of Victoria, Melbourne, Australia

RG   Record Group

RH-Oxford   Bodleian Library of Commonwealth and African Studies at Rhodes House, Oxford University

SA   South Australia

SLSA   State Library of South Australia (Mortlock), Adelaide

SLV   State Library of Victoria, Melbourne

SRG   Society Record Group

SRSA   State Records of South Australia, Adelaide

SROWA   State Records Office of Western Australia, Perth

VPRS   Victoria Public Record Series

WA   Western Australia

WSA   Wyoming State Archives, Cheyenne

Prologue

The title of this prologue derives from a series of fifteen articles written by the Australian anthropologist Daisy Bates about herself that ran in the *Melbourne Herald* in 1936. The series was called "White Mother to a Black Race." See CRS A1, 1936/1738, NAA-ACT.

1. Tucker, *If Everyone Cared*, 20–21, 41.
2. Tucker, *If Everyone Cared*, 14, 17, 65, 63, 34–35, 81–82, 91–92, 92–93, 94.
3. Read, *The Stolen Generations*; Human Rights and Equal Opportunity Commission, *Bringing Them Home*. Aboriginal autobiographies as well as scholarly works on the Stolen Generations are quoted and cited throughout the book.
4. Sekaquaptewa, *Me and Mine*, 91–92.
5. Quoted in James, *Pages from Hopi History*, 125.
6. For some notable samples from the vibrant scholarly literature on the Indian boarding schools, see D. W. Adams, *Education for Extinction*; Archuleta, Child, and Lomawaima, *Away from Home*; Trafzer, Keller, and Sisquoc, *Boarding School Blues*; Child, *Boarding School Seasons*; Ellis, *To Change Them Forever*; Lomawaima, *They Called It Prairie Light*; Coleman, *American Indian Children at School*; Riney, *The Rapid City Indian School*; Trennert, *The Phoenix Indian School*. More general histories of Indian education that include material on the boarding schools include Reyhner and Eder, *American Indian Education*; Szasz, *Education and the American Indian*; DeJong, *Promises of the Past*.
7. One significant exception is Child, *Boarding School Seasons*.
8. In addition to Sekaquaptewa, see, for example, La Flesche, *The Middle Five*; Qoyawayma, *No Turning Back*. Many other Indian autobiographies are cited throughout the book.

9. *The Indian's Friend* 16, no. 5 (January 1904): 5.
10. Stoler, *Carnal Knowledge.*
11. Stoler, *Carnal Knowledge,* 10.
12. For another comparative study of the Indian boarding schools, see Coleman, *American Indians, the Irish, and Government Schooling.*

1. Gender and Settler Colonialism

1. Pettit, *Utes.*
2. Stasiulis and Yuval-Davis, "Introduction: Beyond Dichotomies-Gender, Race, Ethnicity and Class in Settler Societies," in *Unsettling Settler Societies,* 3. For examples of colonies that combined resource extraction with settlement, see Gutiérrez, *When Jesus Came.* For a colony that changed over time, see Perry, *On the Edge of Empire.*
3. Wolfe, "Logics of Elimination," 2. See also Wolfe, "Land, Labor, and Difference," 872. Given Wolfe's formulation, it is no wonder that many scholars are locked in an intense debate as to whether settler colonies such as Australia and the United States practiced genocide against indigenous peoples. For more on these debates, see Moses, *Genocide and Settler Society*; "Special Section: 'Genocide'?"; Bartrop, "The Holocaust, the Aborigines, and the Bureaucracy of Destruction"; Gigliotti, "Unspeakable Pasts as Limit Events"; A. Palmer, *Colonial Genocide.*
4. Kociumbas, "Genocide and Modernity in Colonial Australia," 91–92.
5. For some examples of recent work that has engaged in studies of comparative settler colonialism, see J. Evans et al., *Equal Subjects, Unequal Rights*; L. Russell, *Colonial Frontiers*; Denoon, *Settler Capitalism*; Wolfe, "Land, Labor, and Difference," 866–1006; Stasiulis and Yuval-Davis, *Unsettling Settler Societies.*
6. D. B. Rose, *Reports from a Wild County,* 5. See also Curthoys, "Constructing National Histories"; Docker and Fischer, "Introduction," in *Race, Colour and Identity,* 8–9; Denoon, *Settler Capitalism,* 216–17.
7. Shammas quoted in Limerick, *Legacy of Conquest,* 48.
8. Pettman, "Race, Ethnicity and Gender in Australia," 67; P. Russell, "Unsettling Settler Society." Robert Hughes's *The Fatal Shore,* which was enormously popular in the United States, is a good example of this type of narrative. Though outstandingly researched and written, the book offers just a few scattered pages on conflict with Aborigines in its 603 pages of text.
9. Testimony of Charles E. C. Lefroy in *Report of the Royal Commission on the Constitution,* 480.
10. Patricia Nelson Limerick has dubbed this characterization of the frontier in American history as "the empire of innocence" in her influential critique of western history. See *Legacy of Conquest,* especially 35–54.

11. Quoted in Moses, "Genocide and Settler Society in Australian History," in *Genocide and Settler Society*, 15.

12. Russell, "Introduction," in *Colonial Frontiers*, 2; Kociumbas, "Genocide and Modernity," 77–78, 84.

13. Limerick, *Legacy*, 186–87.

14. Opening Remarks of C. A. Abbott, Minister for Home Affairs, *Conference . . . to consider the report and recommendations . . . by J. W. Bleakley*, April 12, 1929, CRS A1/15, 33/8782, NAA-ACT.

15. Pettman, "Race, Ethnicity and Gender in Australia," 68.

16. P. Deloria, *Playing Indian*; M. Jacobs, *Engendered Encounters*, especially 149–79.

17. Macintyre and Clark, *The History Wars*, 43–44, 137. See also Attwood and Foster, *Frontier Conflict*; Attwood, *Telling the Truth about Aboriginal History*.

18. Reynolds, "Aborigines and the 1967 Referendum." My thanks to Ann Curthoys for tracing this lecture for me. For a critique of scholarly histories that grapple with Australia's colonial past, see Windschuttle, *The Fabrication of Aboriginal History*.

19. Nash, Crabtree, and Dunn, *History on Trial*, x, 3–6.

20. Nash et al., *History on Trial*, 122–27, quotes on 124, 125. For more on another museum exhibit that engendered acrimonious debate about the meaning and interpretation of U.S. history, see Linenthal and Engelhardt, *History Wars*.

21. For critiques of the focus on white women in the American (and Canadian) West, see Elizabeth Jameson and Susan Armitage, "Introduction," in *Writing the Range*, 3–16; Jensen and Miller, "The Gentle Tamers Revisited"; Perry, *On the Edge of Empire*, 9. For Australia, see McGuire, "The Legend of the Goodfella Missus"; P. Russell, "Unsettling Settler Society," 25–27. For more on how American feminist scholars have been slow to analyze the United States as an empire, see Janiewski, "Engendering the Invisible Empire."

22. McGrath, "Being Annie Oakley."

23. Curthoys, "Colonialism, Nation, and Gender in Australian History," 173; Jolly, "Colonizing Women," 104.

24. For some recent notable works on the American West, see Jameson and Armitage, *Writing the Range*; González, *Refusing the Favor*; Ruiz, *From out of the Shadows*; Pascoe, *Relations of Rescue*. In Australia, for works that examine the experiences of nonwhite women and the intersections of gender and race, see Saunders and Evans, *Gender Relations in Australia*; Haskins, *One Bright Spot*; McGrath, "*Born in the Cattle.*" For a comparative U.S.-Australia study, see Ellinghaus, *Taking Assimilation to Heart*.

25. See Stoler, *Carnal Knowledge* and "Tense and Tender Ties."

26. Hine and Faragher, *The American West*, 29–38.

27. Hine and Faragher, *The American West*, 43–49, 93–95, 133–58.

28. L. Russell, "'Dirty Domestics and Worse Cooks';" Macintyre, *A Concise History of Australia*, 38. Later, when pastoralists moved to the outback, many also relied on indigenous men's and women's knowledge and skills. White men also formed relationships with Aboriginal women. See McGrath, *"Born in the Cattle."*

29. Calloway, *First Peoples*, 149. So far, I have not found sources for the Australian context that discuss the effects of these new extractive industries on indigenous economies.

30. L. Ackerman, *A Necessary Balance*. American scholarship on American Indian women has focused on changes in their economic status after colonial contact; to date, I have not found a comparable body of research in Australian historiography.

31. Devens, *Countering Colonization*, 17–18.

32. Perdue, *Cherokee Women*, 65–85; Johnston, *Cherokee Women in Crisis*, 36–38; Peters, *Women of the Earth Lodges*.

33. Strobel, *Gender, Sex, and Empire*, 3–6 ; Stoler, *Carnal Knowledge*, especially 41–111; Perry, *On the Edge of Empire*, 48–78.

34. Hurtado, *Intimate Frontiers*; R. Evans, "'Don't You Remember Black Alice.'"

35. Hamilton, "Bond-Slaves of Satan," 252; McGrath, *"Born in the Cattle,"* 68–94.

36. For more on the fur trade in North America, see Van Kirk, *Many Tender Ties*; J. Brown, *Strangers in Blood*; Sleeper-Smith, *Indian Women and French Men*. For the sealing industry in Australia, see L. Russell, "Dirty Domestics."

37. Hurtado, *Intimate Frontiers*, 13–16; C. Berndt, "Mondalmi," 35.

38. Hamilton, "Bond-Slaves of Satan," 238, 241, n. 5.

39. C. Berndt, "Mondalmi," 35.

40. Devens, *Countering Colonization*, 24–30; K. L. Anderson, *Chain Her by One Foot*, 37, 162–63. For Franciscan friars' attempts to undermine Indian gender systems in early New Mexico and California, see Gutiérrez, *When Jesus Came*, 71–79; Hurtado, *Intimate Frontiers*, 1–19.

41. Scanlon, "'Pure and Clean and True to Christ';" Hamilton, "Bond-Slaves of Satan," 236–58; Grimshaw and Nelson, "Empire, 'the Civilizing Mission' and Indigenous Christian Women in Colonial Victoria."

42. Sources on early Virginia are numerous. A classic examination of the colony is E. Morgan, *American Slavery, American Freedom*. An update of Morgan with a gendered twist is K. Brown, *Good Wives, Nasty Wenches, and Anxious Patriarchs*.

43. For an overview of American Indian history in colonial America, see Calloway, *First Peoples*, 67–210. See also Cave, *The Pequot War*; Gleach, *Powhatan's World and Colonial Virginia*; Lepore, *In the Name of War*; Axtell, *The Invasion Within*.

44. Macintyre, *A Concise History*, 17–40.

45. Macintyre, *A Concise History*, 31, 41, 82, 108–15.

46. Calloway, *First Peoples*, 161–64. See also Calloway, *The American Revolution in Indian Country*.

47. Calloway, *First Peoples*, 211–32. See also Edmunds, *The Shawnee Prophet*; Horsman, *Expansion and American Indian Policy*; Perdue and Green, *The Cherokee Removal*.

48. Hine and Faragher, *The American West*, 333–37.

49. Calloway, *First Peoples*, 276–349. See also Utley, *The Indian Frontier of the American West*; Weeks, *Farewell My Nation*.

50. Macintyre, *A Concise History*, 59, 77; Denoon, *Settler Capitalism*, 52. See also McGrath, *Contested Ground*; Broome, *Aboriginal Australians*.

51. Reynolds, *Frontier*, 30, 37, 53, 67, quote on 40; R. M. Berndt and C. Berndt, *The World of the First Australians*, 490–514; Goodall, *Invasion to Embassy*, 65.

52. Macintyre, *A Concise History*, 62, 67–68; McGrath, "Tasmania I"; Reynolds, "Genocide in Tasmania?"

53. R. Evans, "'Plenty Shoot 'Em';" Palmer, *Colonial Genocide*.

54. Macintyre, *A Concise History*, 68–69, 79–81; Mattingley and Hampton, *Survival in Our Own Land*.

55. Macintyre, *A Concise History*, 97–99; Denoon, *Settler Capitalism*, 82, 102.

56. Grimshaw et al., *Creating a Nation*, 142–44, 150.

57. Calloway, *First Peoples*, 11; Prucha, *Atlas of Indian Affairs*, 142.

58. Pettman, "Race, Ethnicity and Gender in Australia," 69; Attwood and Foster, *Frontier Conflict*, 5. Precolonial Aboriginal population estimates are controversial; see Kociumbas, "Genocide and Modernity," 82–84; Rowse, "Notes on the History of Aboriginal Population of Australia."

59. Namias, *White Captives*; Carter, *Capturing Women*; Schaffer, "Colonizing Gender in Colonial Australia"; Threadgold, *Feminist Poetics*, 134–67, especially 151–52, 159.

60. Perry, *On the Edge of Empire*, 19.

61. M. M. Bennett, *The Australian Aboriginal as a Human Being*, 115; Hamilton, "Bond-Slaves of Satan," 252, 255; Hurtado, *Intimate Frontiers*, 80–81, 86–90.

62. This was particularly true among fur trading families. See Van Kirk, *Many Tender Ties*, 145–242; Hurtado, *Intimate Frontiers*, 41–44; Perry, *On the Edge of Empire*, 97–123.

63. Bell, *Daughters of the Dreaming*, 45–46, 59.

64. Perdue, *Cherokee Women*.

65. Johnston, *Cherokee Women in Crisis*, 40–49; Perdue, *Cherokee Women*, 159–84;

Coleman, *Presbyterian Missionary Attitudes toward American Indians*, 92–97; Hamilton, "Bond-Slaves of Satan"; Grimshaw et al., *Creating a Nation*, 141–42; Grimshaw and Nelson, "Empire, 'the Civilizing Mission' and Indigenous Christian Women."

2. Designing Indigenous Child Removal Policies

1. General Sheridan made this "only good Indian" comment in 1869 in reply to a Comanche chief who, when he surrendered, asked Sheridan, "Why am I and my people being tormented by you? I am a good Indian." Sheridan responded, "The only good Indians I ever saw were dead." See Weeks, *Farewell My Nation*, 147–48.

2. Victoria Haskins and I first asserted this argument in our article, "Stolen Generations and Vanishing Indians: The Removal of Indigenous Children as a Weapon of War in the United States and Australia, 1870–1940." This chapter builds, in part, on our joint article as well as M. Jacobs, "Indian Boarding Schools in Comparative Perspective."

3. Stoler, *Carnal Knowledge*, 19; see also 139. Moreover, colonial authorities in the Dutch East Indies (Indonesia) also removed métis children from their native mothers (121).

4. Quoted in *The Indian's Friend* 3, no. 7 (March 1891): 4. For more on the history of U.S. policy during this time, see Fletcher, *Indian Education and Civilization*, 167–73.

5. Pratt, *Battlefield and Classroom*, 121, 163.

6. Quoted in DeJong, *Promises of the Past*, 110.

7. Pratt, *Battlefield and Classroom*, 188–90, 196–204; Folsom, *Ten Years' Work for Indians*; Graber, *Sister to the Sioux*, 16–22.

8. *The Indian's Friend* 3, no. 11 (July 1891): 2; *The Indian Craftsman* (Carlisle Indian School's journal, which later became *The Red Man*) 1, no. 1 (February 1909): back cover; Robert Utley, introduction to Pratt, *Battlefield and Classroom*, xiii; Pratt, *Battlefield and Classroom*, 230–31.

9. Hoxie, *A Final Promise*; Prucha, *American Indian Policy in Crisis*; Prucha, *The Churches and the Indian Schools*; Mathes, "Nineteenth-Century Women and Reform."

10. Quoted in Fletcher, *Indian Education*, 170.

11. D. W. Adams, *Education for Extinction*, 57, 58; DeJong, *Promises of the Past*, 107–9; E. C. Adams, *American Indian Education*, 57.

12. "Location, Capacity, Enrollment, and Average Attendance, United States Indian Schools," compiled by H. B. Peairs, 1911, included in Box 160, Folder 005/860, Correspondence with Supervisor of Schools, H. B. Peairs, 1910–13, Consolidated

Ute Agency Decimal Files, 1879–1952 (hereafter Ute Agency), RG 75, Records of the BIA, NARA-DEN.

13. Hoxie, "From Prison to Homeland," 59.

14. On Victoria, see Haebich, *Broken Circles*, 165; Human Rights and Equal Opportunity Commission, *Bringing Them Home*, 58–59; Broome, "Victoria," 158. For New South Wales, see Goodall, "New South Wales," 76–77; Edwards and Read, introduction to *The Lost Children*, xii–xiii. On Western Australia, see Haebich, *For Their Own Good*, 1–46.

15. Haebich, *Broken Circles*, 161–64; Buti, *Separated*, 59–63; Brock, "Aboriginal Families and the Law," 136. Katherine Ellinghaus provides a useful comparative analysis of Australian state policies of protection in *Taking Assimilation to Heart*, 189–212.

16. The website of the Australian Institute for Aboriginal and Torres Strait Islander Studies (AIATSIS) includes all the state legislation relevant to Aboriginal child removal. See http://www1.aiatsis.gov.au/exhibitions/legislations/legislation_hm.html.

17. Haebich, *Broken Circles*, 165. For more on how these policies affected indigenous families, see Grimshaw and Nelson, "Empire."

18. Human Rights Commission, *Bringing Them Home*, 40.

19. Kidd, *The Way We Civilise*, 47–54; Human Rights Commission, *Bringing Them Home*, 72–76; Haebich, *Broken Circles*, 168–79.

20. Haebich, *For Their Own Good*, 47–89, 11–13, 153–87, 255–67, 276–83, 344–51; Buti, *Separated*, 80–92, 98–105, 109–12; Haebich, *Broken Circles*, 186–89; Beresford and Omaji, *Our State of Mind*, 37–38; Human Rights Commission, *Bringing Them Home*, 102–6.

21. Neville, *Australia's Coloured Minority*, 180–81.

22. Human Rights Commission, *Bringing Them Home*, 133–34. For the use of "dog tags," see MacDonald, *Between Two Worlds*, 40; Paisley, "Race Hysteria," 44.

23. Commonwealth of Australia, *Aboriginal Welfare*, 14; Haebich, *Broken Circles*, 194–96.

24. "Report on the Administration of the Northern Territory for year ended 30 June 1932," CRS A1, 1932/10562, NAA-ACT.

25. "Aborigines Act of 1890," Item #2, Regulations, 1871–1937, CRS B313, NAA-VIC, emphasis added.

26. Human Rights Commission, *Bringing Them Home*, 40–41, 43–44; Haebich, *Broken Circles*, 181–86; Goodall, "New South Wales," 76–77.

27. South Australia, *Report of the Protector of Aborigines* for 1908, 4; Hall *A Brief History*, 8; Mattingley and Hampton, *Survival in Our Own Land*, 45–46; Brock, "Ab-

original Families," 138–39, 141; Haebich, *Broken Circles*, 197–202; Human Rights Commission, *Bringing Them Home*, 120–21.

28. SA, *Report of the Protector of Aborigines* for 1908, 4; Hall, *A Brief History*, 8; Mattingley and Hampton, *Survival*, 45–46; Brock, "Aboriginal Families," 138–39, 141; Haebich, *Broken Circles*, 197–202; Human Rights Commission, *Bringing Them Home*, 120–21.

29. Human Rights Commission, *Bringing Them Home*, 40–41, 43–44; Haebich, *Broken Circles*, 181–86; Goodall, "New South Wales," 76–77; Haskins, *One Bright Spot*, 29.

30. "Aborigines Act of 1915," Item #2, Regulations, 1871–1937, CRS B313, NAA-VIC.

31. Maykuttener, "Tasmania: 2," 350–51; Human Rights Commission, *Bringing Them Home*, 94–97; Haebich, *Broken Circles*, 179–81.

32. Read, *The Stolen Generations*, 28; Edwards and Read, *The Lost Children*, ix; Read, "How Many Separated Children?"

33. Testimony of J. W. Bleakley, July 3, 1913, in "Progress Report of the Royal Commission on the Aborigines," 98.

34. Testimony of J. Gray, July 23, 1913, in "Progress Report of the Royal Commission on the Aborigines," 121.

35. Chief Secretary's Dept. re. Visit of Mr. Gordon Sprig to Lake Tyers Aboriginal Station, [1927], Item #93, CRS B356, NAA-VIC.

36. For Australian criticism of the treatment of Aborigines, see Reynolds, *This Whispering in Our Hearts*. For Britain's early humanitarian criticism of the treatment of indigenous inhabitants in its colonies, see Reynolds, "Genocide in Tasmania?" 136, 139–40, 147; Reynolds, *Aborigines and Settlers*, 151–56; Goodall, *Invasion to Embassy*, 45. For criticism of violence used against Aborigines in Queensland, see Kidd, *The Way We Civilise*, xv–xvii, 25–29, 41–47.

37. T. J. Morgan, "Indian Contract Schools," *Baptist Home Mission Monthly* 18, no. 2 (December 1896): 391.

38. Haebich, *Broken Circles*, 138–41; Kidd, *The Way We Civilise*, 41–45. See also Moses, "Genocide and Settler Society in Australian History," 7; R. Evans, "'Plenty Shoot 'Em.'"

39. T.J. Morgan, "A Plea for the Papoose," *Baptist Home Mission Monthly* 18, no. 12 (December 1896): 402, 403.

40. Quoted in "The Indian Institute," *The Indian's Friend* 12, no. 2 (October 1899): 9.

41. SA, *Report of the Protector of Aborigines*, 1911, 1.

42. Quoted in "Looking After Aborigines," *Adelaide Advertiser*, August 30, 1933, CRS A1, 1933/243, NAA-ACT.

43. Thomas Morgan, "The Education of American Indians," paper read before the Lake Mohonk Conference, n.d., Box 160, Folder 005/810 "Correspondence in/

out: School Curriculum: Textbooks, teaching methods, 1889–1926, Ute Agency, RG 75, NARA-DEN. See also Ellinghaus, *Taking Assimilation*, 105–19.

44. Secretary for Prime Minister to A. N. Brown, n.d., CRS A431, 48/961, NAA-ACT.

45. T. J. Morgan, "A Plea for the Papoose," 404.

46. T. J. Morgan, "A Plea for the Papoose," 404.

47. Commonwealth of Australia, *Aboriginal Welfare*, 17.

48. For the example of how the Omahas chose village sites and strictly regulated the placement of tepees within their villages, see Fletcher and La Flesche, *The Omaha Tribe*, 95, 137–41.

49. For more on the deplorable conditions in some of these communities, see Reynolds, *With the White People*, 135–39, 154. Heather Goodall notes that in Australia all parties referred to an "Aboriginal living area on land not reserved for Aborigines" as camps. See Goodall, *Invasion to Embassy*, xv. Given how little land was reserved for Aborigines, such a usage of the term connoted that Aborigines had become impermanent dwellers on the land rather than its rightful owners.

50. Crane, *Indians of the Enchanted Desert*, 157–80, quotes on 173; James, *Pages from Hopi History*, 166.

51. Commonwealth of Australia, *Aboriginal Welfare*, 19.

52. Extract from letter from police officer at Oodnadatta, December 29, 1930, GRG 52/1/1931, SRSA.

53. Daisy Bates, "Adelina-Halfcaste," 1913, Folio 85/165, MS 365, Daisy Bates papers, NLA.

54. Quoted in Mattingley and Hampton, *Survival*, 166. Almost assuredly Watson's desire to raise the son of his sister derived from his Aboriginal kinship system that regarded the bond between a child and its maternal uncle as extremely significant. See McKnight, *Going the Whiteman's Way*, 46–49.

55. Huffer with Roughsey, *The Sweetness of the Fig*, 48. Peggy Brock has also argued that women's control of conception and the matrilineal descent system present among the Adnjamathanha people of South Australia made it possible for women to easily integrate "half-caste" children into that group as well. See Brock, introduction to *Women, Rites and Sites*, xxi–xxii.

56. Turner, *Ooldea*, 68–69.

57. Cawood to Dept. of Home and Territories, September 19, 1927, CRS A1, 1927/29982, NAA-ACT.

58. Letter from F. A. Hagenauer to "Sir," January 2, 1888, Item #181, CRS B313/1, NAA-VIC.

59. Quoted in Thonemann, *Tell the White Man*, 59, 61. Although this book uses an outdated and derogatory term, "lubra," for an Aboriginal woman, much of the

material that Buludja related to Thonemann is of value. In *People, Countries, and the Rainbow Serpent* David McKnight observes that the Lardil readily adopted Aboriginal children who were sent from the mainland to Mornington Island (115). For more on Aboriginal kinship systems, see Keen, *Aboriginal Economy and Society*, 174–209.

60. Quoted in Walter Dyk, "Preface," in *Left Handed*, xii.

61. Testimony of Mr. W. Goodall, May 28, 1877, *Report of the Commissioners, Royal Commission on the Aborigines*, 65.

62. See Stoler, *Carnal Knowledge*, 83, 79.

63. AFA, *63rd Annual Report*, 1921, 5, 6.

64. Morgan, "A Plea for the Papoose," 408.

65. Quoted in clipping enclosed with letter from R. S. Fellowes to Fletcher, February 3, 1884, Box 1, Alice Cunningham Fletcher and Francis La Flesche papers, NAA.

66. SA, *Report of the Protector of Aborigines*, 1910, 2.

67. Broome, *Aboriginal Australians*, 77, 78; Barwick, "Aunty Ellen," 182–83; Goodall, *Invasion to Embassy*, 77–79.

68. Broome, *Aboriginal Australians*, 77, 78; Barwick, "Aunty Ellen," 182–83.

69. Broome, *Aboriginal Australians*, 81–83. For more on Cumeroogunga, see Attwood, *Rights for Aborigines*, 31–32; Goodall, *Invasion to Embassy*, 117–24, 126–31, 247–58.

70. McLoughlin, *Cherokee Renascence in the New Republic*.

71. Debo, *And Still the Waters Run*.

72. *Conference of Representatives . . . to consider the Report . . . by J. W. Bleakley*, April 12, 1929, 9, CRS A1/15, 33/8782, NAA-ACT.

73. Commonwealth of Australia, *Aboriginal Welfare*, 3, 33–34. Marilyn Lake has found quite solid evidence that Australian nation builders looked to the experience of the United States during Reconstruction in formulating their White Australia policy. Again, however, Australian nation builders looked to America's policy regarding African Americans, not American Indians. See Lake's "White Man's Country." See also Lake and Reynolds, *Drawing the Global Colour Line*.

74. Stoler, *Carnal Knowledge*, 78. Tony Ballantyne has also studied the "mobile character of racial knowledge and discourses about cultural difference within the British empire," not only between metropole and colony, but between disparate colonies. In one case, he studies the circulation of conceptions of "Aryanism" from British India to the New Zealand frontier in the second half of the nineteenth century. See his "Race and the Webs of Empire."

75. Brooks, *Captives and Cousins*, 1–40; Namias, *White Captives*, 3–7; S. Jones, *The Trial of Don Pedro*, 19–21.

76. Brooks, *Captives and Cousins*; S. Jones, *Trial of Don Pedro*, 28–35, quote on 31; S. Jones, "'Redeeming' the Indian."

77. Fuchs and Havighurst, *To Live on This Earth*, 2. For more on French missionary efforts, see Axtell, *The Invasion Within*, 3–127. For the Franciscans in New Mexico, see Gutiérrez, *When Jesus Came*, 46–94. For the Franciscans in California, see Hurtado, *Intimate Frontiers*, 1–19; Jackson and Castillo, *Indians, Franciscans, and Spanish Colonization*.

78. E. Adams, *American Indian Education*, 15–16, 17.

79. Quoted in DeJong, *Promises of the Past*, 111. Other European missionary organizations declined to remove Indian children from their families. The German Moravians, for example, who opened missions among the Delawares (Lenape) and other Indians in the northeastern American colonies beginning in the 1740s, ministered to entire families, and according to Amy Schutt, appeared to enjoy great success in conversion due to their respect for Indian families' wishes. See Schutt, "What will become of our young people?'"

80. S. Jones, *Trial of Don Pedro*, 52, 100, 99. See also S. Jones, "'Redeeming' the Indian," 229. Thanks to Matthew Garrett as well for sharing his unpublished paper, "Buying Indian Captives: Mormon Motivations, 1850–1890."

81. Quoted in S. Jones, *Trial of Don Pedro*, 100.

82. Quoted in Trafzer and Hyer, *"Exterminate Them,"* 157, 158. See also Almaguer, *Racial Fault Lines*, 107–50; Hurtado, *Indian Survival on the California Frontier*.

83. Brewer, *Up and Down California*, 493.

84. Nearly every scholarly work on slavery mentions the threat of or actual separation of slave children from their mothers as a tactic masters used to compel slave women's obedience or to punish them. For a firsthand account, see H. Jacobs, *Incidents in the Life of a Slave Girl*.

85. Hawes, *The Children's Rights Movement*, 2.

86. Tiffin, *In Whose Best Interest?* 39.

87. Gordon, *The Great Arizona Orphan Abduction*, 10; Hawes, *Children's Rights Movement*, 18–19, 22–23, 33; Tiffin, *In Whose Best Interest?* 18; Platt, *The Child Savers*.

88. Tiffin, *In Whose Best Interest?* 38–39, 66–69.

89. Holt, *The Orphan Trains*; Gordon, *Great Arizona Orphan Abduction*, 9–10.

90. Quoted in Platt, *The Child Savers*, 62–63.

91. Quoted in E. Rose, *A Mother's Job*, 40.

92. E. Rose, *Mother's Job*, 40.

93. Quoted in Ashby, *Saving the Waifs*, 31, 34, 54, 65, quote 58.

94. Tiffin, *In Whose Best Interest?* 110.

95. E. Rose, *Mother's Job*, 35.

96. On the categorization of many immigrants as nonwhite, see Ignatiev, *How the Irish Became White*; Jacobson, *Whiteness of a Different Color*; Roediger, *The Wages of Whiteness*.

97. For an excellent discussion of the removal of both Aboriginal and white children in NSW up to 1915, see J. M. Wilson, "'You took our children,'" 51–84. See also Link-Up (NSW) and Wilson, *In the Best Interest of the Child?* 49.

98. Haebich, *Broken Circles*, 65, 79–94; Human Rights Commission, *Bringing Them Home*, 91–92. For more on kidnapping Aboriginal children throughout the Australian colonies, see Reynolds, *Aborigines and Settlers*, 33–34, 53–54; Reynolds, *With the White People*, 165–88; Reynolds, *Frontier*, 74–75.

99. Human Rights Commission, *Bringing Them Home*, 71–72, 119–20.

100. J. M. Wilson, "'You took our children,'" 53–55, Link-Up and Wilson, *In the Best Interest?* 49–50; Human Rights Commission, *Bringing Them Home*, 101–2, 120; Haebich, *Broken Circles*, 94–117.

101. Link-Up and Wilson, *In the Best Interest?* 49–50; Human Rights Commission, *Bringing Them Home*, 101–2.

102. Haebich, *Broken Circles*, 70–76, 94–109; McGrath, "Tasmania I," 316–22; Human Rights Commission, *Bringing Them Home*, 91–92. For more on Tasmania's early violent history, see Reynolds, "Genocide in Tasmania?"

103. Quoted in Hall, *A Brief History*, 4; Mattingley and Hampton, *Survival*, 45. For debates in NSW, see J. M. Wilson, "'You took our children,'" 55–59. For Victoria, see Human Rights Commission, *Bringing Them Home*, 57–58.

104. Broome, *Aboriginal Australians*, 76–77; Human Rights Commission, *Bringing Them Home*, 39–40.

105. Van Krieken, *Children and the State*, 49; Haebich, *Broken Circles*, 77–78.

106. Goodall, "'Saving the Children,'" 6; van Krieken, *Children and the State*, 49–60; Haebich, *Broken Circles*, 151–54; Human Rights Commission, *Bringing Them Home*, 44.

107. Buti, *Separated*, 54–55; van Krieken, *Children and the State*, 61–63. For Queensland, see Kidd, *The Way We Civilise*, 18–21.

108. Goodall, "'Saving the Children,'" 6; van Krieken, *Children and the State*, 72–79; Haebich, *Broken Circles*, 151–54; Human Rights Commission, *Bringing Them Home*, 44.

109. Buti, *Separated*, 54–55; van Krieken, *Children and the State*, 87–88. The similarity of American and Australian schemes for dealing with "delinquent" working-class children may derive from the long-standing transnational debates about child welfare that were "bound to modernizing political rationalities." See Stoler, *Carnal Knowledge*, 120.

110. Buti, *Separated*, 55; Haebich, *Broken Circles*, 152–53.

111. Barbalet, *Far from a Low Gutter Girl*, 190, 191, 193–94, 195, 212; van Krieken, *Children and the State*, 61–63, 95–97.

112. Buti, *Separated*, 23–38, 56–57.

113. Buti, *Separated*, 92–94. See also Haebich, *Broken Circles*, 250–51.

114. Haebich, *Broken Circles*, 159; Haebich, *For Their Own Good*, 111; van Krieken, *Children and the State*, 8, 97, 107–9.

115. Buti, *Separated*, 92–94.

116. In "Identifying the Process: The Removal of Half-Caste Children from Aboriginal Mothers," Suzanne Parry also makes the point that child removal was linked to nation building in Australia.

117. Lake and Reynolds, *Drawing the Global Colour Line*, 147–50; Elder, "Immigration History," 107; R. Evans, "'Pigmentia,'" 114; Ellinghaus, *Taking Assimilation*, xxx.

118. Grimshaw et al., *Creating a Nation*, 206, 279.

119. R. Evans, "'Pigmentia,'" 111.

120. Takaki, *Strangers from a Different Shore*, 110–12, 203–8; Chan, *Asian Americans*, 38, 39, 47, 54–55; Daniels, *Coming to America*, 245–46.

121. López, *White by Law*.

122. Daniels, *Coming to America*, 282–84, 292–94; Ngai, "The Architecture of Race in American Immigration Law."

123. Ngai, "The Strange Career of the Illegal Alien."

124. Calloway, *First Peoples*, 374, 435.

125. On the ties between whiteness and Australian nationalism, see McGregor, "'Breed Out the Colour.'"

126. L. H. Morgan, *Ancient Society*.

127. McGregor, *Imagined Destinies*; Reynolds, *Frontier*, 115–29; Haebich, *Broken Circles*, 132–33.

128. Quoted in McGregor, *Imagined Destinies*, 157. Basedow also served periodically as chief medical inspector and chief protector of Aborigines in the Northern Territory, in addition to acting as a local correspondent for the Royal Anthropological Institute of Great Britain and Ireland.

129. Hill, *The Great Australian Loneliness*, 171, 174.

130. Quoted in *Proceedings of the 18th Annual Meeting of the Lake Mohonk Conference*, 1900, 73.

131. Quoted in Mark, *A Stranger in Her Native Land*, 133.

132. Quoted in Morris, "Jane Ada Fletcher," 76.

133. "Report on Lake Tyers Aboriginal Station," August 19, 1925, Item 53, CRS B356, NAA-VIC, emphasis in original.

134. Quoted in Haebich, *For Their Own Good*, 80.

135. Testimony of Charles E. C. Lefroy, in *Report of the Royal Commission on the Constitution*, 479.

136. Wolfe, "Logics of Elimination," 2. See also Wolfe, "Land, Labor, and Difference," 872.

137. Hill, *Great Australian Loneliness*, 150.

138. Quoted in "Discussion on Natives," *The Ladder*, no. 3 (February 1937): 16, 17, 18, available in Series 12, Box 30, Item 191, MS 2004, Bessie Rischbieth papers, NLA.

139. Commonwealth of Australia, *Aboriginal Welfare*, 11.

140. Beresford and Omaji, *Our State of Mind*, 30–55; Haebich, *For Their Own Good*, 182–83, 215. Neville never commanded the fiscal resources necessary to carry out his plan to the fullest. See McGregor, "'Breed Out the Colour,'" 289.

141. Cecil Cook, *Report on the Administration of the Northern Territory* (1933), CRS A1, 1933/6909, NAA-ACT. Like Neville, Cook was impeded in his goals by lack of funding. McGregor estimates that in the eleven years of his administration, he engineered no more than fifty marriages between half-caste women and white men. See McGregor, "'Breed Out the Colour,'" 289.

142. Quoted in Read, "Northern Territory," 280.

143. NSW, *Report of the Board for the Protection of Aborigines*, 1921, 5.

144. NSW, *Report of the Board for the Protection of Aborigines*, 1925–26, 2. Victoria Haskins argues that although the NSW 1915 Act originally targeted lighter-skinned Aboriginal girls, it soon targeted *all* Aboriginal girls. See Haskins, *One Bright Spot*, 31–32.

145. Commonwealth of Australia, *Aboriginal Welfare*, 18. For more on the relationship of "breeding out the colour" schemes to the eugenics movement, see McGregor, "'Breed Out the Colour,'" 297–99. McGregor points out that avowed eugenicists generally opposed the policy of "breeding out the colour." For more on the eugenics movement in Australia, see Garton, "Sound Minds and Healthy Bodies."

146. Quoted in "Bonus Offered for Marrying Half-Castes: Australia's Plan to Breed Out Black Strain," news clipping, June 8, 1933, Box 30, Series 12, Item 162, Rischbieth papers.

147. Araunah, "The Native Problem," newspaper clipping, December 17, 1931, in Box 30, Series 12, Rischbieth papers. For more on the racial science that believed Aborigines to be a stem of the Caucasian race, see McGregor, "'Breed Out the Colour,'" 290–91.

148. Commonwealth of Australia, *Aboriginal Welfare*, 18.

149. McGregor, "'Breed Out the Colour,'" 289–90; Tony Austin, introduction to Ruddick, "'Talking about Cruel Things,'" 11.

150. Quoted in Austin, *I Can Picture the Old Home*, 141. For more on Cook, see McGregor, *Imagined Destinies*, 153, 155–56, 167–73. For taboos against relationships between white women and Aboriginal men, see Ellinghaus, *Taking Assimilation*, 149–66.

151. Goodall, "'Saving the Children,'" 7, 9; Goodall, "New South Wales," 77, 80. See also McGregor, *Imagined Destinies*, 154.

152. Katherine Ellinghaus has reached similar conclusions in her book *Taking Assimilation to Heart* and article "Indigenous Assimilation and Absorption in the United States and Australia."

153. Quoted in DeJong, *Promises of the Past*, 110, emphasis added.

154. Neville, *Australia's Coloured Minority*, 42.

155. T. J. Morgan, "Report of the Commissioner of Indian Affairs," *Baptist Home Mission Monthly* 14, no. 1 (January 1892): 29.

156. Quoted in Prucha, *American Indian Policy in Crisis*, 153.

157. Charles Bartlett Dyke, "Essential Features in the Education of the Child Races," speech, National Education Association Conference, Denver CO, 1909, Box 1, Folder 27, MS 120 Papers of Estelle Reel, EWSHS. In *A Final Promise*, Frederick Hoxie has also noted a shift among white reformers from a belief that changing the environment of Indian children could bring them up to the status of whites to a notion that Indian children were destined by their racial inheritance to inferiority.

158. Quoted in Lomawaima, "Estelle Reel," 14.

159. Gallagher, *Breeding Better Vermonters*, 7.

160. Elaine Goodale Eastman, "The Education of Indians," *The Arena*, October 1900, 414, Box 1, Folder 32, Reel papers, EWSHS. Nevertheless, as Katherine Ellinghaus uncovered, Eastman still seems to have been influenced by eugenic thought. In her biography of Pratt, Eastman argued for the genetic superiority of children of the "first cross," like those of her own with her husband. See Ellinghaus, *Taking Assimilation*, 100.

161. On missionaries' general opposition to the policy, see McGregor, "'Breed Out the Colour,'" 289.

162. Ellinghaus, *Taking Assimilation*, especially 214.

163. Quoted in Prucha, *American Indian Policy in Crisis*, 148. See also 132–68.

164. Quoted in Prucha, *American Indian Policy in Crisis*, 153.

165. Prucha, *American Indian Policy in Crisis*, 158–59.

166. Article reprinted in Turner, *Pearls from the Deep*, 79.

167. Turner, *Ooldea*, 168.

168. In my reading of Australian history, Christianity did not have the foundational

role that it did in American history. Whereas religious revivals frequently swept across America, and often spurred social movements that in turn influenced government policy, religion seems to have had much less influence and to have had more of a perfunctory character in Australian life. See Macintyre, *A Concise History*, 49, 116.

169. I explore this extensively in my book *Engendered Encounters: Feminism and Pueblo Cultures, 1879–1934*, especially 82–105, as does Philip Deloria in *Indians in Unexpected Places*. For Australia, see Macneil, "Time after Time." See also D. B. Rose, *Reports from a Wild County*, 16.

170. WA, *Annual Report of the Chief Protectors of Aborigines*, 1936, 16.

171. Stoler also finds concern among Dutch colonial authorities with fair-skinned métis children living as poor Indonesians. See Stoler, *Carnal Knowledge*, 70.

172. For more on "the seasonal round" of many Aboriginal people, see Keen, *Aboriginal Economy and Society*, 103. For American Indians' continued use of this as a modern economic strategy, see O'Neill, *Working the Navajo Way*; Hosmer and O'Neill, *Native Pathways*; Littlefield and Knack, Native *Americans and Wage Labor*.

173. On BIA attempts to stop giveaways, see M. Jacobs, *Engendered Encounters*, 109, 111. Ian Keen writes that traditional Aboriginal economies (and the same could be said for American Indian economies) were at odds with capitalism because they limited demand, or "wants," and were based on gifts, not commodities. See *Aboriginal Economy and Society*, 4–5.

174. Pratt to Fletcher, August 7, 1891, Box 1, Fletcher and La Flesche papers.

175. Quoted in D. W. Adams, *Education for Extinction*, 53.

176. Quoted in Mattingley and Hampton, *Survival*, 157.

177. Quoted in "Rights of the Indian," *Post*, April 26, 1902, Box 1, Folder 42, Reel papers, EWSHS.

178. Quoted in Turner, *Lazarus at the Gate*, 44.

179. *Course of Study of the Indian Schools*, 49, 87, included in Box 1, Folder 13, Reel papers, EWSHS.

180. Stoler, *Carnal Knowledge*, 95.

181. Walden, "'That Was Slavery Days.'"

182. *Course of Study of the Indian Schools*, 189.

183. Victoria Haskins also points out that Aboriginal women had long worked independently as domestic servants before the NSW Aborigines Protection Board set up its apprenticeship scheme. She contends, "Apprenticeship meant that both the earning capacity and reproductive capacity of Aboriginal girls were denied to their communities." See "'A Better Chance'?" 39.

184. Goodall, "New South Wales," 78–80; Goodall, *Invasion to Embassy*, 121–23.
185. Quoted in Prucha, *American Indian Policy in Crisis*, 160.
186. For a general overview of assimilation policy, including allotment, see Hoxie, *The Final Promise*. The act provided eighty acres of land to single Indian women, and the Burke Act of 1906 made it possible for Indians deemed "competent" to sell their lands instead of the government holding their lands in trust for twenty-five years.
187. Goodall, "New South Wales," 82.
188. Morgan quoted in *The Indian's Friend* 4, no. 5 (January 1892): 20.
189. Quoted in Pratt, *Battlefield and Classroom*, 122–23, 158. The adjutant general approved of reuniting the prisoners with their families, but the BIA refused to comply with their wishes.
190. Pratt, *Battlefield and Classroom*, 202; also see 220 and 227.

3. The Great White Mother

The title of this chapter derives from an article in the Women's National Indian Association's publication, *The Indian's Friend* 16, no. 5 (January 1904): 5.

1. Threadgold, *Feminist Poetics*, 134–67, especially 151–52, 159. Threadgold argues that white male Australian nation builders conceived of both white women and Aborigines as in need of the protection of a white, masculine state. In fact, Threadgold asserts, nation builders constructed white women as threatened by Aboriginal men and therefore in need of sequestration away from the public realm of politics and voting. See also Lake, "The Politics of Respectability"; Lake, "Colonised and Colonising," especially 379; and Lake, "Frontier Feminism." For the United States, see Bederman, *Manliness and Civilization*, 170–215; Kaplan, *The Anarchy of Empire*, especially 92–145.
2. Gordon, *Pitied but Not Entitled*, 55. Gordon cites the last three of these as the central tenets of maternalism.
3. Gordon, *Pitied but Not Entitled*; Michel, *Children's Interests/Mother's Rights*; Mink, *The Wages of Motherhood*; Ladd-Taylor, *Mother-Work*; Skocpol, *Protecting Soldiers and Mothers*. Most scholarship on maternalism has looked at women in the eastern United States, but a few scholars have examined maternalism in the West. See K. Anderson, "Changing Woman"; Cahill, "'Only the Home Can Found a State,'" 16–19, 77–82, 227–77; Pascoe, *Relations of Rescue*.
4. Quoted in Skocpol, *Protecting Soldiers and Mothers*, 438, 450. *The Delineator* was subtitled *A Journal of Fashion, Culture, and Fine Arts* and ran from 1873 to 1937.
5. Lake, *Getting Equal*, 49–51; H. Jones, *In Her Own Name*, 235–57.
6. "The Unmarried Mother and Her Child," resolution adopted at 10th International Congress, Paris, 1926, reprinted in *The Dawn* 9, no. 1 (July 19, 1927): 11.

7. Quoted in Lake, *Getting Equal*, 84.

8. H. Jones, *In Her Own Name*, 253–55.

9. Lake, *Getting Equal*, 72–76.

10. Key, *The Century of the Child*, 44.

11. Quoted in Lake, *Getting Equal*, 85, 86. Australia passed a law in 1934 granting equal custody rights to men and women.

12. Quoted in E. Rose, *A Mother's Job*, frontispiece.

13. "Mrs. John Jones," *The Dawn*, May 14, 1925, 5.

14. Quoted in Pascoe, *Relations of Rescue*, 50.

15. "Articulate Women: Mrs. John Jones Interviewed," *The Dawn*, July 19, 1927, 14.

16. Lake, *Getting Equal*, 31–36, 56–63.

17. Pascoe, *Relations of Rescue*.

18. Gordon, *Pitied but Not Entitled*, 70–80, 107–8; Lake, *Getting Equal*, 72–79. Nevertheless, as Gordon makes clear, in the United States mother's pensions and the later ADC program never provided enough money for women to support themselves independently. Maternalists and policy makers alike did not wish to encourage single motherhood and instead envisioned that single mothers would soon become dependent on a man again in a conventional marriage. See 7–8, 49–51, 289–91.

19. Quinton, "Care of the Indian." See also Prucha, *American Indian Policy in Crisis*, 134–38; Mathes, "Nineteenth Century Women and Reform"; Wanken, "Woman's Sphere and Indian Reform"; Cahill, "'Only the Home Can Found a State,'" 86–143.

20. WNIA, *Annual Meeting and Report of the WNIA* (hereafter *WNIA Report*), 1883, 8–9.

21. *WNIA Report* (1884), 20–21; *WNIA Report* (1885), 32.

22. *Report of the Missionary Committee*; *The Indian's Friend* 9, no. 7 (March 1897): 4.

23. *WNIA Report* (1883), 10, 11.

24. Quoted in *Proceedings of the 18th Annual Meeting of the Lake Mohonk Conference* (hereafter *Lake Mohonk Proceedings*) (1900), 110–11.

25. *WNIA Report* (1883), 18; *WNIA Report* (1894), 16–17.

26. For Quinton's support of boarding schools, see *The Indian's Friend* 3, no. 10 (June 1891): 4.

27. *WNIA Report* (1884), 53.

28. Welter, "'She Hath Done What She Could'"; Brumberg, "Zenanas and Girlless Villages"; Flemming, *Women's Work for Women*; Hunter, *The Gospel of Gentility*; Burton, *Burdens of History*; Grimshaw, *Paths of Duty*.

29. *WNIA Report* (1884), 53. White women missionaries in Canada similarly used maternal metaphors to describe their mission and relationships with indigenous people. See Rutherdale, "Mothers of the Empire."

30. Paisley, *Loving Protection?* 35, 36–37. Lake claims the WNPA did not take up the Aboriginal issue until 1927. See Lake, *Getting Equal*, 111–12.

31. Grimshaw, "Gender, Citizenship and Race."

32. *Conference of Representatives . . . to consider the Report . . . by J. W. Bleakley* (April 12, 1929), 40, CRS A1/15, 33/8782, NAA-ACT.

33. Bennett to Rischbieth, March 6, 1932, Series 12, Item 23, Box 30, MS 2004, Bessie Rischbieth papers, NLA.

34. Details on Quinton's background and work with the WNIA can be found in Quinton, "Care of the Indian"; Quinton, "The Women's National Indian Association"; Mathes, "Nineteenth Century Women"; Wanken, "Woman's Sphere."

35. Mark, *A Stranger in Her Native Land*, 3–42.

36. Mark, *Stranger in Her Native Land*, 54–122, 169–203.

37. Mark, *Stranger in Her Native Land*, 104–5.

38. Quinton, "Care of the Indian," 376.

39. Mark, *Stranger in Her Native Land*, 147–53, 207, 245–65, 307–15, 329–32.

40. Dolores Janiewski explores these and other tensions in Fletcher's career in "Giving Women a Future."

41. Biographical File, Estelle Reel, WSA; Beach, *Women of Wyoming*, 40.

42. Van Pelt, "Estelle Reel," 53.

43. *Course of Study of the Indian Schools*, included in Box 1, Folder 13, MS 120, Papers of Estelle Reel, EWSHS.

44. "Death Takes Mrs. Cort F. Meyer at Age of Ninety-six," *Toppenish Review*, August 6, 1959, Biographical File, Estelle Reel, WSA. For more on Reel, see Lomawaima, "Estelle Reel."

45. See, for example, "Miss Reel's Report on Indian Schools in the West," *The Indian's Friend* 11, no. 6 (February 1899): 7–8; "The Indian Institute," *The Indian's Friend* 12, no. 1 (September 1899): 7–8; "The Indian Institute (Conclusion)" *The Indian's Friend* 12, no. 2 (September 1899): 9–11; *The Indian's Friend* 13, no. 4 (December 1900): 1; "The Present Indian Policy," *The Indian's Friend* 18, no. 1 (September 1905): 2; *The Indian's Friend* 22, no. 9 (May 1910): 1.

46. "Mrs. Cort Meyer Prepared Own Obituary," *Toppenish Review*, August 6, 1959, Box 1, Folder 6, Reel papers, EWSHS.

47. Quinton, "Women's National Indian Association," 71, 73.

48. Mrs. Egerton Young, "The Transformed Indian Woman," *The Indian's Friend* 10, no. 7 (March 1898): 10.

49. For more on Cooke's background, see Paisley, *Loving Protection?* 21–22; Paisley, "'For a Brighter Day'"; Lake, *Getting Equal*, 111; Holland, "'Saving the Aborigines,'" 42–43, 63.

50. For more on Rischbieth, see Paisley, *Loving Protection?* 16–18, quote on 17; Lake, *Getting Equal*, 50–51, 64–66, 77, 118–19.

51. For more on Jones, see "Articulate Women"; "Women and Parliament," *The Dawn*, August 21, 1929, n.p.; Paisley, *Loving Protection?* 18–20; Lake, *Getting Equal*, 112–14; Holland, "'Saving the Aborigines,'" 56–57.

52. For more on Bennett, see Holland, "Feminism, Colonialism and Aboriginal Workers"; Holland, "Whatever her race, a woman is not a chattel'"; Holland, "'Saving the Aborigines,'" 10–11, 76–86; Paisley, *Loving Protection?* 10–15; Paisley, "'Unnecessary Crimes and Tragedies'"; Lake, *Getting Equal*, 110–16; Lake, "Feminism and the Gendered Politics of Antiracism," 99–100.

53. Jones to Rischbieth, August 27, 1930, and September 24, 1930, Series 5, Item 1097, Rischbieth papers.

54. Bennett to Rischbieth, October 20, [1930], Series 12, Box 30, Rischbieth papers.

55. Jones to Rischbieth, June 24, 1931, Series 7, Item 126, Rischbieth papers.

56. Jones to Rischbieth, May 18, 1932, Series 7, Item 158, Rischbieth papers.

57. J. Anderson, "'A glorious thing,'" 229. For more on Bates, see Bates, *The Passing of the Aborigines*; Salter, *Daisy Bates*; White, "Daisy Bates"; Hill, *Kabbarli*.

58. Marcus, *The Indomitable Miss Pink*; Marcus, "The Beauty, Simplicity and Honour of Truth."

59. Quoted in Mark, *Stranger in Her Native Land*, 50.

60. Quoted in "The Indian Institute," 7.

61. Memorandum, "Control of Aboriginals, Proposals Made by Mrs. Daisy Bates," June 1929, CRS A1, 1935/1066, NAA-ACT. For more on white women's maternalism and colonialism, see Jolly, "Colonizing Women," especially 113–15; Ramusack, "Cultural Missionaries"; McGuire, "The Legend of the Goodfella Missus," especially 125; Thorne, "Missionary-Imperial Feminism."

62. Untitled article, *The Weekly News*, August 9, 1933, Box 30, Series 12, Item 51, Rischbieth papers.

63. Memorandum, "Control of Aboriginals, Proposals Made by Mrs. Daisy Bates."

64. *The Indian's Friend* 6, no. 10 (June 1894): 9. For more on representations of Indian women as beasts of burden, see Smits, "The 'Squaw Drudge.'" Alice Fletcher took a rare opposing view of American Indian women. See Draft of publication: "The Indian Woman and Her Problems" [1899], Box 6, Alice Cunningham Fletcher and Francis La Flesche papers, NAA; Janiewski, "Giving Women a Future," 330.

65. Mrs. John Jones, "Australia, Aborigines," in *Proceedings of the British Commonwealth League Conference (hereafter BCL Proceedings)* (1936), 27. See also Holland, "'Saving the Aborigines,'" 95.

66. Young, "The Transformed Indian Woman," 9.

67. Boydston, *Home and Work*; Simonsen, *Making Home Work*.

68. Roessel, *Women in Navajo Society*, 105.

69. Kaberry, *Aboriginal Woman*, 36.

70. Laura Klein and Lillian Ackerman refer to "a balanced reciprocity" in their introduction to *Women and Power in Native North America*, 14; Carol Devens discusses "a vital symmetry" in *Countering Colonization*; L. Ackerman, *A Necessary Balance*. Catherine Berndt uses the term "interdependent independence"; see "Retrospect, and Prospect," 6. See also Shoemaker, *Negotiators of Change*; K. L. Anderson, *Chain Her by One Foot*; Johnston, *Cherokee Women in Crisis*, 3–5, 11–35; Keen, *Aboriginal Economy and Society*, 306–7, 318–27, 330–31; D. B. Rose, *Dingo Makes Us Human*, 28, 49–51.

71. Kaberry, *Aboriginal Woman*, 94.

72. Holland, "'Saving the Aborigines,'" 87–89.

73. Mary Bennett, letter to the editor, *A.B.M. Review* 19, no. 7 (October 20, 1932): 124.

74. No author given, "The Australian Aborigine Woman: Is She a Slave?" speech, n.d. [ca. 1930s], Box 31, Series 12, Item 316, Rischbieth papers. See also Holland, "'Saving the Aborigines,'" 71–76, 87–89; Scanlon, "'Pure and Clean and True to Christ.'"

75. *The Indian's Friend* 38, no. 3 (January 1926): 7.

76. McKnight, *Going the Whiteman's Way*, 193; Keen, *Aboriginal Economy*, 190, 349, 355, 373; D. B. Rose, *Dingo Makes Us Human*, 123–24, 126, 174–75, 178.

77. Keen, *Aboriginal Economy*, 247.

78. Kaberry, *Aboriginal Woman*, 271; Choo, *Mission Girls*, 203; D. B. Rose, *Dingo Makes Us Human*, 140.

79. R. M. Berndt and C. Berndt, *The World of the First Australians*, 199–200; Choo, *Mission Girls*, 193; Kaberry, *Aboriginal Woman*, 100–108; McKnight, *Going the Whiteman's Way*, 60–61; D. B. Rose, *Dingo Makes Us Human*, 133–34. For a more extended discussion of Aboriginal marriage practices, see Keen, *Aboriginal Economy*, 178–207.

80. For one example of a book that attempts this, for just one group of Aboriginal people, see McKnight, *Going the Whiteman's Way*.

81. Deloria, *Waterlily*, 13, 14, 135–41. For more on the complicated nature of indigenous gender relations in Australia, see Hamilton, "A Complex Strategical Situation," 85; C. Berndt, "Mythical Women," 14; Choo, *Mission Girls*, 218; D. B. Rose, *Dingo Makes Us Human*, 134; R. M. Berndt and C. Berndt, *World of First Australians*, 207; Keen, *Aboriginal Economy*, 247, 253, 268–69. For American Indian gender relations, see L. Ackerman, *A Necessary Balance*, especially 93, and sources above in note 71.

82. Carter, *Capturing Women*, 158–93; Burton, *Burdens of History*; Pascoe, *Relations of Rescue*; Welter, "'She Hath Done What She Could'"; Brumberg, "Zenanas and Girlless Villages."

83. Mohanty, "Under Western Eyes."

84. Mary Bennett, "The Aboriginal Mother in Western Australia in 1933," paper read at the BCL Conference, London, 1933, Box 30, Series 12, Item 213, Rischbieth papers.

85. Hill, *The Great Australian Loneliness*, 230, 231.

86. *The Indian's Friend* 2, no. 10 (June 1890): 1.

87. Susan Thorne noted a similar tendency among London Missionary Society women toward "heathen" women. See her "Missionary-Imperial Feminism," 54–56.

88. *Report of the Missionary Committee of the* WNIA (1889), 10, 11.

89. *WNIA Report* (1884), 33–34.

90. Stewart, *A Voice in Her Tribe*, 11–12.

91. On Navajo cradleboards, see Benedek, *Beyond the Four Corners*, 99–100.

92. Quoted in Bishop, "'A woman missionary,'" 76.

93. R. M. Berndt and C. Berndt, *World of the First Australians*, 159; Hamilton, *Nature and Nurture*, 29.

94. Daisy Bates, "Suggestions for the Betterment of Aborigines and Castes," 1939, Box 33, Folio 65/4, Daisy Bates papers, MS 365, NLA.

95. *The Indian's Friend* 9, no. 9 (May 1897): 4.

96. M. M. Bennett, *Hunt and Die*, 5. For more on historical interpretations of infanticide, see L. Russell, "'Dirty Domestics and Worse Cooks,'" 31–34.

97. Perdue, *Cherokee Women*, 33.

98. Memorandum, "Control of Aboriginals, Proposals Made by Mrs. Daisy Bates." Bates repeated her assertion that "baby cannibalism was rife" in *The Passing of the Aborigines*, 107–8.

99. J. Anderson, "A glorious thing," 222.

100. White, "Daisy Bates," 62.

101. Litchfield, *Far-North Memories*, 58.

102. M. D. Jacobs, *Engendered Encounters*, 110.

103. Linda Gordon makes this point regarding child savers in urban areas in *Heroes of Their Own Lives*, 166. Colonizers promoted the patriarchal nuclear family in other colonies as well. See Emberley, "The Bourgeois Family."

104. Quoted in *Lake Mohonk Proceedings* (1897), 101.

105. *WNIA Report* (1890), 19.

106. Turner, *Lazarus at the Gate*, 54–55.

107. Rowse, *White Flour, White Power*.

108. Loulie Taylor, "What a Diocesan Officer Saw on an Indian Reservation," *The Woman's Auxiliary* 67, no. 3 (March 1902): 208–9, in Box 64, Archives of the Episcopal Diocese of Idaho, MS 91, Special Collections, Boise State University, Idaho.

109. Turner, *Lazarus at the Gate*, 32.

110. For more on the significance of the home to American white middle-class women, see Pascoe, *Relations of Rescue*, 32–40; Simonsen, *Making Home Work*.

111. *The Indian's Friend* 12, no. 4 (December 1899): 10.

112. Turner, *Lazarus at the Gate*, 54.

113. Cahill, "'Only the Home Can Found a State,'" 43–85; Simonsen, *Making Home Work*, 71–109.

114. *The Indian's Friend* 2, no. 11 (July 1890): 2.

115. Quoted in "Education for Indian Girls," *The Woman's Journal*, January 19, 1901, Box 2, Folder 1, Reel papers, EWSHS.

116. For the Selection Acts, see Macintyre, *A Concise History of Australia*, 97–101. For the Homestead Act, see Hine and Faragher, *The American West*, 333–37.

117. Hill, *Great Australian Loneliness*, 132.

118. For more on the linkages between white women, home, and empire building, see Blunt and Dowling, *Home*, 140–95.

119. Paisley, *Loving Protection?* 33–47; Lake, *Getting Equal*, 110–35; Woollacott, *To Try Her Fortune*, 105–38.

120. Bennett to Pink, December 18, 1937, I.F.(a)(2), Pink papers, AIATSIS; M. M. Bennett, *The Australian Aboriginal as a Human Being*, 11, 50. For Du Bois's remark, see *The Souls of Black Folk*, foreword.

121. Tyrrell, *Woman's World, Woman's Empire*, 3, 29; Boyd, *Emissaries*; Grimshaw, "Gender, Citizenship and Race," 201–2.

122. J. Ackermann, *Australia from a Woman's Point of View*, 209.

123. Quoted in Burton, *Burdens of History*, 190. See also Tyrrell, *Woman's World*, 221–41.

124. *The Indian's Friend* 3, no. 10 (June 1891): 4.

125. *The Indian's Friend* 1, no. 5 (January 1889): 1.

126. "Our Duty toward Dependent Races," draft of lecture, n.d., Box 11, Fletcher and La Flesche papers.

127. Draft of publication, "Going Home with the Indians," 1882, Box 6, Fletcher and La Flesche papers.

128. Field diary, September–November 1881, includes draft of letter to Robert Lincoln, secretary of war, Box 11, Fletcher and La Flesche papers. Fletcher needed his permission because Pratt had gained permission from the secretary to bring only eight children from Sitting Bull's band to Carlisle.

129. Lillian Gray, "Estelle Reel: Superintendent of Indian Schools," *The New Orleans Item*, May 10, 1903, Box 1, "Articles" folder, Estelle Reel papers, H6–110, WSA. This article was syndicated and put under several other bylines in many other papers.

130. "Woman's Great Work for the Government," draft of article, n.d., Box 1, "Articles" folder, Reel papers, WSA.

131. "Her Work for the Indians: Miss Estelle Reel, Genl Supt of Indian Schools, talks interestingly regarding Indian matters, favors compulsory education and industrial training," n.d., Box 1, "Articles" folder, Reel papers, WSA.

132. *Report of the Superintendent of Indian Schools* (1900), 15, in Box 2, Folder 72, Reel papers, EWSHS.

133. Letter from Reel and Committee at Industrial School at Grand Junction to the Supts of Indian Boarding and Training Schools, February 8, 1900, Box 1, Folder 19, Reel papers, EWSHS.

134. "Her Work for the Indians."

135. Quoted in "National Councils of Women: Treatment of Aboriginals," *The Age*, October 24, 1924, in CRS A1, 1927/2982, NAA-ACT.

136. Letter from E. M. Gibbin, Tasmanian Women's Non-Party Political League, to Senator Payne, October 6, 1924, CRS A1 1927/2982, NAA-ACT.

137. Letter from E. G. Walker, WNPA, SA, to minister of home and territories, November 7, 1924, CRS A1 1927/2982, NAA-ACT; see also letter from E. M. Gibbin, Tasmanian Women's Non-Party Political League, to Senator Payne, October 6, 1924; "The Alice Springs Bungalow," *Hobart Mercury*, December 27, 1924; "National Councils of Women: Treatment of Aboriginals," *The Age*, October 24, 1924; "Half-Castes and Other Hybrids," *Adelaide Advertiser*, November 8, 1924; "Half-Castes at Alice Springs," *Adelaide Advertiser*, October 18, 1924; all included in CRS A1 1927/2982, NAA-ACT.

138. Draft of letter from Cooke to minister, ca. 1924, File 18, GRG 52/32, Constance Cooke papers, SRSA.

139. Sexton to minister for home and territories, October 28, 1924, CRS A1 1927/2982, NAA-ACT.

140. Letter to the editor from Alfred Giles, [October 6,] 1924, clipping in File 15, GRG 52/32, Cooke papers, SRSA.

141. "The Alice Springs Bungalow," *Hobart Mercury*, December 27, 1924, CRS A1, 1927/2982, NAA-ACT.

142. Mr. Howse for prime minister to premier of SA, August 30, 1927, CRS A1 1927/2982, NAA-ACT.

143. Constance Cooke, speech, BCL *Proceedings* (1927), 29, 30.

144. Committee Minutes, August 10, 1932, 116/2/2, League of Women Voters of SA papers, SRG 116, SLSA.

145. Quoted in McGregor, *Imagined Destinies*, 174.

146. Quoted in McGregor, *Imagined Destinies*, 177.

147. Pink to Mrs. Menzies, August 28, 1940, Box 22, Series 8, Folder 43, E. W. P. Chinnery papers, MS 766, NLA.

148. Olive Pink, "A Policy for the Aborigines by White Fellow-Australians," May 24, 1939, I.c.(a)(1), Olive Pink papers, MS 2368, AIATSIS.

149. J. C. Lovegrove to director of Native affairs, November 21, 1940; Ted Strehlow to Chinnery, February 8, 1941; "Notes on Precautions regarding entry of Europeans into areas reserved for Natives," ca. 1941; all in Box 22, Series 8, Folder 43, Chinnery papers.

150. Olive Pink, "The Australian Full Bloods," ca. 1937, I.c.(c)(2), Pink papers.

151. Quoted in McGregor, *Imagined Destinies*, 241.

152. Quoted in Constance T. Cooke, "The Status of Aboriginal Women in Australia," ca. 1928, 14, SRG 139/1/195, AFA papers, SLSA.

153. Hill, *Great Australian Loneliness*, 230. For more on Hill, see Griffiths, *Hunters and Collectors*, 190–92.

154. Bennett to editor, *Western Australian*, ca. 1940, CRS A659, 40/1/524, NAA-ACT.

155. J. Anderson, "A glorious thing," 220–21.

156. Quoted in Bishop, "'A woman missionary,'" 46–47.

157. M. M. Bennett, "The Aboriginal Mother in Western Australia in 1933."

158. M. M. Bennett, *Australian Aboriginal as a Human Being*, 126.

159. *Conference to consider the Report by J. W. Bleakley*, 41. For more on the campaign for women protectors, see Holland, "'Saving the Aborigines,'" 151–204.

160. Helen Baillie, "The Great Need of Trained Women Protectors for the Aboriginal and Half-Caste Women and Children of Australia," paper written for BCL conference, 1937, CRS A659, 40/1/524, NAA-ACT.

161. Quoted in broadcast interview with Ernest Mitchell by Katherine Prichard, "The Aborigines and their Problems," ca. 1939, Box 14, Series 9, Folder 5, Katherine Prichard papers, MS 6201, NLA.

162. Quoted in Baillie, "Protection of Aborigines," BCL *Proceedings* (1937), 41.

163. Quoted in Bishop, "'A woman missionary,'" 47.

164. "Report on the Half Castes and Aboriginals of the Southern Division of the Northern Territory, with special reference to the Bungalow at Stuart and the Hermannsburg Mission Station," n.d. [ca. 1930], CRS A1, 1930/1542, NAA-ACT.

165. Women Protectors for Aborigines Urged," *The Herald*, June 5, 1936).

166. Commonwealth of Australia, "Aboriginal Welfare," 4.

167. File 139/1/25, AFA papers. See also Haskins, "The Call for a Woman Visitor"; Holland, "The Campaign for Women Protectors," 36–37.
168. Quinton, "Care of the Indian," 387.
169. Mark, *Stranger in Her Native Land*, 116–20, 194–95, quote on 85.
170. *Conference to consider the Report by J. W. Bleakley*, 41. One exception to white women's near exclusion from policy making is Constance Cooke, who was invited by the federal government to participate in a conference on Aboriginal issues in 1929 and also was appointed to the SA government's Advisory Council of Aborigines that same year. Nevertheless, Cooke's role was small in comparison to that of white women in the United States. See Paisley, "For a Brighter Day," 173–74.
171. Neville, *Australia's Coloured Minority*, 39–40. In her comparison of U.S. and Australian assimilation policies, Katherine Ellinghaus argues not only that white women had little influence on the Australian state governments but also that there was virtually "no influential reform movement" in Australia on a par with the Indian Rights Association or the Women's National Indian Association. See *Taking Assimilation to Heart*, xxviii.
172. J. Jones, *Soldiers of Light and Love*; Pascoe, *Relations of Rescue*; Ruiz, *From out of the Shadows*, 33–50; Deutsch, *No Separate Refuge*, 63–85; Van Nuys, *Americanizing the West*.
173. Turner, *Lazarus at the Gate*, 35.
174. Quoted in Paisley, "'For a Brighter Day,'" 172.
175. WNIA *Report* (1914), 16.
176. Turner, *Lazarus at the Gate*, 33.
177. Turner, *Lazarus at the Gate*, 33.

4. The Practice of Indigenous Child Removal

1. Patrick Wolfe has made a similar point in his writings. See, for example, *Settler Colonialism*, 168–69. Victoria Haskins and I have also explored this issue in our article, "Stolen Generations and Vanishing Indians."
2. Pratt, *Battlefield and Classroom*, 197–203, quote on 197.
3. Pratt, *Battlefield and Classroom*, 221–25, 226–27, 238–39, quote on 222.
4. T. J. Morgan to U.S. Indian Agents, November 29, 1892, Box 159, Folder 005/806, Ute Agency, 1879–1952, RG 75, Records of the BIA, NARA-DEN.
5. Seaman, *Born a Chief*, 106, 96, 97.
6. Seaman, *Born a Chief*, 112.
7. Pratt, *Battlefield and Classroom*, 230.
8. Quoted in *Lake Mohonk Proceedings* (1898), 54, 55. For more on Dawson, see Simonsen, *Making Home Work*, 151–81.

9. Rev. Lee I. Thayer, "School Work at Two Gray Hills Mission," *Baptist Home Mission Monthly* 28, no. 2 (February 1908): 75.

10. Quoted in *The Indian's Friend* 4, no. 4 (December 1891): 17.

11. Battey, *The Life and Adventures*, 122.

12. "Angel DeCora: An Autobiography," *The Red Man* 3, no. 7 (March 1911): 279–80.

13. Qoyawayma, *No Turning Back*, 17–18, 22.

14. R. Mitchell, *Tall Woman*, 61–62.

15. Transcript of interview with Charlie Cojo, October 3, 1940, 36, MS 216, Dorothea C. Leighton and Alexander Leighton Collection, Archives and Special Collections, Cline Library, NAU.

16. Quoted in Gabriel, *Marietta Wetherill*, 198.

17. *The Indian's Friend* 10, no. 1 (September 1897): 10.

18. Pratt to Fletcher, October 31, 1883, Box 1, Alice Cunningham Fletcher and Francis La Flesche papers, NAA. For more on the conflict between Protestant and Catholic missions over Indian education, see Prucha, *The Churches and the Indian Schools* and *American Indian Policy in Crisis*.

19. Letter from McKean to CIA Burke, March 11, 1926, Box 2, Folder 150, Ute Agency, RG 75, NARA-DEN. For more on Ute resistance to boarding schools, see Osburn, *Southern Ute Women*, 27–29.

20. Qoyawayma, *No Turning Back*, 21, 24.

21. Qoyawayma, *No Turning Back*, 49, 54.

22. Life Story of Bill Sage (a pseudonym), Draft 2, part 1, 33, Box 1, Folder 3, MS 216, Leighton Collection.

23. Stewart, *A Voice in Her Tribe*, 15.

24. *The Indian's Friend* 10, no. 1 (September 1897): 10. See also Ball with Henn and Sánchez, *Indeh*, 219. Ball notes that at Mescalero, after building a boarding school on the reservation in 1884, agents took children forcibly to school and "incarcerated" them there. "To prevent their escape the windows were nailed shut" (219).

25. "Miss Reel's Report on Indian Schools in the West," *The Indian's Friend* 11, no. 6 (February 1899): 7.

26. Atkins to C. F. Stollsteimer, Agent, S. Ute Agency, February 29, 1888, and Morgan to Agent Bartholomew, March 13, 1890, Box No. 159, Folder 005/806, Ute Agency, RG 75, NARA-DEN.

27. Osburn, *Southern Ute Women*, 26.

28. See Plummer to Mrs. Whyte, December 18, 1893, and January 8, 1894, Plummer to Henry Dodge, n.d. (1893), and Plummer to Frank Walker, December 20, 1893, and January 19, 1894, all in Navajo Agency, Fort Defiance, Box 7, Vol. 20, Letters Sent, RG 75, NARA-LAG.

29. Lame Deer with Erdoes, *Lame Deer*, 22.

30. Quoted in Gabriel, *Marietta Wetherill*, 198.

31. T. J. Morgan to C. E. Vandever, January 4, 1890, Letters Received File, August 1888–93, Navajo Agency, Fort Defiance, RG 75, NARA-LAG.

32. David Shipley to CIA, July 8, 1891, Box 6, Vol. 15, Letters Sent, Navajo Agency, Fort Defiance, RG 75, NARA-LAG; James, *Pages from Hopi History*, 111.

33. Plummer to Charles Goodman, December 26, 1893, Box 7, Vol. 20, Letters Sent, Navajo Agency, Fort Defiance, RG75, NARA-LAG. See also Plummer to Thomas Keam, December 26, 1893, in same collection.

34. Plummer to CIA, January 8, 1894, and Plummer to Goodman, January 8, 1894, Box 7, Vol. 20, Letters Sent, Navajo Agency, Fort Defiance, RG 75, NARA-LAG.

35. Herbert Welsh to Plummer, February 8, 1894, Box 25, Letters Received, 1888–1935, Navajo Agency, Fort Defiance, RG 75, NARA-LAG.

36. James, *Pages from Hopi History*, 112–13. For a detailed account of both the Hopis' and Navajos' travails with the federal government regarding the removal of their children, see M. Jacobs, "A Battle for the Children."

37. Clipping, "Shoshones Have an Aversion to White Man's Education," *Denver Times*, October 3, 1900, in Box 1, Folder 32, Reel papers, EWSHS.

38. *Congressional Record*, 49th Congress, Sess. 1., Ch. 333, 1886, p. 45.

39. Atkins to C. F. Stollsteimer, July 6, 1886, Box 159, Folder 005/806, Ute Agency, RG 75, NARA-DEN.

40. As an example, see Supervisor of Indian Schools to Superintendent "Stacker" [Stacher], July 26, 1922, Box 84, Eastern Navajo Agency Subject Files, Pueblo Bonito Boarding School, RG 75, NARA-LAG.

41. Morgan to Bartholomew, September 5, 1890, Box 159, Folder 005/806, Ute Agency, RG 75, NARA-DEN.

42. E. C. Adams, *American Indian Education*, 55.

43. *Congressional Record*, 51st Congress, Sess. 2, Ch. 543, 1891, p. 1014.

44. *Congressional Record*, 52nd Congress, Sess. 2, Ch. 209, 1893, p. 635.

45. Morgan to Bartholomew, March 2, 1892, Box 160, Folder 005/806, Ute Agency, RG 75, NARA-DEN.

46. Morgan to Bartholomew, November 14, 1892, Box 160, Folder 005/806, Ute Agency, RG 75, NARA-DEN.

47. Lummis, *Bullying the Moqui*, 1–12; Lummis, *Mesa, Cañon, and Pueblo*.

48. Clippings: Charles Lummis, "Plain Talk on Pueblos, II," *Boston Evening Transcript*, September 3, 1892; "Want His Childrens [*sic*]" n.d. [ca. 1892], *Albuquerque Citizen*; in "Newspaper Articles on the Treatment of Indians" scrapbook, uncatalogued section, Charles Lummis Papers, ANC/SM.

49. "Plain Talk on Pueblos, I"; see also clipping, "A Heavy Load," no publication cited, August 12, 1892; "A Tyrant in Office" [about T. J. Morgan], *St. Louis Republic*, August 12, 1892, in "Newspaper Articles on the Treatment of Indians" scrapbook, Lummis papers.

50. Letter from Lummis to editor, *Albuquerque Times*, n.d. [1892], in "Newspaper Articles on the Treatment of Indians" scrapbook, Lummis papers.

51. Quoted in James, *Pages from Hopi History*, 122.

52. Browning to U.S. Indian Agents, April 21, 1893, Box 160, Folder 005/806, Ute Agency, RG 75, NARA-DEN.

53. *Congressional Record*, 53rd Congress, Sess. 2, Ch. 290, 1894, pp. 313–14.

54. Browning to Day, August 27, 1895, Box 160, Folder 005/806, Ute Agency, RG 75, NARA-DEN.

55. M. Jacobs, "Battle for the Children."

56. *Congressional Record*, 59th Congress, Sess. 1, Ch. 3504, 1906, p. 328.

57. E. Adams, *American Indian Education*, 61–62.

58. For example, see correspondence between supervisor, Indian Schools, Southwest District, with Supt. Stacker [Stacher] in 1922, Box 84, File: "Pueblo Bonito Boarding School," Eastern Navajo Agency, RG 75, NARA-LAG.

59. W. A. Jones to Agent, Fort Defiance, November 26, 1901, Box 25, Folder: "Letters received from CIA, 1889–1901," Navajo Agency–Fort Defiance, Letters Received, August 1888–January 1935, RG 75, NARA-LAG.

60. CIA Francis Leupp mentioned and condemned this practice in his Education Circular 127, August 14, 1905, Box 13, Folder: Education: 4/25/04–11/19/10, Fort Apache, Letters Received from CIA, 1899–1910, RG 75, NARA-LAG.

61. Hagan, *Theodore Roosevelt*, 54–58.

62. Education Circular 127, August 14, 1905, Box 13, Folder: Education: 4/25/04–11/19/10, Fort Apache, Letters Received from CIA, 1899–1910, RG 75, NARA-LAG, emphasis in original.

63. Francis Leupp, *Report of the* CIA (Washington DC: Government Printing Office, 1908), 16–17, in Box 2, Folder 6, Reel papers, EWSHS.

64. *Report of the* CIA (1908), 18.

65. "The Improvements at Carlisle Indian School: By the Superintendent," *The Indian Craftsman* 1, no. 1 (February 1909): 1.

66. *Report of the* CIA (1908), 15.

67. H. B. Peairs, chief supervisor of education, U.S. Indian Service, Circular No. 30, July 28, 1928, Folder 2/1, AZ 132, Berard Haile papers, University of Arizona Library Special Collections, Tucson.

68. Iverson, *Diné*, 172–76; Iverson, *The Navajo Nation*, 40–41.

69. Tiffin, *In Whose Best Interest?* 145.

70. Hoxie, *A Final Promise.*

71. Lomawaima, "Domesticity in the Federal Indian Schools," 237.

72. Neville, *Australia's Coloured Minority*, 178, 179.

73. Quoted in Whittington, *Sister Kate*, 420.

74. Read, "How Many Separated Children?"; Hall, *A Brief History*, 12.

75. Burgoyne, *The Mirning*, 65–66.

76. Quoted in Whittington, *Sister Kate*, 417.

77. Interview with Sam Lovell by Colleen Hattersley, August 17, 2000, corrected transcript, 2, TRC-5000/156, Bringing Them Home Oral History Project (hereafter BTH project), NLA.

78. Hegarty, *Is That You Ruthie?* 8–14.

79. Quoted in Mattingley and Hampton, *Survival in Our Own Land*, 161.

80. Testimony of William Garnet South, July 22, 1914, Minutes of Evidence of Aborigines Royal Commission, in "Final Report of the Royal Commission on the Aborigines," 23.

81. Brock, "Aboriginal Families and the Law," 141–42.

82. M. Morgan, *A Drop in the Bucket*, 106–7.

83. Goodall, "New South Wales," 79–80, 84–85, quotes on 80, 85.

84. Interview with Mary King by Colleen Hattersley, March 20, 2001, uncorrected transcript, 7, 8, TRC-5000/244, BTH Project.

85. Testimony of J. Gray, July 23, 1913, in "Progress Report of the Royal Commission on the Aborigines," 1913, 120–21.

86. Report of Constable Loftins, July 27, 1896, B 313/1, Item 130, NAA-VIC.

87. Turner, *Ooldea*, 74–76, quote on 76.

88. Mattingley and Hampton, *Survival*, 99.

89. Interview with Victoria Archibald by Robert Willis, May 22, 2000, edited transcript, 6, TRC-5000/144, BTH Project.

90. Interview with Nita Marshall by Colleen Hattersley, August 27, 2000, corrected transcript, 3–4, TRC5000/163, BTH Project.

91. Broadcast interview with Ernest Mitchell by Katherine Prichard, "The Aborigines and Their Problems," ca. 1939, Box 14, Series 9, Folder 5, MS 6201, Katherine Susannah Prichard papers, NLA.

92. Plummer to CIA, date illegible [1894], Box 8, Vol. 20, Letters Sent, Navajo Agency, Fort Defiance, RG 75, NARA-LAG.

93. C. Berndt, "Mondalmi," 37.

94. Letters from K. M. to secretary of the Board of Protection of Aborigines, July 1, 1912, and March 10, 1914, VPRS 1694, Unit 5, PROV.

95. Quoted in Mattingley and Hampton, *Survival*, 168.

96. Quoted in Mattingley and Hampton, *Survival*, 159–60.

97. Quoted in Haskins, "On the Doorstep," 17.

98. Rose Foster to Board for Protection of Aborigines, June 20, 1918, VPRS 1694, Unit 6, PROV. The records are silent as to whether the board granted Foster's request.

99. Odegaard to Martens, October 2, 1933, CRS A1, 1936/3096, NAA-ACT.

100. Martens to Nelson, October 13, 1933, CRS A1, 1936/3096, NAA-ACT.

101. Cook to administrator of NT, November 13, 1933, CRS A1, 1936/3096, NAA-ACT.

102. Cook to administrator of NT, March 24, 1936, CRS A1, 1936/3096, NAA-ACT.

103. Clipping: "The Odegaard Case," *Northern Standard*, August 11, 1936, in CRS A1, 1936/3096, NAA-ACT.

104. Clipping: "Writ of Habeas Corpus," *Northern Standard*, September 11, 1936, in CRS A1, 1936/3096, NAA-ACT.

105. "Writ of Habeas Corpus."

106. Mattingley and Hampton, *Survival*, 52. Queensland also allowed for exemption from its Aboriginal Act for those "half-castes" who were living a European lifestyle. See Haebich, *Broken Circles*, 172. WA allowed for exemptions to the act, but rarely granted them. See Haebich, *For Their Own Good*, 89, 126–27, 163.

107. Battey, *Life and Adventures*, 66–70.

108. DeHuff to Geronimo Castillo, August 7, 1925, Box 84, "Pueblo Bonito Boarding School" file, Eastern Navajo Agency, RG 75, NARA-LAG.

109. DeHuff to Stacher, January 8, 1926, Box 84, "Pueblo Bonito Boarding School" file, Eastern Navajo Agency, RG 75, NARA-LAG.

110. "Warrto" to Stacher, n.d., Box 84, "Pueblo Bonito Boarding School" file, Eastern Navajo Agency, RG 75, NARA-LAG.

111. Stacher to Supt. Perry, May 29, 1926, Box 84, "Pueblo Bonito Boarding School" file, Eastern Navajo Agency, RG 75, NARA-LAG.

112. See, for example, Supt. [Stacher] to Supt. Paquette, June 12, 1920, Box 84, "Pueblo Bonito Boarding School" file, Eastern Navajo Agency, RG 75, NARA-LAG.

113. Gates to Lummis, December 27, 1902, with report on Hopi affairs, uncatalogued section, Lummis papers.

114. Leo Crane, untitled, undated manuscript, 416–418, Folder 5, MS 256, Leo Crane Collection, Archives and Special Collections, Cline Library, NAU.

115. Stacher to Supt. Perry, May 29, 1926, Box 84, "Pueblo Bonito Boarding School" file, Eastern Navajo Agency, RG 75, NARA-LAG.

116. *The Indian's Friend* 7, no. 3 (November 1894): 1; *The Indian's Friend* 7, no. 7 (March 1895): 6; *The Indian's Friend* 8, no. 7 (March 1896): 1; *The Indian's Friend* 8, no. 11 (July 1896): 10; *The Indian's Friend* 8, no. 12 (August 1896): 6.

117. Quoted in James, *Pages from Hopi History*, 181.

118. *The Indian's Friend* 9, no. 8 (April 1897): 10; *The Indian's Friend* 3, no. 10 (June 1891): 4; *The Indian's Friend* 3, no. 11 (July 1891): 2.

119. B. N. Dow to Nicholls, May 19, 1919, Series 7, Correspondence, MS 855, Records of the APNR, University of Sydney Archives. For more on the events at Cumeroogunga (spelled in many different ways), see Barwick, "Aunty Ellen," 190–91; Attwood, *Rights for Aborigines*, 31–53.

120. Testimony of Matthew Kropinyeri, March 11, 1913, with addendum, May 6, 1913, Progress Report of the Royal Commission on the Aborigines, 1913, in *Proceedings of the Parliament of South Australia*, no. 26 (1913), 37.

121. Testimony taken on June 13, 1914, Minutes of Evidence of Aborigines Royal Commission, "Final Report of the Royal Commission on the Aborigines," in *Proceedings of the Parliament of South Australia* (1916), 16.

122. W. W. Coon to CIA, September 25, 1923, Box 44, Folder 150, Code: 147–150, Sacramento Area Office, 1910–1958, RG 75, Records of the BIA, NARA-SB.

123. Norman Harris to Australian Aborigines Amelioration Association, June 9, 1933, and June 19, 1933, copied in "Evidence [to Moseley Commission]," Series 11, Duguid Family papers, MS 5068, NLA. Many white parents sought to bar Aboriginal children from attending public schools with their own children. See Ellinghaus, *Taking Assimilation to Heart*, 111–13.

124. Haskins, *One Bright Spot*, 92.

125. K. Bennett, *Kaibah*, 22–24.

126. Riney, "'I Like the School.'"

127. Simmons, *Sun Chief*, 89, 90, 100, 101.

128. Child, *Boarding School Seasons*, 14–25.

129. Hyer, *One House*, 57, 68–69.

5. Intimate Betrayals

1. Pratt, *Battlefield and Classroom*, 220, 231.

2. Buffalohead and Molin, "'A Nucleus of Civilization,'" 68–69.

3. Pratt to Fletcher, June 9 and June 19, 1882, Box 1, Fletcher and La Flesche papers.

4. Pratt to Fletcher, June 28, 1882, Box 1, Fletcher and La Flesche papers.

5. Pratt to Fletcher, June 19, 1882, Box 1, Fletcher and La Flesche papers.

6. Pratt to Fletcher, June 28, 1882, Box 1, Fletcher and La Flesche papers.

7. For Omaha beliefs that Fletcher was "paid by the head," I rely on informal conversations with Mark Awakuni-Swetland, who teaches Omaha-language classes at the University of Nebraska, Lincoln.

8. Armstrong to Fletcher, July 19, 1882, Box 1, Fletcher and La Flesche papers.

9. H. Price to Fletcher, July 29, 1882, Box 1, Fletcher and La Flesche papers.

10. H. Price to Fletcher, October 27, 1882, Box 1, Fletcher and La Flesche papers.

11. Pratt to Fletcher, July 22, 1882, Box 1, Fletcher and La Flesche papers.

12. Andrews to Fletcher, August 17, 1882, Box 1, Fletcher and La Flesche papers.

13. Field Diary, September–November 1881, includes draft of letter to Robert Lincoln, secretary of war, Box 11, Fletcher and La Flesche papers.

14. Pratt to Fletcher, November 13, 1882, Box 1, Fletcher and La Flesche papers.

15. Quoted in Buffalohead and Molin, "'A Nucleus of Civilization,'" 68–69.

16. "Extract from Miss Fletcher's Letter," *Morning Star* 3, no. 3 (October 1882), Box 5, Fletcher and La Flesche papers. In another draft, Fletcher placed the date of departure as August 16. See "Drafts of publication," untitled, 1882, Box 6.

17. Because I am discussing so many members of the La Flesche family I depart here from the standard style and use their first names to distinguish among them.

18. Mark, *A Stranger in Her Native Land*, 45–47, 67–68.

19. Rosalie La Flesche Farley to Fletcher, June 28, 1885, Box 1, Fletcher and La Flesche papers.

20. Rosalie La Flesche Farley to Fletcher, July 7, 1885, Box 1, Fletcher and La Flesche papers.

21. Noah La Flesche to Fletcher, July 16, 1885, Box 1, Fletcher and La Flesche papers.

22. Mark, *Stranger in Her Native Land*, 127.

23. St. Cyr to Fletcher, June 28, 1885, Box 1, Fletcher and La Flesche papers.

24. St. Cyr to Fletcher, June 28, 1885, Box 1, Fletcher and La Flesche papers.

25. St. Cyr to Fletcher, July 20, 1885, Box 1, Fletcher and La Flesche papers.

26. Sheridan to Fletcher, October 23, 1885, Box 1, Fletcher and La Flesche papers. He wrote her again on April 10, 1886, with the same request.

27. John Big Elk to Fletcher, n.d. [ca. 1885], Box 1, Fletcher and La Flesche papers.

28. Webster to Fletcher (included with letter from John Copley), May 6, 1885, Box 1, Fletcher and La Flesche papers. Copley, seemingly a white friend of Webster's, added, "John Webster and his family are greatly distressed over the death of Noah. I never saw such grief manifested by Indians before. . . . I believe it would be a good thing for them if Etta could come home. . . . Were it not for the hope that Mrs. Webster has that she will see her daughter, I do not think she could bear up at all. This loss is almost too much for them."

29. Webster to Fletcher, n.d. [ca. 1885], Box 1, Fletcher and La Flesche papers.

30. James Springer and Lena (signed Lenora) Springer to Pratt, November 20, 1883, Box 1, Fletcher and La Flesche papers.

31. Pratt to Lenora and James Springer, November 27, 1883, Box 1, Fletcher and La Flesche papers.

32. Fletcher to James and Lena/Lenora Springer, December 6, 1883, Box 2, Fletcher and La Flesche papers.

33. Pratt to Fletcher, December 8, 1883, Box 1, Fletcher and La Flesche papers.

34. "Mrs. Hamilton" to Willie Springer, July 12, 1885, Box 1, Fletcher and La Flesche papers.

35. *WNIA Report*, 1884, 9.

36. Campbell to minister of the interior, August 12, 1934, CRS A1/15, 34/6800, NAA-ACT.

37. "'I Want My Baby!,'" *Adelaide Sun*, April 12, 1924, clipping in file from Mr. Taplin to chief protector, SRG 139/1/40, AFA papers, SLSA. Karpanny's name also appears as Karpany, Karpenny, and Karpani in official correspondence.

38. C. E. Taplin to Mr. Garnett, April 21, 1924, SRG 139/1/40, AFA papers.

39. H. E. Read to Rev. Sexton, April 28, 1924, SRG 139/1/40, AFA papers.

40. "'I Want My Baby!'"

41. "'I Want My Baby!'"

42. Garnett to Sexton, May 2, 1924, and May 7, 1924, SRG 139/1/40, AFA papers.

43. Testimony given on July 29, 1914, Minutes of Evidence of Aborigines Royal Commission, "Final Report of the Royal Commission on the Aborigines," in *Proceedings of the Parliament of South Australia* (1916), 32.

44. Turner, *Pearls from the Deep*, 35.

45. Turner, *Pearls from the Deep*, 32–34, quote on 34.

46. Turner, *Lazarus at the Gate*, 64, 65.

47. Turner, *Lazarus*, 81.

48. Turner, *Pearls from the Deep*, 53–59, quotes on 56, 59.

49. Turner, *The "Good Fella Missus,"* 6; Cartwright, *Missionaries*, 1–2; Bishop, "'A woman missionary,'" 12–15. Bishop explains that the mission society Lock belonged to changed its name four times between 1894 and 1929. From 1908 to 1929 it was known as the Australian Aborigines' Mission. From 1929 on, it was called the United Aborigines' Mission (v).

50. Quoted in Bishop, "'A woman missionary,'" 179, 180, 270.

51. Turner, *Pearls from the Deep*, 5–8, 8–11, quotes on 7, 9.

52. Lock to Cooke, September 18, 1929, GRG 52/32/32, SRSA.

53. Lock to Bennett, August 1929, GRG 52/32/31, SRSA.

54. Lock to Mr. Sexton, June 1, 1927, SRG 139/1/102, AFA papers.

55. Quoted in Bishop, "'A woman missionary,'" 186.

56. Annie Lock to Mrs. Angelo, July 9, 1914, Accession #652, Item #753/1914, SROWA; see also Bishop, "'A woman missionary,'" 98, 118, 189.

57. Quoted in Bishop, "'A woman missionary,'" 268.

58. Quoted in Bishop, "'A woman missionary,'" 265. See also 102–3, 137. Chief Protector McLean opposed Lock's suggestion.

59. Lock to Miss Evans, July 1, 1928, CRS A1/15, 1929/984, NAA-ACT.

60. Quoted in Bishop, "'A woman missionary,'" 122 n 54.

61. Lock to Bennett, August 1929, GRG 52/32/31, SRSA.

62. Lock to Bennett, August 1929, GRG 52/32/31, SRSA.

63. Lock to Cooke, December 16, 1929, GRG 52/32/35 SRSA.

64. Cartwright, *Missionaries*, 5–7; Turner, *"Good Fella Missus,"* 32, 36–38. The official count of Aborigines killed in retribution was thirty-four, but Lock later estimated that over seventy were killed. See Cartwright, *Missionaries*, 14.

65. Turner, *"Good Fella Missus,"* 44–51, quotes on 48, 50, 51; Cartwright, *Missionaries*, 9–13; M. M. Bennett, *The Australian Aboriginal as a Human Being*, 84–85; Bishop, "'A woman missionary,'" 126–30.

66. Lock to Cooke, September 18, 1929, GRG 52/32/32, SRSA. In 1929 Lock claimed to have worked for twenty-six years among eight different Aboriginal groups.

67. Lock to Mr. Sexton, June 1, 1927, SRG 139/1/102, AFA papers; see also Cartwright, *Missionaries*, 2–4.

68. Lock to Protector of Aborigines, December 12, 1927, CRS A1/15, 1929/984, NAA-ACT.

69. Public service inspector, Brisbane, to Department of Home Affairs, December 21, 1928, CRS A1/15, 28/11056, NAA-ACT.

70. Cawood to secretary, Home and Territories Dept., November 8, 1928, CRS A1/15, 1929/984, NAA-ACT.

71. Stott to Cawood, March 2, 1928, CRS A1/15, 1929/984, NAA-ACT.

72. Stott to Cawood, March 2, 1928, CRS A1/15, 1929/984, NAA-ACT.

73. Lock to Mr. J. A. Carrodus, July 17, 1928, CRS A1/15, 1929/984, NAA-ACT.

74. Report by Annie Lock, November 25, 1928, CRS A1/15, 1929/984, NAA-ACT.

75. Sworn Statement by Lock to Board of Inquiry, January 8, 1929, quoted in Cartwright, *Missionaries*, 9–10.

76. Report by Annie Lock.

77. Stott to Cawood, March 2, 1928, CRS A1/15, 1929/984, NAA-ACT.

78. Murray to "Sir," October 19, 1928, CRS A1/15, 1929/984, NAA-ACT.

79. Stott to Cawood, March 2, 1928, CRS A1/15, 1929/984, NAA-ACT.

80. Cartwright, *Missionaries*, 5–7; Turner, *"Good Fella Missus,"* 32, 36–38.

81. Clippings: "Grim Struggle for Abo. Girls," *Labor Daily* (Sydney), November 19, 1928; "Crowd Objects to Police Taking Abo. Children," *Guardian* (Sydney), November 19, 1928; both in CRS A1/15, 1929/984, NAA-ACT.

82. Joan Kingsley Strack's experience with the Aborigines Protection Board in NSW

over the employment and wages of her Aboriginal servants is somewhat akin to Annie Lock's experience with Dolly and Betsy. As with Lock, Strack's case demonstrates how strained white women's relationships with the state were in Australia over matters of Aboriginal affairs. See Haskins, *One Bright Spot*.

83. Lock to Bennett, August 1929, GRG 52/32/31, SRSA.
84. Lock to Bennett, August 1929, GRG 52/32/31, SRSA; see also Turner, *"Good Fella Missus,"* 51.
85. Turner, *"Good Fella Missus,"* 52–67, quotes on 54, 67.
86. Bishop, "'A woman missionary,'" 30–34; Turner, *"Good Fella Missus,"* 74–91, quote on 91. Cartwright tells the story with slightly different details (*Missionaries*, 18–21). According to him, Lock set up a school not for the Curtises but for another half-caste station owner nearby, George Hayes. Turner mistakenly claims that Lock stayed at Boxer Creek for six years.
87. Report by Mr. Sexton on visit to Ooldea, October 4, 1934, 139/1/337, AFA papers.
88. Daisy Bates to H. C. Brown, secretary for minister of the interior, July 20, 1934, CRS A1, 1935/1066, NAA-ACT.
89. Bishop, "'A woman missionary,'" 22, 34–37, 95–96, quotes on 36, 270; Cartwright, *Missionaries*, 1, 21; Turner, *Ooldea*, 4–36.

6. Groomed to Be Useful

1. Quoted in Edwards and Read, *The Lost Children*, 5.
2. Stewart, *A Voice*, 15.
3. Stewart, *A Voice*, 15–16.
4. Quoted in Edwards and Read, *The Lost Children*, 5.
5. Quoted in Hyer, *One House*, 8–9.
6. Pratt, *Battlefield and Classroom*, 232.
7. Zitkala-Ša, *American Indian Stories*, 54, 55–56. This story originally appeared in the *Atlantic Monthly* in 1900.
8. Fletcher and La Flesche, *The Omaha Tribe*, 122, 124.
9. Quoted in Mattingley and Hampton, *Survival*, 101.
10. Quoted in Golden, *Red Moon*, 190.
11. Quoted in Golden, *Red Moon*, 192.
12. Hunt, *A Colonial Lexicon*, 121–22.
13. Quoted in Golden, *Red Moon*, 192.
14. Stewart, *A Voice*, 16.
15. Interview with Jim Hart by David Woodgate, October 26, 2000, uncorrected transcript, 4, TRC5000/186, BTH, NLA.
16. Quoted in Golden, *Red Moon*, 190.

17. For another analysis of "racializing bodies" at Indian schools in New Mexico, see P. Mitchell, *Coyote Nation*, 26–51.

18. Interview with Marjorie Woodrow by Colleen Hattersley, September 29, 1999, corrected transcript, 11, TRC-5000/43, BTH Project.

19. Quoted in Ball et al., *Indeh*, 144.

20. Fletcher and La Flesche, *The Omaha Tribe*, 115–22, quote on 117.

21. McDonald with Finnane, *When You Grow Up*, 4.

22. Brandl, "A Certain Heritage," 37. For more on the importance of naming among the Lardil of Mornington Island, see McKnight, *People, Countries*, 54–75; for naming among other Aboriginal groups, see Keen, *Aboriginal Economy and Society*, 140–41.

23. E. C. Deloria, *Waterlily*, 34.

24. Hegarty, *Is That You Ruthie?* 35–36.

25. Life Story, "Bill Sage," Draft 2, part 1, 36–37, Box 1, Life Stories, Folder 3, MS 216, Dorothea C. Leighton and Alexander Leighton Collection, Archives and Special Collections, Cline Library, NAU.

26. Pratt, *Battlefield and Classroom*, 237, 240.

27. Lame Deer with Erdoes, *Lame Deer*, 23.

28. Quoted in Hyer, *One House*, 11.

29. Stewart, *A Voice*, 17.

30. Interview with Victoria Archibald by Robert Willis, May 22, 2000, edited transcript, 8, TRC-5000/144, BTH Project.

31. Oates, "Emily Margaret Horneville," 109–10.

32. Boyer and Gayton, *Apache Mothers and Daughters*, 16–22, quotes on 17, 22.

33. Quoted in G. Wilson, *Buffalo Bird Woman's Garden*, 16, 22.

34. Turner, *Lazarus at the Gate*, 22–23.

35. Interview with Sandra Hill by John Bannister, n.d., ca 1999, unedited transcript, 14, TRC-5000/64, BTH Project.

36. Huffer with Roughsey, *The Sweetness of the Fig*, 36.

37. Golden, *Red Moon*, 9.

38. Lame Deer with Erdoes, *Lame Deer*, 24.

39. Pratt, *Battlefield and Classroom*, 234.

40. Fear-Segal, "The Man on the Bandstand," 99–122.

41. Interview with Lyn Hobbler by Lloyd Hollingsworth, November 21, 1999, uncorrected transcript, 12, TRC-5000/65, BTH Project.

42. Interview with Jean Sibley by Phillip Connors, November 6, 1999, uncorrected transcript, 3, TRC-5000/148, BTH Project.

43. Interview with Ruth Elizabeth Hegarty by Helen Curzon-Siggers, December 14,

1999, unedited draft, 2–3, 17, TRC-5000/79, BTH Project. See also Hegarty, *Is That You Ruthie?*

44. Interview with Doris Pilkington by John Bannister, June 6 and 26, 2001, uncorrected transcript, 17, TRC-5000/278, BTH Project.

45. Roessel, *Women in Navajo Society*, 169.

46. Zitkala-Ša, *American Indian Stories*, 41–42.

47. Qoyawayma, *No Turning Back*, 50.

48. Quoted in Edwards and Read, *The Lost Children*, 50.

49. Quoted in Whittington, *Sister Kate*, 417.

50. Huffer and Roughsey, *Sweetness of the Fig*, 36–37.

51. Roessel, *Women in Navajo Society*, 168.

52. Pratt, *Battlefield and Classroom*, 238.

53. Spack, "English, Pedagogy, and Ideology," 7.

54. Quoted in Golden, *Red Moon*, 189.

55. Quoted in Benedek, *Beyond the Four Corners*, 113.

56. Quoted in Benedek, *Beyond the Four Corners*, 104, 105.

57. Quoted in Mattingley and Hampton, *Survival*, 102.

58. Keen, *Aboriginal Economy and Society*, 211. For American Indians, see Basso, *Wisdom Sits in Places*.

59. Quoted in Miller, *Koori*, 159, 162.

60. Quoted in Spack, "English, Pedagogy, and Ideology," 18.

61. Simon Redbird, "An Indian's View of the Indian Problem," in *Report of the 26th Annual Meeting of the Lake Mohonk Conference* (1908), 48, 49.

62. Interview with Hilda Evans by John Bannister, February 29, 2000, corrected transcript, 19, TRC-5000/96, BTH Project.

63. Quoted in Edwards and Read, *The Lost Children*, 79–80.

64. Cummings, *Take This Child*, 24.

65. Interview with Hegarty, BTH Project. See also Hegarty, *Is That You Ruthie?* 44–45.

66. Interview with Sandra Hill, 11–12, BTH Project.

67. Coleman, *American Indian Children at School*, 89–90.

68. Interview with Annie Mullins by Lyn McLeavy, September 30, 2000, transcript, 12, TRC-5000/280, BTH Project.

69. Ruddick, "'Talking about Cruel Things,'" 18, 19.

70. Huffer with Roughsey, *Sweetness of the Fig*, 37.

71. Quoted in Mattingley and Hampton, *Survival*, 163.

72. Affidavit of Laura Dandridge, July 13, 1903, 1.1.1008, Charles Lummis papers, ANC/SM.

73. Cummings, *Take This Child*, 24.

74. Lame Deer with Erdoes, *Lame Deer*, 146, 24, 17.

75. R. M. Berndt and C. Berndt, *The World of the First Australians*, 165, 339. See also Hamilton, *Nature and Nurture*, 10; McKnight, *Going the Whiteman's Way*, 28.

76. Supt. Stacher to Col. R. E. Twitchell, October 31, 1923, Eastern Navajo Agency, Box 83, Subject Files ca. 1909–ca. 1935, File: Schools, RG 75, BIA, NARA-LAG.

77. Life Story, "Bob," Drafts 1 and 2, 7–8, Folder 11, MS 216, Leighton Collection.

78. Quoted in Mary Bennett, "The Charges Made by the Native Welfare Council of Western Australia," February 18, 1945, 3, 4, Series 11, MS 5068, Duguid Family papers, NLA.

79. Stewart, *A Voice*, 18.

80. Quoted in Robinson, "Aborigines and White Popular Culture," 58. See also Hegarty, *Is That You Ruthie?* 41–43.

81. K. Bennett, *Kaibah*, 227. This particular incident incited the families of the runaway girls to come to the school and take their children back.

82. Hegarty, *Is That You Ruthie?* 77.

83. Human Rights and Equal Opportunity Commission, *Bringing Them Home*, 163, 162.

84. Sekaquaptewa, *Me and Mine*, 106.

85. Letter from James Allen to Ute Agent, November 6, 1884, Box 159, Folder 005/806 Correspondence: Pupils in Albuquerque Indian School, 1883–1912, Ute Agency, 1879–1952, RG 75, BIA, NARA-DEN. For more on the hunger that many Indian children experienced, see Hyer, *One House*, 1–28.

86. Interview with Marjorie Woodrow, BTH Project. Many other interviewees in this project as well as many Aboriginal autobiographers mention the inadequate food, in particular, "weevily porridge." See also Ruddick, "'Talking about Cruel Things,'" 16.

87. Quoted in Whittington, *Sister Kate*, 423.

88. Interview with Ruth Elizabeth Hegarty, BTH Project.

89. Ruddick "'Talking about Cruel Things,'" 15.

90. Seaman, *Born a Chief*, 91–92.

91. Affidavit of Laura Dandridge, Lummis papers.

92. Quoted in M. Bennett, "The Charges Made by the Native Welfare Council," Duguid papers.

93. "Statistics for Phoenix Indian Industrial School," 1903, Box 143, File: Annual Report FY 1903, Phoenix Indian School Central Classified Files, 1891–1951, RG 75, BIA Records, NARA-LAG.

94. Affidavit of Mary E. Keough, August 27, 1903, 1.1.689, Lummis papers.

95. Blake cited in Haebich, *Broken Circles*, 402–3.

96. Stewart, *A Voice*, 16.

97. R. Mitchell, *Tall Woman*, 133.

98. Gabriel, *Marietta Wetherill*, 200.

99. Supt. Bryan to C. M. Stollsteimer, May 2, 1885, Box 159, Folder 005/806 Correspondence: Pupils in Albuquerque Indian School, 1888–1925, Ute Agency, RG 75, NARA-DEN.

100. Quoted in Whittington, *Sister Kate*, 423.

101. Golden, *Red Moon*, 55.

102. Golden, *Red Moon*, 127.

103. Lame Deer with Erdoes, *Lame Deer*, 24.

104. Kidd, *Black Lives*, 19–20.

105. Interview with Sam Lovell by Colleen Hattersley, August 17, 2000, corrected transcript, 33, TRC-5000/156, BTH Project.

106. Quoted in Ball et al., *Indeh*, 144.

107. Letter from Supt. McKean to CIA, November 12, 1925, Box 159, Folder 005/806 Correspondence: Pupils at Southern Ute Boarding School, 1888–1925, Ute Agency, RG 75, NARA-DEN.

108. Supt., Carlisle to "Sir," July 24, 1909, Box 46, Folder: Carlisle School, 1909–1919, Flathead Agency, Indian Boarding School Correspondence, 1905–1945, A-C, RG 75, NARA-DEN.

109. Child, "Runaway Boys, Resistant Girls," 53.

110. Goodall, "New South Wales," 80; Goodall, "'Saving the Children,'" 8.

111. Acting Indian Agent to Commissioner of Indian Affairs, December 18, 1893, Box 7, Vol. 20, Letters Sent, Navajo Agency, Fort Defiance, RG 75, NARA-LAG.

112. Seaman, *Born a Chief*, 125–52, quote on 127.

113. Pilkington, *Rabbit Proof Fence*, 106.

114. Quoted in Edwards and Read, *The Lost Children*, 86. Bore water is untreated, usually brackish well water usually used for livestock.

115. Quoted in Edwards and Read, *The Lost Children*, 86, 89.

116. Lame Deer with Erdoes, *Lame Deer*, 25, 26.

117. Battey, *The Life and Adventures*, 40–41, 60–62.

118. See, for example, Peavey and Smith, "World Champions"; Bloom, "'Show what an Indian can do.'"

119. Cummings, *Take This Child*, 100.

120. Quoted in Ball et al., *Indeh*, 146, 147. See also P. Deloria, "'I Am of the Body'"; Rader, "'The Greatest Drama.'"

121. Interview with Sam Lovell, BTH Project.

122. Interview with Ruth Hegarty, 15, 22, BTH Project.

123. Stewart, *A Voice*, 18.

124. Huffer with Roughsey, *Sweetness of the Fig*, 37.

125. Sekaquaptewa, *Me and Mine*, 94, 103–4.

126. Interview with Doris Pilkington, 69, BTH Project.

127. Interview with Victoria Archibald, 10, BTH Project.

128. Spack, "English, Pedagogy, and Ideology," 16.

129. Stewart, *A Voice*, 18, 19.

130. Sexton to Senator Pearce, July 20, 1925, CRS A1, 1935/2364, NAA-ACT.

131. Hegarty, *Is That You Ruthie?* 6–7, 64–65.

132. Ruddick "'Talking about Cruel Things,'" 16.

133. La Flesche, *The Middle Five*, 117–18.

134. Roessel, *Women in Navajo Society*, 168, 169.

135. Interview with Leonard Ogilvie by John Bannister, May 31, 2001, uncorrected transcript, 11, TRC-5000/274, BTH Project.

136. Interview with Alfred Neal by Lloyd Hollingsworth, September 25, 1999, uncorrected transcript, 11, TRC-5000/140, BTH Project.

137. Interview with Martin Dodd by Sue Anderson, June 8, 2000, uncorrected transcript, 22, TRC-5000/128, BTH Project.

138. Life Story, Bill Sage, Draft 2, part 1, 41, Box 1, Life Stories, Folder 3, Leighton papers.

139. Quoted in Edwards and Read, *The Lost Children*, 45, 47, 44, 46.

140. Eastman, *From the Deep Woods*, 137–38.

141. Stewart, *A Voice*, 20.

142. Quoted in Horne and McBeth, *Essie's Story*, xxxiii–xxxiv.

143. Hegarty, *Is That You Ruthie?* 4.

144. Stewart, *A Voice*, 33, 35, 36.

145. Life Story, Bill Sage, Draft 2, part 1, 44, 45, 46, Folder 3, Box 1, Life Stories, Leighton papers.

146. Life Story, Bill Sage, Draft 2, part 1, 63, 64–65, Folder 3, Box 1, Life Stories, Leighton papers.

147. Interview with Laurette Butt by Helen Curzon-Siggers, July 5, 2000, unedited draft, 38, TRC-5000/154, BTH Project.

148. Interview with Doris Pilkington, 5, BTH Project.

149. Interview with Sandra Hill, 15, 5, 15, 22, BTH Project.

150. Interview with Helen Baldwin by Helen Curzon-Siggers, September 10, 1999, unedited draft, 2, 69, TRC-5000/39, BTH Project.

151. Interview with Doris Pilkington, BTH Project.

152. Interview with Doris Pilkington, 28, TRC-5000/278 BTH Project.

153. Interview with Geoffrey Parfitt by John Bannister, October 11, 2000, uncorrected transcript, 25, 28, TRC-5000/213, BTH Project.
154. Quoted in Edwards and Read, *The Lost Children*, 130.
155. Life Story, "Bob," Folder 11, Drafts 1 and 2, MS 216, Leighton papers. For an earlier unedited version of this interview, see Interview with R. P., Box 4, Folder 102, Opinions and Attitudes of Navajos, June 16 1940–May 5, 1940.
156. *WNIA Report*, 1894, 32.
157. Interview with Leonard Ogilvie, 24, BTH Project.
158. Interview with Helen Baldwin, 69, BTH Project.
159. Quoted in Whittington, *Sister Kate*, 421.
160. Interview with Laurette Butt, 48, BTH Project.
161. Zitkala-Ša, *American Indian Stories*, 97.
162. Quoted in Mattingley and Hampton, *Survival*, 162.
163. Stewart, *A Voice*, 34–35.

7. Maternalism in the Institutions

1. Antonio Buti defines these duties of guardianship, as set down by English common law, in *Separated*, 23–38. For the post–World War II era, Denise Cuthbert also argues that the state co-opted the child-rearing labor of white women to raise and "de-Aboriginalise the Indigenous children placed in their care." See Cuthbert, "Mothering the 'Other,'" 33, 36, 39, 40.
2. Pratt, *Battlefield and Classroom*, 121, 231–36, quote on 236.
3. Quinton, "Care of the Indian," 373.
4. D. W. Adams, *Education for Extinction*, 82, 83.
5. Cahill, "'Only the Home Can Found a State,'" 161, 387.
6. Quoted in Meriam et al., *The Problem of Indian Administration*, 361.
7. Testimony of Julia Carroll, in U.S. Senate, Committee on Indian Affairs, *Survey of Conditions of Indians*, part 4, p. 1600; Cahill, "'Only the Home Can Found a State,'" 77–78, 82, 234–35. For more on the field matron program, see Emmerich, "'To respect and love'"; Bannan, "'True Womanhood.'"
8. Meriam et al., *Problem of Indian Administration*, 361–62.
9. Cole, "'Would have known it by the smell of it,'" 157.
10. Ellinghaus, *Taking Assimilation to Heart*, 165.
11. Neville, *Australia's Coloured Minority*, 116.
12. Quoted in R. H. Weddell to Dept. of Interior, September 19, 1932, CRS AI, 1934/7281, NAA-ACT.
13. Bishop, "'A woman missionary,'" 18, 22.
14. For more on white women who worked in the BIA schools, see Cahill, "'Only the Home Can Found a State,'" especially 227–77.

15. D. W. Adams, *Education for Extinction*, 85–87, 90.

16. E. A. Brown, *Stubborn Fool*, 203.

17. Scrapbook and Visitor's Book, Ida Standley, D5465, SLSA; Sydney *Land*, October 11, 1929, in CRS A1/15, 1935/7458, NAA-ACT.

18. Interview with Eileen Park by Helen Chryssides, February 29, 1988, 3, NTRS 226, TS 474, NTAS.

19. Austin, *I Can Picture the Old Home*, 78–79, 156.

20. M. H. Ellis, "Black Australia. Alice Springs Bungalow. A Place of Squalid Horror," clipping from *Adelaide Advertiser*, n.d. [ca. 1924], CRS A1, 1927/2982, NAA-ACT; Clipping, "Honored by Royalty," ca. 1929, in Scrapbook and Visitor's Book, Ida Standley; "Royal Recognition," *Melbourne Herald*, November 9, 1929, in CRS A1/15, 1935/7458, NAA-ACT.

21. Entry of William Jones, constable, April 17, 1916, in Scrapbook and Visitor's Book, Ida Standley; "Mother of Alice Springs," *Smith's Weekly* (Sydney), July 13, 1929, and "The 'Beloved Lady' of Alice Springs," *Melbourne Herald*, May 31, 1929, both in CRS A1/15, 1935/7458, NAA-ACT.

22. *Report of the Superintendent of Indian Schools for* 1898 (1899), 33, in Box 2, Folder 70, Papers of Estelle Reel, MS 120, EWSHS.

23. *Course of Study of the Indian Schools*, 220, in Box 1, Folder 13, Reel papers, EWSHS.

24. Dissette to Herbert Welsh, January 5, 1899, Indian Rights Association papers, Reel 14.

25. *The Indian's Friend* 13, no. 4 (December 1900): 12.

26. Gilman, *Herland*. Gilman promoted her maternalist vision in other writings as well, including *Women and Economics* in 1898, *Concerning Children* in 1900, and *The Home: Its Work and Influence* in 1903. Although Gilman was an American author, Marilyn Lake asserts that Australian feminists read and were influenced by her. See *Getting Equal*, 87–93.

27. J. Hill, "Our Colored Problems," *The Dawn* 15, no. 3 (September 20, 1933): 2.

28. Whittington, *Sister Kate*, 337, 343, 345, 361.

29. Sister Kate to Miss Cass, February 13, 1934, Item 62, Subject Files: Native Welfare, 1931–1937, Women's Service Guild (WSG) Papers, Accession #1949A, MS 393, Battye Library, WA.

30. Whittington, *Sister Kate*, 1, 276–279, 306–7, 309, 336.

31. Sister Kate to editor, *West Australian*, June 15, 1939, and entire file, Accession #993, Item 240/1934, "Sister Kate's Home for Quarter-Caste Children," SROWA; Whittington, *Sister Kate*, 361–69.

32. Quoted in Whittington, *Sister Kate*, 366, 351.

33. Quoted in Whittington, *Sister Kate*, 321.

34. Buffalohead and Molin, "'A Nucleus of Civilization,'" 59–94.

35. *Proceedings of the 11th Annual Meeting of the Lake Mohonk Conference* (1893), 27.

36. Lomawaima, "Estelle Reel," 14.

37. Quoted in Whittington, *Sister Kate*, 330.

38. "Sister Kate's New Work," *West Australian*, June 24, 1934, clipping in 2004/12/162, Box 30, Bessie Rischbieth papers, MS 2004, NLA.

39. Quoted in Buffalohead and Molin, "'A Nucleus of Civilization,'" 69.

40. Buffalohead and Molin, "'A Nucleus of Civilization,'" 76, 87.

41. Quoted in Golden, *Red Moon*, 199.

42. Alice Awa to Laura Dandridge, February 1, 1903, uncatalogued section, Charles Lummis papers, ANC/SM.

43. Emma Chooro to Laura Dandridge, February 1, 1903, uncatalogued section, Lummis papers.

44. Lame Deer with Erdoes, *Lame Deer*, 25.

45. Haskins, *One Bright Spot*, 111.

46. Interview with Clarence Smith by Helen Chryssides, February 24, 1988, tape 1, 3, NTRS 226, TS 486, NTAS.

47. Interview with Eileen Park, NTAS.

48. Interview with Eileen Park, NTAS.

49. Interview with Emily Liddle (née Perkins) by Francis Good, June 7, 1991, tape 1, 11, NTRS 226, TS 660, NTAS.

50. Interview with Clarence Smith, tape 1, p. 3.

51. Whittington, *Sister Kate*, 371, 374–75, 422, 419. Sister Kate tried to limit contact between children and their relations beginning in the early 1940s. See her correspondence with Commissioner of Native Affairs Bray (Neville's successor), Accession #993, Item #305/1938, "Home for Quarter-Caste Children (Sister Kate's)—Queens Park—General Correspondence," SROWA.

52. Whittington, *Sister Kate*, 423, 318, 328–29.

53. Interview with Gerald Warber by John Bannister, March 26, 2000, corrected transcript, 7, 11, 13, TRC-5000/101, BTH Project.

54. Interview with Hilda Evans by John Bannister, February 29, 2000, corrected transcript, 11, 15, TRC-5000/96, BTH Project.

55. Interview with Ada Wade by Vicki MacDonald, November 24, 1981, tape 1, 4, 7, NTRS 226, TS 348, NTAS.

56. Interview with Emily Liddle, tape 2, 1.

57. Hegarty, *Is That You Ruthie?* 60, 47–48.

58. "Angel DeCora: An Autobiography," *The Red Man* 3, no. 7 (March 1911): 280,

285. For more on DeCora, see Archuleta, "'The Indian Is an Artist'"; Simonsen, *Making Home Work*, 183–214.

59. Quoted in Mrs. William Dietz, "Native Indian Art," in *Lake Mohonk Proceedings* (1908), 17–18.

60. *Lake Mohonk Proceedings* (1895), 63.

61. Quoted in Dietz, "Native Indian Art," in *Lake Mohonk Proceedings* (1908), 16, 17. While at Carlisle, DeCora met and married William Dietz, who worked on *The Red Man*. DeCora died on February 7, 1919, of pneumonia, in Northampton, Massachusetts. See "Angel DeCora Dietz," obituary, *The Indian's Friend* 31, no. 5 (May 1919): 5.

62. See Blunt and Dowling, *Home*, for more on the multiple meanings of home in a number of contexts. For more on motherhood, see Jetter, Orleck, and Taylor, *The Politics of Motherhood*; Glenn, Chang, and Forcey, *Mothering*.

63. Turner, *Ooldea*, 87.

64. WNIA *Report*, (1891), 12.

65. Lillian Gray, "Estelle Reel: Superintendent of Indian Schools," *New Orleans Item*, May 10, 1903, Box 1, "Articles" folder, Estelle Reel papers, H6-110, WSA.

66. *Course of Study of the Indian Schools*, 93.

67. *Lake Mohonk Proceedings* (1898), 94.

68. *Lake Mohonk Proceedings* (1893), 28–29.

69. Elizabeth G. Bender, "Training Indian Girls for Efficient Home Makers," *The Red Man* 8, no. 5 (January 1916): 154–55.

70. Zitkala-Ša, *American Indian Stories*, 59–61.

71. Quoted in *Lake Mohonk Proceedings* (1898), 54.

72. Sybil Carter, "Work for Indian Women," in *Lake Mohonk Proceedings* (1894), 23–24. For white women's shifting conceptions of domesticity in relation to the assimilation of American Indians, see Simonsen, *Making Home Work*.

73. Quoted in Lomawaima, "Estelle Reel," 16.

74. Lomawaima, "Domesticity in the Federal Indian Schools."

75. Hunt, *A Colonial Lexicon*, 119, 130.

76. Margaret Beauregard, "An Indian Girl on Wifehood," *The Indian's Friend* 23, no. 3 (October 1910): 11.

77. Quoted in Osburn, *Southern Ute Women*, 46.

78. "The Modern Indian Girl," *Indian Craftsman* 2, no. 3 (November 1909): 23.

79. Turner, *Lazarus at the Gate*, 65.

80. Daisy Bates, "Suggestions for the Betterment of Aborigines and Castes," ca. 1929, CRS A1, 1935/1066, NAA-ACT.

81. Hegarty, *Is That You Ruthie?* 57, 58.

82. Farley to Fletcher, July 24, 1885, Box 1, Alice Cunningham Fletcher and Francis La Flesche papers, NAA.

83. For puberty ceremonies among Australian Aboriginal peoples, see Keen, *Aboriginal Economy and Society*, 267–68; R. M. Berndt and C. Berndt, *The World of the First Australians*, 216; Brock, introduction to *Women, Rites and Sites*, xvii–xx; Fay Gale, "Roles Revisited: The Women of Southern South Australia," in Brock, *Women, Rites and Sites*, 120–35. For accounts of the Navajo girl's puberty ceremony, see Stewart, *A Voice in Her Tribe*, 19–20; Frisbie, *Kinaaldá*.

84. Hegarty, *Is That You Ruthie?* 60–62, quotes on 62, 60.

85. Roessel, *Women in Navajo Society*, 170. See also Lomawaima, *They Called It Prairie Light*, 91; Lomawaima, "Domesticity," 232.

86. Roessel, *Women in Navajo Society*, 170–71.

87. Golden, *Red Moon*, 154, 155, 156. See also E. A. Brown, *Stubborn Fool*, 225–26, for another such example.

88. Quoted in Buffalohead and Molin, "'A Nucleus of Civilization,'" 65. See also Ellinghaus, *Taking Assimilation*, 28–32.

89. Scanlon, "'Pure and Clean,'" 90–93. Scanlon documents several other instances in which missionaries intervened in marriage practices of Aboriginals, yet he does not study the role of white women in the process. For more on attempts by Catholic missionaries to control Aboriginal marriage, see Choo, *Mission Girls*, 186–243.

90. Huffer with Roughsey, *The Sweetness of the Fig*, 37–38.

91. Beresford and Omaji, *Our State of Mind*, 44.

92. Turner, *Ooldea*, 102–6, quotes on 104, 105.

93. *The Indian's Friend* 38, no. 3 (January 1926): 7.

94. Daisy Bates, "Efforts Made by Western Australia towards the Betterment of Aborigines," ca. 1911, CRS A1, 1911/7900, NAA-ACT.

95. Huffer with Roughsey, *Sweetness of the Fig*, 41–42.

96. Huffer with Roughsey, *Sweetness of the Fig*, 85.

97. McKnight, *Going the Whiteman's Way*, xx, 76–77, 222–23.

98. Petition of Half-Caste women to Moseley Commission, 2004/12/234, Box 30, Rischbieth papers.

99. Petition of Half-Caste women to Moseley Commission.

100. Petition of Half-Caste women to Moseley Commission. See also Choo, *Mission Girls*, 118–21.

101. "Woman Fights for Her Race," *The Herald* (Sydney), January 23, 1935, clipping in CRS A1/15, Item 35/3951, NAA-ACT.

102. "Aboriginal Woman's Charges," *The Herald* (Sydney), January 23, 1935, clipping in CRS A1/15, Item 35/3951, NAA-ACT.

103. Helen Baillie, "Aboriginal Woman Speaks for Her Race," obituary, *Woman To-day* 1, no. 5 (December 1936): 6, 24.

104. Quoted in Paisley, "Feminist Challenges to White Australia," 268. On Gibbs's relationship with Strack (or "Ming"), see Haskins, *One Bright Spot*, 167–78.

105. "Indian Welfare Work Will Be Undertaken," *General Federation News* 2 (August 1921): 1, 9.

106. E. C. Deloria, "Health Education for Indian Girls," 63, 64, 66.

107. Marie L. Baldwin, "Modern Home-Making and the Indian Woman," presentation to the First Annual Conference of the American Indian Association [later the Society of American Indians], October 12–15, 1911, 1, 5, 6, Society of American Indians papers, Part II, Series 2, Reel 9. Part of Baldwin's speech was reprinted in *The Indian's Friend* 24, no. 8 (April 1912): 10.

108. "Native Indian Art," *The Indian's Friend* 20, no. 2 (October 1907): 8.

109. Quoted in Dietz, "Native Indian Art," in *Lake Mohonk Proceedings* (1908), 17–18.

110. Baldwin, "Modern Home-Making and the Indian Woman," 1.

111. WNIA *Report* (1897), 26.

112. "Indian Childhood," address given at Hampton Commencement by Lucy Conger, reprinted in *The Indian's Friend* 16, no. 1 (September 1903): 2, 11.

113. Johnston, *Cherokee Women in Crisis*, 132–34. There is evidence that some American Indian women today also base their activism on this type of maternalism. See Udel, "Revision and Resistance."

114. Quoted in Edwards and Read, *The Lost Children*, 130, 132.

115. Margaret Tucker, speech, International Women's Day (March 8), n.d., Series 5, Box 3, Folder 20, Vroland family papers, NLA.

116. Quoted in Mattingley and Hampton, *Survival*, 163.

117. Anna Morgan, "Under the Black Flag," *Labor Call*, September 20, 1934.

118. Quoted in broadcast interview with Ernest Mitchell by Katherine Prichard, "The Aborigines and Their Problems," ca. 1939, Box 14, Series 9, Folder 5, MS 6201, Katherine Susannah Prichard papers, NLA.

8. Out of the Frying Pan

1. NSW, *Report of the Board for the Protection of Aborigines*, 1915–16 (1916), 3.

2. *Course of Study of the Indian Schools*, 189, included in Box 1, Folder 13, Papers of Estelle Reel, MS 120, EWSHS.

3. Address before Dept. of Indian Education, Charleston SC, included as appendix to *Report of the Superintendent of Indian Schools* (1900), 57, in Box 2, Folder 72, Reel papers, EWSHS.

4. Colson, "A Study of Acculturation among Pomo Women," 60, 84.

5. "Report by Mr. F. C. Urquhart on Half-Caste Problem of the Northern Territory," August 1, 1922, CRS A1, 1930/1542, NAA-ACT.

6. See entire file, CRS A1, 1933/7568, NAA-ACT.

7. Mrs. John Jones, "The Case for the Australian Aboriginals in Central and Northern Australia," June 19, 1930, in *Proceedings of British Commonwealth League Conference* (1930), 35.

8. Interview with Dorothea Lyons by Helen Wilson, August 27, 1980, NTRS 226, TS 84-1/2, 4, 29, NTAS.

9. Excerpt from Report on Land, NT, n.d., NTRS 281, Correspondence, Photographs, and Reports of Dr. Cecil E. Cook, 1927–1939, NTAS. See also Cook to "Ellen," November 15, 1980, in same file. In many colonial sites with tropical climates officials evinced concern about whether white women would lose their ability to reproduce over time. See Stoler *Carnal Knowledge*, 73. The presence of Aboriginal women as domestic servants to carry out the strenuous work seemingly eased such concerns.

10. Trennert, *The Phoenix Indian School*, 52–54, 70–73; Reel quoted on 72.

11. For general coverage of the decline of white, native-born women in domestic service and the predominance of nonwhite women in the field, see DuBois and Dumenil, *Through Women's Eyes*, 285, 543. For more on domestic service specifically in the early twentieth century, see P. Palmer, *Domesticity and Dirt*.

12. Moore, *To Place Our Deeds*; Lemke-Santangelo, *Abiding Courage*.

13. For domestic service in the San Francisco Bay Area, see Glenn, *Issei, Nisei, War Bride*, 105–9. For more on the restrictions on Asian immigration, see Takaki, *Strangers from a Different Shore*. For the repatriation of Mexican Americans in the 1930s, see Balderrama and Rodriguez, *Decade of Betrayal*.

14. Walden, "'That Was Slavery Days,'" 200.

15. Lebergott, *Manpower in Economic Growth*, 304–5, 476–77, 506, 526, 542.

16. Report on Los Angeles Outing Center by John Holst, November 12, 1928, Box 1, Folder 15-0 "Outing Los Angeles," Coded Correspondence of Supervisor Holst, 1928–1929; "Contract" between Mrs. James Chelwood and Carson Indian School, June 16, 1927, Box 1, Folder: "Outing Contracts, 1927," Records of Berkeley Outing Matron and Placement Officer, 1916–33 (hereafter Records of Berkeley Outing Matron), both in BIA, California, RG 75, NARA-SB.

17. Bonney to Mrs. Young, May 7, 1883, Box 1, MS 4558, Alice Cunningham Fletcher and Francis La Flesche papers, NAA.

18. Mrs. Young to Pratt, May 12, 1883, Box 1, Fletcher and La Flesche papers.

19. See Haskins, *One Bright Spot*, 50–51.

20. "'Black-White' Children," newspaper clipping, CRS A1 1934/6800, NAA-ACT.

21. Sleswick to Perkins, July 7, 1934; Smith to Perkins, August 26, [1934]; CRS A1/15, 34/6800, NAA-ACT.

22. Griffiths to Perkins, July 20, 1934 CRS A1 1934/6800, NAA-ACT.

23. Baker to Perkins, July 19, 1934; CRS A1 1934/6800, NAA-ACT.

24. Philp to Perkins, July 6, 1934, CRS A1 1934/6800, NAA-ACT.

25. Barnes to Mission, August 13, 1934, CRS A1/15, 34/6800, NAA-ACT.

26. Testimony of J. W. Bleakley, July 3, 1913, Progress Report of the Royal Commission on the Aborigines, in *Proceedings of the Parliament of South Australia*, no. 26 (1913), 95.

27. P. Palmer, *Domesticity and Dirt*, 53.

28. Hondagneu-Sotelo, *Doméstica*, 22–23.

29. This was the case for Joan Kingsley-Strack, described in Haskins, *One Bright Spot*, 40.

30. Interview with Ruby Roney by Ian Marshall for ABC Radio, 1974, NTRS 226, TS 735, Tape 1, Side B, 21-22, NTAS.

31. Trennert, *Phoenix Indian School*, 87–90.

32. Trennert, *Phoenix Indian School*, 90–92.

33. Haskins, "'A Better Chance?'" especially 42, 44; Walden, "'That Was Slavery Days,'" 203.

34. Haskins, "'A Better Chance?'" 53.

35. See for example, Ada Bronham, Letter to the editor, *The West Australian*, ca. 1932, clipping in Box 30, 2004/12/265, MS 2004, Bessie Rischbieth papers, NLA.

36. Whittington, *Sister Kate*, 422; M. Morgan, *A Drop in the Bucket*, 161.

37. Mrs. J. Litchfield to minister of the interior, August 23, 1938, CRS A1, 1938/23077, NAA-ACT.

38. Report on Los Angeles Outing Center by John Holst.

39. Roster of women servants and employers, GRG 52/1/1935, File 29, SRSA.

40. Ward, *Wandering Girl*, 11, 12, 13, 18, 19, 71.

41. Report of M. C. Williams, November 4, 1931, GRG 52/1, File 37, SRSA.

42. Quoted in Austin, *I Can Picture the Old Home*, 81.

43. Interview with Victoria Archibald by Robert Willis, May 22, 2000, edited transcript, 16–18, TRC-5000/144, BTH Project.

44. "Alleged Libel," *Northern Standard*, August 4, 1936, newspaper clipping in CRS A1, 1937/16237, NAA-ACT. See also Haskins, *One Bright Spot*, 81–92, for another documented case of sexual abuse.

45. Walden, "'To send her to service,'" 13.

46. Interview with Dorothea Lyons, 4, NTAS.

47. Interview with Dorothea Lyons, 5, NTAS.

48. Interview with Eileen Park by Helen Chryssides, February 29, 1988, 10, NTRS 226, TS 474, NTAS.
49. Ward, *Wandering Girl*, 139.
50. Interview with Emily Liddle (née Perkins) by Francis Good, June 7, 1991, tape 2, p. 3, NTRS 226, TS 660, NTAS.
51. Huggins, "'Firing On in the Mind,'" 9.
52. Walden, "'That Was Slavery Days,'" 203.
53. Mahood, *Craft for a Dry Lake*, 123, 124.
54. Quoted in Parreñas, *Servants of Globalization*, 76.
55. Huggins, "White Aprons, Black Hands," 189.
56. Huggins, "'Firing On in the Mind,'" 16–17.
57. Hegarty, *Is That You Ruthie?* 124–28, quotes on 126, 128.
58. Memorandum, July 10, 1925, CRS A1, 1927/1106, NAA-ACT.
59. Memorandum re. Sarah Breaden, March 30, 1928, CRS A1, 1927/1106, NAA-ACT.
60. Fitz to Mr. Stott, February 22, 1927, CRS A1 1936/7846, NAA-ACT.
61. Quoted in Edwards and Read, *The Lost Children*, 90.
62. Interview with Penny Everaardt by Rob Willis, October 26, 1999, uncorrected transcript, 6, TRC-5000/48, BTH Project.
63. Daisy Bates, "Suggestions for the Betterment of Aborigines and Castes," ca. 1929, CRS A1, 1935/1066, NAA-ACT.
64. See Relocation, Training, and Employment Assistance Case Records, 1933–1946, Outing Girls, Sacramento Agency, BIA Records, California, RG 75, NARA-SB (hereafter Case Records, Outing Girls). These records contain sensitive material that may embarrass or offend the Indian women or their descendants. Therefore, to respect the identity of these women, their families, and their descendants, I have used pseudonyms for each young woman, followed by her tribal identity if specified in the records. The notes give the initials of each young woman.
65. Mr. Royce to CIA, August 31, 1916, Box 10, Investigative Records of Col. L. A. Dorrington, Special Agent, 1913–1923, RG 75, BIA Nevada, NARA-SB.
66. Dorrington to Cato Sells, August 5, 1916, Box 10, Investigative Records of Colonel Dorrington, RG 75, NARA-SB.
67. Cato Sells to Supt. Royce, June 8, 1918, and Supt. Royce to Cato Sells, June 26, 1918, Box 10, Investigative Records of Colonel Dorrington, RG 75, NARA-SB.
68. Cato Sells to Supt. Royce, September 12, 1918, Box 10, Investigative Records of Colonel Dorrington, RG 75, NARA-SB.
69. Royce to Supervisor Holst, July 23, 1929, Box 1, Folder: "Los Angeles Berkeley Outing Centers," Supervisor of Indian Education 1928–1929; Royce to Moore, June 10, 1930, Box 3, Folder: "Outing Center—Berkeley," Supervisor of Indian

Education, Administrative Subject Records, 1929–1932, both in RG 75, BIA California, NARA-SB.

70. See Van Every to Bertha Eckert, National Board, YWCA, October 5, 1937, J. B. file, Box 1, Case Records, Outing Girls; list of Indian Girl's Work Committee, April 15, 1942, courtesy of YWCA of Oakland. According to Phyllis Palmer, the YWCA was "the women's organization that was most persistently concerned with the problems of domestic service." Thus it is no surprise that the outing matrons had connections with the YWCA and some sympathy for the young domestic servants. See P. Palmer, *Domesticity and Dirt*, 113.

71. Lombard, "The Migration of Women from the Ukiah Valley," 25; Patterson, "Indian Life in the City," 408.

72. Royce to Snyder, April 9, 1930, Box 3, Folder: "Outing Center-Berkeley"; Supervisor of Indian Education, Administrative Subject Records, 1929–1932, both in RG 75, NARA-SB. For an example of a young Indian woman who found domestic work on her own, see Sarris, *Mabel McKay*, 64.

73. A. Be. to Royce, October 6, 1931, A. Be. file, Box 1, Case Records, Outing Girls.

74. Fl. A. file, Box 1, Case Records, Outing Girls.

75. M. Bl. to Royce, August 12, 1930, M. Bl. file, Box 1, Case Records, Outing Girls.

76. Chronology, March 5, 1939, I. B. file, Box 1, Case Records, Outing Girls.

77. J. J. to Royce, September 23, 1931, J. J. file, Box 2, Case Records, Outing Girls.

78. E. J. file, Box 2, Case Records, Outing Girls.

79. Patterson, "Indian Life in the City," 410; A YWCA promotional brochure of 1930 boasts that sixty "individual Indian girls attended winter and summer programs, clubs, parties, Sunday afternoon services and out-door expeditions." See also Oakland YWCA, "A Review of the year 1939," 13–14. Both of these items are courtesy of the Oakland Public Library.

80. M. C. file, Box 1, Case Records, Outing Girls.

81. M. and A. D. to Royce, Mt. Diablo Country Club, ca. 1929, A. D. file, Box 2, Case Records, Outing Girls.

82. M. to A., March 23, 1929, M. J. file, Box 2, Case Records, Outing Girls.

83. Fl. A. file, Box 1, Case Records, Outing Girls.

84. Files of Ev. A., El. A, and P. Ar., Box 1, Case Records, Outing Girls.

85. Report on Los Angeles Outing Center by John Holst; "Contract" between Mrs. James Chelwood and Carson Indian School.

86. Taft to Traxler, November 13, 1933, H. E. file, Box 2, Case Records, Outing Girls.

87. See Clark-Lewis, *Living In, Living Out*.

88. I. S. file, Box 4, Case Records, Outing Girls.

89. Harrington to Royce, n.d., Box 1, Folder: "Outing Contracts, 1932," Records of the Berkeley Outing Matron.

90. Chronology, P. Ar. file, Box 1, Case Records, Outing Girls. For more on employers who expected "rituals of deference," see Rollins, *Between Women*, 156–70, 178–203; Romero, *Maid in the U.S.A.*, 97–119; and Parreñas, *Servants of Globalization*, 195.

91. Cresap to Royce, July 3, 1930, Box 1, Folder: "Outing Contracts, 1930," Records of the Berkeley Outing Matron.

92. P. Ar. to Van Every, October 30, 1934, chronology, P. Ar. file, Box 1, Case Records, Outing Girls.

93. P. A. to Van Every, October 30, 1934, P. Ar. file, Box 1, Case Records, Outing Girls.

94. F. C. to Royce, n.d., Box 1, Folder: "Outing Contracts, 1932," Records of the Berkeley Outing Matron.

95. Stoler, *Carnal Knowledge*, 165.

96. V. F. to "Dearie," May 3, 1928, V. F. file, Box 2, Case Records, Outing Girls.

97. Royce to Mrs. C. B., October 24, 1932, A. Be. file, Box 1, Case Records, Outing Girls.

98. Royce to L. R., Reno, March 12, 1929, A. D. file, Box 2, Case Records, Outing Girls.

99. V. F. to Dearie, May 3, 1928, V. F. file, Box 2, Case Records, Outing Girls.

100. Chronology, March 22, 24, and 26, 1937, P. Ar. file, Box 1, Case Records, Outing Girls.

101. Supt. Snyder to Daniel Robertson, May 15, 1925, G. W. file, Box 4, Case Records, Outing Girls.

102. J. W. to Royce, July 6, 1925, G. W. file, Box 4, Case Records, Outing Girls.

103. Chronology, March 6, 1938, Fl. A. file, Box 1, Case Records, Outing Girls.

104. S. C. to Van Every, July 18, 1936, S. C. file, Box 1, Case Records, Outing Girls.

105. Royce to Emmett McNeilly, February 16, 1929, A. H. file, Box 2, Case Records, Outing Girls.

106. I. T. to John Collier, August 6, 1933, I. T. (S.) file, Box 4, Case Records, Outing Girls.

107. Collier to I. T., August 24, 1933, I. T. (S.) file, Box 4, Case Records, Outing Girls.

108. Chronology, October 13, 1941, I. T. (S.) file, Box 4, Case Records, Outing Girls.

109. Katherine Ellinghaus mentions that many young women who were outed from Carlisle also became pregnant. See *Taking Assimilation to Heart*, 32.

110. S. A. M. file, Box 1; A. Be. file, Box 1; B. L. file, Box 3, Case Records, Outing Girls.

111. M. B. file, Box 1, Case Records, Outing Girls.

112. Katherine Martin to Royce, August 8, 1932, and September 5, 1932, S. B. file, Box 1, Case Records, Outing Girls.

113. Royce to Mrs. Holcomb, July 27, 1931, E. M. file, Box 3, Case Records, Outing Girls.

114. Notes on "outing form," March 1, 1934, March 23, [1934], and March 26, 1934, J. G. file, Box 2, Case Records, Outing Girls.

115. R. R. Miller to director, Indian Bureau, June 10, 1932, G. W. file, Box 4, Outing Records.

116. Royce to Snyder, July 16, 1932, G. W. file, Box 4, Outing Records.

117. Royce to Snyder, July 16, 1932, G. W. file, Box 4, Outing Records.

118. Haskins, *One Bright Spot*, 228–39.

119. Supt. Ray Parrett to Royce, October 7, 1925, L. M. file, Box 3, Case Records, Outing Girls.

120. E. W. to Royce, July 19, 1928, E. W. file, Box 4, Case Records, Outing Girls.

121. Chronology, March 28, 1938, Fl. A. file, Box 1, Case Records, Outing Girls.

122. Patterson, "Indian Life in the City," 410; Lombard, "Migration of Women," 32–33; Colson, "A Study of Acculturation," 85–86.

9. Challenging Indigenous Child Removal

1. Anne Bon to Mr. Bowles, October 3, 1918, Series B337/0, Item 377, NAA-VIC.

2. Anne Bon to chief secretary, February 20, 1934, Series B313/1, Item 67, NAA-VIC.

3. L. A. Cameron to Captain Page, June 25, 1886, Series B313/1, Item 220, NAA-VIC. See also Holland, "'Saving the Aborigines,'" 161.

4. Hatton to prime minister, March 22, 1921, CRS A1, 1921/6686, NAA-ACT. For more on Hatton, see Maynard, "'Light in the darkness,'" 3–27.

5. Hatton to prime minister, March 22, 1921, CRS A1, 1921/6686, NAA-ACT.

6. Hatton to prime minister.

7. Hatton to prime minister.

8. Secretary for prime minister to Hatton, May 2, 1921, CRS A1, 1921/6686, NAA-ACT.

9. Quoted in Maynard, "'Light in the darkness,'" 19.

10. Native Welfare Council of WA, "The Tragedy of Native Affairs," n.d. (ca. 1944), Series 11, Duguid Family papers, MS 5068, NLA.

11. Interview with Eileen Heath by John Bannister, November 30, 2000, December 7 and 8, 2000, uncorrected transcript, 13, 25, 26, 22, TRC-5000/197, BTH Project.

12. Interview with Leonard Ogilvie by John Bannister, May 31, 2001, uncorrected transcript, 11, TRC-5000/274, BTH project; interview with Doris Pilkington by John Bannister, June 6 and 26, 2001, uncorrected transcript, no page recorded, TRC-5000/278, BTH Project.

13. Haskins, *One Bright Spot*; Haskins, "'Lovable Natives' and "Tribal Sisters.'"

14. M. M. Bennett, *Christison of Lammermoor*, 229.

15. Mary Bennett, speech to wsg, December 11, 1931, 2004/12/302, MS 2004, Bessie Rischbieth papers, NLA.

16. Holland, "'Saving the Aborigines,'" 120.

17. M. Morgan, *A Drop in the Bucket*, 135–42, 106–7. For more on the issue of controlling marriage at Mt. Margaret, see Holland, "'Whatever her race,'" 144–148.

18. "White Men's Offence against Natives," *Daily News (Perth)*, December 12, 1933, includes coverage of Bennett's speech to wsg, Accession # 993, Item 3 166/1932, SROWA.

19. Bennett to Duguid, January 3, 1935, Series 11, Duguid papers.

20. Morgan, *A Drop in the Bucket*, 106–7, 91–101, 107.

21. Morgan, *A Drop in the Bucket*, 161, 100, 91–92, 157.

22. Mary Bennett, "The Aboriginal Mother in Western Australia in 1933," paper read at the BCL Conference, London, 1933, Box 30, 2004/12/213, Rischbieth papers.

23. Quoted in Lake, *Getting Equal*, 120.

24. Mary Bennett, speech to wsg, December 11, 1931, emphasis in original.

25. Bennett to Pink, September 12, 1937, I. F. (a) (2), Olive Pink papers, MS 2368, AIATSIS, emphasis in original.

26. Quoted in *Lake Mohonk Proceedings* (1899), 69, 72. For more on Collins, see Clow, "Autobiography of Mary C. Collins," especially 17–18.

27. Quoted in *Lake Mohonk Proceedings* (1899), 69, 71.

28. *The Indian's Friend* 38, no. 3 (January 1926): 7.

29. "Navaho Needs," *The Indian's Friend* 17, no. 9 (May 1905): 11.

30. Graber, *Sister to the Sioux*, 29, 31–39, 116–19, 123–24, 127–28, 129–30. For more on Eastman, see Ellinghaus, *Taking Assimilation*, 81–104.

31. Graber, *Sister to the Sioux*, 123, 43, 90, 104–5.

32. Golden, *Red Moon*, 146.

33. E. A. Brown, *Stubborn Fool*, 232.

34. E. A. Brown, *Stubborn Fool*, 104, 114, 115.

35. Testimony of Mrs. Julia C. Carroll, in U.S. Senate, Committee on Indian Affairs, *Survey of Conditions of Indians*, part 4, pp. 1601, 1602, 1603, 1600.

36. Dandridge to Gates, December 28, 1902, 1.1.1625A, Charles Lummis papers, ANC/SM.

37. Bertha Wilkins, "Some Indian Schools," *Pittsburgh Chronicle*, n.d. (1899); uncatalogued sections of Sequoyah League, Lummis papers.

38. Quoted in "The Indian Institute," *The Indian's Friend* 12, no. 2 (October 1899): 10.

39. E. A. Brown, *Stubborn Fool*, 137, 233–34, 256–57.

40. Golden, *Red Moon*, 156.

41. E. A. Brown, *Stubborn Fool*, 257–58.

42. Cecile Carter to Lummis, August 14, 1903, 1.1.689, Lummis papers.

43. Dandridge to Gates, December 28, 1902, 1.1.1625A, Lummis papers. It is possible that Dandridge was not "white"; in one document, authorities referred to her as a "mulatto woman." See excerpts from report of James Jenkins, Indian inspector, on the Charges Preferred Against the Management of the Moqui Indian Reservation, August 15, 1903, "Review of Testimony on which charges were based," 23, uncatalogued section, Lummis papers.

44. Testimony of Mrs. Ina M. Livermore, in U.S. Senate, Committee on Indian Affairs, *Survey of Conditions of Indians*, 1609.

45. Quoted in James, *Pages from Hopi History*, 123–24, 125, 126–27, 128. Kolp's affidavit is also included in Lummis, *Bullying the Moqui*, 42–50.

46. Burton to Kolp, January 28, 1903, 1.1.2525, Lummis papers.

47. Quoted in James, *Pages from Hopi History*, 126, 129.

48. Gabriel, *Marietta Wetherill*, 199, 200.

49. For more on Lummis, see Lummis, *Bullying the Moqui*, 1–12; Lummis, *Mesa, Cañon, and Pueblo*.

50. Gates to Lummis, December 5, 1902, 1.1.1625A, Lummis papers.

51. Gates to Lummis, December 27, 1902, with report on Hopi affairs, uncatalogued section, Lummis papers.

52. Lummis to C. Hart Merriam, November 25, 1902, 1.1.3060A, Lummis papers.

53. Gates to Lummis, December 27, 1902, Lummis papers.

54. Excerpts from report of James Jenkins, 23–24, Lummis papers.

55. Lummis, *Bullying the Moqui*, 86, 94.

56. See Kroeber to DuBois, December 4, 1902, December 15, 1902, December 22, 1902, February 6, 1903, February 19, 1903, March 14, 1903, May 19, 1906, May 29, 1906, June 20 and 27, 1906; Wissler to DuBois, June 23, 1905; all in Constance Goddard DuBois Papers, #9167, Division of Rare Books and Manuscript Collections, Cornell University Library, formerly located at the Huntington Free Library, Bronx, New York.

57. Constance Goddard DuBois, "A New Phase of Indian Education," *City and State*, June 7, 1900, 362, 363; Box 1, Folder 30, Newspaper Clippings, MS 120, Estelle Reel papers, EWSHS.

58. Quoted in D. W. Adams, *Education for Extinction*, 135.

59. Philp, *John Collier's Crusade*, 1–91; Kelly, *The Assault on Assimilation*, 124–348; Collier, *From Every Zenith*. For the activism of this new generation of feminists in New Mexico, see M. Jacobs, *Engendered Encounters*.

60. Wiegel to E. E. McKean, November 27, 1925, Box 1, Folder 096, Organizations Interested in Indians, Correspondence 1925–1927, Colorado Federation of Women's Clubs, Ute Agency, Decimal File 1879–1952, RG 75, BIA Records, NARA-DEN.

61. Wiegel to McKean, May 8, 1926, Box 1, Folder 096, Ute Agency, RG 75, NARA-DEN.

62. Meriam et al., *The Problem of Indian Administration*, 11–13, 32, 206–7, 210, 316–18, 325, 330–31, 332, 382, 375–76, 15, 576, 403.

63. Fuchs and Havighurst, *To Live on This Earth*, 12, 227.

64. President Huntley, AFA, Report re. visit to Pt. McLeay, November 25 and 26, 1921, 139/1/13, AFA papers, SRG 139, SLSA.

65. Sexton to "Sir," November 29, 1921, 139/1/13, AFA papers.

66. Sexton to Senator Pearce, October 28, 1924, 139/1/44, AFA papers.

67. This conflict over lady visitors is detailed in correspondence between the AFA and WNPA in 1391/1/66 and 139/1/25, AFA papers, as well as in the Committee Minutes, April 8, 1925, May 13, 1925, and November 11, 1925, 116/2/1 and 116/2/2, LWVSA papers, SRG 116, SLSA. See also Haskins, "The Call for a Woman Visitor." For opposition to moving the Bungalow, see Sexton to Abbot, April 19, 1929, 139/1/143, AFA papers.

68. Rev. William Morley, Testimony before Royal Commission on the Constitution, in *Report of the Royal Commission on the Constitution*, 1600. At other times, according to Victoria Haskins, Morley was much weaker in his opposition to Aboriginal child removal. When Joan Kingsley Strack sought to mobilize the APNR on behalf of her wronged domestic servants, Morley was evasive and obstructionist. See Haskins, *One Bright Spot*, 130–31, 144, 148–50.

69. "Australian Aboriginals," a statement by the Aborigines' Protection League (1929), 3, 4, CRS A1/15 1932/4262, NAA-ACT.

70. "The Proposed Aboriginal State-Manifesto," by the Aborigines' Protection League, 1929, CRS A1/15 1932/4262, NAA-ACT.

71. Paper by Bennett delivered to BCL, ca. 1934, included in letter from Hal Colebetch, agent general, to premier, WA, June 18, 1934, Accession # 993, Item 3 166/1932, SROWA.

72. Morgan, *A Drop in the Bucket*, 154–55; Holland, "'Whatever her race,'" 142; Paisley, "'Unnecessary Crimes and Tragedies,'" 138.

73. "Welfare of Blacks," *Argus (Melbourne)*, December 15, 1933, 9.

74. Letter to the editor/petition from women's groups, October 2, 1933, Box 30, Series 12, Item 56, Rischbieth papers.

75. State general secretary, WSG, to ASAPS, London, June 21, 1934, WSG Papers, Accession # 1949 A, MS 393, Item 62, Subject Files: Native Welfare, 1931–1937, Battye Library, Perth, Western Australia.

76. Statement for Royal Commission, Welfare of Aborigines, Perth, 1934, from WSG of WA, Series 11, Duguid papers.

77. WSG to Bennett, February 5, 1934, and Bennett to Cass, February 12, 1934, WSG papers; Holland, "'Saving the Aborigines,'" 123, quote on 126; Holland, "Wives and Mothers." There is debate among Australian historians as to the nature of white women's activism. In contrast to Holland's and my interpretation, Marilyn Lake argues that "the maternalist orientation of the women's movement between the wars led feminists to champion the rights of Aboriginal women—and these feminists were the first organized political group to oppose the removal of Aboriginal children from their mothers." See Lake, *Getting Equal*, 13–14; Lake, "Response."

78. Transcripts of Evidence for Royal Commission into Treatment of Aborigines (1934), 214, 225, 227, 228, Accession # 987, Box #2, SROWA, emphasis in original.

79. Excerpt of Mary Bennett's testimony to the Moseley Commission, "The Native Administration Act of WA," 1934, Series 11, Folder: "Royal Commission," Duguid papers.

80. Transcripts of Evidence, 229.

81. Transcripts of Evidence, 303.

82. Mrs. Nesbitt-Landon's Evidence before the Royal Commission, April 5, 1934, Series 11, Duguid papers.

83. Holland, "'Saving the Aborigines,'" 123.

84. Frank Davies Collie to May Vallance, March 26, 1934, WSG papers.

85. *Report of Royal Commission Appointed to Investigate, Report, and Advise upon Matters in Relation to the Condition and Treatment of Aborigines* (January 1935), 17–18, 23, 24, 72, 63–64, Accession # 987, Box #2, Folder 8, SROWA.

86. Bennett to Rischbieth, November 16, 1934, Box 30, Series 12, Item 81c, Rischbieth papers.

87. Bennett to Jones, included in letter from Jones to Harris, December 30, 1936, MSS Brit. Emp. s.22 G378, ASAPS papers, RH-Oxford.

88. Discussion regarding "Aborigines Education in Australia," June 14, 1934, in *Proceedings of British Commonwealth League Conferences*, 1934, 50.

89. Discussion regarding "Aborigines Education in Australia," 52.

90. Holland, "'Saving the Aborigines,'" 121, 132–40, 148–49; Lake, *Getting Equal*, 130–31.

91. Victorian Aboriginal Group, 7th Annual Report, 1936, 9212/3655/1A, Amy Brown papers, SLV; Holland, "'Saving the Aborigines,'" 180.

92. Baillie, *The Call of the Aboriginal*, 7. See also Helen Baillie to Mr. Parker, April 30, [1934], B313/1, Item 245, NAA-VIC.

93. Baillie to Harris, November 24, [1937], B/ ASAPS papers.

94. *Telegraph (Sydney)*, January 24, 1938. On Bennett's attendance, see "Mission Station Gets a Please Explain," *Daily News (Perth)*, January 21, 1938, Accession # 993, Item 3 166/1932, SROWA; Holland, "'Saving the Aborigines,'" 142.

95. Helen Baillie to Mr. King, December 29, [ca. 1938], Box 8, File "Aborigines," Tom and Mary Wright Collection, Z267, NBAC.

96. Quoted in "Protectors in Conference," *The Ladder*, no. 6 (June 1938): 3, available in Series 12, Box 30, Item 191, Rischbieth papers. For the official report of the conference, see Commonwealth of Australia, *Aboriginal Welfare*.

97. "Protectors in Conference," 3, 4, 5.

98. Bennett to Neville, February 14, 1938, Accession # 993, Item 3 166/1932, SROWA, emphasis in original.

99. M. Jacobs, *Engendered Encounters*.

100. M. Jacobs, *Engendered Encounters*, 56–81.

101. M. Jacobs, *Engendered Encounters*, 56–81; Holland, "'Saving the Aborigines,'" 143–44.

102. M. Jacobs, *Engendered Encounters*, particularly 82–148; Lake, *Getting Equal*, 95, but see also 49–109 for an in-depth discussion of feminism in Australia in the interwar years.

103. M. Jacobs, *Engendered Encounters*, especially 56–81.

Epilogue

1. Bennett to Hon. Emil Nulsen, May 28, 1942, Series 11, Duguid family papers, MS 5068, NLA.

2. McGregor, *Imagined Destinies*, 181–223; McGregor, "Governance, Not Genocide," 290–311; Beresford and Omaji, *Our State of Mind*, 61.

3. "Outline of Policy for the Welfare and Development of Aboriginals and Part Aboriginals of the Northern Territory," with letter from H. I. V. Johnson to Bessie Rischbieth, December 10, 1947, Box 30, Series 12, Item 119, Bessie Rischbieth papers, MS 2004, NLA.

4. Beresford and Omaji, *Our State of Mind*, 61–100, 158–88. See also Cuthbert, "Mothering the 'Other,'" 40.

5. For one example, see Hyer, *One House*.

6. S. Jones, "'Redeeming' the Indian," 240.

7. Crow Dog with Erdoes, *Lakota Woman*, 16.

8. For an overview of some post–World War II American Indian movements, see Smith and Warrior, *Like a Hurricane*.

9. Attwood and Markus, *The Struggle for Aboriginal Rights*; Attwood, *Rights for Aborigines*.

10. Lake, "Feminism and the Gendered Politics of Antiracism"; Holland, "'Saving the Aborigines,'" 231.

11. Holt, *Indian Orphanages.*

12. Chisholm, "Aboriginal Children."

13. Read, *The Stolen Generations.* For the origins of Link-Up, see Link-Up (NSW) and Wilson, *In the Best Interest of the Child?* 2–7.

14. For an overview of reconciliation efforts since the 1990s and the emergence of child removal as a significant issue in this process, see Beresford and Omaji, *Our State of Mind,* 234–54.

15. Currie, "Bringing Them to Court," 17. Thanks to Rosanne Kennedy for sharing part of this thesis with me.

16. "The Stolen Generation Stakes a Claim," *Law Spot,* April 1999, http://www .law4u.com/au. See also Caroline Milburn, "Stolen Generation Despairs of Apology, Begins Test Case," *The Age (Melbourne),* February 6, 1999; Caroline Milburn, "Aborigines Seek Pay for the Pain," *The Age,* March 2, 1999; Caroline Milburn, "Racism Claim on PM 'Appalling,'" *The Age,* March 3, 1999; Michael Duffy, "Stolen Truths Are Hard to Pin Down," *Daily Telegraph (Sydney),* September 11, 1999. See also Behrendt, "Genocide."

17. "Controversial 'Rabbit-Proof' Posters Appear in U.S.," *Sydney Morning Herald,* November 28, 2002, smh.com.au.

18. Sharon Waxman, "Abuse Charges Hit Reservation; Church-Run Schools Cited in Wide-Ranging Lawsuit," *Washington Post,* June 2, 2003, A01.

19. Chet Brokaw, "Lawsuits Allege Abuse at Native Boarding Schools," *Lincoln (NE) Journal Star,* July 14, 2004. Former students of the boarding schools have also established a Boarding School Healing Project: http://www.maquah.net/BIA/ BoardingSchoolHealingProject.html (accessed June 23, 2006).

20. "Indian Affairs Head Apologizes for Agency's 'Legacy of Racism,'" *Las Cruces (NM) Sun-News,* September 9, 2000.

21. Posting from Harold Prins, Kansas State University, on H-Amindian, October 2, 2000, in possession of the author.

22. Quoted in Orleck and Jetter, "Reclaiming Culture and the Land," 77–78.

Bibliography

Unpublished Sources

Aborigines' Advancement League papers, Society Record Group 250/2/2, State Library of South Australia (Mortlock), Adelaide.

Aborigines' Friends' Association papers, Society Record Group 139, State Library of South Australia (Mortlock), Adelaide.

Anti-Slavery and Aborigines Protection Society papers, MSS. Brit. Emp. S.22 G378, Bodleian Library of Commonwealth and African Studies at Rhodes House, Oxford University, England.

Association for Protection of Native Races, Records, MS S55, University of Sydney Archives, Australia.

Daisy Bates papers, MS 365, National Library of Australia, Canberra.

Bringing Them Home Oral History Project, National Library of Australia, Canberra.

Interview with Victoria Archibald by Robert Willis, TRC-5000/144.

Interview with Helen Baldwin by Helen Curzon-Siggers, TRC-5000/39.

Interview with Laurette Butt by Helen Curzon-Siggers, TRC-5000/154.

Interview with Martin Dodd by Sue Anderson, TRC-5000/128.

Interview with Hilda Evans by John Bannister, TRC-5000/96.

Interview with Penny Everaardt by Rob Willis, TRC-5000/48.

Interview with Jim Hart by David Woodgate, TRC-5000/186.

Interview with Eileen Heath by John Bannister, TRC-5000/197.

Interview with Ruth Elizabeth Hegarty by Helen Curzon-Siggers, TRC-5000/79.

Interview with Sandra Hill by John Bannister, TRC-5000/64.

Interview with Lyn Hobbler by Lloyd Hollingsworth, TRC-5000/65.

Interview with Mary King by Colleen Hattersley, TRC-5000/244.

Interview with Sam Lovell by Colleen Hattersley, TRC-5000/156.

Interview with Nita Marshall by Colleen Hattersley, TRC-5000/163.

Interview with Annie Mullins by Lyn McLeavy, TRC-5000/280.

Interview with Alfred Neal by Lloyd Hollingsworth, TRC-5000/140.

Interview with Leonard Ogilvie by John Bannister, TRC-5000/274.

Interview with Geoffrey Parfitt by John Bannister, TRC-5000/213.

Interview with Doris Pilkington by John Bannister, TRC-5000/278.

Interview with Jean Sibley by Phillip Connors, TRC-5000/148.

Interview with Gerald Warber by John Bannister, TRC-5000/101.

Interview with Marjorie Woodrow by Colleen Hattersley, TRC-5000/43.

E. W. P. Chinnery papers, MS 766, National Library of Australia, Canberra.

Leo Crane Collection, MS 256, Archives and Special Collections, Cline Library, Northern Arizona University, Flagstaff.

Constance Goddard DuBois Papers, #9167, Division of Rare Books and Manuscript Collections, Cornell University Library, Ithaca, New York (formerly located at the Huntington Free Library, Bronx, New York).

Duguid Family papers, MS 5068, National Library of Australia, Canberra.

Episcopal Diocese of Idaho, Archives, MS 91, Special Collections, Boise State University, Idaho.

Alice Cunningham Fletcher and Francis La Flesche papers, MS 4558, National Anthropological Archives, Smithsonian Institution, Washington DC.

Berard Haile papers, AZ 132, University of Arizona Library Special Collections, Tucson.

Indian Rights Association papers. Historical Society of Pennsylvania, Philadelphia. Glen Rock NJ: Microfilming Corporation of America, 1974.

League of Women Voters of South Australia (formerly Women's Non-Party Association) papers, State Record Group 116, State Library of South Australia (Mortlock), Adelaide.

Dorothea C. Leighton and Alexander Leighton Collection, MS 216, Archives and Special Collections, Cline Library, Northern Arizona University, Flagstaff.

Charles Lummis papers, Braun Library, Autry National Center's Southwest Museum of the American Indian, Los Angeles, California.

Papers of Carlos Montezuma, microfilm edition, ed. John Larner. Wilmington DE: Scholarly Resources, 1983.

National Archives and Records Administration, Rocky Mountain Region, Denver, Colorado.

    Records of the Bureau of Indian Affairs, Record Group 75:

        Consolidated Ute Agency

        Flathead Agency, Indian Boarding School Correspondence, 1905–1945

        Santa Fe Indian School Superintendent's Correspondence with Day School Employees, 1900–1916

National Archives and Records Administration, Pacific Region, Laguna Niguel, California.

    Records of the Bureau of Indian Affairs, Record Group 75:

Eastern Navajo Agency

Fort Apache Agency

Navajo Agency, Fort Defiance

Phoenix Indian School Central Classified Files, 1891–1951

National Archives and Record Administration, Pacific Region, San Bruno, California.

Records of the Bureau of Indian Affairs, Record Group 75:

Coded Correspondence of Supervisor Holst, 1928–1929

Records of Berkeley Outing Matron and Placement Officer, 1916–1933

Relocation, Training, and Employment Assistance Case Records, 1933–1946, Outing Girls, Sacramento, California Agency, Sacramento Area Office, 1910–1958

Bureau of Indian Affairs, Nevada: Investigative Records of Col. L. A. Dorrington, Special Agent, 1913–1923

National Archives of Australia, Australian Capital Territory, Canberra.

Commonwealth Record Series A1, A431, A659

National Archives of Australia, Victoria, Melbourne.

Commonwealth Record Series B313, B337, B356

Northern Territory Archives Service, Darwin, Australia.

Northern Territory Record Service 226, Typed transcripts of oral history interviews with TS prefix-1979-ct:

Interview with Emily Liddle (nee Perkins) by Francis Good, TS 660

Interview with Eileen Park by Helen Chryssides, TS 474

Interview with Ruby Roney by Ian Marshall for ABC Radio, TS 735

Interview with Dorothea Lyons by Helen Wilson, TS 84

Interview with Clarence Smith by Helen Chryssides, TS 486

Interview with Ada Wade by Vicki MacDonald, TS 348

Correspondence, Photographs, and Reports of Dr. Cecil E. Cook, 1927–1939, NTRS 281.

Oakland, California YWCA, miscellaneous items, Oakland Public Library.

Olive Pink papers, MS 2368, Australian Institute for Aboriginal and Torres Strait Islander Studies, Canberra.

Katherine Susannah Prichard papers, MS 6201, National Library of Australia, Canberra.

Public Record Office of Victoria, Melbourne.

Victoria Public Record Series 1694

Estelle Reel papers, MS 120, Eastern Washington State Historical Society, Northwest. Museum of Arts and Culture, Spokane.

Estelle Reel papers, H6-110, Wyoming State Archives, Cheyenne.

Bessie Rischbieth papers, MS 2004, National Library of Australia, Canberra.

Scrapbook and Visitor's Book, Ida Standley, D5465, State Library of South Australia (Mortlock), Adelaide.

Society of American Indians papers, microfilm edition. Wilmington DE: Scholarly Resources, 1986.

State Records of South Australia, Adelaide.

Government Record Group 52/1, 52/32

State Records Office of Western Australia, Perth.

Accession #652, #987, #993

Jessie Street papers, MS 2683, National Library of Australia, Canberra.

Anton Vroland papers, MS 3991, National Library of Australia, Canberra.

Women's Service Guild papers, Accession #1949A, MS 393, Battye Library, Perth, Western Australia.

Tom and Mary Wright Collection, Z267, Noel Butlin Archives Centre, Australian National University, Canberra.

Published Sources

A.B.M. Review, 1932. Serial publication of Anglican Church of Australia, Australian Board of Missions.

Aborigines' Friends' Association, *Annual Reports*. Adelaide: Aborigines' Friends' Association, 1921.

Baptist Home Mission Monthly. Serial publication of the American Baptist Home Mission Society, 1892, 1894, 1896, 1908.

Congressional Record, Washington DC, 1886, 1891, 1893, 1894, 1906.

The Dawn, 1925, 1927, 1929, 1933. Serial publication of the Women's Service Guilds of Australia, League of Women Voters of Australia.

Indian Craftsman, 1909 (later became *The Red Man*).

The Indian's Friend, 1890–92, 1894–1900, 1903–5, 1907, 1910, 1912, 1919, 1926. Serial publication of the Women's National Indian Association.

New South Wales, *Reports of the Board for the Protection of Aborigines*. Sydney: Government Printer, 1916, 1921, 1925–26.

Proceedings of the Annual Meetings of the Lake Mohonk Conference. Lake Mohonk NY: Lake Mohonk Conference, 1893–95, 1897, 1898, 1899, 1900, 1908.

Proceedings of British Commonwealth League Conferences. London: British Commonwealth League, 1927, 1934, 1936, 1937.

The Red Man, 1909, 1911, 1916 (formerly known as *The Indian Craftsman*).

Reports of the Commissioner of Indian Affairs. Washington DC: Government Printing Office, 1908.

Reports of the Superintendent of Indian Schools. Washington DC: Government Printing

Office, 1899, 1900.

South Australia, *Reports of the Protector of Aborigines*. Adelaide: Government Printer, 1909.

Western Australia. *Annual Reports of the Chief Protectors of Aborigines*. Perth: Government Printer, 1936.

Women's National Indian Association. *Annual Meeting and Report of the WNIA*. Philadelphia: Women's National Indian Association, 1883–85, 1890–91, 1894, 1897, 1914.

Ackerman, Lillian. *A Necessary Balance: Gender and Power among Indians of the Columbia Plateau*. Norman: University of Oklahoma Press, 2003.

Ackermann, Jessie. *Australia from a Woman's Point of View* London: Cassell, 1913.

Adams, David Wallace. *Education for Extinction: American Indians and the Boarding School Experience, 1875–1928*. Lawrence: University Press of Kansas, 1995.

Adams, Evelyn C. *American Indian Education: Government Schools and Economic Progress*. Morningside Heights NY: King's Crown Press, 1946.

Almaguer, Tomás. *Racial Fault Lines: The Historical Origins of White Supremacy in California*. Berkeley: University of California Press, 1994.

Anderson, Jim. "'A glorious thing is to live in a tent in the infinite': Daisy Bates." In *Uncommon Ground: White Women in Aboriginal History*, ed. Anna Cole, Victoria Haskins, and Fiona Paisley, 217–31. Canberra: Aboriginal Studies Press, 2005.

Anderson, Karen. "Changing Woman: Maternalist Politics and 'Racial Rehabilitation' in the U.S. West." In *Over the Edge: Remapping the American West*, ed. Valerie J. Matsumoto and Blake Allmendinger, 148–59. Berkeley: University of California Press, 1999.

Anderson, Karen L. *Chain Her by One Foot: The Subjugation of Women in Seventeenth-Century New France*. New York: Routledge, 1991.

Archuleta, Margaret. "'The Indian Is an Artist': Art Education." In *Away from Home: American Indian Boarding School Experiences, 1879–2000*, ed. Margaret Archuleta, Brenda Child, and Tsianina Lomawaima, 84–97. Phoenix AZ: Heard Museum, 2000.

Archuleta, Margaret, Brenda Child, and Tsianina Lomawaima, eds. *Away from Home: American Indian Boarding School Experiences, 1879–2000*. Phoenix AZ: Heard Museum, 2000.

Ashby, LeRoy. *Saving the Waifs: Reformers and Dependent Children, 1890–1917*. Philadelphia: Temple University Press, 1984.

Attwood, Bain. *Rights for Aborigines*. Crows Nest, New South Wales: Allen & Unwin, 2003.

———. *Telling the Truth about Aboriginal History*. St. Leonards, New South Wales: Allen and Unwin, 2005.

Attwood, Bain, and S. G. Foster, eds. *Frontier Conflict: The Australian Experience*. Canberra: National Museum of Australia, 2003.

Attwood, Bain, and Andrew Markus, eds. *The Struggle for Aboriginal Rights: A Documentary History*. Crows Nest, New South Wales: Allen & Unwin, 1999.

Austin, Tony. *I Can Picture the Old Home So Clearly: The Commonwealth and Half-Caste Youth in the Northern Territory, 1911–1939*. Canberra: Aboriginal Studies Press, 1993.

Axtell, James. *The Invasion Within: The Contests of Cultures in Colonial North America*. New York: Oxford University Press, 1985.

Baillie, Helen. "Aboriginal Woman Speaks for Her Race," *Woman Today* 1, no. 5 (December 1936): 6, 24.

——. *The Call of the Aboriginal*. Melbourne: n.p., 1933.

Balderrama, Francisco, and Raymond Rodriguez. *Decade of Betrayal: Mexican Repatriation in the 1930s*. Albuquerque: University of New Mexico Press, 1995.

Ball, Eve, with Nora Henn and Lynda A. Sánchez. *Indeh: An Apache Odyssey*. Norman: University of Oklahoma Press, 1980.

Ballantyne, Tony. "Race and the Webs of Empire: Aryanism from India to the Pacific." *Journal of Colonialism and Colonial History* 2, no. 3 (2001), online journal.

Bannan, Helen M. "'True Womanhood' on the Reservation: Field Matrons in the U.S. Indian Service." Working Paper no. 18. Southwest Institute for Research on Women, Tucson, 1984.

Barbalet, Margaret. *Far from a Low Gutter Girl: The Forgotten World of State Wards: South Australia 1887–1940*. Melbourne: Oxford University Press, 1983.

Bartrop, Paul. "The Holocaust, the Aborigines, and the Bureaucracy of Destruction: An Australian Dimension of Genocide." *Journal of Genocide Research* 3, no. 1 (2001): 75–87.

Barwick, Diane. "Aunty Ellen: The Pastor's Wife." In *Fighters and Singers: The Lives of Some Australian Aboriginal Women*, ed. Isobel White, Diane Barwick, and Betty Meehan, 173–99. Sydney: Allen & Unwin, 1985.

Basso, Keith. *Wisdom Sits in Places: Landscape and Language among the Western Apache*. Albuquerque: University of New Mexico Press, 1996.

Bates, Daisy. *The Passing of the Aborigines: A Lifetime Spent among the Natives of Australia*. London: John Murray, 1938.

Battey, Thomas C. *The Life and Adventures of a Quaker among the Indians*. Boston: Less and Shepard, 1875.

Beach, Mrs. Alfred H. (Cora M.). *Women of Wyoming*. Vol. 1. Casper WY: S. E. Boyer, 1927.

Bederman, Gail. *Manliness and Civilization: A Cultural History of Gender and Race in the United States*, 1880–1917. Chicago: University of Chicago Press, 1995.

Behrendt, Larissa. "Genocide: The Distance between Law and Life." *Aboriginal History* 25 (2001): 132–47.

Bell, Diane. *Daughters of the Dreaming*. 2nd ed. St Leonards, New South Wales: Allen & Unwin, 1993.

Benedek, Emily. *Beyond the Four Corners of the World: A Navajo Woman's Journey*. New York: Knopf, 1996.

Bennett, Kay. *Kaibah: Recollection of a Navajo Girlhood*. Los Angeles: Westernlore Press, 1964.

Bennett, Mary Montgomery. *The Australian Aboriginal as a Human Being*. London: Alston Rivers, 1930.

———. *Christison of Lammermoor*. London: Alston Rivers, 1927.

———. *Human Rights for Australian Aborigines: How Can They Learn without a Teacher?* Brisbane: Truth and Sportsman, 1957.

———. *Hunt and Die: The Prospect for the Aborigines of Australia*. London: Anti-Slavery Society, 1950.

Beresford, Quentin, and Paul Omaji. *Our State of Mind: Racial Planning and the Stolen Generations*. Fremantle WA: Fremantle Arts Centre Press, 1998.

Berndt, Catherine. "Mondalmi: One of the Saltwater People." In *Fighters and Singers: The Lives of Some Australian Aboriginal Women*, ed. Isobel White, Diane Barwick, and Betty Meehan, 19–39. Sydney: Allen & Unwin, 1985.

———. "Mythical Women, Past and Present." In *We Are Bosses Ourselves: The Status and Role of Aboriginal Women Today*, ed. Fay Gale, 13–21. Canberra: Australian Institute of Aboriginal Studies, 1983.

———. "Retrospect, and Prospect: Looking Back Over Fifty Years." In *Women, Rites and Sites*, ed. Peggy Brock, 1–20. Sydney: Allen & Unwin, 1989.

Berndt, Ronald M., and Catherine H. Berndt. *The World of the First Australians: Aboriginal Traditional Life, Past and Present*. Canberra: Aboriginal Studies Press, 1999.

Betzinez, Jason, with Wilbur Sturtevant Nye. *I Fought with Geronimo*. Lincoln: University of Nebraska Press, 1959.

Bishop, Catherine E. "'A woman missionary living amongst naked blacks': Annie Lock, 1876–1943." MA thesis, Australian National University, 1991.

Bloom, John. "'Show what an Indian can do': Sports, Memory, and Ethnic Identity at Federal Indian Boarding Schools." *Journal of American Indian Education* 35 (spring 1996): 33–48.

Blunt, Alison, and Robyn Dowling. *Home*. New York: Routledge, 2006.

Boyd, Nancy. *Emissaries: The Overseas Work of the American YWCA, 1895–1970*. New

York: Woman's Press, 1986.

Boydston, Jeanne. *Home and Work: Housework, Wages, and the Ideology of Labor in the Early Republic.* New York: Oxford University Press, 1990.

Boyer, Ruth McDonald, and Narcissus Duffy Gayton. *Apache Mothers and Daughters: Four Generations of a Family.* Norman: University of Oklahoma Press, 1992.

Brandl, Maria. "A Certain Heritage: Women and Their Children in North Australia." In *We Are Bosses Ourselves: The Status and Role of Aboriginal Women Today*, ed. Fay Gale, 29–39. Canberra: Australian Institute of Aboriginal Studies, 1983.

Brewer, William. *Up and Down California in 1860–1864.* Ed. Francis Farquhar. Berkeley: University of California Press, 1966.

Brock, Peggy. "Aboriginal Families and the Law in the Era of Segregation and Assimilation, 1890s–1950s." In *Sex, Power and Justice: Historical Perspectives of Law in Australia*, ed. Diane Kirkby, 133–49. Melbourne: Oxford University Press, 1995.

——, ed. *Women, Rites and Sites.* Sydney: Allen & Unwin, 1989.

Brooks, James F. *Captives and Cousins: Slavery, Kinship, and Community in the Southwest Borderlands.* Chapel Hill: University of North Carolina Press, 2002.

Broome, Richard. *Aboriginal Australians: Black Responses to White Dominance, 1788–1994.* 2nd ed. St Leonards, New South Wales: Allen & Unwin, 1994.

——. "Victoria." In *Contested Ground: Australian Aborigines and the British Crown*, ed. Ann McGrath, 121–67. St Leonards, New South Wales: Allen & Unwin, 1995.

Brown, Estelle Aubrey. *Stubborn Fool: A Narrative.* Caldwell ID: Caxton Printers, 1952.

Brown, Jennifer. *Strangers in Blood: Fur Trade Company Families in Indian Country.* Norman: University of Oklahoma Press, 1996.

Brown, Kathleen. *Good Wives, Nasty Wenches, and Anxious Patriarchs: Gender, Race, and Power in Colonial Virginia.* Chapel Hill: University of North Carolina Press, 1996.

Brumberg, Joan Jacobs. "Zenanas and Girlless Villages: The Ethnology of American Evangelical Women, 1870–1910." *Journal of American History* 69 (September 1982): 347–70.

Buffalohead, Roger W., and Paulette Fairbanks Molin. "'A Nucleus of Civilization': American Indian Families at Hampton Institute in the Late Nineteenth Century." *Journal of American Indian Education* 35, no. 3 (spring 1996): 59–94.

Burgoyne, Iris Yumadoo Kochallalya. *The Mirning We Are the Whales.* Broome, Western Australia: Magabala Books, 2000.

Burton, Antoinette. *Burdens of History: British Feminists, Indian Women, and Imperial Culture.* Chapel Hill: University of North Carolina Press, 1994.

Buti, Antonio. *Separated: Aboriginal Childhood Separations and Guardianship Law.* Sydney: Sydney Institute of Criminology, 2004.

Cahill, Cathleen. "'Only the Home Can Found a State': Gender, Labor, and the United States Indian Service, 1869–1928." PhD diss., University of Chicago, 2004.

Calloway, Colin G. *The American Revolution in Indian Country: Crisis and Diversity in Native American Communities*. New York: Cambridge University Press, 1995.

——. *First Peoples: A Documentary Survey of American Indian History*. Boston: Bedford/St. Martin's Press, 1999.

Carter, Sarah. *Capturing Women: The Manipulation of Cultural Imagery in Canada's Prairie West*. Montreal: McGill-Queen's University Press, 1997.

Cartwright, Max. *Missionaries, Aborigines and Welfare Settlement Days in the Northern Territory*. Alice Springs, Northern Territory: Max Cartwright, 1995.

Cave, Alfred. *The Pequot War*. Amherst: University of Massachusetts Press, 1996.

Chan, Sucheng. *Asian Americans: An Interpretive History*. Boston: Twayne, 1991.

Child, Brenda. *Boarding School Seasons: American Indian Families, 1900–1940*. Lincoln: University of Nebraska Press, 1998.

——. "Runaway Boys, Resistant Girls: Rebellion at Flandreau and Haskell, 1900–1940." *Journal of American Indian Education* 35 (spring 1996): 49–57.

Chisholm, Richard. "Aboriginal Children and the Placement Principle." *Aboriginal Law Bulletin* 2, no. 31 (April 1988): 4–7.

Choo, Christine. *Mission Girls: Aboriginal Women on Catholic Missions in the Kimberley, Western Australia, 1900–1950*. Crawley: University of Western Australia Press, 2001.

Clark-Lewis, Elizabeth. *Living In, Living Out: African American Domestics in Washington, D.C., 1910–1940*. Washington DC: Smithsonian Institution Press, 1994.

Clow, Richmond, ed. "Autobiography of Mary C. Collins, Missionary to the Western Sioux." *South Dakota Historical Collections* 41 (1982): 1–66.

Cole, Anna. "'Would have known it by the smell of it': Ella Hiscocks." In *Uncommon Ground: White Women in Aboriginal History*, ed. Anna Cole, Victoria Haskins, and Fiona Paisley, 153–71. Canberra: Aboriginal Studies Press, 2005.

Cole, Anna, Victoria Haskins, and Fiona Paisley, eds. *Uncommon Ground: White Women in Aboriginal History*. Canberra: Aboriginal Studies Press, 2005.

Coleman, Michael C. *American Indian Children at School, 1850–1930*. Jackson: University Press of Mississippi, 1993.

——. *American Indians, the Irish, and Government Schooling*. Lincoln: University of Nebraska Press, 2007.

——. *Presbyterian Missionary Attitudes toward American Indians, 1837–1893*. Jackson: University Press of Mississippi, 1985.

Collier, John. *From Every Zenith: A Memoir*. Denver CO: Sage, 1963.

Colson, Elizabeth, ed. *Autobiographies of Three Pomo Women*. Berkeley: University of California, Department of Anthropology, 1974.

———. "A Study of Acculturation among Pomo Women." MA thesis, University of Minnesota, 1940.

Commonwealth of Australia. *Aboriginal Welfare: Initial Conference of Commonwealth and State Aboriginal Authorities.* Canberra: Government Printer, 1937.

Course of Study of the Indian Schools of the United States, Industrial and Literary. Washington DC: Government Printing Office, 1901.

Crane, Leo. *Indians of the Enchanted Desert.* Boston: Little, Brown, 1925.

Crow Dog, Mary, with Richard Erdoes. *Lakota Woman.* New York: HarperCollins, 1991.

Cummings, Barbara. *Take This Child: From Kahlin Compound to the Retta Dixon Children's Home.* Canberra: Aboriginal Studies Press, 1990.

Currie, Carmen. "Bringing Them to Court: Law, Litigation and the Stolen Generations. A Feminist Cultural Critique." Honours thesis, Australian National University, 1999.

Curthoys, Ann. "Colonialism, Nation, and Gender in Australian History." *Gender and History* 5, no. 2 (summer 1993): 165–76.

———. "Constructing National Histories." In *Frontier Conflict: The Australian Experience,* ed. Bain Attwood and S. G. Foster, 185–200. Canberra: National Museum of Australia, 2003.

Cuthbert, Denise. "Mothering the 'Other': Feminism, Colonialism and the Experiences of Non-Aboriginal Adoptive Mothers of Aboriginal Children." *Balayi: Journal of Indigenous Cultural Issues* 1, no. 1 (2000): 31–49.

Daniels, Roger. *Coming to America: A History of Immigration and Ethnicity in American Life.* 2nd. ed. Princeton NJ: Visual Education Corporation, 2002.

Debo, Angie. *And Still the Waters Run.* Princeton NJ: Princeton University Press, 1940.

DeJong, David H. *Promises of the Past: A History of Indian Education in the United States.* Golden CO: North American Press, 1993.

Deloria, Ella Cara. "Health Education for Indian Girls." *Southern Workman* 53 (February 1924): 63–68.

———. *Waterlily.* Lincoln: University of Nebraska Press, 1988.

Deloria, Philip. "'I Am of the Body': Thoughts on My Grandfather, Culture, and Sports." *South Atlantic Quarterly* 95, no. 2 (1996): 321–39.

———. *Indians in Unexpected Places.* Lawrence: University of Kansas Press, 2004.

———. *Playing Indian.* New Haven: Yale University Press, 1998.

Denoon, Donald. *Settler Capitalism: The Dynamics of Dependent Development in the Southern Hemisphere.* Oxford: Clarendon Press, 1983.

Deutsch, Sarah. *No Separate Refuge: Culture, Class, and Gender on an Anglo-Hispanic*

Frontier in the American Southwest, 1880–1940. New York: Oxford University Press, 1987.

Devens, Carol. *Countering Colonization: Native American Women and Great Lakes Missions,* 1630–1900. Berkeley: University of California Press, 1992.

Docker, John, and Gerhard Fischer, eds. *Race, Colour and Identity in Australia and New Zealand.* Sydney: University of New South Wales Press, 2000.

DuBois, Ellen Carol, and Lyn Dumenil. *Through Women's Eyes: An American History with Documents.* Boston: Bedford/St. Martin's Press, 2005.

Du Bois, W. E. B. *The Souls of Black Folk.* 1903. New York: Fawcett, 1961.

Dyk, Walter, ed. *Left Handed, Son of Old Man Hat: A Navajo Autobiography.* Lincoln: University of Nebraska Press, 1967.

Eastman, Charles Alexander. *From the Deep Woods to Civilization.* 1916. Lincoln: University of Nebraska Press, 1977.

Edmunds, R. David. *The Shawnee Prophet.* Lincoln: University of Nebraska Press, 1983.

Edwards, Coral, and Peter Read, eds. *The Lost Children: Thirteen Australians Taken from Their Aboriginal Families Tell of the Struggle to Find Their Natural Parents.* Sydney: Doubleday, 1989.

Elder, Catriona. "Immigration History." In *Australia's History: Themes and Debates,* ed. Martyn Lyons and Penny Russell, 98–115. Sydney: University of New South Wales Press, 2005.

Ellinghaus, Katherine. "Indigenous Assimilation and Absorption in the United States and Australia." *Pacific Historical Review* 75, no. 4 (2006): 563–85.

———. *Taking Assimilation to Heart: Marriages of White Women and Indigenous Men in the United States and Australia,* 1887–1937. Lincoln: University of Nebraska Press, 2006.

Ellis, Clyde. *To Change Them Forever: Indian Education at the Rainy Mountain Boarding School,* 1893–1920. Norman: University of Oklahoma Press, 1996.

Emberley, Julia V. "The Bourgeois Family, Aboriginal Women, and Colonial Governance in Canada: A Study in Feminist Historical and Cultural Materialism." *Signs* 27, no. 1 (autumn 2001): 59–85.

Emmerich, Lisa. "'To respect and love and seek the ways of white women': Field Matrons, the Office of Indian Affairs, and Civilization Policy, 1890–1938." PhD diss., University of Maryland, 1987.

Evans, Julie, Patricia Grimshaw, David Philips, and Shurlee Swain. *Equal Subjects, Unequal Rights: Indigenous Peoples in British Settler Colonies,* 1830–1910. Manchester, England: Manchester University Press, 2003.

Evans, Raymond. "'Don't You Remember Black Alice, Sam Holt?' Aboriginal Women in Queensland History." *Hecate* 8, no. 2 (1982): 7–21.

——. "'Pigmentia': Racial Fears and White Australia." In *Genocide and Settler Society: Frontier Violence and Stolen Indigenous Children in Australian History*, ed. A. Dirk Moses, 103–24. New York: Berghahn Books, 2004.

——. "'Plenty Shoot 'Em': The Destruction of Aboriginal Societies along the Queensland Frontier." In *Genocide and Settler Society: Frontier Violence and Stolen Indigenous Children in Australian History*, ed. A. Dirk Moses, 150–73. New York: Berghahn Books, 2004.

Fear-Segal, Jacqueline. "The Man on the Bandstand at Carlisle Indian Industrial School: What He Reveals about Children's Experiences." In *Boarding School Blues: Revisiting American Indian Educational Experiences*, ed. Clifford Trafzer, Jean Keller, and Lorene Sisquoc, 99–122. Lincoln: University of Nebraska Press, 2006.

"Final Report of the Royal Commission on the Aborigines." In *Proceedings of the Parliament of South Australia*, no. 21. Adelaide: Government Printer, 1916. (Included in an addendum to proceedings and also printed as a separate document. See also "Progress Report.")

Flemming, Leslie A., ed. *Women's Work for Women: Missionaries and Social Change in Asia*. Boulder CO: Westview Press, 1989.

Fletcher, Alice Cunningham. *Indian Education and Civilization*. Bureau of Education Special Report. Washington DC: Government Printing Office, 1888.

Fletcher, Alice Cunningham, and Francis La Flesche. *The Omaha Tribe*. Introduction by Robin Ridington. Vol. 1. Lincoln: University of Nebraska Press, 1992. (Originally published as the twenty-seventh annual report of the Bureau of American Ethnology for 1905–6.)

Folsom, Cora. *Ten Years' Work for Indians at Hampton Institute, Virginia*. Hampton VA: The Institute, 1888.

Frisbie, Charlotte Johnson. *Kinaaldá: A Study of the Navaho Girl's Puberty Ceremony*. Middletown CT: Wesleyan University Press, 1967.

Fuchs, Estelle, and Robert J. Havighurst. *To Live on This Earth: American Indian Education*. Albuquerque: University of New Mexico Press, 1972.

Gabriel, Kathryn, ed. *Marietta Wetherill: Life with the Navajos in Chaco Canyon*. Albuquerque: University of New Mexico Press, 1992.

Gale, Fay, ed. *We Are Bosses Ourselves: The Status and Role of Aboriginal Women Today*. Canberra: Australian Institute of Aboriginal Studies, 1983.

Gallagher, Nancy. *Breeding Better Vermonters: The Eugenics Project in the Green Mountain State*. Hanover NH: University Press of New England, 1999.

Garton, Stephen. "Sound Minds and Healthy Bodies: Re-considering Eugenics in Australia, 1914–1940." *Australian Historical Studies* 26, no. 103 (October 1994): 163–81.

Gigliotti, Simone. "Unspeakable Pasts as Limit Events: The Holocaust, Genocide, and the Stolen Generations." *Australian Journal of Politics and History* 49, no. 2 (2003): 164–81.

Gilman, Charlotte Perkins. *Herland, The Yellow Wallpaper, and Selected Writings.* New York: Penguin, 1999.

Gleach, Frederic. *Powhatan's World and Colonial Virginia: A Conflict of Cultures.* Lincoln: University of Nebraska Press, 1997.

Glenn, Evelyn Nakano. *Issei, Nisei, War Bride: Three Generations of Japanese American Women in Domestic Service.* Philadelphia: Temple University Press, 1986.

Glenn, Evelyn Nakano, Grace Chang, and Linda Rennie Forcey, eds. *Mothering: Ideology, Experience, and Agency.* New York: Routledge, 1994.

Golden, Gertrude. *Red Moon Called Me: Memoirs of a Schoolteacher in the Government Indian Service.* San Antonio TX: Naylor, 1954.

González, Deena. *Refusing the Favor: The Spanish-Mexican Women of Santa Fe, 1820–80.* New York: Oxford University Press, 1999.

Goodall, Heather. *Invasion to Embassy: Land in Aboriginal Politics in New South Wales, 1770–1972.* St. Leonards, New South Wales: Allen & Unwin, 1996.

———. "New South Wales." In *Contested Ground: Australian Aborigines and the British Crown*, ed. Ann McGrath, 55–120. St Leonards, New South Wales: Allen & Unwin, 1995.

———. "'Saving the Children': Gender and the Colonization of Aboriginal Children in New South Wales, 1788 to 1990." *Aboriginal Law Bulletin* 2, no. 44 (June 1990): 6–9.

Gordon, Linda. *The Great Arizona Orphan Abduction.* Cambridge MA: Harvard University Press, 1999.

———. *Heroes of Their Own Lives: The Politics and History of Family Violence, Boston 1880–1960.* New York: Viking, 1988.

———. *Pitied but Not Entitled: Single Mothers and the History of Welfare.* Cambridge MA: Harvard University Press, 1994.

Graber, Kay, ed. *Sister to the Sioux: The Memoirs of Elaine Goodale Eastman, 1885–1891.* Lincoln: University of Nebraska Press, 1985.

Griffiths, Tom. *Hunters and Collectors: The Antiquarian Imagination in Australia.* Cambridge, England: Cambridge University Press, 1996.

Grimshaw, Patricia. "Gender, Citizenship and Race in the Woman's Christian Temperance Union of Australia, 1890 to the 1930s." *Australian Feminist Studies* 13, no. 28 (1998): 199–214.

———. *Paths of Duty: American Missionary Wives in Nineteenth-Century Hawaii.* Honolulu: University of Hawaii Press, 1989.

Grimshaw, Patricia, Marilyn Lake, Ann McGrath, and Marian Quartly. *Creating a Nation*. Victoria, Australia: Ringwood McPhee Gribble, 1994.

Grimshaw, Patricia, and Elizabeth Nelson. "Empire, 'the Civilizing Mission' and Indigenous Christian Women in Colonial Victoria." *Australian Feminist Studies* 16, no. 36 (2001): 295–309.

Gutiérrez, Ramón. *When Jesus Came the Corn Mothers Went Away: Marriage, Sexuality, and Power in New Mexico, 1500–1846*. Stanford: Stanford University Press, 1991.

Haebich, Anna. *Broken Circles: Fragmenting Indigenous Families, 1800–2000*. Fremantle WA: Fremantle Arts Centre Press, 2000.

———. *For Their Own Good: Aborigines and Government in the Southwest of Western Australia, 1900–1940*. Nedlands: University of Western Australia Press, 1988.

Hagan, William T. *Theodore Roosevelt and Six Friends of the Indian*. Norman: University of Oklahoma Press, 1997.

Hall, Andrew. *A Brief History of the Laws, Policies, and Practices in South Australia which led to the Removal of Many Aboriginal Children: A Contribution to Reconciliation*. 2nd ed. Adelaide: Department of Human Services, 1998.

Hamilton, Annette. "Bond-Slaves of Satan: Aboriginal Women and the Missionary Dilemma." In *Family and Gender in the Pacific: Domestic Contradictions and the Colonial Impact*, ed. Margaret Jolly and Martha Macintyre, 236–58. Cambridge, England: Cambridge University Press, 1989.

———. "A Complex Strategical Situation: Gender and Power in Aboriginal Australia." In *Australian Women: Feminist Perspectives*, ed. Norma Grieve and Patricia Grimshaw, 69–85. Melbourne: Oxford University Press, 1981.

———. *Nature and Nurture: Aboriginal Child-Rearing in North-Central Arnhem Land*. Canberra: Aboriginal Studies Press, 1981.

Haskins, Victoria. "'A Better Chance'?: Sexual Abuse and the Apprenticeship of Aboriginal Girls under the NSW Aborigines Protection Board." *Aboriginal History* 28 (2004): 33–58.

———. "The Call for a Woman Visitor to 'Half-Caste' Girls and Women in Domestic Service, Adelaide, 1925–1928." *Frontiers* 28, nos. 1 and 2 (2007): 124–64.

———. "'Lovable Natives' and 'Tribal Sisters': Feminism, Maternalism, and the Campaign for Aboriginal Citizenship in New South Wales in the Late 1930s." *Hecate* 24, no. 2 (1998): 8–21.

———. "On the Doorstep: Aboriginal Domestic Service as a 'Contact Zone.'" *Australian Feminist Studies* 16, no. 34 (2001): 13–25.

———. *One Bright Spot*. New York: Palgrave, 2005.

Haskins, Victoria, and Margaret Jacobs. "Stolen Generations and Vanishing Indians:

The Removal of Indigenous Children as a Weapon of War in the United States and Australia, 1870–1940." In *Children and War*, ed. James Marten, 227–24. New York: New York University Press, 2002.

Hawes, Joseph. *The Children's Rights Movement: A History of Advocacy and Protection.* Boston: Twayne, 1991.

Hegarty, Ruth. *Is That You Ruthie?* St. Lucia: University of Queensland Press, 1999.

Hill, Ernestine. *The Great Australian Loneliness.* 1940. Melbourne: Robertson and Mullens, 1952.

———. *Kabbarli: A Personal Memoir of Daisy Bates.* Sydney: Angus and Robertson, 1973.

Hine, Robert V., and John Mack Faragher. *The American West: A New Interpretive History.* New Haven CT: Yale University Press, 2000.

Holland, Alison. "The Campaign for Women Protectors: Gender, Race and Frontier between the Wars." *Australian Feminist Studies* 16, no. 34 (March 2001): 27–42.

———. "Feminism, Colonialism and Aboriginal Workers: An Anti-Slavery Crusade." *Labour History*, no. 69 (November 1995): 52–64.

———. "Post-War Women Reformers and Aboriginal Citizenship: Rehearsing an Old Campaign?" In *Citizenship, Women and Social Justice*, papers presented at the 1998 International Federation for Research in Women's History, ed. Joy Damousi and Katherine Ellinghaus, 20–29. Melbourne: University of Melbourne, History Department, 1999.

———. "'Saving the Aborigines,' The White Woman's Crusade: A Study of Gender, Race, and the Australian Frontier, 1920s-1960s." PhD diss., University of New South Wales, 1998.

———. "Whatever her race, a woman is not a chattel': Mary Montgomery Bennett." In *Uncommon Ground: White Women in Aboriginal History*, ed. Anna Cole, Victoria Haskins, and Fiona Paisley, 129–52. Canberra: Aboriginal Studies Press, 2005.

———. "Wives and Mothers Like Ourselves? Exploring White Women's Intervention in the Politics of Race, 1920s-1940s." *Australian Historical Studies* 117 (2001): 292–310.

Holt, Marilyn Irvin. *Indian Orphanages.* Lawrence: University Press of Kansas, 2001.

———. *The Orphan Trains: Placing Out in America.* Lincoln: University of Nebraska Press, 1992.

Hondagneu-Sotelo, Pierrette. *Doméstica: Immigrant Workers Cleaning and Caring in the Shadows of Affluence.* Berkeley: University of California Press, 2001.

Horne, Esther Burnett, and Sally McBeth. *Essie's Story: The Life and Legacy of a Shoshone Teacher.* Lincoln: University of Nebraska Press, 1998.

Horsman, Reginald. *Expansion and American Indian Policy, 1783–1812*, reprint ed. Norman: University of Oklahoma Press, 1992.

Hosmer, Brian, and Colleen O'Neill. *Native Pathways: American Indian Culture and Economic Development in the Twentieth Century*. Boulder: University Press of Colorado, 2004.

Hoxie, Frederick. *A Final Promise: The Campaign to Assimilate the Indians, 1880–1920*. New York: Cambridge University Press, 1984.

———. "From Prison to Homeland: The Cheyenne River Indian Reservation before World War I." In *The Plains Indians of the 20th Century*, ed. Peter Iverson, 55–76. Norman: University of Oklahoma Press, 1985.

Huffer, Virginia, with Elsie Roughsey. *The Sweetness of the Fig: Aboriginal Women in Transition*. Sydney: University of New South Wales Press, 1980.

Huggins, Jackie. "'Firing On in the Mind': Aboriginal Domestic Servants in the Inter-War Years." *Hecate* 8, no. 2 (1987–88): 5–23.

———. "White Aprons, Black Hands: Aboriginal Women Domestic Servants in Queensland." *Labour History*, no. 69 (November 1995): 188–95.

Hughes, Robert. *The Fatal Shore: The Epic of Australia's Founding*. New York: Knopf, 1986.

Human Rights and Equal Opportunity Commission. *Bringing Them Home: Report of the National Inquiry into the Separation of Aboriginal and Torres Strait Islander Children from Their Families*. Canberra: Commonwealth of Australia, 1997.

Hunt, Nancy Rose. *A Colonial Lexicon of Birth Ritual, Medicalization, and Mobility in the Congo*. Durham NC: Duke University Press, 1999.

Hunter, Jane. *The Gospel of Gentility: American Women Missionaries in Turn-of-the-Century China*. New Haven CT: Yale University Press, 1984.

Hurtado, Albert. *Indian Survival on the California Frontier*. New Haven CT: Yale University Press, 1988.

———. *Intimate Frontiers: Sex, Gender, and Culture in Old California*. Albuquerque: University of New Mexico Press, 1999.

Hyer, Sally. *One House, One Voice, One Heart: Native American Education at the Santa Fe Indian School*. Santa Fe: Museum of New Mexico Press, 1990.

Ignatiev, Noel. *How the Irish Became White*. New York: Routledge, 1995.

"Indian Welfare Work Will Be Undertaken." *General Federation News* 2 (August 1921): 1, 9.

Iverson, Peter. *Diné: A History of the Navajos*. Albuquerque: University of New Mexico Press, 2002.

———. *The Navajo Nation*. Westport CT: Greenwood Press, 1981.

Jackson, Robert H., and Edward Castillo. *Indians, Franciscans, and Spanish Colonization: The Impact of the Mission System on California Indians*. Albuquerque: University of New Mexico Press, 1999.

Jacobs, Harriet. *Incidents in the Life of a Slave Girl.* Ed. Nell Irvin Painter. New York: Penguin Classics, 2000.

Jacobs, Margaret. "A Battle for the Children: American Indian Child Removal in Arizona in the Era of Assimilation." *Journal of Arizona History* 45, no. 1 (spring 2004): 31–62.

——. *Engendered Encounters: Feminism and Pueblo Cultures,* 1879–1934. Lincoln: University of Nebraska Press, 1999.

——. "Indian Boarding Schools in Comparative Perspective: The Removal of Indigenous Children in the U.S. and Australia, 1880–1940." In *Boarding School Blues: Revisiting the American Indian Boarding School Experience,* ed. Clifford Trafzer, Jean Keller, and Lorene Sisquoc, 202–31. Lincoln: University of Nebraska Press, 2006.

Jacobson, Matthew Frye. *Whiteness of a Different Color: European Immigrants and the Alchemy of Race.* Cambridge MA: Harvard University Press, 1998.

James, Harry C. *Pages from Hopi History.* Tucson: University of Arizona Press, 1974.

Jameson, Elizabeth, and Susan Armitage, eds. *Writing the Range: Race, Class, and Culture in the Women's West.* Norman: University of Oklahoma Press, 1997.

Janiewski, Dolores. "Engendering the Invisible Empire: Imperialism, Feminism, and U.S. Women's History." *Australian Feminist Studies* 16, no. 36 (2001): 279–93.

——. "Giving Women a Future: Alice Fletcher, the 'Woman Question,' and "Indian Reform." In *Visible Women: New Essays on American Activism,* ed. Nancy Hewitt and Suzanne Lebsock, 327–44. Urbana: University of Illinois Press, 1993.

Jebb, Mary Anne, and Anna Haebich. "Across the Great Divide: Gender Relations on Australian Frontiers." In *Gender Relations in Australia: Domination and Negotiation,* ed. K. Saunders and R. Evans, 20–41. Sydney: Harcourt Brace Jovanovich, 1992.

Jensen, Joan, and Darlis Miller. "The Gentle Tamers Revisited: New Approaches to the History of Women in the American West." *Pacific Historical Review* 49 (May 1980): 173–213.

Jetter, Alexis, Annelise Orleck, and Diane Taylor, eds. *The Politics of Motherhood: Activist Voices from Left to Right.* Hanover NH: University Press of New England, 1997.

Johnston, Carolyn Ross. *Cherokee Women in Crisis: Trail of Tears, Civil War, and Allotment,* 1838–1907. Tuscaloosa: University of Alabama Press, 2003.

Jolly, Margaret. "Colonizing Women: The Maternal Body and Empire." In *Feminism and the Politics of Difference,* ed. Sneja Gunew and Anna Yeatman, 103–27. Boulder CO: Westview Press, 1993.

Jones, Helen. *In Her Own Name: A History of Women in South Australia from 1836.* Kent Town South Australia: Wakefield Press, 1994.

Jones, Jacqueline. *Soldiers of Light and Love: Northern Teachers and Georgia Blacks, 1865–1873.* Chapel Hill: University of North Carolina Press, 1980.

Jones, Sondra. "'Redeeming' the Indian: The Enslavement of Indian Children in New Mexico and Utah." *Utah Historical Quarterly* 67, no. 3 (summer 1999): 220–41.

———. *The Trial of Don Pedro León Luján: The Attack against Indian Slavery and Mexican Traders in Utah.* Salt Lake City: University of Utah Press, 2000.

Kaberry, Phyllis. *Aboriginal Woman Sacred and Profane.* London: George Routledge and Sons, 1939.

Kaplan, Amy. *The Anarchy of Empire in the Making of U.S. Culture.* Cambridge MA: Harvard University Press, 2002.

Keen, Ian. *Aboriginal Economy and Society: Australia at the Threshold of Colonisation.* South Melbourne: Oxford University Press, 2004.

Kelly, Lawrence C. *The Assault on Assimilation: John Collier and the Origins of Indian Policy Reform.* Albuquerque: University of New Mexico Press, 1983.

Key, Ellen. *The Century of the Child.* New York: G. P. Putnam's Sons, 1909.

Kidd, Rosalind. *Black Lives, Government Lies.* Sydney: University of New South Wales Press, 2000.

———. *The Way We Civilise: Aboriginal Affairs—The Untold Story.* St. Lucia: University of Queensland Press, 1997.

Klein, Laura, and Lillian Ackerman, eds. *Women and Power in Native North America.* Norman: University of Oklahoma Press, 1995.

Kociumbas, Jan. "Genocide and Modernity in Colonial Australia, 1788–1850." In *Genocide and Settler Society: Frontier Violence and Stolen Indigenous Children in Australian History,* ed. A. Dirk Moses, 77–102. New York: Berghahn Books, 2004.

Ladd-Taylor, Molly. *Mother-Work: Women, Child Welfare, and the State, 1890–1930.* Urbana: University of Illinois Press, 1994.

La Flesche, Francis. *The Middle Five: Indian Schoolboys of the Omaha Tribe.* Lincoln: University of Nebraska Press, 1978.

Lake, Marilyn. "Colonised and Colonising: The White Australian Feminist Subject." *Women's History Review* 2, no. 3 (1993): 377–86.

———. "Feminism and the Gendered Politics of Antiracism, Australia 1927–1957: From Maternal Protectionism to Leftist Assimilationism." *Australian Historical Studies* 29, no. 110 (April 1998): 91–108.

———. "Frontier Feminism and the Marauding White Man." *Journal of Australian Studies* no. 49 (1996): 12–20.

———. *Getting Equal: The History of Australian Feminism.* Sydney: Allen & Unwin, 1999.

———. "The Politics of Respectability: Identifying the Masculinist Context." *Historical Studies,* no. 86 (1986): 116–31.

——. "Response: Women and Whiteness." *Australian Historical Studies* 117 (2001): 338–42.

——. "White Man's Country: The Trans-National History of a National Project." *Australian Historical Studies* 34, no. 122 (2003): 346–63.

Lake, Marilyn, and Henry Reynolds. *Drawing the Global Colour Line: White Men's Countries and the Question of Racial Equality*. Carlton, Victoria: Melbourne University Press, 2008.

Lame Deer with Richard Erdoes. *Lame Deer: Seeker of Visions*. New York: Washington Square Press, 1972.

Lebergott, Stanley. *Manpower in Economic Growth: The American Record since 1800*. New York: McGraw Hill, 1964.

Lemke-Santangelo, Gretchen. *Abiding Courage: African American Migrant Women and the East Bay Community*. Chapel Hill: University of North Carolina Press, 1996.

Lepore, Jill. *In the Name of War: King Philip's War and the Origins of American Identity*. New York: Knopf, 1998.

Limerick, Patricia Nelson. *Legacy of Conquest: The Unbroken Past of the American West*. New York: Norton, 1987.

Linenthal, Edward T., and Tom Engelhardt, eds. *History Wars: The* Enola Gay *and Other Battles for the American Past*. New York: Henry Holt, 1996.

Link-Up (NSW) and Tikka Jan Wilson. *In the Best Interest of the Child? Stolen Children: Aboriginal Pain/White Shame*. Aboriginal History Monograph 4. Canberra: Aboriginal History, 1997.

Litchfield, Jessie. *Far-North Memories: Being the Account of Ten years Spent on the Diamond-Drills, and of Things that Happened in Those Days*. Sydney: Angus and Robertson, 1930.

Littlefield, Alice, and Martha C. Knack, eds. *Native Americans and Wage Labor: Ethnohistorical Perspectives*. Norman: University of Oklahoma Press, 1996.

Lomawaima, K. Tsianina. "Domesticity in the Federal Indian Schools: The Power of Authority over Mind and Body." *American Ethnologist* 20, no. 2 (May 1993): 227–40.

——. "Estelle Reel, Superintendent of Indian Schools, 1898–1910: Politics, Curriculum, and Land." *Journal of American Indian Education* 35 (spring 1996): 5–31.

——. *They Called It Prairie Light: The Story of the Chilocco Indian School*. Lincoln: University of Nebraska Press, 1994.

Lombard, Juliette. "The Migration of Women from the Ukiah Valley in California to the San Francisco Bay Region." MA thesis, Columbia University, 1942.

López, Ian F. Haney. *White by Law: The Legal Construction of Race*. New York: New York University Press, 1996.

Lummis, Charles F. *Bullying the Moqui*. Ed. Robert Easton and Mackenzie Brown. Prescott AZ: Prescott College Press, 1968.

———. *Mesa, Cañon, and Pueblo*. New York: Century, 1925.

MacDonald, Rowena. *Between Two Worlds: The Commonwealth Government and the Removal of Aboriginal Children of Part Descent in the Northern Territory*. Alice Springs, Northern Territory: IAD Press, 1995.

Macintyre, Stuart. *A Concise History of Australia*. Cambridge, England: Cambridge University Press, 1999.

Macintyre, Stuart, and Anna Clark. *The History Wars*. Melbourne: Melbourne University Press, 2003.

Macneil, Rod. "Time after Time: Temporal Frontiers and Boundaries in Colonial Images of the Australian Landscape." In *Colonial Frontiers: Indigenous-European Encounters in Settler Societies*, ed. Lynette Russell, 47–67. Manchester, England: Manchester University Press, 2001.

Mahood, Kim. *Craft for a Dry Lake*. Sydney: Anchor Books, 2000.

Marcus, Julie. "The Beauty, Simplicity and Honour of Truth: Olive Pink in the 1940s." In *First in Their Field: Women and Australian Anthropology*, ed. Julie Marcus, 110–35. Melbourne: Melbourne University Press, 1993.

———, ed. *First in Their Field: Women and Australian Anthropology*. Melbourne: Melbourne University Press, 1993.

———. *The Indomitable Miss Pink: A Life in Anthropology*. Sydney: University of New South Wales Press, 2001.

Mark, Joan. *A Stranger in Her Native Land: Alice Fletcher and the American Indians*. Lincoln: University of Nebraska Press, 1988.

Mathes, Valerie. "Nineteenth-Century Women and Reform: The Women's National Indian Association." *American Indian Quarterly* 14 (1990): 1–18.

Mattingley, Christobel, and Ken Hampton, eds. *Survival in Our Own Land: "Aboriginal" Experiences in "South Australia" since 1836*. Kew: Australian Scholarly Publishing, 1998.

Maykuttener (Vicki Matson-Green). "Tasmania: 2." In *Contested Ground: Australian Aborigines and the British Crown*, ed. Ann McGrath, 338–58. St Leonards, New South Wales: Allen & Unwin, 1995.

Maynard, John. "'Light in the darkness': Elizabeth McKenzie Hatton." In *Uncommon Ground: White Women in Aboriginal History*, ed. Anna Cole, Victoria Haskins, and Fiona Paisley, 3–27. Canberra: Aboriginal Studies Press, 2005.

McDonald, Connie Nungulla, with Jill Finnane. *When You Grow Up*. Broome, Western Australia: Magabala Books, 1996.

McGrath, Ann. "Being Annie Oakley: Modern Girls, New World Woman." *Frontiers* 28, nos. 1 and 2 (2007): 203–31.

——. *"Born in the Cattle": Aborigines in Cattle Country.* Sydney: Allen & Unwin, 1987.

——, ed. *Contested Ground: Australian Aborigines and the British Crown.* St Leonards, New South Wales: Allen & Unwin, 1995.

——. "Tasmania I." In *Contested Ground: Australian Aborigines and the British Crown,* ed. Ann McGrath, 306–37. St Leonards, New South Wales: Allen & Unwin, 1995.

McGregor, Russell. "'Breed Out the Colour' or the Importance of Being White." *Australian Historical Studies* 33, no. 120 (2002): 286–302.

——. "Governance, Not Genocide: Aboriginal Assimilation in the Postwar Era." In *Genocide and Settler Society: Frontier Violence and Stolen Indigenous Children in Australian History,* ed. A. Dirk Moses, 290–311. New York: Berghahn Books, 2004.

——. *Imagined Destinies: Aboriginal Australians and the Doomed Race Theory,* 1880–1939. Melbourne: Melbourne University Press, 1997.

McGuire, Margaret. "The Legend of the Goodfella Missus." *Aboriginal History* 14, nos. 1 and 2 (1990): 124–51.

McKnight, David. *Going the Whiteman's Way: Kinship and Marriage among Australian Aborigines.* Hants, England: Ashgate, 2004.

——. *People, Countries, and the Rainbow Serpent: Systems of Classification among the Lardil of Mornington Island.* New York: Oxford University Press, 1999.

McLoughlin, William. *Cherokee Renascence in the New Republic.* Princeton NJ: Princeton University Press, 1986.

Meriam, Lewis. *The Problem of Indian Administration: Report of a Survey Made at the Request of Hubert Work, Secretary of the Interior, and Submitted to him, February 21, 1928.* Baltimore: Johns Hopkins University Press, 1928.

Michel, Sonya. *Children's Interests / Mother's Rights: The Shaping of America's Child Care Policy.* New Haven CT: Yale University Press, 1999.

Miller, James. *Koori: A Will to Win.* London: Angus & Robertson, 1985.

Mink, Gwendolyn. *The Wages of Motherhood: Inequality in the Welfare State,* 1917–1942. Ithaca NY: Cornell University Press, 1995.

Mitchell, Pablo. *Coyote Nation: Sexuality, Race, and Conquest in Modernizing New Mexico,* 1880–1920. Chicago: University of Chicago Press, 2005.

Mitchell, Rose. *Tall Woman: The Life Story of Rose Mitchell, a Navajo Woman, c. 1874–1977.* Ed. Charlotte Frisbie. Albuquerque: University of New Mexico Press, 2001.

Mohanty, Chandra Talpade. "Under Western Eyes: Feminist Scholarship and Colonial Discourses." *Feminist Review,* no. 30 (autumn 1988): 61–88.

Moore, Shirley Ann Wilson. *To Place Our Deeds: The African American Community in Richmond, California,* 1910–1963. Berkeley: University of California Press, 2000.

Morgan, Edmund. *American Slavery, American Freedom: The Ordeal of Colonial Virginia*. New York: Norton, 1975.

Morgan, Lewis Henry. *Ancient Society: Researches in the Lines of Human Progress from Savagery through Barbarism to Civilization*. Chicago: Charles H. Kerr, 1877.

Morgan, Margaret. *A Drop in the Bucket: The Mount Margaret Story*. Box Hill, Victoria: United Aborigines Mission, 1986.

Morgan, Sally. *My Place*. New York: Little, Brown, 1990.

Morris, Miranda. "Jane Ada Fletcher and the Little Brown Piccaninnies of Tasmania." In *First in Their Field: Women and Australian Anthropology*, ed. Julie Marcus, 66–83. Melbourne: Melbourne University Press, 1993.

Moses, A. Dirk, ed. *Genocide and Settler Society: Frontier Violence and Stolen Indigenous Children in Australian History*. New York: Berghahn Books, 2004.

Namias, June. *White Captives: Gender and Ethnicity on the American Frontier*. Chapel Hill: University of North Carolina Press, 1993.

Nash, Gary B., Charlotte Crabtree, and Ross E. Dunn. *History on Trial: Culture Wars and the Teaching of the Past*. New York: Knopf, 1997.

Neville, A. O. *Australia's Coloured Minority: Its Place in the Community*. Sydney: Currawong Publishing, 1947.

Ngai, Mae M. "The Architecture of Race in American Immigration Law: A Reexamination of the Immigration Act of 1924." *Journal of American History* 86, no. 1 (June 1999): 67–93.

——. "The Strange Career of the Illegal Alien: Immigration Restriction and Deportation Policy in the United States, 1921–1965." *Law and History Review* 20, no. 1 (spring 2003): 69–109.

Oates, Lynette. "Emily Margaret Horneville of the Muruwari." In *Fighters and Singers: The Lives of Some Australian Aboriginal Women*, ed. Isobel White, Diane Barwick, and Betty Meehan, 106–22. Sydney: Allen & Unwin, 1985.

O'Neill, Colleen. *Working the Navajo Way: Labor and Culture in the Twentieth Century*. Lawrence: University of Kansas Press, 2005.

Orleck, Annelise, and Alexis Jetter, eds. "Reclaiming Culture and the Land: Motherhood and the Politics of Sustaining Community." An interview with Winona LaDuke. In *The Politics of Motherhood: Activist Voices from Left to Right*, ed. Alexis Jetter, Annelise Orleck, and Diana Taylor, 77–83. Hanover NH: University Press of New England, 1997.

Osburn, Katherine M. B. *Southern Ute Women: Autonomy and Assimilation on the Reservation, 1887–1934*. Albuquerque: University of New Mexico Press, 1998.

Paisley, Fiona. "Feminist Challenges to White Australia, 1900–1930s." In *Sex, Power, and Justice: Historical Perspectives of Law in Australia*, ed. Diane Kirkby, 252–69. Melbourne: Oxford University Press, 1995.

——. "'For a Brighter Day': Constance Ternent Cooke." In *Uncommon Ground: White Women in Aboriginal History*, ed. Anna Cole, Victoria Haskins, and Fiona Paisley, 172–96. Canberra: Aboriginal Studies Press, 2005.

——. *Loving Protection? Australian Feminism and Aboriginal Women's Rights, 1919–1939.* Carlton South, Victoria: Melbourne University Press, 2000.

——. "Race Hysteria, Darwin 1938." *Australian Feminist Studies* 16, no. 34 (2001): 43–59.

——. "'Unnecessary Crimes and Tragedies': Race, Gender, and Sexuality in Australian Policies of Aboriginal Child Removal." In *Gender, Sexuality and Colonial Modernities*, ed. Antoinette Burton, 134–47. London: Routledge, 1999.

Palmer, Alison. *Colonial Genocide.* Adelaide: Crawford House, 2000.

Palmer, Phyllis. *Domesticity and Dirt: Housewives and Domestic Servants in the United States, 1920–1945.* Philadelphia: Temple University Press, 1989.

Parreñas, Rhacel Salazar. *Servants of Globalization: Women, Migration and Domestic Work.* Stanford: Stanford University Press, 2001.

Parry, Suzanne. "Identifying the Process: The Removal of Half-Caste Children from Aboriginal Mothers." *Aboriginal History* 19, no. 2 (1995): 141–53.

Pascoe, Peggy. *Relations of Rescue: The Search for Female Moral Authority in the American West, 1874–1939.* New York: Oxford University Press, 1990.

Patterson, Victoria. "Indian Life in the City: A Glimpse of the Urban Experience of Pomo Women in the 1930s." *California History* 71 (fall 1992): 403–11, 453.

Peavey, Linda, and Ursula Smith. "World Champions: The 1904 Girls' Basketball Team from Fort Shaw Indian Boarding School." *Montana, the Magazine of Western History* 51, no. 4 (winter 2001): 2–25.

Perdue, Theda. *Cherokee Women: Gender and Culture Change, 1700–1835.* Lincoln: University of Nebraska Press, 1998.

Perdue, Theda, and Michael Green, eds. *The Cherokee Removal: A Brief History with Documents.* Boston: Bedford/St. Martin's Press, 1995.

Perry, Adele. *On the Edge of Empire: Gender, Race, and the Making of British Columbia, 1849–1871.* Toronto: University of Toronto Press, 2001.

Peters, Virginia Bergman. *Women of the Earth Lodges: Tribal Life on the Plains.* North Haven CT: Archon Books, 1995.

Pettit, Jan. *Utes: The Mountain People.* Boulder CO: Johnson Books, 1990.

Pettman, Jan Jindy. "Race, Ethnicity and Gender in Australia." In *Unsettling Settler Societies: Articulations of Gender, Race, Ethnicity and Class*, ed. Daiva Stasiulis and Nira Yuval-Davis, 65–94. London: Sage, 1995.

Philp, Kenneth R. *John Collier's Crusade for Indian Reform, 1920–1954.* Tucson: University of Arizona Press, 1977.

Pilkington, Doris. *Rabbit Proof Fence*. New York: Miramax Books, 2002.

Platt, Anthony M. *The Child Savers: The Invention of Delinquency*. Chicago: University of Chicago Press, 1969.

Pratt, Richard Henry. *Battlefield and Classroom: Four Decades with the American Indian, 1867–1904*. New Haven CT: Yale University Press, 1964.

"Progress Report of the Royal Commission on the Aborigines." In *Proceedings of the Parliament of South Australia*, vol. 2, no. 26. Adelaide: Government Printer, 1913.

Prucha, Francis Paul. *American Indian Policy in Crisis: Christian Reformers and the Indian, 1865–1900*. Norman: University of Oklahoma Press, 1976.

———. *Atlas of Indian Affairs*. Lincoln: University of Nebraska Press, 1990.

———. *The Churches and the Indian Schools, 1888–1912*. Lincoln: University of Nebraska Press, 1979.

Qoyawayma, Polingaysi, as told to Vada Carlson. *No Turning Back: A Hopi Indian Woman's Struggle to Live in Two Worlds*. Albuquerque: University of New Mexico Press, 1964.

Quinton, Amelia Stone. "Care of the Indian." In *Woman's Work in America*, ed. Annie Nathan Meyer, 373–91. New York: Henry Holt, 1891.

———. "The Women's National Indian Association." In *The Congress of Women: Held in the Woman's Building, World's Columbian Exposition, Chicago, U.S.A.*, 1893, ed. Mary Kavanaugh Oldham Eagle, 71–73. Chicago: Monarch, 1894.

Rader, Benjamin. "'The Greatest Drama in Indian Life': Experiments in Native American Identity and Resistance at Haskell Institute Homecoming of 1926." *Western Historical Quarterly* 35, no. 4 (2004): 429–53.

Ramusack, Barbara. "Cultural Missionaries, Maternal Imperialists, Feminist Allies: British Activists in India, 1865–1945." *Women's Studies International Forum* 13, no. 4 (1990): 309–21.

Read, Peter. "How Many Separated Children?" *Australian Journal of Politics and History* 49, no. 2 (2003): 155–63.

———. "Northern Territory." In *Contested Ground: Australian Aborigines and the British Crown*, ed. Ann McGrath, 269–305. St Leonards, New South Wales: Allen & Unwin, 1995.

———. *The Stolen Generations: The Removal of Aboriginal Children in New South Wales 1883 to 1969*. 2nd ed. Sydney: New South Wales Department of Aboriginal Affairs, 1998.

Report of the Commissioners, Royal Commission on the Aborigines. Melbourne: Government Printer, 1877.

Report of the Missionary Committee of the Women's National Indian Association. Philadelphia: Women's National Indian Association, 1889.

Report of the Royal Commission on the Constitution. Canberra: Government Printer, 1929.

Report of the Select Committee of the Legislative Council on Aborigines, Victoria, 1858–1859. Melbourne: Government Printer, 1859.

Reyhner, John, and Jeanne Eder. *American Indian Education: A History*. Norman: University of Oklahoma Press, 2004.

Reynolds, Henry, ed. *Aborigines and Settlers: The Australian Experience*, 1788–1939. North Melbourne: Cassell Australia, 1972.

———. "Aborigines and the 1967 Referendum: Thirty Years On." Lecture presented to Department of Senate Occasional Lecture Series at Parliament House, 14 November 1997, Canberra. Available online at http://www.aph.gov.au/senate/pubs/pops/pops31/co5.pdf. Accessed July 1, 2008.

———. *Frontier: Aborigines, Settlers, and Land*. 1987. St. Leonards, New South Wales: Allen & Unwin, 1996.

———. "Genocide in Tasmania?" In *Genocide and Settler Society: Frontier Violence and Stolen Indigenous Children in Australian History*, ed. A. Dirk Moses, 127–49. New York: Berghahn Books, 2004.

———. *This Whispering in Our Hearts*. St. Leonards, New South Wales: Allen & Unwin, 1998.

———. *With the White People: The Crucial Role of Aborigines in the Exploration and Development of Australia*. Ringwood, Victoria: Penguin Books, 1990.

Riney, Scott. "'I Like the School So I Want to Come Back': The Enrollment of American Indian Students at the Rapid City Indian School." *American Indian Culture and Research Journal* 22, no. 2 (1998): 171–92.

———. *The Rapid City Indian School*, 1898–1933. Norman: University of Oklahoma Press, 1999.

Robinson, Gwen. "Aborigines and White Popular Culture in the 1930s in Queensland." *Hecate* 15, no. 1 (1989): 54–63.

Roediger, David. *The Wages of Whiteness: Race and the Making of the American Working Class*. London: Verso, 1991.

Roessel, Ruth. *Women in Navajo Society*. Rough Rock, Navajo Nation AZ: Navajo Resource Center, Rough Rock Demonstration School, 1981.

Rollins, Judith. *Between Women: Domestics and Their Employers*. Philadelphia: Temple University Press, 1985.

Romero, Mary. *Maid in the U.S.A.* New York: Routledge, 1992.

Rose, Deborah Bird. *Dingo Makes Us Human: Life and Land in an Australian Aboriginal Culture*. Cambridge England: Cambridge University Press, 2000.

———. *Reports from a Wild Country: Ethics of Decolonisation*. Sydney: University of New South Wales Press, 2004.

Rose, Elizabeth. *A Mother's Job: The History of Day Care, 1890–1960*. New York: Oxford University Press, 1999.

Rowse, Tim. "Notes on the History of Aboriginal Population of Australia." In *Genocide and Settler Society: Frontier Violence and Stolen Indigenous Children in Australian History*, ed. A. Dirk Moses, 312–25. New York: Berghahn Books, 2004.

———. *White Flour, White Power: From Rations to Citizenship in Central Australia*. Cambridge England: Cambridge University Press, 1998.

Ruddick, Daisy, as told to Kathy Mills and Tony Austin. "'Talking about Cruel Things': Girls' Life in the Kahlin Compound." *Hecate* 15, no. 1 (1989): 8–22.

Ruiz, Vicki. *From out of the Shadows: Mexican Women in Twentieth-Century America*. New York: Oxford University Press, 1998.

Russell, Lynette, ed. *Colonial Frontiers: Indigenous-European Encounters in Settler Societies*. Manchester, England: Manchester University Press, 2001.

———. "'Dirty Domestics and Worse Cooks': Aboriginal Women's Agency and Domestic Frontiers, South Australia, 1800–1850." *Frontiers* 28, nos. 1 and 2 (2007): 18–46.

Russell, Penny. "Unsettling Settler Society." In *Australia's History: Themes and Debates*, ed. Martyn Lyons and Penny Russell, 22–40. Sydney: University of New South Wales Press, 2005.

Rutherdale, Myra. "Mothers of the Empire: Maternal Metaphors in the Northern Canadian Mission Field." In *Canadian Missionaries, Indigenous Peoples: Representing Religion at Home and Abroad*, ed. Alvyn Austin and Jamie S. Scott, 46–66. Toronto: University of Toronto Press, 2005.

Salter, Elizabeth. *Daisy Bates: Great White Queen of the Never Never*. Sydney: Angus and Robertson, 1971.

Sarris, Greg. *Mabel McKay: Weaving the Dream*. Berkeley: University of California Press, 1994.

Saunders, K., and R. Evans, eds. *Gender Relations in Australia: Domination and Negotiation*. Sydney: Harcourt Brace Jovanovich, 1992.

Scanlon, Tony. "'Pure and Clean and True to Christ': Black Women and White Missionaries in the North." *Hecate* 7, nos. 1 and 2 (1986): 82–105.

Schaffer, Kay. "Colonizing Gender in Colonial Australia: The Eliza Fraser Story." In *Writing Women and Space: Colonial and Postcolonial Geographies*, ed. Alison Blunt and Gillian Rose, 101–20. New York: Guilford Press, 1994.

Schutt, Amy. "'What will become of our young people?' Goals for Indian Children in Moravian Missions." *History of Education Quarterly* 38, no. 3 (fall 1998): 268–86.

Seaman, David, ed. *Born a Chief: The Nineteenth Century Hopi Boyhood of Edmund Nequatewa*. Tucson: University of Arizona Press, 1993.

Sekaquaptewa, Helen, as told to Louise Udall. *Me and Mine: The Life Story of Helen Sekaquaptewa*. Tucson: University of Arizona Press, 1969.

Shoemaker, Nancy, ed. *Negotiators of Change: Historical Perspectives on Native American Women*. New York: Routledge, 1995.

Simmons, Leo, ed. *Sun Chief: The Autobiography of a Hopi Indian*. New Haven CT: Yale University Press, 1942.

Simonsen, Jane E. *Making Home Work: Domesticity and Native American Assimilation in the American West, 1860–1919*. Chapel Hill: University of North Carolina Press, 2006.

Skocpol, Theda. *Protecting Soldiers and Mothers: The Political Origins of Social Policy in the United States*. Cambridge MA: Harvard University Press, 1992.

Sleeper-Smith, Susan. *Indian Women and French Men: Rethinking Cultural Encounter in the Western Great Lakes*. Amherst: University of Massachusetts Press, 2001.

Smith, Paul Chaat, and Robert Allen Warrior. *Like a Hurricane: The Indian Movement from Alcatraz to Wounded Knee*. New York: New Press, 1996.

Smits, David D. "The 'Squaw Drudge': A Prime Index of Savagism." *Ethnohistory* 29 (fall 1982): 281–306.

Spack, Ruth. "English, Pedagogy, and Ideology: A Case Study of the Hampton Institute, 1878–1900." *American Indian Culture and Research Journal* 24, no. 1 (2000): 1–24.

"Special Section: 'Genocide'?: Australian Aboriginal History in International Perspective." *Aboriginal History* 25 (2001): 1–172.

Stasiulis, Daiva, and Nira Yuval-Davis, eds. *Unsettling Settler Societies: Articulations of Gender, Race, Ethnicity and Class*. London: Sage, 1995.

Stewart, Irene. *A Voice in Her Tribe: A Navajo Woman's Own Story*. Ed. Doris Ostrander Dawdy. Socorro NM: Ballena Press, 1980.

Stoler, Ann Laura. *Carnal Knowledge and Imperial Power: Race and the Intimate in Colonial Rule*. Berkeley: University of California Press, 2003.

———. "Tense and Tender Ties: The Politics of Comparison in North American History and (Post) Colonial Studies." In *Haunted by Empire: Geographies of Intimacy in North American History*, ed. Ann Laura Stoler, 23–67. Durham NC: Duke University Press, 2006.

Strobel, Margaret. *Gender, Sex, and Empire*. Washington DC: American Historical Association, 1993.

Szasz, Margaret Connell. *Education and the American Indian: The Road to Self-Determination, 1928–1973*. Albuquerque: University of New Mexico Press, 1974.

Takaki, Ronald. *Strangers from a Different Shore: A History of Asian Americans*. Boston: Little, Brown, 1989.

Thonemann, H. E. *Tell the White Man: The Life Story of an Aboriginal Lubra*. Sydney: Collins, 1949.

Thorne, Susan. "Missionary-Imperial Feminism." In *Gendered Missions: Women and Men in Missionary Discourse and Practice*, ed. Mary Taylor Huber and Nancy C. Lutkehaus, 39–65. Ann Arbor: University of Michigan Press, 1999.

Threadgold, Terry. *Feminist Poetics: Poiesis, Performance, Histories*. London: Routledge, 1997.

Tiffin, Susan. *In Whose Best Interest? Child Welfare Reform in the Progressive Era*. Westport CT: Greenwood Press, 1982.

Trafzer, Clifford E., and Joel R. Hyer, eds. *"Exterminate Them": Written Accounts of the Murder, Rape, and Slavery of Native Americans during the California Gold Rush, 1848–1868*. East Lansing: Michigan State University Press, 1999.

Trafzer, Clifford, Jean Keller, and Lorene Sisquoc, eds. *Boarding School Blues: Revisiting the American Indian Boarding School Experience*. Lincoln: University of Nebraska Press, 2006.

Trennert, Robert A., Jr. *The Phoenix Indian School: Forced Assimilation in Arizona, 1891–1935*. Norman: University of Oklahoma Press, 1988.

Tucker, Margaret. *If Everyone Cared*. Melbourne: Grosvenor Books, 1977.

Turner, Violet E. *The "Good Fella Missus."* Adelaide: Hunkin, Ellis, & King, 1938.

——. *Lazarus at the Gate*. Adelaide: United Aborigines' Mission, 1937.

——. *Ooldea*. Melbourne: S. John Bacon, 1950.

——. *Pearls from the Deep: The Story of Colebrook Home for Aboriginal Children, Quorn, South Australia*. Adelaide: United Aborigines' Mission, 1936.

Tyrrell, Ian. *Woman's World, Woman's Empire: The Woman's Christian Temperance Union in International Perspective, 1880–1930*. Chapel Hill: University of North Carolina Press, 1991.

Udel, Lisa J. "Revision and Resistance: The Politics of Native Women's Motherwork." *Frontiers* 22, no. 2 (2001): 43–62.

U.S. Senate. Committee on Indian Affairs. *Survey of Conditions of Indians in United States*. Hearings before a Subcommittee. 70th Congress, 2nd session. Washington DC: Government Printing Office, 1929.

Utley, Robert. *The Indian Frontier of the American West, 1847–1890*. Albuquerque: University of New Mexico Press, 1984.

Van Kirk, Sylvia. *Many Tender Ties: Women in Fur Trade Society, 1670–1870*. Norman: University of Oklahoma Press, 1983.

van Krieken, Robert. *Children and the State: Social Control and the Formation of Australian Child Welfare*. Sydney: Allen & Unwin, 1991.

Van Nuys, Frank. *Americanizing the West: Race, Immigrants, and Citizenship,* 1890–1930. Lawrence: University Press of Kansas, 2002.

Van Pelt, Lori. "Estelle Reel, Pioneer Politician." *True West* 47 (April 2000): 50.

Walden, Inara. "'That Was Slavery Days': Aboriginal Domestic Servants in New South Wales in the Twentieth Century." *Labour History,* no. 69 (November 1995): 196–209.

——. "'To Send Her to Service': Aboriginal Domestic Servants." *Aboriginal Law Bulletin* 3, no. 76 (October 1995): 12–14.

Wanken, Helen M. "Woman's Sphere and Indian Reform: The Women's National Indian Association, 1879–1901." PhD diss., Marquette University, 1981.

Ward, Glenyse. *Wandering Girl.* Broome, Western Australia: Magabala Books, 1987.

Weeks, Philip. *Farewell My Nation: The American Indian and the United States,* 1820–1890. Arlington Heights IL: Harlan Davidson, 1990.

Welter, Barbara. "'She Hath Done What She Could': Protestant Women's Missionary Careers in the Nineteenth Century." *American Quarterly* 30 (1978): 624–38.

White, Isobel. "Daisy Bates: Legend and Reality." In *First in Their Field: Women and Australian Anthropology,* ed. Julie Marcus, 46–65. Melbourne: Melbourne University Press, 1993.

White, Isobel, Diane Barwick, and Betty Meehan, eds. *Fighters and Singers: The Lives of Some Australian Aboriginal Women.* Sydney: Allen & Unwin, 1985.

Whittington, Vera. *Sister Kate: A Life Dedicated to Children in Need of Care.* Nedlands: University of Western Australia Press, 1999.

Wilson, Gilbert. *Buffalo Bird Woman's Garden: Agriculture of the Hidatsa Indians.* 1917. St. Paul: Minnesota Historical Society Press, 1987.

——. *Waheenee: An Indian Girl's Story.* 1921. Lincoln: University of Nebraska Press, 1981.

Wilson, Jan McKinley. "'You took our children': Aboriginal Autobiographical Narratives of Separation in New South Wales, 1977–1997." PhD diss., Australian National University, 2002.

Windschuttle, Keith. *The Fabrication of Aboriginal History:* Vol. 1, *Van Diemen's Land,* 1803–1847. Sydney: Macleay Press, 2002.

Wolfe, Patrick. "Land, Labor, and Difference: Elementary Structures of Race." *American Historical Review* 106 (June 2001): 866–1006.

——. "Logics of Elimination: Colonial Policies on Indigenous Peoples in Australia and the United States." Lecture delivered at University of Nebraska, Lincoln, February 21, 1999.

——. *Settler Colonialism and the Transformation of Anthropology: The Politics and Poetics of an Ethnographic Event.* London: Cassell, 1999.

Woollacott, Angela. *To Try Her Fortune in London: Australian Women, Colonialism, and Modernity*. New York: Oxford University Press, 2001.

Zitkala-Ša (Gertrude Bonnin Simmons). *American Indian Stories*. Foreword by Dexter Fisher. Lincoln: University of Nebraska Press, 1981.

Index

Page numbers in italics refer to illustrations. Locations are identified by Aus (Australia), GB (Great Britain), or US (United States).

AAPA (Australian Aboriginal Progressive Association), 375
Abbott, Lyman, 83
Abenakis, 76
Abeita, Juan Rey, 164–65
Aboriginal Child Placement Principle, 429–30
Aboriginal children, 337; and child-family contact, 267; and child removal post–World War II, 426; and education, 41–42; and estrangement from indigenous life, 274–75; and fear of other Aborigines, 271; and kidnapping, 58–59; as labor source, 59. *See also* child removal
Aboriginal child welfare systems, 32
Aboriginal Fellowship Group, 419
"The Aboriginal Mother in Western Australia" (Bennett), 410
Aboriginal peoples, 33; adaptation to white society, 49; assumed extinction of, 67–68; biological absorption of, 26; as British subjects, 16; camps

of, 43, 448n49; and child rearing, xxii, 121–23, 432; and child removal policies, xxiv–xxv; children, 233; and citizenship, 64; debate over race of, 71–72; and disease, 222; favoring education, 187–88; and government aid, 32; hiding children, 174; and hunting/gathering strategies, xxi–xxii; and labor, 33; marriage practices of, 117, 379; missions for, 36–37; and Moseley Commission, 416; portrayed as a burden to white society, 48–49; and poverty, 32, 45; and resistance to child removal, 173–75, 179, 187; settlements for, xxi, 36–37; and slavery, 410; stereotypes of, 139, rights of; traditional territories, 36–37. *See also* Aboriginal women
Aboriginal policies: and national identity building, 63; and search for models, 51–52, 449n73, 449n74; and white women, 88, 145–46, 465n170
Aboriginal Protection and Restriction of the Sale of Opium Act (1897), 33–34
Aboriginals Ordinance (1919), 431
Aboriginal women, 128, 348; and food production, xxi–xxii, 23; as institutional workers, 299–302; portrayed

acceptance of, 190–91, 431; and Indian staff, 191; length of attendance, 39; Meriam Report findings, 406–7; and missionaries, 93; and morals, 132; on-reservation, 186–87; physical abuse at, 391, 396, 399; punishment at, 400, 478n81; quotas for, 162, 168, 197; and Estelle Reel, 135; and student documentation, 38. *See also* names of boarding schools

Board of Indian Commissioners, 73

Boas, Franz, 320, 424

Bomaderry Children's Home (New South Wales), 249–50, 270–71, 324

Bon, Anne, 372

Bonney, Mary Lucinda, 97, 335

Brace, Charles Loring, 56

Brandl, Maria, 237

breakdown of indigenous culture: and child removal policies, 279; and Christian proselytizing, 249–50; and extractive colonialism, 12–13; and land appropriation, 248–49; and missionaries, 14, 23, 126; and reformers, 77; and settler colonialism, 84

"breeding out the color." *See* absorption policy

Bringing Them Home (Human Rights and Equal Opportunity Commission), xxvi, xxvii, 377, 430

British Commonwealth League. *See* BCL

Bronham, Ada, 419

Brookings Institution, 406

Broome, Richard, 60

Broome, Western Australia, 177–78, 316

Brown, Estelle Aubrey, 286, 389–90, 393–95

Browning, Daniel, 166

Brusnahan, Margaret, 229, 253, 325

Buffalo Bird Woman. *See* Maxi'diwiac

Buffalohead, Roger, 295

bullying, 266

Buludja (Mangari woman), 47

Bungalow institution, 70, 137–39, 225, 268, 287, 296–97, 297, 299, 331; and plan to relocate, 409

Bungalow institution at Jay Creek, 297

Bureau of Indian Affairs. *See* BIA

Burgess, Marianna, 198

Burgoyne, Iris, 171, 173

Burke Act (US, 1906), 456n186

Burton, Charles, xxviii, 392, 395, 398–400

Buti, Antonio, 61, 62

Butt, Laurette, 275, 278

Caddo Indians, 184, 265

Cahill, Cathleen, 284

Calfee, F. S., Mrs. (field matron), 123

California Children's Home Society, 365–66

The Call of the Aboriginal (Baillie), 419

Calloway, Colin, 13

camps, Aboriginal, 43, 448n49

cannibalism, 124–25

Cape Bedford, Queensland, 234

Carlisle Institute, 28, 99, 100, 151, 152, 153, 160; and assimilation, 196; and changing body shape, 309; compared to prison, 244; Angel DeCora at, 300–301; and Alice Fletcher, 132, 199; and institution experiences, 231; quotas at, 197; recruitment for, 195; and Richard Henry Pratt, 231; and runaways, 262; and student deaths, 203

Carroll, Julia, 284, 390–91

Department of the Native Affairs (Aus), 415

Devanny, Jean, 422

Devens, Carol, 13, 14

De Vries, Nancy, 251, 264, 351

Dilth-cleyhen (Apache girl), 241–42, 246

disease: at boarding schools, 154–55, 167, 229, 259–60, 404, 406; and indigenous peoples, 21, 154, 222; at institutions, 229, 259–60

disobedience, as coping strategy, 306–7

dispersal policies (Aus), 33, 45

Dissette, Mary, 289–90

"diverted mothering," 349, 365

division of labor: and gender, 10, 22–23, 114, 246, 281; and trade, 13

Dodd, Martin, 270

Dolly (Aboriginal girl), 221, 227; and Lock, 220–26

domesticity, teaching of, 302–7

domestic service, 329–69; and absorption policy, 368; and assimilation, 330, 368, 487n9; and conflict between employer and employee, 342, 345, 358–61; conflict with matrons, 361–62; duties, 357; as economic strategy, 368; and employer's control of domestic workers, 350–52, 362, 364; employer's expectations, 358–59; and employer status, 337–39; and family contact, 367; and homesickness, 367; and marriage, 364; and maternalism, 335; and motherhood, 363–66, 491n109; and physical abuse, 343–44; and placement services, 354–55; reasons for taking jobs in, 355–57; and relationships between indigenous domestic workers and white children, 347, 348, 349, 359–60; and relationships between indigenous domestic workers and white employers, 330, 335–37, 342, 347; and sexual abuse, 340, 346; and skin color, 336; and social life, 356–57, 364; as tool of assimilation, 330; training for, 329–30, 339; wages, 333–34, 351, 357–58, 359, 415

Donaldson, Thomas, 166

Doomadgee Mission, Queensland, 252

DuBois, Constance, 167, 401–4, 402; influence of ethnology on, 422

Dulhi Gunyah orphanage, 214

Durack, Mary, 291

Dyke, Charles Bartlett, 74–75

Eastman, Charles, 76, 271, 388, 427

Eastman, Elaine Goodale, 76, 385–88

economic systems, of indigenous peoples, 79–80, 242

education: and biological determinism, 74; and child removal policies (US), 41; indigenous practices, 240–41; at institutions, 261–62; and WNIA, 94–95

Edwards, Coral, 38, 430

Elkin, A. P., 110–11

Ellinghaus, Katherine, 76, 285

Elong, Catherine, 316

environmental determinism, 67, 74

Ernabella Mission, South Australia, 279

"Essential Features in the Education of the Child Races" (Dyke), 74–75

Etahdleuh (Indian prisoner of war), 153

ethnically mixed children, 22, 72, 414, 448n55; and absorption policy, 69; and cannibalism, 125; and child removal policies, 137–41, 171, 317; from Cumeroogunga, 50; and dispersal

CPSIA information can be obtained at www.ICGtesting.com
Printed in the USA
BVOW05s1333050814

361635BV00003B/3/P